PROPORTIONALITY IN CRIME CONTROL AND CRIMINAL JUSTICE

This edited volume seeks to reassess the old and to analyse and develop novel approaches to the notion of proportionality in criminal matters and the new security architecture. The discourse is not limited to conventional constitutional constellations and standard problems of sentencing in traditional criminal proceedings. Rather, the book offers an interdisciplinary and cross-jurisdictional exploration of highly topical, proportionality-related issues pertinent to penal theory and legal philosophy, criminalisation policies, security and anti-terrorism strategies, alternative types of justice delivery, and supranational enforcement as well as human rights and international criminal and humanitarian law.

In today's global risk society, with its numerous visible and invisible enemies of the state and the individual, balancing freedom and security has become nothing less than an attempt at untying a Gordian knot. Against this background, the proportionality of measures of crime prevention and repression is unquestionably an issue of utmost importance, which basic research and legal policy in rule-of-law based systems are urgently called to address.

The timely and fascinating contributions in this book, covering jurisdictions from both the common law and the civil law as well as hybrid and international jurisdictions, will appeal to academics, researchers, policy advisers and practitioners working in the areas of national and international criminal law, comparative criminal justice/criminology and legal philosophy as well as constitutional and security law.

Proportionality in Crime Control and Criminal Justice

Edited by
Emmanouil Billis,
Nandor Knust
and
Jon Petter Rui

•HART•
OXFORD • LONDON • NEW YORK • NEW DELHI • SYDNEY

HART PUBLISHING
Bloomsbury Publishing Plc
Kemp House, Chawley Park, Cumnor Hill, Oxford, OX2 9PH, UK
1385 Broadway, New York, NY 10018, USA
29 Earlsfort Terrace, Dublin 2, Ireland

HART PUBLISHING, the Hart/Stag logo, BLOOMSBURY and the Diana logo are trademarks of Bloomsbury Publishing Plc

First published in Great Britain 2021

Reprinted 2021

A catalogue record for this book is available from the British Library.

Library of Congress Cataloging-in-Publication data

Names: Effectiveness and Proportionality: Modern Challenges in Security Law and Criminal Justice (2019 : Freiburg im Breisgau, Germany) | Billis, Emmanouil, 1983- editor. | Knust, Nandor, 1975- editor. | Rui, Jon Petter, editor. | Max-Planck-Institut zur Erforschung von Kriminalität, Sicherheit und Recht, sponsoring body.

Title: Proportionality in crime control and criminal justice / edited by Emmanouil Billis, Nandor Knust and Jon Petter Rui.

Description: Oxford, UK ; New York, NY : Hart Publishing, an imprint of Bloomsbury Publishing, 2021. | Based on papers presented at "the international workshop at the Max Planck Institute for the Study of Crime, Security and Law in Freiburg, Germany, in October 2019" | Includes bibliographical references and index.

Identifiers: LCCN 2021000164 (print) | LCCN 2021000165 (ebook) | ISBN 9781509938605 (hardback) | ISBN 9781509947065 (paperback) | ISBN 9781509938629 (pdf) | ISBN 9781509938612 (Epub)

Subjects: LCSH: Criminal law—Congresses. | Proportionality in law—Congresses.

Classification: LCC K5014.8 .E34 2021 (print) | LCC K5014.8 (ebook) | DDC 345—dc23

LC record available at https://lccn.loc.gov/2021000164

LC ebook record available at https://lccn.loc.gov/2021000165

ISBN: HB: 978-1-50993-860-5
ePDF: 978-1-50993-862-9
ePub: 978-1-50993-861-2

Typeset by Compuscript Ltd, Shannon
Printed and bound in Great Britain by TJ International Ltd, Padstow, Cornwall

FOREWORD

In democratic states governed by the rule of law and human rights, governmental power must be limited to those measures that are necessary in light of the legitimate aim pursued. The principle of proportionality is applied in many domains of the law; however, one may say that its application in the field of crime control and criminal justice has taken on particular importance. For example, the highly complex forms of espionage and terrorism threatening our democratic societies require states to take effective measures to defend themselves and their citizens, but states cannot be permitted to arbitrarily take any measure they choose in this fight. In this context, the assessment of the proportionality of the state measures in question is crucial.

The present volume, which gathers 17 impressive papers from diverse legal disciplines, enriches legal scholarship on this topic by exploring the concept of proportionality from different perspectives. Having participated in the international workshop at the Max Planck Institute for the Study of Crime, Security and Law in Freiburg, Germany, in October 2019, where the first drafts of these papers were presented, I am very pleased to be able to contribute to the volume by way of this foreword.

My presentation in Freiburg reflected on the challenge the European Court of Human Rights ('the Court') faces in national security and terrorism cases whenever it is called to assess the proportionality of certain measures a government has adopted. National security may be invoked as a ground for enabling states to exercise exceptional powers, limiting the protection normally afforded to fundamental rights.

While the Court's case law does not provide a precise definition of the concept of national security, one can say that it includes the protection of state security and constitutional democracy against espionage, terrorism, support for terrorism, separatism and incitement to breach military discipline. The question I posed was: How does the Court approach a proportionality assessment in these types of cases?

As we all know, the principle of proportionality is not explicitly mentioned in the European Convention on Human Rights (ECHR). Nevertheless, the search for a fair balance between the demands of the general interest of the community, on the one hand, and fundamental rights of the individual, on the other, is inherent in the Convention's entire system.[1] To achieve this balance requires a proportionality assessment.

[1] *Soering v United Kingdom* App no 14038/88 (ECtHR, 7 July 1989) [89].

Reliance on the principle of proportionality is most evident with respect to the so-called qualified rights. Under the second paragraphs of Articles 8–11 ECHR, a state may restrict the protected rights to the extent 'necessary in a democratic society' for certain listed public interest purposes, national security being the first among them. The Court interpreted this to mean that the restrictions must be 'proportionate to the legitimate aim pursued'.[2]

In my presentation, I described the proportionality test applied by the Court with respect to these qualified rights as 'the general proportionality criterion'. However, a proportionality assessment may also be possible with respect to other provisions of the Convention. For example, national security considerations may be relevant to the exceptions allowed to the right to life under Article 2 ECHR. Lethal force may be used in contexts such as absolute necessity, legitimate defence or defence of a person against national security-related violence, most frequently terrorist attacks, the arrests of suspects or the prevention of their escape, or the quelling of a riot or insurrection against a state institution. I termed this the 'absolute proportionality criterion'. Furthermore, in the national security context and particularly in mass surveillance cases, there is a call for the Court to develop what can be termed a 'strict or intermediate proportionality criterion'. This is a standard of scrutiny positioned between the general criterion, on the one hand, and the absolute model derived from Article 2 ECHR, on the other.

The classical formulation of the proportionality test applied in the Court's case law consists of four independent but closely interrelated components: first, there must be a reasonable relationship between the means and the ends; secondly, there must also be a fair balance between the demands of the general interest and the interest of the individual concerned; thirdly, the limitation must not impair the very essence of the right; and fourthly, these components are relative to the scope of the margin of appreciation afforded to the state in the field in question.

The first three I called 'functional' components of the proportionality model. In other words, they constitute the model itself as implemented in practice. The last one is an institutional component informed by the principle of subsidiarity. The margin of appreciation in a particular case informs the scope and content of the first three components. The wider the margin, the more deference is given to the national authority when it comes to the Court's review.

In case of an application against it, a state's position before the Court is stronger if the domestic institutions themselves already addressed the issue of the proportionality of the interference with the applicant's right. If a prior assessment at the national level is lacking, a violation may be found simply because the respondent government did not demonstrate a proportionality assessment at the domestic level.

In the particular context of national security and terrorism, I used the example of mass or bulk surveillance of signals communication for national security or

[2] *Handyside v United Kingdom* App no 5493/72 (ECtHR, 7 December 1976) [49].

counter-terrorism purposes. Regimes providing for the acquisition of surveillance material must be 'in accordance with the law'; in other words, they must have some basis in domestic law, must be accessible to the person concerned and must be foreseeable as to their effects.[3] Furthermore, they must be proportionate to the legitimate aim pursued, and adequate and effective safeguards must exist against abuse. In particular, the procedures for supervising the ordering and implementation of the measures in question must be such as to keep the 'interference' to what is 'necessary in a democratic society'.[4]

Two important cases are currently pending before the Grand Chamber on mass surveillance. In *Big Brother Watch and Others v United Kingdom*[5] and *Centrum för rättvisa v Sweden*[6] the Court is reviewing the issues at hand on the basis of a legislative proportionality assessment already performed by the British and Swedish legislatures respectively. Since these cases are still pending, we will have to await the Grand Chamber's precise take on this point.

The Court has always been acutely conscious of the difficulties faced by the states in protecting their populations from terrorist violence, which constitutes, in itself, a grave threat to human rights.[7] In recent years it has also expressly acknowledged – in response to complaints invoking a wide range of Convention Articles – the very real threat that Contracting States currently face on account of international terrorism.[8]

In this context, the Court has considered it legitimate for Contracting States to take a firm stand against those who contribute to terrorist acts. Due to the special nature of global terrorism, and in particular the complexity of global terror networks, the Court accepts that taking such a stand for the prevention of violent acts endangering the lives of innocent people requires a flow of information between the security services of many countries in all parts of the world. That said, it is for the Court to assess whether or not the legislative context regulating this information flow also provides considerable safeguards against abuse. If it considers that it does, then the Court may accept that the resulting interference was kept to what is 'necessary in a democratic society'.

The present volume provides an in-depth exploration of these and other relevant issues from a variety of different angles. It offers its readers ample material for coming to grips with the proportionality concept, from general core principles to its specific use in contemporary criminal and security matters.

Robert Spano
President of the European Court of Human Rights

[3] *Roman Zakharov v Russia* App no 47143/06 (ECtHR GC, 4 December 2015) [228].
[4] ibid [232].
[5] *Big Brother Watch and Others v United Kingdom* App nos 58170/13, 62322/14 and 24960/15 (ECtHR, 13 September 2018).
[6] *Centrum för rättvisa v Sweden* App no 35252/08 (ECtHR, 19 June 2018).
[7] *Öcalan v Turkey* App no 46221/99 (ECtHR GC, 12 May 2005) [179].
[8] See, eg, *Othman (Abu Qatada) v United Kingdom* App no 8139/09 (ECtHR, 17 January 2012) [183].

CONTENTS

LIST OF CONTRIBUTORS

Ilias Anagnostopoulos is Professor of Criminal Law and Criminal Procedure Law at the National and Kapodistrian University of Athens and head of the Athens-based law firm Anagnostopoulos, focusing on all aspects of white-collar crime.

Lorena Bachmaier Winter is Professor of Law at the Complutense University of Madrid.

Emmanouil Billis is Research Group Leader at the Max Planck Institute for the Study of Crime, Security and Law, in Freiburg (formerly Max Planck Institute for Foreign and International Criminal Law).

Michael Bothe is Professor Emeritus of Public Law at the University of Frankfurt.

Johan Boucht is Professor of Criminal Law at the University of Oslo and Professor of Police and Prosecution Law at the University of Bergen.

Nestor Courakis is Professor Emeritus of Criminology and Penology at the National and Kapodistrian University of Athens and Professor of Criminal Law and Criminal Justice at the University of Nicosia.

R A Duff is Professor Emeritus of Philosophy at the University of Stirling and Professor Emeritus at the University of Minnesota Law School.

Thomas Elholm is Professor of Criminal Law at the University of Copenhagen.

Emanuela-Chiara Gillard is Senior Research Fellow at the Oxford Institute for Ethics, Law and Armed Conflict and Associate Fellow with the International Law Programme at Chatham House.

John Jackson is Professor of Comparative Criminal Law and Procedure at the University of Nottingham.

Konstanze Jarvers is Senior Researcher at the Max Planck Institute for the Study of Crime, Security and Law, in Freiburg (formerly Max Planck Institute for Foreign and International Criminal Law).

Nandor Knust is Associate Professor of Law at the University of Tromsø.

Russell A Miller is the J.B. Stombock Professor of Law at the Washington & Lee University School of Law, Virginia.

Christos Mylonopoulos is Professor of Criminal Law at the National and Kapodistrian University of Athens, Founder and President of the European and International Criminal Law Institute (Athens) and Member of the European Academy of Sciences and Arts (Salzburg).

Vagia Polyzoidou is Assistant Professor of Law at the University of Nicosia.

Ralf Poscher is Director (Department of Public Law) at the Max Planck Institute for the Study of Crime, Security and Law, in Freiburg (formerly Max Planck Institute for Foreign and International Criminal Law).

Julian V Roberts is Professor of Criminology in the Faculty of Law, University of Oxford.

Jon Petter Rui is Professor of Law at the University of Tromsø.

Richard Vogler is Professor of Comparative Criminal Law and Criminal Justice at the University of Sussex.

Thomas Weigend was Professor of Criminal Law at the University of Cologne until 2016.

Lucia Zedner is Senior Research Fellow in Law at All Souls College and Professor in the Faculty of Law, University of Oxford, and Conjoint Professor in the Faculty of Law, University of New South Wales.

PART I

Conceptualising Proportionality

1

The Typology of Proportionality*

EMMANOUIL BILLIS, NANDOR KNUST AND JON PETTER RUI

This volume is the product of a two-year study on proportionality in crime control and criminal justice, conceived and organised by the Max Planck Society's Otto Hahn Research Group on Alternative and Informal Systems of Crime Control and Criminal Justice. The book comprises 17 chapters by 21 leading international scholars in the fields of legal theory and philosophy, constitutional and public security law, human rights and humanitarian law, (national, international and supranational) criminal law, criminal justice and criminology. The overall goal is to contribute to the theoretical exploration and practical evolution of the proportionality concept. To this end, the emphasis is on aspects of proportionality that might (or should) serve both as guidelines (in terms of effectiveness and efficiency) and substantial limitations (in terms of human rights and humanitarian grounds) on the use of the legislative, executive and judicial instruments of crime control and criminal justice by individual states and the international community. The first drafts of the papers that form the chapters of this book were presented and extensively discussed during an international workshop convened for this purpose at the Max Planck Institute for the Study of Crime, Security and Law (formerly Max Planck Institute for Foreign and International Criminal Law) in Freiburg (Germany) and co-funded by the Max Planck Society (Otto Hahn Award Programme), the University of Bergen and the Research Council Norway. Drawing on the debates and outcomes of the workshop, the final versions of the chapters were prepared and systematically edited not with the (virtually infeasible) purpose of providing an exhaustive and generally (vertically and horizontally) applicable theory of proportionality. Rather, the shared objective was to raise basic (doctrinal and pragmatic) questions, to identify the colliding dynamics, major obstacles and key challenges and to comprehensively

* This book would not have been possible without the fruitful exchanges with, the continuous encouragement by and the collaborative spirit of the contributing authors. The editors' special appreciation goes to Lucia Zedner for her advice and support during the project's initial phases and to Antony Duff for his invaluable comments on early drafts of the research proposal. Last but not least, we are very grateful to Eftychia Bampasika for her outstanding research assistance.

discuss the proposed solutions with respect to the application and enforcement of proportionality criteria and guarantees in contemporary criminal and security matters. It is a common presumption that our modern risk societies are faced with a plethora of visible and invisible enemies. Balancing freedom and security in this globalised (legal) world has indeed turned into nothing less than an attempt at untying a Gordian knot. Against this background, the proportionality of measures of crime prevention and repression is unquestionably an issue of utmost importance, which basic research and legal policy are urgently called to address.

I. Proportionality in Crime Control and Criminal Justice: Challenges and Dilemmas

The editing of the present volume coincided with the outbreak of the coronavirus (COVID-19) pandemic.[1] This novel – even for today's scientifically and technologically highly advanced societies – situation arose at the same time as recently (re-)emerging ('cold' and 'hot') wars and their destructive humanitarian and environmental repercussions, large-scale financial crises with international impact, constantly increasing social inequalities, widespread (in many instances, systemic and gravely violent) incidents of racism and xenophobia and the societal responses thereto in the form of massive distrust and protest movements. The unique conglomeration of symmetric and asymmetric challenges for nation states, the international community of nations and the individual and society (majorities and minorities) as a whole has prompted governments and organisations worldwide to reconsider their official priorities and strategies in the fields of socio- and geopolitics, economics, international relations and, not least, security and criminal justice – not always for the advancement of individual and human rights. The resulting universal consequences in almost every field of social life could not but affect our research as well, particularly with respect to basic viewpoints on the issues addressed here. Due to their diachronic importance for liberal states and democratic legal orders, the volume's main orientation points and thematic questions remained unchanged. This notwithstanding, specific theses and assumptions, especially those debating the relationship between fundamental

[1] Regarding the 'Coronavirus disease (COVID-19) pandemic', see the official updates provided by the World Health Organization, available at: www.who.int/emergencies/diseases/novel-coronavirus-2019. For an interesting collection of legal publications and other research initiatives related to the coronavirus crisis, see www.law.mpg.de. For a summary of the main challenges faced by the judicial systems, including with respect to maintaining the rule of law, protecting human rights and reviewing the proportionality of the emergency rights-restrictive measures, see European Commission for the Efficiency of Justice (CEPEJ) of the Council of Europe Declaration, 'Lessons Learnt and Challenges Faced by the Judiciary during and after the Covid-19 Pandemic', 10 June 2020, CEPEJ (2020)8rev, available at: rm.coe.int/declaration-en/16809ea1e2.

personal freedoms and security, had to be (implicitly or explicitly) re-evaluated in light of recent developments and setbacks in criminal justice and the global security architecture. Still, in the midst of momentous events of unprecedented global proportions, one insight was reaffirmed: the significance of the proportionality concept for preventing arbitrary coercion, preserving vested human rights and guaranteeing the rule of law.

A. Balancing Constellations: Old and New

The raison d'être of public authority, that is, the safeguarding of freedom and human dignity of all individuals, is best reflected in the notions of the social contract and the rule of law. A fundamental *negative* obligation of liberal rule-of-law states and international communities is to limit official (coercive) conduct that restricts human freedoms and poses a direct threat to human dignity. This is mainly achieved by incorporating the (constitutional) definition of individual and human rights into the law. At the same time, modern democratic states and institutions have the *positive* obligation to actively guarantee the unobstructed exercise of these rights. As a result, they are often required to implement security and coercive measures so as to prevent risks that might compromise freedom and human dignity and to protect the public from harm threatened from within and/or from outside a specific area. The control of crime is one major challenge in this respect. The administration and delivery of criminal justice is another: in addition to the provision of preventive instruments of crime control it is also necessary to maintain operational law enforcement and judicial systems geared to providing an effective and fair response to serious infringements of freedoms, individual rights and collective legal interests by other individuals and entities.

Individual freedoms and human rights guarantees, effective security and prevention mechanisms and operational justice systems may very well be essential in maintaining social peace. But there are two faces to Janus: the positive obligation to actively protect freedom and human dignity often clashes with the negative obligation to safeguard people's fundamental rights from institutional interferences. Thus, positive and negative obligations must be constantly weighed and measured against each other. How to arrive at the proper balance is the most difficult question driving pertinent legal research and policy.[2] In contemporary legal systems the competing interests may be balanced at three different levels: the legislative, the executive (administrative/law-enforcing) and the judicial. In search

[2] According to Zedner, particularly in terms of balancing between security and liberty, 'the metaphor of balancing is problematic. The idea of balance, though well-established in political and legal debate, is perilous because it pays too little attention to exactly which threats suffice to tip the scales, what factors are to be balanced, how they should be weighed and in whose interests'; see Lucia Zedner's chapter 7 in this volume (with further references). On the 'necessity of balancing', see Christos Mylonopoulos' chapter 4 in this volume.

of adequate weighing tools and factors, the application of so-called proportionality tests has been extensively explored in the field of constitutional law,[3] whereas in the fields of crime control and criminal justice the scope and limits of the proportionality concept have attracted less doctrinal analysis (save for sentencing issues)[4] or empirical attention.[5]

Its importance not only for individual subjects but also for the systemic integrity of law enforcement and criminal justice cannot be historically denied,[6] but the notion of a proportionate balancing of interests is only one of the many factors which the three branches of public power are called to consider and weigh against each other when designing, applying and enforcing measures of security and crime repression. Although equally difficult to define and verify (at least in empirical terms), a higher-profile concept is that of *effectiveness*. Ever-present in policy programmes and socio-legal debates, effectiveness constitutes an essential part of contemporary crime control strategies, conflict resolution mechanisms and sanction models. Two different ways to examine the effectiveness–proportionality relationship in this context are as a dipole, on the one hand, and as interdependent concepts, on the other. Depending on one's perspective, proportionality can indeed be viewed as being at odds with, setting limits on, or presenting obstacles to the effectiveness of crime control and criminal justice instruments. A more analytical approach, however, suggests that effectiveness actually depends on the

[3] See, eg, R Alexy, 'Constitutional Rights and Proportionality' (2014) 22 *Revus – Journal for Constitutional Theory and Philosophy of Law* 51; A Barak, *Proportionality. Constitutional Rights and Their Limitations* (Cambridge, Cambridge University Press, 2012); D M Beatty, *The Ultimate Rule of Law* (Oxford, Oxford University Press, 2010); G Huscroft, B W Miller and G Webber (eds), *Proportionality and the Rule of Law. Rights, Justification, Reasoning* (Cambridge, Cambridge University Press, 2014); K Möller, 'Proportionality: Challenging the Critics' (2012) 10 *International Journal of Constitutional Law* 709; E T Sullivan and R S Frase, *Proportionality Principles in American Law. Controlling Excessive Government Actions* (New York, Oxford University Press, 2009), which also includes a chapter on American criminal justice. See also the comparative and empirical analyses in M Kremnitzer, T Steiner and A Lang (eds), *Proportionality in Action: Comparative and Empirical Perspectives on the Judicial Practice* (Cambridge, Cambridge University Press, 2020). For further references, see Ralf Poscher's chapter 3 in this volume.

[4] See, eg, N Lacey and H Pickard, 'The Chimera of Proportionality: Institutionalising Limits on Punishment in Contemporary Social and Political Systems' (2015) 78 *Modern Law Review* 216; Y Lee, 'Why Proportionality Matters' (2012) 160 *University of Pennsylvania Law Review* 1835; T Miceli, 'On Proportionality of Punishments and the Economic Theory of Crime' (2018) 46 *European Journal of Law and Economics* 303; J Ryberg and J V Roberts (eds), *Popular Punishment. On the Normative Significance of Public Opinion* (Oxford, Oxford University Press, 2014); J Staihar, 'Proportionality and Punishment' (2015) 100 *Iowa Law Review* 1209; M Thorburn, 'Proportionate Sentencing and the Rule of Law' in L Zedner and J V Roberts (eds), *Principles and Values in Criminal Law and Criminal Justice* (Oxford, Oxford University Press, 2012) 269–84; A von Hirsch, *Deserved Criminal Sentences* (Oxford, Hart Publishing, 2017); A von Hirsch and A Ashworth, *Proportionate Sentencing: Exploring the Principles* (Oxford, Oxford University Press, 2005). In this volume, Julian Roberts' chapter 12 summarises some key components and factors of proportional sentencing and analyses the role of sentencing guidelines in promoting proportionality. In the broader field of punishment, Johan Boucht's chapter 13 in this volume explores the proportionality of the various types of asset confiscation proceedings.

[5] *cf* the bibliography at the end of this volume.

[6] *cf* Nestor Courakis' and Vagia Polyzoidou's chapter 6 in this volume on the historical evolution of the proportionality principle in the field of criminal law and punishment. On the historical origins of proportionality from a constitutional law perspective, see Barak (n 3) 175ff.

proportionality (suitability, necessity and appropriateness) of measures pursuing legitimate aims of criminal policy, and that effectiveness is itself an integral element of proportionality.[7] According to another opinion, the question whether effectiveness and proportionality are in conflict with each other should not be given so much weight. To some extent, particularly in terms of the necessity and appropriateness of the measures at hand, effectiveness and proportionality can be in conflict, and, occasionally, it might appear inevitable to sacrifice one value over the other. Setting aside any symptomatic political eagerness to advertise and promote effectiveness, however, following this approach, balancing and evaluating should be focused on *efficiency* rather than the (supposed) effectiveness of crime control and criminal justice measures; in this case efficiency includes (and, thus, cannot conflict with) proportionality.[8]

Different notions of the balancing processes and the relationship between proportionality and other policy goals may lead to different strategies as to how to configure or reconfigure crime-fighting techniques. Yet, a common prerequisite of, and simultaneously a further challenge for, operational crime control and criminal justice systems is the continuous identification and evaluation of the pragmatic dilemmas faced by legal orders and societies in terms of safeguarding and, in times of conflict, prioritising fundamental norms and values. Traditional risks include potential collisions of rights of different persons as well as of individual and societal interests, notably those concerning personal freedoms, on the one hand, and individual or collective (subjective or objective)[9] security, on the other. It is an undisputed achievement of liberal legal orders that, at least in theory, they have been reserving the use of criminal law, punishment and other powerful coercive instruments – supposedly the most effective and efficient[10] tools of enforcement and conflict resolution – as a response only to the most severe (types) of infringements in this context and, for that matter, have been equipping citizens with sufficient rule-of-law guarantees against the arbitrary exercise of institutional powers. In this sense, the criminal law principle of *ultima ratio* is based, inter alia, on notions of proportionality, leniency and justness; in turn, proportionality encompasses the idea of *ultima ratio*.[11] Of key importance in this regard is the acknowledgment that, today more than ever, liberties must be safeguarded and people must be kept safe not only from crime but also from 'evils that emanate from the state itself'.[12]

[7] See Zedner's chapter 7, focusing on counter-terrorism measures. *cf* also Thomas Elholm's and Konstanze Jarvers' chapters 5 and 11 in this volume.

[8] See R A Duff's chapter 2 in this volume: 'A means of preventing some mischief, or achieving some good, is efficient if and only if it is "suitable", in that it will contribute to the end; *and* "necessary", in that no other less costly way of achieving the end is available (if a less costly means is available, this means is not cost-effective – ie, not efficient); *and* "proportionate *stricto sensu*", in that the mischief to be averted, or the good to be achieved, is significant enough to justify these costs.'

[9] *cf* Zedner's and Elholm's chapters 7 and 5 in this volume.

[10] *cf*, however, Thomas Weigend's chapter 15 in this volume.

[11] *cf* chapters 11, 15 and 7 by Jarvers, Weigend and Zedner respectively.

[12] Duff, chapter 2 in this volume.

These observations are also significant with respect to newly emerging and less traditional risk constellations. Characteristic examples involve polemic labels such as 'war on terror' and 'invisible enemies'. Such phenomena may refer to anything, from international terrorism, terrorists in the making, financiers and ideological supporters of terrorism, to the imperceptible structures of (transnational) organised crime and money laundering, to the sophisticated and virtually untraceable cyberattacks against economic establishments and state institutions. In response to these latest kinds of threats, governments, international organisations and cooperating private actors tend to act proactively, resorting not only to the traditional means of criminal law but also to technologically advanced and operationally flexible preventive and security practices[13] of a permanent or exceptional (turning into permanent) nature. They exhibit an extended range of rights-intrusive characteristics and, more often than not, they are not directed against a particular suspicious behaviour or target but against broad categories of 'pre-suspects', likely security or safety liabilities and 'potential' criminals.

Prevention, security and safety have been generalised priorities also with respect to literally *invisible* threats such as the coronavirus during the COVID-19 pandemic. At first sight, the extensive executive and rights-restrictive measures taken in such situations aim not at controlling crime per se but rather at constraining a widespread exceptional and exogenous hazard. Irrespective of whether one adopts an absolutist or a relativist approach to the protection of fundamental rights against state interferences,[14] the coronavirus crisis has revealed that, in light of an imminent risk to the health and lives of millions or billions of people, the proportionality of imposed limitations often plays a secondary role in both the legal-policy agendas and socio-legal debates. Still, massive administrative restrictions of liberty, movement and privacy rights cannot but also affect the form and operation of current and future crime control and criminal justice systems; and in these systems, where, as mentioned, the most coercive measures ought to be used only as a last resort, the notion of proportionality is immanent. But what exactly is the correlation? Drawing on various official COVID-19 management strategies, we can abstract at least two examples:

First, even emergency and temporary, yet highly intrusive, measures – especially when accompanied by the usual didactic political narrative ('stay safe',

[13] In this volume, see especially the examples in the chapters by Zedner (counter-terrorism measures, eg, suspicionless stops and searches; criminalisation of viewing terrorism-related material online – ch 7), John Jackson (net-widening, guilt by association and reverse burdens of proof in the context of anti-terrorist offences – ch 8), Richard Vogler (use of big data by police and security services – ch 9) and Lorena Bachmaier Winter (mass surveillance and interception of communications – ch 16). For more examples drawn from the 'new security architecture', see U Sieber, 'The New Architecture of Security Law – Crime Control in the Global Risk Society' in U Sieber, V Mitsilegas, C Mylonopoulos, E Billis and N Knust (eds), *Alternative Systems of Crime Control. National, Transnational, and International Dimensions* (Berlin, Duncker & Humblot, 2018) 3–34.

[14] *cf* the discussion in Russell Miller's chapter 10 in this volume.

'stay secure') – may facilitate the ultimate transition from the 'criminal law of the act'[15] to the 'criminal law of the enemy'[16] and to what could be characterised as the 'criminal law of the disobedient'. While fighting an *invisible* global threat, new *visible* enemies of the state and society may arise even in the form of formerly law-abiding citizens, who ought to be controlled and, if necessary, socially distanced or isolated: they are the 'disobedient' – individuals who fail to comply with preventive measures such as the wearing of face masks, quarantine restrictions, personal data registrations, health-check and vaccination requirements. These persons may not only be faced with extraordinary and, in most cases, urgently planned and (in terms of their effectiveness, efficiency and proportionality) insufficiently debated criminal law consequences;[17] as a result of the latter they may also be officially stigmatised as additional risks to the community's security and wellbeing. In turn, attempts to contain this secondary risk source may progressively result in the adoption of stricter coercive measures of general application, penalising further aspects of social life and eventually challenging the application of the *ultima ratio* principle.

Second, as in the cases of mass surveillance or collection and analysis of big data for security reasons, the extended application of highly evolved electronic and artificial intelligence (AI) technologies for the bulk registration, analytic observation and/or tracking of actual or potential health hazards (and 'non-compliant' individuals) may interfere with the privacy rights of large sections of populations not even remotely linked to criminal behaviour of any kind.[18] The national, supranational and international responses to the major terrorism incidents of the past two decades illustrate that nothing may be as permanent as a 'temporary'

[15] ie, fragmentary criminalisation of acts/omissions and harms of a specific minimum gravity as opposed to the criminalisation of thoughts or intentions. *cf* the examples on the design of preparatory terrorism offences in Jackson's chapter 8.

[16] *cf* G Jakobs, 'Bürgerstrafrecht und Feindstrafrecht' (2004) (3) *Höchstrichterliche Rechtsprechung Strafrecht* 88.

[17] On the importance of the means by which such legislation is promulgated and applied, and particularly on procedural effectiveness and pre-legislative scrutiny, *cf* Zedner's chapter 7.

[18] See, eg, the 'unprecedented move to use data secretly gathered to combat terrorism for public health efforts' in Israel (www.nytimes.com/2020/03/16/world/middleeast/israel-coronavirus-cellphone-tracking.html); the deployment of police robots on lockdown patrol in Tunisia (www.bbc.com/news/world-africa-52148639) and of drones for the same purpose in Spain (www.businessinsider.com/spanish-police-using-drones-to-ask-people-stay-at-home-2020-3?r=US&IR=T); the use of smartphone 'selfie apps' to keep track of quarantined people in Poland (www.france24.com/en/20200320-selfie-app-to-keep-track-of-quarantined-poles) and of contact-tracing apps in Singapore (www.latimes.com/world-nation/story/2020-03-24/coronavirus-singapore-trace-together); or the use of electronic wristbands to monitor COVID-19 patients in quarantine in Bahrain (www.wearable-technologies.com/2020/04/bahrain-to-use-electronic-wristbands-to-monitor-covid-19-patients-in-quarantine/) and to enforce quarantine on arriving passengers in Hong Kong (www.cnbc.com/2020/03/18/hong-kong-uses-electronic-wristbands-to-enforce-coronavirus-quarantine.html). For further examples of such (mandatory or voluntary) measures during the coronavirus crisis, see *The Guardian* report 'Growth in Surveillance May Be Hard to Scale Back after Pandemic, Experts Say', 14 April 2020, available at: www.theguardian.com/world/2020/apr/14/growth-in-surveillance-may-be-hard-to-scale-back-after-coronavirus-pandemic-experts-say.

security programme.[19] Emergency legislation declaring war on terror and justifying mass surveillance as an exceptional but necessary tool for the purpose of fulfilling the legitimate policy aim of security may easily end up promoting a permanent framework of general and 'blindly' intrusive measures of crime prevention and repression.[20] Accordingly, the urgent needs for protection created by exosystemic and unpredictable large-scale crises such as the COVID-19 pandemic may not only justify exceptional measures aimed at keeping the population safe and secure by restraining, inter alia, well-established privacy rights. Depending on ruling authorities and dominant ideologies, there is always the, hopefully remote but surely dystopian, possibility that they might also serve as a Trojan Horse for establishing an indelible reality of endless people-tracking and state supervision with immediate consequences in the fields of crime control and criminal justice.[21] After all, taking into account the current multifaceted societal challenges described above, there is no question that safety and security have a comforting effect – even when promoted at the expense of privacy. Under these circumstances, the social acceptance not only of state-imposed but also of 'voluntary' or 'quasi-voluntary' surveillance systems, for example of advanced location- and contact-tracing smartphone applications, can be expected to be broad; and this despite the fact that, at least at this early stage of technical development and in view of the insufficient legal guarantees put in place so far, such AI-based applications are hardly free from the dangers of manipulation, discrimination, non-transparency and lack of accountability.[22] Considering the (implicitly or explicitly) uneven allocation of weight to the different interests on both sides of the scale (life and health versus personal privacy), the degree of public acceptance of such control measures and mechanisms may eventually turn out to be comparable to, or even higher than, the one enjoyed by other ('voluntary' turning into coercive) systems such as the Chinese social credit. In fact, if the surveys are a true reflection of social reality, the social credit system already appears to meet with high approval in the relevant population.[23]

Overall, it is in contexts like these where emotive rhetorical strategies designed to increase public acceptance and policy programmes symbolically oriented toward sending ideological signals of social unity (or social marginalisation for

[19] Paraphrasing M Friedman and R Friedman, *Tyranny of the Status Quo* (San Diego, CA, Harcourt Brace Jovanovich, 1984) 115.

[20] *cf* the problems raised in Bachmaier Winter's chapter 16.

[21] See, eg, the interesting examples given by Y N Harari, 'The World after Coronavirus', *Financial Times*, 20 March 2020, available at: www.ft.com/content/19d90308-6858-11ea-a3c9-1fe6fedcca75.

[22] See, eg, European Institute of Innovation & Technology, 'The European Struggle with COVID-19 Contact Tracing Apps', 29 April 2020, available at: eit.europa.eu/news-events/news/european-struggle-covid-19-contact-tracing-apps. For an overview of the problems and challenges of artificial intelligence in terms of proportionality, see E Billis, N Knust and J P Rui, 'Künstliche Intelligenz und der Grundsatz der Verhältnismäßigkeit' in H Kudlich, M Engelhart and B Vogel (eds), *Festschrift für Ulrich Sieber* (Berlin, Duncker & Humblot, 2020 forthcoming).

[23] On the social credit system, its dangers and its peculiar public acceptance, see the analysis and references in Vogler's chapter 9.

that matter) may reach their peak. Aspects of symbolic application of criminal law and other control measures – which do not necessarily rely on scientific proof and reasoning but primarily aim at evoking certain emotions – can be found in even the most liberal of democratic societies.[24] It is doubtful whether symbolically grounded instruments of crime control and criminal justice are, by definition, able to fulfil the rational requirements of proportionality. Rather than concentrating on effectiveness and proportionality (suitability, necessity and appropriateness) in terms of protecting certain legal interests from specific dangers, they usually resort to vague justifications involving broadly defined 'moral beliefs' and 'collective sentiments'. Thus, emphasis is placed on social solidarity, social cohesion and coherence, comfort and compliance, ethical virtuousness and moral order, the feelings of safety, security and togetherness, common national values, etc.

Interestingly, as we can witness, for example, during the current COVID-19 pandemic, when it comes to enforcing exceptionally coercive measures in order to address security challenges and safety risks of such global proportions, even the most extreme policies which resort to the rhetorical devices of panic and fear need (to appear) to be supported by sufficient scientific data. Nonetheless, however thorough the scientific risk assessment may be, it cannot always offer absolute certainty regarding the actual effectiveness of the proposed legal responses and, most importantly, regarding the magnitude of their potential collateral impact on other legally regulated aspects of social life. To the extent that field-specific science cannot be definite, both its blind pursuit and its political instrumentalisation may raise serious proportionality issues in terms of the restrictions imposed. In old and new risk and balancing constellations alike, not to assign proportionality its proper weight – symbolically and pragmatically – as both a temperate (*μηδὲν ἄγαν*)[25] method of controlling public power and a rational factor of social legitimacy, means not only to compromise traditional criminal law principles and human rights policies but also to jeopardise the functionality of legal systems in the long term.

B. Proportionality and Social Legitimacy

Proportionality can have a strong legitimising effect in terms of enhancing public acceptance of measures of crime prevention and repression. Legitimacy traditionally rests on the de facto prevalent notion of the validity of decisions and their legal bases.[26] In functionally differentiated societies and their corresponding plurality of self-referential observations, the legitimacy of a decision-maker's actions can no longer be based on references to external sources (religion, a

[24] See the examples and analysis in Elholm's chapter 5.

[25] (Mēdèn ágan) 'nothing in excess'. See also in this volume chapter 14 by Michael Bothe and Emanuela-Chiara Gillard as well as chapter 6 by Courakis and Polyzoidou.

[26] N Luhmann, *Legitimation durch Verfahren* (Frankfurt am Main, Suhrkamp Verlag, 1983) 27, 28.

certain God, a higher virtuousness, etc); rather, it originates from within, it refers to itself and its interconnectedness. Thus, legitimation is at the same time self-legitimation: decision-makers as well as addressees of decisions must meet a certain cognitive expectation and are expected to learn through decisions. Accordingly, decisions can be regarded as legitimate on the assumption that any third party normatively expects that those affected by them will cognitively adjust to what the decision-makers communicate as normative expectations. The institutional aspect of legitimacy resides therefore in the presumption of acceptance.

Legitimacy is not just a social construct; it also depends on the perceptions of individuals within their belief systems. The normative reality produced and nurtured by the state has no legitimising power if its citizens do not believe in it. At the same time, a system is only legitimate as long as people trust its rightful existence and function. Thus, obtaining and maintaining legitimacy is about shaping beliefs by gaining acceptance with respect to a particular content and by making legitimation a strategic process involving justifications as well as efforts to influence public opinion.[27] This has become apparent, for example, with respect to the measures adopted against the 'war on terror' and, more recently, in the context of the COVID-19 crisis management.

According to Max Weber there are three pure types of legitimate domination (authority):

> The validity of the claims to legitimacy can be based on:
>
> 1. Rational grounds – resting on a belief in the legality of enacted rules and the right of those elevated to authority under such rules to issue commands (legal authority).
> 2. Traditional grounds – resting on an established belief in the sanctity of immemorial traditions and the legitimacy of those exercising authority under them (traditional authority); or finally,
> 3. Charismatic grounds – resting on devotion to the exceptional sanctity, heroism or exemplary character of an individual person, and of the normative patterns or order revealed or ordained by him (charismatic authority).[28]

Even if there are indications of a return to charismatic and traditional grounds today, such as in the context of the alt-right movements[29] and the COVID-19 crisis, rational grounds continue to form the main basis of legitimate authority, particularly in terms of measures of crime control and criminal justice. Legal-rational legitimation focuses on laws and regulations as guarantees that rationality applies to the system's bureaucratic structure as a whole. As long as the general public is

[27] *cf* the analysis in Vogler's chapter 9 in this volume.

[28] M Weber, *Wirtschaft und Gesellschaft*, 5th edn (Tübingen, Mohr, 1980) 124, English translation in G Roth and C Wittich (eds), *Max Weber's Economy and Society* (Berkeley CA, University of California Press, 1978) 215.

[29] The alt-right, an abbreviation of alternative right, is a loosely connected far-right, white nationalist movement based in the United States.

convinced of 'rationality' and its proper implementation in the bureaucratic structure, individuals will continue to grant legitimacy to a system that works according to a principle they embrace. By integrating additional exosystemic information, the concept of proportionality promotes and supports 'rationality'; in its function as an essential guarantee of fairness and procedural justice it serves as one more piece of the puzzle in the scheme of checks and balances applied for reviewing the imposition of coercive measures.[30]

In the system of crime control and criminal justice, legitimacy is also established through procedures. Legally regulated procedures aim at the distribution of decisions and policies on highly complex topics through the reduction of complexity.[31] Unlike self-evident scientific truths, the social recognition of policies, rules and regulations that have been adopted requires special justification.

In highly individualised societies, legitimacy is difficult to achieve by taking into account each individual opinion on every possible topic. Actual social systems are incapable of coping with the immense plurality of individual opinions and topics. Thus, there is a systemic necessity for reducing complexity and plurality.[32] This objective requires a social system in the form of a procedure where the generally binding recognition of decisions is institutionalised. A procedure in this sense corresponds to an interactive social system for producing collectively binding and acceptable decisions within a given time. In legal, administrative and political contexts, procedures are designed to resolve conflicts by providing the affected parties with an active role in the interactive information exchange, with the purpose of producing a comprehensible outcome. Each participant has the chance to incorporate his/her ideas and information into the procedure in order to integrate all perspectives and evidence into the decision-making system. By their selective actions, the parties involved proceed towards a concrete result by continuing to exclude more and more alternative ways of proceeding. The legal norms providing the procedural framework must not be equated with the proceedings themselves. The procedural rules merely reduce complexity by restricting the types of conduct open to the parties involved. It is precisely the function of legally regulated procedures to leave different possibilities of conduct at the parties' disposal so as to enable them to adopt behavioural roles.[33] The integration of proportionality into the procedure facilitates, along with additional impulses and 'external' assessment factors, the production of a decision through the procedure itself.

Nevertheless, the procedure is less about generating a factual consensus of all parties and more about decoupling the general acceptance of procedurally

[30] See the examples analysed in the chapters by Duff (ch 2), Elholm (ch 5), Jackson (ch 8), Vogler (ch 9) and Zedner (ch 7).

[31] On the role of procedure in the legal and political system in general, see Luhmann (n 26).

[32] For a detailed discussion on complexity and the legal system, see N Luhmann, *Rechtssoziologie*, 3rd edn (Opladen, Westdeutscher Verlag, 1987) 31–39.

[33] N Luhmann, *Das Recht der Gesellschaft* (Frankfurt am Main, Suhrkamp Verlag, 1995) 333; Luhmann (n 32) 141–45, 173–78, 218.

generated decisions from the willingness of those directly affected to agree.[34] Proportionality assumes a corrective function within this process by producing a decision based on legal-rational grounds, which those involved and those affected by 'rationality' and 'traceability' can comprehend.

The concept of proportionality also plays an essential role in the 'creation of law' by the courts with respect to the application of their procedures and the resulting decisions. In applying proportionality tests the courts do not merely engage in a cognitive act but carry out a proper assessment.[35] The extensive application of proportionality within the legal system indicates a broader interpretation by the courts of their law-constitutive role by extending their sphere of control.[36] Applying proportionality criteria generates for the courts the possibility to take law-constitutive decisions on topics with immediate impact on the political system, thus causing irritations within other social systems.

One example where this can be observed is in the context of modern warfare. Today, the law and the legal system are shaping the institutional, logistical and physical landscape of war.[37] The proportionality principle is of vital importance in international humanitarian law for the legal evaluation of military actions by courts and tribunals. By using proportionality assessments, the courts can feed 're-coded' content and interpretations into the decision-making process and, thus, into the legal system, which normally fall within the scope of the political or administrative powers. This type of structural coupling of the legal with the political system is primarily known from constitutional law.[38] However, in terms of the general application of proportionality by the courts, the coupling is not permanent. The content of other social systems is only fed into the legal system if a court has the corresponding decision-making competence and if this is done 'lawfully'. As such, this can be regarded as the activity of a structurally determined and environmentally adapted system, which is bound to its task and self-preservation by a reference test of the system and its environment. The idea behind this coupling is to limit irritations from the external environment on the legal system and, at the same time, to guide the impulses.[39] This fundamental operational unity of the legal system against the influences of the political and the economic system is created by the functional differentiation according to which each system operates on its own. Only in certain interrelationships, provided specifically for this purpose, can the interaction be selectively carried out via

[34] For a detailed analysis in the context of post-conflict situations, see N Knust, *Strafrecht und Gacaca* (Berlin, Dunker & Humblot, 2013).

[35] See M Cohen-Eliya and I Porat, 'Proportionality and the Culture of Justification' (2011) 59 *American Journal of Comparative Law* 463–90; A von Bogdandy and I Venzke, *In wessen Namen? – Internationale Gerichte in Zeiten globalen Regierens* (Berlin, Suhrkamp Verlag, 2014) 142.

[36] von Bogdandy and Venzke (n 35) 142.

[37] See D Kennedy, *Of War and Law* (Princeton NJ, Princeton University Press, 2006). On international humanitarian law and proportionality, see Bothe's and Gillard's chapter 14 in this volume.

[38] See Luhmann, *Das Recht der Gesellschaft* (n 33) 468–81.

[39] For details, see ibid 440–96.

clearly defined linkages.[40] The proportionality test constitutes such a selective linkage, providing a very limited and strictly defined 'gateway' for the legal system to actively interact with other social systems such as politics, the economy, etc. Proportionality schemes furnish the legal system with new information that is re-coded into a code (legal–illegal) on which the operation or evaluation of the legal system can be based. The huge impact of proportionality on the legal system may be observed wherever the principle is more vigorously debated: before constitutional courts, courts of last resort and international courts. By facilitating the interaction and cross-evaluation between different social systems while strengthening the checks and balances of both the legal and the political systems, proportionality is indispensable for obtaining and maintaining social legitimacy.

II. Conceptualising and Applying Proportionality: Typological Considerations

A. 'Proportionality' or 'Proportionalities'?

(i) Proportionality Types and Models

Is there only one or are there different types of proportionality aimed at fulfilling these crucial functions of administering crime control and delivering criminal justice? Is there actually a 'global proportionality paradigm'[41] that categorises legal systems according to their approach to the interpretation of rights and the implementation of rights restrictions?

Obviously, essentially diverse legal traditions and systems may develop different ways to define, substantiate and appraise abstract concepts. Different notions of proportionality may also be noted in different areas of the law in one and the same system, for example constitutional law, administrative law and criminal law, or within different disciplines in the same legal field, for example substantive law (eg, with respect to criminalisation[42] and the limits of self-defence[43]), procedure (eg, regarding the applicability conditions for coercive measures such as searches, communication interceptions, arrest warrants and pre-trial detentions)[44] and sentencing (eg, concerning the assessment of the seriousness of crimes and penalties).[45]

[40] ibid 468–81.
[41] Miller, chapter 10 in this volume.
[42] *cf* Duff's, Elholm's and Jarvers' chapters 2, 5 and 11 respectively.
[43] See Courakis' and Polyzoidou's chapter 6. In the context of *ius ad bellum*, see Bothe's and Gillard's chapter 14.
[44] *cf* the examples in the chapters by Anagnostopoulos (ch 17), Bachmaier Winter (ch 16), Jackson (ch 8), Vogler (ch 9) and Zedner (ch 7) in this volume.
[45] On the absolute and relative seriousness of crimes (ordinal and cardinal proportionality), see Roberts' chapter 12. *cf* also Duff's and Weigend's chapters 2 and 15 respectively.

The best-known 'overall' dichotomy in this context is between *retrospective* and *prospective* proportionality, which primarily serves purposes of conceptualisation and analysis and focuses on the diversity of objects and functions of proportionality assessments:

> Retrospective proportionality is the proportionality of a present response to a past event. The obvious example is that of present punishment to past crime. ... Retrospective proportionality figures in several ways in the criminal law – not only in sentencing. ... Prospective proportionality, by contrast, is of means to ends, of present action to the goal that it is intended to serve. ... This species of proportionality is central to discussions of proportionality as a constitutional principle.[46]

On some occasions, the dividing lines between the two types are blurred and considerations of the one may interfere with or also be relevant to the other.[47] This may allow for a variety of methods to implement proportionality, without necessarily impacting on the definition of its individual elements or affecting its (cross-systemically) unchanged conceptual core: the notions of *μηδέν ἄγαν* and *ultima ratio*. Neither does the dichotomy directly address key proportionality issues such as problems of balancing and incommensurability – but it does offer an analytical framework for discussing possible solutions.

At a more abstract level, it is theoretically possible, based on the observation of actual legal systems or groups of systems, to categorise the various approaches to the interpretation of rights and the implementation of rights restrictions into general proportionality models. One prominent example is the distinction between systems that adopt an absolutist approach to the interpretation and application of fundamental rights, rejecting any form of proportionate balancing of interests, and systems that always engage in proportional adjudication when a conflict over rights arises.[48] Notwithstanding the ongoing 'battle' between contextualist comparatists and functionalist comparatists, ideal-typical constructs such as those just mentioned should not be perceived as something more or something less than they really are: a tool for designing the framework for further comparisons – and a fictional standard against which real similarities and differences between phenomena can be measured for illustrative purposes.[49] Whether and to what degree the

[46] Duff, chapter 2 in this volume. In his chapter 13, Boucht also uses the terms backward-looking and forward-looking as well as 'quantification proportionality' and 'norm proportionality'. Elholm notes in his chapter 5: 'The distinction between retrospective and prospective concepts is important in order to illustrate two different ways of operating with proportionality in rule-of-law states. However, the distinction should not be exaggerated: the two approaches derive from the same principle and are closely related, using partly the same tools to measure proportionality, for example, the notions of *de minimis* and appropriateness.' For a historical account, involving also the notions of retributivism and utilitarianism/consequentialism, see Courakis' and Polyzoidou's chapter 6.

[47] See the detailed analysis in Duff's chapter 2; see also Boucht's chapter 13.

[48] See the analysis in Miller's chapter 10.

[49] See E Billis, 'On the Methodology of Comparative Criminal Law Research: Paradigmatic Approaches to the Research Method of Functional Comparison and the Heuristic Device of Ideal Types' (2017) 24 *Maastricht Journal of European and Comparative Law* 864, 872ff with references to Max Weber's theory on ideal types.

hypothetical statements in the theoretical extreme models correspond to the actual reality of particular systems is a matter of empirical proof and should not allow for prejudices and rushed conclusions when conceptualising and applying proportionality.

This is not to say that paradigms do not vary in terms of how proportionality assessments are theoretically synthesised and practically implemented in various constellations within the same legal system, within diverse national legal orders of the same or different traditions, or within the plurality of international legal disciplines and jurisdictions. In this context, particular attention must be paid to the ways in which institutional and procedural aspects may interact and affect the definition and application of the proportionality concept. Assessments may differ in terms of function, focus, direction and content between *legislative proportionality* and *proportionality in adjudication* – usually, however, the first will determine the normative scope of the latter and the latter will have a de facto informative impact on the first.[50] Along with the extensive variety of legal sources, cultural backgrounds and systemic idiosyncrasies, it is the diversity of missions and democratic functions assigned to legislative organs, international, supranational, constitutional and supreme courts, ordinary criminal and sentencing courts, law enforcement authorities, sentencing and oversight commissions and other judicial, administrative or political bodies responsible for designing, implementing and/or reviewing crime control strategies that dynamically informs the content and normative significance of proportionality.[51]

(ii) The Paradigm of the ECtHR's Proportionality Concept

Take, for example, the mission and inherent (operational) limitations of an international human rights adjudicating body like the European Court of Human Rights (ECtHR). Despite the fact that the majority of the rights and freedoms of the European Convention on Human Rights (ECHR) are not absolute, in the sense that states can restrict them given certain conditions, there is no explicit reference to the term 'proportionality' in the ECHR provisions determining these conditions.

> Nevertheless, the search for a fair balance between the demands of the general interest of the community, on the one hand, and fundamental rights of the individual, on the

[50] See Billis, Knust and Rui (n 22).

[51] The chapters in the present volume touch on these institutional and procedural matters in different jurisdictions, eg, with respect to: the functional role, focus and influence of constitutional and supreme courts in terms of implementing and enforcing proportionality in different security- and criminal justice-related constellations (Boucht (ch 13), Elholm (ch 5), Jackson (ch 8), Miller (ch 10), Zedner (ch 7)); the mission, scope of action and systemic limitations of international, supranational and human rights organisations and courts in terms of proportionality considerations (Anagnostopoulos (ch 17), Bachmaier Winter (ch 16), Bothe and Gillard (ch 14), Boucht (ch 13), Elholm (ch 5), Weigend (ch 15)); the objectives, advantages and shortcomings of parliaments, legislative councils and sentencing commissions regarding proportionality debates and strategies (Roberts (ch 12), Zedner (ch 7)); and the discretion of prosecuting and law enforcement authorities regarding proportionality decisions (Duff (ch 2), Jarvers (ch 11)).

> other, is inherent in the Convention's entire system. To achieve this balance requires a proportionality assessment.[52]

More concretely, the ECHR has no provision on the proportionality of offences and penalties. The ECtHR's main position regarding this kind of proportionality is that, while on rare and unique occasions 'a grossly disproportionate sentence would violate Article 3 of the Convention', it is not for the Court to decide on the appropriate penalty for a particular offence, since

> as a rule issues relating to just and proportionate punishment are the subject of rational debate and civilised disagreement. Accordingly, Contracting States must be allowed a margin of appreciation in deciding on the appropriate length of prison sentences for particular crimes.[53]

Furthermore, proportionality considerations are relevant, even if not expressly stated in the Convention, with respect to the conditions, scope and severity of restrictions imposed by the states on the rights to life (Article 2), to liberty and security (Article 5)[54] and to respect for private and family life (Article 8) as well as the freedoms of thought, conscience and religion (Article 9), of expression (Article 10) and of assembly and association (Article 11). Article 2 ECHR prescribes three distinct legitimate aims justifying interfering with the right to life and the interference must be 'absolutely necessary'. Article 5 ECHR provides for several legitimate aims justifying interfering with the right to personal liberty and security, but the provision's wording does not require that such interference be necessary. Articles 8–11 ECHR provide that the protected rights and freedoms may only be restricted according to law if the states anchor the interference to one of the prescribed legitimate aims and if the interference is 'necessary in a democratic society'.[55] Finally, according to Article 15 ECHR, a derogation from the

[52] Robert Spano in the foreword to this volume.

[53] *Vinter and Others v United Kingdom* App nos 66069/09, 130/10 and 3896/10 (ECtHR GC, 9 July 2013) [102], [105] with further references. On the scope of the proportionality review and the 'fair balance' requirement in the ECtHR case law regarding cases of asset confiscation under Article 1 ECHR-Protocol No 1, see Boucht's chapter 13. See also the analysis in V Mitsilegas and E Billis, 'Article 49 – Principles of Legality and Proportionality of Criminal Offences and Penalties' in S Peers, T Hervey, J Kenner and A Ward (eds), *The EU Charter of Fundamental Rights. A Commentary*, 2nd edn (Oxford, Hart Publishing, 2021 forthcoming).

[54] See also Art 2(3) ECHR-Protocol No 4 (freedom of movement); Art 1(2) ECHR-Protocol No 7 (procedural safeguards relating to expulsion of aliens).

[55] The list of legitimate aims consists of: the protection of the interests of national security, public safety and the economic well-being of the country, the prevention of disorder or crime, the protection of health or morals and the protection of the rights and freedoms of others (Art 8(2) ECHR); the protection of the interests of public safety, of public order, health or morals and of the rights and freedoms of others (Art 9(2) ECHR); the protection of the interests of national security, territorial integrity and public safety, the prevention of disorder or crime, the protection of health or morals, the protection of the reputation or rights of others, the prevention of the disclosure of information received in confidence and maintaining of the authority and impartiality of the judiciary (Art 10(2) ECHR); and the protection of the interests of national security and public safety, the prevention of disorder or crime, the protection of health or morals and the protection of the rights and freedoms of others (Art 11(2) ECHR).

corresponding Convention obligations is possible in times of war or other public emergency 'to the extent strictly required by the exigencies of the situation';[56] moreover, Article 18 ECHR states that the restrictions permitted under the ECHR on its rights and freedoms shall not be applied for purposes other than those for which they have been prescribed.[57]

One example of contemporary significance in the context of rights restrictions is the regulation and limitation of state interferences with the fundamental right of Article 8 ECHR in cases of mass surveillance for security purposes. It is difficult to deny the need for thorough proportionality checks of such highly intrusive measures, especially in view of the significant socio-legal and human rights challenges described above. Nevertheless, relevant ECtHR case law reveals a rather restrained approach to limiting states' powers.[58] This is rooted in the subsidiary role politically assigned to the ECtHR,[59] which is functionally complemented by the margin-of-appreciation doctrine; in accordance with the latter, national authorities have a certain discretion in choosing the necessary means for achieving the legitimate aim (in this particular scenario: to protect 'national security'). Accordingly, the Court focuses its control in terms of the 'Conventionality' of interferences (a) on the presence of a legitimate aim leading to the restriction of rights, (b) on the fulfilment of the usual legality requirements (foreseeability, accessibility) of the imposed measures and (c) on the adequacy and effectiveness of the existing safeguards (eg, oversight mechanisms) against potential abuses of power. These safeguards, put in place by the national authorities, must be adequate guarantees for keeping the interferences caused by bulk surveillance measures to what is 'necessary in a democratic society'.[60] However, in terms of the actual assessment of the proportionality elements and the balancing between the competing interests of privacy and security, the ECtHR gives precedence to the domestic evaluations.[61]

[56] For a proportionality analysis and ECtHR case-law references regarding the adoption of emergency legislation (anti-terrorism measures) derogating from the provisions of Art 5 ECHR, see Jackson's chapter 8; *cf* also Zedner's chapter 7.

[57] See also Art 17 ECHR (prohibition of abuse of rights): 'Nothing in this Convention may be interpreted as implying for any State, group or person any right to engage in any activity or perform any act aimed at the destruction of any of the rights and freedoms set forth herein or at their limitation to a greater extent than is provided for in the Convention.'

[58] For a detailed examination of the respective challenges for the rule of law and the shortcomings of the relevant ECtHR case law in that respect, see Bachmaier Winter's chapter 16.

[59] On the recent political declarations of the Member States of the Council of Europe highlighting the subsidiary function of the ECtHR, most notably within the framework of the High Level Conferences of Interlaken, Izmir, Brighton, Brussels and Copenhagen, see, eg, J P Rui, 'The Interlaken, Izmir and Brighton Declarations: Towards a Paradigm Shift in the Strasbourg Court's Interpretation of the European Convention of Human Rights?' (2013) 31 *Nordic Journal of Human Rights* 28–54; R Spano, 'Universality or Diversity of Human Rights? Strasbourg in the Age of Subsidiarity' (2014) 14 *Human Rights Law Review* 487, 498–99; L R Glas, 'From Interlaken to Copenhagen: What Has Become of the Proposals Aiming to Reform the Functioning of the European Court of Human Rights?' (2020) 20 *Human Rights Law Review* 121–51.

[60] See Spano's foreword.

[61] See Bachmaier Winter's chapter 16.

To this end, the Court currently employs a process-based review system, which shifts

> the Court's primary methodological focus from its own independent assessment of the 'Conventionality' of the domestic measure towards an examination of whether the issue has been properly analysed by the domestic decision-maker in conformity with already embedded principles and the States' obligations to secure Convention rights to peoples within their jurisdictions.[62]

Another example raising serious proportionality questions, illustrating this kind of approach, is the restriction on the right to respect for private life (Article 8 ECHR) of women who wish to wear a full-face veil for reasons related to their beliefs, and of their freedom to manifest those beliefs (Article 9 ECHR). In a significant Grand Chamber judgment of 2014 concerning a legislative ban on wearing clothing designed to conceal the face in public places, accompanied by criminal sanctions in case of refusal to comply with this measure, the ECtHR took into account the subsidiary role of the Convention system and stated that:

> [129] The State should thus, in principle, be afforded a *wide margin of appreciation* in deciding whether and to what extent a limitation of the right to manifest one's religion or beliefs is *'necessary'* ... [131] The Court's task is to determine whether the measures taken at national level were justified in principle and proportionate ... [139] in view of its impact on the rights of women who wish to wear the full-face veil for religious reasons, a blanket ban on the wearing in public places of clothing designed to conceal the face can be regarded as proportionate only in a context where there is a general threat to public safety ... [152] As to the fact that criminal sanctions are attached to the ban, this no doubt increases the impact of the measure on those concerned. It is certainly understandable that the idea of being prosecuted for concealing one's face in a public place is traumatising for women who have chosen to wear the full-face veil for reasons related to their beliefs. It should nevertheless be taken into account that the sanctions provided for by the Law's drafters are among the lightest that could be envisaged, since they consist of a fine ... [153] The question whether or not it should be permitted to wear the full-face veil in public places constitutes a *choice of society* ... [154] In such circumstances, the Court has a duty to exercise a degree of *restraint* in its review of Convention compliance, since such review will lead it to assess a *balance* that has been struck by means of a *democratic process* within the society in question. The Court has, moreover, already had occasion to observe that in *matters of general*

[62] R Spano, 'The Future of the European Court of Human Rights – Subsidiarity, Process-Based Review and the Rule of Law' (2018) 18 *Human Rights Law Review* 473, 480–81. On this procedural approach of the ECtHR, see also O de Schutter and F Tulkens, 'Rights in Conflict: The European Court of Human Rights as a Pragmatic Institution' in E Brems (ed), *Conflicts between Fundamental Rights* (Antwerp, Intersentia, 2008) 188–89; Rui (n 59); Spano (n 59) 498–99; O M Arnardóttir, 'The "Procedural Turn" under the European Convention on Human Rights and Presumptions of Convention Compliance' (2017) 15 *International Journal of Constitutional Law* 9–35; J Gerards and E Brems, 'Procedural Review in European Fundamental Rights Cases: Introduction' in J Gerards and E Brems (eds), *Procedural Review in European Fundamental Rights Cases* (Cambridge, Cambridge University Press, 2017) 1–14; T Kleinlein, 'The Procedural Approach of the European Court of Human Rights: Between Subsidiarity and Dynamic Evolution' (2019) 68 *International & Comparative Law Quarterly* 91–110; Glas (n 59).

> *policy*, on which opinions within a democratic society may reasonably differ widely, the *role of the domestic policy-maker should be given special weight* … [157] Consequently, having regard in particular to the breadth of the margin of appreciation afforded to the respondent State in the present case, the Court finds that the ban imposed by the Law of 11 October 2010 can be regarded as proportionate to the aim pursued, namely the preservation of the conditions of 'living together' as an element of the 'protection of the rights and freedoms of others' … [158] The impugned limitation can thus be regarded as 'necessary in a democratic society' … [159] Accordingly, there has been no violation either of Article 8 or of Article 9 of the Convention (emphasis added).[63]

Generally, the main responsibility for securing respect for the ECHR's rights and freedoms, and, consequently, for applying any rights restrictions only in accordance with the (proportionality) conditions provided by the Convention system itself lies with the Member States of the Council of Europe (Article 1 ECHR). Regarding authorised state interferences with protected rights, the first and *primary* evaluator of their proportionality will be, in most cases, the democratic law-maker. The competent national courts are the *secondary* evaluator of the proportionality of the restrictive measures. The ECtHR is in this scenario a potential *third* evaluator, however one that lacks both the direct democratic legitimacy of national parliaments and the direct constitutional legitimacy of national courts. Subsidiarity, margin of appreciation and a process-based review characterise the exercise of the ECtHR's control over national legal orders regarding the proportionate implementation of rights restrictions. Raising the status of the margin of appreciation to a quasi-autonomous (institutional) component that informs the scope and content of the remaining functional components of the proportionality test[64] sharply distinguishes the ECtHR's complex concept from other adjudication models of proportionality. Nonetheless, such an approach is exclusively tailored to the limited jurisdiction and enforcing capacities of this particular human rights court. It should in no way lead to an undermining of the core content and importance of proportionality as an indispensable principle or rule for safeguarding fundamental rights and freedoms from abuses of state power in modern legal systems.

B. Principle or Rule?

(i) Terminology and Content

In legal philosophy, *principles versus rules* constitutes a familiar and much debated distinction, primarily with regard to the binding nature of constitutional rights and the corresponding margin of limitations.[65] In terms of crime control and criminal

[63] *S.A.S. v France* App no 43835/11 (ECtHR GC, 1 July 2014). For an extensive comparative analysis, see Elholm's chapter 5.

[64] See Spano's foreword.

[65] See Miller's and Mylonopoulos' chapters 10 and 4 respectively.

justice semantics, the different labels associated with proportionality – principle, rule, concept, notion, etc – are often used interchangeably. In substance, proportionality is, first and foremost, recognised as a basic 'technique of legal reasoning'[66] and a tool of checks and balances that limits the exercise of public power. Labelling may depend on the normative choices of legal systems when appraising proportionality in the 'hierarchy' of rule-of-law guarantees. If rights are always absolute, there is in fact no need for a proportionality 'principle' or 'rule'. If, however, rights are in one way or another limitable, a fair balancing of the competing interests will on many occasions be invoked as a central factor of operability and integrity of the legal systems as well as of social legitimacy. Proportionality may then be treated as a guiding principle and optimisation requirement[67] and/or as a generally applicable rule that determines the outcome of conflicts and can be further specified in the form of various tests and assessment types.

In constitutional contexts relevant to crime control, such as in assessing the proportionality of intrusive security measures, law-makers, (constitutional) courts and scholars tend to resort to the term 'principle'.[68] In national criminal law and justice, most characteristically regarding the requirement of proportionate sentencing, both the terms 'principle' and 'concept', as well as 'proportionality' as a stand-alone word, are widely used.[69] At the levels of international humanitarian and criminal law – notwithstanding the considerable enforcement challenges – various international conventions, statutes and court judgments include normative aspects of the general 'principle of proportionality' in times of war, important notions of 'sentencing proportionality' before international courts as well as 'proportionality rules of engagement' in the context of armed conflicts.[70] Furthermore, at the level of the international human rights system of the ECHR, the Convention text does not expressly refer to any form of proportionality, as mentioned above; nevertheless, by establishing dynamic standards of review to fit the Court's *sui generis* mission and functions, ECtHR case law has proclaimed its importance as a human rights principle and general requirement that shapes and sets limits to the restriction of rights.[71] Finally, the example of the EU legal framework is in this context informative with respect to supranational systems.

(ii) The Paradigm of the EU Proportionality Concept

In the complex supranational system of the European Union, the general principle of proportionality plays a central role in limiting the action of EU organs.

[66] Bothe and Gillard, chapter 14 in this volume.

[67] *cf* Mylonopoulos, chapter 4 in this volume (with further references).

[68] See, eg, the chapters by Duff (ch 2), Elholm (ch 5), Miller (ch 10) and Poscher (ch 3) in this volume.

[69] See, eg, the chapters by Boucht (ch 13), Courakis and Polyzoidou (ch 6), Duff (ch 2), Elholm (ch 5), Jarvers (ch 11), Roberts (ch 12) and Zedner (ch 7).

[70] For specific references, see Mitsilegas and Billis (n 53); see also Billis, Knust and Rui (n 22). In this volume, see Bothe's and Gillard's chapter 14 and Weigend's chapter 15.

[71] For references, see Spano's foreword and Bachmaier Winter's chapter 16. See also Mitsilegas and Billis (n 53).

According to Article 5(1) of the Treaty on European Union (TEU), the use of Union competences is governed by the 'principles of subsidiarity and proportionality'; according to Article 5(4) TEU, under the principle of proportionality, the content and form of EU action shall not exceed what is necessary to achieve the objectives of the EU Treaties.[72] Furthermore, with respect to national action and legislation falling within the scope of or implementing EU law, the Court of Justice of the EU (CJEU) has ruled on more than one occasion that the principle of proportionality is one of the general principles of EU law and requires that measures implemented through provisions of EU law be appropriate for attaining the legitimate objectives pursued by the legislation at issue and must not go beyond what is necessary to achieve them.[73]

In the field of criminal law and justice in particular, Article 49 of the Charter of Fundamental Rights of the European Union (the 'Charter') enshrines the 'principles of legality and proportionality of criminal offences and penalties'.[74] Legality and proportionality had long been established as general principles of the EU legal system even prior to the adoption of the Charter.[75] Article 49 primarily sets concrete normative limits on the state and the EU's power to criminalise; it applies at the stage of adoption of EU legislation in criminal matters, at the stage of interpretation of EU criminal law by the CJEU and national courts, at the stage of implementation of EU law by Member States, and at the stage of scrutiny of national criminalisation and the assessment of its compliance with EU law.[76] In terms of secondary EU law, the proportionality notion can also be located in the generic requirement in EU criminal law instruments for Member States to adopt penalties that are effective, proportionate and dissuasive.[77]

Finally, at the more general level of the protection and lawful restriction of fundamental rights, the Charter states in Article 52(1) that any limitation on the exercise of the rights and freedoms recognised by the Charter must be provided for by law and must respect the essence of those rights and freedoms; subject to the principle of proportionality, limitations may only be imposed if they are necessary and genuinely meet objectives of general interest recognised by the Union or the need to protect the rights and freedoms of others.[78] From this perspective as

[72] According to Art 5(4) TEU, the institutions of the Union shall apply the principle of proportionality as laid down in the Protocol on the application of the principles of subsidiarity and proportionality; according to Art 5 of this Protocol, draft legislative acts by EU institutions must be justified with regard to, and contain a detailed statement making it possible to appraise compliance with, the principle of proportionality. On the so-called 'emergency brake' under Arts 82(3) and 83(3) of the Treaty on the Functioning of the European Union (TFEU) and on other institutional aspects of the proportionality review system, see Mitsilegas and Billis (n 53).

[73] See extensive references in Mitsilegas and Billis (n 53).

[74] According to Art 49(3) of the Charter, the severity of penalties must not be disproportionate to the criminal offence.

[75] According to the Charter Explanations, Art 49(3) 'states the general principle of proportionality between penalties and criminal offences which is enshrined in the common constitutional traditions of the Member States and in the case-law of the Court of Justice of the Communities'.

[76] See Mitsilegas and Billis (n 53).

[77] ibid (with further references).

[78] See, further, Bothe's and Gillard's chapter 14.

well, these components that largely make up the EU concept of proportionality are commonly regarded as essential rule-of-law elements in the constitutional and criminal justice traditions of the EU Member States and beyond.[79]

C. Components of the Proportionality Assessment

Principle or rule, constitutional, security or criminal law, prospective or retrospective interference, legislative or adjudicative evaluation: a core of minimum components appears to remain consistent in the context of the variety of constellations and types of proportionality (means–ends) assessments, even if – depending on actual circumstances, legal-policy priorities, systemic idiosyncrasies and institutional particularities – the degree of emphasis given to each individual element may vary.[80] Notwithstanding the plurality of possible formulations of the precise tests[81] and field-specific criteria[82] of proportionality, these are the consolidated general components:

- the existence of a legitimate aim for adopting a certain measure;
- the suitability/adequacy of the measure for reaching this particular aim;
- the necessity of the measure in view of the aim (requirement of the least intrusive measure); and
- the appropriateness (proportionality *stricto sensu*) of the measure in terms of its right-limiting effects balanced against the benefits of the aim pursued.

This line of assessment may be applied in the areas of crime control and criminal justice with respect to preventive and security measures (for example, administrative rights restrictions accompanied by criminal sanctions), coercive instruments of criminal prosecution and procedure and punishment issues alike.[83] It is recognised, more or less, in the constitutional orders of many national legal systems.[84]

[79] For a detailed analysis of the specific proportionality provisions and its different aspects and components under EU law, see Mitsilegas and Billis (n 53). On the application of the principle to cooperative inter-state arrangements established under mutual recognition in criminal matters, see Anagnostopoulos' chapter 17; see also, inter alia, D Helenius, 'Mutual Recognition in Criminal Matters and the Principle of Proportionality. Effective Proportionality or Proportionate Effectiveness?' (2014) 5 *New Journal of European Criminal Law* 349–69.

[80] *cf* Billis, Knust and Rui (n 22) with further references.

[81] See, eg, the various definitions, references and case studies in the chapters by Bachmaier Winter (ch 16), Boucht (ch 13), Duff (ch 2), Elholm (ch 5), Mylonopoulos (ch 4) and Zedner (ch 7) in this volume.

[82] See, eg, the different constellations examined in the chapters by Anagnostopoulos (judicial assistance and extradition (ch 17)), Boucht (asset confiscation proceedings (ch 13)), Jackson (penal and non-penal anti-terrorism measures (ch 8)), Roberts (sentencing in common law systems (ch 12)) and Weigend (sentencing before international criminal courts (ch 15)).

[83] *cf* also Duff's chapter 2.

[84] See, eg, the references in Billis, Knust and Rui (n 22) and the comparative analyses in Kremnitzer, Steiner and Lang (n 3). In this volume, see also Miller's and Poscher's chapters 10 and 3 respectively.

And it may be detected, with variations, in international contexts as well.[85] As to the ECHR system, while the ECtHR has not yet taken a clear position regarding the cumulative applicability of the aforementioned requirements,[86] scholars seem to agree that a systematic read of the Court's judgments allows, to a certain degree at least, for the identification and use of all four components.[87] Finally, the EU proportionality test, as applied by the CJEU, appears to be focusing on the elements of suitability and necessity; the question whether the requirement of proportionality *stricto sensu* is (or must be) included in the relevant evaluations has not yet been conclusively answered.[88]

While issues of suitability, necessity and effectiveness/efficiency usually prevail in legal-policy debates, most of the theoretical and practical difficulties in appraising proportionality (or disproportionality)[89] are associated with the element of appropriateness; indeed, the actual balancing of the conflicting interests and all major value judgements occur at the level of proportionality *stricto sensu*.[90] Due to the complexity of the different weighing factors, proportionality *stricto sensu* has in fact come under criticism. 'Some claim that it attempts to balance incommensurable items. ... Others assert that balancing is irrational.'[91] To address these concerns, various approaches and solutions have been proposed, including the use of common and independent standards of value (such as Barak's criterion of 'social importance'), mathematic equations and numerical comparisons of individual aspects such as the weight of and interference with colliding principles (as expressed, for example, in the famous Alexy formula), comparisons between degrees of realisation of the competing interests, fuzzy logic and comparative concepts as well as hermeneutics.[92] Still, despite these theoretical attempts and

[85] See Bothe's and Gillard's chapter 14.

[86] For the relevant terminology used in the ECtHR case law, see, eg, L Lavrysen, 'System of Restrictions' in P van Dijk, F van Hoof, A van Rijn and L Zwaak (eds), *The Theory and Practice of the European Convention on Human Rights*, 5th ed (Cambridge, Intersentia, 2018) 307ff; W A Schabas, *The European Convention on Human Rights. A Commentary* (Oxford, Oxford University Press, 2015) 406; Mitsilegas and Billis (n 53).

[87] See, eg, J McBride, 'Proportionality and the European Convention on Human Rights' in E Ellis (ed), *The Principle of Proportionality in the Laws of Europe* (London, Hart Publishing, 1999) 23ff; Barak (n 3) 183–84; J Gerards, 'How to Improve the Necessity Test of the European Court of Human Rights?' (2013) 11 *International Journal of Constitutional Law* 466ff; E Brems and L Lavrysen, '"Don't Use a Sledgehammer to Crack a Nut": Less Restrictive Means in the Case Law of the European Court of Human Rights' (2015) 15 *Human Rights Law Review* 139ff; Schabas (n 86) 406. For a differing analysis, see J Christoffersen, *Fair Balance: Proportionality, Subsidiarity and Primarity in the European Convention on Human Rights* (Leiden, Martinus Nijhoff Publishers, 2009) 112–91. *cf* also Spano's foreword and Bachmaier Winter's chapter 16 in this volume.

[88] See Mitsilegas and Billis (n 53) with references to case law and academic discussion.

[89] On the difficulty of providing a positive definition of proportionality, see Duff's chapter 2. *cf* also the negative formulation of Art 49(3) of the Charter of Fundamental Rights of the European Union, stating that the severity of penalties must not be disproportionate to the criminal offence.

[90] See chapters 2 and 4 by Duff and Mylonopoulos respectively.

[91] A Barak, 'Proportionality and Principled Balancing' (2010) 4 *Law & Ethics of Human Rights* 1, 15–16 (with references).

[92] See the detailed analyses in Poscher's and Mylonopoulos' chapters 3 and 4 with further references.

constructions, incommensurability has not yet ceased to be a 'central and unassailable problem'[93] in terms of defining and applying proportionality.

These barriers encountered in the conceptual synthesis and practical implementation of the proportionality components definitely add to the ambiguities caused by the many ways in which proportionality assessments can be institutionally enforced at national, international and supranational levels. Moreover, rapid technological advancements, which, inter alia, enable the automatic 'real-time' processing of large volumes of personal data worldwide and often assign the decision-making process to autonomous electronic systems,[94] constitute further pragmatic challenges to the proportionality endeavour in general. But this is not to say that proportionality considerations are rendered useless en masse. On the contrary: these are precisely the circumstances where intemperate, excessive and non-accountable responses to trivial and grave threats alike may have the most adverse consequences for the preservation of the rule of law and the effective safeguarding of human rights. Systematically identifying the constituent aspects of the modern dilemmas in crime control and criminal justice and agreeing on (the necessity of) a foundational framework of non-excessiveness and oversight to address them are essential steps for generating a detailed outline for moderate action. The multifaceted exploration of the broad thematic areas covered by the contributions in the present volume aims to enrich the proportionality debate in this respect.

III. Outline

The chapters in this volume seek to reassess the old approaches and to analyse and develop novel approaches to the notion of proportionality in criminal matters and in the new security architecture. The discourse is not limited to conventional constitutional constellations and standard problems of sentencing in traditional criminal proceedings. The book examines a wide range of highly topical, proportionality-related issues pertinent to penal theory and legal philosophy, criminalisation policies, security and anti-terrorism strategies, alternative types of justice delivery and supranational enforcement, as well as human rights and international criminal and humanitarian law. The theoretical positions and/or practical paradigms analysed in the individual contributions cover common law and civil law as well as hybrid and international jurisdictions.

The volume is divided into three parts. The first part ('Conceptualising Proportionality') addresses general definitional aspects of the proportionality concept in security and criminal matters, in particular its legal-philosophical, constitutional, socio-legal and historical-theoretical foundations. Duff discusses

[93] Poscher, chapter 3 in this volume.

[94] *cf* Billis, Knust and Rui (n 22).

the overall role that proportionality (both retrospective and prospective), effectiveness and efficiency considerations play in decisions about criminalisation, policing, prosecution, sentencing and the imposition of preventive/security measures. Based on the German example, Poscher focuses on the problem of the legal bindingness of constitutional rights and on the proportionality principle as a potential answer to this hermeneutical issue. Mylonopoulos identifies the epistemological merits of fuzzy logic and comparative concepts in establishing a rational measure of proportionality. Elholm showcases the major challenges that rational argumentation and proportionality are faced with in the new era of symbolic legislation in the fields of crime prevention and criminal law. Finally, Courakis and Polyzoidou examine the factors that influenced the historical evolution of the proportionality concept with respect to criminal law and punishment.

The second part ('Applying Proportionality: National Paradigms') explores the mission, function and practical application of proportionality norms and tests at different levels and phases of various national models and systems of crime control and criminal justice. In view of recent developments in UK counter-terrorism laws and policies, Zedner argues that procedural justice, proportionality and the respect for rights are the requirements for effective counter-terrorism rather than obstacles to it. Jackson examines a similar context by looking at the various facets of proportionality in the UK's penal and non-penal responses to Northern Irish and Islamic terrorism. Vogler's chapter reviews, inter alia, the latest data-based surveillance and policing practices in the US, the UK and China to identify the impact of using 'big data' in crime control and criminal justice on the effectiveness of the proportionality equation. Miller compares the (merits of the) different approaches of the German Federal Constitutional Court and the US Supreme Court regarding the proportionality review of national security practices and surveillance measures. Jarvers uses the example of the Italian legal system to address the question whether measures of abstract and concrete decriminalisation can lead to a more proportionate and, at the same time, a more effective criminal justice system. Focusing on common law systems, Roberts' chapter explains how not just statutory law and appellate review but also sentencing guidelines can promote proportionality in judicial decision-making about sentencing. Boucht concludes the second part by exploring the possibilities and difficulties in applying proportionality to different types of asset confiscation (ordinary criminal, extended criminal and non-conviction-based confiscation).

The third and final part of the book ('Applying Proportionality: International Paradigms') is devoted to central questions of proportionality in constellations of international, supranational, human rights and international humanitarian law. Bothe and Gillard provide a systematic overview of the ways in which the proportionality principle is normatively materialised and practically implemented in the fields and subcategories of international and supranational law. Weigend's analysis focuses on the importance and role of proportionality in sentencing considerations before international criminal tribunals. Bachmaier Winter addresses recent ECtHR case law on mass surveillance policies and identifies its shortcomings with respect to the proportionality assessment of highly intrusive security and criminal investigation measures. In the book's final chapter, Anagnostopoulos takes three actual cases as examples to discuss basic issues concerning the disproportionate use of the European Arrest Warrant as the EU's main legal instrument of judicial cooperation in criminal matters.

2

Proportionality and the Criminal Law: Proportionality of What to What?*

R A DUFF

I. Introduction: Prospective and Retrospective Proportionality

My task in this chapter is to sketch some of the ways in which proportionality considerations figure within the criminal law, and more broadly in the field of criminal justice, understood as including governmental efforts to prevent crime and to protect security.

We should begin by noting the familiar distinction between prospective and retrospective proportionality. Retrospective proportionality is the proportionality of a present response to a past event. The obvious example is that of present punishment to past crime: the severity of an offender's punishment must be proportionate to the seriousness of the crime for which it is imposed. Writers sometimes talk of 'retributive' rather than 'retrospective' proportionality,[1] but retributive proportionality is simply one species of retrospective proportionality, which is concerned with the appropriateness of many kinds of response. If someone does me a favour, gratitude and thanks are appropriate, but should be proportionate to the favour. It would be inappropriate, because disproportionately ungrateful, to offer only a brief 'Thank you' to someone who has saved my life. It would be inappropriate to keep expressing profuse thanks to, or to press gifts of gratitude on, someone who returns my lost umbrella: unless the umbrella was of significant value to me, such a response would be disproportionately fulsome.[2]

* Thanks to the participants in the Freiburg workshop, and especially to the editors, for helpful comments on an earlier version of this chapter.

[1] See, eg, E T Sullivan and R S Frase, *Proportionality Principles in American Law: Controlling Excessive Government Actions* (New York, Oxford University Press, 2009) 6. For a historical perspective, see Nestor Courakis' and Vagia Polyzoidou's chapter 6 in this volume.

[2] It is perhaps more natural to talk of what is 'disproportionate' only in relation to what is excessive – of punishments that are too severe, or expressions of gratitude that are overly fulsome; it seems less natural to talk of unduly lenient sentences, or unduly ungrateful thanks, as 'disproportionate'. But the same principle of proportionality is at work in both cases.

As we will see in section II, retrospective proportionality figures in several ways in the criminal law – not only in sentencing.

Prospective proportionality, by contrast, is of means to ends, of present action to the goal that it is intended to serve. Suppose a pharmaceutical company discovers an effective cure for common colds, and urges a national health service to make it generally available: the health service might refuse to offer it because, although effective, it is too expensive, since it would cost €10,000 per treatment; the benefits gained by curing this mild ailment are insufficient to justify such a cost; the cost is disproportionate to the end.[3] This species of proportionality is central to discussions of proportionality as a constitutional principle.

In this chapter, I first discuss the significance of retrospective proportionality within the criminal law – not just in relation to sentencing, but also in relation to trials, to prosecutorial and police practice and to criminalisation (section II). I then show how prospective proportionality also bears on the criminal law, and how retrospective and prospective proportionality are intertwined (section III). In section IV, I turn to the role of prospective proportionality in judging the legitimacy (perhaps indeed the constitutional validity) of measures that governments might take in order to prevent crime or protect security. One question here concerns the possible tension between demands for effective protection and considerations of proportionality; another concerns the possible tension between criminal law, to which retrospective proportionality is central, and non-criminal types of preventive measure, as responses to various kinds of threat – notably the threat of terrorism.

II. Retrospective Proportionality in the Criminal Law

Theorists' discussions of proportionality in criminal law often focus (almost obsessively) on retrospective proportionality in sentencing: on the meaning and strength of the demand that the severity of a punishment should be proportionate to the seriousness of the crime for which it is imposed. Can we find appropriate metrics for crimes' seriousness, and for punishments' severity, to construct some kind of proportionality calculus? Can we assess not only relative (ordinal) proportionality, which compares the punishment imposed on this offender for this offence with those imposed on other offenders for other offences, but absolute (cardinal) proportionality, to decide what punishment is appropriate for any

[3] This is an instance of what Sullivan and Frase (n 1 at 7) call 'ends-benefits' proportionality. Another dimension of prospective proportionality is what they call 'alternative-means' proportionality, which would come into play if another, equally effective but cheaper, cure for the common cold was available: see section IV below. On retrospective and prospective proportionality, see also Johan Boucht's chapter 13 in this volume. For a typological overview on proportionality, see Emmanouil Billis', Nandor Knust's and Jon Petter Rui's chapter 1 in this volume. On 'means-to-ends proportionality' in the context of anti-terrorism laws and measures, see Lucia Zedner's chapter 7 in this volume.

given offence taken by itself? Can we thereby render practicable not only the demand that similarly serious offences receive similarly severe sentences (and more serious offences receive harsher sentences), but also a demand that punishments be absolutely proportionate to crimes? How stringent are the demands of proportionality: can we justifiably impose punishments that are, retrospectively, disproportionately severe, in order to prevent future crime, so long as such punishments are prospectively proportionate to their preventive aims; or punishments that are, retrospectively, disproportionately lenient, on the grounds that a retrospectively proportionate punishment would be (prospectively) unnecessary or harmful?[4] I will not enter these debates here, but will simply make two unargued suggestions.[5]

First, attempts to make proportionality a reasonably precise, positive guide to sentencing are doomed to failure: we cannot plausibly aspire to identify *the* proportionate punishment for a given offence or offender either in relative terms (the sentence that is proportionate given the sentences imposed on others) or in absolute terms (the sentence that is intrinsically apt for this case). To do that we would need to construct a single scale of seriousness on which to locate every offence, and a single scale of severity on which to locate every sentence: but neither of these enterprises is achievable. The most we can hope to do is to mobilise a rough principle of *dis*proportionality: that sentences should not be (manifestly) disproportionate to the seriousness of the crimes for which they are imposed; that offenders should not suffer punishments that are clearly harsher, or milder, than their offence deserves. This would lead us towards some form of 'limiting retributivism': considerations of proportionality (grounded in the idea of penal desert) do not determine *the* appropriate punishment, but rather set limits within which the sentence may be determined by reference to other kinds of consideration.[6]

Second, if we are too concerned about proportionality, or insist too firmly that sentences must be not merely not clearly disproportionate, but positively proportionate, we are likely to distort deliberations about sentencing. For we are likely to focus on measuring the severity of sentences, and on making available kinds of sentence which can be compared to each other on a single metric of severity: but this will distract us from thinking about the *meaning* of the sentence (about what different modes of punishment say to and about the offender and the offence) and might make us reluctant to contemplate new modes of punishment (such as different kinds of community service or of rehabilitative programmes) if they cannot readily be measured on the scale of seriousness. We might do better to look for punishments that are *appropriate* to the offence and to the offender: for although

[4] For recent discussions, see A von Hirsch and A Ashworth, *Proportionate Sentencing* (Oxford, Oxford University Press, 2005); M Tonry (ed), *Of One-eyed and Toothless Miscreants: Making the Punishment Fit the Crime?* (New York, Oxford University Press, 2019). See also Julian Roberts' chapter 12 in this volume.

[5] See RA Duff, *Punishment, Communication and Community* (New York, Oxford University Press, 2001) ch 4.

[6] See, eg, R S Frase, *Just Sentencing* (Oxford, Oxford University Press, 2012).

formal proportionality (or non-disproportionality) is an aspect of appropriateness, appropriateness is also a matter of meaning – of substantive fittingness, rather than just of formal or abstract proportionality.

However, considerations of retrospective proportionality are also relevant to other parts of the criminal process that culminates in punishment. They may be relevant to the verdict that completes a criminal trial. This possibility is made explicit in the American Model Penal Code's '*De Minimis*' provisions, according to which a court should

> dismiss a prosecution if … the defendant's conduct … did not actually cause or threaten the harm or evil sought to be prevented by the law defining the offense or did so only to an extent too trivial to warrant the condemnation of conviction.[7]

If the defendant's conduct did 'cause or threaten the harm or evil' targeted by the law, but to an utterly 'trivial' extent, she is formally guilty of the offence, but hers is a 'merely technical violation … of law' for which she should not be convicted.[8] Why not? Because there could not be a criminal conviction that was light enough in its meaning or impact to match the triviality of the wrong. We can reduce the impact of a conviction, for instance by allowing courts to grant an absolute discharge that precludes both punishment and the acquisition of a criminal record;[9] but a formal criminal conviction nonetheless gives the matter a degree of seriousness that might be disproportionate to the seriousness of the wrong – making the wrong appear more serious than it was.

It is worth noticing that what the Model Penal Code prescribes for '*De Minimis*' cases is not an acquittal, but a dismissal of the prosecution: this implies that the prosecution should not have been brought – that prosecution itself was disproportionate to the defendant's trivial crime; and this implies that prosecutors should attend to considerations of proportionality in deciding whether to pursue a case. For prosecution itself is burdensome, for the defendant and for others involved in the process: it gives the affair a formal seriousness by portraying the defendant's alleged conduct as a wrong serious enough to merit a criminal conviction. If the wrong was quite trivial, then to prosecute it is to respond with disproportionate severity. A similar point applies to policing: if police officers become aware of a technical breach of the criminal law, they must decide whether it is worth investigating further with a view to possible prosecution; and one good reason not to investigate further is that the offence was too trivial to warrant such a response – further investigation would be disproportionate to the (non-)seriousness of the crime.

(My comments in the previous paragraph beg some important questions about the role of discretion in systems of criminal justice: for instance, those who

[7] Model Penal Code §2.12.

[8] American Law Institute, *Model Penal Code and Commentaries, Commentary vol 1*, revised edn (Philadelphia PA, American Law Institute, 1985) 399. See, eg, J Nemerofsky, 'What is a "Trifle" Anyway?' (2002) 37 *Gonzaga Law Review* 315, 327–28.

[9] Powers of Criminal Courts (Sentencing) Act 2000 s 14.

support a 'legality principle' of mandatory prosecution, rather than an 'opportunity principle' of discretionary prosecution, would object to the suggestion that prosecutors should feel free to decide whether to pursue a case in which there is strong enough evidence of an accused person's legal guilt. There is, of course, much more to be said than can be said here about the kinds and extent of discretion that officials in a democratic system of criminal justice should enjoy, and about how any such discretion can be made accountable. However, first, the discretion not to pursue cases that are manifestly trivial seems one of the less disturbing kinds of official discretion. Second, I think that a strong argument can be made in democratic political theory for giving officials, and indeed lay citizens, a significant measure of accountable discretion that makes them co-agents rather than simply servants of the law.[10])

As we will see, considerations of prospective proportionality are also relevant here. This is because, first, in asking whether an offence is serious enough to merit investigation or prosecution, we are asking whether this would be a sensible use of resources: whether such expenditure of resources would be (dis)proportionate to the end to be achieved. Second, it might be argued that even if prosecution would be disproportionate to the (non-)seriousness of the offence, its beneficial consequences could justify it. Thus, according to the 'broken windows' theory,[11] what matters is not (just) whether the criminalised conduct contributes to some serious harm, but whether criminalising it would help to avert such harm, by displaying 'zero tolerance' towards even trivial crimes. Such arguments raise questions about the relationship between prospective and retrospective proportionality: can we justify retrospectively disproportionate measures as prospectively proportionate means to a valuable end?

Finally, retrospective proportionality also figures at the start of the enterprise of criminal law, when legislatures decide whether to criminalise a given type of conduct. Considerations of prospective proportionality are salient here: legislatures must ask whether criminalisation will be a proportionate means to whatever ends criminalisation should serve. Considerations of retrospective proportionality are also relevant, however, since another important question is whether the conduct under discussion constitutes a serious enough mischief or wrong to warrant criminalisation as a response. For instance, in societies with a practice of queuing, queue-jumping is a public or social wrong, which, even if it does not cause harm, can cause inconvenience and offence, and takes unfair advantage of others' queue-respecting conduct: it might thus, depending on our principles

[10] For some useful discussions of prosecutors' roles in democratic systems, see M Langer and D Sklansky (eds), *Prosecutors and Democracy* (Cambridge, Cambridge University Press, 2017): see in particular the 'Epilogue' at 316–18 on 'mandatory prosecution', with further references. For a sketch of the 'strong argument' in favour of discretion, see R A Duff, *The Realm of Criminal Law* (Oxford, Oxford University Press, 2018) especially ch 5.

[11] See M D Reisig, 'Community and Problem-Oriented Policing' in M Tonry (ed), *The Oxford Handbook of Crime and Criminal Justice* (Oxford, Oxford University Press, 2011) 538.

of criminalisation,[12] satisfy the criteria for being in principle criminalisable. But it is too trivial a wrong or mischief to warrant criminalisation: to criminalise it, to make it liable to police intervention and to prosecution, would exaggerate its seriousness – it would be a disproportionately excessive response to so trivial a mischief.

(In these contexts too, what does the work is not proportionality, but disproportionality. We do not select a response on the grounds that it is proportionate; we rather rule out certain responses as being disproportionate.)

I have so far been discussing the role of retrospective proportionality within the criminal justice system. However, prospective proportionality is also often relevant; and we must note the ways in which retrospective and prospective proportionality can interweave, and conflict.

III. Prospective (and Retrospective) Proportionality in the Criminal Law

Prospective proportionality is expressed by the 'Proportionality Principle' – a principle much discussed by constitutional theorists. There are three familiar elements to the Proportionality Principle.[13] First, there must be a 'rational connection' between means and end: the means must be 'suitable' to, must actually serve, that end. Second, the proposed measure must be 'necessary': there must be no other available means to the end that would be less costly (we must attend, as always, not only to material or financial costs, but also to moral costs – the ways in which the measure constrains freedom or impinges on rights, for instance). Third, the measure must be proportionate in the 'narrow' sense, '*stricto sensu*': we must balance the costs of the measure against the benefits or value secured by the end.[14] Some add a fourth element, that the means must be intended to serve a 'proper purpose',[15] and measures will indeed satisfy a plausible proportionality test only if they serve some proper purpose. However, that is not a requirement distinct from the other three:[16] though we can assess 'suitability' and 'necessity' without making any judgement on the value of the end at which the measure is directed, the assessment of 'proportionality *stricto sensu*' must include an evaluation of the worth of

[12] On which, see Duff (n 10) especially ch 6.

[13] A Barak, *Proportionality: Constitutional Rights and their Limitations* (Cambridge, Cambridge University Press, 2012) Introduction.

[14] *cf* 'intermediate scrutiny' in American law (*Central Hudson Gas and Electric Corporation v Public Service Commission of New York* 447 US 557 (1980)), and see D N Husak, *Overcriminalization: The Limits of the Criminal Law* (Oxford, Oxford University Press, 2007) 127–29, applying this idea to criminalisation.

[15] See, eg, Barak (n 13) 3.

[16] See R Alexy, 'Proportionality and Rationality' in V C Jackson and M Tushnet (eds), *Proportionality: New Frontiers, New Challenges* (Cambridge, Cambridge University Press, 2018) 13, 19–20.

the end or purpose; a purpose that is not 'proper' cannot justify any burdensome or right-limiting means, since it has no positive value to balance against those burdens or limits.[17]

The end to which the means must be prospectively proportionate might be a further good to which those means are instrumental: we ask, for instance, whether the prevention of future crime is a valuable enough end to justify the criminalisation, prosecution and punishment of this kind of conduct as a means. Or it might be a good internal to the criminal justice system, so that the relationship of means to end is not instrumental, but constitutive. If it is a proper aim of the criminal law, for instance, to ensure that public wrongdoers are called to formal account for their crimes,[18] or that they suffer the retribution they deserve,[19] criminalisation and prosecution are means to that end: but the end is achieved in the very completion of the process of criminalisation – in the trial, conviction and punishment of the wrongdoer; it is not a further outcome to which that process is an instrumental means. In both cases, however, we must ask whether the means proposed are proportionate, or not disproportionate, to the end to be achieved.

The administration of criminal justice is a costly, burdensome business. It imposes burdens on those whom it convicts and punishes: both the intended burdens of punishment and the further burdens imposed by the 'collateral consequences' of conviction and punishment, which might include exclusions from various important aspects of civic life, such as employment, housing and welfare.[20] It also imposes burdens on others who become entangled with it, for instance as witnesses or suspects or defendants, and on the families of those who are arrested, convicted and punished. It requires substantial resources to maintain its operations. It also involves moral costs and burdens: criminalisation impinges on citizens' liberty by ruling out certain kinds of conduct as criminal, and thus rendering them liable to its coercive attentions; it impinges drastically on the rights and liberties not just of those who are punished,[21] but of those who are questioned, arrested or prosecuted; it is inevitably prone to errors, which result in the conviction and punishment of some innocents. Even if we believe that a system of criminal law can serve ends that are important enough to justify such costs and burdens, and indeed is necessary as a means to those ends, we must therefore ask of all aspects of such a system whether they contribute enough to those ends to justify their costs.

[17] I cannot discuss the problems of 'balancing', of how we are to weigh possibly incommensurable goods and evils against each other, here – though I will comment later on one limitation to the idea of balancing.

[18] See Duff (n 10) ch 1.

[19] See M S Moore, *Placing Blame: A Theory of Criminal Law* (Oxford, Oxford University Press, 1997) ch 1.

[20] Z Hoskins, *Beyond Punishment? A Normative Account of the Collateral Legal Consequences of Conviction* (New York, Oxford University Press, 2019).

[21] Hence the attraction of talking of a 'right not to be punished'; see Husak (n 14) 92–103.

Thus legislators must ask whether the end to be achieved by criminalising a certain type of conduct is important enough to justify so costly a measure – or whether those costs would be disproportionate to the end; police officers must decide how best to deploy their limited resources, and thus whether it is worth investigating this crime, or this type of crime, further; prosecutors must decide how to deploy *their* resources, and whether it is worth prosecuting this (type of) crime or this offender;[22] and in determining sentencing policy or guidelines, or determining the sentences to be imposed on individual offenders, sentencing authorities must ask whether the end to be achieved can justify such costly means. Such questions must be asked whether that end is extrinsic or internal to the criminal justice system.

(How costly the means are will depend on the character of the criminal justice system in question. Thus, how costly punishment is, in the ways noted above, depends on the nature of the punishment, on how it is administered, on what further consequences flow from it; how costly the criminal process is depends on how it is conducted – including the range of rights and protections that it affords defendants.)

Now if the ends to be achieved are internal to the practice of criminal justice (ends such as holding wrongdoers to appropriate public account or punishing the guilty), prospective and retrospective proportionality might seem to be in harmony: if a given kind of wrongdoing is serious enough to warrant criminalisation, prosecution, conviction and punishment as a matter of retrospective proportionality, achieving that aim is surely sufficiently important to justify the costs and burdens that those means involve. But matters are not that simple, even if we think only about the relation between means and such internal ends, since the means might still be disproportionately burdensome relative to the end. An extreme example is that of capital punishment: even someone who believes that the death penalty is a retrospectively proportionate punishment for certain kinds of murder might also believe that the various costs of maintaining a system of capital punishment (the material costs, but also the moral costs for all those involved, and the certainty of mistaken convictions) are so significant that they are not worth incurring even for the sake of that (supposedly) valuable end. More generally, even those who believe that the state has a duty to punish wrongdoers, for instance to ensure that they suffer the retribution they deserve, will also believe that given the material and moral costs of effective criminalisation, many wrongs should, on balance, not be criminalised: for effective criminalisation requires significant resources that might be better spent on

[22] This is one aspect of the questions that prosecutors in England & Wales must ask in deciding whether to bring a case to trial. They must satisfy themselves not only that they have enough admissible evidence to give 'a realistic prospect of conviction', but also whether prosecution would be 'in the public interest'; one factor bearing on the latter question is whether 'prosecution is proportionate to the likely outcome' – whether the 'cost … [would be] excessive when weighed against any likely penalty'; see *Code for Crown Prosecutors* (October 2018) paras 4.9–4.14 (available at: www.cps.gov.uk/publications/code_for_crown_prosecutors/).

other things, and impinges on other values such as liberty and privacy that might matter more.[23]

The Proportionality Principle requires us, of course, to ask not only whether the end to be achieved is valuable enough to justify such costly means, but also whether there are other less costly means of achieving that same end – whether these means are 'necessary'.[24] If one aim of criminalisation and prosecution is to prevent or deter certain kinds of conduct, we must ask whether there are less costly ways of achieving that goal – for instance by a system of non-criminal regulation; if an aim is that wrongdoers be called to public account, we must ask whether that could be achieved at lesser material and moral cost by, for instance, practices of restorative justice.[25]

I have been talking as if retrospective and prospective proportionality are clearly distinct species of proportionality: as if we can ask separately whether a given measure is, on the one hand, retrospectively proportionate to a past event to which it is a response, and on the other hand, whether it is prospectively proportionate to whatever end it is intended to achieve. This is partly true: as we will see, there can be conflict between a demand for efficient prevention of future crimes (as a matter of prospective proportionality) and a demand for retrospective proportionality of present punishment to past crimes. But it is also true that retrospective and prospective proportionality are interconnected, since the seriousness of the wrong or harm to be addressed bears on both. The more serious the wrong or harm, the more important it is to provide a retrospectively proportionate response to it, and the more burdensome that response can justifiably be: that is why we have stronger reason to criminalise rape than to criminalise littering – to devote greater resources to prosecuting rape and to impose harsher punishments on rapists. But the more serious the wrong or harm, the more important it also is to take steps (including responsive steps) to prevent or deter its future occurrence, and the more costly those steps can justifiably be: that is also why we have stronger reason to criminalise rape, and to devote more resources to prosecuting and punishing rapists than we do for those who drop litter.

Whether we have to judge the seriousness of the wrong to which we must respond (and determine what kind of response would be not disproportionate) or the importance of the end to be achieved (and determine what means would be not disproportionate), we face familiar dangers: dangers not just of misjudgements, but of distributive injustice, since the relevant costs and benefits, the burdens that we are to impose, are not typically distributed evenly. I will return to such issues in section IV, but should note here some ways in which they figure within the criminal law.

[23] *cf* Moore (n 19) ch 18.

[24] See also Sullivan and Frase (n 1) Introduction, on 'alternative-means' proportionality as distinct from 'ends-benefits' proportionality.

[25] See further Duff (n 10) ch 7.2. We must ask, however, whether proposed alternatives to criminalisation are indeed alternative means to the same end(s) or alternatives that also involve changing the ends that are to be pursued.

First, our assessments of the (relative) seriousness of a kind of wrong or harm, and thus of how important it is to respond to it, can be distorted. Members of disadvantaged groups may complain, with reason, that the polity and its criminal law do not take wrongs that are committed against them seriously enough: that they are slow to criminalise those wrongs; that police are slow to investigate them; that their perpetrators are too lightly punished as compared with the way in which wrongs against other groups are treated; that crimes against more favoured groups, against the rich and powerful, are treated with disproportionate seriousness. If we are to make well-grounded judgements about proportionality, we must make sure that we identify the relevant mischief or end, and have the proper measure of it: we must, for instance, attend to the kinds of harm that are not captured by a purely material or financial metric.

Second, particular groups can also be unjustly disadvantaged when the cost or burden that they suffer is given insufficient weight in the proportionality assessment, so that the end benefit to be achieved (a benefit in which they might not fully share) is too easily judged to justify the burdensome means. Thus, the criminalisation of various kinds of conduct in which homeless people are most likely to engage (offences of 'vagrancy' of different types) might produce noticeable benefits of convenience and comfort for those who are not homeless as they move around 'their' streets, but it is too easy for those considering such criminalisation to ignore, or under-value, the effects that this will have on the homeless people whose conduct is criminalised.[26]

Third, if we find that the means necessary to achieve some valued end become, as we see it, too expensive, there are various ways in which we might respond. We might rethink our commitment to the end: if its pursuit is that expensive, is it really worth it? We might provide more resources for its pursuit, which would be to decide that the expensive means are not *too* expensive. Or we might try to make the means cheaper, but here we might fall into one of the first two dangers. For instance, contested criminal trials are expensive, and criminal justice systems come under serious pressure as they try to deal with massive numbers of cases. That pressure could be alleviated by putting more resources into the system; but that would require a problematic shifting of resources from other areas of government expenditure, or significant increases in taxation. It could instead be alleviated by reducing the scope of the criminal law – by reducing the number of crimes or by diverting more crimes from the criminal process; but that might be unpopular with politicians who fear a supposedly punitive public. It could instead be alleviated by making the criminal process cheaper – by, for instance,

[26] See G F Evangelista and S Jones (eds), *Mean Streets: A Report on the Criminalisation of Homelessness in Europe* (Belgium, European Federation of National Organisations working with the Homeless, 2013), available at: www.housingrightswatch.org/sites/default/files/Mean%20Streets%20-%20Full.pdf. For further examples concerning the 'symbolic' use of the criminal law, see Thomas Elholm's chapter 5 in this volume.

reducing the 'due process' protections afforded to defendants, thus making trials quicker and easier, or by encouraging (if not coercing) plea bargains that avert the need for a trial at all. This is a route that is too often followed,[27] but it is liable to bear extremely harshly (in material and moral terms) on defendants – whose interests it is all too easy for policy-makers and practitioners to ignore or under-value. Similarly, prisons – if properly run – are expensive institutions, which impose heavy costs on the polity if large numbers of offenders are imprisoned. One way to mitigate this problem (if we are not to pump substantial additional resources into the prison system) is to send fewer offenders to prison or to shorten sentences for those imprisoned. But another – too often preferred – way is to make prisons cheaper to run by cutting the resources provided *per capita*; an obvious effect of this is to make life in various ways much worse for prisoners, whose interests are too often ignored or under-valued. If we try to reduce the cost of the means, we are also likely to – more or less covertly – change the end: thus, a pervasive system of coercive plea bargaining is liable to replace the aim of identifying the guilty, or of calling them to public account, with the aim of processing large numbers of people through a system concerned simply with social control.[28]

IV. Proportionality and Efficacy

Though the criminal law obviously serves prospective goals, such as the prevention of certain kinds of wrongful or harmful conduct, its operations are essentially responsive. By defining certain kinds of conduct as criminal, it provides for alleged commissions of such crimes to be investigated, and for perpetrators to be tried, convicted and punished: its focus is backwards, on past crimes and on who committed them. So although, as we have seen, considerations of prospective proportionality are relevant in criminal law, retrospective proportionality is more saliently relevant: the first and obvious question to ask about proportionality is whether this criminal law response (criminalisation, investigation, prosecution, conviction, punishment) is retrospectively proportionate to the wrong to which it is a response. When we look beyond the criminal law, however, to the wider structures of governmental activity in which it is set, prospective proportionality becomes more salient. This is particularly, and for our purposes most significantly, true when we consider the state's preventive responsibilities in relation to the kinds

[27] See generally W Stuntz, *The Collapse of American Criminal Justice* (Cambridge MA, Belknap Press, 2011); S Bibas, *The Machinery of Criminal Justice* (Oxford, Oxford University Press, 2012).

[28] See, eg, M Feeley and J Simon, 'Actuarial Justice: The Emerging New Criminal Law' in D Nelken (ed), *The Futures of Criminology* (London, Sage, 1994). On the problems of plea bargaining, see further E Billis and N Knust, 'Alternative Types of Procedure and the Formal Limits of National Criminal Justice: Aspects of Social Legitimacy' in U Sieber, V Mitsilegas, C Mylonopoulos, E Billis and N Knust (eds), *Alternative Systems of Crime Control* (Berlin, Duncker & Humblot, 2018) especially 40–48.

of conduct with which criminal law is also concerned.[29] For whilst the criminal law is a responsive institution, grounded in the state's duty to respond appropriately to certain kinds of wrongdoing, the state also has a significant responsibility to protect citizens against those kinds of wrongdoing and against the harms that they cause, by preventing such wrongs – or, more realistically, by reducing their incidence to tolerable levels.[30] Criminal law, in its preventive dimension, is one of the ways in which this responsibility can be discharged, but it is far from the only, or most effective, way: other, more overtly preventive or forward-looking kinds of measure are also important, and we must ask about the ways in which they are subject to demands of proportionality.

To give the discussion a manageable focus, I will concentrate on the threat of terrorist attacks, against which the state clearly has a responsibility to protect its citizens, and on the goal of 'security' (understood typically, but as we will see incompletely, as security against such attacks). Similar issues arise with many kinds of crime, but it will be simpler to concentrate on just one. Criminal law clearly can and does deal with terrorist activities:[31] many of them constitute familiar crimes (such as murder or criminal damage), and it is also an increasingly common strategy to create specific terrorist-related offences, including some that criminalise conduct quite remote from the commission of terrorist attacks,[32] as well as making special provisions for the sentencing of terrorist offenders.[33] Such provisions raise obvious questions of retrospective proportionality: are the kinds of conduct that are criminalised and punished serious enough, in their wrongful or harmful character, to warrant this type of response, or is the criminal law's response disproportionately severe? But they also highlight the potential for conflict between retrospective and prospective proportionality: for it might be argued in defence of such measures that whilst they may be retrospectively disproportionate, they are prospectively proportionate as means of protection against the serious threat of terrorism; and that given the seriousness of the threat, such retrospective disproportionality is justifiable.

We must also, however, look at measures outside the criminal law, and measures that implicate the criminal law only indirectly, where the most salient questions

[29] In talking of 'the state' and its responsibilities I do not assume it to be the main political authority: the state is (it should be) simply the set of institutional structures through which a political community organises and governs itself. The state's responsibilities are the responsibilities delegated to it by the polity.

[30] On 'reductivism', see N Walker, *Punishment, Danger and Stigma* (Oxford, Oxford University Press, 1980) 26; this label makes it clear that preventing *all* future crimes is not a realistic goal.

[31] I leave aside here the issue of whether we should treat all kinds of terrorist activity within the framework of criminal law; or whether it sometimes becomes more appropriate to treat it within the framework of war and the laws of war.

[32] Plenty of examples can be found in English legislation such as the Terrorism Acts of 2000 and 2006.

[33] For just one recent instance, the Terrorist Offenders (Restriction of Early Release) Act 2020 places more restrictive conditions for early release from a prison sentence on those sentenced for terrorist offences than apply to other prisoners: the aim is clearly prospective – the effective prevention of future attacks.

rather concern prospective proportionality – although, as we will see, they also raise retrospective questions. By 'measures that implicate the criminal law only indirectly' I mean measures that initially impose non-criminal restrictions on those suspected of involvement in terrorism, but make it a criminal offence to breach those restrictions.[34]

Preventive measures – especially those that involve coercion or other kinds of burden – invite proportionality assessments that are most obviously prospective: are these means proportionate to the preventive end that they are meant to serve? One question that the editors of this volume asked the contributors to consider in this context is whether efficacy and proportionality constitute a 'dipole': that is, do they predictably, or inevitably, come into conflict? It will be as well to deal first (briefly) with this question, before moving on to some of the more significant problems raised by the application of the proportionality principle in this context: the quick answer is that they do indeed conflict, but that efficacy is not what matters here.[35]

Efficacy concerns the first dimension of prospective proportionality noted in section III above:[36] does the measure serve, is it an effective way of achieving, the specified end? It does not directly fall within the reach of the second dimension, since a means can be effective even if there are other means that are as effective but less costly; nor does it fall within the reach of the third dimension, since the costs of an effective means might far outweigh the benefits it brings: efficacy and proportionality can thus conflict. It might then seem that when they do conflict, one will have to be sacrificed or compromised: effective means of preventing terrorist attacks and achieving security may be disproportionate; in that case we must either forswear effective prevention, thus sacrificing security, or compromise proportionality at the expense of justice.

It is clearly true in general that efficacy and proportionality can conflict. For instance, an effective way to prevent offensive behaviour by passengers on aircraft and the inconvenience and annoyance that such behaviour causes would be to sedate all passengers and strap them in their seats: but even if such a measure were necessary, in that no other less burdensome way to achieve that goal was available, it would be disproportionate in the 'strict' sense; the intended end is not valuable enough, the mischief to be averted is not serious enough, to justify such means. Similarly, a €10,000 cure for common colds might be effective, and be 'necessary' in that no other cure is as effective, but unjustifiable because disproportionate:[37] a cold is not a significant enough evil to warrant expending so much on curing it.

[34] See, for just one instance, the Terrorism Prevention and Investigation Measures Act 2011; A Ashworth and L Zedner, *Preventive Justice* (Oxford, Oxford University Press, 2014) ch 4 on 'civil preventive orders' (and the whole book on the problems raised by 'preventive justice').

[35] See Lucia Zedner's chapter 7 in this volume, on the relationship between effectiveness and proportionality.

[36] See text to nn 13–14 above.

[37] See text to n 3 above; suppose that the cure costs €10,000 per dose, and that patients must take a dose every day for a month. Whether it is disproportionate depends of course on how burdensome

(We might be tempted to talk here of using a sledgehammer to crack a nut:[38] suppose that I could 'cure' the cramp I occasionally suffer in my leg only by having the leg amputated. The metaphor is in one way inapt: for presumably the desired end is not to destroy the nut but to shell it in order to eat it; and a sledgehammer hardly serves that end, since it will reduce the nut to tiny fragments in which shell and kernel are inextricably mixed. But it provides an apt reminder that an insufficiently careful search for more effective means might, as we will see, lead to means that actually destroy or compromise the end that we should be pursuing.)

However, the simple answer to the worry that efficacy and proportionality may conflict is that our concern should be with efficiency, not efficacy; and that efficiency cannot conflict with proportionality, since it includes it. (I emphasise the 'should' here: governments eager to be seen to be 'doing something' about a perceived threat or enemy are in fact all too likely to focus on efficacy, or apparent efficacy, at the cost of efficiency.) A means of preventing some mischief, or achieving some good, is efficient if and only if it is 'suitable', in that it will contribute to the end; *and* 'necessary', in that no other less costly way of achieving the end is available (if a less costly means is available, this means is not cost-effective – ie, not efficient); *and* 'proportionate *stricto sensu*', in that the mischief to be averted, or the good to be achieved, is significant enough to justify these costs. It is efficient if and only if it is prospectively proportionate.[39]

Is this then to say that there is no problem here: that since efficiency is clearly a demand on every prospective enterprise, in every attempt to achieve an end proportionality is demanded too? Matters are not, alas, that simple, since whether we talk of efficiency or proportionality, further serious problems arise. It is to these – focusing still on the use of constraining legal measures to avert terrorist attacks and thus protect security – that we must now turn.

Matters are, at least in theory, tolerably clear if two conditions are met: first, that both the end and the costs incurred by the means are clearly specifiable and comparable; second, that the costs are borne by those who will also enjoy the benefits of the end (those who will share in the good, or in the security from evil, that is to be achieved).[40] However, all too often one or both of them are not met.

paying €300,000 would be: a sufficiently wealthy person who is sufficiently averse to the mild discomfort of a cold might regard it as a price worth paying.

[38] See Konstanze Jarvers' chapter 11 in this volume, applying this saying to questions of criminalisation.

[39] It might be said that a measure can be an efficient means to a worthless or evil end – in which case it would be wrong to identify efficiency with proportionality, since the Proportionality Principle includes an implicit requirement that the end be valuable (see text to nn 15–16 above). But so does efficiency: we can judge a means to an evil end to be efficient only if we judge it from the perspective of one who espouses the end as good.

[40] The first of these conditions concerns the possibility of 'balancing', which I cannot discuss here: all I can do is declare my belief that we will not make real progress by searching for a 'Weight Formula' (*cf* Alexy, n 16), although the language of 'balancing' might lead us down that road; and that if we ask instead, with less apparent precision but I think with greater clarity, whether the end is worth the cost of the means, we can begin to explore in a more discursive manner the ways in which we do manage to answer that question.

As to the ends, and focusing again on security, we need to ask various questions.[41] First, is security to be understood in 'subjective' terms, as a matter of feeling secure, or not feeling threatened; or in 'objective' terms, of being in fact safe from the threat in question; or should the state aim to protect both kinds of security?[42]

Second, against what do we need to be or feel secure? The obvious answer is 'terrorist attacks'; or, more generally, all kinds of crime that threaten our wellbeing. But that answer focuses on only one kind of human threat; we also surely need to be, and feel, secure against evils that emanate from the state itself – various kinds of state coercion, in particular coercion that is 'arbitrary' in the sense that it is not a rational, foreseeable response to our voluntary actions, but results from discretionary decisions by government officials.[43] This highlights one of the ways in which measures that are intended to serve a valuable end might undermine it, if it is understood in richer or broader terms: if measures intended to promote security against terrorist attacks expose us to the risk of various kinds of 'arbitrary' governmental coercion, including detention if we are suspected of terrorist involvement, they promote one dimension of security, but undermine another.[44]

Third, whose security is protected – and do the costs involved in the means of protection fall on those who are to benefit? It might seem obvious that the answer must be 'everyone', and that is true if we focus on security against typically indiscriminate terrorist attacks. But complaints about crime prevention policies are often based on their discriminatory impact: either because the protections they provide are focused on some groups rather than on others who are just as vulnerable, as when the police make greater efforts to prevent burglary in wealthier neighbourhoods; or because the preventive measures are focused especially on certain groups, as when 'stop and search' is used disproportionately against young black males.[45] Complex questions inevitably arise in these contexts. For instance, it might seem sensible to focus preventive measures on areas in which there are

[41] Lucia Zedner has provided some of the most insightful discussions of the issues here: see, eg, L Zedner, 'Securing Liberty in the Face of Terror: Reflections from Criminal Justice' (2005) 32 *Journal of Law and Society* 507; L Zedner, *Security* (London, Routledge, 2009).

[42] See P Ramsay, *The Insecurity State: Vulnerable Autonomy and the Right to Security in the Criminal Law* (Oxford, Oxford University Press, 2012).

[43] *cf* P Pettit, *Republicanism: A Theory of Freedom and Government* (Oxford, Oxford University Press 1997) ch 2, on 'non-domination' – not being vulnerable to arbitrary interference by others. See also H L A Hart, 'Legal Responsibility and Excuses' in H L A Hart, *Punishment and Responsibility*, 2nd edn (Oxford, Oxford University Press, 2008) 28, at 44–49, on the law as a 'choosing system' that provides us with predictability insofar as it enables us to 'determine by [our] own choice[s] what the future shall be' (at 45).

[44] See the chapters by John Jackson (on anti-terrorism measures and preventive detention (ch 8)) and by Richard Vogler (on big data surveillance (ch 9)) in this volume.

[45] On stop and search in England, see B Bowling and C Phillips, 'Disproportionate and Discriminatory: Reviewing the Evidence on Police Stop and Search' (2007) 70 *Modern Law Review* 936; A Parmar, 'Stop and Search in London: Counter-Terrorist or Counter-Productive?' (2011) 21(4) *Policing and Society* 369.

greater risks of greater harms, so that they bring greater preventive benefits: but if a result of this is that other areas and their inhabitants receive consistently lower levels of protection, they might reasonably complain of unfairness.[46] It might also seem sensible, if we focus on efficiency, to target for pre-emptive measures such as 'stop and search' members of groups among whom there is the highest incidence of the kinds of crime at which the measures are aimed: but we must ask whether such statistic-based policy is fair to those who are targeted. Another apt illustration of this problem is the way in which imprisonment is often portrayed as an effective way of preventing crime simply by taking offenders 'out of circulation', or incapacitating them: for whilst those in prison are (usually) incapacitated from committing crimes against those not in prison, they are all too able to commit crimes against fellow prisoners and prison officers. It is hard not to suspect that those who are to be protected are the 'law-abiding citizens' who need protection against criminal 'enemies' who are less worthy of protection.[47]

These points, which are independent of further questions that we need to ask about the relationship between security and other important state goals, might be portrayed as questions about the metric of proportionality: is a measure that significantly benefits one group at the cost of burdens imposed on others 'proportionate' just so long as the benefits outweigh the burdens (and no less burdensome means are available); or does proportionality also depend on the distribution of those burdens? But I suspect that we should not try to make the idea of proportionality do so much work: we should rather recognise that proportionality, understood as efficiency, is just one among other criteria for the justifiability of coercive governmental measures.[48]

As to the costs of preventive measures, I have already noted the danger of attending only to 'costs' that can be measured in quantifiable (most obviously monetary) terms; we need to attend to the relative impact of materially similar costs on differently situated people, and to what we can call the moral costs – the ways in which measures that are intended to serve one value can undermine other values. A familiar way to illustrate this point is to talk about how liberty and security can conflict – the ways in which measures intended to increase security can impinge on liberty; but this example highlights a further problem, about the relationship between apparently conflicting values.[49] For if we understand liberty in republican terms, as non-domination,[50] we will realise that liberty includes a

[46] Suppose that police focus their anti-burglary activities on wealthier neighbourhoods, in which burglaries are more frequent: in purely economic terms this might be efficient and proportionate; but this is to ignore the non-material harms of burglary, its plausibly greater impact on those who are already poor and the question of distributive justice.

[47] *cf* (of course) G Jakobs, 'Bürgerstrafrecht und Feindstrafrecht' (2004) (3) *Höchstrichterliche Rechtsprechung Strafrecht* 88.

[48] Thus, it is worth noting that Bowling and Phillips (n 45) treat disproportionality and injustice (unjust discrimination) as distinct complaints.

[49] See Zedner, 'Securing Liberty' (n 41).

[50] See n 43 above.

certain kind of security – security against arbitrary interference or coercion; and if we understand security to include security against arbitrary state coercion, we will see that it includes an important kind of liberty, that of non-domination.

I have already noted, as an issue that we cannot pursue here, the question of 'balancing': how are we to 'weigh' costs against benefits, when different, and possibly incommensurable, values are involved on either side? But a further question is whether weighing or balancing is always the appropriate concept (or metaphor): in particular, some 'costs' might figure not as disvalues that can be weighed against, and may be outweighed by, the benefits, but rather as categorical constraints on what may be done even in pursuit of a valuable end. This point is especially important when the 'costs' are infringements or limitations on rights. For if rights are really 'trumps', they do not merely outweigh the benefits that their violation might bring (which would be to suggest that if the benefits were great enough they might outweigh the rights); they rule out the pursuit of those (or any) benefits by these means.[51] We then face questions about whether any rights are not merely categorical but absolute – never to be infringed come what may; and questions about whether in emergencies we might be morally forced to violate even an absolute right.[52] We cannot pursue these issues here, but should simply note that they mark a further limit on the role of proportionality, and of the 'balancing' or 'weighing' that it seems to involve, as a measure of justifiability: if a measure violates an absolute right, the problem is not that it is disproportionate, but that it is unjust; and even if a right is categorical without being absolute, it is not clear whether the question of whether it is justifiably infringed can be settled by appealing to proportionality alone.

I should again emphasise here a further issue about the distribution of costs and benefits. A measure that imposes proportionate costs for the sake of some benefit, a measure that is an efficient means to that benefit, is likely to seem warranted if those who bear the costs also share in the benefits: *we* should accept these costs for the sake of the benefits they bring *us*. We should, for instance, accept airport security measures to which all passengers are subject, if they are a proportionate means of reducing the threat of terrorist attacks – perhaps even if they involve infringements of privacy that would usually constitute rights violations. Matters are different when particular groups are targeted for enhanced measures on the basis of, for instance, their ethnicity or supposed religion: such measures might be efficient, and in that sense proportionate, if the statistical incidence of terrorist activity is higher among members of those groups; they might be more efficient, more cost-effective, than untargeted measures; but they raise familiar worries about distributive justice. Such worries become significantly greater when those

[51] For a concise exposition of this Dworkinian idea, see R M Dworkin, 'Rights as Trumps' in J Waldron (ed), *Theories of Rights* (Oxford, Oxford University Press, 1984) 153.

[52] For a helpful discussion of the issues about the structure of moral thought in this context, see M Kramer, *Torture and Moral Integrity: A Philosophical Inquiry* (Oxford, Oxford University Press, 2014) ch 1.

on whom the costs fall most heavily do not even share in the benefits, or benefit less than others on whom the costs do not fall so heavily – for instance if security for 'law-abiding citizens' is provided by incapacitative modes of detention that then expose those subjected to them to greater risk of attack from fellow inmates. This is simply to note that if we understand proportionality in consequentialist terms that balance costs and benefits, we must also recognise the importance of the objection that a *purely* consequentialist calculus is liable to sacrifice some for the sake of (to use some as a means to) the benefit of others.

This leads back to the relationship between prospective and retrospective proportionality. Criminal law is a primarily responsive practice, which is therefore subject most obviously to the demands of retrospective proportionality, as we saw in section II. However, I noted there that considerations of prospective proportionality are also relevant, and a correlative point can be made here about preventive measures: since they are essentially forward-looking, they are most obviously subject to the demands of prospective proportionality; but considerations of retrospective proportionality may also be relevant.

Consider preventive detention – a drastic mode of preventive coercion. Suppose (though this itself controversial) that it satisfies the requirements of prospective proportionality if it is focused on those whom courts have reason to believe are likely to engage in terrorist activity: the burdens, moral and material, of the detention are proportionate to the preventive benefits to be gained. But, it is objected, such prospectively proportionate measures are distributively unjust because they are targeted on particular groups, who are then used as means to the end of security. That objection might be met if the measures are imposed only on those who have been convicted of a relevant crime, and their severity is retrospectively proportionate to that crime. Matters become harder if the period of detention supposedly required for security exceeds the limits set by retrospective proportionality: can we treat the commission of that past crime as a licence to impose a retrospectively disproportionate length of detention, if it is prospectively proportionate to the end to be achieved?[53] Matters become yet more difficult if efficient prevention is taken to require the detention of those who have not been convicted of any relevant offence, but are judged to be 'dangerous':[54] for they are being treated as if they are guilty of a relevant crime, without having been convicted by due process in a criminal court, which seems clearly at odds with the presumption of innocence. Another preventive tactic is the creation of new offences that criminalise conduct remote from, but in some way related or preparatory to, the target mischief, and

[53] For a subtle attempt to justify some kinds of extended preventive sentence as still being retrospectively proportionate, see A Walen, 'A Punitive Precondition for Preventive Detention: Lost Status as an Element of a Just Punishment' (2011) 63 *San Diego Law Review* 1229: someone who commits a relevantly serious kind of crime loses his immunity to 'long-term preventive detention'; he is liable to be thus detained if this is necessary for (and prospectively proportionate to) preventive purposes.

[54] See Ashworth and Zedner (n 34) especially ch 7; also relevant here are the kinds of 'hybrid' measure noted above (n 34) that attach criminal sanctions to breaches of 'civil preventive orders'.

the imposition of harsh sentences for such offences:[55] such measures might be prospectively proportionate, but they raise very obvious questions of retrospective proportionality – not just about whether such sentences are proportionate to the seriousness of the offences as defined, but whether criminalisation itself is a retrospectively proportionate response to such conduct.

I have not tried here to resolve the various problems I have identified about proportionality and the criminal law. My aim has rather been, more modestly, to clarify the roles played by both prospective and retrospective proportionality within the criminal law and in the broader field of criminal justice; to clarify what each kind of proportionality involves, and how they relate to each other – how they can interweave, but also conflict; and to bring out some of the ways in which they are related to other important political values – in particular the values of distributive justice.

[55] See nn 32–33; Ashworth and Zedner (n 34) ch 5. See also Lucia Zedner's and John Jackson's chapters 7 and 8 in this volume.

3

Proportionality and the Bindingness of Fundamental Rights*

RALF POSCHER

The proportionality principle has developed over time to become *a* – and in some jurisdictions, such as Germany, *the* – central standard of constitutional law and human rights. The principle has witnessed a meteoric rise both in Germany and abroad. It has also been incorporated into international human rights law. I will focus on the German development for three reasons of increasing importance. First, pragmatism: I am most familiar with the situation in Germany. Second, history: the international success story of the proportionality principle – at least as portrayed by Aharon Barak – originated in Germany. Third, analysis: German constitutional history reveals most clearly and explicitly the functional, systematic problem that the principle of proportionality is designed to solve.

I. The Hermeneutic Problem of Binding Constitutional Rights

The principle of proportionality owes its acclaim to a problem that lawyers who have grown up with the principle no longer recognise – evidence of how effectively the principle has solved the problem. That said, the problem is fundamental, as it concerns nothing less than the binding nature of constitutional rights with regard, in particular, to the legislature. Most constitutional and international fundamental and human rights guarantees at least aspire to be binding on the legislature, as well as other branches of government. Article 1(3) of the German Basic Law (*Grundgesetz*, German Constitution) states this explicitly: 'The following fundamental rights shall bind the *legislature*, the executive, and the judiciary as directly applicable law' (emphasis added). This formulation is a

* This chapter draws in large part on a more comprehensive contribution to M Herdegen, J Masing, R Poscher and K Gärditz, *Handbuch des Verfassungsrechs in transnationaler Perspektive* (München, CH Beck, 2021 forthcoming).

response to earlier doctrines concerning fundamental rights, such as during the late period of constitutionalism and the Weimar Republic, when constitutional protections and fundamental rights were regarded as mere political declarations. In contrast, the founding mothers and fathers of the Basic Law sought to create a constitutional system in which the legislature was bound to uphold fundamental rights.

Yet this is easier said – as in Article 1(3) Basic Law – than doctrinally done. Most of the fundamental rights enshrined in the Basic Law are subject to the possibility of legislative restrictions that allow the legislature to limit the same fundamental rights it is bound to uphold. For example, while Article 14(1) Basic Law states: 'Property and the right of inheritance shall be guaranteed', it goes on to note: 'Their *content* and *limits* shall be defined by the laws' (emphasis added). So, how can the legislature, which is expressly authorised to define the 'contents and limits' of property, simultaneously be bound by Article 14(1) Basic Law, as required by Article 1(3)? Similarly, although Article 5(1) Basic Law protects freedom of speech, Article 5(2) allows free speech to be restricted by general laws. What does it mean for the legislature to be bound to uphold freedom of speech if, at the same time, it is permitted to limit free speech by means of general laws?[1] Constitutional doctrine and practice in the Weimar Republic[2] wrestled with this problem, but ultimately none of the proposed solutions was accepted. As a result, the opinion was widely held that fundamental rights were not binding on the legislature,[3] and, since the executive and the courts were bound by the laws of the legislature anyway, fundamental rights were felt to be of little import other than as a reminder to obey the statutory law.

The German Federal Constitutional Court (Bundesverfassungsgericht) has taken a markedly different approach, correctly assuming that the Basic Law intends

[1] Art 5 Basic Law: '(1) Every person shall have the right freely to express and disseminate his opinions in speech, writing and pictures … (2) These rights shall find their limits in the provisions of general laws, in provisions for the protection of young persons and in the right to personal honour.' (translation available at: www.gesetze-im-internet.de/englisch_gg/englisch_gg.html).

[2] For suggestions, see, eg, C Schmitt, *Verfassungsrechtliche Aufsätze aus den Jahren 1924–1954* (Berlin, Duncker & Humblot, 1958) 140ff; on further approaches to the institutional guarantee during the Weimar period, see U Mager, *Einrichtungsgarantien: Entstehung, Wurzeln, Wandlungen und grundgesetzgemäße Neubestimmung einer dogmatischen Figur des Verfassungsrechts* (Tübingen, Mohr Siebeck, 2003) 34ff; see also A Hensel, 'Die Rangordnung der Rechtsquellen' in G Anschütz and R Thoma (eds), *Handbuch des deutschen Staatsrechts* (Tübingen, Mohr Siebeck, 1932) 316, fn 2, who called for the legislature, 'when exercising the proviso, to leave the value of the fundamental rights decision untouched'. On the essence guarantee of the Basic Law, see H Dreier, 'Die Zwischenkriegszeit' in D Merten and H-J Papier (eds), *Handbuch der Grundrechte I* (Heidelberg, CF Müller, 2004) 33f; R Smend, 'Das Recht der freien Meinungsäußerung' (1928) 4 *Veröffentlichungen der Vereinigung der Deutschen Staatsrechtslehrer (VVDStRL)* 44, 52; F Poetzsch-Heffter, *Handkommentar der Reichsverfassung vom 11. August 1919: Ein Handbuch für Verfassungsrecht und Verfassungspolitik*, 3rd edn (Berlin, Liebmann, 1928) 427; B Remmert, *Verfassungs- und verwaltungsrechtsgeschichtliche Grundlagen des Übermaßverbotes* (Heidelberg, Müller Juristischer Verlag, 1995).

[3] On the period of constitutionalism, see R Wahl, 'Der Grundsatz der Verhältnismäßigkeit: Ausgangslage und Gegenwartsproblematik' in D Heckmann, R P Schenke and G Sydow (eds), *Verfassungsstaatlichkeit im Wandel: Festschrift für Thomas Würtenberger zum 70. Geburtstag* (Berlin, Duncker & Humblot, 2013) 824–26.

for its fundamental rights to be binding on the legislature. The Court made this particularly clear in one of its earliest decisions, stating:

> In the literature, the objection has been frequently raised that the fundamental right is 'toothless' because it is subject to general legal limitations. However, it is often overlooked that legislative power under the Basic Law is subject to far greater restrictions than it was under the Constitution of 1919. At that time, many of the fundamental rights were, in fact, 'toothless'. In contrast, the current Basic Law has established a value-based order that limits public power.[4]

Article 1(3) Basic Law enshrines this intent to bind: 'The following fundamental rights shall bind the legislature, the executive, and the judiciary as directly applicable law.' But given the fact that most fundamental rights in the Basic Law – much like in the Weimar Constitution – contain explicit provisos that reserve to the legislature the power to limit or even define them (*Gesetzesvorbehalt, reserva de ley, reserve de loi, riserva di legge*), how should the intent to bind the legislature to observe fundamental rights be implemented? The central hermeneutic challenge posed by Article 1(3) Basic Law has been how to enrich the doctrinal content of fundamental rights, despite the seemingly expansive provisos, in order to ensure their binding force – especially on the legislature.

II. The Solution Presented in the *Pharmacy Decision* of 1958

In 1958, the German Federal Constitutional Court ruled on the constitutional complaint of a pharmacist whose application to open a pharmacy in Traunreut, a small town in Bavaria that already had a pharmacy, had been denied. His application was denied in accordance with the Bavarian Pharmacy Act, which provided for a demand-oriented system for the opening of new pharmacies. The government maintained that there was no demand for a second pharmacy in Traunreut: one pharmacy seemed sufficient. In ruling on the complaint, the Federal Constitutional Court did not see the government's decision as the problem but rather the Act itself. It therefore undertook a review of the Bavarian Pharmacy Act and its effect on the fundamental freedom of occupation. In so doing, the Court was faced with the problem described above: according to Article 12(1) Basic Law, the fundamental freedom of occupation can be limited by statutory law, and the Bavarian Pharmacy Act was such a law.[5] As such, how could it possibly be unconstitutional? Facing this challenge, the Federal Constitutional Court pronounced one of the

[4] BVerfGE (Federal Constitutional Court Reports) 6, 32 (40) [16 January 1957] (translation by the author).

[5] Art 12 Basic Law: '(1) All Germans shall have the right freely to choose their occupation or profession, their place of work and their place of training. The practice of an occupation or profession may be regulated by or pursuant to a law.'

most consequential decisions of its entire history: it introduced the principle of proportionality into constitutional law and, at the same time, required the legislature to adhere to this principle.[6]

The decision had sweeping repercussions. The Federal Constitutional Court gave itself extensive powers of review over the legislature. This power has fundamentally shaped both its role vis-à-vis the other branches of government and the further development of the Basic Law. The Court was obviously well aware of this, as it is the only decision in which it has expressly discussed its claim to judicial review of legislation in accordance with the proportionality standard, which includes review of the necessity of the law:[7]

> It has been argued that it is beyond the competencies of this Court to rule on such matters: that this Court cannot judge whether a particular legislative measure is necessary because it cannot know whether there are other equally effective options at hand; this can only be known if the entire range of political options and possibilities that are open to the legislature are known. This view, which seeks to place narrow constraints on the review competencies of the Federal Constitutional Court, is based on the theory that extensive powers of review encroach on the legislature and violate the principle of the separation of powers. This Court does not agree with this interpretation.[8]

The Federal Constitutional Court appealed to the role conferred upon it by the Basic Law to protect and uphold fundamental rights, holding that, without the power of a proportionality review, it could not effectively fulfil this role vis-à-vis the legislature.[9] The Federal Constitutional Court saw the responsibility to ensure that the fundamental rights of the Basic Law not be viewed as 'idle' rights, which had been the fate of the fundamental rights of the Weimar Constitution.[10]

Doctrinally, the principle of proportionality is located in Article 1(3) Basic Law. Sometimes this is expressed by stating that the principle of proportionality flows

[6] But see also the previous concise statements of the same senate of the Court in BVerfGE 7, 320 (323f) [10 March 1958], in which a law was rejected because it did not meet the 'necessary and adequate means' test.

[7] This judgment was not entirely positively received. See, eg, H Ehmke, 'Prinzipien der Verfassungsinterpretation: Mitbericht von Professor Dr. Horst Ehmke, Freiburg' (1963) 20 *Veröffentlichungen der Vereinigung der Deutschen Staatsrechtslehrer (VVDStRL)* 53, 92ff.

[8] BVerfGE 7, 377 (409f) [11 June 1958]; the representatives of the opposing view were not named in the decision. Corresponding positions can be found in E Kaufmann, 'Die Grenzen der Verfassungsgerichtsbarkeit' (1952) 9 *Veröffentlichungen der Vereinigung der Deutschen Staatsrechtslehrer (VVDStRL)* 1, 9f, opposing a balancing test; U Scheuner, 'Die Rechtsprechung des Bundesverfassungsgerichts und das Verfassungsrecht der Bundesrepublik' (1952) 67 *Deutsches Verwaltungsblatt* 613, 615, opposing a suitability test; O Pohl, *Ist der Gesetzgeber bei Eingriffen in die Grundrechte an den Grundsatz der Verhältnismäßigkeit gebunden?* (Köln, Dissertation Universität Köln, 1959) 116ff already in support of such a test; R von Krauss, *Der Grundsatz der Verhältnismäßigkeit: In seiner Bedeutung für die Notwendigkeit des Mittels im Verwaltungsrecht* (Hamburg, Kommissionsverlag Ludwig Appel, 1955) 42ff.

[9] BVerfGE 7, 377 (410f) [11 June 1958].

[10] BVerfGE 7, 377 (404f) [11 June 1958]; see already BVerfGE 6, 32 (40f) [11 January 1957], in which the Weimar problem was identified even more expressly.

directly from the fundamental rights per se.[11] A later anchoring of the principle also in the rule of law[12] has since allowed for its application beyond fundamental rights.[13] In the *Pharmacy Decision*, the principle of proportionality was framed in terms of a suitability test, a necessity test, which was controversial in 1958, and an appropriateness control. The appropriateness control takes the form of the so-called tiered theory, which the Federal Constitutional Court developed to assess infringements that affect the fundamental freedom of occupation.[14] In addition to suitability and necessity, the appropriateness control compares infringements of varying intensity with the regulatory goals of the legislative infringement. Objective restraints on freedom of occupation, such as the concession system of the Bavarian Pharmacy Act, are admissible only if they are absolutely essential to prevent a demonstrable or highly probable serious danger to the community. The Bavarian law failed this legal test.

With the *Pharmacy Decision*, the Federal Constitutional Court structured the principle of proportionality as a control standard and established its applicability to the legislature. It has never once looked back. Beginning in 1959, the principle stopped being viewed as something that applies to specific fundamental rights and instead started being seen as a 'general principle of proportionality' that permeates the Basic Law.[15] With the proportionality principle in hand, the Federal Constitutional Court could enforce the bindingness of fundamental rights with regard to the legislature as required by Article 1(3) Basic Law. Systematically, the introduction of the proportionality principle into constitutional law is a doctrinal legal construction that gives meaning to Article 1(3) Basic Law in the face of provisos that allow the legislature to 'define and limit' fundamental rights by means of

[11] BVerfGE 19, 342 (348f) [15 December 1965]; BVerfGE 61, 126 (134) [19 October 1982]; BVerfGE 76, 1 (50f) [12 May 1987]; see also BVerfGE 90, 145 (173) [9 March 1994]. For additional references on the current state of the discussion, see P Reimer, 'Verhältnismäßigkeit im Verfassungsrecht: Ein heterogenes Konzept' in M Jestaedt and O Lepsius (eds), *Verhältnismäßigkeit: Zur Tragfähigkeit eines verfassungsrechtlichen Schlüsselkonzepts* (Tübingen, Mohr Siebeck, 2016) 61ff.

[12] BVerfGE 23, 127 (133) [5 March 1968]; BVerfGE 61, 126 (134) [19 October 1982]; BVerfGE 80, 103 (106f) [9 May 1989].

[13] BVerfGE 138, 1 (19f) [19 November 2014]; B Grzeszick, 'Art. 20 GG' in T Maunz and G Dürig (eds), *Grundgesetz: Kommentar* (München, Beck, 2019) Art 20 no 109.

[14] See BVerfGE 13, 97 (104) [17 July 1961]: tiered theory of the *Pharmacy Decision* as 'the result of the strict application of the principle of proportionality'.

[15] BVerfGE 10, 141 (173) [27 October 1959]; see also BVerfGE 10, 221 (225) [17 November 1959]. The principle was also immediately generalised in the literature. For a prime example, see P Lerche, *Übermaß und Verfassungsrecht: Zur Bindung des Gesetzgebers an die Grundsätze der Verhältnismässigkeit und der Erforderlichkeit* (Köln, Heymann, 1961); under the term 'practical concordance' (*praktische Konkordanz*) which was particularly true of proportionality in the narrow sense, see K Hesse, *Grundzüge des Verfassungsrechts der Bundesrepublik Deutschland* (Karlsruhe, Müller, 1967) 28f; on developments in this area, O Lepsius, 'Chancen und Grenzen des Grundsatzes der Verhältnismäßigkeit' in M Jestaedt and O Lepsius (eds), *Verhältnismäßigkeit: Zur Tragfähigkeit eines verfassungsrechtlichen Schlüsselkonzepts* (Tübingen, Mohr Siebeck, 2016) 5f; K Stern, 'Zur Entstehung und Ableitung des Übermaßverbotes' in P Badura (ed), *Wege und Verfahren des Verfassungslebens: Festschrift für Peter Lerche zum 65. Geburtstag* (München, Beck, 1993) 171f.

statutory law. Methodologically, it is the result of a hermeneutic effort undertaken by the Court.

III. The Proliferation of the Principle of Proportionality

The Basic Law is not the only legal text guaranteeing fundamental rights that must confront the structural problem of how to balance binding constitutional obligations, on the one hand, with the legislative power to enact freedom-limiting statutes, on the other. Like the Basic Law, many other constitutional as well as international and European human rights documents recognise the legislative need to, at times, constrain fundamental rights. It is therefore not surprising that the principle of proportionality has become the main international standard for determining permissible statutory limitations on fundamental rights. This makes it one of the internationally most widely-received principles of German constitutional law. The following diagram (Figure 1), created by Aharon Barak, illustrates the international migration and proliferation of the principle of proportionality[16] and highlights the role played by the Federal Constitutional Court, which led the development in Germany, in this process:[17]

The substantial influence exerted by the Federal Constitutional Court's jurisprudence can be explained by the fact that it garnered attention not only from its German-speaking neighbours but also from countries located farther afield in eastern and southern Europe as well as in Asia and South America. In common law jurisdictions, the 1986 decision handed down by the Canadian Supreme Court in *R v Oakes* proved to be particularly influential in the reception of the principle of proportionality.[18] In essence, the *Oakes* test, which is used to determine the constitutionality of legislative infringements on guaranteed fundamental rights, corresponds to the principle of proportionality and has now been widely accepted throughout the Commonwealth. Since the 1970s, the principle of proportionality has also been used by the European Court of Human Rights (ECtHR) to determine the types of legislative interventions that are '*necessary* in a democratic society' (emphasis added):[19] this has led to the principle's secondary reception in many

[16] A Barak, *Proportionality. Constitutional Rights and Their Limitations* (Cambridge, Cambridge University Press, 2012) 178ff. On comparative legal aspects, see also Lepsius (n 15) 25ff; J Greene, 'Rights as Trumps?' (2018) 132 *Harvard Law Review* 28, 58f.

[17] Barak (n 16) 182.

[18] *R v Oakes*, [1986] 1 SCR 103.

[19] *Case 'Relating to certain aspects of the laws on the use of languages in education in Belgium' v Belgium* App nos 1474/62, 1677/62, 1691/62, 1769/63, 1994/63 and 2126/64 (ECtHR, 23 July 1968); *Handyside v United Kingdom* App no 5493/72 (ECtHR, 7 December 1976); *Dudgeon v United Kingdom* App no 7525/76 (ECtHR, 22 October 1981). See J Saurer, 'Die Globalisierung des Verhältnismäßigkeitsgrundsatzes' (2012) 43 *Der Staat* 3, 9ff; B Baade, *Der Europäische Gerichtshof für Menschenrechte als Diskurswächter: Zur Methodik, Legitimität und Rolle des Gerichtshofs im demokratisch-rechtsstaatlichen Entscheidungsprozess* (Berlin, Springer, 2017) 111ff; J Christoffersen, *Fair Balance: Proportionality, Subsidiarity and Primarity in the European Convention on Human Rights* (Leiden, Martinus Nijhoff Publishers, 2009) 31ff.

Figure 1 The migration of proportionality

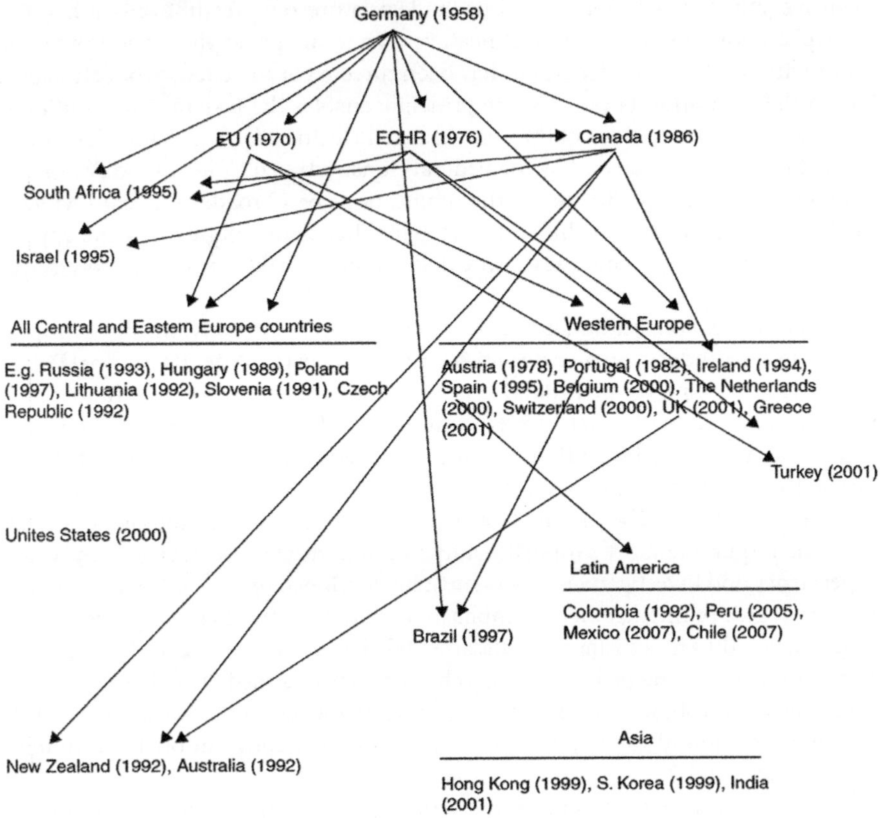

Member States of the Council of Europe. In the European Union, the principle is expressly stated in Article 52(1) of the Charter of Fundamental Rights:[20] 'Subject to the principle of proportionality, limitations may be made only if they are necessary and genuinely meet objectives of general interest recognised by the Union or the need to protect the rights and freedoms of others.'

IV. Constitutional Justification of the Proportionality Control

The principle of proportionality requires that legitimate purposes be pursued by legitimate means that are suitable, necessary and appropriate in relation to

[20] On the importance of the principle of proportionality in EU law prior to the entry into force of the Charter of Fundamental Rights, see O Koch, *Der Grundsatz der Verhältnismäßigkeit in der Rechtsprechung des Gerichtshofs der Europäischen Gemeinschaften* (Berlin, Duncker & Humblot, 2003).

the intensity of the infringement of the fundamental right concerned. Such an intensive, albeit structured control of the legislature requires not only a historical explanation but, above all, justification. While the principle is widespread, it is not without its critics. Criticism has been directed at the effect proportionality has on the separation of powers: the principle enables the Federal Constitutional Court to override decisions of the democratically legitimated legislature. However, while the criticism discussed by the Federal Constitutional Court in the *Pharmacy Decision* was generally directed at the implications of a broader judicial review,[21] the focus of later criticism shifted to the actual balancing required by the appropriateness criterion, sometimes also called proportionality in the narrow sense (*stricto sensu*).[22]

Today, many constitutional decisions rely almost exclusively on the appropriateness test. In its decision on new anti-terror powers in the Federal Criminal Police Office Act, for example, the Federal Constitutional Court mentions the fundamental rights affected by the Act in mere summary fashion; subsequently, the Court determines that the constitutionality of the powers conferred by the Act depends on their proportionality. In a short discussion, the suitability and necessity of the Act are then affirmed, before the Court comments that: 'Limitations arise mainly from the requirements of proportionality in the narrow sense. Consequently, the supervisory and investigative powers must be developed *appropriately* with regard to their degree of infringement' (emphasis added).[23] Of the 244 paragraphs of the ruling devoted to its substantive fundamental rights reasoning, 236 deal with the appropriateness of the provisions. In light of criticism aimed at such an extensive balancing approach, why have judicial proportionality controls – in all their different nuances – found their way into so many different constitutional and human rights jurisdictions?

A legal realist explanation could simply point to the attractiveness of the proportionality control to the courts that claim it. It provides constitutional and other courts with a broad and flexible power of judicial review with which to overturn legislative decisions. But even if the temptations associated with judicial power are part of the explanation, it would be strange if courts could assert this power in so many jurisdictions without losing acceptance if there were no underlying reasons of political morality upon which the proportionality control could lean. Theories of democracy certainly cannot explain the widespread use of the proportionality control: as critics never tire of emphasising, the democratic legitimacy of courts is much less than that of parliaments when it comes to balancing conflicts of interest. Thus, there must be other normative foundations of the liberal

[21] E Forsthoff, *Der Staat der Industriegesellschaft: Dargestellt am Beispiel der Bundesrepublik Deutschland* (München, CH Beck, 1971) 137ff.

[22] B Schlink, *Abwägung im Verfassungsrecht* (Berlin, Duncker & Humblot, 1976) 134ff; A T Aleinikoff, 'Constitutional Law in the Age of Balancing' (1987) 96 *Yale Law Journal* 943, 1004; S Tsakyrakis, 'Proportionality: An Assault on Human Rights?' (2009) 7 *International Journal of Constitutional Law* 468; DM Beatty, *The Ultimate Rule of Law* (Oxford, Oxford University Press, 2010) 160ff.

[23] BVerfGE 141, 220 (267) [20 April 2016].

constitutional state upon which the courts can base their use of the proportionality control over the more democratically legitimated legislature.

A deeper reason is seen in the fact that in a liberal constitutional state, the individual can call upon the democratically elected legislature to justify the need to infringe on fundamental rights: the right to a justification is a counterpart of the democratic process.[24] This type of justification can be based on recognition approaches in ethics,[25] in which the right to justification is the fundamental recognition of the other as a rational subject.[26] Democracy is not legitimised as a power struggle that enables the interests of the majority to override those of the minority: it is a search for reasonable consensus on the common good, which, on the basis of diverging interests, must be solved using the majority criterion. But it remains the case that democratic decisions must be justified as reasonable. Due to a number of potential pathologies of the democratic process – such as unreflected path dependencies, ideological influences or special interests that do not promote the common good – the fulfilment of this need for reasonableness and justification is not guaranteed by the parliamentary discussion and decision process alone. Judicial review based on the principle of proportionality demands that this justification be given. Such review does engage in legal interpretation; it does not operate in a hermeneutical mode but as an instrumental and normative rationality control. It does not demand a justification with reference to an authoritative text[27] but rather an instrumental and normative justification of governmental measures on the basis of rational standards.

Due to the jurisdiction of the courts, the right to justification is also taken seriously from an institutional perspective – just as the democratic principle is institutionalised in the parliament, the proportionality standard institutionalises the right to a justification in the courts. The principle of proportionality requires representatives of the majority to provide a rational justification for their decision; the proportionality requirement forces the majority to present this justification to an appropriate and independent constitutional institution. As such, constitutional courts use the principle of proportionality *reactively*. It is not their place

[24] M Kumm, 'The Idea of Socratic Contestation and the Right to Justification: The Point of Rights-Based Proportionality Review' (2010) 4 *Law & Ethics of Human Rights* 141, 157ff; see also N Petersen, *Verhältnismäßigkeit als Rationalitätskontrolle: Eine rechtsempirische Studie verfassungsgerichtlicher Rechtsprechung zu den Freiheitsgrundrechten* (Tübingen, Mohr Siebeck, 2015) 32ff; A Arnauld, 'Zur Rhetorik der Verhältnismäßigkeit' in M Jestaedt and O Lepsius (eds), *Verhältnismäßigkeit: Zur Tragfähigkeit eines verfassungsrechtlichen Schlüsselkonzepts* (Tübingen, Mohr Siebeck, 2016) 289.

[25] A Honneth, *Kampf um Anerkennung: Zur moralischen Grammatik sozialer Konflikte*, Sonderausgabe (Frankfurt am Main, Suhrkamp, 2003) 174ff, on the importance of the legal recognition for self-respect.

[26] R Forst, *Das Recht auf Rechtfertigung: Elemente einer konstruktivistischen Theorie der Gerechtigkeit* (Frankfurt am Main, Suhrkamp, 2007) 9ff, 68ff, 291ff, on the importance of justification for human rights.

[27] On the intentional reference to texts as a defining aspect of hermeneutic justification of legal interpretation and legal construction, see R Poscher, 'The Hermeneutic Character of Legal Construction' in S Glanert and F Girard (eds), *Law's Hermeneutics: Other Investigations* (New York, Routledge, 2017) 207ff.

to substitute their idea of proportional balancing for that of more democratically legitimated institutions but rather to use the principle of proportionality to force such institutions to show that their decisions are rationally justifiable. The extent to which the principle of proportionality satisfies this reactive profile depends not least on how rationally effective it proves to be.

V. Proportionality in the Narrow Sense

The criteria of suitability and necessity, on the one hand, fare quite well as a rationality standard; on the other hand, they only prevent the legislature or the executive from doing something stupid, namely, choosing a means that does not advance the designated purpose or being heavy-handed and choosing a means that could be substituted by another one that would achieve the purpose at least as well but be less intrusive with regard to the fundamental rights in question. This does not mean that the legislature or the administration does not sometimes miss the mark of such a purely instrumental rationality standard, but most – at least of the controversial – decisions go further and engage in an appropriateness control that involves the balancing of the aims pursued by the state and the liberty interests of the affected citizens. Thus, whether the principle of proportionality can be legitimated by the right of rational justification depends to a large extent on the performance of proportionality in the narrow sense, as the appropriateness criterion is also called.

A. Incommensurability as a Problem of Proportionality

So, it comes as no surprise that criticism of the principle of proportionality has, first and foremost, been concerned with the lack of rationalisability regarding the balancing of interests demanded by the appropriateness criterion, due to the incommensurability of the state interests and the liberty interests involved. In order to judge the relative value of goods, it appears that we need a uniform standard of value: if we want to assess the relative financial strength of two federal states, for example, their tax revenues, assets and liabilities can be compared in euros, using a monetary calculation. In constitutional law, however, there is no uniform standard of value with which to evaluate interests of security, on the one hand, and freedom, on the other – competing interests that have frequently been weighed against one another in recent case law. Aharon Barak proposed the use of 'social importance' as a unified value scale.[28] But while it is true that we can compare different legal positions once we have converted them into the currency of social

[28] Barak (n 16) 348ff.

importance, Timothy Endicott rightly notes that for such a conversion to occur, we must have first solved their incommensurability, the elimination of which is intended to serve as a uniform measure of social importance.[29] An econometric solution would be to overcome incommensurability by empirically questioning the holders of fundamental rights about their willingness to pay for the goods that are to be weighed against each other. But the methodological difficulties of this approach are almost insurmountable;[30] moreover, such investigations are not practicable for constitutional law jurisprudence. Thus, the incommensurability of the positions to be compared seems to be the central and unassailable problem of the principle of proportionality.

B. Proportionality as a Solution to the Incommensurability Problem

If a different perspective is taken, however, the script can be flipped: incommensurability is not the problem of the principle of proportionality; instead, proportionality is the solution to the problem of incommensurability.[31] Precisely because we are unable to compare two legal positions using a common standard, we must compare the degree of proportional realisation of each of the positions with respect to its own scale. Comparing degrees of realisation allows for the comparison of the incommensurable.[32] Bruce Chapman uses the example of a dog show to explain this:[33] poodles and German shepherds cannot be compared. But for both the poodle and the German shepherd, judges can decide on the extent to which they approximate to the ideal representation of their breed. Using this method, a decision can be reached about which dog deserves first place. This also works if, when judging the poodle, only its appearance is considered, while, when judging the German shepherd, its functionality as a guard dog is also taken into account.

Such comparisons of proportionate realisation can even achieve numerical exactness. For example, in the decathlon, incommensurable achievements are evaluated numerically. To tally the diverse results (ie, how many centimetres more in the long jump compared to how many seconds less in the 1,500 metres) into a single overall score, the metrics for each event are fed into a more complex formula using a discipline-specific constant. This formula is based on the world record and

[29] T Endicott, 'Proportionality and Incommensurability' in G Huscroft, B W Miller and G Webber (eds), *Proportionality and the Rule of Law: Rights, Justification, Reasoning* (Cambridge, Cambridge University Press, 2014) 318.

[30] See Petersen (n 24) 58 ff.

[31] B Chapman, 'Law, Incommensurability, and Conceptually Sequenced Argument' (1998) 146 *University of Pennsylvania Law Review* 1487.

[32] For a formalised treatment, see P-E N Veel, 'Incommensurability, Proportionality, and Rational Legal Decision-Making' (2010) 4 *Law & Ethics of Human Rights* 177, 195ff; on this, Petersen (n 24) 65ff.

[33] Chapman (n 31) 1492.

the average of the achievements of the 30 best specialists and the 100 best decathletes as calculated in 1984.[34]

Likewise, the relative weight of the curtailment of fundamental rights, on the one hand, and the realisation of public interests, on the other, can be compared. To what extent will a fundamental right be curtailed in relation to its ideal realisation? To what extent will a public interest be promoted in relation to its ideal realisation? The comparison of the two degrees of realisation will allow for a decision in favour of the value that is realised to a higher degree.

Of course, it is rightly argued that such far-reaching expectations – which are associated with this reversal of the perspective – are hampered by considerable uncertainties and normative assumptions.[35] For the decathlon example, Weyma Lübbe rightly points out that the point values are not used to measure but rather to define – and thus construct – the best decathlete.[36] Accordingly, the conversion formulas are controversial because they can result in a different weighting of disciplines.[37] Correspondingly, controversial assumptions can be made when constructing the ideal types that form the basis for the degree of realisation of a certain fundamental freedom or state purpose. Not only the construction of ideal types but also the assignment of degrees of realisation is associated with the need to make value judgements for which intersubjective agreement cannot be guaranteed. It will be difficult to reach consensus on the degree to which a surveillance measure infringes on personal freedom or privacy and the degree to which it promotes national security. The degree-of-realisation model also presupposes the equivalence of the legal goods being compared: this is not self-evident, even if individual fundamental rights are not ranked and the public interest is not broken down into the individual fundamental rights that it affects.

Nevertheless, the idea captures something that goes on when we engage in the innumerable small and large balancing decisions between incommensurables with which we are confronted every day.[38] They range all the way from banal decisions between incommensurable restaurants, Italian or Chinese, to life-shaping decisions between two incommensurable careers, such as academia or private practice. In cases of *clear* disproportionality, a proportional comparison of the degrees of realisation can likely count on broad intersubjective agreement. If the Italian restaurant is really bad and the Chinese really good, the decision is easy – even though Italian and Chinese cuisines are incommensurable. And to

[34] On the metrics, see M Fröhlich, F Gassmann, S Becker, M Backfisch and E Emrich, '30 Jahre Bewertungstabelle im Zehnkampf: Ist eine Revision nötig?' (2016) 57 *Leipziger Sportwissenschaftliche Beiträge* 81.

[35] Petersen (n 24) 66f.

[36] W Lübbe, 'Abwägen: Warnung vor einer Metapher der normativen Urteilsbildung' (2018) *Information Philosophie* 26, 28.

[37] Fröhlich, Gassmann, Becker, Backfisch and Emrich (n 34).

[38] This is also pointed out by J Waldron, 'Fake Incommensurability: A Response to Professor Schauer' (1993) 45 *Hastings Law Journal* 813, 817ff, who therefore distinguishes between strong and weak incommensurability, reserving the strong for so-called tragic decisions.

take an actual constitutional case: if a lumbar puncture – a risky and invasive procedure – is sought by the prosecution for the purpose of proving the culpability of a person suspected of having committed a minor offence, then we would consider the prosecution's wish disproportionate to the degree of impairment that would be suffered by the accused, should the procedure be carried out.[39] It seems equally possible to argue in a similar way with respect to data retention laws that comprehensively monitor the internet behaviour of the entire population: while broad data retention laws may be proportional when considered from the perspective of the need to protect the population from terrorism and violent organised crime, this would hardly be the case if measured against the need to prosecute copyright infringements.[40] Rationally speaking, a disproportional data protection law enacted in order to enable the prosecution of copyright infringements would suggest that, during the legislative process, well-organised, special copyright interests prevailed over the interest in protecting the fundamental rights of the majority of the population.

Clear disproportionalities mask subtler differences in valuation and allow for an intersubjectively convincing judgement. In cases in which there is no gross imbalance, however, the intersubjective differences in valuation will make themselves known. Yet the imponderability of comparing incommensurable goods lies deeper than the difficulty of *inter*subjective agreement. The intricacies of *intra*subjective judgements on incommensurable alternatives are discussed in theories of evaluative reason. They take very different approaches to explaining the difficulties posed for intrasubjective judgements in cases of incommensurability. Career decisions provide a standard example of such difficulties. For many, the decision to pursue a career either as a researcher or as a practising lawyer may be clear, but some individuals will no doubt be plagued by major decision-making difficulties. How do we explain the corresponding difficulties when weighing up these options?

Epistemic theories maintain that in all cases of evaluative comparison, one alternative is better than the other, but that we find it difficult, if not impossible, to recognise which one it is.[41] Semantic theories do not consider the issue to be the difficult decision itself but rather the vagueness of the linguistic expressions with which we describe the choices as better or worse or equally good. Maybe the terms 'better', 'worse' and 'equally good' are vague.[42] Conversely, incomparabilists deduce the incomparability of the alternatives from incommensurability.[43] Incommensurability pushes our evaluative reason to its limits – at least in cases

[39] BVerfGE 16, 194 (202) [10 June 1963].

[40] On this consequence of data retention, see BVerfGE 125, 260 (271) [2 March 2010].

[41] D Regan, 'Value, Comparability, and Choice' in R Chang (ed), *Incommensurability, Incomparability, and Practical Reason* (Cambridge MA, Harvard University Press, 1997) 129.

[42] J Broome, 'Is Incommensurability Vagueness?' in R Chang (ed), *Incommensurability, Incomparability, and Practical Reason* (Cambridge MA, Harvard University Press, 1997) 67.

[43] This view seems to prevail; see, eg, J Raz, *The Morality of Freedom* (Oxford, Clarendon Press, 1986) para 13; for additional references, see R Chang, 'The Possibility of Parity' (2002) 112 *Ethics* 659, 660.

where we experience lasting difficulties in choosing between two or more alternatives. We must therefore assume that a rational decision is no longer possible in such cases.[44] Just as it does not make sense to compare the colour green to the number 13, it does not make sense to compare incommensurable career alternatives. They are just different.

Ruth Chang added another proposal to the discussion, one based on the phenomenology of corresponding decision-making situations. According to Chang, it is a mistake to assume that our evaluative judgements about incommensurable alternatives have the same structure as those about commensurable ones. Commensurable comparisons are based on a trichotomy of evaluative alternatives: the common standard of 'better, worse or equally good'. Yet for Chang, it remains open whether this trichotomy also applies to evaluative judgements about incommensurables, or whether the phenomenology of our decision-making practice suggests that there is yet another evaluative value, namely, that one of two incommensurable alternatives can be not only better, worse or equally good but also 'on a par'.[45]

The trichotomy can only explain the difficulty of deciding between two career alternatives by assuming that the alternatives are equally good. But then it would be permissible to make the decision by tossing a coin. This may be an adequate decision-making technique if the careers are indeed equally good; for example, deciding to work at a law firm 'A' or 'B' where the conditions of employment differ only slightly – a corner office with a sunrise or sunset view, Coca Cola or Pepsi as a client, a Mercedes or BMW as a company car – but are nevertheless equivalent. However, this does not seem to apply to every decision between incommensurable alternatives. Choosing between a career in academia and one in private practice by tossing a coin would be inappropriate due to the importance of the decision. In addition, if our difficulties were to be explained by the alternatives being equally good, a slight change in one of the relevant conditions of the alternatives would make the decision straightforward. If both career paths offered a starting salary of €100,000 per annum, for example, then an increase of €10,000 at the law firm would necessarily result in the latter becoming the better offer and the decision to forgo a career in academia an easy one. Yet this does not seem to correspond to the phenomenology of the decision-making situation.

The assumption of incomparability is also difficult to reconcile with the phenomenology of our decision-making behaviour. If one of the alternatives is considerably devalued or upgraded, then (as the court decisions in cases of clear disproportionality show) we can certainly make comparative judgements. If our decision-maker could pursue an academic career only as a private, self-funded scholar with little to no chance of entering the circles of professional academic debate, and if the law firm option was coupled with a path to a high-ranking judicial

[44] Raz (n 43) 324.
[45] Chang (n 43) 659; R Chang, *Making Comparisons Count* (Hoboken NJ, Routledge, 2014) 123ff.

post where adjudication is practised at an academic level, then the comparison between the two alternatives would clearly favour private practice. However, why should an alteration – for the better or for the worse – in some aspects of the alternatives change not only the result of the comparison but also the comparability *as such* of the alternatives?

The 'on a par' category describes incommensurable alternatives that require us to make a kind of existential decision with which we commit ourselves to certain values associated with the chosen alternative. Only through and after this decision can we deem one of the two alternatives 'better'. Indeed, it is through this decision-making process that our autonomy is manifested and our personality developed. If all of our decisions were determined by evaluative reason, as epistemic theories assume, then there would be no room for freedom.[46]

Ultimately, all theories of evaluative value judgements speak against the mathematical formalisation of intrasubjective decisions on incommensurable alternatives. For incomparabilists, any comparison is anyhow out of the question, especially a mathematical one. However, this also applies to epistemic and semantic theories, insofar as they assume that reason offers a solution, but we cannot recognise or describe it. We can only calculate with known and describable amounts. One of the consequences of Chang's reasoning is that decision-making formalisations based on the aforementioned trichotomy cannot be applied to evaluative judgements about incommensurable alternatives.[47] This is all the more true when incommensurable alternatives must be compared at an *inter*subjective level as is the case when the proportionality principle is applied in the context of human rights and constitutional law, since the issues encountered already at the *intra*subjective level multiply – even exponentially. Thus, contrary to the formula suggested by Robert Alexy, it does not seem possible to assign meaningful numerical properties to individual aspects for their eventual numerical comparison.[48] The advantage of the considerations that led to the formula lies not in the formalisation itself but rather in the analysis of the individual components that are used to reach the formalisation. In this respect, the epistemic component of our balancing decisions deserves special mention. In the case law of the German Federal Constitutional Court, these epistemic components are

[46] Chang, *Making Comparisons* (n 45) 170ff.

[47] Chang (n 43) 660ff; Chang, *Making Comparisons* (n 45) 25ff.

[48] R Alexy, 'On Balancing and Subsumption: A Structural Comparison' (2003) 16 *Ratio Juris* 433, 443–48:

$$(P)\ W_{i,j} = \frac{I_i \cdot W_i \cdot R_i}{I_j \cdot W_j \cdot R_j} \quad (P)\ W_{i,j} = \frac{I_i \cdot W_i \cdot R_i}{I_j \cdot W_j \cdot R_j}$$

(P) $W_{i/j}$ = Weight of a principle i in a concrete case relative to a colliding principle j
$I_{i/j}$ = Intensity of the interference with a principle i / j
$W_{i/j}$ = abstract weight of a principle i / j
$R_{i/j}$ = Degree of reliability of the empirical assumptions about 'I'

not openly considered; instead, they are incorporated into risk assessments and probability judgements.[49]

The phenomenology of our evaluative judgements on incommensurable alternatives thus especially argues against overstraining the intersubjective reliability of the balancing process. There are cases, such as the one concerning the lumbar puncture, in which the imbalance of the relative degrees of realisation of the different legal positions seems evident. Although the range of such cases cannot be accurately defined – since intersubjective agreement about degrees of realisation and initial values is itself a gradual phenomenon – it is hardly controversial that the Federal Constitutional Court has occasionally stepped beyond these boundaries. In such cases, it is questionable what role the Federal Constitutional Court should play when it comes to the right to justification. From the perspective of the right to justification, there is much to be said for restricting the disproportionality control to self-evident cases; from this perspective, existential decisions involving conflicts between incommensurable democratic values should be left to other, more politically legitimate actors, such as the legislature.[50]

C. The Re-Entry of Hermeneutics

Vis-à-vis the legislature, in particular, the Federal Constitutional Court has gone beyond this narrowly defined role of the right to justification. This could be taken to mean that the Court has simply exceeded its legitimacy, and there certainly are judgments of the Court that are otherwise difficult to explain. It could also be, however, that at least some of the Court's judgments conceal other phenomena that suggest more than a mere disproportionality control. In order to identify them, it is helpful to remember how the principle of proportionality entered constitutional law in the first place. It came about to solve a hermeneutical problem: what does it mean for fundamental rights to be binding on a legislature that is, by the same rights, empowered to define and limit them?

An answer to this was provided by the instrumental and normatively rational principle of proportionality, of which the remark by Matthias Kumm, that it is itself not hermeneutic in nature, is certainly correct.[51] Yet already in the hour of its birth as a constitutional principle, the Federal Constitutional Court used the proportionality principle to further its hermeneutical task, which emanates from the provision of direct bindingness in Article 1(3) Basic Law. In the

[49] This is rightly pointed out by T Mori, 'Wirkt in der Abwägung wirklich das formelle Prinzip?' (2019) 58 *Der Staat* 555, 562ff.

[50] See also M Kumm, 'Political Liberalism and the Structure of Rights: On the Place and Limits of the Proportionality Requirement' in G Pavlakos (ed), *Law, Rights and Discourse: The Legal Philosophy of Robert Alexy* (Oxford, Hart Publishing, 2007) 164f, who argues for a limitation of the proportionality test to an institutional division of labour between courts and political institutions.

[51] Kumm (n 24) 142f.

Pharmacy Decision, the Federal Constitutional Court developed its tiered theory of freedom of occupation within its balancing considerations, a theory that relies on the distinction between the choice of occupation and the exercise of that occupation, alluded to in the text of the norm, which also distinguishes between the choice and the exercise of an occupation. It thus tries to effectuate the bindingness of Article 12 Basic Law with respect to the legislature via hermeneutically guided balancing considerations within its appropriateness test. In functional terms, the tier-based approach derived from the *Pharmacy Decision* is similar to various tests developed in the US for regulating limitations on freedom of expression. Thus, early proportionality jurisprudence foreshadowed a re-entry of hermeneutics into the rationality control established with the proportionality test.

First, the principle of proportionality is hermeneutically developed from the bindingness clause of Article 1(3) Basic Law; second, within the principle of proportionality – which only calls for an instrumental and normative rationality control – the hermeneutical task is taken up again in the context of the appropriateness criterion. The appropriateness test is thus the place where hermeneutical construction of doctrinal standards for specific fundamental rights occurs. These doctrinal standards elaborate the specific way in which these rights are directly binding. This can be seen in the doctrinal construction of statutory limits on property rights that require compensation even though they do not amount to an expropriation in the sense of Article 14(3) Basic Law,[52] for which compensation is explicitly demanded. This construction was developed within the framework of the appropriateness criterion, though not as a result of a rationality control, but rather hermeneutically from the legal provisions in Article 14 Basic Law on the substance and value guarantee of property ownership.[53] With the doctrinal development of the compensation requirement, appropriateness is hermeneutically re-specified for the purposes of Article 14 Basic Law.

This can also be seen regarding many of the organisational and procedural measures required by the Court in the context of the appropriateness test for the protection of various fundamental rights.[54] They are better explained hermeneutically rather than as expressions of a comparative rationality control of degrees of

[52] Art 14 Basic Law: '(1) Property and the right of inheritance shall be guaranteed. Their content and limits shall be defined by the laws. (3) Expropriation shall only be permissible for the public good. It may only be ordered by or pursuant to a law that determines the nature and extent of compensation.'

[53] BVerfGE 58, 300 (330ff) [15 July 1981]; see also BVerfGE 35, 79 (120ff) [29 May 1973]; BVerfGE 53, 30 (65) [20 December 1979]; BVerfGE 61, 1 (44) [22 June 1982].

[54] H Goerlich, *Grundrechte als Verfahrensgarantien: Ein Beitrag zum Verständnis des Grundgesetzes für die Bundesrepublik Deutschland* (Baden-Baden, Nomos, 1981); H Bethge, 'Grundrechtsverwirklichung und Grundrechtssicherung durch Organisation und Verfahren: Zu einigen Aspekten der aktuellen Grundrechtsdiskussion' (1982) *Neue Juristische Wochenschrift* 1; K Redeker, 'Grundgesetzliche Rechte auf Verfahrensteilhabe: Bemerkungen zu einem status activus processualis' (1980) *Neue Juristische Wochenschrift* 1593; F Ossenbühl, 'Grundrechtsschutz im und durch Verfahrensrecht' in K Eichenberger and G Müller (eds), *Staatsorganisation und Staatsfunktionen im Wandel: Festschrift für Kurt Eichenberger zum 60. Geburtstag* (Basel, Helbing & Lichtenhahn, 1982) 183.

realisation. The Basic Law itself provides for procedural safeguards, especially – but not only – in the form of prior judicial approval, for particularly severe encroachments on especially sensitive fundamental rights, such as deprivation of liberty or searches of the home. In the meantime, this thought has been taken up in the context of other particularly intrusive infringements of other fundamental rights that are not equipped with explicit procedural safeguards. Like the general guarantee of personal freedom in Article 2(1) Basic Law, the Basic Law also provides for the protection of the right to life and physical integrity in Article 2(2)[55] with a proviso that allows for limitations by an ordinary statutory law. Does this mean that the right to freedom from serious infringements of physical integrity, such as compulsory medical treatment, enjoys the same degree of legal protection as the arbitrary general freedom to ride a horse in the woods?[56] When the Federal Constitutional Court requires strict procedural standards and judicial approval for compulsory medical treatment, it gives an answer to the question of what the bindingness of the guarantee to life and physical integrity means in the face of a proviso that seems to require only an ordinary statutory law to justify infringements on life, physical integrity and personal liberty. Hermeneutically, the doctrinal construction of procedural safeguards that go beyond a simple statutory law could point to Article 104 Basic Law,[57] where comparable procedural safeguards for severe infringements on personal liberty are explicitly required in the habeas corpus tradition. Personal liberty, it should be noted, is guaranteed in the same article and indeed the same paragraph as the rights to life and physical integrity.[58]

The same applies to online searches and the monitoring of telecommunications.[59] Both are severe infringements on the fundamental right to privacy. In its spatial dimension, privacy is protected by Article 13 Basic Law,[60] which guarantees the inviolability of the home. For searches of the home, as a very severe infringement, Article 13(2) Basic Law requires prior judicial authorisation. When the Federal Constitutional Court demands a prior independent authorisation of online searches and monitoring of telecommunications in the context of its appropriateness considerations, it can draw hermeneutically on the procedural safeguards that the Basic Law itself provides for severe infringements

[55] Art 2 Basic Law: '(1) Every person shall have the right to free development of his personality insofar as he does not violate the rights of others or offend against the constitutional order or the moral law. (2) Every person shall have the right to life and physical integrity. Freedom of the person shall be inviolable. These rights may be interfered with only pursuant to a law.'

[56] BVerfGE 80, 137 (154ff) [6 June 1989].

[57] Art 104(2) Basic Law: 'Only a judge may rule upon the permissibility or continuation of any deprivation of liberty. If such a deprivation is not based on a judicial order, a judicial decision shall be obtained without delay.'

[58] BVerfGE 128, 282 (315ff) [23 March 2011].

[59] BVerfGE 120, 274 (331ff) [27 February 2008].

[60] Art 13 Basic Law: '(1) The home is inviolable. (2) Searches may be authorised only by a judge or, when time is of the essence, by other authorities designated by the laws and may be carried out only in the manner therein prescribed.'

of privacy in Article 13 Basic Law. Thus, it updates the bindingness of the Basic Law's privacy protections for new types of sometimes even more invasive, technology-enhanced infringements of privacy.

The ability of appropriateness to function as a gateway for the further doctrinal construction of the binding nature of fundamental rights becomes particularly clear where the principle of proportionality reaches its limits. This seems to have happened with regard to national security law, especially concerning risk prevention.[61] How can the mere collection of data not be suitable, necessary and appropriate to prevent terrorist events such as the 2001 attacks on September 11 and those in Madrid, London and Paris in 2004 and 2005? In the view of the enormity of the threatened harm, the comparative weight assigned to privacy rights has to fade into insignificance. The risk prevention dynamic has already resulted in calls to elevate the proportionality standard by demanding that its operability, too, be guaranteed. Precautionary measures would then be unconstitutional, not only when they are disproportionate but also when they are always proportionate.[62] If this correctly describes the situation, it is not surprising that discussions of reasonableness consume such large portions of the Federal Constitutional Court's security law jurisprudence.

When the Federal Constitutional Court sets 'concrete danger' as a standard appropriate for particularly intensive[63] or particularly extensive[64] security measures[65] or develops detailed procedural requirements for the protection of the core area of the general right of personality,[66] these doctrinal constructions may not be regarded merely as the result of a comparison of different degrees of realisation of national security and fundamental rights. Rather, they are the result of a constructive doctrinal effort to solve the original hermeneutical problem of the legislature's commitment to fundamental rights in view of the failure, or at least the poor performance, of the principle of proportionality as a mere rationality control. Considerations of appropriateness in such instances are concerned with normative rationality control but also, and most importantly, with the specification of how the legislature is bound by a specific fundamental right. The binding nature of fundamental rights continues to be doctrinally developed within the proportionality principle, which in turn is a doctrinal development to effectuate the legal bindingness of fundamental rights required by Article 1(3) Basic Law.

[61] U Volkmann, 'Anmerkung zur BVerfGE Rasterfahndung' (2006) 61 *Juristenzeitung* 906, 919; O Lepsius, 'Die Grenzen der präventivpolizeilichen Telefonüberwachung' (2006) *Jura* 929, 931.

[62] C Enders, 'Sozialstaatlichkeit im Spannungsfeld von Eigenverantwortung und Fürsorge' (2004) 64 *Veröffentlichungen der Vereinigung der Deutschen Staatsrechtslehrer (VVDStRL)* 7, 46ff.

[63] BVerfGE 115, 320 (361f) [4 April 2006]; BVerfGE 125, 260 (330) [2 March 2010]; BVerfGE 141, 220 (217) [20 April 2016].

[64] BVerfGE 115, 320 (362ff) [4 April 2006].

[65] On the different levels of dangerousness, see R Poscher, 'Eingriffsschwellen im Recht der inneren Sicherheit: Ihr System im Licht der neueren Verfassungsrechtsprechung' (2008) 41 *Die Verwaltung* 345.

[66] R Poscher, 'Menschenwürde und Kernbereichsschutz: Von den Gefahren einer Verräumlichung des Grundrechtsdenkens' (2009) 64 *Juristenzeitung* 269.

This reasoning is not limited to the situation of the legislature and its constitutionally binding obligations; indeed, the Federal Constitutional Court has used the concept of appropriateness to further doctrinally develop the constraints that fundamental rights place on specialist courts. An example can be seen in decisions on freedom of expression, in which public officials and the courts are required to interpret contested utterances in a way that is sympathetic to the exercise of free speech. In other words, they have to presume that such utterances are intended to have a meaning that is compatible with the law.[67] It would be neither purposively irrational nor, in a normatively proportional sense, inappropriate to base the interpretation of an utterance on the addressee's point of view. The appropriateness criterion, however, not only serves the purpose of a comparative analysis of degrees of realisation but also provides the framework for specifying the directly binding nature of the obligation of Article 5(1) Basic Law on public officials and the courts by forcing them to seek an interpretation of utterances that is sympathetic to the exercise of freedom of speech. Just as the interpretation of the generality requirement in Article 5(2) Basic Law[68] for laws that curtail freedom of speech, in the sense of a content neutrality requirement, strengthens the bindingness of the right on the legislature, so the principle of proportionality serves as a framework within which the presumption of the constitutionality of utterances can contribute to strengthening the bindingness of the right to freedom of speech on the administration and the courts.

These examples of the re-entry of hermeneutics into the discussion of proportionality are not exhaustive.[69] However, they are an indication that this perspective on the appropriateness considerations of the Federal Constitutional Court might be more fertile than trying to understand them as balancing degrees of realisation. They point to a research programme that could also prove to be productive from a comparative perspective, since proportionality may assume a comparable function in other constitutional or human rights systems as well. Binding constitutional obligations and proportionality are thus recursively linked. The principle of proportionality responds to the hermeneutical problem of how to ensure the constitutional bindingness of fundamental rights in the face of wide-ranging provisos that allow for the statutory limitations of these rights. Within the principle of proportionality, the answer to this question is then hermeneutically re-specified for each fundamental right within the appropriateness criterion. The appropriateness test serves to make the constitutional bindingness of each fundamental right more concrete and thus more effective.

[67] BVerfGE 82, 43 (53f) [19 April 1990]; BVerfGE 94, 1 (9) [13 February 1996].

[68] Art 5(2) Basic Law: 'These rights shall find their limits in the provisions of general laws, in provisions for the protection of young persons and in the right to personal honour.'

[69] For additional examples, see C Bumke, *Der Grundrechtsvorbehalt* (Baden-Baden, Nomos, 1998) 101, 231.

4

The Contribution of Fuzzy Logic and Comparative Concepts to the Rational Application of Proportionality *Stricto Sensu*

CHRISTOS MYLONOPOULOS

I. The Difficulty of an Exhaustive Definition

According to a generally accepted definition, the principle of proportionality, which, over the last decades, has received ever-increasing international recognition in legislation, theory and practice,[1] consists of three sub-principles: *suitability*, *necessity* and *proportionality in the narrow sense*.[2] This chapter focuses on the definitional and commensurability issues that arise with regard to proportionality in the narrow sense (proportionality *stricto sensu*).

In the field of criminal law, the principle appears mainly – but not exclusively – in the relationship between the offence and the sanction provided for by the law or imposed by the judge. As far as the legislator is concerned, a criminal sanction is deemed to violate the proportionality principle (in the sense that it does not comply with the prerequisite of proportionality in the narrow sense) if it is *in an obvious and intolerable way* disproportionate to the gravity of the offence.[3] In this case the upper limit of the permissible sentence is barred on the basis of the so-called *prohibition of exaggeration* (*Übermaßverbot*). This *negative approach*

[1] D M Beatty, *The Ultimate Rule of Law* (Oxford, Oxford University Press, 2004); A Stone Sweet and J Mathews, 'Proportionality Balancing and Global Constitutionalism' (2008) 47 *Columbia Journal of Transnational Law* 68.

[2] H-J Koch and H Rüßmann, *Juristische Begründungslehre. Eine Einführung in die Grundprobleme der Rechtswissenschaft* (München, CH Beck, 1982) 105.

[3] 'Nicht außer Verhältnis zum verfolgten Zweck steht'. See BVerfGE (German Federal Constitutional Court Reports) 50, 217 (227) [6 February 1979]; BVerfGE 109, 133 [5 February 2004]; W Höffling, 'Grundrechtstatbestand – Grundrechtsschranken – Grundrechtsschrankenschranken' (1994) *Jura* 169; T Reuter, 'Die Verhältnismässigkeit im engeren Sinne – Das unbekannte Wesen' (2009) *Jura* 511.

to the third component of the proportionality concept is rather expanded: Lübbe-Wolff gives an example of proportionality in the narrow sense, stating that 'the prejudice to the freedom or property right must not be inadequate in comparison with the weight of interests supposed to justify the intervention'.[4] As it is said, a state measure is appropriate when the infringement of the citizen's right is *not disproportionate* to the aim pursued. Thus, a 'reasonable relationship' must be established between the burden imposed on the citizen and the community interests.

In the field of administrative law, the approach to the concept is similar. The position adopted in the rulings of the Court of Justice of the European Union (CJEU) is that

> proportionality inquiry concerns three stages: whether the measures adopted by the EU institutions aren't excessive compared to what is appropriate and necessary to achieve the desired end (suitability); whether they are necessary to achieve the pursued objective (necessity); and whether they impose a burden excessive compared to the aim sought to be achieved (proportionality *stricto sensu*).[5]

The same applies to the decisions of the European Court of Human Rights (ECtHR). Thus, the ECtHR stated in the *Sunday Times* case:

> It must now be decided whether the 'interference' complained of corresponded to a 'pressing social need', whether it was 'proportionate to the legitimate aim pursued', whether the reasons given by the national authorities to justify it are 'relevant and sufficient'.[6]

From the above current and very widely adopted definitions, the following provisional conclusions may be drawn:

- First provisional conclusion: Defining proportionality through '*proportionality in the narrow sense*' is obviously *unavailing*. Proportionality *stricto sensu* is nothing more than proportionality *within* the proportionality, ie, the definition of the proportionality concept contains the *definiendum* in the *definiens* and is therefore a *circular definition*, which is entirely unsuitable as an exhaustive *total definition*. It is a mere *functional definition* with poor informative value, and it tells us little about the essence of the concept.[7] This approach reflects the position (if we may paraphrase US Supreme Court Justice Potter Stewart): 'I cannot

[4] G Lübbe-Wolff, 'The Principle of Proportionality in the Case-Law of the German Federal Constitutional Court' (2014) 34 *Human Rights Law Journal* 12, 13.

[5] P Craig and G de Búrca, *EU Law: Text, Cases, and Materials*, 5th edn (Oxford, Oxford University Press, 2015) 545.

[6] *The Sunday Times v United Kingdom* App no 6538/74 (ECtHR, 26 April 1979); *cf* J Gerards, 'How to Improve the Necessity Test of the European Court of Human Rights' (2013) 11 *International Journal of Constitutional Law* 466, 466–68.

[7] C Mylonopoulos, *Poiniko Dikaio: Geniko Meros* (Criminal Law: The General Part), vol I (Athens, PN Sakkoulas, 2007) 14.

define disproportionality, but I know it when I see it.' Obviously, the problem is to put into words what we perceive as disproportionate.

- Second provisional conclusion: There is no clear distinction between proportionality and disproportionality. In the absence of a clearer approach, the prevailing view is that proportionality *stricto sensu* is given when the infringement of one right is *not excessive* in comparison with the weight of the protected interest. Hence, it is implicitly claimed that between the certain non-violation and the certain violation of proportionality, a grey zone exists, a kind of *terra nullius*, within which we cannot reliably argue whether the intervention is proportionate or not. In other words, it cannot be firmly established whether a variable is disproportionate until a certain point and then it abruptly starts being proportionate. This means that a clear boundary distinction between the two concepts (proportionality–disproportionality) is missing, which, by applying an accurate and thorough analysis, could hypothetically be detected. The transition from proportionality to disproportionality is not immediate but *gradual*. The proportionality–disproportionality pair of concepts is on a continuous line that renders any boundaries between them rather vague.
- Third provisional conclusion: The above entails that proportionality and disproportionality cannot be *classificatory concepts*. Classificatory concepts have sharp outlines and are therefore not suited to the treatment of variables with fluid contours. Applying such concepts in cases like this causes, in Radbruch's words, 'violence to real life'[8] and constitutes, according to Hempel and Oppenheim, an 'artificial and theoretically sterile procedure'.[9]

II. Rules and Principles

If we wish to advance our analysis, we must consider the fundamental distinction between rules and principles. Legal rules can either be violated or not. A legal rule cannot be more or less violated. By contrast, legal measures do not need to satisfy the proportionality principle in a univocal way, since legal principles can be satisfied to varying degrees, ie, they can be satisfied *gradually*.

Indeed, nowadays, the existence of an essential distinction between rules and principles is clear. As Alexy states:

> Rules are norms that require something definitively. They are *definitive commands*. Their form of application is subsumption. If a rule is valid and if its conditions of

[8] G Radbruch, 'Klassenbegriffe und Ordnungsbegriffe im Rechtsdenken' (1938) 12 *Internationale Zeitschrift für Theorie und Praxis* 46.

[9] C G Hempel, 'Typologische Methoden in den Sozialwissenschaften' in E Topisch (ed), *Logik der Sozialwissenschaften*, 8th edn (Köln, Kiepenheuer & Witsch, 1972) 87; see also C Mylonopoulos, *Komparative und Dispositionsbegriffe im Strafrecht* (Frankfurt am Main, Peter Lang, 1998) 32ff.

> application are fulfilled, it is definitively required that exactly what it demands be done. If this is done, the rule is complied with; if this is not done, the rule is not complied with. By contrast, principles are *optimization requirements*. As such, *they demand that something be realised 'to the greatest extent possible* given the legal and factual possibilities' (emphasis added).[10]

In the same way Dworkin observes that

> [t]he difference between legal principles and legal rules is a logical distinction … Rules are applicable in an all-or-nothing fashion. If the facts a rule stipulates are given, then either the rule is valid in which case the answer it supplies is valid or it is not.[11]

A principle, on the contrary, states a reason that argues in one direction but does not necessitate a particular decision. So, according to Dworkin, 'all that is meant when we say that a particular principle is a principle of law, is that the principle is one which officials must take into account, if it is relevant, as a consideration inclining in one direction or another.'[12] Therefore: the more a legal activity complies with a principle, the more this principle is satisfied and vice versa. The crucial question, of course, is: to what extent must a principle be observed in order for us to say that it is satisfied?

The answer is not easy. It is common knowledge that the *antagonism* between the various principles of law constitutes a basic characteristic of any legal order. This is also the case in the field of criminal law, where the multiplicity and heterogeneity of purposes and needs means they are in a permanently antagonistic relationship with one another. Within a legal order, rules and principles serving a particular aim have to be measured against (and/or counterbalanced by) others – for example, safety versus freedom. Hence, the need arises to obtain partial satisfaction whenever full satisfaction is impossible. In such cases, no goal or principle can be entirely satisfied. The criminal law requires the criminal process to fulfil conditions beyond its possibilities according to its functional destination.[13] In these cases, *balancing* becomes indispensable.

The usefulness of balancing conceived as a value judgement has already been pointed out with regard to proportionality in the narrow sense. According to Lübbe-Wolff, this third level of proportionality ('*adequacy*') is the point where a balancing operation must be performed. The question to be answered here is whether the objective promoted by restricting or otherwise invading the fundamental right in question and the extent to which the objective is promoted by the

[10] R Alexy, 'Constitutional Rights and Proportionality' (2014) 22 *Revus – Journal for Constitutional Theory and Philosophy of Law* 51, 52. See also R Alexy, *A Theory of Constitutional Rights* (Oxford, Oxford University Press, 2002 [1st German edn 1985]) 47–49.

[11] R Dworkin, *Taking Rights Seriously* (London, Duckworth, 1987) 24–26.

[12] ibid.

[13] U Neumann, *Wahrheit im Recht: Zur Problematik und Legitimität einer fragwürdigen Denkform* (Baden-Baden, Nomos, 2004) 31ff; E Savigny, 'Die heterogene Basis als wissenschaftstheoretisch bedeutsames Merkmal der strafrechtsdogmatischen Argumentation' in U Neumann, J Rahlf and E Savigny (eds), *Juristische Dogmatik und Wissenschaftstheorie* (München, CH Beck, 1976) 144.

intrusion are worth the loss. As she argues, 'the value of the portion of the fundamental right which has been taken away must be compared with the value of the associated gain for the interest or concern promoted by that taking'.[14]

III. Balancing and Weighing Up

The necessity of balancing is founded on the need to determine the appropriate degree of satisfaction of one principle relative to the requirements of other principles. Thus, balancing becomes 'the specific form of application of principles',[15] in the sense that it 'expresses what *optimization* relative to the legal possibilities means' (emphasis added).[16] Therefore, the greater the degree of non-satisfaction of, or detriment to, one principle, the greater the importance of satisfying the other. The rule of balancing was further elaborated by Alexy in a so-called *Weight Formula*:[17]

The Weight Formula defines the weight of a principle *Pi* in a concrete case, that is, the concrete weight of *Pi* relative to a colliding principle *Pj* (*Wi, j*), as the quotient of, first, the product of the intensity of the interference with *Pi* (*Ii*) and the abstract weight of *Pi* (*Wi*) and the degree of reliability of the empirical assumptions concerning what the measure in question means for the non-realisation of *Pi* (*Ri*), and, second, the product of the corresponding values with respect to *Pj*, now related to the realisation of *Pj*. It runs as follows:

$$W_{i,j} = \frac{I_i \cdot W_i \cdot R_i}{I_j \cdot W_j \cdot R_j}$$

Nevertheless, the use of this formula enables us to obtain very limited informative content. As Alexy correctly observes, weighing up is connected to graduation. He further admits that between compared variables a continuous scale exists. Nevertheless, he proceeds to the contention that the application of his 'weight formula' presupposes the use of arithmetical values, which renders the formula useless. Thus, he comes to the conclusion that weighing up is impossible in legal reasoning. However, this last conclusion is susceptible to further analysis. It is indeed true that the introduction of arithmetical values could be arbitrary. But the impossibility of using this formula does not mean that a weighing up is equally impossible. Alexy himself rightly observes that 'the weight formula … makes clear which points are decisive and how these points are related to one another'.[18]

[14] Lübbe-Wolff (n 4) 15.

[15] Alexy, 'Constitutional Rights and Proportionality' (n 10) 52.

[16] Alexy, 'Constitutional Rights and Proportionality' (n 10) 54.

[17] R Alexy, 'On Balancing and Subsumption. A Structural Comparison' (2003) 16 *Ratio Juris* 433; R Alexy, 'The Weight Formula' in J Stelmach, B Brożek, W Załuski (eds), *Studies in the Philosophy of Law: Frontiers of the Economic Analysis of Law* (Krakow, Jagiellonian University Press, 2007) 9–27.

[18] R Alexy, 'The Construction of Constitutional Rights' (2010) 4 *Law & Ethics of Human Rights* 21, 32.

The identification of the decisive points could be useful because it is in these points that rational discourse and inquiry could establish a greater degree of certainty.

IV. The Standards

This certainty could be obtained through a *weighing up*. In the case of the enactment of a criminal sanction, if we wish to ascertain whether it satisfies the proportionality principle, we must first focus on cases in which compliance with the *Übermaßverbot* is definitely undisputed and then on those in which compliance is definitely disputed. In other words, we have to focus on *standards which provide us with certainty*. The reason is obvious: in these cases, we can obtain a greater degree of certainty about proportionality. The next step is to bridge this specific variable and the sanction under consideration.

Weighing up is not unknown in legal theory and practice. For instance, drug addiction is assessed using this criterion: the more indications are available, the more legitimate our contention that the application of this criterion is valid. In the same manner, the law weighs the antagonistic values or principles against each other, for example the protection of minors against the freedom of the arts, liberty against security, etc.[19]

But weighing up also has a normative foundation. It is well known that when two antagonistic legal principles collide, weighing up is not just a possibility but inevitably necessary. It is necessary because of the limited range of legal possibilities, which requires one of the colliding principles to yield somewhat to enable the partial satisfaction of the other principle. In this case 'the legal possibility of the realization of the first principle depends on the contrary one'.[20] This point of view is not new. *Proportionality renders necessary the weighing up, and weighing up is inherent in any statement about proportionality*: the proportionality principle requires the optimisation of the relationship between two antagonistic principles and the weighing up derives quasi *eo ipso* from it.[21]

In this connection the use of *comparative concepts* and preference rules could be useful indeed. This, however, presupposes additional information, which would allow us to decide with absolute certainty whether a concept is concurrent. In analytic philosophy this information is called a 'point of departure',[22] a *standard*,[23] which permits us to gauge the degree of similarity between the standard or 'point of departure' and the case in question.

[19] C Mylonopoulos, 'Bargain Practices and the Fundamental Values of the ECHR' in U Sieber, V Mitsilegas, C Mylonopoulos, E Billis and N Knust (eds), *Alternative Systems of Crime Control. National, Transnational, and International Dimensions* (Berlin, Duncker & Humblot, 2018) 89.

[20] R Alexy, *Theorie der Grundrechte* (Frankfurt am Main, Suhrkamp, 1986) 101.

[21] ibid 101, 147.

[22] E Sapir, 'Grading, A Study in Semantics' (1944) 11 *Philosophy of Science* 93.

[23] See K Baier, *Der Standpunkt der Moral. Eine rationale Grundlegung der Ethik* (Düsseldorf, Patmos Verlag, 1974) 64; N Cooper, 'Scale Words' (1967) 27 *Analysis* 153, 154; Mylonopoulos (n 9) 50.

V. Fuzzy Logic and Comparative Concepts

The central thesis of the fuzzy logic theory is, according to its founder, Lofti Zadeh, that everything, *truth included*, is a matter of degree.[24] According to Bart Kosco, the binary logic is an instrument which sacrifices accuracy for simplicity and works fine at extremes but fails everywhere else. As Kosco says, 'legal decisions are also fuzzy and relative. The scales of justice tip to varying degrees. Courts convict persons who commit crimes with enough intent and acquit those who commit them with enough diminished capacity'.[25] The main contribution of the fuzzy logic theory consists in pointing out that fuzzy sets are not classes with sharp contours, but that they have a continuity of an *affinity degree* or 'degree of belonging' (*Zugehörigkeitsgrad*). The usefulness of fuzzy logic for legal theory is therefore that it enables us to treat concepts that are vague and lack sharp outlines in a rational way.[26] Fuzzy logic focuses on linguistic variables which are capable of obtaining *a gradually increasing degree* of correctness of using a word in the language based on a possibility distribution. As such, the linguistic value of, for example, the distinction between a 'light', a 'medium' and a 'cruel' sanction does not need to be 'confined' to these three concepts, where, let's say, a 'moderate' sanction after a certain point abruptly stops being 'moderate' and starts being 'cruel'. It is distributed instead across a gradual scale, enabling us to find out *which option is more convincingly arguable.*

This brings us to the next crucial question: *how can we decide which one is more convincingly arguable* (*vertretbar*)? Since fuzzy logic demonstrated that the passage from one gradable concept to another cannot be abrupt, the use of classificatory concepts is unproductive. By contrast, the use of comparative concepts seems to be much more fruitful and promising. *The great usefulness of comparative concepts consists in that they allow us to know to what degree a quality may be ascribed to a subject,*[27] so that objects possessing a quality to a greater or lesser degree may be ranked accordingly.[28] Such ascriptions are founded on statements

[24] L A Zadeh, 'Fuzzy Logic' (1988) 21 *Computer* 83, 84; *cf* L A Zadeh, 'Fuzzy Sets' (1965) 8 *Information and Control* 338.

[25] B Kosco, *Fuzzy Thinking. The New Science of Fuzzy Logic* (London, HarperCollins, 1994) 36–37. See also the pioneering works of L Philipps, 'Auf die Entsprechung kommt es an! Die Logik der je/desto-Sätze im Recht' in L Philipps, *Endliche Rechtsbegriffe mit unendlichen Grenzen. Rechtslogische Aufsätze* (Bern, Editions Weblaw, 2012) 127; *cf* H J Zimmermann, *Fuzzy Sets Theory and its Applications*, 2nd edn (New York, Springer Science+ Business Media, 1991); Mylonopoulos (n 9) 59.

[26] M Caudill, 'Using Neural Sets: Fuzzy Decisions' (1990) 5 *AI Expert* 59, 60; Mylonopoulos (n 9) 59.

[27] G Otte, 'Komparative Sätze im Recht. Zur Logik eines beweglichen Systems' in A Hans (ed), *Jahrbuch für Rechtssoziologie und Rechtstheorie*, vol 2 (Düsseldorf, Bertelsmann Universitätsverlag, 1972) 303ff, especially 311; E Savigny, *Grundkurs im wissenschaftlichen Definieren* (München, Deutscher Taschenbuch Verlag, 1970); Mylonopoulos (n 9) 54.

[28] M Herberger and S Dieter, *Wissenschaftstheorie für Juristen. Logik, Semiotik, Erfahrungswissenschaften* (Frankfurt am Main, Alfred Metzner Verlag, 1980) 279; W Stegmüller, *Probleme und Resultate der Wissenschaftstheorie und analytischen Philosophie, Theorie und Erfahrung*, vol 2a (Berlin, Springer, 1973) 213; L Kuhlen, *Typuskonzeptionen in der Rechtstheorie* (Berlin, Duncker & Humblot, 1977) 39.

in the form of: the more of variable *a*, the more of quality *b* may be ascribed to the subject. For instance, the greater a person's duty to forestall the consequences of an action, the graver his/her negligence. The greater a person's participation in the political, financial and social life of a country, the more this person must tolerate the violation of his/her privacy.

This approach was adopted by the Federal Constitutional Court of Germany in the so-called *Esra* decision,[29] commented on in an exemplary way by Lothar Philipps.[30] According to this decision, in a case where the Court of First Instance had to decide whether the ban on circulating a novel constituted a particularly grievous violation of the constitutional guarantee of the freedom of the arts, the Federal Constitutional Court held that there is a reciprocal relationship between the extent to which the author creates an aesthetic work of art removed from reality and the intensity of the violation of the right of personality. The more the original and the fictive personages coincide, the more serious the violation of the right to personality. The more the artistic presentation infringes on particularly protected dimensions of the right of personality, the stronger the fictionalisation must be to exclude a violation of the right of personality.

The advantage of comparative concepts consists in this: they allow us to argue with clarity which option is preferable. Although prima facie they seem to be vague and to cause uncertainty, exactly the opposite is the case: to say whether a variable is more important, more severe, less effective, and so on than another is an absolutely clear statement when we are dealing with a possibility distribution.

VI. The Commensurability Question

However, it is often argued in this context that a balancing process is unreliable (if not impossible), because the values compared are incommensurable.[31] The main argument is that the preference for one over the other element compared is irrational,[32] allowing courts to make political decisions behind the veil of legal reasoning.[33]

This latter observation reveals that, in reality, the incommensurability objection is not a matter of deficient rationality or even the lack of a common denominator, but rather the question is whether the common denominator used

[29] Bundesverfassungsgericht, Beschluss des Ersten Senats vom 13. Juni 2007 – 1 BvR 1783/05.

[30] Philipps (n 25) 127ff.

[31] J Alder, 'The Sublime and the Beautiful: Incommensurability and Human Rights' (2006) *Public Law* 697, 717–18. See more on the whole discussion in N Petersen, 'Proportionality and the Incommensurability Challenge: Some Lessons from the South African Constitutional Court' (2013) *New York University Public Law and Legal Theory Working Papers* 1.

[32] J Habermas, *Between Facts and Norms: Contributions to a Discourse Theory of Law and Democracy*, trans by W Rehg (Cambridge MA, MIT Press, 1996) 259.

[33] F Venter, 'The Politics of Constitutional Adjudication' (2005) 65 *Zeitschrift für ausländisches öffentliches Recht und Völkerrecht* 129, 165.

for the weighing up is legal or non-legal. The criticism is obviously directed at the fact that a political common denominator could be arbitrarily introduced, which would undermine proportionality. However, this concern is unfounded. In terms of the application of proportionality standards, the question is not whether a legal measure or a judicial decision may be classified as disproportionate or proportionate; it is equally not a conceptual-logic relationship. On the contrary, it is a normative gradual relationship, ie, a comparison between values.[34] The values compared are assessed according to the degree to which they promote the central ideal behind all fundamental constitutional values, ie, human dignity. Hence, Alexy was right in stating that *the* common point of view is the point of view of the Constitution.[35]

From this point of view, several efforts were made to reduce the gravity of a criminal offence to a common denominator and thus to convert it to a measurable entity. These efforts, made by distinguished scholars such as Andrew von Hirsch, Niels Jareborg, Andrew Ashworth, Ingeborg Puppe, Joel Feinberg and others, reflect the methodological concepts of Jeremy Bentham, who first tried to create a rational system of criminal justice by introducing the concepts of 'moral arithmetic' and 'parameters of ordinal proportionality'.

Court decisions provide the opportunity for more tangible case studies. For example, the US Supreme Court's approval of a decision where the defendant was sentenced to *life imprisonment* for fraud to the value of about USD 120 on the ground that he was a recidivist can be seen as a clear case of disproportionality (*Rummel v Estelle* (1980)); similarly the decision in *Harmelin v Michigan* (1991), in which the defendant was sentenced to life imprisonment for possession of 672 grams of cocaine).[36] By contrast, in *Solem v Helm* (1983), the US Supreme Court came to the conclusion that life imprisonment for stealing USD 100 imposed on a defendant who had already been convicted three times in the past for burglary and driving under the influence of alcohol was 'intolerably disproportional' and constituted 'cruel and unusual punishment' under the US Constitution.[37] Such decisions may be used as indisputable '*points of departure*'. On the basis of them we can argue whether the qualification of a treatment or of a state measure as 'disproportionate' is *more justified* (in the sense of *convincingly arguable* or '*vertretbarer*') than the opposite and vice versa. This conclusion is evidently easier than the direct *subsumption* (classification) of a case under the concept of 'disproportionality'.

[34] C Mylonopoulos, 'Das Verhältnis von Vorsatz und Fahrlässigkeit und der Grundsatz in dubio pro reo' (1987) 99 *Zeitschrift für die gesamte Strafrechtswissenschaft* 685, 716.

[35] Alexy, 'The Weight Formula' (n 17).

[36] *Rummel v Estelle* 445 US 263 (1980); *Harmelin v Michigan* 501 US 957 (1991).

[37] *Solem v Helm* 463 US 277 (1983). See L L Weinreb, *Criminal Law: Cases, Comment, Questions*, 7th edn (New York, Foundation Press, 2003) 717.

5

The Emotional Component of Proportionality

THOMAS ELHOLM

I. Principle of Proportionality – The Main Contention

The principle of proportionality has evolved into a key legal principle in many jurisdictions all over the (Western) world, particularly within the last five to six decades. It also found a prominent place in legal instruments of regional and international organisations such as the European Union (EU) and the Council of Europe. The development was driven by legal practitioners, court decisions and legal scholars. The facets and details vary from jurisdiction to jurisdiction, from one legal field to another and from scholar to scholar, but the core of the principle seems to be the same.

Starting with the *Pharmacy Decision* (*Apotheken-Urteil*) of 1958 and developed in a number of landmark decisions over the years, the German Federal Constitutional Court (Bundesverfassungsgericht) laid down the foundations of the principle of proportionality with its three-step theory and the sub-principles of suitability, necessity and appropriateness (proportionality *stricto sensu*).[1] According to this now well-established theory, in a state based on the rule of law, any measure interfering with individual rights requires a legitimate aim, and the measure must be effective (adequate or suitable) and necessary in order to achieve the aim (including the *de minimis* requirement). Also, the measure must be appropriate or proportionate *stricto sensu*: a measure is only proportionate in the narrow sense if the disadvantages associated with the measure are not completely out of proportion to the advantages associated with it. Thus, all advantages and disadvantages of the measure must be weighed: the importance of the individual right and the amount of interference in the right are weighed against the state's legitimate need to interfere.[2] These key features of the principle can be also traced

[1] See *Apotheken-Urteil*, BVerfGE (Federal Constitutional Court Reports) 7, 377 [11 June 1958] (available at: www.servat.unibe.ch/dfr/bv007377.html# with further case-law references). For further details, see Ralf Poscher's chapter 3 in this volume.

[2] See A Barak, *Proportionality. Constitutional Rights and their Limitations* (Cambridge, Cambridge University Press, 2012).

and have been elaborated in the case law of the Court of Justice of the European Union (CJEU) and the case law of the European Court of Human Rights (ECtHR). The principle applies to all levels, all measures and all state powers: legislators, courts and administration.

One distinction frequently drawn in the proportionality debate is between retrospective and prospective proportionality.[3] Prospective proportionality is about means and ends, particularly the proportionate means of achieving a legitimate aim as described above. Retrospective proportionality is primarily concerned with the relationship between the seriousness of the crime and the severity of the punishment. This has been extensively elaborated in scholarly research. The distinction between retrospective and prospective concepts is important in order to illustrate two different ways of operating with proportionality in rule-of-law states. However, the distinction should not be exaggerated: the two approaches derive from the same principle and are closely related, using partly the same tools to measure proportionality, for example the notions of *de minimis* and appropriateness.

In the following, both aspects of the principle will be considered by arguing that proportionality, whether retrospective or prospective, is primarily a rational concept that has been challenged by contemporary criminal law legislation adopted primarily with the aim of expressing certain moral beliefs, sentiments or feelings. This chapter will discuss certain aspects of these emotional components in terms of the proportionality principle, particularly in relation to criminalisation and sentencing.[4] The main contention will be that in present criminal law legislation the emotional component quite often trumps the rational reasoning and foundation of the principle.

II. Rationality – The Point of Departure

The point of departure for the present analysis is the distinction between reasoning based on rational arguments, on the one hand, and reasoning based on emotions, sentiments or taste (preferences and perceptions), on the other. This is an analytical distinction (and probably an exaggerated one), since there are many ways in which emotions and sentiments could be regarded as rational.[5] However, the

[3] See, eg, Antony Duff's chapter 2 in this volume.

[4] Thus, this chapter does not encompass the principle of proportionality in terms of procedural criminal law or administrative law measures.

[5] As Siehr rightly pointed out, law and politics cannot be clearly distinguished in the legislative process by the conception of rationality and irrationality; see A Siehr, 'Symbolic Legislation and the Need for Legislative Jurisprudence: The Example of the Federal Republic of Germany' (2008) 2 *Legisprudence* 271, 279. For contributions to revising conceptions of rationality, see also C Jolls, C Sunstein and R Thaler, 'A Behavioral Approach to Law and Economics' (1998) 50 *Stanford Law Review* 1471ff and M Kelman, 'Behavioral Economics as Part of a Rhetorical Duet: A Response to Jolls, Sunstein, and Thaler' (1998) 50 *Stanford Law Review* 1577ff.

distinction is important to illustrate the current trend in criminal policy in many European countries, a trend which might constitute a challenge to the principle of proportionality.

Another point of departure is the assumption that proportionality notions are first and foremost based on rational arguments and argumentation. The concepts of effectiveness, suitability and necessity are all inherently rational ideas based on rational arguments, knowledge and possibly evidence. Meaningful proportionality reasoning cannot disregard facts and knowledge about the effects of the means applied and the ends pursued, and any argumentation must strive to be consistent and coherent[6] – otherwise the functioning of the principle in legal argumentation by courts etc threatens to be undermined by a collision with its own logic.

By contrast, a non-rational viewpoint is characterised by assessments based on matters of taste, sentiments or feelings. Such an argumentation does not necessarily mean rejecting facts and knowledge altogether, and the preferred taste or sentiment might be labelled right and reasonable according to rational standards. However, an irrational approach gives taste or feelings priority, and this will ultimately trump any opposing fact. As John Stuart Mill pointed out: 'so long as an opinion is strongly rooted in the feelings, it gains rather than loses in stability by having a preponderating weight of argument against it.'[7] The non-rational approach based on taste, sentiments or feelings is often (but not always) accidental and arbitrary.

Applying the proportionality principle as developed by legal scholars and practitioners during the last few decades means striving to achieve a functional, consistent and coherent set of viewpoints based on rational arguments. Although the test of appropriateness (proportionality *stricto sensu*) might involve elements of taste or beliefs, it is often also conceptualised as a rational feature.[8]

The importance of the proportionality principle increased during the second half of the twentieth century as a reaction to the ideology of treatment of offenders that dominated the criminal law systems of many Western European countries at the beginning of and up into the mid-twentieth century. Andrew Ashworth, Andrew von Hirsch, Tatjana Hörnle and Nils Jareborg are some of the scholars who played a central role in the development of the thoughts and ideas on proportionality. Their work, which is examined below, is characterised, among many other things, by the effort to conceptualise proportionality as a tool for finding a reasonable justification for punishment.[9]

[6] See also Barak (n 2) 391f and 541f.

[7] J S Mill, *The Subjection of Women* (London, 1869) 1.

[8] A Aarnio, *The Rational as Reasonable. A Treatise on Legal Justification* (Dordrecht, D Reidel Publishing Company, 1987) 195.

[9] See, eg, A von Hirsch and A Ashworth, *Proportionate Sentencing: Exploring the Principles* (Oxford, Oxford University Press, 2005); A von Hirsch, 'Proportionality in the Philosophy of Punishment' (1992) 16 *Crime and Justice* 55ff; T Hörnle, *Tatproportionale Strafzumessung* (Berlin, Duncker & Humblot, 1998); and A von Hirsch and N Jareborg, 'Gauging Criminal Harm: A Living-Standard Analysis' (1991) 11 *Oxford Journal of Legal Studies* 1ff.

From a broad perspective, criminal policy in many Western countries changed over the last 100 years. The following assessment is characteristic of the Nordic countries[10] but undoubtedly applies to many other European countries as well: during the first half of the twentieth century, the prevailing ideology was treatment, leading to a broad variety of responses including sometimes long-term deprivations of liberty even for minor offences in order to treat ('cure') the offender. The ideology of treatment rests upon a rational, evidence-based approach, where the effect and effectiveness of the treatment are at the epicentre.

However, during the second half of the twentieth century, it became clear that treatment in many cases did not significantly prevent recidivism; the percentage of re-offending remained high. The support for the ideology of treatment gradually started to decline.[11] This decline was probably accelerated by the fact that treatment is often costly. At the same time, the idea of a more just and more proportionate sentencing system started to emerge. Although the ideology of treatment has not disappeared and is still a significant feature of most Western sentencing systems, especially regarding young offenders and substance abusers, proportionality has since become a strong counterbalancing ideology.[12]

Particularly during the second half of the twentieth century, we notice a shift in sentencing ideology: the growing influence of the proportionality principle in sentencing systems throughout the Western world.[13] This shift was fuelled by a critique based on knowledge and evidence revealing the poor and costly effects of treatment, on the one hand, and rational arguments for a more just and proportionate sentencing practice, on the other. European countries became concerned about disparities in sentencing,[14] and the response to this concern took the shape of a rational, knowledge-based and evidence-oriented criminal policy:

> [E]ach member state should have a coherent and rational crime policy … Responses to crime should have clearly identified aims and be integrated within a coherent and rational crime policy … governments should take advice from and actively co-operate with professionals directly concerned with the implementation of the policy; they should at the same time take advice from scientists.[15]

[10] B Kyvsgaard, '100 års nordisk kriminalpolitik. Indlæg ved Svensk Kriminalistforenings 100-års jubilæum' (2012) 2 *Nordisk Tidsskrift for Kriminalvidenskab* 128; D Victor, 'Från behandlingsideologi till nyklassicism' (2012) 2 *Nordisk Tidsskrift for Kriminalvidenskab* 114.

[11] See R Martinson, 'What works? – Questions and Answers about Prison Reform' (1974) 35 *The Public Interest* 22ff. The conclusion of the article is often restated as 'Nothing works!', but the message has been modified by R Martinson, 'New Findings, New Views: A Note of Caution Regarding Sentencing Reform' (1979) 7(2) *Hofstra Law Review* 242ff. From a Nordic perspective, see J Andenæs, 'Nyere forskning om almenprevensjonen – status og kommentar' (1977) *Scandinavian Journal of Criminal Law and Criminology* 61ff.

[12] See also a similar description concerning Norway in T A Busch, 'Noen utviklingstrekk I norsk kriminalpolitikk basert på 40 år I påtalemyndigheten' (2018) 4 *Tidsskrift for strafferett* 265, 272.

[13] See the historical overview by Nestor Courakis and Vagia Polyzoidou in chapter 6 of this volume.

[14] Regarding the concern for disparity, see Council of Europe Recommendation No R (92)17 of the Committee of Ministers to Member States Concerning Consistency in Sentencing (19 October 1992).

[15] Council of Europe Recommendation No R (96)8 of the Committee of Ministers to Member States on Crime Policy in Europe in a Time of Change (5 September 1996) paras 5 and 6.

The EU Commission also adopted policy papers with a similar approach:

> [C]riminal law must always remain a measure of last resort. This is reflected in the general principle of proportionality … For criminal law measures supporting the enforcement of EU policies, the Treaty explicitly requires a test of whether criminal law measures are 'essential' to achieve the goal of an effective policy implementation … To establish the necessity for minimum rules on criminal law, the EU institutions need to be able to rely on clear factual evidence about the nature or effects of the crime in question.[16]

Thus it is no coincidence that the requirements of effectiveness and necessity are the cornerstones of the ideology supporting the principle of proportionality: they form the essential critique of the ideology of treatment and are closely linked to the rational, knowledge-based and evidence-oriented criminal policy of that period. Interestingly, both ideologies, treatment and proportionality, focus on the *effects* of punishment and both consider crime prevention to be the overall aim of criminal law. While the ideology of treatment focuses on the positive crime-preventive effects, the ideology of proportionality focuses on the negative effects, trying to set limits by requiring measures of criminal law to be legitimate, suitable, necessary and appropriate. Nevertheless, both ideologies rely on rational conceptions, giving weight to facts and knowledge about the effects of criminal law and punishment.

III. A Modern Challenge to the Rational Approach

A new shift in criminal policy seems to have started at the beginning of the twenty-first century. This new trend emphasises the emotional aspects of legislation and neglects, to some extent, facts, effects and effectiveness of criminal law and punishment. It is characterised by the importance given to the expressive function of criminal law, by the desire of the legislator to send signals and by symbolic statements expressing common moral beliefs or values. Certainly, such expressive functions were always inherent in criminal law, but they were often assigned a secondary role, as criminal law's instrumental function of regulating citizens' behaviour was prioritised. In line with the new trend described here, facts, effects and effectiveness do not become entirely irrelevant, but they are no longer decisive for the legislator.[17]

[16] European Commission, 'Towards an EU Criminal Policy: Ensuring the effective implementation of EU policies through criminal law', 20 September 2011, COM(2011) 573 final.

[17] It is important to add that this is not true for every new legislative act. Indeed, some of the legislation adopted is absolutely based on knowledge and facts. As rightly pointed out by Jacobsen concerning Norwegian criminal policy, the non-rational (populistic) approach to criminal law is only significant for some of the new provisions and measures, while other initiatives are indeed rational and evidence-based; see J Jacobsen, 'Is the Last Laugh on Liszt? – The Development of the Norwegian Criminal Sanctions' (2020) 132(1) *Zeitschrift für die gesamte Strafrechtswissenschaft* 223. The same can be said from the perspective of Danish criminal policy.

Some illustrative examples of the subordinated role lately assigned to facts and effects can be observed in Denmark. In a bill of 1999, the former Danish Minister of Justice, Frank Jensen (Social Democrats), proposed a ban on masked demonstrators. The reason was that some anarchists had used masks at demonstrations to make it difficult for the police to identify the participants. The proposed bill was criticised for being practically useless. Frank Jensen stated to a Danish newspaper when the bill was proposed in parliament:

> You could say that we remain concerned over our inability to enforce a ban, but that we are still sending a clear signal. It is important to stress that this is a matter of signal legislation, and that we are well aware that the anarchists are highly unlikely to respect it.[18]

A few years later, the former Danish Minister of Justice, Lene Espersen (Conservative), proposed a new, special provision concerning female genital mutilation. At that time, female genital mutilation was already a criminal offence under the Danish Criminal Code section 245 on aggravated assault, but when the new bill was passed, a special provision was introduced in section 245A regarding female genital mutilation. The bill at issue states that:

> Female genital mutilation is currently a criminal offence … but we propose that a new, special criminal code provision be incorporated in order to reflect society's condemnation of the practice.[19]

In other words, it was the law-makers' 'need' to signal or mark society's condemnation of female genital mutilation that led to the adopting of the new provision in section 245A of the Criminal Code. However, this provision did not add anything new. The criminalisation of the conduct and the penalty scale remained unchanged. Section 245A has only been applied in one or two criminal cases since the provision was introduced in 2003.[20] The ban on masks from 1999 is also still in force, but the effects are hard to measure.

This kind of legislation has been called 'symbolic' or 'signal' legislation. The phenomenon is not new. According to Blankenburg, in case of 'symbolic acts of legislation' the legislator has a normative claim but is not willing (or not able) to take responsibility for its effectiveness.[21] The discrepancy between the aim and

[18] Quoted in *Politiken*, 17 November 1999, 1, 7.

[19] See Bill No L 183, parliamentary year 2003 (L 183, FT 2003).

[20] The Council of Europe Convention on preventing and combating violence against women and domestic violence does not require a specific criminal law provision on female genital mutilation, but the States must 'exercise due diligence to prevent, investigate, punish and provide reparation for acts of violence covered by the scope of this Convention'; see Art 5(2). On the tension between cultural traditions of minorities and protection (by criminal law provisions) of vulnerable groups like women and children, see C Rigoni, 'Crime, Diversity, Culture and Cultural Defence' in H N Pontell (ed), *Oxford Research Encyclopedia of Criminology and Criminal Justice* (Oxford, Oxford University Press, 2018) especially the section entitled 'Criminalization'.

[21] E Blankenburg, 'Über die *Unwirksamkeit* von Gesetzen' (1977) 63 *Archiv für Rechts- und Sozialphilosophie* 43. One of the first examples is provided by the Norwegian sociologist, W Aubert, who demonstrated the ineffectiveness of the 'housemaids' law' in terms of improving the working conditions of housemaids but the effectiveness in solving a parliamentarian conflict, see W Aubert,

the effects of a legislative act is characteristic of symbolic legislation. According to Noll, it is a feature of symbolic legislation that the legislator, despite the law's ineffectiveness, holds on to it for reasons that lie beyond the law itself.[22] This implies another characteristic feature of symbolic laws: there is often a discrepancy between the official or explicit aim of the legislative act and its hidden or implicit aim. This was pointed out by Hassemer, who stated that laws with a latent function prevailing over the manifest function are symbolic laws.[23]

The above-mentioned elements noted by Blankenburg, Noll and Hassemer combined can result in the assessment that criminal law is symbolic when the expressive function exceeds the capability to ensure an effective protection of the legal interest (*Rechtsgut*).[24] This, I would say, is the core of symbolic legislation (with the first two components mentioned below being mandatory for the 'definition'):

1) The expressive or symbolic function is the primary aim of the law (the 'symbolic message' can be either manifest or latent).
2) The effects of the law, including the negative side-effects, play only a secondary role for the legislator, if any.
3) The true scope of the (underlying) problem, which is the official reason for adopting the new legislation, is of no interest to the legislator.

This is, of course, a vague definition, and the fact that there is no exact definition naturally weakens the whole idea as an analytical tool.[25] The increased emphasis on the expressive function of criminal law, its signals and symbolic value has, nevertheless, become visible in many ways. Obviously, the perception of this phenomenon depends on the definition of what can be labelled 'symbolic'.[26] However, taking the three criteria mentioned above into consideration, at least some of the following legislative acts could be said to be examples of primarily expressive or symbolic legislation.

In 2019 Austria adopted a bill imposing restrictions on wearing a headscarf ('religiously influenced clothing') by schoolchildren.[27] A member of the Austrian

T Eckhoff and K Sveri, *En lov i søkelyset, sosialpsykologisk undersøkelse av den norske hushjelplov* (Oslo, Akademisk forlag, 1952).

[22] P Noll, 'Symbolische Gesetzgebung' (1981) 100 *Zeitschrift für Schweizerisches Recht* 355.

[23] W Hassemer, 'Symbolisches Strafrecht und Rechtsgüterschutz' (1989) (9) *Neue Zeitschrift für Strafrecht* 556. Lauterwein points out that a legal act is symbolic if the latent or immanent function exceeds the manifest or explicit function, see C Lauterwein, *Symbolische Gesetzgebung. Eine Untersuchung am Beispiel Strafrecht* (München, Verlag Ernst Vögel, 2006) 48.

[24] Lauterwein (n 23) 48.

[25] Besides the references in this chapter, a similar draft definition of the concept of symbolic legislation can be found in T Elholm, 'The Symbolic Purpose of Criminal Law' in S Reindl-Krauskopf, I Zerbes, W Brandstetter, P Lewisch and A Tipold (eds), *Festschrift für Helmut Fuchs* (Wien, Verlag der Österreichischen Akademie der Wissenschaft, 2014) 137.

[26] As rightly pointed out by Hassemer, a law is not either symbolic or not symbolic but rather more or less symbolic, see W Hassemer (n 23) 555. One could also say that the law could be primarily symbolic in one context but merely instrumental in another.

[27] Parlament, 495/A XXVI. GP., 22 November 2018.

Parliament called this a measure with symbolic effect.[28] In 2018 Hungary adopted a new provision forbidding rough sleeping. If the police order a homeless person to move into a shelter and they fail to comply three times within nine days, they can be imprisoned.[29] In 2018 Denmark introduced restrictions on rough sleeping, too, authorising the police to hand down an administrative fine and to ban people from sleeping in the streets in certain areas, if they are deemed to cause what is called 'insecurity' among the public by sleeping in 'camps'.[30] In 2003 France adopted a special provision on occupying a building hallway to crack down on youngsters who used to gather in such places, which subsequently led to the obstruction of free movement in the lobbies of buildings.[31] In 2005 Germany introduced an amendment to the law of assembly to prohibit the deployment of neo-Nazi symbols in certain places in order to set an example against right-wing extremism. Under Article 8 (Freedom of Assembly) of the German Constitution (Grundgesetz) the scope of application of this particular provision is limited, and the amendment was therefore characterised as symbolic.[32] In Norway, in a period of 13 years, from 2000 to 2013, the punishment for raping a sleeping person was increased twelve-fold.[33] Further examples of symbolic legislation from Denmark are the Act of 2017 criminalising begging, where such conduct makes other people feel 'uncomfortable' or 'insecure'.[34] More so, in 2018 Denmark adopted a ban on the concealment of one's face (with burqa, niqab, ski mask, etc) in public places.[35] A Danish research project from 2010 estimates that a considerable number of the changes to the Danish Criminal Code from 2000 to 2009 could be labelled as symbolic in the above-mentioned sense.[36] From an international perspective, legislation on hate crimes has been defined as symbolic.[37]

[28] 'Maßnahme mit Symbolkraft' (*Parlamentskorrespondenz* Nr 33, 16 January 2019).

[29] The Hungarian Constitution had to be changed, *cf* Art 22 Constitution and the law on misdemeanours.

[30] Section 22 para 2 of the Danish Police Act. See Bill No L 118 of 13 December 2017.

[31] Art 126-3 French Construction and Housing Code. See further T Elholm and R Colson, 'The Symbolic Purpose of EU Criminal Law' in R Colson and S Field (eds), *EU Criminal Justice and the Challenges of Diversity: Legal Cultures in the Area of Freedom, Security and Justice* (Cambridge, Cambridge University Press, 2016) 52. Part of this chapter is based on the article mentioned here.

[32] According to Siehr, 'mainly of symbolic value', see Siehr (n 5) 280. In a similar context, the criminalisation of the '*Auschwitzlüge*' (Holocaust denial) has also been called symbolic by Lauterwein (n 23) 38.

[33] See Jacobsen (n 17). See also, from the prosecutorial perspective (the author is Attorney General of Norway), Busch (n 12) 265, 273.

[34] Section 197 para 2 of the Danish Criminal Code (the provision was in force until July 2020). In practice, the punishment will be 14 days of imprisonment, with no possibility of suspension, for first-time offenders caught begging in pedestrian zones, at stations or in public transport. See Bill No L 215 of 2 July 2017.

[35] Act No 717 of 8 August 2018. According to the *travaux préparatoires*, this kind of behaviour constitutes a threat to the 'cohesiveness' of society, see Bill No L 219 of 11 April 2018. The French legislator used a similar argument in the Explanatory Memorandum to the Bill prohibiting the concealment of one's face in public places of May 2010 ('cohesion of the Nation'), see text to nn 41–42 below.

[36] Elholm (n 25) 137.

[37] See J B Jacobs and K A Potter, 'Hate Crimes: A Critical Perspective' (1997) 22 *Crime and Justice* 1–50.

One characteristic of the legal provisions described here is the radical change in the perception of criminal law and the discourse about criminal law. Instead of focusing on effects and effectiveness – many of these laws are neither crime preventive nor are they in a position to solve the underlying societal problem – such provisions are adopted with the primary aim of sending signals and flashing symbolic statements that express common moral values. The political debate on the legitimacy of law is shifting from rational arguments about effectiveness, suitability and appropriateness to emotionally-based needs of signalising certain ideas and perceptions or values.

IV. What are the Legislators Trying to Express and Why?

If expression is the primary aim of some criminal laws, then what are the legislators seeking to express? Drawing inspiration from Durkheim, one could say that in many Western countries today criminal laws are adopted with the primary aim – either manifest or immanent – to express and promote specific moral beliefs or values. According to Durkheim, punishment and criminal law cannot be regarded as merely technical tools to prevent and combat crime. They are first and foremost symbols expressing certain common beliefs, sentiments or moral values.[38] By punishing the offender, society is not only taking revenge and trying to prevent criminal behaviour, but also – and primarily – reaffirming and strengthening the moral order, the shared moral beliefs, says Durkheim.

This idea is also present today, for example in the *travaux préparatoires* of the French law prohibiting the wearing of clothing concealing one's face in public places. On 11 May 2010 the French National Assembly adopted, by a unanimous vote, a 'Resolution on attachment to respect for Republic values at a time when they are being undermined by the development of radical practices'. According to the National Assembly's Resolution, 'radical practices undermining dignity and equality between men and women, one of which is the wearing of the full veil, are incompatible with the values of the Republic'.[39]

According to Durkheim, criminal law holds a special position in the legal system: violations of criminal law are (often) associated with strong sentiments or emotions deeply rooted in society; criminal law is not just any kind of law but

[38] Durkheim calls this 'conscience collective', see, eg, E Durkheim, *The Division of Labor in Society*, trans by G Simpson (New York, Macmillan, 1933) 79. Durkheim's theory of punishment runs through several of his works, also *De la division du travail social*, trans by G Simpson (Paris, Alcan, 1893). It is developed at length in *L'Éducation morale* (Cours dispensé en 1902–1903 à la Sorbonne) (Paris, Alcan, 1934) (*Moral Education*, trans by E K Wilson (New York, Dover Publications, 2011)) and in the article 'Deux lois de l'évolution pénale' in (1899–1900) 4 *Année sociologique* 65–95, reprinted as ch 4, 'The Evolution of Punishment' in S Lukes and A Scull (eds), *Durkheim and the Law*, 2nd edn (London, Palgrave Macmillan, 2013).

[39] Quoted by the ECtHR in the *S.A.S. v France* case (n 42 below), at [24].

the kind of law which citizens are often passionate about, and therefore violations of criminal law become important manifestations of common moral beliefs.[40] At the same time, criminal law marks a shared sense of justice, which could be regarded as a kind of glue holding society together. This idea is also apparent in the French bill prohibiting the wearing of clothing concealing one's face in public places (Loi 2010-1192):

> France is never as much itself, faithful to its history, its destiny, its image, than when it is united around the values of the Republic: liberty, equality, fraternity. Those values form the foundation-stone of our social covenant; they guarantee the cohesion of the Nation.[41]

This reasoning informed the response of the French Government in defending the prohibition of concealing one's face in public before the ECtHR (in *S.A.S. v France*), according to which the law was legitimate and necessary in order to ensure the 'living together' and 'the observance of the minimum requirements of life in society';[42] in other words: the necessity to obey (to some extent) society's common moral values. Unfortunately, according to Durkheim, manifestations of common moral values most often take place at the expense of marginalised social groups (the poor, the unemployed, the homeless, immigrants, etc); in fact, the purpose of such laws is precisely to mark a distance from these groups. This was exactly one of the allegations against the French law on concealing one's face in public places.[43]

Durkheim's theory was developed in the nineteenth century. Society has changed radically since then. His theory has also been subject to much criticism.[44] Yet, some core elements of Durkheim's theory might still be useful today for understanding the current development of criminal justice systems in Europe,[45] albeit that other factors such as the following may also explain why criminal law legislation has become increasingly symbolic:

> [T]he essential attractiveness of the punitive response is that it can be represented as an authoritative intervention to deal with a serious, anxiety-ridden problem. Such action gives the appearance that 'something is being done' here, now, swiftly and decisively. Like the decision to wage war, the decision to inflict harsh punishment exemplifies the sovereign mode of state action. No need for cooperation, no negotiation, no question

[40] Durkheim, *The Division of Labor in Society* (n 38) 64 and 79. Durkheim calls this 'manifestations of conscience collective'.

[41] Explanatory Memorandum to Loi 2010-1192, impact assessment, May 2010. Quoted in the judgment of the ECtHR in the *S.A.S. v France* case (n 42 below), at [25].

[42] See especially *S.A.S. v France* App no 43835/11 (ECtHR GC, 1 July 2014) [82] and [140].

[43] See *S.A.S. v France* (n 42) especially [97] and [13]–[14] of the opinion of the two dissenting judges.

[44] See D Garland, 'Durkheim's Theory of Punishment: A Critique' in D Garland and P Young (eds), *The Power to Punish* (London, Heinemann, 1983); D Garland, *Punishment and Modern Society – A Study in Social Theory* (Chicago IL, The University of Chicago Press, 1993) 50.

[45] The expressive function of criminal law is advocated by J Feinberg, *Doing and Deserving: Essays in the Theory of Responsibility* (Princeton NJ, Princeton University Press, 1970) 98. See also Elholm and Colson (n 31) 58.

> of whether or not it might 'work'. Punishment is an act which exemplifies what absolute power is all about ... Accompanying these punitive policies is a certain criminology ... It is a criminology of the alien other which represents criminals as dangerous members of distinct racial and social groups which bear little resemblance to 'us'. It is, moreover, a 'criminology' which trades in images, archetypes and anxieties, rather than in careful analyses and research findings – more a politicized discourse of the unconscious than a detailed form of knowledge – for power.[46]

> [A] strong urge of control ... makes way for a nervous need for ... quick fixes. In this way, criminal law is more and more frequently being used as a means to mark the different practices of life-styles with which we do *not* wish to identify ourselves ... many widely divergent actions are being experienced as threats to our collective self-image.[47]

> There are signs that criminal law is being used as a 'symbolic' element at the discursive (political) level to convey a message of 'security' to the citizenry, regardless of whether it can be made more or less effective in a generalised way.[48]

> Symbolic laws might be enacted for different reasons. Alibi laws are introduced to give the appearance that something has been done and that the polity is taking care of the regulated matter ... The effective content of the law is unimportant, for what counts in these situations is the appearance of justice.[49]

The prominent role of criminal law and the fact that criminal law violations are often associated with strong sentiments or emotions deeply rooted in society makes criminal justice a preferred tool among politicians. Legislation must often be adopted fast, in the wake of dramatic (or at least dramatised) crime stories, under pressure of public opinion and occasionally of victims' associations or other influential groups.[50] Criminal law is often considered useful to demonstrate decisiveness or the ability to act against a serious threat, to convey a sense of security in troubled times, to calm anxiety or to signal disapproval of certain beliefs, cultures or social groups.[51] In relation to security and security laws, whenever these functions prevail and the purpose of laws and measures is more symbolic than concrete, this practice has been labelled 'security theatre':

> Sometimes it seems those in charge – of governments, of companies – need to do something in reaction to a security problem. Most people are comforted by action, whether good or bad. There are times when a player creates compelling security theater.[52]

[46] D Garland, 'The Limits of the Sovereign State, Strategies of Crime Control in Contemporary Society' (1996) 36(4) *The British Journal of Criminology* 445, 460.

[47] F de Jong, 'Symbolic and Diabolic Forces in Criminal Law' (2016) 81 *Pompe Reeks* 31.

[48] S Jones (ed), *Mean Streets: A Report on the Criminalisation of Homelessness in Europe, FEANTSA* (Belgium, European Federation of National Organisations Working with the Homeless, 2013) 20.

[49] V Zoppei, *Anti-Money Laundering Law: Socio-Legal Perspectives on the Effectiveness of German Practices* (The Hague, TMC Asser Press, 2017) 18.

[50] On counter-terrorism measures, see Lucia Zedner's chapter 7 in this volume.

[51] See, eg, R Hefendehl, 'Enron, WorldCom, and the Consequences: Business Criminal Law Between Doctrinal Requirements and the Hopes of Crime Policy' (2004) 8 *Buffalo Criminal Law Review* 54.

[52] B Schneier, *Beyond Fear. Thinking Sensible about Security in an Uncertain World* (New York, Copernicus Books, 2003) 38.

Insecurity, anxiety, fear of crime, etc are all challenges with a strong emotional element,[53] encompassing an uneasy sentiment or feeling, which politicians or society generally attempt to soothe by expressive criminal law initiatives; sometimes this may even result in legislative hyperinflation or 'security frenzy'.[54] While Durkheim reminds us that criminal law has always had an inherent *emotional element*, it has now become an *emotional tool* frequently utilised by politicians to provide psychological satisfaction to the majority.

V. Why is this a Challenge to Proportionality?

Elevating the expression of certain moral beliefs or shared values to the primary aim of criminal law, especially in times when politicians are under constant pressure to act, has consequences in terms of content and construction of criminal law provisions. The above-mentioned examples from different countries illustrate this: loosely defined offences (eg, how should 'insecurity' be assessed?) and abstract ideas about the protected legal interests may overlap with criminal legislation already in force, are often difficult to apply in practice and usually have little or no effect on the problem they are officially called to address (eg, homelessness, poverty).[55]

Such characteristics are not a problem – or at least not an important one – if the primary aim of the legislation is the expression of moral beliefs and values. However, they may constitute a considerable problem from the perspective of a rationally founded principle of proportionality. Loosely defined offences create difficulties in terms of determining the legitimate aim. It can be difficult to identify the legal interest to be protected or the actual threat, such as in the Danish examples of the ban on concealing the face in public on grounds of the 'cohesiveness of society'[56] and the criminalisation of begging and rough sleeping when such conduct is creating 'a feeling of insecurity'.[57] In such cases it is unclear which legal interest the legislation is meant to protect and how exactly the proscribed behaviour poses a threat to this interest.[58] The German Federal Constitutional Court found the headscarf ban disproportionate for lack of 'a sufficiently specific danger'.[59]

Furthermore, making the expressive function the primary aim of criminal law urges politicians to adopt new legislation again and again to convey empowerment

[53] See, eg, de Jong (n 47) 29 on anxiety: he describes how, primarily from a psychological perspective, anxiety might increase in times where criminality is decreasing.

[54] In Denmark, for example, the number of yearly changes to the Criminal Code has increased threefold from the end of the 20th century to the present. For Norway, see, eg, Busch (n 12) 272. See also on counter-terrorism Lucia Zedner's chapter 7 in this volume. See further Elholm and Colson (n 31) 52.

[55] On counter-terrorism measures, see Lucia Zedner's chapter 7 in this volume.

[56] In Nazi Germany taking the '*völkische Werte*' into account was considered necessary to secure the cohesiveness of society, see Lauterwein (n 23) 23.

[57] Section 22 para 2 of the Danish Police Act. See Bill No L 118 of 13 December 2017.

[58] See also the separate opinion by Nussberger and Jäderblom in *S.A.S. v France* (n 42) [3]–[12].

[59] Bundesverfassungsgericht, Order of 27 January 2015, 1 BvR 471/10 and 1 BvR 1181/10, [115].

and reaffirm common moral beliefs. Thus, new provisions may often overlap with criminal legislation already in force, as in the Danish example of female genital mutilation described above. From the perspective of proportionality, this is problematic in terms of both effectiveness and necessity.

Criminal laws primarily aimed at expressing certain moral beliefs or values are often difficult to apply in practice.[60] Politicians wish to send clear signals by enacting new legislation, but when the law comes to be enforced, it may not be clear to the police and the courts how to implement the law in practice.[61] Some provisions may cause problems in terms of legal interpretation, for example because of the loosely defined criminalised conduct or because there must obviously be exemptions from the rules,[62] but the legal practitioners have no (real) guidelines on how to enforce them. Other prohibitions may be difficult to enforce simply because citizens will not listen to the signals, as demonstrated in the Danish example of the ban on masks at demonstrations, or because they have little choice to conform, as illustrated in the example of the homeless people sleeping in 'camps'. Therefore, criminal law with an expressive aim has sometimes little or no effect on the problem it *officially* declares to address:

> In addition, those laws would be disproportional because they are not appropriate for achieving their declared outcomes. Even an attempt at implementing them would require a useless effort that might cause collateral damages and costs.[63]

It seems obvious that laws which are not enforced or may not even be enforceable can hardly be suitable, necessary and appropriate. If non-enforceable laws are enforced anyway, they might create negative side-effects or might have no real effect in terms of their declared outcomes. Expressive criminal law with an immanent or latent purpose also faces a clear problem of proportionality: how can the law's aim be found to be legitimate (or even illegitimate), suitable and necessary, if there are blurry borders between manifest and immanent purposes?

> The … development is caused by the … new understanding of the function of criminal law … which is misused not as ultima ratio of the state for the protection of legal good but as a cheap and at the same time apparently effective magic bullet in order to

[60] Elholm (n 25) 147.

[61] Legal counsellor to homeless people Maja Løvbjerg Hansen gave an interview to Danish national television (TV-Avisen, 18:30) on 14 February 2020 regarding the legislation of 2018 on rough sleeping in 'camps' which makes people feel uneasy or insecure (and with respect to which 550 administrative fines and 22 zone-bans have been handed down so far). Hansen stated that police and prosecutors are not sure how to apply this particular act of legislation. Having helped the homeless to bring several cases to court, she gives an example of two homeless persons being fined for sleeping too close to each other, thereby creating 'a camp', even though there is no clear definition on how close people must sleep together in order to constitute 'a camp'. Also, the UK police have struggled to understand how to enforce the Coronavirus Act 2020, see, eg, V Dodd and L O'Carroll, 'UK Police Warned against "Overreach" in Use of Virus Lockdown Powers', *The Guardian*, 31 March 2020, available at: www.theguardian.com/uk-news/2020/mar/30/uk-police-guidelines-coronavirus-lockdown-enforcement-powers-following-criticism-lord-sumption.

[62] See, eg, Le Conseil constitutionnel, Decision of 7 October 2010, No 2010-613 DC (Loi interdisant la dissimulation du visage dans l'espace public), at [5], noting an exception for public places of worship.

[63] See Zoppei (n 49) 20 regarding anti-money laundering provisions.

> re-establish trust in economy. This new symbolic function enjoys a boom not only in United States but in Europe as well.[64]

This is not only a problem of 'bad legislation'. When considerations about effects, suitability, necessity and appropriateness of a law are trumped by the need to express certain moral beliefs or values, the discourse on criminal law is changing. The rational discourse based on knowledge is displaced by the presumed sentiment or taste of the majority of the population, which is regarded as a sufficient source of legitimation for the adoption of new legislation. Facts and knowledge about the consequences of the legislation become secondary; the primary and legitimising aim is the expressive function, which tends to provide the majority with some psychological satisfaction by, for example, upholding common values, handling the problem or soothing anxiety and insecurity. As a result it seems reasonable – as the Danish examples show – to openly reject knowledge and evidence about the likely effects of a legal provision and simply refer to the need to express certain beliefs. Changing the discourse from a rational, knowledge-based approach to a matter of taste or public belief (of the majority) seems difficult to align with the principle of proportionality.

VI. Any Role Left for Proportionality?

If we focus on the kind of legislation described above, what about the principle of proportionality? There seem to be two quite different ways of reasoning: one, to simply brush this kind of legislation aside, calling it disproportionate or 'bad legislation' right from the start, or else to apply a 'reluctant' version of the principle of proportionality, whereby the legislator is given a wide margin of appreciation and where only manifestly disproportionate acts may be considered in violation of the proportionality principle.

These two ways of reasoning can be illustrated by the different approaches taken by the German Federal Constitutional Court and the French Constitutional Court. The German Court in its 2015 judgment on the headscarf ban for educational staff conducted an in-depth analysis of proportionality. The Court came up with the conclusion that the wearing of headscarves presented no sufficiently specific danger to the protected legal interest or legal good. Hence, the legislation was in violation of the principle of proportionality and the German Constitution.[65] Taking the principle of proportionality seriously by conducting an in-depth analysis based on rational arguments and evidence does actually put modern legislation to test. It is highly likely that many cases of criminal laws with a primarily expressive or symbolic aim would be deemed disproportionate using the proportionality test applied by the German Federal Constitutional Court.

[64] Hefendehl (n 51) 72.
[65] Bundesverfassungsgericht, Order of 27 January 2015, 1 BvR 471/10 and 1 BvR 1181/10.

The French Constitutional Court took a different approach in its 2010 judgment on the ban on concealing the face in public. The Court did not apply an in-depth analysis of the proportionality principle, dedicating only a few lines to the matter. With a general reference to the purpose of the law, the Court found that 'Parliament has enacted provisions which ensure a conciliation which is not disproportionate between safeguarding public order and guaranteeing constitutionally protected rights.'[66] This approach is manifestly different from the German approach. Apparently, the French Court did not conduct an in-depth analysis of proportionality, it did not measure the 'specific danger' to the protected legal interest; it did not discuss the legitimacy of the aim and – so it seems at least – did not conduct the tests of suitability, necessity and appropriateness. Instead, the Court applied a rather general or abstract test about manifestly disproportionate laws, leaving broad discretion to the legislator. Under this approach, the principle of proportionality is rather toothless, and expressive or symbolic criminal law provisions are likely not to be declared disproportionate. The situation could be similar in countries such as Denmark, where there is no constitutional court and where the national supreme courts are very reluctant to review the constitutionality of legislation.

Is there, then, a third way of reasoning? The question arises because, as already pointed out, the German approach (although admirable) might face considerable practical problems outside of Germany, while the French approach might leave the principle of proportionality somewhat 'toothless'. It could be argued that the ECtHR in its judgment on the aforementioned case of *S.A.S. v France* took a middle course.

The ECtHR's judgment in the *S.A.S.* case – regarding the same 2010 French law mentioned above on the concealment of one's face in public places – is a fine illustration of the important considerations embedded in the proportionality principle. Even though no violation of the European Convention on Human Rights (ECHR) was found in the end, the Court did pursue an in-depth analysis of proportionality, carefully laying open and balancing against each other the important arguments of both sides. This is a clear recognition of the principle of proportionality. Even though the wide margin of appreciation recognised by national legislators and the principle of subsidiarity led the majority of the ECtHR judges to conclude that there was no violation of the ECHR, the judgment can be seen as a warning to national legislators not to disregard the principle of proportionality. This is underlined by the fact that the French Government tried hard to proffer rational arguments of legitimacy and proportionality in favour of the legislation.

Particularly the opinions of the two dissenting judges in the *S.A.S.* case showcased the potential of the principle of proportionality by highlighting the problematic consequences of letting 'abstract principles' (in this case the

[66] Le Conseil constitutionnel, Decision of 7 October 2010, No 2010-613 DC (Loi interdisant la dissimulation du visage dans l'espace public), at [5].

invoked principle of 'living together') trump the individual rights of Article 8(2) and Article 9(2) ECHR. Should this approach be transferred to the examples of symbolic legislation mentioned above, many of the laws with notions such as the 'feeling of safety' and 'societal coherence' as their primary aim would scarcely be considered legitimate.

VII. The Emotional Element Embedded in Proportionality

Looking at the judgment in the *S.A.S.* case, the path taken by the ECtHR is not so very different from those taken by the French and the German Constitutional Courts: either the legislation will be violating the principle of proportionality because it does not have a legitimate aim and is not suitable, necessary and appropriate, or the judges will be recognising the (legitimate) need of a state to express certain moral beliefs ('values of the Republic') and allowing the legislator a wide margin of appreciation to act accordingly. Simply put: the first solution dismisses the emotional component, while the second solution leaves it up to the legislator's choice. The question is: what is in the emotional component and how can it be weighed against the other elements of proportionality?

Some legal scholars and sociologists argued against a unilateral instrumentalisation of criminal law. They pointed out that criminal law entails something else or something more – an ethical or moral element or an element of social identity – which cannot be reduced to a question of prevention. Garland argues (drawing on Durkheim and Foucault) that punishment should be considered in the same way as other social institutions through which society defines and expresses itself:

> To think of punishment in this way is to question the narrow, instrumental self-description that modern penal institutions generally adopt … and instead to suggest more socially conscious and morally charged perceptions of penal affairs.[67]

It could be argued that the principle of proportionality *already* has an emotional element, an embedded notion of common moral beliefs or sense of justice, which is indeed related to the feelings or the taste of the general public. Hörnle points out, for example, that a theory of sentencing based on the idea of proportionality cannot be exclusively construed on the basis of rational, purpose-oriented considerations. She refers to Durkheim when she claims that there is an 'emotionally anchored component' in the principle of proportionality, which seems to play and must play a role.[68] Others might perceive such an emotional element in the tradition, the convention or the culture of a society, all of which – in theories of

[67] D Garland, 'Sociological Perspectives on Punishment' in A von Hirsch and A Ashworth (eds), *Principled Sentencing. Readings on Theory and Policy* (Oxford, Hart Publishing, 1998) 391.

[68] Hörnle (n 9) 112.

proportionality – are relevant for cardinal proportionality[69] or may be regarded as part of the test of appropriateness (proportionality *stricto sensu*).

Regarding security and security laws, the distinction between subjective and objective security is often highlighted. Subjective security obviously incorporates an emotional element of psychological security and reassurance of the individual.[70] The question arises to what extent the pursuit of subjective security might be a legitimate aim in addition to objective security. While some accept that subjective security is a legitimate aim of security laws, some argue that subjective security is not sufficient reason to intrude upon the rights of others.[71]

Although there seems to be a recognition of an emotionally anchored component embedded in the principle of proportionality, the component has not been extensively analysed or elaborated. Even though the ECtHR in the *S.A.S.* case proceeded to a careful analysis of the principle of proportionality, it somehow avoided or bypassed closer scrutiny of the emotional component. The majority of the ECtHR judges focused on the legislator's wide margin of appreciation. This becomes evident, for example, when the 'choices of society' are addressed:

> It can thus be said that the question whether or not it should be permitted to wear the full-face veil in public places constitutes a choice of society … In such circumstances, the Court has a duty to exercise a degree of restraint in its review of Convention compliance, since such review will lead it to assess a balance that has been struck by means of a democratic process within the society in question. The Court has, moreover, already had occasion to observe that in matters of general policy, on which opinions within a democratic society may reasonably differ widely, the role of the domestic policy-maker should be given special weight. [ECtHR *S.A.S. v France*, paragraphs [153]–[154]].

The margin of appreciation policy-makers are enjoying in matters of general policy could conceivably be perceived as the 'place' or 'space' for the emotional component, for expressing and enforcing common moral values within the principle of proportionality. However, if the protection of common moral values, including abstract notions such as the 'living together principle', constitutes a legitimate aim according to the principle of proportionality, what limitations can the remaining aspects of the proportionality principle possibly set? If abstract principles and common moral beliefs are the primary and legitimate aim of new legislation, there is a risk that the tests of suitability, necessity and appropriateness become empty gestures, which will – especially if a wide margin of appreciation is applied – inevitably lead to the following conclusion:

> Consequently, having regard in particular to the breadth of the margin of appreciation afforded to the respondent State in the present case, the Court finds that the ban imposed by the Law of 11 October 2010 can be regarded as proportionate to the aim

[69] See von Hirsch and Ashworth (n 9) 142.
[70] L Zedner, *Security* (London, Routledge, 2009) 16ff. See also Schneier (n 52) 17ff.
[71] J Waldron, 'Safety and Security' (2006) 85 *Nebraska Law Review* 452ff and J Waldron, *Torture, Terror and Trade-offs: Philosophy for the White House* (Oxford, Oxford University Press, 2010).

> pursued, namely the preservation of the conditions of 'living together' as an element of the 'protection of the rights and freedoms of others' ... The impugned limitation can thus be regarded as 'necessary in a democratic society'. This conclusion holds true with respect both to Article 8 of the Convention and to Article 9. [ECtHR *S.A.S. v France*, paragraphs [157]–[158]].

The two dissenting ECtHR judges in the *S.A.S.* case came to a different conclusion. They questioned the aim of the legislation. They found that the aim of 'living together' through 'the observance of the minimum requirements of life in society' was an abstract principle, which could hardly legitimise the limitation of individual fundamental rights:

> While it is perfectly legitimate to take into account the specific situation in France, especially the strong and unifying tradition of the 'values of the French Revolution' as well as the overwhelming political consensus which led to the adoption of the Law, it still remains the task of the Court to protect small minorities against disproportionate interferences. [ECtHR *S.A.S. v France*, joint partly dissenting opinion of judges Nussberger and Jäderblom, paragraph [20]].

Thus, while the two dissenting judges also recognised a certain emotional component (the moral beliefs and values common in French society), they found the legislation to be disproportionate: first, because there should not be such a wide margin of appreciation in a case like this; second, because the consequences for the persons concerned were considerable; and third, because the possibility of applying less restrictive measures was not pursued.

It could be argued that the emotional elements are closely linked to the idea of positive general prevention. In that case, the argument would be that a legal provision is proportionate if an effect on the moral *habitus* (or the stabilisation of the system of norms[72]) is measurable or at least likely to occur.

> Criminal law has a strong symbolic component that explains its general-preventive function. This symbolic dimension does not yet exhaust the purpose of criminal law, which is usually directed at an instrumental function of solving social conflicts through the protection of determined interests. Constitutions often contain principles that are purely symbolic, the vague formulation of which might be filled with a different content, according to social progress ... yet they are accepted as expressions and confirmations of shared values. Hence, the symbolic effectiveness of the law can be a positive thing.[73]

If this assumption is correct, symbolic laws might have a crime-preventive effect, which could also be considered in terms of proportionality (effectiveness and the like). However, emphasising the symbolic or expressive function of criminal law and integrating the 'symbolic effectiveness' into the proportionality test would

[72] A von Hirsch and T Hörnle, 'Positive Generalprävention und Tadel' in A von Hirsch (ed), *Fairness, Verbrechen und Strafe: Strafrechtstheoretische Abhandlungen* (Berlin, Berliner Wissenschafts-Verlag, 2005) 9.

[73] Zoppei (n 49) 18.

potentially legitimise per se expressive and symbolic criminal law legislation: the more expressive, the stronger the preventive effect (at least potentially). Moreover, the assumption would hardly add much to the actual application of proportionality tests. Most likely, it would be impossible to measure the (positive) general preventive effect, while there would always be room for claiming that new legislation has *potential* for a positive general preventive effect.[74] Thus, there is a risk that it will be meaningless to have a proportionality test based on the positive general preventive effect. Furthermore, von Hirsch and Hörnle warn against an instrumentalisation of the positive general prevention theory, arguing that the legitimation of criminal law should not be found (solely) in the preventive effects but in the fact that a response to crime in the form of proportionate censure is reasonable and desirable.[75]

VIII. Conclusion

Proportionality is first and foremost a rational concept based on rational reasoning and knowledge. The more emotional and non-rational aspects of criminal law are recognised and emphasised, the feebler the proportionality idea becomes. Certainly, the principle of proportionality does contain emotional components, but these are vaguely elaborated and very difficult to apply in the balancing of interests. Proportionality considerations seem to either capitulate to emotionally-based legislation or to lead to declaring such legislation void.

A shift in criminal policy occurred at the beginning of the twenty-first century in several European countries. New legislation with a strong symbolic function is being adopted, signalising common moral values and sentiments. This kind of legislation challenges the principle of proportionality for a number of reasons. The symbolic or expressive aim of such legislation is often blurry and vaguely defined, lacking a specific protected legal interest as grounds for legitimacy (see, for example, the abstract notions of 'living together', 'feeling of security' or 'cohesiveness of society') or failing to identify specific dangers to the legal interest. Occasionally the legislative aim is hidden, and sometimes the latent or underlying aim outweighs the officially declared aim. Given such aims, symbolic legislation could be regarded simultaneously as suitable, necessary and appropriate but not suitable, not necessary and not appropriate. Furthermore, symbolic legislation is often adopted in times of crisis or 'panic', putting the proportionality values to test. Moreover, symbolic laws are usually difficult to apply and enforce, once again calling the proportionality (suitability and necessity) of the provisions at hand into question. The fact that symbolic laws in some cases specifically address and limit

[74] See also von Hirsch and Hörnle (n 72) 20.
[75] ibid 29.

the living conditions and rights of vulnerable groups of people or minorities adds to the problem of appropriateness.

These issues are apparent in the aforementioned judgments of the German and the French Constitutional Courts on the respective cases regarding the concealment of one's face in public places. They are also underlined in the ECtHR judgment in *S.A.S. v France*, where the majority of judges seemed to accept the proportionality of the French law, primarily based on the wide margin of appreciation of the Council of Europe Member States and the fact that the ECtHR is bound by the principle of subsidiarity. The problems outlined above are definitely also visible in the reasoning of the two dissenting judges in the *S.A.S.* judgment.

Is there still room for the principle of proportionality when legislation becomes primarily symbolic? The answer depends, of course. There are constitutional courts, like the German Federal Constitutional Court, where the principle of proportionality is highly regarded and respected and whose strict approach thereto is likely to lead in most cases to the conclusion that many symbolic laws are in violation of the principle. Other courts take a more reluctant approach to the principle, risking that proportionality tests become 'toothless'. Following this approach, and especially regarding the margin of appreciation of legislators, reluctant courts will most probably find that symbolic laws are not manifestly disproportionate.

However, the practical significance of the principle of proportionality should not be rejected even in times of symbolic legislation. It seems that the French Government in the *S.A.S.* case tried hard to advance rational arguments to support the new legislation as legitimate and proportionate. Thus, the government indirectly recognised the principle's validity and importance. Furthermore, the judgment of the ECtHR in the *S.A.S.* case recognises and clearly showcases the important considerations embedded in the proportionality principle. The Court pursued a balanced approach, carefully laying open and analysing the important arguments of both sides. Even though no violation of the ECHR rights was found in this case, the Court's reasoning could have an impact on future legislation. Proportionality tests may help reveal to us when rationality and logic are left aside and the legislator is stepping into the realm of feelings, sentiments and symbolism. This awareness is useful and may potentially impact legislation as well. Finally, even a more reluctant application of the principle might set some outer limits on symbolic legislation, for example by helping to identify certain aims as *too* vague, a danger to the legal interest as *too* unspecific or a certain measure as *manifestly* inappropriate.

Thus, a reluctant approach to the test of proportionality could also be meaningful. In the end, a democratic legislator must enjoy a certain margin of appreciation regarding the adoption of new legislation, leaving room for common moral beliefs and sentiments to be expressed and enforced through the law. From this point of view, an emotional component is already and necessarily embedded in the principle of proportionality. However, this element remains rather vaguely defined, analysed and applied.

Future legal research on the principle of proportionality could make up for this. A point of departure could be the thoughts from Durkheim's theory, combined with the present ideas of proportionality: to balance the rights of minorities, including individual rights, against the need of the majority to express certain values and sentiments. The principle of proportionality must be designed to gauge the reasonable proportion of the need to express values – and maybe even the extent to which the expression of feelings by the majority legitimises the adoption of new legislation.[76] This is a slightly different approach to proportionality from the one mentioned in the introduction. An approach with an – as yet rather unexplored – emotional component to the principle of proportionality.

[76] See also Lucia Zedner's chapter 7 in this volume and Rigoni (n 20).

6

The Principle of Proportionality: Tracing its Historical Evolution*

NESTOR COURAKIS AND VAGIA POLYZOIDOU

I. Introductory Remarks on the Factors Influencing the Principle's Evolution

The working hypothesis for this chapter is that we can distinguish between *two forms of the principle of proportionality* in the field of criminal law and punishment: strict and broad proportionality. *'Strict' proportionality* is the symmetry between (a) the gravity of the crime and/or the criminal's culpability or guilt and (b) the severity of the sanction. *'Broad' proportionality*, by contrast, comprises, apart from the gravity of the crime and/or the culpability of the criminal, several additional, individual criteria, ie, the circumstances of the crime, the specific characteristics of the criminal (for example, a criminal record) and the preventive aims which a sanction must achieve. However, broad proportionality does not necessarily lead to a milder punishment due to mitigating factors; it may also result in a harsher punishment, for example for a repeat offender or due to aggravating factors.

Our focus here is to examine the different *factors that may influence* the evolution of the principle of proportionality and, consequently, result in the emergence of strict or broad forms of the principle. The aim of this chapter is therefore not merely to present the historical evolution of the proportionality concept but also to evaluate, by integrating the historical information into a more general context, the influence of particular factors on the above-mentioned two forms of the principle. In other words, the aim is to examine the reasons why there are certain periods in history where the principle takes a strict form of retribution, even of retaliation (*lex talionis*: 'an eye for an eye'), while at other times it is more individualised and incorporates the full spectrum of facts.

* This chapter benefited from the comments of two outstanding colleagues: Antony Duff and Georgios Giannoulis.

Against this backdrop, the main factors influencing the evolution of the principle of proportionality are the opposite pairs of (a) liberalism versus authoritarianism and (b) realism versus idealism, especially in its later form of utilitarianism versus retributivism. More precisely:

Liberalism answers the question of to what extent the members of a given society respect human freedom, human dignity and human rights. At the opposite end is *authoritarianism*: in societies and countries where the individual human value is considered unimportant – as in the case of authoritarian and totalitarian regimes – the principle of proportionality has a very limited role to play, if any. The punishments these regimes impose can be particularly cruel, not only for their opponents but also for individuals whose actions merely fail to match the regime's ideology and '*Weltanschauung*' (*cf* Orwell's '1984'). By contrast, it is a characteristic of modern liberalism that after the end of the Second World War, in the then prevailing spirit of social justice,[1] a plethora of transnational and national legal orders adopted not only various human rights declarations and conventions but specifically also the principle of proportionality.[2] Moreover, concrete criteria were adopted for testing proportionality in relation to the limits of public power; the most well-known being necessity, suitability and proportionality *stricto sensu*.[3] Consequently, after 1945 the principle was gradually consolidated in its 'broad' sense and also permeated by a humanitarian spirit in favour of the offender.

Apart from the antipodes of liberalism versus authoritarianism, which bear, to a certain degree, on the field of politics, there is another pair of factors

[1] *cf* N Courakis and T Gavrielides, 'Beyond Restorative Justice. Social Justice as a New Objective for Criminal Justice' in T Gavrielides (ed), *Routledge International Handbook of Restorative Justice* (London, Routledge, 2019) 43–55, 46.

[2] Today, the principle of proportionality is present in almost every legal order. It is remarkable how this principle manages to draw the approaches of the civil law and the common law systems closer together. At the European level, this is largely due to the jurisprudence of the European Court of Human Rights and the Court of Justice of the European Union. *cf* Art 49(3) of the European Union Charter of Fundamental Rights: 'The severity of penalties must not be disproportionate to the criminal offence', which is considered as embodying a binding rule of primary European law, see M Böse, 'The Principle of Proportionality and the Protection of Legal Interests' (2011) 1 *European Criminal Law Review* 35–41, 35. Furthermore, in Art 5(4) of the Treaty of European Union we may find some sort of definition of the principle's function at EU level: 'Under the principle of proportionality, the content and form of Union action shall not exceed what is necessary to achieve the objectives of the Treaties'. See also, at a more general level, I Porat and M Cohen-Eliya, *Proportionality and Constitutional Culture* (Cambridge, Cambridge University Press, 2013) 3; N Emiliou, *The Principle of Proportionality in European Law: A Comparative Study* (London, Kluwer Law International, 1996) 191–94; L Bachmaier Winter, 'The Role of the Proportionality Principle in Cross-Border Investigations Involving Fundamental Rights' in S Ruggeri (ed), *Transnational Inquiries and the Protection of Fundamental Rights in Criminal Proceedings* (Berlin, Springer, 2013) 85–110.

[3] *cf* R Alexy, 'Constitutional Rights and Proportionality' (2014) 22 *Revus – Journal for Constitutional Theory and Philosophy of Law* 51–65, 52–54; F Urbina, 'A Critique of Proportionality' (2012) 57 *American Journal of Jurisprudence* 49. The forms of the proportionality principle mentioned here originate in administrative and constitutional law but have been equally adopted in other legal areas, among them criminal law. On the interactive correlations between these areas of the law, *cf* P Asp, 'Two Notions of Proportionality' in N Kimmo (ed), *Festschrift in Honour of Raimo Lahti* (Helsinki, Publications of the Faculty of Law – University of Helsinki, 2007) 207–19.

with a philosophical background influencing the evolution of the principle of proportionality, namely idealism versus realism, which often takes the form of retributivism versus utilitarianism.[4] *Idealism* prioritises ideas like 'justice', which must be served at all costs, even at the expense of practical considerations. This position is typified by the opinion of the German philosopher Immanuel Kant, which holds that a criminal must not be punished for reasons of intimidation (for in that case human value would be instrumentalised in the service of an aim), but 'for the sole reason that he has committed a crime' (*weil er verbrochen hat*), thereby removing from his person and/or from his material goods the protection previously afforded to him by society.[5] Similarly for Hegel, who holds that the elimination of the crime and the restoration of the law violated by the crime can only be achieved by offending the will that has realised the crime, ie, by inflicting punishment on the offender.[6] From the point of view of Kantian idealism, the nature of proportionality is definitely 'strict', amounting to retribution, whereby the death penalty for murderers becomes the rule.

At the other end of the scale, after the beginning of the seventeenth century intellectuals like Grotius, Montesquieu, Beccaria and Bentham manifested, in a spirit of *realism*, a strong concern for reforming the penal systems of their time, making them more rational and efficient, mainly by taking measures for preventing crime in the future.[7] From this realistic and utilitarian point of view, the principle of proportionality acquired a primary role in the penal system and in some cases (Bentham) even assumed a 'broad' character materially different from the strict notion of retribution. In a way, the opposition between idealism and realism may also take the form of a confrontation between the deontological approach, focusing on moral considerations, and the consequentialist approach, focusing on the supposed effects of punishment.[8]

It is noteworthy that the contrast between retributivism and utilitarianism had already been highlighted in antiquity in the form of a corresponding polarity between the retrospective and the prospective approaches, when Plato in his dialogue '*Protagoras*' (324 b) stated two basic aims of punishment: the one looking to the past and emphasising punishment for the evildoer 'for the reason that he has done wrong' (here the aim of punishment is *retrospective* based on retribution

[4] Some authors talk in this context about a 'fight' between retributivism and utilitarianism, with which the late history of proportionality is inseparably linked, see A von Hirsch, 'Neoclassicism, Proportionality, and the Rationale for Punishment: Thoughts on the Scandinavian Debate' (1983) 29(1) *Crime & Delinquency* 52–70.

[5] I Kant, 'Metaphysik der Sitten, Rechtslehre II, Teil I, Abschnitt E (1798)' in W Weischedel (ed), *Kant Werke, Bd 7* (Darmstadt, Wissenschaftliche Buchgesellschaft, 1975) 309–499, 453.

[6] G W F Hegel, 'Grundlinien der Philosophie des Rechts (1821), §§99, 100' in H Reichelt (ed) (Frankfurt am Main, Ullstein, 1972) 95–97.

[7] According to N Lacey, 'The Metaphor of Proportionality' (2016) 43(1) *Journal of Law and Society* 27–44, 31, traces of proportionality may be found in the works of Montesquieu – and in all principal founders of the political projects of the Enlightenment and its long aftermath.

[8] *cf* A von Hirsch, 'Proportionality in the Philosophy of Punishment' (1992) 16 *Crime & Justice* 55–98, 57.

for what happened in the past), and the other looking to the future and taking into account 'that the man who is punished, and he who sees him punished, may be deterred from doing wrong again' (here the aim of punishment is *prospective* and contemplates some future benefits for the criminal and society).[9]

The above-mentioned two main pairs of influencing factors on the evolution of the principle of proportionality evidently *do not necessarily coincide* and must be examined at different and autonomous levels. Realism in particular, especially in the form of utilitarianism, has little to do with liberalism. In fact, it was developed during the time of Beccaria, not so much out of humanitarian concern for the liberties of criminal offenders but rather to ensure the efficiency and preventive effect of punishment. Indeed, the proportionality of punishments in relation to the gravity of crimes was mainly considered – in the modern sense of ordinal proportionality – a means for evaluating different crimes and punishing them accordingly. In the spirit of the philosophers who suggested this idea, such as Montesquieu and Beccaria, a criminal would prefer stealing to robbing, provided the punishment for theft is lighter than that for robbery.[10] As Jean-Paul Marat, the French revolutionary leader, pointed out,

> a strict punishment for an insignificant breach of law does not simply entail damage to the validity of the respective authority. It is also a multiplication of crimes; it is to push the evil-doers to the extremities. What could then restrain them? Whatever they do, they have nothing more to fear.[11]

At the same time, idealism, especially in the form of retribution, has nothing to do with authoritarianism. Kant and Hegel are listed among the liberal thinkers of the Enlightenment. Even nowadays, when the idea of 'just deserts' (retributivism) increases the current of retribution, no one would suggest that this idea is devoid of concern for human dignity and human liberties – on the contrary.

II. The Seven Stages Marking the Evolution of the Principle

Based on these pairs of factors influencing the evolution of the proportionality principle in the field of criminal law and punishment, it is evident that

[9] On the distinction between prospective and retrospective proportionality, *cf* for example, A von Hirsch, 'Ein grundrechtliches Verbot exzessiver Strafen? – Versuch einer Begründung' in U Neumann and F Herzog (eds), *Festschrift für Winfried Hassemer* (Heidelberg, CF Müller Verlag, 2010) 373–82, 377; G Giannoulis, *Studien zur Strafzumessung* (Tübingen, Mohr Siebeck, 2014) 44. In a way, this distinction between backward- and forward-looking approaches is prevalent in the scientific debate even today, with retributivism in its various forms exemplifying the former, while utilitarianism is the most familiar example of the latter (though it might be better to talk more generally of 'consequentialism').

[10] *cf* Montesquieu, *De l'esprit des lois* (Paris, Garnier Frères, 1927 [1748]) at VI and XVI, and C Beccaria, *On Crimes and Punishments* (Milan, 1764) at XXVII (Of the Mildness of Punishments), available at: www.laits.utexas.edu/poltheory/beccaria/delitti/index.html.

[11] J-P Marat, *Plan de législation criminelle. Introduction, notes, postface de Daniel Hamiche* (Paris, Aubier Montaigne, 1974) 70.

from antiquity and until the eighteenth century there are no significant examples of 'broad' proportionality at the legislative level and its implementation by the courts. Due also to the non-liberal regimes in many societies of that period, *retaliation* (*lex talionis*) is the rule. However, at the *theoretical level*, leading philosophers or religious leaders of that period, who certainly did not adopt the principle of *lex talionis*, expressed interesting, temperate and lenient ideas. Among them Socrates,[12] Cicero,[13] Seneca[14] and Jesus Christ.[15] Saint Paul,[16] Saint Augustine[17] and Saint Thomas Aquinas,[18] as heads of the Christian religion, all stressed the *importance of moderation* (argument of 'ratio', ie, rate, proportion, measure and the Greek axiom of *μηδὲν ἄγαν*, meaning 'never too much')[19] and of 'lenient' proportionality in dealing with others, friends or enemies, and therefore also with criminals. In a sense, this approach could be considered as having laid the foundation for the modern principle of proportionality.

A main precursor of the principle of proportionality is undoubtedly Aristotle. The Greek philosopher examines this issue in the Fifth Book of *Nicomachean Ethics*, where he meticulously analyses the essence of 'justice'. There, he perceives proportionality as a constituent element of justice in both its Aristotelian forms,

[12] As Socrates declared in Plato's *Gorgias* (380 BC), 'it is better to suffer injustice than to commit it'.

[13] Cicero in his book *On Obligations* (*De Officiis*), 44 BC, I, XI, explains that 'there is a limit to retribution and to punishment; or rather, I am inclined to think, it is sufficient that the aggressor should be brought to repeat his wrong-doing, in order that he may not repeat the offence and that others may be deterred from doing wrong' (*cf* also ibid I, XI, 34: 'we must resort to force only in case we may not avail ourselves of discussion').

[14] It is interesting to remember here how Seneca argues with rational reasoning about clemency of punishments in his essay 'Of Clemency' (*De Clementia*), 55–56 AD, I, XXII: 'It is conducive, however, to good morals in a state, that punishment should seldom be inflicted: for where there is a multitude of sinners men become familiar with sin, shame is less felt when shared with a number of fellow-criminals, and severe sentences, if frequently pronounced, lose the influence which constitutes their chief power as remedial measures'.

[15] Jesus Christ had the courage to reject openly the mosaic axiom of retaliation ('an eye for an eye') and to proclaim instead the command: 'Offer no resistance to one who is evil. When someone strikes you on [your] right cheek, turn the other one to him as well' (Matthew 5:25).

[16] Saint Paul, *Second Letter to Timothy* (Epistles, II Timothy 2:24): 'And the servant of the Lord must not strive; but be gentle unto all men, apt to teach, patient'.

[17] In a letter to Boniface in AD 418, Saint Augustine stated with regard to Christians who go to war the following: 'Let the manner of your life be adorned by chastity, sobriety, and moderation' (Letter 189, para 7), available at: newadvent.org/fathers/1102189.htm. Besides, Saint Augustine in his *City of God*, XIX, 7, correlates moderation with just wars and explains that 'it is the wrongdoing of the opposing party which compels the wise man to wage just war', available at: newadvent.org/fathers/120119.htm.

[18] Saint Thomas Aquinas referred to the idea of moderation in the context of self-defence. In his monumental work *Summa Theologiae* (II, II, Question 64.7) he explains that force, when used in self-defence, must not be excessive (the same must also apply to self-defence among states – ibid Question 40.1): 'Wherefore if a man, in self-defence, uses more than necessary violence, it will be unlawful: whereas if he repel force with moderation his defence will be lawful, because according to the jurists [*Cap. Significasti, De Homicid. volunt. vel casual.], "it is lawful to repel force by force, provided one does not exceed the limits of a blameless defence."'; available at: www.ccel.org/a/aquinas/summa/SS/SS064.html.

[19] *cf* A E Ienilieieva, *Basic Approaches to the History of the Principle of Proportionality* (Simferopol, Taurida National V I. Vernadsky University, 2013) 12ff, available at: academia.edu/9262757.

ie, commutative and distributive justice:[20] in *commutative or corrective justice*, the main objective is for the *civil judge* to restore in correct proportions the balance of gains and losses (damage), which is upset when, for example, a thief illegally obtains another's property (*arithmetic proportionality*).[21] This procedure applies to contracts or torts and does not take into consideration the qualities of the two parties, who are regarded as equal. In *distributive justice* what matters is the legislative distribution of benefits and burdens according to the qualities of the persons involved, who are therefore considered of different value (*geometric proportionality*).[22] As a consequence of the latter, we could say that the legislator must articulate criminal sentencing rules by using as a starting point the idea that punishment must be inflicted in proportion to the nature of the crime and the personal characteristics of the criminal ('broad' proportionality). Yet, Aristotle does not actually draw this conclusion. On the contrary, he insists on the importance of the Pythagorean idea of retaliation ('proportionate reciprocity')[23] as the limit up to which a retributive response to crime could be extended. However, in a different work, the *Magna Moralia* (Great Ethics), which some scholars attribute to Aristotle, the rule of proportionality is even more strictly defined. This treatise suggests that it is not fair, if somebody cuts out the eye of another person, merely to gouge the eye of the offender in return but that the latter has to suffer more than this if proportionality is to be maintained.[24] In any event, this isolated rigid approach should be taken with a grain of salt, bearing in mind that Aristotle particularly appreciates the *notion of equity* (*epieikeia*) as a means to correct the inclemencies of a strict law.[25]

In the following, we will outline the seven most important stages of the proportionality principle's evolution in the history of criminal law starting with the roots of the principle and continuing with the consolidation of the principle in modern times. We examine these stages through the prism of the above-mentioned pairs of determining factors. The evolutionary stages obviously involve different societies with different mentalities and degrees of socio-economic development. Hence, the stages presented here constitute only a *typical model* of how they *could* evolve under normal conditions over the course of time, from archaic communities to contemporary complex societies; however, the presentation of the last four stages focuses particularly on the penal history of the Western world.

[20] *cf* E Engle, 'The General Principle of Proportionality and Aristotle' in L Huppes-Cluysenaer and N Coelho (eds), *Aristotle and The Philosophy of Law: Theory, Practice and Justice* (Dordrecht, Springer, 2013) 265–76, 268. See also E Engle, 'The History of the General Principle of Proportionality: An Overview' (2012) 10 *Dartmouth Law Journal* 1.

[21] Aristotle, 'Nicomachean Ethics' Book V.3, 1131 b 25ff, 272–73, in the edition of the Loeb Classical Library with a translation by H Rackham (Cambridge MA, Harvard University Press, 1968).

[22] ibid Book V.2, 1131 a 10ff, 266–67ff.

[23] ibid Book V.5, 1132 b 32ff, 280–81.

[24] Aristotle, *Magna Moralia*, Book I, ch 33 'Justice' 1194 a 30ff, available at: ia800503.us.archive.org/35/items/magnamoralia00arisuoft/magnamoralia00arisuoft.pdf.

[25] Aristotle (n 21) Book V.10, 1137 b 31ff.

III. Roots of the Principle

A. Archaic Communities

The first stage of evolution refers to archaic communities. During this period certain *serious offences* directed against the community as such and/or its political and religious leaders or deities (high treason, desertion, sacrilege, etc; hence crimes which may be called 'public') are met with *harsh punishments.* By contrast, *offences against the life, corporal integrity, honour or property of another person* are usually considered a matter between the parties themselves which is addressed in a spirit of *revenge* by the entire family group (clan) of the victim. The revenge could last for years and, initially, had no limits – only later did it acquire elements of *retaliation* (*'an eye for an eye'*) according to a primitive form of 'strict' proportionality based on the damage caused. Yet, in place of killing members of the opponent's family, the victim or his family could accept compensation in goods from the other party, calculated on a scale proportionate to the offence. Such acts of reconciliation could even extend to contracting a marriage between members of the two rival families. It should be pointed out that the custom of revenge, known as 'blood feud' or 'vendetta',[26] still resonated until recently in various isolated communities of Corsica, Sardinia, Southern Italy, Southern Greece, Northern Albania and elsewhere.

The principle of retaliation ('an eye for an eye') as a kind of 'strict' and measured proportionality involving private persons is further reflected in certain *archaic legal texts*, such as the Babylonian *Code of Hammurabi* (circa 1760 BC),[27] the *Pentateuch* of the Jews (circa sixth century BC)[28] and the Roman codification *Lex Duodecim tabularum* (Law of Twelve Tablets, circa 450 BC).[29]

[26] *cf* lexical entry 'feud' in en.wikipedia.org/wiki/Feud.

[27] It is interesting that retributive penalties are differentiated in this Code on the basis of the social status of offender and offended. For example, according to Art 196, 'if a seignior has destroyed the eye of a member of the aristocracy, they shall destroy his eye', while according to Art 198, 'if he [=a seignior] has destroyed the eye of a commoner, he shall pay one mina of silver'; J B Pritchard (ed), *The Ancient Near East. An Anthology of Texts and Pictures* (Princeton NJ, Princeton University Press, 1958) 161.

[28] Retaliation ('an eye for an eye') is mentioned more specifically in Exodus, 21:23ff, in Leviticus, 24:21 and in Deuteronomy, 19:21. According to M Fish, 'An Eye for an Eye: Proportionality as a Moral Principle of Punishment' (2008) 28(1) *Oxford Journal of Legal Studies* 57–71, 60, 'the original meaning of "an eye for an eye" in the Pentateuch related to monetary compensation for the injured eye, rather than infliction of an identical (or even similar) injury on the wrongdoer'.

[29] Two typical retributive examples from the Table VIII (Torts or Delicts) of this Roman codification in the form of 'mirror punishments' [=meaning a precise reflection of the crime] are the following: No 2: 'If anyone has broken another's limb there shall be retaliation in kind unless he compounds for compensation with him'; No 10: 'Whoever destroys by burning a building or a stock of grain placed beside a house … shall be bound, scourged, burned to death, provided that knowingly and conscious he has committed the crime; but if this deed is by accident, that is, by negligence, either he shall repair the damage or if he is unable he shall be corporally punished more lightly' (available at: avalon.law.yale.edu/ancient/twelve_tables.asp).

It appears also in Aesop's *Fables*, where retaliation is common practice, within specific limits.[30]

B. The System of Compensations

The system of compensations (second stage) starts to preponderate with the emerging importance of commercial transactions. The penal response is now bifurcated: *offences against private persons*, such as murder, manslaughter, bodily harm, rape and theft are valued and *paid for in cash* or *in kind* proportionate to the damage caused (interestingly enough, a part of the money goes to the chief or the community and the rest to the victim). By contrast, serious *public offences* continue to be *harshly punished* during this stage, as before. This duality of penal responses is observed, for example, in a law enacted by *Salian Francs*, a group of Germanic peoples, in around 500 AD.[31] Generally speaking, during the first two stages of evolution, proportionality equals pure retaliation or compensation as far as private offences go but is ignored regarding serious public offences, which are addressed with particular harshness.

C. State Sovereignty and the Absence of Proportionality in Punishment

The third stage of evolution is marked by the decline of autonomous communities and the corresponding strengthening of the authoritarian state. All private offences are considered disturbances of the peace and serenity in the surrounding region and are therefore treated as public offences. This evolution, which is henceforth connected with cruel punishments for every kind of offence, private or public, typically occurs in legal orders related to the Roman Empire,[32] the reign

[30] A kind of retaliation in these fables is certainly demonstrated in the case of the fox, who served his guest, the stork, broth on a marble slab; as a result, the stork remained hungry. In return, and in a kind of retribution, the stork, after inviting the fox to dinner, served crumbles of food in a narrow-mouthed jug; this time it was the fox who could not eat anything at all. *cf* the text of the fable in L Gibbs, *Aesop's Fables* (New York, Oxford University Press, 2002) 81ff; see also: mythfolklore.net/aesopica/oxford/156.htm. At a more general level about retaliation in Ancient Greece, *cf* C Gill, N Postlethwaite and R Seaford (eds), *Reciprocity in Ancient Greece* (Oxford, Oxford University Press, 1998) especially 213–14.

[31] There are two characteristic provisions of this Salic Law (*Lex Salica*) on murder. In title XLI ('concerning the murder of free men'): 'If any one shall have killed a free Frank, or a barbarian living under the Salic law, and it have been proved on him, he shall be sentenced to 8.000 denars'. In title LXII ('concerning wergild'): 'If any one's father have been killed, the sons shall have half the compounding money (*wergild*); and the other half the nearest relatives, as well on the mother's as on the father's side, shall divide among themselves' (available at: avalon.law.yale.edu/medieval/salic.asp).

[32] For example, the distinction between public offences (*crimina*) and private offences (*delicta*) was abolished during the period of the Roman Empire, as manifested in the two last books of the Justinian Pandects (*Digesta*), which are traditionally called '*libri terribiles*' (terrible books) exactly because the

of the German Emperor Charles V and his *Constitutio Criminalis Carolina*[33] and also during the French '*ancien régime*' until its fall in 1789. A typical example of the role of criminal law during this period can be found in a French Edict of 1534 stating that 'punishments are enacted in order to provoke fear, terror and to set an example to all subjects of the state' (*Les peines sont edictées pour donner crainte, terreur et exemple à tous*).[34]

In a way, the mission of punishments at that time, as Michel Foucault pertinently stressed, was to demonstrate the great distance ('dissymmetry') separating the little criminal man from the omnipotent state, against which he had dared to raise his insignificant stature.[35] In fact, punishments with disproportionate suffering, such as the dismemberment of the traitor by four horses riding in different directions, turned from time to time into a popular spectacle,[36] as mentioned by Foucault in '*Surveiller et Punir*' (Discipline and Punish).[37] Nevertheless, it is remarkable that *punishments were not the same for all citizens*. For example, in the Roman Empire and also in the Byzantine Empire of the Justinian era, an important distinction was made between high-class citizens, the so-called *honestiores* (the more honourable), who principally received a rather favourable penal treatment, and low-class subjects, the so-called *humiliores* (the more lowly), for whom cruel punishments and tortures were the rule.[38] Thus, during this dark period, punishments are based on the general idea that the life and value of human beings, at least of the more humble among them and certainly of the criminals, are insignificant and, consequently, taking their lives for even minor causes is entirely justified. Under such circumstances, there is really no place for a proper enactment and application of the principle of proportionality. Nevertheless, deadly force in the context of self-defence (a relic of the archaic institution of retaliation for private offences) continued to be permitted during this period. Such acts were considered justified by the right of every person to defend him-/herself in case of an attack, but only within proportional limits, ie, provided that the person defends his/her own life or corporal integrity.[39]

punishments mentioned there are atrocious, irrespective of whether the offence is public or private. For details on the issue of punishments during the Roman Empire, see mainly T Mommsen, *Römisches Strafrecht* (Leipzig, Duncker & Humblot, 1899 and reprinted in Graz, 1955) especially 895ff.

[33] The *Constitutio Criminalis Carolina* is the first modern codification of penal provisions (on felonies). In spite of its subsidiary position in relation to local law, it succeeded in remaining in force in German territories for centuries. Some of its provisions include punishments fixed on a retaliatory basis, for example in the cases of perjury and false accusation, for which the punishment is the same evil which the offender intended to cause another person (Arts CVII and CX).

[34] See J-P Duroché and P Pédron, *Droit pénitentiaire*, 2nd edn (Paris, Vuibert, 2013) ch 2 section 5.17.

[35] M Foucault, *Surveiller et Punir. Naissance de la Prison* (Paris, Gallimard, 1975) 52.

[36] This penalty of dismemberment was also provided for traitors in Art CXXXI *Constitutio Criminalis Carolina*. Other cruel penalties of that period, apart from the death penalty, were branding, whipping, maiming and pillorying.

[37] Foucault (n 35) 9.

[38] *cf Digesta* 48, 19, 9.11 and 48.19, 15. See also P Garnsey, *Social Status and Legal Privilege in the Roman Empire* (Oxford, Clarendon Press, 1970).

[39] See Art 140ff *Constitutio Criminalis Carolina* (a similar provision existed already in the Justinian Code 8.4.1: *moderatio inculpatae tutelae*); *cf* C F von Scherenberg, *Die sozialethischen Einschränkungen*

D. The Rational Approach by the School of Natural Law (Grotius)

In reaction to the authoritative practices of the previous, state-oriented period, some scholars, and particularly the Dutchman Hugo Grotius in the seventeenth century, undertook the task of approaching punishment from a more rational perspective. In this fourth stage of evolution, Grotius sought to base his argumentation on Natural Law, focusing mainly on issues of international criminal law and of the so-called Just War. More specifically, he famously defined *punishment*, in his treatise *The Rights of War and Peace* (1625), as an evil, inflicted by way of a symmetrical response to an evil action of the offender (*malum passionis, quod infligitur ob malum actionis*).[40] On this basis, he further established as the aim of punishment the *prevention of a future mischief*, by promoting the welfare of the offender, his victim and of society as a whole.[41] Grotius even accepted that punishment can be more lenient, if this is in accordance with the aims of punishment.[42] One may therefore speak of a 'broad' and prospective concept of proportionality.

IV. Consolidation of the Principle in Modern Times

A. New Ideas in the Age of Enlightenment

During the eighteenth century, the notion of proportionality enters its fifth stage of evolution and gradually becomes the primary principle to be discussed and promoted by the liberal intellectuals of the Enlightenment, in connection with the necessary penal system reforms of that time. First, Montesquieu in two of his works (1721 and 1748) declares that punishments in Europe should be inflicted in a temperate manner and with the least burdens for the citizens.[43] In particular, in terms of the evaluation scale, *punishments must be proportionate to the gravity of the crimes*, so that criminals avoid committing dangerous crimes and have recourse to minor offences. Thus, Montesquieu emphasised the direct correlation between (a) the crime's harmfulness and the offender's culpability and (b) the

der Notwehr (Frankfurt am Main, Peter Lang, 2009) 16 and N Courakis, *Zur sozialethischen Begründung der Notwehr* (Baden-Baden, Nomos, 1978) 55 and fn 21.

[40] H Grotius, *The Rights of War and Peace* (*De jure belli ac pacis*, 1625) Book II, ch XX, I (available at: oll.libertyfund.org/titles/grotius-the-rights-of-war-and-peace-1901-ed).

[41] ibid, Book II, ch XX, Vff.

[42] ibid, Book II, chs XX, XXVIII.

[43] Montesquieu, *Lettres persanes* (Cologne, Pierre Marteau, 1721), Lettre no LXXX (available at: vousnousils.fr/casden/pdf/id00233.pdf).

response to the crime in the form of punishment, whereby the death penalty is also acceptable for serious crimes.[44] In the light of this, the nature of proportionality is 'strict'.

Several years later, in 1764, Cesare Beccaria, in his influential book *On Crimes and Punishments*, undertakes the hard work of systematising and updating, with fresh and rational ideas, the knowledge of his time about liberal penal policy. Beccaria sets as the starting point for his reasoning *Rousseau's idea of the social contract*, pursuant to which citizens sacrifice some of their liberties in return for safety. From this axiom he draws the conclusion that these relinquished parts of liberty constitute the foundation of the state's right to punish (*jus puniendi*). Hence, 'all that extends beyond this [=limit of absolute necessity to ensure the objective of common salvation], is abuse, not justice'.[45] Penal legislation is primarily aimed at preventing new offences (*prospective aim of punishment*); this can be achieved when penalties are proportionate to offences in terms of their social harm, so that the offender may be induced to choose to commit a lesser offence with a more lenient punishment.[46] In this context Beccaria rejects the old-fashioned notion of retaliation, opting in its place for a more rational approach to proportionality. Consequently, Beccaria rejects the punishments of death, infamy, general confiscation and torture (at XVIff). Accordingly, the legislator must give priority to mild penalties, which prevent crime in the long term.[47] Clearly, Beccaria rejects the idea of retaliation ('an eye for an eye') and his idea of proportionality assumes a more moderate, 'broad' and prospective[48] character.

The ideas of Jeremy Bentham move in the same liberal direction. In his *Treatise on Civil and Penal Legislation* (1820), he proclaims that a legislator must seek, by means of norms, to ensure, in intensity and duration, the greatest possible happiness and satisfaction for the greatest number of people. In practice, this can be achieved through the so-called '*felicific calculus*', weighing each time the pros and cons of one or more future actions against the degree of happiness they can provide.[49] As far as punishments are concerned, they are evils justified only if they produce other benefits or satisfactions to an equal or greater degree[50] by exceeding the harm of the crimes they are meant to prevent.

[44] Montesquieu (n 10) chs VI, XVI and XIX.

[45] Beccaria (n 10) ch II; *cf* F Venturi, *Utopia and Reform in the Enlightenment* (Cambridge, Cambridge University Press, 1971) 100ff.

[46] Beccaria (n 10) ch XXVII.

[47] *cf* Beccaria (n 10) ch XXIII.

[48] It is prospective rather than retrospective, but its prospectivity still seems narrowly focused on rational deterrence.

[49] J Bentham, *Traités de législation civile et pénale*, vol 1 (Paris, 1820) ch V, 28ff, available at: isidore.science/document/ark:/12148/bpt6k5696197f.

[50] von Hirsch (n 8) 55–98, 58 and J Goh, 'Proportionality – An Unattainable Ideal in the Criminal Justice System' (2013) 2 *Manchester Student Law Review* 41, 48, available at: hummedia.manchester.ac.uk/schools/law/main/research/MSLR_Vol2_FullWebVersion.pdf.

Bentham defines, inter alia, the following as criteria for legislative proportionality:[51]

- A crime must be punished according to its magnitude (harmfulness), which means that a more harmful crime must elicit a stricter punishment; in this way, a criminal may, if he so chooses, opt for the crime with the lighter punishment.
- The harm inflicted by the punishment on the criminal must exceed the benefits of committing the crime.
- The punishment must be inflicted according to the personal characteristics of the criminal (family, financial situation, etc) and the specific circumstances which may act upon his sensitivity to punishment (for example, different pecuniary penalties for different perpetrators according to their financial status).

Bentham pays particular attention to the circumstances of the criminal event as well as to the characteristics of the offender. As a result, he evidently adopts a 'broader' notion of proportionality compared to Montesquieu or Beccaria. Regarding punishments per se, he insists that they must be *those that are absolutely necessary* in view of the purpose they serve. Further, Bentham does not support penalties inflicted for reasons of revenge, and therefore also rejects the death penalty.[52]

By contrast, regarding retribution, a few further ideas by its main advocate, Immanuel Kant, may be helpful at this point for clarifying his position on the principle of proportionality. Kant's starting point is the need for recognition of human dignity as the supreme value of every human being.[53] He also makes clear that culpability or guilt is a necessary condition for a conviction. As a consequence, punishment should be a response to a crime only when the accused is declared guilty.[54] Proportionality comes into play when a penalty/sentence is imposed on the offender as a guilty person and according to his inner wickedness (*innere Bösartigkeit*)[55] and subsequent blameworthiness [=responsibility for wrongful conduct]. Kant contends that punishment should depend on the criminal's own deserts rather than on the penalty's societal benefits.[56] In a way, retaliation (*lex talionis*) as an absolute form of retribution expresses 'the principle of equality, by which the pointer of the scale of justice is made to incline no more to one side than the other'.[57] In Kant's opinion, if the guilty are not punished, then justice is not

[51] Bentham (n 49).

[52] Bentham (n 49) chs II, III, IX, 187ff.

[53] *cf* J Rachels, 'Kantian Theory: The Idea of Human Dignity' in J Rachels, *The Elements of Moral Philosophy* (New York, Random House Inc, 1986), available at: public.callutheran.edu/~chenxi/phil345_022.pdf.

[54] Actus reus is not enough unless it is accompanied with mens rea (purpose or negligence).

[55] Kant (n 5) 455. As Tonry noticed, Kant referred to offenders' 'inner wickedness' and A von Hirsch wrote of their 'just deserts', while others refer to blameworthiness, wrongfulness or moral culpability, see M Tonry (ed), *Proportionality Theory in Punishment Philosophy: Fated for the Dustbin of Otiosity? Of One-eyed and Toothless Miscreants: Making the Punishment Fit the Crime?* (New York, Oxford University Press, 2019).

[56] von Hirsch (n 8) 59.

[57] Kant (n 5) 454.

done and the idea of law and justice itself is undermined. As he mentioned in his famous '*Inselbeispiel*' (Island example), even in the case of a society which is about to be dissolved, its members should not fail, before its dissolution, to execute the last murderers on death row, so that justice be done and the souls of the murdered can find serenity.[58]

Among the theoretical positions of the period, utilitarian ideas exercised a strong influence over legislation or declarations enacted at the end of the eighteenth century. Most were marked by the notion of proportionality and by its limits and were based on the intrinsic character of punishment itself, mainly in the form of what we would actually call 'necessity testing'. This is the case, for example, with the Constitution of the United States (Eighth Amendment) of 1791[59] (rooted in the British Magna Carta of 1215 and the Bill of Rights of 1689) and with the French Declaration on the Rights of Man and Citizen of 1789.[60] Some years later, the Prussian Civil Code 1794 (*Allgemeines Landrecht für die Preußischen Staaten*)[61] also incorporated a provision stating that [only] 'necessary measures' (*die nöthigen Anstalten*) should be taken by the state police in order to maintain public peace, security and order. It should be noted that many scholars consider this provision the first modern crystallisation of the proportionality principle in public law. Around the same time, in the field of penal law, prominent social activists, such as Thomas Jefferson in American Virginia (1776)[62] and Jean-Paul Marat in France (1782),[63] produced drafts of penal legislation, where the principle of proportionality formed the basis of a rational and thus efficient sanction system.

In spite of all these remarkable ideas, the major penal codifications adopted immediately afterwards took a *particularly punitive approach* to criminals.

[58] Kant (n 5) 455.

[59] See the Eighth Amendment of the US Constitution: 'excessive bail shall not be required, nor excessive fines imposed, nor cruel and unusual punishments inflicted', compared with the relevant provision in s 12 of the Canadian Charter of Rights and Freedoms, which also refers to 'cruel and unusual punishments', and also with Art 3 of the European Convention on Human Rights: 'No one shall be subjected to torture or to inhuman or degrading treatment or punishment'. In both British and US common law, the Magna Carta of 1215 (mainly because of its chapter 20, which sets the rule that 'amercements' may not be excessive) is sometimes considered to be the modern legal source of the principle of proportionality.

[60] Indeed, Art 8 of the French Declaration on the Rights of Man and Citizen 1789 included a provision, according to which: 'The Law must prescribe only the punishments that are strictly and evidently necessary' ('… *des peines strictement et évidemment nécessaires*'), thus presaging what we actually call the necessity test of proportionality; on this notion, *cf* G Gerapetritis, *Proportionality in Administrative Law* (Athens, Ant N Sakkoulas, 1997) 54.

[61] See Part II title 17 para 10 of the 'Allgemeines Landrecht' of 1794. According to Porat and Eliya (n 2 at p 3), the principle of proportionality first arose in Germany, specifically in Prussia, the politically and intellectually dominant German Land in the 18th and 19th centuries. However, strictly speaking, necessity is not the same as proportionality. To use an example from the German legal discussion on defensive violence, if the only way to prevent a thief from stealing apples from an orchard would be to shoot and kill him/her, shooting him/her would then be 'necessary' but would certainly also be disproportionate.

[62] JP Boyd (ed), *The Papers of Thomas Jefferson vol 2 (A Bill for Proportioning Crimes and Punishments in Cases Heretofore Capital)* (Princeton NJ, Princeton University Press, 1950) 492–507.

[63] Marat (n 11) 70.

Proportionality was merely meant as a restraining mechanism to keep penalties within specific, but nonetheless strict, limits. As an example, the French Penal Code of 1791 punished bigamy with 12 years of incarceration with hard labour ('*fers*'), while abortion and false testimony were punished with 20 years of the same penalty.[64] The death penalty was also a fundamental part of the penal arsenal of this Code, constituting the state's response to 32 types of crime.[65] The same is true for the Napoleonic Penal Code of 1810, whose harsh and authoritative character was to some extent moderated only many years later, in 1832 and in 1863.

For the so-called Classical School of Penal Law, the criminal offender, at the theoretical level, never ceased to be a rational human being and a reasonable man, who makes his choices with free will and faces a punishment proportionate to his culpability or guilt. It is true that the penal system during that period 'focused not only on doing justice but also on disciplining the subjects of punishment in a more systematic way, notably through the modernisation and expansion of the prison' (instead of corporal punishments).[66]

B. Taking into Account the Personal Characteristics of the Offender

As a reaction to the Classical School and its formalism, but also under the influence of the teachings of Darwin, Marx and Comte, a new current of thought started gaining ground from the end of the nineteenth century. At the forefront was the Italian Positive School, whose ideas set the framework for a new, sixth stage in this historical evolution. This School's main contribution is its emphasis on the different categories for classifying criminals, namely: criminals by birth, by accident and by emotion, as well as habitual and insane offenders. Indeed, the

[64] French Penal Code 1791: Part II, Title II, section I, Art 33 (bigamy); Part II, Title II, section I, Art 17 (abortion); Part II, Title II, section II, Art 48 (false testimony).

[65] H Remy, *Les principes généraux du Code Pénal de 1791* (Thèse Paris, 1910) 54ff. We may say that in that Code serious crimes received harsher punishments (in modern terminology: ordinal proportionality) and that the overall punishment scale was equally much harsher (cardinal proportionality).

[66] N Lacey and H Pickard, 'The Chimera of Proportionality: Institutionalising Limits on Punishment in Contemporary Social and Political Systems' (2015) 78(2) *Modern Law Review* 216–40, 223. Yet, in practice, the *criminal was considered something like an enemy of society* and had to suffer greatly in prison to 'pay off' his mischief. Even at the end of the nineteenth century, the situation had not changed. A characteristic testimony of this gloomy mentality of retaliation is the poem *The Ballad of Reading Gaol*, composed by the prominent Irish author, Oscar Wilde, during his incarceration for a sexual offence (gross indecency) in the prison of Reading in the years 1895–97. Indicative are the following two verses:

> With midnight always in one's heart, And twilight in one's cell,
> We turn the crank, or tear the rope, Each in his separate Hell,
> And the silence is more awful far Than the sound of a brazen bell.
> And never a human voice comes near To speak a gentle word:
> And the eye that watches through the door Is pitiless and hard:
> And by all forgot, we rot and rot, With soul and body marred.

personal particularity of each criminal was considered to influence their motivation, their degree of 'dangerousness' for society and, consequently, the way in which society should respond in a kind of 'social defence' against the most dangerous among them. For the main proponents of this School, ie, Lombroso, Garofalo and Ferri, the criminal was not necessarily a reasonable human being. In most cases the criminal acts emotionally; hence, his punishment had to be determined not on the basis of his supposed 'rationality', free will and culpability or guilt, as was the opinion of the Classical School, but in view of his *social responsibility* and 'dangerousness'. From this perspective, the previous notion of proportionality as the relationship between gravity of crime and/or culpability or guilt of the criminal, on the one hand, and the severity of the sanction, on the other, played a rather minimal role.

The Positivists, however, did enrich the discussion on the issue of proportionality in two interesting ways. First, they stressed the importance of taking into account – at the legislative and judicial levels – the *offender's personal characteristics* and the specific circumstances under which he committed a crime in order to take social defence measures; this consideration is evidently significant for a 'broader' meaning of proportionality. Second, they correlated the type of punishment with the type of the offender, proposing *interesting new penal measures* – the first hints of the 'alternative penalties' that developed thereafter – such as work in an agricultural colony (*lavoro all' aperto*) as a penalty for 'offenders by accident', namely for those whose crime was due to the 'temptations' from the environment in which they lived. These proposals gave rise to what later (after 1945) would be called the 'welfare model of criminal policy', with emphasis on the 'rehabilitative ideal'[67] (individualisation of sanctions). As a result, the increase in types of penalties and aims of punishment due to the Positivists had a positive impact on the principle of proportionality, particularly in the sense of greater flexibility and a broadening in its application, especially for less serious offences and where the offender could therefore be treated more mildly.[68]

C. Twentieth Century: New Wine in Old Bottles?

Finally, during the seventh stage of its history, the pendulum in terms of the principle of proportionality swings to the other side. Particularly after 1975, the 'justice model of criminal policy' gradually becomes predominant in Europe and the United States and displaces the welfare model, which had been dominant until then. According to this new model, the rights of the accused and convicted must

[67] Lacey and Pickard (n 66) 224–26, referring to D Garland, *The Culture of Control* (Oxford, Oxford University Press, 2001) and D Garland, *Punishment and Welfare* (Aldershot, Gower, 1985).

[68] However, as far as retrospective proportionality is concerned, it could be argued that introducing such new types of penalties actually makes it harder to achieve proportionality by making it harder to measure the relative severity of different kinds of punishment.

be carefully respected, judges' discretion must be constrained, sanctions must be proportionate to the severity of the offences and imprisonment must be only a measure of last resort (*ultima ratio/ultimum refugium*) of the machinery of the penal system, whereas alternative punishments must have priority with respect to minor offences. These ideas have been consolidated in international conventions, such as the UN Convention on the Rights of the Child (1989), especially in Articles 37–40, and have been repeatedly included in soft-law instruments of the UN[69] and the Council of Europe.[70]

As regards the theoretical approaches of the principle's evolution in the twentieth century, there are many important contributions, mainly related to sentencing and the aims of punishment, such as the communicative theory of punishment and criminalisation by Antony Duff.[71] However, the scope of this chapter allows only a brief outline of the historical evolution of the principle of proportionality. In an effort to restrain ourselves, we singled out three penologists and philosophers of penal law whose contributions on this very principle opened up new avenues in the relevant discussion, namely Andrew von Hirsch, Joel Feinberg and H L A Hart.

Von Hirsch[72] elaborated the important notion of 'just deserts'[73] in sentencing, which is based on the idea that the distribution and the quantum of punishment

[69] *cf* UN Standard Minimum Rules for the Administration of Juvenile Justice. The Beijing Rules, Rule 17.1 (a) and (b) (available at: ohchr.org/Documents/ProfessionalInterest/beijingrules.pdf).

[70] For example, the Council of Europe's recommendation on Consistency in Sentencing [Recommendation No R (92) 17, Appendix] states: 'A.4. Whatever rationales for sentencing are declared, disproportionality between the seriousness of the offense and the sentence should be avoided'. Similarly in B.5.*a*, noting that 'Custodial sentences should be regarded as a sanction of last resort' (available at: rm.coe.int/16804d6ac8).

[71] R A Duff, *Punishment, Communication and Community* (Oxford, Oxford University Press, 2003) ch 4. Already in his earlier study, R A Duff, 'Penal Communications: Recent Work in the Philosophy of Punishment' (1996) 20 *Crime and Justice* 1–97, 58 summarises the relation of his theory to the principle of proportionality as follows: 'If punishment is to communicate to a wrongdoer the censure his crime deserves, then since the severity of the punishment expresses the strength of the censure, communicative honesty requires the severity of the punishment must be at least relatively proportionate to the seriousness of the crime. It follows that, whatever the absolute levels of punishment, proportionality is respected only when equally guilty offenders (those equally culpable of equally serious crimes) are punished with equal severity, while those guilty of more serious offenses are punished more severely than those who are less culpable.' For the modification of Duff's initial approach of punishment, *cf* the discussion of Antony Duff and Sandra Marshall with Konstantinos Papageorgiou, Dimitris Kioupis and Tonia Tzannetaki in *The Art of Crime*, May 2018 (available at: theartofcrime.gr/may-2018/).

[72] *cf* in particular A von Hirsch, 'The "Desert" Model for Sentencing: Its Influence, Prospects, and Alternatives' (2007) 74(2) *Social Research: An International Quarterly* 413–34 and A von Hirsch and A Ashworth, *Proportionate Sentencing: Exploring the Principles* (Oxford, Oxford University Press, 2005).

[73] 'Just deserts' is referred to as the 'retribution' type of sentencing, (desert < Middle English < Old French *deserte*, noun use of feminine past participle of *deservir*: *to deserve*). The notion is also used in political philosophy. John Rawls argued that a person does not morally deserve the fruits of his/her talents and/or efforts, such as a good job or a high salary, which are purely the result of the 'natural lottery', see in J Rawls, *A Theory of Justice* (Cambridge MA, Harvard University Press, 1971) para 17. These views were objected to by the libertarian R Nozick in *Anarchy, State and Utopia* (Oxford, Blackwell, 1974) 228, while J Hampton intervened in the discussion by proposing the parameter of moral responsibility in J Hampton, *Political Philosophy* (Oxford, Westview Press, 1997) 150.

must be linked to the offender's desert,[74] and that, consequently, just deserts are in direct relation to the principle of proportionality.[75] Following this approach, the severity of punishment should be measured by how much punishment is deserved,[76] ie, by the seriousness of the convicted person's criminal conduct. This measurement is conducted according to the principle of culpability or guilt (*Schuldprinzip*), which means that it would be impermissible, in the opinion of von Hirsch,[77] to adopt a severe response to minor crimes simply because the offender might commit major crimes in the future.[78] The 'just deserts' notion is consistent with the so-called 'equity factors', which, for example, can lead to the prisoner's early release from the penal institution for reasons of health after the initial sentence; however, such moderations of punishment should not be primarily based on the judge's discretion but on specific legal provisions[79] (a list of equity factors is included in the desert-orientated Swedish Criminal Code, chapter 29, section 5). Nevertheless, 'just deserts' is not in principle opposed to the so-called 'limiting retributivism', which is supported by Tonry, Morris, Frase and others,[80] but can accept such limitations only to a certain extent. Furthermore, the notion of 'just deserts' also limits criminalisation with regard to the seriousness and quality of offences at issue. For example, it cannot be acceptable to criminalise conduct which merely bears on social mores.[81] Finally, a basic distinction in the desert theory is between ordinal proportionality – concerning the relative seriousness of offences and the relative severity of punishments among themselves – and cardinal proportionality, which connects the ordinal ranking to a scale of punishments (anchoring the penalty scale).[82]

Another prominent scholar who discussed the problem of proportionality in the context of punishment is Joel Feinberg. Feinberg gives the impression of adopting a position closer to utilitarian (liberal, of course) proportionality, given that he uses the severity of crime as a measure not for requital or revenge but

[74] von Hirsch (n 9) 375; *cf* Lacey and Pickard (n 66) 225.

[75] *cf* A Ashworth and J Horder, *Principles of Criminal Law*, 7th edn (Oxford, Oxford University Press, 2013) 19–20.

[76] A von Hirsch, *Doing Justice: The Choice of Punishments* (New York, Hill & Wang, 1976) and von Hirsch (n 8) 55–98.

[77] A von Hirsch, *Past and Future Crimes* (Manchester, Manchester University Press, 1985); *cf* the interview by Georgios Giannoulis with A von Hirsch in *The Art of Crime*, May 2017 (available at: theartofcrime.gr/may-2017/).

[78] *cf* M Sumner, 'Retribution' in E McLaughlin and J Muncie (eds), *The Sage Dictionary of Criminology* (London, Sage, 2013) 456–58, 458.

[79] *cf* von Hirsch and Ashworth (n 72) app 1, 165–79.

[80] *cf* N Morris, 'Punishment, Desert and Rehabilitation' in H Gross and A von Hirsch, *Sentencing* (Oxford, Oxford University Press, 1981) 268–69; see also a differentiating opinion of R S Frase, 'Limiting Retributivism' in M Tonry (ed), *The Future of Imprisonment* (New York, Oxford University Press, 2004) 83–120. According to this theory, desert remains a cardinal principle, but functions only as an upper, and, more controversially, a lower limit on just punishment.

[81] *cf* N Androulakis, 'Abschied vom Rechtsgut – Einzug der Moralität?' in U Neumann and F Herzog (eds), *Festschrift für Winfried Hassemer* (Heidelberg, CF Müller Verlag, 2010) 279.

[82] A Ashworth, *Sentencing and Criminal Justice*, 6th edn (Cambridge, Cambridge University Press, 2015) 94; *cf* Lacey and Pickard (n 66) 227ff.

in order to maximise society's benefit;[83] however, this is only the first impression. Despite some objections he raised to the pure idea of retribution,[84] Feinberg rather seems to belong himself to the retributivists. He recognises the *gravity of crime as a measure for the severity of punishment* and relates the concept of proportionality to the wrongdoer's degree of responsibility for his deed and to the degree of his blameworthiness, as determined by his motives and circumstances.[85] Furthermore, he criticises strict moralism and opposes (with some hesitation) the strict moralist view according to which we have good reasons to criminalise and punish any and every kind of moral wrongdoing; this view, however, is quite consistent with holding, as Feinberg does, that we have reason to criminalise and punish those kinds of moral wrongdoing that cause (or might cause) harm or serious offence.[86]

Connected to this is the 'expressive' idea that the severity of punishment should reflect society's 'level of condemnation or disapproval' of the conduct.[87] Accordingly, criminal punishment must be distinguished from other official sanctions – such as administrative ones – on the basis of moral wrongdoing. Feinberg refers to *punishment as a conventional device for expressing emotions* (ie, resentment and indignation, disapproval and reprobation) on the part of the punishing authority itself or of those 'in whose name' punishment is inflicted.[88] Yet, in Feinberg's mind, punishment is also a notion connected to *equality and fairness*, in the sense that the state should treat equals equally and unequals unequally.[89]

Finally, H L A Hart undertook in 1968[90] the difficult task of overcoming the polarity between retributivism and utilitarianism in search of a synthesis and a coherent reconciliation of their different approaches. He recognised the parallel utility of these two schools and their relevant contribution to the implementation of proportionality. In Hart's opinion, the two theories do not fight for control over the same field, as long as utilitarianism gives the answer to '*what is the main*

[83] J Feinberg, *Offense to Others – The Moral Limits of the Criminal Law*, vol 2 (Oxford, Oxford University Press, 1985) 66–67.

[84] For example, that causing harm to the offender does not mean that it affects only him/her (it strikes also his/her family) or that choosing the right amount of suffering in a given case is almost utopic, see A Corlett, 'The Philosophy of Joel Feinberg' (2006) 10 *The Journal of Ethics* 131–91, 140–42.

[85] J Feinberg, *Harmless Wrongdoing – The Moral Limits of the Criminal Law*, vol 4 (New York, Oxford University Press, 1990) 148ff.

[86] J Feinberg, *Harm to Others – The Moral Limits of the Criminal Law*, vol 1 (New York, Oxford University Press, 1984) 203. B Herman, 'Feinberg on Luck and Failed Attempts' (1995) 37(1) *Arizona Law Review* 143–50, 143 reminds us of one of Feinberg's positions: 'punishment is a legal sanction whose severity ought to be a function of the moral gravity of the criminal action'.

[87] J Feinberg, 'The Expressive Function of Punishment' (1965) 49(3) *The Monist* 397–423, 399.

[88] ibid 400ff.

[89] Feinberg (n 86) 149ff. See also K O'Day, 'Some Thoughts on Joel Feinberg's Modest Proposal: Is it Really Such a Modest Proposal After All?' (1995) 37(1) *Arizona Law Review* 243–50, 243.

[90] For what follows, see in particular H L A Hart, *Punishment and Responsibility* (Oxford, Clarendon Press, 1968) 8–27, 161–69, 186–237; *cf* M J Fish, 'An Eye for an Eye: Proportionality as a Moral Principle of Punishment' (2008) 28(1) *Oxford Journal of Legal Studies* 57–71, 66ff and A von Hirsch, 'Proportionality in the Philosophy of Punishment' (1992) 16 *Crime & Justice* 55–98, 62ff.

aim of punishment?' (ie, why punishment should exist at all) and retributivism to the '*problem of the criteria of distribution*' (ie, what are the criteria to determine the grade and extent a punishment should take).[91] Hence, utilitarianism and retributivism could live in harmony if we accept that the general justifying aim of punishment is utilitarian, while punishment should be dispensed on retributive basis. Following similar observations expressed by Jean-Paul Marat and others, Hart further stated that a penal system which imposes severe punishments for minor crimes runs the risk of being discredited and ridiculed.[92]

V. Concluding Remarks on the Principle's Future Perspectives

Proportionality started out as retrospective retaliation and gradually obtained the more refined and sophisticated status of retribution,[93] especially concerning notions like self-defence and just war. Then, thanks to the realist ideas of Grotius and the utilitarian ideas of the philosophers of the Enlightenment, such as Montesquieu and Beccaria, it was connected to the prospective ideas of setting limits to acts of the police and, more generally, to the state's powers, hence also in the context of *jus puniendi*. Nowadays, the principle is treated as a synonym for justice and fairness, and has been widely approved in all modern legal systems – an evolution which, however, muddies the formerly clear content of the principle and creates serious difficulties in its interpretation. Similar problems arise due to the direct connection of the principle with the different aims of punishment and the opposing factors that exercise influence on its validity and content, namely liberalism versus authoritarianism and realism versus idealism – the latter pair especially in the form of retributivism versus utilitarianism. However, these difficulties can actually prove to be useful, in the sense that different views offer different ways of approaching the principle according to the various needs and the different historical, social and political characteristics of each society or individual.[94]

The evolution of the principle will be ongoing. It seems that it will absorb – in the spirit of objectivity and harmonisation – the various recent interpretations of retributivism and utilitarianism, which in our times can indeed be considered as nothing more than new wine in old bottles. Hence, future research should focus

[91] Hart (n 90) especially 9ff. According to Joshua Dressler, Hart's theory could be practically useful by 'applying the principles of retribution as a limit upon utilitarianism', ie, if 'harm sets the ceiling of punishment, while blamelessness sets the floor' in J Dressler, 'The Jurisprudence of Death by Another: Accessories and Capital Punishment' (1979–1980) 51 *University of Colorado Law Review* 17–75, especially 35ff.

[92] Hart (n 90) 20–30.

[93] *cf* Feinberg (n 86) 160.

[94] *cf* Lacey and Pickard (n 66) 216–40.

on two fields: first, on finding objective criteria that reflect the values of the society in question by which we can measure the gravity of crimes, so as to construct retrospective proportionality on a safe basis rather than on elastic and fluid conceptions;[95] secondly, on establishing a kind of 'synthesis' which might balance the two opposing approaches of retributivism and utilitarianism and exploit all their advantages[96] – a synthesis based mainly on the idea of 'just punishment'.[97]

Regarding the latter issue, Hart has already paved the way with his fundamental distinction between the question regarding the main aim of punishment and questions regarding the level and extent of punishment. Following this approach, retributivism could provide the upper limit in sentencing, ie, the limit up to which a punishment can be extended depending on what the guilty offender deserves. In other words, retributivism can be particularly helpful in defining the gravity of crime and the corresponding *uppermost level ('ceiling') of a punishment*, as already suggested by Grotius three centuries ago: *puniendus nemo est ultra meritum*[98] (we must not punish beyond what someone deserves). At the same time, utilitarianism can determine the *inner content, kind and concrete severity of the punishment*, in view of the personal characteristics and specific circumstances of the criminal and crime, and in connection with the aims of punishment. Within this framework of synthesis, Joel Goh[99] once undertook an interesting endeavour to fill the gap between retributivism and utilitarianism by proposing in 2013 a scheme of four criteria of proportionality. The first pair of these criteria concerns retributivism: (a) *defining retributivism*, which means, as a first step, determining punishment as precisely as possible in view of the severity of the offence; (b) *limiting retributivism*, which allows, in a second step, consideration of other sentencing goals by merely placing retributive outer limits on the range of potential sentences.[100] The second pair of criteria refers to utilitarianism: (a) *ends proportionality*, which examines whether the costs of pursuing the goals of the criminal sentence outweigh the benefits to be derived from it, both to society and the individual offender; and (b) *means proportionality*, which

[95] T Sellin and M E Wolfgang, *The Measurement of Delinquency* (New York, Wiley, 1978), proposed back in 1964 a method (the magnitude estimation method) on how to evaluate the seriousness of crimes. Besides, we have other interesting relevant assessments by committees such as the Sentencing Advisory Council of Victoria in 2012, or by judicial initiatives such as the Magistrates' Courts Sentencing Guidelines in 2008. For a normative approach, *cf* A von Hirsch and N Jareborg, 'Gauging Criminal Harm. A Living-Standard Analysis' (1991) 11(1) *Oxford Journal of Legal Studies* 1ff; von Hirsch and Ashworth (n 72) 186ff.

[96] A Kolber, 'The Comparative Nature of Punishment' (2009) 89 *Boston University Law Review* 1565–1608, 1566, 1607, 1608; J Amankonah, *Crime and Punishment, Examining Proportionality Issues within Criminal Law* (LLM thesis in University of South California, 2012) 1ff.

[97] On the content of this notion, *cf* M Tonry, 'Fairness, Equality, Proportionality, and Parsimony: Towards a Comprehensive Jurisprudence of Just Punishment' in A du Bois-Pedain and A E Bottoms (eds), *Penal Censure. Engagements Within and Beyond Desert Theory* (Oxford, Hart Publishing, 2019).

[98] Grotius (n 40) chs II, XX, XXVIII. As concerns the lower limit, see comments above (n 80) on limiting retributivism.

[99] Goh (n 50) 41–72.

[100] ibid 46–47.

assesses whether alternative, less costly sanctions are available for achieving the same intended benefit.

Besides, Antony Duff proposed already in 1996 an interesting sort of synthesis in the domain of sentencing and, more precisely, of what we call 'strict' and 'broad' proportionality within the context of retributivist theory:[101]

> We face … a conflict between two different concepts of 'doing justice'. We can try to do formal justice, administering (as far as we can) formally equal quanta of censure to equally culpable criminals. Or we can try to do substantive justice by finding punishments that are substantively apposite to the offender and her crime. The former aim demands that we seek proportionate equality between criminals across the whole penal system, the latter aim that we seek the substantively apposite punishment for the particular case: but it is impossible consistently to pursue both aims together. We might try to reduce the tension between these aims: for instance, by suggesting that the formal principle of proportionality should figure only as a negative constraint on sentencing, precluding manifestly disproportionate sentences, rather than as a positive ambition requiring us to impose demonstrably proportionate sentences.

Furthermore, interesting ideas about the essence of the principle of proportionality and the feasible ways to combine its different elements can also be traced in the modern discussion about the right to self-defence and its prerequisites, defining the amount of force employed by the defender that can be considered proportionate to the aggressive force threatened.[102] A synthesis of opposing theories could also be attempted at the level of the aims of punishment. In our opinion, it seems reasonable for the main positions of retributivists and utilitarians to find a common denominator in the theory of 'positive general prevention', which was proposed by Johannes Andenaes[103] and further elaborated, among others, by Claus Roxin[104] and Günther Jakobs.[105] According to Jakobs, the emphasis is on the idea that, through punishment, members of *society should be educated in accepting and practising legal provisions* (*Einübung in die Normenanerkennung*). More specifically, this educational aim is geared to create these conditions so that citizens: (a) have confidence in the legal provisions, (b) act according to the law, and (c) accept the consequences of their acts. Evidently, these elements of the aim of 'positive general prevention' seem to deal not only with the classical utilitarian approach of prevention but also with the position of certain retributivists that law

[101] R A Duff, 'Penal Communications: Recent Work in the Philosophy of Punishment' (1996) 20 *Crime and Justice* 1–97, especially 64 and 65.

[102] *cf* N Courakis, 'Self-Defense as a Domain of Moderate Paternalism: The Need for Social Solidarity and Cohesion' in C Papacharalambous (ed), *Paternalism and Criminal Law. Modern Problems of an Old Query* (Athens, Sakkoulas, 2018), 135–45, especially 140ff.

[103] *cf* J Andenaes, *Punishment and Deterrence* (Ann Arbor MI, University of Michigan Press, 1974) 111–28.

[104] C Roxin, 'Zur jüngsten Diskussion über Schuld, Prävention und Verantwortlichkeit im Strafrecht' in A Kaufmann (ed), *Festschrift für Paul Bockelmann* (München, CH Beck, 1979), 279–309.

[105] G Jakobs, *Strafrecht, Allgemeiner Teil: Die Grundlagen und ihre Zurechnumg* (Berlin, De Gruyter, 1991) 13ff.

must be respected and justice must be done. However, positive general prevention as an aim, as described above, is strictly forward-looking: it cannot encompass the backward-looking concerns of retributivism. Retributivists of course do care that justice is done; but, as Nozick also argues,[106] theoretically this is done in and by the very imposition of punishment, not as a contingent consequence.

The present outline of the historical evolution of the principle of proportionality has revealed specific aspects of the past and present which may shed some light on certain elements of the principle's evolution in the future. The main outcome is that there is a further need for a synthesis of the opposing approaches. Yet, at a strictly practical level this synthesis will not be easy, for, as an old proverb says, 'the devil is in the details', ie, in the implementation. For example, if an offence occurs frequently and in a way that is disturbing to the citizens, such as the staining of the facades of buildings by graffiti with no artistic value, the question arises: is it legitimate for a judge to impose a harsh penalty simply for reasons of deterrence, ie, as a means to send a message to the members of society that this kind of offence will no longer be tolerated? To this question, which can be integrated into the discussion about the so-called 'punishment-of-the-innocent' issue,[107] the utilitarian answer could be rather positive. By contrast, Kant's idealistic approach would surely be negative, given that with such a judgment a person would cease to be a goal in him-/herself (human dignity!) and would simply become the means to realise another goal, ie, deterring others.

In trying to tackle this question, it would be useful to distinguish between the competences of the judge and the legislator: the judge, when deciding on the sentence to be imposed within the statutory limits, must not, for any reason whatsoever, exceed the limit of what an offender deserves as punishment at a personal level of deterrence. Whereas the legislator, on an abstract basis and with an eye to the future, is undoubtedly legitimised to enact a law which will provide higher penalties for socially disruptive behaviour, provided these penalties are not excessive and, in particular, do not lead to harsher punishments for less serious crimes. Only in this way does criminal policy seem to comply with effectiveness as well as with the rule of law.

[106] R Nozick, *Philosophical Explanations* (Oxford, Clarendon Press, 1981) 374: 'The wrongdoer has become disconnected from correct values, and the purpose of punishment is to (re)connect him. It is not that this connection is a desired further effect of punishment: the act of retributive punishment itself effects this connection'.

[107] *cf* von Hirsch (n 8) 58.

PART II

Applying Proportionality: National Paradigms

7

Ends and Means: Why Effective Counter-Terrorism Requires Respect for Proportionality and Rights*

LUCIA ZEDNER

I. Introduction

The gravity of the threat posed by terrorism places a premium on effective action by the state, such that the constraints imposed by the proportionality principle and human rights sometimes appear as an unwarranted impediment to the successful pursuit of security. This chapter critically examines the common characterisation of effectiveness and proportionality as dipoles to suggest a more complex, interdependent relation between the two. It illustrates this proposition by reference to recent developments in UK counter-terrorism law. It proposes a more nuanced, heterogeneous conception of effectiveness that takes into account factors beyond the single goal of public protection. Rather than regard proportionality as a limit on – or at odds with – effectiveness, it suggests that effective counter-terrorism depends also on ensuring the legitimacy, suitability, necessity and appropriateness of the means by which laws are promulgated, applied and enforced. Indeed, it seeks to argue that effectiveness is an integral element of prospective proportionality. Taking the objective of counter-terrorism to be, above all, the security of the liberal state, it argues that regard for the rule of law, due process, principled limits and rights is integral to the legitimacy and effectiveness of security laws and measures.

The proposition that effective counter-terrorism aims not only at reducing the risk of terrorism but also at upholding the security of the liberal state requires closer attention to the relationship between effectiveness and proportionality. This chapter questions the contention, voiced by police, security officials

* I am very grateful to Elspeth Windsor for her excellent research assistance, to Thomas Elholm and the editors for their invaluable comments on earlier drafts and to Jo Choulerton for superb copy-editing.

and politicians, that proportionality constraints and rights protections hinder their efforts to counter terrorism effectively. Although the problem of mediating between effectiveness and proportionality is commonly recast as requiring a balance between security and liberty,[1] the metaphor of balancing is problematic. The idea of balance, though well-established in political and legal debate,[2] is perilous because it pays too little attention to exactly which threats suffice to tip the scales, what factors are to be balanced, how they should be weighed and in whose interests.[3] While public safety may appear to be an incontrovertible good, the collective interest in security is always liable to outweigh individual interests and to license laws and measures that are disproportionate, discriminatory and rights-eroding.[4] This risk is compounded by the fact that each new terrorist atrocity prompts demands for immediate state action that, at least in the UK, results in yet more counter-terrorist legislation, introducing new and ever-more extensive measures with little regard for whether they duplicate existing laws, are necessary, or are likely to be effective.

This chapter contests the claim that proportionality and respect for rights are obstacles to effective counter-terrorism, and it takes issue with the proposition that they should be regarded as mere side-constraints upon new laws and policy developments.[5] Instead, following Duff (1996), and Duff and Marshall (2000), it argues that a better ethical perspective is 'one which denies the sharp distinction between "ends" and "means".'[6] This approach calls for closer attention to 'the very ends' that laws and measures are designed to serve and rejects a 'crudely utilitarian' approach that assumes happiness, or – in respect of counter-terrorism – security, is the only good worthy of pursuit. Instead, Duff and Marshall suggest we adopt, 'a morally rich account of the relevant goods and harms – for instance one that includes such familiar liberal values as freedom, autonomy and privacy as goods, and their loss or infringement as harms.'[7] Significantly, they insist that

[1] D Luban, 'Eight Fallacies About Liberty and Security' in R A Wilson (ed), *Human Rights in the War on Terror* (Cambridge, Cambridge University Press, 2005); C Gearty, 'Human Rights in an Age of Counter-Terrorism: Injurious, Irrelevant or Indispensable?' (2005) 58 *Current Legal Problems* 25–46.

[2] As R Dworkin critically observes in *Taking Rights Seriously* (Boston MA, Harvard University Press, 1977) 198.

[3] L Zedner, 'Securing Liberty in the Face of Terror: Reflections from Criminal Justice' (2005) 32 *Journal of Law and Society* 507–33.

[4] J Waldron, 'Security and Liberty: The Image of Balance' (2003) 11 *Journal of Political Philosophy* 191–210; H Fenwick, 'The Anti-Terrorism, Crime and Security Act 2001: A Proportionate Response to 11 September?' (2002) 65 *Modern Law Review* 724–62; C Michaelsen, 'The Proportionality Principle, Counter-Terrorism Laws and Human Rights: A German-Australian Comparison' (2010) 2 *City University of Hong Kong Law Review* 19–43, 20–24.

[5] See, eg, J Braithwaite and P Pettit, *Not Just Deserts* (Oxford, Oxford University Press, 1990).

[6] R A Duff, 'Penal Communications: Recent Work in the Philosophy of Punishment' (1996) 20 *Crime and Justice: A Review of Research* 1–97; R A Duff and S E Marshall, 'Benefits, Burdens and Responsibilities: Some Ethical Dimensions of Situational Crime Prevention' in A von Hirsch, D Garland and A Wakefield (eds), *Ethical and Social Perspectives on Situational Crime Prevention* (Oxford, Hart Publishing, 2000) 19.

[7] Duff and Marshall (n 6) 18.

the articulation of these ends should not leave open the question of the means by which to achieve them.[8] Their approach builds upon Duff's earlier injunction to 'look more carefully ... at the relations between those means and the values that they are meant to serve.'[9] To do so is to reject a purely consequentialist account of effectiveness, which would permit the introduction of any means likely to enhance greater public safety, but which offers few restraints upon new laws deemed to be effective according to this narrow metric.

To prioritise effective security as the sole end of counter-terrorism risks granting the state untrammelled licence to exercise coercive power. While asserting non-consequentialist side-constraints, such as human rights and proportionality, places limits on the pursuit of security and promises some protection against excessive state power, the effectiveness of those side-constraints tends to be limited. Part of the problem is that even fundamental rights protections can be satisfied by minor adjustments to coercive measures,[10] and some, such as the right to privacy, are qualified even on the face of the right.[11] Although side-constraints offer some limits on consequentialism, such mixed theories[12] leave unanswered the dilemma of how to resolve conflicts between the general justifying aim of prevention and limiting constraints upon pursuit of this goal.

One way out of this dilemma is to conceive the goal of security less as a 'pure safety conception' that pursues a narrow idea of public protection, and instead to follow Waldron in asking, 'Is a population more secure simply by virtue of people being safer, i.e., simply in terms of a diminution in the prospect of their being killed or harmed?'[13] Waldron contends that, 'we should not be satisfied with the pure safety conception' because it focuses on individualised injury or loss but 'fails to capture the connection between the idea of security and the idea of social order.'[14] This approach requires us to consider more deeply the nature and quality of the order we seek to preserve, and, in particular, the principles and values essential to protect the liberal legal order in a free and democratic society. The means by which this legal order is secured should, as Duff suggests, be 'intrinsically appropriate' to the end sought and should inform our conception of the

[8] Duff (n 6) 20.

[9] Duff (n 6) 20.

[10] For example, the quashing of a terrorism Control Order in *Secretary of State for the Home Department v JJ* [2006] EWCA (Civ) 1141 (upheld by the House of Lords in 2007), on the grounds that an 18-hour curfew constituted an unwarranted *deprivation* of liberty, was hailed as a triumph for human rights. However, its effect was that the Home Office introduced 14-hour curfews, as they were held to be mere *restrictions* on liberty and therefore ECHR-compliant.

[11] Under Art 8 ECHR, the right to private and family life may be subject to interference 'in the interests of national security, public safety or the economic well-being of the country, for the prevention of disorder or crime, for the protection of health or morals, or for the protection of the rights and freedoms of others'.

[12] Such as that developed in H L A Hart, *Punishment and Responsibility*, 2nd edn (Oxford, Oxford University Press, 2008) 8–13.

[13] J Waldron, 'Safety and Security' (2006) 85 *Nebraska Law Review* 454–507, 461ff.

[14] ibid 462.

end itself.[15] To avoid adopting means that are inappropriate or even contrary to securing the liberal legal order requires closer attention to what the constitution of law demands.[16]

To permit counter-terrorism laws to pursue security by the introduction of measures that are disproportionate is to trample upon fundamental principles of criminal law, justice and the rule of law.[17] This chapter, therefore, considers a more complex conception of security which emphasises the relationship between means and ends. This requires attention to the substantive content, form and impact of laws and measures to ensure that they are consistent with and appropriate to the ends sought. And it extends the enquiry laterally and temporally to consider the processes by which laws are subject to public consultation, pre-legislative scrutiny, parliamentary debate and post-legislative oversight and review.[18] Only by ensuring proper regard for fundamental principles such as transparency and democratic accountability in the legislative process, and by guaranteeing fairness, impartiality and respect for rights in the justice system can the legitimacy of the liberal legal order be secured.[19]

This more extensive enquiry into the relationship between means and ends recognises that the justice of security laws, indeed all laws, is inseparable from the justice of the procedures by which they are instituted and applied.[20] Procedure matters because it is what stands between the individual citizen and the over-extension of state power.[21] While all offenders are liable, by virtue of their offence, to suffer some measure of forfeiture of their rights as full citizens, those suspected of planning future acts of terrorism are much more likely to be regarded as 'enemies of the state' to whom the usual procedural and rights protections do

[15] Duff (n 6) 46.

[16] R A Duff, L Farmer, S E Marshall, M Renzo and V Tadros (eds), *The Constitution of the Criminal Law* (Oxford, Oxford University Press, 2013); M Thorburn, 'Constitutionalism and the Limits of the Criminal Law' in R A Duff, L Farmer, S E Marshall, M Renzo and V Tadros (eds), *The Structures of the Criminal Law* (Oxford, Oxford University Press, 2011) 88.

[17] M C Melia, 'Terrorism and Criminal Law: The Dream of Prevention, the Nightmare of the Rule of Law' (2011) 14 *New Criminal Law Review* 108–22.

[18] J Blackbourn, 'Accountability, Counter-Terrorism and Civil Liberties' (2018) 29 *King's Law Journal* 297–323, 301–4.

[19] L Zedner, 'Security against Arbitrary Government in Criminal Justice' in A du Bois-Pedain, M Ulväng and P Asp (eds), *Criminal Law and the Authority of the State* (Oxford, Hart Publishing, 2017); T R S Allan, 'Procedural Fairness and the Duty of Respect' (1998) 18 *Oxford Journal of Legal Studies* 497. *cf* further E Billis and N Knust, 'Alternative Types of Procedure and the Formal Limits of National Criminal Justice: Aspects of Social Legitimacy' in U Sieber, V Mitsilegas, C Mylonopoulos, E Billis and N Knust (eds), *Alternative Systems of Crime Control* (Berlin, Duncker & Humblot, 2018) 49–57.

[20] T R S Allan, *Constitutional Justice: A Liberal Theory of the Rule of Law* (Oxford, Oxford University Press, 2003) 81.

[21] L Zedner and C-F Stuckenberg, 'Due Process' in K Ambos, R A Duff, J Roberts, T Weigend and A Heinze (eds), *Core Concepts in Criminal Law and Criminal Justice: Volume 1, Anglo-German Dialogues* (Cambridge, Cambridge University Press, 2020) 304–42.

not apply.[22] The potentially catastrophic harms inflicted by terrorist atrocities are commonly deemed to license emergency powers, extraordinary laws and exceptional measures.[23] In respect of preventive measures and preparatory and pre-inchoate offences, these intrusions on individual liberties are justified less by past wrongdoing than by reference to the risk of future harm.[24] Here the principles of preventive justice[25] require strict limits upon coercive laws and measures, including the principles of necessity, *ultima ratio*, the least restrictive appropriate measure and parsimony, such that any interference in individual rights is the minimum consistent with the end of security.[26] In upholding these principles, the role of the state is central: as Thorburn has argued, '[t]he ground of the liberal constitutional state's legitimacy is the simple fact that it – and it alone – can provide the conditions of freedom for all'.[27] Effective counter-terrorism, thus understood, is not simply a question of maximising its capacity to silence the ticking bomb, but its ability to do so in a way consistent with the liberal legal order.

In what follows, the chapter first considers what it means to speak of the effectiveness of counter-terrorism and suggests the need for a multifaceted conception that takes into account a wider array of variables and values than the 'pure safety' goal of public protection. It argues that this conception should extend to concern for 'procedural effectiveness', namely conformity of the means with the requirements of due process and the rule of law essential to the liberal legal order. The next section asks to what, precisely, does proportionality refer? While in respect of punishment, proportionality connotes equivalence between gravity of the offence and severity of sentence, in respect of counter-terrorist laws and measures a more complex, forward-looking metric is required. The chapter considers several variables including the proportionality of substantive laws to the risk, likelihood and impact of prospective harms. It goes on to suggest that prospective proportionality requires closer attention to the goals of counter-terrorism beyond the pursuit of 'pure safety', and that this necessitates a clearer articulation of the role of the courts in defining, upholding and enforcing proportionality constraints. Finally, the chapter considers the implications of this analysis of ends and means for the relationship between effectiveness and proportionality, and it concludes that effective counter-terrorism requires respect for process, proportionality

[22] C Gomez-Jara Diez, 'Enemy Combatants Versus Enemy Criminal Law' (2008) 11 *New Criminal Law Review* 529–62; L Zedner, 'Curtailing Citizenship Rights as Counterterrorism' in B Goold and L Lazarus (eds), *Security and Human Rights*, 2nd edn (Oxford, Hart Publishing, 2019).

[23] B Ackerman, 'The Emergency Constitutions' (2004) 113 *Yale Law Journal* 1029–91.

[24] J Monahan, 'The Individual Risk Assessment of Terrorism: Recent Developments' in G LaFree and J D Freilich (eds), *The Handbook of the Criminology of Terrorism* (London, Wiley, 2017) 520–34.

[25] A Ashworth and L Zedner, *Preventive Justice* (Oxford, Oxford University Press, 2014) ch 11; K Hardy, 'Preventive Justice Principles for Countering Violent Extremism' in T Tulich, R Ananian-Welsh, S Bronitt and S Murray (eds), *Regulating Preventive Justice: Principle, Policy and Paradox* (London, Routledge, 2017) 117–35.

[26] Ashworth and Zedner (n 25) 254.

[27] Thorburn (n 16) 88.

and rights. To do otherwise, it suggests, is not only ethically objectionable, but more likely to do harm than good.

II. Effectiveness and Counter-Terrorism

A. Complexities of Conventional Measures of Effectiveness

Counter-terrorism laws and measures are justified primarily by the pressing need to tackle the threat terrorism poses to person and property. Yet, systematic evaluation of whether counter-terrorist measures are effective is surprisingly scarce.[28] One obstacle is that the effectiveness of security measures is measured primarily by an absence: when they operate effectively, the anticipated harm does not occur, so success is achieved when nothing happens. Even to deploy this absence as a measure of success relies upon a counterfactual claim that, were it not for state intervention, unknown and possibly unknowable harms would otherwise eventuate. In respect of conventional crimes where numbers of incidents are large and, in some measure, predictable, it is possible to estimate the likelihood of a risk and thereby to calculate the effectiveness of any given strategy, law or measure in averting it. In respect of security, however, Monahan has 'found scant empirical evidence of the validity of putative risk factors for terrorism', not least because the numbers are too small to estimate the actuarial risks of terrorist attack accurately.[29] If it is not possible to predict the risks of a terrorist attack occurring, then logically, neither is it possible to know whether counter-terrorist laws and measures have been effective in reducing those risks. Even greater problems arise in respect of attempts to counter radicalisation, because the concept of radicalisation itself lacks clarity,[30] and the processes by which individuals are radicalised and by which they may be restrained remain unclear.[31]

Against this background of radical uncertainty, significant difficulties arise in establishing that counter-terrorism laws and measures meet the requirements of suitability, necessity and appropriateness (proportionality *stricto sensu*). Nonetheless, adherence to these standards has a vital role to play in enhancing the legitimacy of counter-terrorism laws by requiring officials and politicians to question superficial claims of effectiveness and to scrutinise more carefully whether new laws and measures are really necessary and likely to succeed in fulfilling their declared aims.[32] All too often, the questions of whether new counter-terrorist laws

[28] F de Londras, 'Evaluation and Effectiveness of Counterterrorism' in J P Burgess, G Reniers, K Ponnet, W Hardyns and W Smit (eds), *Socially Responsible Innovation in Security: Critical Reflections* (London, Routledge, 2018) 117–28.

[29] Monahan also found that 'risk factors for lone-actor terrorism may differ dramatically from risk factors for group-based terrorism'; Monahan (n 24) 521–22.

[30] P Neumann, 'The Trouble with Radicalization' (2013) 89 *International Affairs* 873.

[31] ibid 874.

[32] Melia (n 17) 113–17.

and measures are indispensable, fit for purpose and no more extensive or intrusive than efficacy requires are disregarded or taken to be self-evident. Several factors explain this relative lack of commitment to addressing questions of the necessity and likely effectiveness of counter-terrorism laws and measures.

First, counter-terrorism legislation is commonly introduced in response to a specific atrocity, new exigency or external pressure. A few examples from the UK will suffice to illustrate the reactive nature of the UK's hyper-legislative response to the threat of terrorism. The Anti-terrorism, Crime and Security Act 2001 followed swiftly on 9/11 and UN Security Council Resolution (UNSCR) 1373 (2001).[33] The Terrorism Act 2006 was enacted in reaction to the 7/7 London bombings in July 2005. The Counter-Terrorism and Security Act 2015 was the UK's response to UNSCR 2170[34] and UNSCR 2178,[35] which were themselves responses to the rise of the so-called Islamic State and multiple Islamist terrorist attacks.[36] Much of this legislation was largely reactive to domestic and international pressure to take action in light of new threats rather than a result of research or considered policy development.[37] Even prior to 9/11, UK counter-terrorist legislation was already very extensive,[38] and rather than identify a particular need for new measures or, indeed, undertake serious evaluation of their likely effectiveness, laws were passed with little scrutiny and less opposition. Who, after all, would dare be 'against' security?

A second reason for the relative lack of investment in evaluation and monitoring of security laws is the lack of clarity about what it means to talk about effective counter-terrorism, which of many metrics of effectiveness should prevail and what relative weight should be assigned to each. In place of generic claims about risk reduction, greater precision is needed to identify the specific aims of any given

[33] UN Security Council Resolution 1373 (2001), available at: www.un.org/sc/ctc/resources/databases/recommended-international-practices-codes-and-standards/united-nations-security-council-resolution-1373-2001/.

[34] UN Security Council Resolution 2170 (2014), available at: www.un.org/en/ga/search/view_doc.asp?symbol=S/RES/2170%282014%29.

[35] UN Security Council Resolution 2178 (2014) called on all Member States to 'prevent the movement of terrorists or terrorist groups by effective border controls', available at: unscr.com/en/resolutions/doc/2178.

[36] In 2015 alone, 151 people were killed and over 360 injured in ISIS terrorist attacks across Europe. See Europol, '211 Terrorist Attacks Carried Out in EU Member States in 2015, New Europol Report Reveals', Press Release, 20 July 2016, available at: www.europol.europa.eu/newsroom/news/211-terrorist-attacks-carried-out-in-eu-member-states-in-2015-new-europol-report-reveals.

[37] Similarly, David Cole identified the need for the US Government to be seen to act, irrespective of clear lacunae in existing laws, as a motivating force behind much legislation in the US in the wake of 9/11; see D Cole, 'The Priority of Morality: The Emergency Constitution's Blind Spot' (2004) 113 *Yale Law Journal* 1753–1800, 1755.

[38] The UK's omnibus Terrorism Act 2000, resulting from a wide-ranging review of terrorism laws by Lord Lloyd of Berwick, consolidated and significantly extended more than 30 years of 'temporary' provisions and 'emergency' powers. See D Anderson, 'Shielding the Compass: How to Fight Terrorism without Defeating the Law' (2013) 3 *European Human Rights Law Review* 233–46, 233; L Zedner, 'Criminal Justice in the Service of Security' in M Bosworth, C Hoyle and L Zedner (eds), *Changing Contours of Criminal Justice* (Oxford, Oxford University Press, 2016) 156.

law or measure, while claims of efficacy should be substantiated by such evidence as is available and, if possible, verifiable. As de Londras reminds us, we should be ready 'to ask whether counter-terrorist financing laws and other measures actually disrupt terrorist financing, whether restrictions on speech really reduce radicalisation, whether citizenship-stripping aids security in any way'.[39] Given that the imperative is to avert attack by any legal means,[40] appropriate measures of effectiveness might include the ability to identify those vulnerable to radicalisation, to spot nascent risks and to impede their development into full-blown threats. A salient example here is the UK Prevent Strategy that, since 2003, has attempted, albeit not without controversy, to tackle the underlying causes of terrorism by deploying 'soft power' to address the social, ideological and other root causes of radicalisation and to protect those deemed vulnerable.[41] Another measure of effectiveness might be the capacity of laws to tackle more proximate hazards to reduce harm to persons and limit damage to property. However, the task of assessing the effectiveness – to say nothing of the ethics – of surveillance measures, defensive street architecture and measures of situational crime prevention is challenging, and these difficulties militate against over-enthusiastic adoption of new counter-terror laws.[42]

Aside from seeking objective security, effectiveness is often assessed by reference to a law's capacity to reassure the public and contribute to improvements in subjective security.[43] While some, like Schneier, dismiss the pursuit of subjective security as political dalliance in symbolic 'security theater',[44] the psychological and the economic impact of public insecurity on commerce, consumption and tourism should not be underestimated.[45] Terrorism seeks, above all, to instil terror. It follows that seeking to enhance individual subjective security and tackling public insecurity – not least the fear that the core values of liberal society will be attacked – are legitimate aims of counter-terrorism. However, it is doubtful whether seeking subjective security in itself suffices to license extensions of state coercive power. As Waldron reminds us, while subjective security is an inherent element of security, it is questionable whether it alone can be regarded as sufficient grounds to justify laws and measures that intrude upon other people's rights.[46]

[39] De Londras (n 28).

[40] Anderson (n 38).

[41] UK Government, *Prevent Strategy*, Cm 8092 (London, HMSO, June 2011), available at: assets.publishing.service.gov.uk/government/uploads/system/uploads/attachment_data/file/97976/prevent-strategy-review.pdf.

[42] J Coaffee, *Terrorism, Risk and the City: The Making of a Contemporary Urban Landscape* (London, Routledge, 2009) ch 2; A von Hirsch, D Garland and A Wakefield (eds), *Ethical and Social Perspectives on Situational Crime Prevention* (Oxford, Hart Publishing, 2000).

[43] L Zedner, *Security* (London, Routledge, 2009) 16–19. On symbolic legislation and proportionality, see Thomas Elholm's chapter 5 in this volume.

[44] B Schneier, *Beyond Fear: Thinking Sensibly about Security in an Uncertain World* (New York, Springer, 2006) 38.

[45] As the COVID-19 crisis 2020 has made all too evident; see Emmanouil Billis', Nandor Knust's and Jon Petter Rui's chapter 1 in this volume.

[46] J Waldron, *Torture, Terror and Trade-offs: Philosophy for the White House* (Oxford, Oxford University Press, 2010) 123–27.

Effective counter-terrorism also requires policies and measures that enhance resilience by safeguarding essential infrastructure and enabling the authorities to respond speedily and efficiently to harms to persons, damage to property and disruption to communications and transport.[47] Given the impossibility of foreseeing and forestalling every attack, a further important aspect of effectiveness is the capacity of laws and counter-terrorist measures to mitigate the impact of attacks and respond efficiently to the harms and damage inflicted. In sum, greater specificity is required to define the metrics needed to assess the effectiveness of each counter-terrorist law and measure, in order to evaluate not only their impact on the risk of attack and level of harm inflicted, but also their capacity to mitigate loss, enhance resilience and restore order.

B. Procedural Effectiveness

So far, we have examined the need to identify more clearly the goals and outcomes of counter-terrorist laws and measures before accepting claims as to their effectiveness. Let us now return to our opening argument, that effectiveness should not be assessed by reference to ends alone but should also have regard to the means by which counter-terrorism legislation is promulgated and applied. This is particularly important given that counter-terrorist laws tend to be introduced in direct and often urgent response to terrorist attacks and new security threats, with the result that little time and thought is given to the propriety of the means by which they are enacted.[48] The pressure on governments to act quickly tends to crowd out the prior question of whether there are existing laws that adequately address the very problems that the proposed laws are intended to resolve. Instead, the starting presumption should be that new legislation is not mandated unless a persuasive case can be made to show that new laws are really needed. It follows that the legislature should take care to resist executive pressure to enact unnecessary, and potentially problematic, duplicative counter-terrorism legislation. Only where pre-legislative scrutiny reveals there is a legal lacuna to be filled and where the necessity test is satisfied should new legislation be contemplated.

Experience suggests, however, that because counter-terrorism legislation is often reactive, time for considered contemplation is limited. In the UK, security

[47] S Walklate and G Mythen, *Contradictions of Terrorism: Security, Risk and Resilience* (London, Routledge, 2015) ch 6; see also Government of Canada, *Building Resilience against Terrorism: Canada's Counter-Terrorism Strategy* (Ottawa, Government of Canada, 2011).

[48] One legal commentator said of the UK Coronavirus Act 2020, 'the very reason why we have emergency legislation is for, well, emergencies, and this is one of them. Yet this should not mean that anything goes, and that grand questions of legitimacy and mundane issues of simple legal efficacy should be ignored. They may be less urgent than the lives at risk, but constitutional and legal propriety still matters.' D Allen Green, 'How the State Came to Criminalise Ordinary Life', *Prospect*, 5 May 2020, available at: www.prospectmagazine.co.uk/magazine/state-law-constitution-police-david-allen-green-coronavirus-covid-19.

legislation is typically introduced under 'emergency', 'fast-track' or other expedited processes that curtail time and opportunity for internal deliberation and external consultation with experts and the wider public. An understandable sense of urgency, combined with governments' desire to be seen to be acting promptly, inhibits careful consideration of whether new laws are necessary. It also limits scope for pre-legislative scrutiny, which might otherwise ensure that the proposed legislation is appropriate and conforms to human rights and constitutional protections, and which allows law-makers to assess the economic, social and other risks consequent on its enactment. Dyzenhaus casts doubt on the common official claim that 'there is no time to debate properly both the extent of the emergency and the appropriate responses to it'.[49] Instead, he promotes a 'culture of justification', which assigns to the legislature a special 'responsibility to ensure that parliament is an institution in which reasons are properly debated, in order that legislation might take forward the rule of law project'.[50] Only when 'the decision maker's reasons are good enough in a democratic society'[51] and legislatures operate as 'reason-giving or reason-demanding institutions in the rule of law project'[52] is due deference owed by the judiciary in its interpretation of emergency legislation. This approach brings other metrics of effectiveness into play: for example, the quality of prior consultation, the adequacy of pre-legislative scrutiny and the calibre of parliamentary debate. Emergency legislation, expedited procedures and curtailed parliamentary debate[53] are liable to impede effective scrutiny and thus undermine legality. Recognition of such hazards kerbs the tendency to focus only on counter-terrorism laws' capacity to pursue safety, and instead shifts attention to the effectiveness of the procedures by which they are developed and enacted.

No less important are the processes by which new counter-terrorism laws and measures are applied and enforced. Demands for the protection of the majority against terror attack should not be permitted to override the right of the individual to enjoy security against the unwarranted or excessive exercise of state coercive power.[54] Effective provisions that uphold due process protections and ensure fair trial rights are essential. Everyday policing entails intrusions upon person and property, such as stop and search, which are legitimate only if they adhere to procedural constraints and accord with legality. By contrast, the investigation and prosecution of terrorism-related offences are often subject

[49] D Dyzenhaus, 'Deference, Security and Human Rights' in B Goold and L Lazarus (eds), *Security and Human Rights* (Oxford, Hart Publishing, 2007) 130.

[50] ibid 143.

[51] ibid 142.

[52] ibid 145.

[53] Ackerman (n 23); P Thomas, 'Emergency and Anti-Terrorist Powers: 9/11: USA and UK' (2003) 26 *Fordham International Law Journal* 1193; C Walker and J Blackbourn, 'Interdiction and Indoctrination: The Counter-Terrorism and Security Act 2015' (2016) 79 *Modern Law Review* 840.

[54] Zedner (n 19).

to lower procedural requirements and the policing of these offences tends to ignore or override such due process protections as do apply. So, for example, section 44 of the Terrorism Act 2000 permitted police to stop and search without any requirement of reasonable suspicion in areas identified by the police as high risk.[55] Section 44 was introduced as a means to increase the effectiveness of policing terrorism but, following legal challenge, it was struck down by the European Court of Human Rights (ECtHR) in the leading case of *Gillan* (2010) on the grounds that it 'amounted to a clear interference with the right to respect for private life'.[56] Significantly, the number of section 44 'suspicion-less stops' in the UK fell from 102,504 in 2009/10, the year prior to the *Gillan* judgment, to just 9,652 in 2010/11.[57] Section 44 was replaced in 2011 by the more limited power under section 47A, which permits police stops only where a 'senior officer reasonably suspects that an act of terrorism "will take place" and reasonably considers that the authorisation is necessary to prevent such an act.'[58] Thus restricted, the section 47A power was used very rarely, just once in 2013 and four times in 2017.[59] This brief history of counter-terrorist police stop powers thus tracks a shift from a 'pure safety conception' of effectiveness under section 44 to the reassertion of 'procedural effectiveness' under section 47A, which placed a far more effective constraint on the exercise of police powers.

To prioritise procedural effectiveness requires state officials to adhere to due process and rights protections not as mere side-constraints on their pursuit of security but as essential to effective counter-terrorism. It acknowledges that the protection of fundamental rights is integral to the very legal order that counter-terrorism laws are designed to protect. This approach requires that laws are necessary, appropriate and compliant with fundamental human rights, and that counter-terrorist powers are applied in accordance with effective means of restraint. Effectiveness of means also requires transparency and accountability; these are provided by parliamentary scrutiny and debate, regular reporting on the use of different counter-terrorism powers and ongoing oversight by an independent reviewer or review body to ensure that counter-terrorism laws accord

[55] A Parmar, 'Stop and Search in London: Counter-Terrorist or Counter-Productive?' (2011) 21 *Policing and Society* 369–82.

[56] *Gillan and Quinton v United Kingdom* App no 4158/05 (ECtHR, 12 January 2010) [63]. Note, however, that the police may still stop without any requirement of reasonable suspicion at the UK border under sch 7 of the Terrorism Act 2000 and sch 3 of the Counter-Terrorism and Border Security Act 2019; see L Zedner, 'The Hostile Border: Crimmigration, Counter-Terrorism or Crossing the Line on Rights?' (2019) 22 *New Criminal Law Review* 318–45.

[57] 'Police use of terrorism stop and search powers drops 90 per cent', *The Daily Telegraph*, 13 October 2011, available at: www.telegraph.co.uk/news/uknews/terrorism-in-the-uk/8824203/Police-use-of-terrorism-stop-and-search-powers-drops-90-per-cent.html.

[58] Section 47A(1)(b) Terrorism Act 2000.

[59] 'Independent Reviewer of Terrorism', (2020) *Report of the Independent Reviewer of Terrorism Legislation on the Operation of the Terrorism Acts*, available at: terrorismlegislationreviewer.independent.gov.uk/wp-content/uploads/2020/03/Terrorism-Acts-in-2018-Report-1.pdf, at 60–63.

with legal principles and the rule of law.[60] It is significant and to be commended that the Independent Reviewer of Terrorism in the UK is officially entrusted to 'monitor UK counter-terrorism legislation for its fairness, effectiveness and proportionality.'[61]

No less important is the use of time-limited restrictions on emergency legislation, and sunset clauses requiring periodic review of the grounds for continuing use of counter-terrorist powers.[62] Such oversight is possible only if information about the exercise of these powers is well-publicised and accessible, and if there are opportunities and public resources to permit legal challenge and judicial review.[63] The interference with rights on such security grounds as are defensible can be justified only when counter-terrorism laws and measures are applied in a manner that is non-discriminatory, fair and clearly directed at a legitimate aim, when they are the least intrusive means possible and proportionate. In the following section, we turn to the question of what precisely proportionality in counter-terrorism requires.

III. Proportionality in Counter-Terrorism

A. Applying Proportionality to Preventive Endeavour

Proportionality is a central concept in penal theory, developed by modern retributivist or desert theorists[64] as a justification for, and important limit on, punishment, and widely used in liberal legal systems as a guide to sentencing. Proportionality requires that the severity of a sentence be set by reference to the gravity of the crime committed and is thus backward-looking. Granted, difficult questions arise as to how gravity should be calculated, what weight should be given respectively

[60] Some countries have designated public officials responsible for ongoing review of terrorism legislation. On the official role of the UK Independent Reviewer of Terrorism Legislation, see: terrorismlegislationreviewer.independent.gov.uk/about-me/ and on the Australian Independent National Security Legislation Monitor, www.inslm.gov.au/.

[61] Home Office, *Independent Reviewer of Terrorism Legislation Recruitment Information Pack* (August 2016), 4: publicappointments.cabinetoffice.gov.uk/wp-content/uploads/2016/08/160805-Independent-Reviewer-of-Terrorism-Legislation-candidate-pack.pdf.

[62] Blackbourn (n 18).

[63] As former President of the UK Supreme Court, Lord Neuberger, has argued, 'unless a right to due process in criminal proceedings, a right to protection against abuses or excesses of the state … is enforceable, it might as well not exist'; see Neuberger, 'Justice in an Age of Austerity', 15 October 2013, available at: www.supremecourt.uk/docs/speech-131015.pdf.

[64] Not least A von Hirsch and A Ashworth, *Proportionate Sentencing* (Oxford, Oxford University Press, 2005); A von Hirsch, 'Proportionality in the Philosophy of Punishment' (1992) 16 *Crime and Justice* 55–98; A Walen, 'Retributive Punishment' in the *Stanford Encyclopedia of Philosophy*, at: plato.stanford.edu/entries/justice-retributive/. See further Antony Duff's chapter 2 in this volume. On the historical evolution of the principle of proportionality in sentencing, see Nestor Courakis' and Vagia Polyzoidou's chapter 6 in this volume. On proportionality as a guide to sentencing in common law systems, see Julian Roberts' chapter 12 in this volume.

to culpability, wrongdoing and harm, and whether desert is an absolute constraint requiring complete equivalence, whether it should set only an upper limit on sentencing[65] or merely delineate a range of 'not-undeserved' punishment.[66]

Proportionality in respect of counter-terrorism – or indeed any other preventive endeavour – is more complex still and raises further questions about the referent objects against which proportionality should be calculated.[67] Does proportionality in prevention require advertence only to wrongs already committed – which, in the terrorist case, may amount to no more than viewing of terrorist-related materials, facilitating their publication or distribution? If proportionality in the preventive realm is necessarily forward-looking, can desert plausibly fulfil the justificatory role that it does in penal theory?[68] In the case of prevention, should proportionality be set in respect of the gravity of the anticipated harm or the probability of it occurring, in which case, what level of risk is required before rights' eroding interventions are permitted? Or should the metric of proportionality be some combination of the two? And how far should proportionality relate to the type and quantum of intervention needed to bring about desired future ends?[69] As the discussion of effectiveness above made clear, setting the goal of pure safety as the dominant metric is problematic. A broader conception of security requires closer regard to the reciprocal relationship between means and ends if it is to minimise the risk of the overreach of state power resulting from pressure to avert terrorist attacks.

As we observed above, there are clear collateral costs to the all-out pursuit of 'pure safety'.[70] First, although security is often set as an undisputed goal, simply enhancing public safety sets too amorphous a metric to provide a tangible quantum by which to measure whether a law or measure is necessary, proportionate and appropriate. Secondly, to set pure safety as the priority risks licensing counter-terrorist laws and measures that may seem proportionate to the potentially catastrophic effects of the most serious attack, but which are insufficiently attentive to the low risk of it occurring. Thirdly, even if it were possible to formulate a calculus that incorporated both the likelihood and the seriousness of harm, estimating prospective gravity would entail too many imponderables[71] to furnish a robust

[65] C Slobogin, 'Limiting Retributivism and Individual Prevention' in F Focquaert, E Shawn and B Wallace (eds), *The Routledge Handbook of the Philosophy and Science of Punishment* (London, Routledge, 2020).

[66] M Tonry (ed), *Why Punish? How Much? A Reader on Punishment* (Oxford, Oxford University Press, 2011); R S Frase, *Just Sentencing: Principles and Procedures for a Workable System* (Oxford, Oxford University Press, 2012).

[67] C Steiker, 'Proportionality as a Limit on Preventive Justice: Promises and Pitfalls' in A Ashworth, L Zedner and P Tomlin (eds), *Prevention and the Limits of the Criminal Law* (Oxford, Oxford University Press, 2013) 195–96, 207–9.

[68] ibid 212.

[69] Ashworth and Zedner (n 25) 18–19.

[70] Waldron (n 13).

[71] As Donald Rumsfeld, the then US Secretary of Defense, infamously declared in the aftermath of 9/11, 'there are known knowns; there are things we know we know. We also know there are known unknowns; that is to say we know there are some things we do not know. But there are also unknown

basis for setting limits. Finally, and most importantly, any metric of proportionality that attended only to end goals would, as argued above, tend to disregard the collateral costs to the liberal legal order, which it is the very purpose of security laws to uphold.

Counter-terrorism policies that fail to consider countervailing costs and risks to social order, trust and justice, as Michaelsen observes, risk losing the 'war on terrorism without firing a single shot.'[72] In practice, however, the goal of public safety tends to prevail in political discourse, policy and practice, even where the consequence is to license laws and measures that are disproportionate to the wrong done, only remotely related to prospective harms and insufficiently attentive to collateral damage. For this reason, the role of courts is crucial as the next sub-section will seek to show.

B. Proportionality, Counter-Terrorism and the Courts

Historically, the role of the courts in the UK in ensuring proportionality of counter-terrorism laws has been hampered by judicial deference to the executive in security matters, largely on the grounds that the executive has greater access to national security intelligence and expert evidence than the courts.[73] Of the Law Lords' acceptance that there was 'a public emergency threatening the life of the nation' in the leading case of *A v SSHD* (2004),[74] Tomkins critically queried 'how did they know?'[75] Although the Court deferred to the executive on the claim that there was such an emergency as to permit derogation from the European Convention on Human Rights (ECHR) under Article 15, it found the indefinite detention of foreign terrorist suspects without trial to be unlawful on grounds of discrimination. Significantly, Lord Bingham went on to insist that, 'the function of independent judges charged to interpret and apply the law is universally recognised as a cardinal feature of the modern democratic state.'[76] Tomkins, and many others, applauded the ruling in *A v SSHD* as marking 'the beginnings of a much belated judicial awakening to the fact that even in the

unknowns – the ones we don't know we don't know'; D Rumsfeld, 'DoD News Briefing', 12 February 2002, available at: archive.defense.gov/Transcripts/Transcript.aspx?TranscriptID=2636.

[72] Michaelsen (n 4) 21.

[73] S Macdonald, 'The Role of the Courts in Imposing Terrorism Prevention and Investigation Measures: Normative Duality and Legal Realism' (2015) 9 *Criminal Law and Philosophy* 265–83, 267.

[74] *A and others v Secretary of State for the Home Department* [2004] UKHL 56 (*Belmarsh case*). See Gearty (n 1).

[75] A Tomkins, 'Readings of A v Secretary of State for the Home Department' (2005) *Public Law* 259–66, 261–62.

[76] *A and others v Secretary of State for the Home Department* [2004] UKHL 56. See also D Feldman, 'Proportionality and Discrimination in Anti-Terrorism Legislation' (2005) 64 *Cambridge Law Journal* 271–73.

context of national security the courts have a responsibility to ensure that the rule of law is respected'.[77]

The subsequent development of a more robust role of the appeal courts in matters of security and greater confidence in judicial expertise in assessing intelligence[78] have emboldened the courts routinely to address the necessity, appropriateness and proportionality of terrorism laws and measures. In *SSHD v AP* (2010), for example, Lord Brown held that the superior courts are 'properly to be regarded as expert tribunals in this difficult and sensitive field'.[79] Thus while the UK's constitutional separation of powers accords to the executive the prerogative to act in matters of national security, the constitutional role of the courts to scrutinise the legality of counter-terrorism laws and their conformity with fundamental rights has been strongly reaffirmed. The principle of proportionality has proven to be an important means of protecting rights by stipulating that restrictions must be proportionate and that any interference requires strong justification. In *Pham* (2015), a case concerning citizenship deprivation on security grounds, the Supreme Court held that proportionality required that there be no 'less onerous means of achieving the same aim' and that due regard must be given to the nature of the right involved, the seriousness of the interference with that right and 'the nature of the justification for that interference'.[80]

In practice, the task of determining whether a counter-terrorist law or measure is proportional to the purported threat also entails practical evaluation of intelligence data and other information, and this raises further issues of transparency and accountability. Relevant considerations include the need to establish that the threat against which the action is taken is genuine, present and sufficiently serious to justify the imposition of the law or measure at issue.[81] In order to make this determination, the court must have 'sufficient material to permit a proper assessment of proportionality',[82] and it must disclose precisely and in full the grounds upon which its decision is based. In terrorist cases, countervailing considerations relating to the security of operations, personnel, informants and regard for the security interests of friendly nations often weigh against open trials and public hearings, to the detriment of transparency and accountability.

In the UK, so-called 'closed material proceedings' are used in security-sensitive immigration and civil cases, in which security-cleared 'special advocates' may see 'closed material' but are not permitted to communicate with their clients once they

[77] Tomkins (n 75) 259. See also John Jackson's chapter 8 in this volume.

[78] Macdonald (n 73) 270.

[79] *Secretary of State for the Home Department v AP* [2010] UKSC 24 [5].

[80] *Pham v Secretary of State for the Home Department* [2015] UKSC 19 [40] and [117].

[81] See *R (on the application of XH) v Secretary of State for the Home Department, R (on the application of AI) v Secretary of State for the Home Department* [2017] EWCA (Civ) 41 [113]–[116].

[82] ibid [125].

have done so.[83] Even criminal trials have been held *in camera* on national security grounds.[84] In the leading case of *Incedal* (2014),[85] the Court of Appeal expressed 'grave concern' over the damage to justice that would be inflicted by holding a criminal trial wholly in secret and insisted that '[o]pen justice is both a fundamental principle of the common law and a means of ensuring public confidence in our legal system.'[86] Despite this, roughly two-thirds of the trial was held *in camera* and the 10 selected journalists allowed to attend were not permitted to report on it. A subsequent bid by several newspaper groups for reporting restrictions to be lifted was dismissed by the Court of Appeal on security grounds.[87]

As we have observed, proportionality requires that measures taken are suitable; interfere with rights no more than is absolutely necessary; constitute the least restrictive measure appropriate; and are not disproportionate to the security threat or danger posed. However, closed material proceedings and secret trials deny journalists, academics and rights organisations the ability to assess whether such measures are proportionate according to these metrics. Their capacity to assess the justice of the trial, the quality of evidence, the proportionality of sentencing and, not least, the ostensible grounds for resorting to secrecy is gravely undermined when transparency and accountability are thus denied. It follows that an essential component of effective procedural proportionality is sufficient disclosure and access to relevant facts to judge whether a law and its application is proportionate or not. It is surely questionable whether the practice of providing only a 'gist' of the core of the case to the defendant can be said to satisfy this requirement.[88]

The difficulty of ensuring proportionality arises not only in relation to procedure but also to the framing of terrorism offences and the sentences attached to them. A prominent example from the UK serves to illustrate the problems raised. Even before 9/11, section 58 of the Terrorism Act 2000 made it a crime to collect, record or possess 'information of a kind likely to be useful to a person committing or preparing an act of terrorism'. However, the courts found it difficult to establish possession. Section 3 of the Counter-Terrorism and Border Security Act 2019 amended section 58 to make it a crime merely to view such material online on a single occasion, and raised the maximum sentence to 15-years' imprisonment.[89] Although the Minister of State for Security insisted that the offence was 'both proportionate and necessary in order to allow the police to take action to protect

[83] A Kavanagh, 'Special Advocates, Control Orders and the Right to a Fair Trial' (2010) 73 *Modern Law Review* 836–57. See also John Jackson's chapter 8 in this volume.

[84] R Goss, 'To the Serious Detriment of the Public: Secret Evidence and Closed Material Procedures' in L Lazarus and J C McCrudden (eds), *Reasoning Rights: Comparative Judicial Engagement* (Oxford, Hart Publishing, 2014) 118–34.

[85] *Guardian News and Media Ltd v AB and CD* [2014] EWCA (Crim) 1861. See discussion in Zedner (n 38) 159–61.

[86] *Guardian News and Media Ltd v AB and CD* [2014] EWCA (Crim) 1861 [10].

[87] *Guardian News and Media Ltd and Others v R and Incedal* [2016] EWCA (Crim) 11.

[88] Kavanagh (n 83).

[89] L Zedner, 'Countering Terrorism or Criminalising Curiosity? The Troubled History of UK Responses to Right-Wing and Other Extremism' (2020) 49(4) *Common Law World Review* (forthcoming).

the public from potentially very serious threats',[90] a 15-year sentence seems grossly disproportionate to the seriousness of viewing such material online on a single occasion. Despite the addition of a 'reasonable excuse defence' during the passage of the bill through parliament (including carrying out work as a journalist or for academic research), the new offence risks the overreach of state power and infringes fundamental rights. To create a 'one click' offence and set penalties so disproportionate to the wrong done is likely to be regarded as unfair. As such, it is liable to undermine public acceptance of the legitimacy of counter-terrorism laws and create a warranted sense of grievance and alienation, particularly in those communities upon whom the burden of counter-terrorism laws falls most heavily.[91] Far from being effective counter-terrorism, such laws are likely to be counterproductive.

IV. Conclusion

This chapter has sought to show that far from being dipoles, effectiveness and proportionality are related and interdependent. Disproportionate counter-terrorism laws and measures are not only unjust, they are liable to be ineffective and, if they are perceived to be illegitimate, may have the opposite of their intended effect. The question therefore arises how best should the hazard of disproportionate laws and measures be averted and by what means? This chapter has contended that core principles of preventive justice and adherence to fundamental legal norms may help to limit the risks of disproportionality and suggest an ethical framework by which to ensure that appropriate limits are imposed.[92] First, the principle of legitimacy requires law-makers to establish that the aim by which a law or measure is justified is a legitimate objective; that the means by which it is pursued are appropriate; and that the means adopted are rationally related to the stated aims.[93] Secondly, the principle of parsimony requires that the means employed be the least intrusive upon individual rights needed to achieve their aim. Thirdly, the principle of *ultima ratio* requires that criminal sanctions, and, in particular, deprivation of liberty, should be a matter of last resort. Finally, the necessity principle requires the level of coercion, infringement of individual rights or deprivation of liberty should be no greater than is strictly necessary to fulfil its aim. These principles should, and, as this chapter has shown, often do inform the jurisprudence of the courts, which has a vital role to play in ensuring that national security policy is lawful and regarded by the public as legitimate.

[90] Counter-Terrorism and Border Security Bill, 11 September 2018, Column 662, available at: hansard.parliament.uk/commons/2018-09-11/debates/156B51AC-2504-442B-BEE4-02B6E2FBB5D5/Counter-TerrorismAndBorderSecurityBill.

[91] Zedner (n 89).

[92] Ashworth and Zedner (n 25) ch 11; Hardy (n 25).

[93] Michaelsen (n 4) 30.

The jurisprudence of the UK courts over recent decades has developed a more demanding proportionality test that requires a rational connection between the laws and measures adopted and their effectiveness in fulfilling their stated aims; that they be necessary; and that there be no less restrictive alternative.[94] This reaffirmation of the judicial role in upholding the rule of law, particularly in cases where interference with human rights is at issue, has proven to be central to the articulation and defence of proportionality in counter-terrorism cases by the courts. While the potentially catastrophic threats posed by terrorism incline governments to adopt whatever lawful means they can to pursue public protection, a fuller, more persuasive conception of security embraces the protection of individual liberties and liberal legal values under the rule of law. This requires that the means adopted accord closely with these ends and, in turn, serve to redefine what it means for a measure to be effective. In sum, proportionality of the substance, means and processes by which security laws are enacted, implemented and enforced should be seen not as a constraint on effective counter-terrorism, but as essential to the very security of the liberal legal order.

[94] *A and others v Secretary of State for the Home Department* [2004] UKHL 56. See Gearty (n 1).

8

Contrasting Penal and Non-Penal Responses to Terrorism: Proportionality and Human Rights in the UK

JOHN JACKSON

I. Introduction

Terrorism is often said to pose such an existential threat to the security of the state that the state is justified in taking exceptional measures outside the criminal justice system in order to counter it. After 9/11 the phrase 'war on terror' famously gained currency in the US, signalling the fact that terrorists were enemies of the state and that the military could take the lead in taking pre-emptive action, without waiting for a crime, probable cause or even reasonable suspicion before taking action. The United Nations (UN) Special Rapporteur on the Protection of Human Rights and Fundamental Freedoms has highlighted the adverse effects of a number of pernicious post-9/11 practices that states have engaged in, such as declaring permanent emergences and establishing special courts, the military commissions in Guantánamo being the most infamous example.[1] The UK, by contrast, with its wealth of experience with conflicts involving terrorism throughout the twentieth century has tended to disavow the language of war. In the aftermath of the London bombing in July 2005, the Director of Public Prosecutions in England and Wales said that 'London is not a battlefield. The innocents who were murdered in 7 July 2005 were not victims of war. … On the streets of London, there is no such thing as a war on terror.'[2] At the same time, as we shall see, the UK has not always used the criminal justice system to combat terrorism.

This chapter aims to audit the UK's record of countering terrorism within the last 50 years against the background of the role that human rights and proportionality have played in curbing executive action. Broadly speaking, it can be claimed

[1] UN Rapporteur, 'Report of the Special Rapporteur on the promotion and protection of human rights and fundamental freedoms while countering terrorism on the human rights challenge of states of emergency in the context of countering terrorism' (2018) A/HRC/37/5.2.

[2] L Bannerman, 'There is No War on Terror in Britain, says DPP', *The Times*, 24 January 2007.

that over the past 50 years or so, there have been two main phases of terrorist activity within the UK: Irish or so-called 'troubles'-based terrorism dating back to the beginning of the 1970s and, more recently, so-called 'jihadi-based' or 'Islamic' terrorism.[3] Although there have been other forms of terrorist action connected to the activities of animal rights campaigners and, more recently, far-right extremists, these have not had the same impact. There is also a considerable contrast to be drawn between the fatalities caused by the two main phases of terrorism. Figures show that from 1970–2017 of the 3,410 fatalities caused by terrorism in the UK, 86 per cent were due to Northern Ireland 'troubles'-based terrorism during 1970–90.[4] From 9/11 2001 until the end of 2017 there were 95 fatalities caused by terrorism in Great Britain; that is an annual average of 5.9 fatalities. Although the fatalities have been far fewer in the latest phase, the indiscriminate and disproportionate impact of 'Islamic' terrorism – the fact that it can occur anywhere, at any time and against anyone, and with the potential to use weapons of mass destruction – has provoked disproportionate reactions in a number of states. As Kahn has put it, in violating the law, such a terrorist is of course a criminal, yet there is a widespread sense that he is more than a criminal and that the techniques of the domestic criminal law are not adequate to the threat.[5]

As we shall see, the initial reaction in the UK to both these kinds of terrorism was one of over-reaction, but over time a more proportionate response was developed. It will be convenient to begin by examining the non-penal executive measures that were taken to combat terrorism in each of the two phases before going on to consider the penal measures. It will be argued that although the non-penal measures introduced at the beginning of each of the two phases were disproportionate in their effect, over time a strict proportionality analysis came to be applied to these measures. A number of measures taken within the criminal justice system, by contrast, have not been subjected to the same rigour, with the result that the criminalisation of terrorism has come at a price in terms of individual rights.

II. Executive Non-Penal Measures in Response to Northern Ireland Terrorism

Following the outbreak of serious violence in Northern Ireland in 1969 the government there pressed for the introduction of internment under special emergency

[3] See S Greer, 'Terrorism and Counter-Terrorism in the UK: From Northern Irish Troubles to Global Islamist Jihad' in G Lennon, C King and C McCartney (eds), *Counter-Terrorism, Constitutionalism and Miscarriages of Justice* (Oxford, Hart Publishing, 2019) 45.

[4] See the University of Maryland's Global Terrorism Database, available at: www.start.umd.edu/research-projects/global-terrorism-database-gtd.

[5] D Kahn, *Sacred Violence: Torture, Terror and Sovereignty* (Ann Arbor MI, University of Michigan, 2008) 6.

powers legislation dating back to the origins of partition. Internment, the name given to executive detention without trial, had represented the primary method of dealing with terrorism in Northern Ireland throughout its history and it was re-introduced by the Northern Ireland Government in 1971 'with reluctant UK government approval'.[6] The strategy badly misfired as it had the effect of escalating the violence instead of reducing it and proved to be a 'recruiting sergeant' for further Irish Republican Army (IRA) volunteers.[7] In the first six months of internment over 2,400 people were detained, most of whom were freed after a short time in custody.[8] Internment was phased out in 1975 but remained on the statute book until 1998, the year of the Belfast peace agreement.

The other major executive non-penal measure that was employed during the years of Northern Ireland terrorism was the use of exclusion orders in response to the spread of IRA terrorism onto the British mainland. In the wake of the Birmingham pub bombings in 1974 which killed 21 people, the UK Government revived a measure that had previously been used in the Second World War to exclude suspected Irish terrorists from the British mainland. Legislation was enacted empowering the Secretary of State to make an order prohibiting a person from being in Great Britain if satisfied that the person was 'concerned in the commission, preparation, or instigation of acts of terrorism'.[9] It was originally claimed that these powers would be used exceptionally against those involved in terrorism who could not be successfully prosecuted. But according to Walker, they were in fact used extensively when it was advantageous to do so and not just when there was no alternative, although they, like internment, ultimately proved counter-productive – displacing terrorism to Northern Ireland was not an effective means of preventing it altogether.[10] It is estimated that nearly 450 exclusion orders were made during the 24 years in which these powers were in operation.[11] They were eventually phased out when Northern Ireland terrorism dissipated in the 1990s due to the peace process and were repealed under the Terrorism Act 2000.

What is striking about these measures is the lack of any effective legal challenge to them and the fact that they were brought to an end as a result of *political* decision-making rather than because of any legal imperative. Domestic judges tended to show a deferential approach towards the legality of executive detention,[12] although in fairness the doctrine of parliamentary (as opposed to

[6] D Bonner, *Executive Measures, Terrorism and National Security* (Aldershot, Ashgate, 2007) 87–88. See Civil Authorities (Special Powers) Act (Northern Ireland) 1922.

[7] Bonner (n 6) 90, citing Standing Advisory Commission on Human Rights, *Report* (1976–77) ch 4.

[8] D McKittrick and D McVea, *Making Sense of the Troubles* (London, Penguin, 2001) 68.

[9] Section 3(3)(b) Prevention of Terrorism (Temporary Provisions) Act 1974.

[10] C Walker, *The Prevention of Terrorism in British Law*, 2nd edn (Manchester, Manchester University Press, 1992) 88–89.

[11] J Blackbourn, 'Excluding Terrorists' in G Lennon, C King and C McCartney (eds), *Counter-Terrorism, Constitutionalism and Miscarriages of Justice* (Oxford, Hart Publishing, 2019) 149.

[12] See the Northern Ireland High Court judgment in *Kelly v Faulkner* [1973] NILR 31. *cf Re McElduff* [1972] NILR 1. See Bonner (n 6) 95–96; S Livingstone, 'The House of Lords and the Northern Ireland Conflict' (1994) 57 *Modern Law Review* 333.

constitutional) sovereignty meant that the courts were considerably constrained in what they could do.[13] The UK was a signatory to the European Convention on Human Rights (ECHR) during this period but when internment was introduced it entered a derogation under Article 15 of the ECHR in respect of Article 5 (right to liberty and security) on the grounds that there was a public emergency which threatened the life of the nation. This was challenged unsuccessfully in *Ireland v United Kingdom* before the European Court of Human Rights (ECtHR), which held that the levels of violence in Northern Ireland were such that there was an emergency affecting the life of the nation and that the measures taken did not go beyond the exigencies of the situation.[14] The Court proclaimed that states had a wide margin of appreciation, but not an unlimited power, to determine what measures were necessary. It was certainly not the Court's function to 'substitute for the British Government's assessment any other assessment of what might be the most prudent or most expedient policy to combat terrorism', nor was it for the Court to engage in a 'retrospective examination of the efficacy of those measures, but of the conditions and circumstances reigning when they were originally taken and subsequently applied'.[15] Adopting this approach, the Court accepted that the limits of the margin of appreciation left to the contracting states by Article 15(1) were not overstepped by the UK when it formed the opinion that extrajudicial deprivation of liberty was necessary.

When the British Government took over direct control of the affairs of Northern Ireland in 1972, it was nevertheless very clear that internment was not working and, after an unsuccessful attempt to seek a truce with the IRA, another strategy had to be devised. An independent Commission under Lord Diplock was established to consider 'whether changes should be made in the administration of justice in order to deal more effectively with terrorism without using internment under the Special Powers Act'.[16] This was the first in a long line of independent reviews of counter-terrorism measures within the UK which paved the way slowly towards more proportionate and human rights compliant methods for dealing with terrorism. The Diplock Commission marked the beginnings of a strategy which became known as 'criminalisation' that gradually superseded the internment approach for dealing with terrorism. Although the jury-less Diplock courts that the Commission recommended were controversial and the emergency legislation that resulted from it gave sweeping powers of arrest and questioning to the security forces,[17] it at least accepted that any criminalisation policy should comply with the minimum standards of Article 6 of the ECHR (right to a fair trial).

[13] See B Dickson, 'The House of Lords and the Northern Ireland Conflict – a Sequel' (2006) 57 *Modern Law Review* 383, 386–87.

[14] *Ireland v United Kingdom* App no 5310/71 (ECtHR, 18 January 1978).

[15] ibid [214].

[16] Lord Diplock, *Report of the Commission to consider legal procedures to deal with terrorist activities in Northern Ireland* (London, HMSO, 1972) Cmnd 5185.

[17] See Northern Ireland (Emergency Provisions) Act 1973.

Long before the enactment of the Human Rights Act 1998 which effectively incorporated the ECHR into UK law, this set an important baseline against which all future legislation directed at containing Northern Ireland terrorism could be judged.

Future independent reviews paid even more regard to the ECHR. The Gardiner Committee which reported in 1975, three years after Diplock, was specifically commissioned to consider measures to deal with terrorism 'in the context of civil liberties and human rights'.[18] Although, like Diplock, the Committee did not feel able to recommend an immediate end to internment, it further entrenched the criminalisation policy by asserting that executive detention could not remain as a long-term policy. Detention could only be tolerated in a democratic society in the most extreme circumstances and must be used with the utmost restraint and retained only as long as strictly necessary. The need for proportionality was echoed 20 years later in the Lloyd report which reviewed all aspects of dealing with terrorism. Its recommendations led to the enactment of the Terrorism Act 2000, which saw an end to internment and exclusion orders.[19] The report set out four guiding principles which introduced the requirement of proportionality into assessing any legislation for dealing with terrorism.[20] These were:

(i) Legislation against terrorism should approximate as closely as possible to the ordinary criminal law and procedure.
(ii) Additional statutory offences and powers may be justified, but only if they are necessary to meet the anticipated threat. They must then strike the right balance between the needs of security and the rights and liberties of the individual.
(iii) The need for additional safeguards should be considered alongside any additional powers.
(iv) The law should comply with the UK's obligations in international law.

III. Executive Non-Penal Measures in Response to Islamic Terrorism

A. Overview

Soon after finally committing itself to an exclusive policy of criminalisation without derogation in its dealings with Northern Ireland terrorism, the British Government shifted tack again when the events of 9/11 focused attention on Islamic

[18] Lord Gardiner, *Report of a Committee to consider, in the context of civil liberties and human rights, measures to deal with terrorism in Northern Ireland* (London, HMSO, 1975) Cmnd 5847.
[19] Lord Lloyd, *Inquiry into Legislation Against Terrorism* (London, HMSO, 1996) Cm 3420.
[20] ibid para 3.1.

terrorism. This was said to pose a terrorist threat 'quite distinct from anything that we have previously faced'.[21] Rather than putting penal measures at the forefront of combatting this threat, the government enacted the Anti-terrorism, Crime and Security Act 2001 which empowered the Secretary of State to issue a certificate for the indefinite detention of suspected international terrorists when it was not possible to deport or remove them from the UK because they might face persecution abroad and removal would therefore breach Article 3 (freedom from torture and inhuman/degrading treatment) of the ECHR. Once again, a derogation was entered in respect to Article 5 of the ECHR and between 2001 and 2005 at least 17 persons were detained in this manner. Certificates of indefinite detention were replaced by control orders under the Prevention of Terrorism Act 2005, which curtailed suspected terrorists' freedom of movement within the UK, and later by terrorism prevention investigation measures under the Terrorism Prevention and Investigation Measures Act 2011 (TPIM Act), which restricted freedom of movement in a less drastic manner.

An important difference when it came to containing the excesses of executive measures against terrorism between twentieth-century Northern Ireland terrorism and twenty-first-century Islamic terrorism, however, has been that while any restraint in the Northern Ireland phase was largely the product of political decisions that the measures were counter-productive (albeit informed by independent reviews), in the case of Islamic terrorism, restraint of the executive measures was more effected by judicial intervention, with much greater attention paid to proportionality analysis. We have seen that legal challenges to the Northern Ireland measures failed before the ECtHR on the ground that Member States had to be given a wide margin of appreciation in deciding what measures were necessary in an emergency. The executive measures against Islamic terrorism, by contrast, attracted much more judicial scrutiny in an era when the Labour Government's policy of 'bringing rights home' under the Human Rights Act 1998 gave human rights an increasing prominence in domestic political and legal discourses.

B. Judicial Control and Proportionality: The Measure of Indefinite Detention

The significance of judicial intervention was highlighted in particular in the House of Lords decision in *A v SSHD*,[22] where a number of appellants who were detained under the Anti-terrorism, Crime and Security Act 2001 claimed that the conditions required for an emergency under Article 15 of the ECHR had not been met in advance, and even if such an emergency existed, the detention

[21] See HL Debs, vol 629, col 142 (27 November 2001) (Lord Goldsmith).

[22] House of Lords, *A v Secretary of State for the Home Department* (*Belmarsh case*) [2004] UKHL 56, [2005] 2 AC 68.

powers introduced under the Act were a disproportionate response. While the House of Lords by a majority of 8–1 considered that there *was* an emergency, when it came to consider whether the measures actually taken were strictly required by the exigencies of the situation, a majority of 8–1 held that they were disproportionate and discriminatory, and the detention power under section 23 of the 2001 Act was declared to be incompatible with Articles 5 (right to liberty) and 14 (freedom from discrimination) of the Convention. Lord Bingham made a distinction between the threshold factual establishment of an emergency, which was an issue on which there could be deference to the executive, and an assessment of the measures selected to address the threat, where a test of strict proportionality must be applied. He accepted the appellants' argument that the proper approach towards the issue of proportionality was for the court to ask itself

> whether: (i) the legislative objective is sufficiently important to justify limiting a fundamental right; (ii) the measures designed to meet the legislative objective are rationally connected to it; and (iii) the means used to impair the right or freedom are no more than is necessary to accomplish the objective.[23]

Walker has pointed out that these tests of proportionality correspond to the tests proposed by Lord Lloyd in his 1996 report on terrorism.[24] The difference, however, is that Lord Lloyd was addressing a largely political audience which was able to ignore him, while Lord Bingham was alluding to a legal test of proportionality which had to be applied by the courts. Sometimes a fourth test is added to the effect that the measures must strike a proper balance between the gains that will accrue and the intensity of the interference with the right.[25] Lord Bingham accepted that it was important to recognise the terrorism dimension but also emphasised the importance of upholding fundamental rights such as Article 5 and Article 6. He cited *Aksoy v Turkey*, where the ECtHR, clearly referring to national courts as well as the Convention organs, held:

> The Court would stress the importance of Article 5 in the Convention system: it enshrines a fundamental human right, namely the protection of the individual against arbitrary interference by the State with his or her right to liberty. Judicial control of interferences by the executive with the individual's right to liberty is an essential feature of the guarantee embodied in Article 5(3), which is intended to minimise the risk of arbitrariness and to ensure the rule of law.[26]

[23] ibid [30].

[24] C Walker, *Blackstone's Guide to the Anti-Terrorism Legislation*, 3rd edn (Oxford, Oxford University Press, 2014) 24.

[25] This fourth test has been adopted by the Canadian Supreme Court and the German Federal Constitutional Court (Bundesverfassungsgericht). See Canadian Supreme Court *R v Oakes* [1986] 1 SCR 103, [71]; and J Sieckmann, *Report: The Principle of Proportionality: A German Perspective* (Venice Commission, 2019). See also R Alexy, *A Theory of Constitutional Rights* (Oxford, Oxford University Press, 2002).

[26] *Aksoy v Turkey* App no 21987/93 (ECtHR, 18 December 1996) [76].

This was an important expression of the view that even in relation to severe threats to the nation such as terrorism, proportionality must take account of the categories of rights that are at stake. It followed that decisions to derogate from fundamental rights such as those in Articles 5 and 6 had to be approached on the basis of a strict test of proportionality. Applying such a test, the majority of the Law Lords considered that the primary weakness in the government's case was the differing treatment accorded to nationals and non-nationals. As Lady Hale put it, as it was not considered necessary to lock up nationals indefinitely, it was not necessary to lock up foreigners.[27]

There can be little doubting the significance of this decision in terms of applying strict proportionality standards towards counter-terrorism measures, as it indicated that this was an area where the courts were not prepared to show the same deference towards the executive as hitherto. As one commentator has put it, it was a 'monumental' case, making it very clear that the new Human Rights Act regime posed a substantial constitutionalist barrier to counter-terrorist state action, notwithstanding executive claims of necessity that had previously more or less determined legality.[28] It is also important to recognise the significance that was attached by the House of Lords to the judgments of the ECtHR, thereby illustrating how the ECtHR and national courts can mutually reinforce each other's decisions. This benign relationship could be seen at work in the immediate aftermath of the House of Lords' decision and, as we shall see, in later judgments ruling on the legality of other executive measures taken against the liberty of the person.

Although the government accepted the Law Lords' declaration of incompatibility in relation to section 23 of the 2001 Act and took steps to repeal it, the House of Lords did not have the power to strike down the legislation and the appellants were not immediately released. The result was that they took their case to Strasbourg where the government informed the ECtHR that it had changed its mind and wished to challenge the House of Lords' judgment. There was thus the curious spectacle of a national government challenging the decision of its own highest court. In *A and Others v United Kingdom*[29] the Grand Chamber of the ECtHR allowed the issue to be re-litigated before it and, in an important unanimous Grand Chamber ruling, it agreed with the House of Lords that there was an 'emergency threatening the life of the nation', but that the measures adopted were disproportionate and discriminatory. It unanimously rejected the government's argument that the House of Lords should have afforded a wider margin of appreciation to the political organs of the state which were in a better place to assess what was required by the exigencies of the situation. The Court stressed that the question of proportionality was 'ultimately a judicial decision'

[27] *A v SSHD* (n 22) [237].

[28] F de Londras, 'Prevention, Detention, and Extraordinariness' in F Ní Aoláin and O Gross (eds), *Guantanamo and Beyond: Exceptional Courts and Military Commissions in a Comparative Perspective* (Cambridge, Cambridge University Press, 2013) 117, 132.

[29] *A and Others v United Kingdom* App no 3455/05 (ECtHR GC, 19 February 2009).

and the House of Lords was correct to apply the strict scrutiny that it did to the detention regime.[30]

The Grand Chamber went on to give an equally important unanimous ruling on the question whether the applicants had been given access to a procedure before national courts to challenge the lawfulness of their detention, as required by Article 5(4) of the ECHR. One of the differences between the internment measures in Northern Ireland and the detention measures under the 2001 Act was in the manner in which particular decisions to detain could be reviewed. The Northern Ireland internment provisions provided for 'quasi-judicial' procedures of review which gave detainees an opportunity to challenge their detention before commissioners but where evidence against them could be heard in their absence. In his 1975 review Lord Gardiner described these procedures as a 'veneer' which bore no resemblance to common law procedures.[31] Those detained under the 2001 Act, by contrast, were able to challenge their detention before a superior court of record, the Special Immigration Appeals Commission (SIAC). Like the Northern Ireland procedures, SIAC was permitted to base its decision on 'closed material' that was not seen by the appellant but in compensation for this, security-cleared 'special advocates' were permitted to view the closed material and represent the interests of the detainees in closed proceedings, although they were unable to communicate with the detainees once they had seen the closed material.[32]

The ECtHR acknowledged that there might be circumstances in which full disclosure of the evidence could not be made. Such circumstances included a 'strong countervailing public interest such as national security, the need to keep secret certain police methods of investigation or the protection of the fundamental rights of another person'.[33] In the present case the ECtHR accepted the urgent need to protect the population of the UK from terrorist attack and that there was a strong public interest in obtaining information about Al-Qaeda and in maintaining the secrecy of the sources of such information. But balanced against these important public interests was the applicants' right under Article 5(4) to procedural fairness and in view of the dramatic impact of the lengthy deprivation of liberty on the applicants' fundamental rights, Article 5(4) must import 'substantially the same fair trial guarantees as Article 6(1) in its criminal aspect'.[34] Against this background, the Court considered:

> [I]t was essential that as much information about the allegations and evidence against each applicant was disclosed as was possible without compromising national security or the safety of others. Where full disclosure was not possible, Article 5(4) required that

[30] ibid [184].
[31] Lord Gardiner (n 18) 152.
[32] See s 6 SIAC Act 1997 and r 36 (2) SIAC (Procedure) Rules 2003. For a comprehensive examination of the role of special advocates, see J Jackson, *Special Advocates in the Adversarial System* (Abingdon (Oxon), Routledge, 2020).
[33] *A and Others v UK* (n 29) [205].
[34] ibid [217].

> the difficulties this caused were counterbalanced so that each applicant still had the possibility effectively to challenge the allegations against him.[35]

The Court accepted that the special advocate procedure could perform an important role in counterbalancing the lack of a full, adversarial hearing by testing the evidence and putting arguments on behalf of the detainee.[36] However, crucially, the 'special advocate could not perform this function in any useful way unless the detainee was provided with sufficient information about the allegations against him to enable him to give effective instructions to the special advocate'.[37] Although this important qualification to the special advocate procedure fell short of enabling applicants to know the *full* case against them, it emphasised the importance of giving applicants a substantial measure of procedural fairness. The Court examined the information that had been provided to each of the applicants in this case and concluded that the case against four of the nine applicants was mainly based on closed material. As there had been insufficient disclosure of information to enable them to make an effective challenge to their detention, the Court found that there was a violation of Article 5(4).

This unanimous ECtHR judgment sent out a strong message that while the Court understands the difficulties states face in protecting their populations from the threat of terrorism, both the substantive executive measures taken to counter this threat and the procedural measures provided for challenging them must be carefully conceived so as to be considered proportionate to the threat faced.[38] This reinforced the strict proportionate approach that the national courts then took towards the further executive measures that the government adopted to replace indefinite detention.

C. Subsequent Developments: Control Orders and TPIMs

The Prevention of Terrorism Act 2005 was passed to replace indefinite detention with 'control orders' that would apply to all those within the UK irrespective of 'nationality or terrorist cause' where the Secretary of State had reasonable grounds to suspect an individual of involvement in terrorism-related activity. The orders imposed restrictions on movement, on use of communications technologies and on associations with particular persons, etc. Although both derogating and non-derogating orders could be made, in practice only non-derogating orders were made, with the government claiming that they did not go beyond the limits of

[35] ibid [218].
[36] ibid [220].
[37] ibid.
[38] S Shah, 'From Westminster to Strasbourg: *A and Others v United Kingdom*' (2009) 9 *Human Rights Law Review* 473, 487.

Article 5 of the ECHR.[39] Once again however, the courts subjected these orders to considerable scrutiny. In *JJ v SSHD*,[40] for example, a majority of the House of Lords held that a control order obligation imposed on six men to observe an 18-hour curfew together with other stringent conditions such as denial of the internet, reporting twice daily to the police, pre-authorisation of visitors, etc, deprived those men of their liberty in violation of Article 5. After some initial hesitation on the question whether the appointment of special advocates alone could sufficiently compensate those who wished to challenge control orders made against them, the House of Lords took the view that the kind of disclosure deemed essential in ECtHR *A and Others v United Kingdom* (sometimes known as 'A-type' disclosure) was additionally required to enable controlled persons to give effective instructions to the special advocate.[41]

Although control orders were heavily criticised by parliamentary groups and were reviewed annually by the Independent Reviewer of Terrorist Legislation, it was judicial intervention that seemed to have a particular chilling effect on their use. In course of the six years of their use (2006–11), only 52 people were subjected to them, despite intelligence estimates in 2007 that 2,000 suspects posed a threat to national security.[42] In 2011 they were replaced by 'terrorism prevention investigation measures' (TPIMs) which ended some of the most controversial aspects of control orders such as the involuntary relocation requirements, although these particular requirements were later on re-established under enhanced powers introduced by the Counter-Terrorism and Security Act 2015. Figures show that TPIMs remain considerably under-utilised, averaging fewer than 10 in any one year.[43] Other executive measures have also been introduced to limit individuals' liberty, such as temporary exclusion orders.[44] But in more recent years there has been a decided shift back to prosecuting suspected terrorists through the criminal courts. In the period 2012–16, only 27 TPIMs were issued as compared with 247 persons prosecuted for terrorism offences.[45] All in all, one can conclude, that in contrast to the executive measures taken to restrict people's liberty during the

[39] Whereas a non-derogating order lasted for 12 months and could be amended or revoked at any time by the Home Secretary, a derogating order lasted for 6 months and required a formal derogation from Art 5 and permission from the High Court for such an order to be made.

[40] House of Lords, *JJ v Secretary of State for the Home Department* [2007] UKHL 45.

[41] House of Lords, *Secretary of State for the Home Department v AF* [2009] UKHL 28, [2010] 2 AC 269. See A Kavanagh, 'Special Advocates, Control Orders and the Right to a Fair Trial' (2010) 73 *Modern Law Review* 836.

[42] C Walker, 'Terrorism Prosecution in the United Kingdom' in F Ní Aoláin and O Gross (eds), *Guantanamo and Beyond: Exceptional Courts and Military Commissions in a Comparative Perspective* (Cambridge, Cambridge University Press, 2013) 225, 247.

[43] G Allen and N Dempsey, *Terrorism in Great Britain: The Statistics* (House of Commons Library, Briefing Paper CBP7613, 2017).

[44] See ss 2–15 Counter-Terrorism and Security Act 2015.

[45] Home Office, *Operation of Police Powers under the Terrorism Act* (Home Office, 2017), available at: www.gov.uk/government/statistics/operation-of-police-powers-under-the-terrorism-act-2000-quarterly-update-to-december-2018.

phase of twentieth-century Northern Ireland terrorism, the executive measures taken to deal with twenty-first-century Islamic terrorism have been enforced in a much more proportionate manner, with the courts exercising considerable human rights oversight.

IV. Penal Measures and Criminalisation

A. The Criminalisation Policy in Northern Ireland

It is commonly argued that criminalisation is a more preferable means of countering terrorism than executive measures, as it is both normatively correct in terms of maintaining the due process constraints of the ordinary criminal law and pragmatically the most effective means of dealing with suspected criminal terrorists.[46] While the policy of criminalisation in Northern Ireland proved more effective in combatting terrorist violence than the previous internment policy, the emergency legislation applied within the criminal process was not always compliant with human rights standards. The abolition of jury trial for terrorist cases and the lowering of the standard of admissibility for confessions from the common law standard of voluntariness to the standard of absence of torture, inhuman and degrading treatment were in keeping with the ECHR. But emergency powers to arrest suspects without reasonable suspicion fell short of the obligations imposed by Article 5, which meant that, quite apart from the continuing use of internment, there was a continuing need to derogate from Article 5.[47] Further powers bestowed under the Prevention of Terrorism (Temporary Provisions) Act 1974 gave security forces the power to arrest and detain persons without a lawyer for 48 hours and, on review by the Secretary of State, to detain them for a further five days before being brought to court. Human rights groups made many criticisms of the emergency legislation that was applied within the criminal justice system, in particular the extensive powers given to the security forces to question suspects before they were brought to court which led to many allegations of abuse. The policy shift away from internment towards using the criminal courts did not in practice lead to ordinary criminal processes being applied.

Although some of these powers were challenged on legal grounds, in this pre-Human Rights Act era, the domestic courts did little to mitigate them. In the absence of constitutional human rights constraints, the domestic courts were required to apply the concept of parliamentary sovereignty which limited the contribution they could make to ensuring the criminal process adhered to human rights standards. So, for example, they upheld the power to arrest on a

[46] See, eg, R Wagstaff, *Terror Detentions and the Rule of Law* (Oxford, Oxford University Press, 2014) xvii.

[47] See s 11 Northern Ireland (Emergency Provisions) Act 1973.

mere suspicion (which did not have to be reasonable) of committing an offence.[48] Even when they could arguably have been more proactive in 'reading in' safeguards to the detention powers, such as the right of access to a lawyer during police interviews, they refused to do so in the absence of any statutory provision to this effect.[49] Dickson has attributed this judicial restraint to an era when the courts did not see themselves as a counter-weight to government power.[50]

As an international human rights court, the ECtHR fared better than the domestic courts in upholding rights whilst also recognising the difficulties that terrorism posed to Member States, at least when the UK withdrew its derogation from Article 5 as it did for the first time from 1984 to 1988. In *Brogan v United Kingdom*, for example, the Court held that the detention of a suspected terrorist without being brought before any judicial authority for four days and six hours under the Prevention of Terrorism (Temporary Provisions) Act 1984 was incompatible with the requirement in Article 5 to bring those arrested 'promptly' before a court.[51] The UK Government had argued that the difficulties faced by the authorities in obtaining evidence that is admissible and usable because suspects are trained in anti-interrogation techniques justified a longer period of detention than for other suspects. The Court acknowledged that the investigation of terrorist offences presented the authorities with special problems and accepted that, subject to the existence of adequate safeguards, the context of terrorism in Northern Ireland had the effect of prolonging the period during which the authorities might, without violating Article 5(3), keep a person suspected of serious terrorist offences in custody before bringing him to court. However, they could not justify dispensing altogether with 'prompt' judicial control, and the scope for flexibility in interpreting and applying the notion of 'promptness' was very limited.

Rather than responding by finding a more proportionate solution, for example in the form of some judicial review after 48 hours, the government decided instead to re-issue a derogation under Article 15, which the ECtHR duly upheld on the basis of needing to give states a wide margin of appreciation when the derogation was challenged in 1993 in *Brannigan and McBride v United Kingdom*.[52]

B. The Terrorism Acts of 2000 and 2006

As with the executive measures mentioned earlier, it was against the background of the peace process in Northern Ireland and the decline in violence, rather than

[48] House of Lords, *McKee v Chief Constable of Northern Ireland* [1984] 1 WLR 1358.

[49] House of Lords, *R v Chief Constable of the RUC ex parte Begley, R v McWilliams* [1997] 1 WLR 1475.

[50] Dickson (n 13).

[51] *Brogan and Others v United Kingdom* App nos 11209/84, 11234/84, 11266/84 and 11386/85 (ECtHR, 29 November 1988).

[52] *Brannigan and McBride v United Kingdom* App nos 14553/89 and 14554/89 (ECtHR, 25 May 1993).

on the basis of any legal imperative, that the government decided to end the emergency regime by withdrawing its notice of derogation under Article 5 in 2001. It commissioned the Lloyd report which recommended dealing with terrorism through permanent criminal processes without the need for emergency legislation, and the ensuing Terrorism Act 2000 set the tone for this new approach. Henceforth all special statutory offences and additional powers to deal with terrorism would become part and parcel of the ordinary law. So instead of continuing with a 7-day detention power, without recourse to the courts, the new Act took the more proportionate approach recommended by Lord Lloyd of requiring judicial involvement at 48 hours, albeit that the application to extend detention could be made ex parte in the absence of the suspect but with an opportunity given to the suspect to make representations to the judicial authority. Although, as we have seen, the government's initial response to Islamic terrorism was to revert to deportation and derogating executive measures, it changed course in 2006 by enacting a new Terrorism Act which introduced a range of new terrorism offences, such as incitement to terrorism and preparation of terrorism, and new police powers, including a 28-day detention power before terrorist suspects had to be charged once a warrant of further detention had been obtained.

C. Procedural Rights and Proportionality

One danger with adopting a criminalisation approach towards counter-terrorism which is highlighted in much of the literature is that special anti-terrorist measures become normalised within mainstream criminal processes.[53] One example of this has been the curtailment of the right of silence by measures first introduced in Northern Ireland in 1988 enabling inferences to be drawn from silence.[54] Although these measures were justified specifically in order to combat the wall of silence that terrorist suspects were putting up against the police when they were questioned in custody, they were applied to *all* suspects in Northern Ireland and the measures were later extended to all suspects in England and Wales.[55] The provisions were challenged in *John Murray v United Kingdom*,[56] where the applicant had been convicted after the trial judge drew strong inferences against him for failing to account for his presence in a house where a man was being kidnapped. The ECtHR held that the right to silence did not entitle an accused to absolute immunity from inferences being drawn from his silence. On the

[53] See, eg, the essays in F Ní Aoláin and O Gross (eds), *Guantanamo and Beyond: Exceptional Courts and Military Commissions in a Comparative Perspective* (Cambridge, Cambridge University Press, 2013).

[54] Criminal Evidence (Northern Ireland) Order 1988. See J Jackson, 'Recent Developments in Criminal Evidence' (1989) 40 *Northern Ireland Legal Quarterly* 105; J Jackson, 'Curtailing the Right of Silence in Northern Ireland: Lessons from Northern Ireland' (1991) *Criminal Law Review* 404.

[55] See ss 34–37 Criminal Justice and Public Order Act 1994.

[56] *John Murray v United Kingdom* App no 18731/91 (ECtHR GC, 8 February 1996).

one hand, it would be incompatible with the immunities to base a conviction solely or mainly on the accused's silence or on a refusal to answer questions. On the other hand, it was equally obvious that these immunities should not prevent an accused's silence from being taken into account in assessing the persuasiveness of the prosecution evidence, in situations which clearly called for an explanation from him, provided adequate safeguards were put in place. One of these safeguards was that before any inferences could be drawn from a suspect's silence in the face of police questioning, a suspect had to be given the opportunity of accessing legal advice. As a consequence of this, the British Government amended the legislation to provide that inferences could not be drawn from suspects who were not given such an opportunity.[57]

Although this is an example of the ECtHR applying proportionate standards towards Article 6, both it and the domestic courts have not always applied these strictly. The *Murray* judgment recognised the importance of suspects obtaining access to a lawyer to advise them of their position when inferences might be drawn from silence but this did not mean that terrorist suspects were entitled as of right to access to a lawyer before they were questioned by the police. The Terrorism Act 2000 subsequently legislated to permit the police to carry out 'safety interviews' with terrorist suspects in the absence of a lawyer where to do so might protect the public.[58] One question that arose before the Grand Chamber of the ECtHR in *Ibrahim and Others v United Kingdom*,[59] was whether it was compatible with Article 6 to use statements made in the absence of a lawyer in safety interviews to convict the applicants who had been arrested on suspicion of having detonated bombs on the London Underground which failed to explode. The Court took the view that there could be no watering down of fair trial rights for the simple reason that the individuals in question were suspected of involvement in terrorism. But it went on to say that in determining whether the proceedings were fair as a whole, the weight of public interest in the investigation and punishment of the particular offence in issue may be taken into consideration, provided that the very essence of an applicant's defence rights is not extinguished. The judges were far from unanimous in determining whether the admission of the applicants' statements constituted a breach of Article 6 and the Court's judgment has been criticised for its lack of clarity on how exactly the balancing act between fair trial rights and the public interest should be carried out.[60] The approach of the Court here is reminiscent of earlier British case law when the Privy Council held that in deciding whether Article 6 can be interfered with, it is necessary to balance

[57] See s 58 Youth Justice and Criminal Evidence Act 1999.

[58] See sch 8 Terrorism Act 2000 and paras 6.7 and 11.2 PACE Code H.

[59] *Ibrahim and Others v United Kingdom* App nos 50541/08, 50571/08, 50573/08 and 40351/09 (ECtHR GC, 13 September 2016).

[60] See R Goss, 'Out of Many, One? Strasbourg's *Ibrahim* Decision' (2017) 80 *Modern Law Review* 1137; D Giannoulopoulos, *Improperly Obtained Evidence in Anglo-American and Continental Law* (Oxford, Hart Publishing, 2019) 180–97.

'the general interest of the community and the personal rights of the individual'.[61] This vague balancing test differs from the stricter approach applied to Article 6 in other cases (for example in relation to the disclosure of sensitive evidence), where the courts have stressed that only measures restricting the rights of the defence which are strictly necessary are permissible under Article 6 and that any difficulties caused to the defence by a limitation to its rights must be sufficiently counterbalanced by the procedures followed by the judicial authorities.[62]

D. Anti-Terrorist Offences and Proportionality: Net-Widening, Guilt by Association and Reverse Burdens of Proof

Leaving aside measures that are taken to deal with terrorism within the criminal process, another area of concern lies in the design of anti-terrorist criminal offences. Walker has highlighted three particular problems that are each relevant to proportionality: net-widening, guilt by association and reverse burdens of proof.[63] An example of net-widening is the use of the term 'terrorism' as defined in section 1 of the Terrorism Act 2000. Suspects can be arrested on suspicion of terrorism even though the term exceeds the boundaries of any single offence. There is no offence of terrorism per se, although a number of special offences are dependent on the concept of terrorism, for example, membership of a terrorist organisation and possession of materials. The offence of membership also runs the risk of guilt by association. Walker claims that these worries have been mitigated by the fact that there have been few prosecutions for membership per se. No such inhibition has existed in the case of precursor or preparatory offences, which entail the criminalisation of conduct which may eventually lead to the commission of a terrorist act. Examples include training for terrorism, possession of items for terrorist purposes, collecting information likely to be useful to terrorism, collecting information about members of the security forces, encouragement of terrorism and dissemination of terrorist publications.[64] The 'ordinary' criminal law has always criminalised behaviour in certain circumstances before it has matured into the completion of an intended criminal act. Examples include attempts, incitement and conspiracy. But all three of these kinds of offences require an *intention* that the primary offence be completed.[65] Walsh has argued

[61] See Privy Council, *Brown v Stott* [2001] 2 WLR 817.

[62] See, eg, *Rowe and Davis v United Kingdom* App no 28901/95 (ECtHR GC, 16 February 2000) [62]; *Jasper v United Kingdom* App no 27052/9 (ECtHR GC, 16 February 2000) [53].

[63] Walker (n 42) 257.

[64] See ss 54, 57 Terrorism Act 2000.

[65] D Walsh, 'Beyond the Ordinary: Criminal Law and Terrorism' in G Lennon, C King and C McCartney (eds), *Counter-Terrorism, Constitutionalism and Miscarriages of Justice* (Oxford, Hart Publishing, 2019) 27, 41.

that counter-terrorism precursor offences are fundamentally different because they can arise at a point in time quite remote from the commission of a primary act of terrorism and the causal relation between them and the commission of a primary offence can be quite loose. Moreover, some of the offences do not require an intent that the conduct proscribed will lead to the commission of a terrorist act. For example, the mental element of encouragement of terrorism and dissemination of terrorist publications can be satisfied by mere recklessness that one's words or conduct will have the indirect effect of encouraging others to commit, prepare or instigate acts of terrorism.

One particular egregious example pinpointed by Duff is the offence of possession under the Terrorism Act 2000 which can be satisfied by possession of an article which merely gives rise to a reasonable suspicion that it is possessed for a terrorist purpose, with the onus then on the accused to prove that his possession of the article was not for a terrorist purpose.[66] An even more egregious example is the offence under the Terrorism Act 2006 (now commonly charged) of engaging in any conduct in preparation for giving effect to an intention to commit acts of terrorism.[67] This penalises conduct that is preparatory to giving effect to an intention to act. There is no requirement that any action should have been taken to expedite a terrorist act. Bad intentions seem to be penalised here rather than harms.[68]

It is true that many of these offences provide a defence for the accused to prove that his conduct was not for a purpose connected with terrorism. In *R v Director of Public Prosecutions ex parte Kebiline*,[69] the House of Lords acted to mitigate the burden on the accused to prove there was no terrorist purpose by reading down the onus of proof to that of a mere evidential burden as opposed to a legal burden, so that the reverse burden was not construed to be contrary to the presumption of innocence under Article 6(2) of the ECHR. In response the government added section 118 to the Terrorism Act 2000 which imposes only an evidential burden on the accused in relation to a number of provisions in the Act that create statutory defences to various offences. This left a question mark hanging over other offences that were *not* listed under section 118. The government here presumably intended a legal burden to be imposed on the accused but in *AG's Ref (No 4 of 2002)*[70] the House of Lords held by a majority that the imposition of a legal burden on a defendant faced with a 'membership' offence to prove that an organisation was not proscribed at the time he became a member and that he had not taken part in any of its activities while it was proscribed was disproportionate to the aim of the offence and such a burden should be read down to an evidential burden.

[66] Section 57 Terrorism Act 2000. See R A Duff, 'Perversions and Subversions of the Criminal Law' in R A Duff, L Farmer, S E Marshall, M Renzo and V Tadros (eds), *The Boundaries of the Criminal Law* (Oxford, Oxford University Press, 2010) 93.

[67] See s 5(1) Terrorism Act 2006.

[68] Walker (n 24) 227.

[69] House of Lords, *R v Director of Public Prosecutions ex parte Kebiline* [2000] 2 AC 326.

[70] House of Lords, *Attorney General's Reference (No 4 of 2002)* [2004] UKHL 43.

This is a good example of the courts taking a strict proportionate approach towards reverse burdens of proof. But there has been less court intervention on the question whether certain precursor offences themselves are a disproportionate response to the threat of terrorism. An argument has been made that the language of some of the offences is insufficiently certain to comply with Article 7 of the ECHR. In one case the Court of Appeal read into the offence of collecting or possessing information likely to be useful to terrorism the requirement that the information possessed or collected be itself intrinsically useful to terrorism.[71] All in all, though, few inroads have been made by the courts into the substance of terrorist offences.

E. Sentencing and Proportionality

Finally, another example where the government is embarking upon potentially disproportionate measures to counter terrorism within the criminal justice system is to be found in the sentencing of those convicted of such offences. In response to recent terror attacks in London carried out by offenders who had been released automatically during the course of their sentence for terrorist offences, the government has ended automatic release for all but the most minor terrorist offenders and made any early release subject to risk assessment by the Parole Board even where persons have already been sentenced and were expecting to be released early.[72] It may be reasonable to require that those sentenced to a terrorist offence are subject to risk assessment before they are released early, on the ground that they pose a greater potential risk to the public than other offenders – although to impose such a requirement on existing prisoners is problematic on the ground that the law is being changed retrospectively. More worrying are the suggestions that have been made that some of those sentenced to terrorist offences should not be eligible for release at all until they are subject to risk assessment.[73] Of course, this already occurs in relation to terrorist offenders who have been sentenced to life sentences but such suggestions extend beyond these offenders and would seem to reintroduce the kind of indeterminate sentences for public protection that were enacted in 2003 for offenders whose offence did not merit a life sentence but who were considered dangerous offenders.[74] These sentences were subjected to much criticism on the grounds that they prioritised public protection at the expense of proportionate and determinate sentencing.[75]

[71] Court of Appeal (England & Wales) *R v K* [2008] EWCA Crim 185.

[72] K Proctor and D Sabbagh, 'Rush to Change Sentencing Laws before Release of Convicted Terrorists', *The Guardian*, 5 February 2020. See Terrorist Offenders (Restriction of Early Release) Act 2020.

[73] S Murphy and R Mason, 'Terror Offenders should be Jailed Indefinitely if Necessary', *The Guardian*, 4 February 2020.

[74] See s 229(1) Criminal Justice Act 2003.

[75] See A Ashworth and L Zedner, *Preventive Justice* (Oxford, Oxford University Press, 2014) 161.

They were phased out in 2012, although thousands continuing to serve such sentences have yet to be released.[76] In the end, the government has decided not to go down the route of imposing indeterminate sentences for dangerous terrorist offenders but is instead proposing a new 'serious terrorism sentence' for dangerous terrorist offenders, mandating a minimum of 14 years in custody with an extended licence period of up to 25 years.[77] Minimum sentences, however, pose their own problems of proportionality in terms of differentiating fairly and proportionately between offenders who commit the same offence but may differ considerably in terms of age and maturity.[78]

V. Conclusions

A number of conclusions can be drawn from this audit of penal and non-penal responses to terrorism in the UK. First of all, it is very evident how over the years much greater attention has been given to individual human rights than at the beginning of the period examined, and this has encouraged greater proportionality analysis. When the Diplock Commission was tasked with looking at criminal measures to deal with terrorism as opposed to executive measures such as internment, it set itself the threshold that nothing recommended should infringe Article 6 of the ECHR. But, as we have seen, some of the emergency powers it recommended directly infringed Article 5. The decision to end internment was not taken on the ground that it was unduly interfering with the right to liberty but purely on the political calculation that it was proving counter-productive in the fight against terrorism. Although we have seen that the ECtHR made some significant interventions during the Northern Ireland phase of terrorism, it was inhibited by the margin of appreciation it gave to derogation notices, and domestic courts were unable to uphold rights when these conflicted with the will of parliament. The enactment of the Human Rights Act 1998 made a crucial difference in bringing rights discourse into the centre of political and legal decision-making. The Act makes it unlawful for public authorities to act in a way which is incompatible with a Convention right and courts now have the power to determine whether a provision of primary legislation is compatible with a Convention right.[79] It is true that after 9/11 the government entered a derogation under Article 15 with respect to Article 5 but this was robustly scrutinised by the Appellate Committee of the House of Lords and although the declaration of incompatibility that was made did not immediately lead to the release of those detained under the Anti-terrorism,

[76] J Grierson, 'IPP Sentencing Regime in England and Wales Called Deeply Harmful', *The Guardian*, 10 November 2019.

[77] See cl 5 Counter-Terrorism and Sentencing Bill 2020.

[78] See U Azmeh, 'Exemplary Sentencing for Terrorist Offenders: The Counter-Terrorism and Sentencing Bill 2020' (2021) 1 *Criminal Law Review* 5.

[79] See ss 4, 6 Human Rights Act 1998.

Crime and Security Act 2001 and some of them were subsequently made the subject of control orders, all the measures that were taken against them were subjected to a strict proportionality analysis by the courts.

Second, the record suggests that over the period examined, the courts became more effective than the executive and legislature in confining security-focused state action to that which was necessary and proportionate. This issue has been much debated in terms of the institutional competence of these branches of government to find the appropriate balance between security and rights.[80] There is a consensus that the executive cannot be trusted to strike a proportionate balance between security exigencies and individual rights. Having said that, it is to be noted that over this period the executive did commission independent reports such as Diplock, Gardiner and Lloyd and in the more recent period of Islamic terrorism these have included reviews conducted by Lords Newton and Macdonald.[81] An important step, praised by the UN Rapporteur,[82] has been the establishment of the Office of the Independent Reviewer of Terrorism Legislation under the Terrorism Act 2006.[83] Even if these watchdogs have not curbed the executive from making derogations under Article 15 and from taking measures thought to be needed, they have at least pressurised the state to provide public rationalisations for measures which can then be further questioned and challenged.[84]

The legislature has had some successes in checking executive proposals, most notably in periodically curbing powers of detention that the Blair Government wanted to grant the police before charge – most dramatically up to 90 days, in the aftermath of the London underground bombings of 7 July 2005. The government had to settle eventually for 28 days under the Terrorism Act 2006 and, as a result of Lord Macdonald's recommendation and further parliamentary scrutiny, this was reduced to 14 days in 2012.[85] But these have been minor successes when set against some egregious examples of poor legislative scrutiny, notably in the era of Northern Ireland terrorism when the Prevention of Terrorism (Temporary Provisions) Act 1974 was enacted within seven days in 1974 and another bill, the Criminal Justice (Terrorism and Conspiracy) Act 1998, was enacted two days after the Omagh car bombing which killed 29 people on 15 August 1998. It is true that parliamentary scrutiny improved in the era of Islamic terrorism. The Joint

[80] F de Londras and F Davis, 'Controlling the Executive in Times of Terrorism: Competing Perspectives on Effective Oversight Mechanisms' (2010) 30 *Oxford Journal of Legal Studies* 19.

[81] Privy Counsellor Review Committee (Lord Newton), *Anti-terrorism, Crime and Security Act Review: Report* (London, Stationery Office, 2003) HC 100; Lord Macdonald, *Review of Counter-Terrorism and Security Powers* (London, Stationery Office, 2011) Cm 8003.

[82] UN Rapporteur (n 1) para 75.

[83] For insight into the reviews carried out by one of the Reviewers, see D Anderson, 'Shades of Independent Review' in G Lennon, C King and C McCartney (eds), *Counter-Terrorism, Constitutionalism and Miscarriages of Justice* (Oxford, Hart Publishing, 2019) 81.

[84] C Walker, 'Counter-Terrorism Laws and their Discontents' in G Lennon, C King and C McCartney (eds), *Counter-Terrorism, Constitutionalism and Miscarriages of Justice* (Oxford, Hart Publishing, 2019) 307, 312.

[85] See s 57 sch 10 pt 4 Protection of Freedoms Act 2012. See Lord Macdonald (n 81) 4.

Committee on Human Rights has played a significant role in scrutinising government legislation. But control orders were hastily enacted after the House of Lords' ruling in *A v SSHD* and the government of the day has mostly got its own way.

Third, throughout the period the ECtHR has progressively made a significant contribution as an international court in setting boundaries where there have been breaches of fundamental human rights, albeit that it has given states a wide margin of appreciation in their decisions to derogate under Article 15. The Court played a role in setting proportionality standards for the government during the years of Northern Ireland terrorism, and in the Human Rights Act era it has played a part in encouraging domestic courts to apply strict proportionality standards towards any limitations on Articles 5 and 6. This mutually reinforcing rights relationship is, however, in danger of being undermined by signs that the ECtHR is back-pedalling on some of its earlier strong jurisprudence, for example in relation to access to a lawyer.[86]

Finally, the courts have on the whole been somewhat more robust in scrutinising executive measures curtailing liberty by reference to Article 5 than in scrutinising criminalisation measures limiting individual rights. As we have seen the courts have applied strict proportionality standards to Article 5 rights, particularly when executive measures have the potential to deprive individuals of their liberty for lengthy periods of time, and have insisted on strict judicial review processes when liberty has been curtailed. With regard to the criminalisation measures, the courts have been stricter in applying proportionality standards to criminal processes than to substantive criminal laws, although we noted that in relation to Article 6 there seems to be some inconsistency in the approach adopted to how fair trial rights should be balanced against security.

If we take a step back and consider the issue of institutional competence, the contrast between the judiciary's stricter scrutiny of executive measures curtailing liberty is not altogether surprising when we consider that there is a long history, going back before the Human Rights Act era, of the courts scrutinising executive actions that curtail individual liberty. In *A v SSHD* Lord Hope referred to the first responsibility of government to protect and safeguard the lives of its citizens and of the duty of the court to protect and safeguard the rights of the individual, particularly liberty.[87] He quoted Baron Hume who in his *Commentaries on the Law of Scotland respecting Crimes* stated that it was obvious that,

> by its very constitution, every court of criminal justice must have the power of correcting the greatest and most dangerous of all abuses of the forms of law – that of the protracted imprisonment of the accused untried, perhaps never intended to be tried.[88]

[86] See in particular *Ibrahim and Others* (n 59) and *Beuze v Belgium* App no 71409/10 (ECtHR GC, 9 November 2018). See J Jackson, 'Common Law Evidence and the Common Law of Human Rights: Towards a Harmonic Convergence?' (2019) 27 *William & Mary Bill of Rights Journal* 689; E Celiksoy, 'Overruling "the *Salduz* Doctrine" in *Beuze v Belgium*: The ECtHR's Further Retreat from the *Salduz* Principles on the Right to Access to Lawyer' (2019) 10 *New Journal of European Criminal Law* 342.

[87] *A v SSHD* (n 22) [99].

[88] ibid [100].

It is therefore not surprising that when it comes to balancing the interests of public safety and individual liberty, the courts apply a strict proportionality analysis towards executive measures designed to protect the former so that sufficient weight is given to the latter. The strict scrutiny given by the courts in the proportionality analysis to procedural rights is also not surprising. Roberts has drawn attention to the fundamental bond that courts owe to the procedures that they operate.[89] Questions of substantive law do not engage the courts' institutional preconditions of existence in quite the same way. A court that enforces an unjust law might still be regarded as a properly constituted tribunal but a court which fails to secure fair processes whether these be in relation to deprivation of liberty or in relation to criminal trials is a 'self-parody and corruption of the core commitments which qualify judicial institutions as *judicial*'.[90] If the courts are inclined to apply a less strict proportionality scrutiny of substantive criminal laws, then this would seem to require greater scrutiny by the executive and legislative branches of the proportionality of these laws. Parliamentary committees, like the courts, have tended to put greater emphasis on legislation affecting executive measures and criminal processes than on the criminal laws themselves. It is perhaps time for the focus to shift towards scrutinising the proportionality of criminal laws at least as zealously.

[89] P Roberts, 'The Priority of Procedure and the Neglect of Evidence and Proof: Finding Facts in International Criminal Law' (2015) 13 *Journal of International Criminal Justice* 479.
[90] ibid 488.

9

Big Data and Criminal Justice. Proportionality, Efficiency and Risk in a Global Context

RICHARD VOGLER

I. Introduction

The use of big data by police and security services seems at first sight to be inherently disproportionate, as the sheer quantity of electronic information available for surveillance spirals exponentially year by year. In a single month, the body-worn cameras of one small US police force can produce seven terabytes of data – the equivalent of 1500 feature-length films[1] – and email traffic available for scrutiny by the world's security systems in 2018 amounted to 381 billion messages per day.[2] Government Communications Headquarters (GCHQ) in the UK has 'attached probes to 200 fibre-optic cables' running between the UK and North America, 'each with a capacity of 10 gigabits per second', allowing access to a flow of 21.6 petabytes per day, representing the 'equivalent to 192 times [the amount of data in] the British Library's entire book collection'.[3] This capacity can only increase over time. Big data is universal, unstructured (or semi-structured), agnostic, and not merely numeric but engaged with a variety of different assembled media.[4] In many ways it defies quantification. In the face of this worldwide tsunami of raw information accessible to electronic surveillance, the measured calculus of Enlightenment proportionality seems an inadequate and anachronistic means of appraisal.

Nevertheless, the concept of proportionality has been invoked repeatedly and insistently in recent attempts to limit the extent and reach of big data surveillance.

[1] Oakland Police Department, CA. See M D Fan, 'Body Cameras, Big Data, and Police Accountability' (2018) 43(4) *Law & Social Inquiry* 1236, 1237.

[2] *Statista*, www.statista.com/statistics/255080/number-of-e-mail-users-worldwide/.

[3] *Open Society Justice Initiative*, www.justiceinitiative.org/litigation/big-brother-watch-v-united-kingdom, quoting *The Guardian* in 2012.

[4] K D Haggerty and R V Ericson, 'The Surveillant Assemblage' (2000) 51(4) *The British Journal of Sociology* 605.

This is true not only in the jurisprudential literature[5] and case law[6] but also in ethical theory, where authors such as Marx,[7] Lyon,[8] Kleinig[9] and Macnish[10] have all emphasised the crucial importance of proportionality for the regulation of surveillance. Macnish has gone so far as to propose that ready-made proportionality doctrines could be imported from 'Just War' theory, proposing a *Jus ad Speculandum* and *Jus in Speculando* to govern big data surveillance, modelled on the principles developed by analysts such as Hurka, for the control of armed force.[11] By contrast, others scholars have suggested that the balancing methodology involved in proportionality assessments is a 'misguided quest for precision and objectivity'[12] concealing by its 'fuzzy and truncated reasoning'[13] an elastic assessment[14] which is inadequate to deal with the complexities of big data policing.[15]

The aim of this short chapter is to identify some of the particular characteristics of the use of big data in criminal justice, which tend to undermine the effectiveness of the proportionality equation in this context. Three important innovations will be discussed. The first is that, unlike most existing criminal justice procedures, the current uses of big data frequently involve a projection into future time and an analysis of inchoate risk. Second, the provision of personal information for use by big data systems is usually, but not exclusively, voluntary. Third, criminal justice in the big data era is no longer a purely state-based competency but must be considered a predominantly commercial, market-driven practice. These changes, taken together, constitute a profound shift in the relationship between the control agencies and the public and, it will be argued, represent a significant threat to proportionality-based measures of control.

[5] See, eg, P de Hert, 'Balancing Security and Liberty Within the European Human Rights Framework. A Critical Reading of the Court's Case Law in the Light of Surveillance and Criminal Law Enforcement Strategies After 9/11' (2005) 1(1) *Utrecht Law Review* 68; J Milaj, 'Privacy, Surveillance, and the Proportionality Principle: The Need for a Method of Assessing Privacy Implications of Technologies Used for Surveillance' (2016) 30(6) *International Review of Law, Computers & Technology* 115.

[6] See, eg, the crucial discussion on the 'bulk interception regime' in *Big Brother Watch and Others v United Kingdom* App nos 58170/13, 62322/14 and 24960/15 (ECtHR, 13 September 2018) [384]–[386].

[7] G Marx, 'Ethics for the New Surveillance' (1998) 14(3) *The Information Society* 171.

[8] D Lyon, 'Facing the Future: Seeking Ethics for Everyday Surveillance' (2001) 3 *Ethics and Information Technology* 171.

[9] J Kleinig, 'The Ethical Perils of Knowledge Acquisition' (2009) 28(2) *Criminal Justice Ethics* 201.

[10] K Macnish, 'An Eye for an Eye: Proportionality and Surveillance' (2015) 18(3) *Ethical Theory and Moral Practice* 529.

[11] ibid 531–32.

[12] S Tsakyrakis, 'Proportionality: An Assault on Human Rights?' (2009) 7(3) *International Journal of Constitutional Law* 468, 468.

[13] F Fontanelli, 'The Mythology of Proportionality in Judgments of the Court of Justice of the European Union on Internet and Fundamental Rights' (2016) 36(3) *Oxford Journal of Legal Studies* 630, 660.

[14] O O'Donovan, *The Just War Revisited* (Cambridge, Cambridge University Press 2003), 61.

[15] E Stoddart, 'Challenging "Just Surveillance Theory": A Response to Kevin Macnish's "Just Surveillance? Towards a Normative Theory of Surveillance"' (2014) 12(1) *Surveillance & Society* 158.

II. Future Participation in Crime

The idea of a presumed shift from offence-based to risk-based practice in criminal justice has become a commonplace in criminological theory. The concept of 'risk society', originally developed by Beck in 1986,[16] was re-imagined by Feeley and Simon in their ground-breaking exploration of actuarial justice in 1992.[17] Other scholars, such as Zedner, have discussed the implications of this 'important temporal shift' in which criminality becomes not so much a completed activity attracting a proportionate, retrospective response, but a risk or a potential future loss. She suggests:

> In important respects we are on the cusp of a shift from a post- to a precrime society, a society in which the possibility of forestalling risks competes with and even takes precedence over responding to wrongs done.[18]

Although the more extreme and dystopian visions of a pre-crime surveillance society have been derided as 'panoptic panic'[19] and Zedner herself has called for caution,[20] the use of big data analytics has given fresh impetus to this approach and Schinkel has explicitly linked his concept of 'prepression' with the growth of the digital archive.[21] According to Mantello:

> In the world of precrime science, the focus of pre-emptive law enforcement shifts from visual evidence taken directly from individuals to algorithmic projections of crimes yet to happen based on real-time data streams and archival criminal meta-data of what others have done in the past.[22]

To achieve this, a new form of criminological knowledge-production has been developed, based around 'meaning extraction', 'sentiment analysis', 'opinion mining' and 'computational treatment of subjectivity'.[23] Our concept of risk itself is changing with the development of 'algorithmic governance',[24] or 'stochastic governance', as Sanders and Sheptycki have described it. This has been defined

[16] U Beck, *Risikogesellschaft: Auf dem Weg in eine andere Moderne* (Frankfurt, Suhrkamp 1986).

[17] M Feeley and J Simon, 'Actuarial Justice. The Emerging New Criminal Law' in D Nelken (ed), *The Futures of Criminology* (London, Sage, 1994).

[18] L Zedner, 'Pre-Crime and Post-Criminology?' (2007) 11(2) *Theoretical Criminology* 261, 262.

[19] J Richards, 'Needles in Haystacks: Law, Capability, Ethics, and Proportionality in Big Data Intelligence-Gathering' in A Bunnik, A Cawley, M Mulqueen and A Zwitter (eds), *Big Data Challenges: Society, Security, Innovation and Ethics* (London, Palgrave Macmillan, 2016) 73.

[20] L Zedner, 'Pre-Crime and Pre-Punishment: A Health Warning: Lucia Zedner Calls for Restraint' (2010) 81 *Criminal Justice Matters* 24.

[21] W Schinkel, 'Prepression: The Actuarial Archive and New Technologies of Security' (2011) 15(4) *Theoretical Criminology* 365.

[22] P Mantello, 'The Machine that Ate Bad People: The Ontopolitics of the Precrime Assemblage' (2016) 3(2) *Big Data & Society* 1, 5.

[23] A Završnik, 'Algorithmic Justice: Algorithms and Big Data in Criminal Justice Settings' (2019) *European Journal of Criminology* 1, 5.

[24] K Hannah-Moffat, 'Algorithmic Risk Governance: Big Data Analytics, Race and Information Activism in Criminal Justice Debates' (2019) 23(4) *Theoretical Criminology* 453.

by them as 'the governance of social order through algorithmic calculation made actionable through policing and regulatory means'.[25] Before considering the relevance of proportionality to pre-emptive law enforcement in this context, it is perhaps worthwhile to examine some of the technologies which have contributed to these dramatic changes.

One of the most significant and exciting prospects opened up by the big data revolution in policing is that officers will in future no longer be dealing with strangers during on-street encounters.[26] Body-worn and facial recognition cameras, combined with instantaneous access to detailed, assembled records and algorithmic risk assessment will, so it is hoped, ensure that stop and search will be a much more targeted and hence proportionate strategy and one which minimises the threat to officers. According to Fan, this new technology represents a significant force-multiplier:

> [t]he advance of technology will permit forensic searches with geospatial and temporal localization and the development of early warning systems for problems such as premature use of force that are more reliable than self-report or citizen reporting.[27]

The whole dynamic of policing, so it is asserted, will move from a reactive to a much more efficient, proactive practice,[28] thereby achieving considerable cost savings,[29] diminishing the use of discretion (for example, police activity based on mere hunches, unreliable informants or intrusive surveillance) and opening up wider opportunities for the accountability of decision-making.[30] As recently as 1994, policing programs, such as the Compstat system, which was introduced in New York City in the 1990s, were simply management tools, linking crime and crime enforcement data in order to identify crime patterns and direct police activity.[31] However, predictive software has evolved dramatically since that time, in terms of both its sophistication and range. For example, the Predpol system,[32] which was developed collaboratively by California police and academic institutions,

[25] C B Sanders and J Sheptycki, 'Policing, Crime and "Big Data"; Towards A Critique of the Moral Economy of Stochastic Governance' (2017) 68(1) *Crime, Law and Social Change* 1, 5.

[26] A Guthrie Ferguson, 'Big Data and Predictive Reasonable Suspicion' (2015) 163(2) *University of Pennsylvania Law Review* 327, 335.

[27] Fan (n 1) 1241.

[28] L Dencik, A Hintz and Z Carey, 'Prediction, Pre-Emption and Limits to Dissent: Social Media and Big Data Uses for Policing Protests in the United Kingdom' (2017) 20(4) *New Media & Society* 1433, 1434; S Sharma and J Nijjar, 'The Racialized Surveillant Assemblage: Islam and the Fear of Terrorism' (2018) 16(1) *Popular Communication* 72, 74.

[29] E Joh, 'The New Surveillance Discretion: Automated Suspicion, Big Data, and Policing' (2016) 10 *Harvard Law and Policy Review* 15, 25; Sanders and Sheptycki (n 25) 335.

[30] Joh (n 29) 25.

[31] D Weisburd, S Mastrofski, A M McNally, R Greenspan and J Willis, 'Reforming to Preserve: Compstat and Strategic Problem Solving in American Policing' (2003) 2(3) *Criminology & Public Policy* 421; S Brayne, 'Big Data Surveillance: The Case of Policing' (2017) 82(5) *American Sociological Review* 977, 981; Dencik, Hintz and Carey (n 28) 1436.

[32] W Hardyns and A Rummens, 'Predictive Policing as a New Tool for Law Enforcement? Recent Developments and Challenges' (2018) 24 *European Journal on Criminal Policy and Research* 201, 209–10.

using seismographic prediction software, was amongst the first to operationalise existing data for algorithmic crime prediction. On the basis of information from a variety of sources, including police records, Predpol's prediction software identifies crime trends in both geospatial and temporal dimensions. According to Sanders and Sheptycki '[l]ikely future crimes show up in tiny red boxes on … maps, directing patrol officers to attend to that location'.[33] According to Predpol's current website, a secure, cloud-based algorithm is used to calculate predictions via three data points – crime type, crime location and crime date/time software. As a result the company claims that their program can '[p]redict where and when specific crimes are most likely to occur'.[34] It can also manage pro-active patrol allocation using crime 'heat-maps' and generate graphical crime analysis.[35] Predpol was aggressively promoted to policing agencies after 2010 and as a result took a very strong market position.[36] However, contract awards have declined since that time, as other competitors have appeared[37] and after research suggested that methodologies similar to that used by Predpol resulted in 'increasingly disproportionate policing of historically over-policed communities'.[38]

Hunchlab is another example of risk-terrain modelling software that calculates the probability of various threat risks (larceny, assault, car-jacking) occurring in specific geographical locations.[39] It builds on existing competencies by adding a wide variety of other data into the calculation, including the proximity of subway stations and bars, the occurrence of public events, such as concerts, sporting or political meetings and even environmental factors such as the weather or the phases of the moon.[40] Its current website claims that Hunchlab is 'not just about anticipating crime, it's about figuring out the best way to respond', while taking account of local community priorities.[41]

Other programs claim to draw on an even wider array of big data sources, including social media and the Internet of Things. Hitachi's Public Safety Visualization Suite (HPSVS), for example, aims to mine and analyse data

> from an array of various nodes such as remote video systems (hotels/city streets/commercial and private properties/transportation lines), gunshot sensors that alert CCTV cameras, vehicle license plate recognition systems, wireless communications, Twitter and other social media, mobile surveillance systems as well as useful data from

[33] Sanders and Sheptycki (n 25) 9.

[34] www.predpol.com/.

[35] ibid.

[36] Sanders and Sheptycki (n 25) 9–10.

[37] A Winston, 'Palantir Has Secretly Been Using New Orleans to Test its Predictive Policing Technology', *The Verge*, 27 February 2018, available at: www.theverge.com/2018/2/27/17054740/palantir-predictive-policing-tool-new-orleans-nopd.

[38] K Lum and W Isaac, 'To Predict and Serve?' (2016) 13(5) *Significance* 14, 19.

[39] Mantello (n 22) 5; Hardyns and Rummens (n 32) 210–11.

[40] Hardyns and Rummens (n 32); R Simmons, 'Quantifying Criminal Procedure: How to Unlock the Potential of Big Data in Our Criminal Justice System' (2016) *Michigan State Law Review* 947, 955.

[41] www.hunchlab.com/.

> smart parking meters, public transit systems, and online newspapers and weather forecasts.[42]

According to publicity material, the outcome of this analysis should enable officers to visualise future threats on a 'single pane of glass'.[43] HPSVS aims to deliver analysis direct to officers in the field as well as allowing data evidence to be tagged and associated with any case.[44]

One of the most important data sources used by many of these programs is provided by Automated Licence Plate Recognition (ALPR). In a society like the US, which is heavily dependent upon motor transport, ALPR systems, such as that developed by Vigilant Solutions, allow very effective tracking and monitoring of vehicles (and hence their owners). Vigilant Solutions in 2015 reported a database of 2.2 billion scans and announced a proposed contract with New York Police Department. Since that time the cloud database of time-stamped and geolocated recordings has expanded to over 13 billion detections in the US, growing at a rate of 250 million a month.[45] Not only can the software identify vehicles which are mobile in the region of a crime scene at the relevant time but it can create a 'virtual fence' around a particular zone, pinpointing vehicles that enter or leave. It can also identify specific addresses (for example, properties potentially associated with drug dealing) which are visited by certain vehicles on a regular basis.[46] According to Linder, ALPR can also be used with a variety of different surveillance systems to create a 'ring of steel' around sensitive locations, such as schools:

> In a webinar ambiguously aimed at both law enforcement and school security officials, Vigilant Solutions pushed for the expansion of school security to include both an outer perimeter of ALPR cameras outside school grounds and an internal perimeter of facial-recognition cameras at 'choke points' in buildings.[47]

Moreover, by pulling in a variety of other public and private data sources through commercial alliances with sister enterprises such as Digital Recognition Network (DRN),[48] Vigilant Solutions can offer a broad range of services to both public policing agencies and private individuals or investigators. Recently, they have added access to body-worn camera video data and a ballistics analysis tool called GunOps for geo- and time-stamping images of spent cartridge casings and matching the markings against existing records.[49]

Body Worn Cameras (BWCs) constitute another crucial addition to the constantly-expanding list of data sources available to these programs, as well

[42] Mantello (n 22) 5.
[43] ibid 5.
[44] www.hitachivantara.com/en-us/pdf/datasheet/hitachi-datasheet-visualization-suite.pdf.
[45] T Linder, 'Surveillance Capitalism and Platform Policing: The Surveillant Assemblage-as-a-Service' (2019) 17(1/2) *Surveillance & Society* 76, 77.
[46] Joh (n 29) 23–24.
[47] Linder (n 45) 78.
[48] ibid 77.
[49] ibid 77.

as providing significant benefits for both police officers and arrestees. Fan has described the adoption of BWCs as 'a paradigm shift' or 'revolution' in policing:[50]

> Putting body cameras on officers potentially transforms the ability to monitor these street-level encounters formerly outside of view … The oft-expressed hope for body cameras is that people on all sides of a police encounter will behave better when they know they are being recorded … The strategy is one of panopticism for police (and the people they encounter) – a mobile technology-assisted update on Jeremy Bentham's concept of the use of a watchtower to elicit good behavior …[51]

Storing and analysing the prodigious amounts of video data generated represents a serious challenge, however. Just one company, Taser's evidence.com, already has more than a petabyte (one million gigabytes) of body camera data, with a video uploaded every 2.9 seconds.[52] There are also concerns over privacy, the security of data, retrospective targeting of officers for infringements and improper usage.[53] Nevertheless, the consequences of the adoption of this technology are only just beginning to be appreciated, and the impact of immediate 'event replay power' on the production of evidence in court is also claimed as a 'paradigm shift'.[54]

It is hoped that, in time, similar levels of accuracy to those achieved by ALRP may be available from another rapidly developing innovation which can be used in conjunction with the others: Facial Recognition Technology (FRT). Purshouse and Campbell have noted the advantages of this technology over closed-circuit television surveillance, since individuals can be identified in real time and the geometric character of their facial images compared to those held on 'watch lists' of persons of interest to the control agencies.[55] A former UK Home Secretary has described the potential of FRT as 'game changing', since it offers to police forces the ability to both accelerate investigations and to vastly expand the surveillance net in respect of a wide range of offences, including online child abuse.[56] Companies such as the Spanish Herta corporation have been providing facial recognition software to a number of national police forces across the world for use in border security, sporting and other events and against violent crime.[57] Programs like Intrado's Beware, are capable of analysing commercial and public records, social media, etc, in order to apply a 'threat rating' to any individual encountered by police.[58]

[50] M D Fan, 'Justice Visualized: Courts and the Body Camera Revolution' (2017) 50(3) *University of California Davis Law Review* 897, 902, 906.

[51] Fan (n 1) 1240–41.

[52] ibid 1237.

[53] ibid.

[54] Fan (n 50) 900–2.

[55] J Purshouse and L Campbell, 'Privacy, Crime Control and Police Use of Automated Facial Recognition Technology' (2019) *Criminal Law Review* 188, 188.

[56] J Grierson, 'Police Trials of Facial Recognition Backed by Home Secretary', *The Guardian*, 12 July 2019, available at: www.theguardian.com/uk-news/2019/jul/12/police-trials-facial-recognition-home-secretary-sajid-javid-technology-human-rights.

[57] Sanders and Sheptycki (n 25) 4.

[58] Joh (n 29) 24–25.

Network theory analysis can also add a new dimension to this data, by providing specific 'heat lists'.[59]

However, the use of FRT raises even more troubling privacy issues than those encountered by the programs mentioned above and has provoked considerable controversy. Widespread concerns have been expressed about the glaring absence of effective legal regimes controlling the use of FRT[60] and its capacity to over-identify certain social groups. Garvie, Bedoya and Frankle have asserted that the facial recognition biometrics of over 50 per cent of American adults had been culled without their consent from driver licence databases, for use in FRT by law enforcement agencies.[61] Such technology, they claim, will 'redefine the nature of public spaces'.[62] Even more serious reservations have been expressed about the technical reliability of FRT. Tests in the UK, using the Japanese Neoface system, indicated an alarming lack of consistency. According to Big Brother Watch in 2018, the overwhelming majority of the police's 'matches' using FRT have been inaccurate and on average 95 per cent of 'matches' wrongly identified innocent people. There were also concerns regarding the composition of the watch lists.[63] Research by Fussey and Murray in 2019,[64] which focused on trials of FRT by the London Metropolitan Police, found that almost 81 per cent of 'matches' were inaccurate. These findings have led to calls for FRT to be abandoned entirely.[65] The UK Information Commissioner, Elizabeth Denham, has expressed concerns about 'a lack of transparency about its use' and Tony Porter, the Surveillance Camera Commissioner, has intervened to stop Greater Manchester Police using FRT at the Trafford shopping centre.[66] Martha Spurrier of the campaign group Liberty has described FRT as 'arsenic in the water of democracy', saying:

> It is one of, if not the, greatest threats to individual freedom, partly because of the intimacy of the information it takes and hands to the state without your consent, and without even your knowledge, and partly because you don't know what is done with that information.[67]

[59] ibid 26.

[60] P Fussey and D Murray, *Independent Report on the London Metropolitan Police Service's Trial of Live Facial Recognition Technology* (Human Rights Centre, University of Essex, 2019); Purshouse and Campbell (n 55).

[61] C Garvie, A Bedoya and J Frankle, *The Perpetual Line-Up: Unregulated Police Face Recognition in America* (Georgetown Law, Center on Privacy & Technology, 2016) 2.

[62] ibid 4.

[63] Big Brother Watch, *Face Off: The Lawless Growth of Facial Recognition in UK Policing* (Big Brother Watch, 2018): www.bigbrotherwatch.org.uk/campaigns/stop-facial-recognition/report/.

[64] Fussey and Murray (n 60).

[65] A Forrest, 'Police Urged to Axe Facial Recognition after Research Finds Four of Five "Suspects" Are Innocent', *Independent*, 3 July 2019, available at: www.independent.co.uk/news/uk/crime/police-facial-recognition-technology-met-suspects-inaccurate-essex-university-a8987356.html.

[66] Grierson (n 56).

[67] I Sample, 'Facial Recognition Tech is Arsenic in the Water of Democracy, Says Liberty', *The Guardian*, 7 June 2019, available at: www.theguardian.com/technology/2019/jun/07/facial-recognition-technology-liberty-says-england-wales-police-use-should-be-banned.

In May 2019, the City authorities in San Francisco voted to ban FRT within their jurisdiction on grounds that the technology was deeply flawed and a serious threat to civil liberties.[68]

Given these concerns about the technology and the great difficulties of quantifying the inchoate risk of potential future events of indeterminate severity, proportionality looks to be an unwieldy tool. In Pratt's formulation: '[as] beauty is in the eyes of the beholder, so is threat in the perception of the defender'.[69] The result has been a sustained attempt to modify proportionality for this new purpose. Rønn and Lippert-Rasmussen, for example, have pointed out that the implications of precautionary intrusion with respect to the proportionality requirement '[have] not previously been specifically addressed in discussions concerning surveillance ethics'.[70] They suggest that the 'moral cost' of surveilling non-liable individuals is very high and therefore there is need for a 'wider' rather than 'narrower' concept of proportionality which distinguishes between foreseeing and intending intrusions by electronic surveillance in these circumstances.[71] Brown and Korff suggest that a new and 'particularly strict' proportionality test which distinguishes between hard (factual) and soft intelligence data and different categories of data subjects, should be applied to preventive and security-based policing.[72] The danger is, however, that such strict tests could be over-inclusive with regard to the regulatory goal pursued and, as Fontanelli puts it, when discussing internet regulation:

> As a result, proportionate balancing is normally and demonstrably impossible to achieve; all solutions are disproportionate. This is so since internet-regulating measures have such a massive inefficiency-creating externality (ie they create useless restrictions for users whose action is irrelevant to the regulatory purpose pursued) that it is impossible to prove their proportionality.[73]

These complexities certainly challenge the relevance and suitability of the proportionality principle, as currently understood, for regulating the predictive use of big data in policing. Such questions are particularly pertinent, since most of the data is collected without direct intrusion into protected spheres of privacy requiring the authority of a judicial warrant. Consequently, it becomes important to ask how any proportionality test should be applied when the potential victims of big data predictions willingly and enthusiastically volunteer themselves for surveillance?

[68] K Paul, 'San Francisco Is First US City to Ban Police Use of Facial Recognition Tech', *The Guardian*, 15 May 2019, available at: www.theguardian.com/us-news/2019/may/14/san-francisco-facial-recognition-police-ban.

[69] Cited in Stoddart (n 15) 161.

[70] K V Rønn and K Lippert-Rasmussen, 'Out of Proportion? On Surveillance and the Proportionality Requirement' (2020) 23 *Ethical Theory and Moral Practice* 181, 181.

[71] ibid.

[72] I Brown and D Korff, 'Terrorism and the Proportionality of Internet Surveillance' (2009) 6(2) *European Journal of Criminology* 119, 130.

[73] Fontanelli (n 13) 649.

III. Voluntary Participation in Surveillance

One of the most striking features of the use of big data in policing is that some of the most sensitive data is provided originally on an entirely voluntary basis. Mantello has described this as 'Ikeaveillance', a practice which 'encourages citizens to do the securitization footwork of the state by offering them the opportunity to participate in do-it-yourself, reward-centered, pro-active, networked and, at times … gamified versions of automated governance.'[74] In exchange for future advantages, particularly access to web-based services, individuals 'voluntarily subscribe to and desire their logic, trading potential disciplinary effects against benefits gained.'[75] For example, by allowing their vehicles to be monitored remotely in relation to their driving style, drivers can claim significant discounts on insurance.[76] Equally, in exchange for voice-activated and enhanced access to the internet, consumers are happy to install listening devices in their houses which have the potential to record any conversation and undertake deep surveillance.[77] Access to detailed personal profiles and location tracking which are volunteered by individuals in exchange for 'free' internet services can of course be marketed to third parties, including criminal justice agencies.[78] Consent to such practices by individuals entering into 'click-wrap' or 'browse-wrap' agreements online may indeed be little more than 'fictional',[79] but nevertheless, such tacit or 'relative consent'[80] has been upheld by many courts as binding.[81] Moreover, this Laputan style of self-imposed discipline – exchanging access to the bright sunshine of the internet for the 'voluntary' acceptance of surveillance and control – can easily morph into compulsion. 'Voluntary subjection to bureaucratic rules', as Peeters and Schuilenburg put it,[82] can quickly become an obligation; a phenomenon which is all too evident in the recent development of 'social credit' in China.

The first stage in this process was the creation in 2015 of a voluntary, opt-in social scoring system called 'Sesame Credit', operated in conjunction with the state by the dominant Chinese e-commerce company, Alibaba. This harvests data on the online social interactions, purchases and financial transactions of volunteer

[74] Mantello (n 22) 2.

[75] R Kitchin and M Dodge, *Code/Space: Software and Everyday Life* (Cambridge MA, MIT Press, 2011) 11.

[76] R Peeters and M Schuilenburg, 'Machine Justice: Governing Security Through the Bureaucracy of Algorithms' (2018) 23(3) *Information Polity* 267–80.

[77] S Zuboff, 'Surveillance Capitalism and the Challenge of Collective Action' (2019) 28(1) *New Labor Forum* 15–16.

[78] M H Maras and A S Wandt, 'Enabling Mass Surveillance: Data Aggregation in the Age of Big Data and the Internet of Things' (2019) 4(2) *Journal of Cyber Policy* 160, 160–63.

[79] M Radin, 'Boilerplate Today: The Rise of Modularity and the Waning of Consent' (2006) 104(5) *Michigan Law Review* 1223, 1231.

[80] N Kim, 'Relative Consent and Contract Law' (2017) 18(1) *Nevada Law Journal* 165.

[81] See the discussion in C Gardiner, 'Principles of Internet Contracting: Illuminating the Shadows' (2019) 48(4) *Common Law World Review* 208.

[82] Peeters and Schuilenburg (n 76) 275.

participants in order to reward them for good citizenship and compliance with government initiatives. The acquisition of socially desirable products such as gardening tools or work shoes is remunerated with extra points while unpaid debts are penalised.[83] Those with high scores obtain enhanced access to personal loans, jobs, visas and more.[84] According to Mantello,

> if a gamer tweets negative criticisms of recent government policies or posts incriminating photos of dysfunctional government services on Facebook their score goes down. But if gamers share state news about the rise of Japanese militarism or US imperialism the score goes up.[85]

However, voluntary participation is only the first stage of this development. In 2014 China's State Council publicised an ambitious and all-inclusive social credit system plan which would eventually be compulsory for all citizens when fully operational by 2020. Drawing on datasets from a wide range of government and commercial sources, information on personal finances, tax payments, traffic violations and social behaviour could be combined with details of online behaviour and general social comportment to produce an individualised score linked to the identity documents of each Chinese citizen.[86] High scores would significantly benefit individuals with easier access to government and commercial facilities, whereas, suggests Creemers, undesired behaviour 'may affect citizens' ability to gain a livelihood, find schools for their children or take out insurance.'[87] In addition, access to transport, personal loans and visas will be curtailed by low scores.

The scheme has attracted considerable scholarly attention[88] as well as journalistic coverage.[89] To many authors, the so-called 'China Model' is nothing more than a 'more appealing term for a comprehensive system of state repression, bolstered by the latest digital technologies'[90] It represents quite simply 'data-driven authoritarianism'[91] or 'digital totalitarianism'[92] and Xinjiang, in particular, has become

[83] Mantello (n 22) 8.

[84] X Qiang, 'The Road to Digital Unfreedom: President Xi's Surveillance State' (2019) 30(1) *Journal of Democracy* 53, 59.

[85] Mantello (n 22) 8.

[86] Qiang (n 84) 59–60.

[87] R Creemers, 'Cyber China: Upgrading Propaganda, Public Opinion Work and Social Management for the Twenty-First Century' (2017) 26(103) *Journal of Contemporary China* 85, 97.

[88] S Hoffman, *Social Credit: Technology-enhanced Authoritarian Control with Global Consequences* (Barton ACT, Australian Strategic Policy Institute, International Cyber Policy Centre, 2018); F Liang, V Das, N Kostyuk, and M Hussain, 'Constructing a Data-Driven Society: China's Social Credit System as a State Surveillance Infrastructure' (2018) 10(4) *Policy & Internet* 415; C Seungeun Lee, 'Datafication, Dataveillance, and the Social Credit System as China's New Normal' (2019) 43(6) *Online Information Review* 952; Qiang (n 84).

[89] See, eg, S Mistreanu, 'Life Inside China's Social Credit System', *Foreign Policy*, 3 April 2018, available at: foreignpolicy.com/2018/04/03/life-inside-chinas-social-credit-laboratory/; A Ma, 'China Ranks Citizens with a Social Credit System – Here's What You Can Do Wrong and How You Can Be Punished', *Independent*, 10 April 2018, available at: www.independent.co.uk/life-style/gadgets-and-tech/china-social-credit-system-punishments-rewards-explained-a8297486.html.

[90] Qiang (n 84) 62.

[91] Lee (n 88) 953.

[92] Qiang (n 84) 63.

'a police state like no other'.[93] However, Chinese social credit, according to Kostka, 'does not require the overt (and unpopular) use of coercion by the state'[94] and is perhaps more accurately described by Hoffman as a 'simultaneous co-optative and coercive' system.[95]

Despite the increasing use of compulsion, social credit is still, apparently, very popular. Using a cross-regional survey, Kostka found in 2019 that there was a 'surprisingly high degree of approval of SCSs [social credit schemes] across respondent groups.'[96] 80 per cent of respondents reported using commercial social credit schemes while only seven per cent were aware of being part of a local-government-run pilot.[97] Whilst younger elite respondents did express some concerns about participation in social credit schemes, older elites (better educated and wealthier) were overwhelmingly positive.[98]

On the face of it, such quasi-voluntary and self-executing sanctioning appears very amenable to proportionality-based regulation and a mathematical proportionality test could simply be embedded in the analytics. However, it is hard to see how this could overcome the complex problem of inherent bias or even how access could be obtained to the precise metrics of the analysis, which may well be hidden from sight entirely behind the veil of corporate secrecy and intellectual property safeguards.

IV. The Domination of the Private Sector

Reliance on the proportionality principle has traditionally been seen as an effective check on state intrusion into the life of the individual. However, almost all of the big data analytical capabilities described above and available to police forces globally, have been produced, advertised and sold by private companies in a highly competitive market, albeit sometimes with public funding support. The data generated by such systems is therefore owned and managed as a corporate resource, available to police forces only to the extent that it is purchased or licensed. Many scholars have noted the 'increasingly porous alliance of law enforcement/security agencies, communications/tech companies, and other corporate enterprises dedicated to constructing a multipurpose, networked juridical and disciplinary precrime assemblage.'[99] Yet in this entirely new relationship, it is the commercial

[93] *The Economist*, 31 May 2018, available at: www.economist.com/briefing/2018/05/31/china-has-turned-xinjiang-into-a-police-state-like-no-other.

[94] G Kostka, 'China's Social Credit Systems and Public Opinion: Explaining High Levels of Approval' (2019) 21(7) *New Media & Society* 1565, 1568.

[95] S Hoffman, 'Managing the State: Social Credit, Surveillance and the CCP's Plan for China' (2017) 17 *China Brief* 21, 24.

[96] Kostka (n 94) 1565.

[97] ibid 1573.

[98] ibid 1584.

[99] Mantello (n 22) 2.

owners of the software, equipment and indeed the raw data itself, rather than their police clients, who are likely to be the dominant partners. As Brauneis and Goodman have noted, '[t]he risk is that the corporation controlling the data and analytics occupies the command center of urban governance while the democratically accountable officials, unable to control the data, move to the periphery.'[100] Attempts to limit the exercise of public authority, according to Fontanelli, are simply not relevant, because of the comparative weakness of the state in this field. 'What needs urgent management', he continues, 'are the interplay between private rights and private interests, and the public policy inputs necessary to arbitrate or moderate between them.'[101]

The consequences of this private sector annexation of crucial areas of policing are profound. The monetisation of data flows must inevitably take precedence over their use for policing,[102] and the priorities of private security, such as risk reduction and avoiding commercial disruption, must take precedence over the detection and punishment of crime.[103] Above all, intellectual property rights will be prioritised over public accountability.[104] Private corporations, unlike state agencies, have no obligation to submit themselves to any proportionality tests. In the view of Ball and Wood, this is an entirely new form of governance, involving:

> systems that allow their use by a corporate-state nexus that seeks both to increase flows that create opportunities for exploitation and profit and at the same time reduce the uncertainties and risks that come from bad circulations – in other words what Foucault … termed 'security'. That this constitutes a kind of emerging neoliberal global government should be clear if one considers 'security' in this sense as the basic function of government.[105]

However, as Deleuze noted several decades ago, the traditional surveillant enclosures – the school, prison and factory associated with Foucault's panopticon – have been superseded by 'societies of control' in which surveillance has become detached from the human gaze.[106] It is, moreover, no longer a function exclusively of state control and governmentality but rather of a dispersive corporate world. Deleuze asserts that 'man is no longer man enclosed, but man in debt',[107] pointing

[100] R Brauneis and E Goodman, 'Algorithmic Transparency for the Smart City' (2018) 20 *Yale Journal of Law and Technology* 103, 117.

[101] Fontanelli (n 13) 658.

[102] Linder (n 45) 77.

[103] E Joh, 'Policing the Smart City' (2019) 15(Special Issue 2) *International Journal of Law in Context* 177, 179.

[104] R Wexler, 'Life, Liberty, and Trade Secrets: Intellectual Property in the Criminal Justice System' (2018) 70 *Stanford Law Review* 1343; Joh (n 103) 178.

[105] K S Ball and D Murakami-Wood, 'Political Economies of Surveillance' (2013) 11(1) *Surveillance & Society* 1, 3.

[106] Cited in M Galič, T Timan and B J Koops, 'Bentham, Deleuze and Beyond: An Overview of Surveillance Theories from the Panopticon to Participation' (2017) 30 *Philosophy & Technology* 9, 19–20.

[107] G Deleuze, 'Postscript on the Societies of Control' (1992) 59 *October* 3, 6.

out gnomically that 'the coils of a serpent are even more complex than the burrows of a molehill.'

Surveillance and the automated analysis of data flows in the contemporary era of 'digital' or 'platform capitalism' have become of central importance to the global economy. Zuboff characterises this as 'a new form of information capitalism (which) aims to predict and modify human behavior as a means to produce revenue and market control.'[108] Her assertion is that surveillance capitalism 'establishes a new form of power in which contract and the rule of law are supplanted by the rewards and punishments of a new kind of invisible hand.'[109] Holding such a surveillance economy to account through legal and contractual proportionality requirements looks increasingly unlikely, even if the owners of the predominantly cloud-based data analytics and the data collection facilities themselves were not multi-national corporations operating outside the jurisdictions which they have under surveillance. In these circumstances, it is not difficult to imagine the coils of Deleuze's serpent freeing themselves easily from the restrictions imposed by state or international oversight based upon proportionality.

V. Conclusion

The great flexibility and effectiveness of proportionality for the purpose of restricting excessive state interference up to the present day has been derived from its double character as both a relational and normative concept.[110] On the one hand, it calculates the ratio between two disparate factors such as the impact on society of a particular type of criminality and a coercive policing response, while, on the other, it establishes a specific relation as a normative standard. Unfortunately, it is not at all clear that this combination of oppositional balancing and norm-setting is the appropriate response to the rapid, complex and rhizomatic development of assembled, algorithmic surveillance.[111]

How can an assemblage of large quantities of diverse data, collected in a variety of different ways by different state and non-state agencies and analysed remotely by an algorithm (which may be technically obscure and constantly changing), be susceptible to regulation by a purely binary formulation? Proportionality balancing is simply incapable of engaging with the concealed biases inherent in the processes. According to Tsakyrakis:

> The most effective critique of balancing concerns the assumption of a common metric in the weighing process. The metaphor says nothing about how various interests are to

[108] S Zuboff, 'Big Other: Surveillance Capitalism and the Prospects of an Information Civilization' (2015) 30(1) *Journal of Information Technology* 75, 75.

[109] ibid 82.

[110] S Uniacke, 'Proportionality and Self-Defense' (2011) 30(3) *Law and Philosophy* 253, 255.

[111] Haggerty and Ericson (n 4) 614.

> be weighted, and this silence tends to conceal the impossibility of measuring incommensurable values by introducing the image of a mechanistic, quantitative common metric.[112]

All of these difficulties are compounded in relation to big data analytics. In particular, the three important characteristics of big data policing which have been discussed above – its focus on inchoate future risks, the largely voluntary provision of data and its domination by the private sector – all contribute to undermining the relevance of the use of conventional proportionality as a measure of control. It is as if the 'upsetting novelty'[113] and the 'idiosyncrasies of human affairs in the digital arena'[114] conspire to exempt this kind of activity from the domain of our traditional protections. Well-meaning attempts to adapt proportionality tests from the laws of war or to propose amendments, as suggested above, do little to improve the applicability of a standard which was designed to control the more traditional and arborescent challenges of a previous era.

In order to exercise some measure of control over the ever-expanding and constantly changing universe of contemporary big data surveillance, new heuristic techniques must be developed, drawing on the strength of past experiences with proportionality but deeply informed by our understanding of digital surveillance. These must establish norms for prediction which are targeted on the elimination of inherent bias, are not defeated by the apparent consent of the data subjects and can reach effectively into the private sector. The cosmopolitan values which are embedded in the proportionality principle are still of fundamental importance, even if the current methodology of balancing must be transcended by more sophisticated and technologically informed methods.

[112] Tsakyrakis (n 12) 471.
[113] Fontanelli (n 13) 638.
[114] ibid 660.

10

Proportionality Paradigm or Paradox? The Proportionality Principle in American and German Security Law Jurisprudence

RUSSELL A MILLER

I. Prelude

Everyone who knows anything about the principle of proportionality as a means for adjudicating constitutional rights knows two things. First, the principle – at least as a form of balancing of interests – has spread from its origins in nineteenth-century Prussian Police Law to conquer the world.[1] Second, the United States has resisted the principle's spread, stubbornly holding to its absolutist approach to interpreting and applying the 1787 Constitution's fundamental rights.[2] These two truisms mark out the boundaries of what is thought to be a global 'proportionality paradigm'.

I only barely exaggerate. Read the opening lines to Columbia Law Professor Jamal Greene's recent, influential *Harvard Law Review* article:

> Two competing frames have emerged for adjudicating conflicts over rights. Under the first frame, rights are absolute but for the exceptional circumstances in which they may be limited. Under the second frame, rights are limited [and proportionally adjudicated] but for the exceptional circumstances in which they are absolute. The first frame describes the approach of the U.S. Supreme Court over roughly the last half century. The second frame describes the approach of the rest of the developed world over the same period.[3]

[1] See, eg, A Barak, *Proportionality. Constitutional Rights and Their Limitations* (Cambridge, Cambridge University Press, 2012); D M Beaty, *The Ultimate Rule of Law* (Oxford, Oxford University Press, 2004).

[2] Barak (n 1) 206–8 ('Commentators cannot point to a single instance in which the concept of proportionality in its entirety – including its four main components – is adopted by the American courts.').

[3] J Greene, 'Rights as Trumps?' (2018) 132 *Harvard Law Review* 28, 30.

What to make of this? Where to begin?

Maybe with the comparative law insight that such sweeping claims about proportionality's ubiquity are possible only if the richly varied world of the law is crudely homogenised. This functionalist manoeuvre requires that the complex concept and practice of proportionality review around the world is banalised and recast as its lowest common denominator: as little more than some kind of judicially-applied balancing.[4]

Maybe by drawing attention to the continental self-satisfaction involved in the claim, which restores the natural order of Europe's civilisational superiority over the barbarian Americans who stole the credit for the French Revolution's achievements for themselves and cleverly rebranded it as an American 'shining city on the hill'.[5]

Or maybe with this surprising insight: it's just not true. At least that is what I found in a study of the national security jurisprudence of the German Federal Constitutional Court and the United States Supreme Court. Those courts, in that distinct legal-policy context, defy the prevailing proportionality paradigm, which holds that Germany leads a world-wide trend towards rights balancing while the United States has opposed that trend with its rights absolutism. In this chapter I suggest that national security jurisprudence in the United States and Germany can be seen to confirm the received understanding. But then I present cases from both courts that show them radically reversing their presumed proportionality polarity. We have America: the land of rights balancing. And we have Germany: the land of rights absolutism. I end by proposing some explanations for this proportionality paradox in the national security context.

II. Proportionality Planet

A. Philosophy

How have we ended up in the proportionality paradigm's dichotomy: most balancing and a few refusing? A dichotomy is to blame. It's dichotomies all the way down.

Dworkin built his theory of rights from a dichotomy, namely, the distinction between principles and rules.[6] It is not very helpful, but he starts by telling us that principles are standards other than rules.[7] He means that principles appeal to

[4] But see J Bomhoff, *Balancing Constitutional Rights* (Cambridge, Cambridge University Press, 2013).

[5] See, eg, A Liptak, '"We the People" Loses Appeal With People Around the World', *New York Times*, 6 February 2012, available at: www.nytimes.com/2012/02/07/us/we-the-people-loses-appeal-with-people-around-the-world.html.

[6] R Dworkin, *Taking Rights Seriously* (Cambridge MA, Harvard University Press, 1977) 22–23.

[7] ibid 24, 28.

justice or morality and therefore have variable weight and significance.[8] They can be calibrated for varying degrees of applicability. Principles can serve as the reason for a legal result. Rules are not principles, Dworkin explains, because rules are all-or-nothing standards.[9] If the elements of a rule are met, then it must be applied and the result is stipulated. In this understanding, rules define specific duties and obligations and the outcomes they produce are not subject to calibration.[10]

Dworkin takes one additional step. He argues that constitutional rights should be treated as rules and not as principles. Dworkin insists that constitutional rights are not just moral claims, but that they establish applicable rules.[11] If rights can be variably applied because they are mere principles, he reasons, then to claim a right against the government is pointless. The government will just wheedle its way out of the 'obligation'. To avoid this, Dworkin insists that constitutional rights must stipulate their outcomes in the manner of a rule. He recognises that this means that an individual's right might prevail over the utilitarian gains for the collective good advanced on behalf of the public by state policy.[12] Dworkin does not blink. Viewing rights as rules naturally involves some sacrifice from the majority. He insists, however, that once the scope of a right (as a rule) is defined, it must be enforced to the fullest and not balanced or adjusted in the way principles can be balanced or adjusted.[13] Dworkin is serious about rights and he wants us to be serious, too. The only way to do this is to regard rights as rules. This is necessary because constitutions pretend to be law and if the rights they prescribe do not produce the intended results (in the form of liberties enjoyed by individuals), then the whole project of law might be cast into doubt.[14] Dworkin says that our only choice – if we hope to preserve the law – is to treat rights as rules, to treat rights as 'trumps'.[15]

It should be clear that this American philosopher's thinking about rights, largely building from the study of the practice of the US Supreme Court, describes and informs the rights absolutism attributed to the United States by the proportionality paradigm. It is a good cultural fit. Note the exaggerated role of the individual, even at the expense of the public good. Could there be anything more American than 'trumps'?[16]

Alexy, the German legal philosopher, more or less agrees with the Dworkinian dichotomy between principles and rules.[17] He parts with Dworkin, however, when

[8] ibid 26.
[9] ibid 24.
[10] ibid.
[11] ibid 191–98.
[12] ibid 190–93.
[13] ibid 198–99.
[14] ibid 204.
[15] ibid xi, xv.
[16] See, eg, S M Walls, *Individualism in the United States* (New York, Bloomsbury Academic, 2015). See also J Rauch, 'How American Politics Went Insane', *The Atlantic*, July/August 2016, available at: www.theatlantic.com/magazine/archive/2016/07/how-american-politics-went-insane/485570/.
[17] R Alexy, *A Theory of Constitutional Rights*, trans J Rivers (Oxford, Oxford University Press, 2002) 44–45.

he claims that some constitutional rights operate in-part as rules and in-part as principles.[18] Alexy's constitutionalism has a different spirit and he is reading a different constitution. Rights as rules *and* principles: that is how the post-War German Constitution (*Grundgesetz* or Basic Law) sees things. Rights function as rules, it is true. But they also function as principles. Alexy points to the many basic rights in the German Constitution that are accompanied by limiting clauses.[19] The text of the Constitution itself anticipates that its rights won't be categorically enforced as rules. Consider Article 5 of the Basic Law, which provides for freedom of opinion in its first paragraph in this absolutist manner: 'Every person shall have the right freely to express and disseminate his opinions in speech, writing and pictures and to inform himself without hindrance from generally accessible sources.'[20] That sounds as much like a 'trump' as the American First Amendment. But the second paragraph of Article 5 reminds us that the right is limitable: 'These rights shall find their limits in the provisions of general laws, in provisions for the protection of young persons and in the right to personal honour.'[21] In this way, a constitutional right has the look of a rule but it must behave like a principle, susceptible to calibration with an eye to the common good. In the case of Article 5 the common good takes the form of the general laws promulgated by the majority in parliament. The right does not stipulate an outcome. The right is not absolute. It must be balanced against other interests.

It should be equally clear that this is the thinking of a German theorist building from a study of the German Constitution. Alexy worries that treating rights as rules 'risks protecting too much'; risks sacrificing too much of the collective good.[22] The community plays an exaggerated role in his thinking in a way that aligns with Germany's more collectivist and consensual social and political style.[23] The only way out, Alexy suggests, is to treat rights as principles that can be satisfied in varying degrees. In this way, proportionality and balancing have a very close connection with constitutional rights.[24]

B. Proportionality in Practice

Even in the area of law enforcement and national security, there is quite a lot of evidence to support the proportionality paradigm: the Germans are in and the Americans are out. Take two quite similar cases from the Constitutional Court and the Supreme Court as examples.

[18] ibid 50–56.
[19] ibid 76–80.
[20] See Art 5(1) Basic Law, translation available at: www.gesetze-im-internet.de/englisch_gg/englisch_gg.html.
[21] Art 5(2) Basic Law.
[22] Alexy (n 17) 76.
[23] See E Langenbacher and D P Conradt, *The German Polity*, 11th edn (London, Rowan & Littlefield, 2017) 96.
[24] Alexy (n 17) 66–67.

The proportionality principle was decisive in the German Federal Constitutional Court's 2005 judgment in the *GPS* case.[25] The case involved German authorities' pursuit of suspected members of the *Antiimperialistische Zellen* (Anti-Imperialist Cell or AIZ).[26] The AIZ claimed to be the heir to the *Rote Armee Fraktion* (Red Army Faction or RAF), a violent left-wing movement that terrorised West Germany with bank robberies, kidnappings, bombings and murders throughout the 1970s and 1980s.[27] The AIZ took up the RAF's violent struggle against the system's elites and the right-wing with a series of bombings, arsons and shootings in the early 1990s.[28] In their pursuit of the AIZ's members, German law enforcement and domestic security forces undertook a comprehensive scheme of surveillance. For several years they maintained personal and video-supported observations of suspected AIZ members.[29] They tapped the suspects' phones.[30] And they followed the suspects' movements with old-school tracking devices attached to their cars.[31] And when the technology became available, for the last three months of their investigation, the authorities secretly attached a more sophisticated and precise GPS tracking system to the suspects' car to shadow them as they drove.[32] The GPS system provided constant information about the suspects' location – within a 50-metre radius – as well as information about the routes they had driven and a precise chronology of the suspects' movements.[33]

As part of their eventual conviction for attempted murder the defendants challenged the use of the GPS system as a severe intrusion on their right to personal privacy secured by Articles 1 and 2 of the Basic Law, which, together, provide a 'right to be let alone'.[34] This right extends outside the intimate family setting and beyond one's home. The defendants complained that the 'technical nature of the GPS-observation, which relied on satellite support, functioned without regard to any substantive suspicion at any given moment, secretly tracking the defendants in order to document their movements over a lengthy period of time'.[35] This, the defendants argued, 'required special statutory authorisation, especially when the GPS surveillance was combined with the other observation measures that constituted an intrusion on the protected spheres of the home and communication'.[36]

The Constitutional Court rejected the defendants' constitutional complaint. The Court recognised the privacy concerns that arise out of a regime of

[25] BVerfGE (Federal Constitutional Court Reports) 112, 304 [12 April 2005].
[26] ibid 306.
[27] ibid.
[28] ibid.
[29] ibid 307.
[30] ibid.
[31] ibid.
[32] ibid 307–8.
[33] ibid 308.
[34] ibid 310. See Arts 1(1), 2(1) Basic Law. See also R A Miller, 'Pantomime of Privacy: Terrorism and Investigative Powers in German Constitutional Law' (2017) 58 *Boston College Law Review* 1545, 1551.
[35] BVerfGE 112, 304 (311) [12 April 2005] (all translations of this case have been made by the author).
[36] ibid.

'total surveillance' like the GPS system deployed against the defendants.[37] But the Court explained that those concerns can be overcome if the authorities implement a number of procedural protections that ensure the proportionality of the privacy intrusion. First, prosecutors must be informed about these investigative measures so that, in the first instance, they can mitigate disproportionate surveillance.[38] Second, the authorities must document these investigative measures in a protocol to permit scrutiny of the intrusive surveillance measures in later proceedings.[39] Third, the legislature must ensure that it monitors developments in technology that might require statutory reform to guarantee the protection of constitutional privacy interests.[40] The Court concluded that these standards had been met in the defendants' case. More significantly, the Court ruled that the ordinary courts had complied with the principle of proportionality when upholding the authorities' use of the GPS system. Those courts were satisfied that the GPS surveillance was only combined with other surveillance measures in a limited fashion and on limited occasions.[41] The Court found that these restraints led to a proportional – and constitutionally acceptable – intrusion on the defendants' privacy rights, especially in light of the immense gravity of the suspected crimes.[42]

The German *GPS* case was a classic exercise in proportionality. The Constitutional Court affirmed the ordinary courts' judgment on the basis of a balancing analysis. On the one hand, the privacy intrusion was limited by adequate procedures. On the other hand, the suspected offence – in this case political terrorism – was extremely weighty.

A few years later the US Supreme Court was confronted with a similar scenario. *US v Jones* (2012) involved a narcotics investigation in which law enforcement agents implemented a wide-ranging scheme of surveillance, including personal and video observation as well as phone taps.[43] Eventually, for a duration and in locations not authorised by a warrant, the authorities tracked Jones' movements with a GPS tracking system that they secretly installed on his car.[44] Over four weeks the agents gathered more than 2,000 pages of data about Jones' movement and location from the GPS device.[45] Jones challenged his conviction on Fourth Amendment grounds, arguing that it was based in-part on evidence obtained by the use of the GPS technology without a judicially issued warrant.[46]

[37] ibid 321.
[38] ibid 320.
[39] ibid.
[40] ibid 320–21.
[41] ibid 321.
[42] ibid.
[43] *United States v Jones*, 565 US 400, 402 (2012).
[44] ibid 402–3.
[45] ibid 403.
[46] The Fourth Amendment provides: 'The right of the people to be secure in their persons, houses, papers, and effects, against unreasonable searches and seizures, shall not be violated, and no warrants shall issue, but upon probable cause, supported by oath or affirmation, and particularity describing the place to be searched, and the persons or things to be seized.'

The Supreme Court agreed with Jones and overturned his conviction. Five of the six justices in the majority saw the authorities' installation of the GPS device on Jones' car as an unreasonable intrusion on his property, which the Fourth Amendment strictly prohibits in the absence of a warrant.[47] Justice Scalia explained that the Constitution guarantees that people should be secure in their 'persons, houses, papers, and effects', and he insisted that this commitment is closely connected to property or 'otherwise [the Fourth Amendment] would have referred simply to "the right of the people to be secure against unreasonable searches and seizures"'.[48] Justice Scalia's opinion seems to confirm the proportionality paradigm, not because he focuses on the property dimensions of the Fourth Amendment's protection, but because he casts that protection in absolute terms. He invoked eighteenth-century English jurisprudence, for example, that held that 'the property of every man is sacred, that no man can set his foot upon his neighbour's close without his leave'.[49] In light of the Fourth Amendment's absolute protection of 'effects' as property, and in light of the conclusion that 'it is beyond dispute that [Jones'] vehicle is an "effect"', then Justice Scalia was compelled to rule that the government's use of the GPS tracking system was unconstitutional.[50]

Justice Scalia's analysis is a classic example of American rights absolutism. It treated the Fourth Amendment right as a rule, the elements of which, when satisfied, stipulate the outcome. The Fourth Amendment serves as a 'trump' to preclude government action.

III. Perverting the Proportionality Paradigm

But the proportionality paradigm already shows signs of strain in the GPS cases. There are hints in the German *GPS* case of 'security absolutism' and in *US v Jones* of 'security balancing'.

The German Court could resort to its typical proportionality balancing analysis because the authorities' use of the GPS tracking device did not involve human dignity concerns or the 'core-area' of privacy. The German Court explained, for example, that the 'infringement of the general right to freely develop one's personality (Article 2(1) in connection with Article 1(1) of the Basic Law) through the application of technical surveillance devices – to the usual extent and intensity – typically does not involve an intrusion of the inviolable core-area of privacy'.[51] The Court has consistently ruled that the Basic Law permits no intrusion on these intimate, deeply personal interests. You read that correctly: 'no intrusion'. Had the

[47] *United States v Jones* (n 43) 404–6, 413.
[48] ibid 404–5.
[49] ibid 405, citing *Entick v Carrington* (1765) 95 Eng Rep 807, 817 (KB).
[50] ibid 404.
[51] BVerfGE 112, 304 (318) [12 April 2005].

circumstances necessitated it, the Court would have been compelled to absolutely enforce the Basic Law's protections.

At the same time, two of the justices who joined the majority in *Jones* were less animated by the absolute protection owed to property interests under the Fourth Amendment. Justices Alito and Sotomayor – in varying ways – objected to the government's use of the GPS tracking device because they felt it was disproportionate in Jones' case.[52] The intrusion was particularly grave, Justice Sotomayor reasoned, because GPS monitoring 'generates a precise, comprehensive record of a person's public movements that reflects a wealth of detail about her familial, political, professional, religious, and sexual associations'.[53] But the gravity of an intrusion upon a constitutional right is not relevant in an absolutist regime. It is only relevant in a balancing regime. Justice Sotomayor concluded that the aggregate of the information collected – or the so-called 'mosaic picture' discernible from the information collected – significantly diminishes the citizen's expectation of privacy.[54] This is especially true because the information can be gathered, stored and recalled at nearly no expense to the state. That might be acceptable, Justice Alito suggested, if GPS tracking is undertaken only when the most serious crimes are suspected.[55] But 'longer term GPS monitoring in investigations of most offenses', Justice Alito reasoned, 'impinges on expectations of privacy'.[56] In those cases GPS tracking would be out of proportion to the state's interest in investigating and interdicting crime. You read that correctly: at least two Supreme Court justices were bothered by the 'disproportionate nature' of the government's action. Justices Sotomayor and Alito were weighing the defendant's constitutional liberty interests against the state's interests in security and law enforcement.

A. Putative Proportionality: Germany

The German Constitution contains a form of rights absolutism that plays a significant role in the security context. On the one hand, German rights absolutism is a consequence of a variety of applications of the Basic Law's protection of 'human dignity'. On the other hand, the Constitutional Court gives absolute protection to the 'core-area' of some constitutional norms.

One version of the German Court's absolutist jurisprudence builds on the Basic Law's hierarchically superior, inviolable protection of human dignity. The Constitutional Court has unambiguously and unwaveringly insisted that Article 1(1) allows for no infringement at all and is not susceptible to proportionality balancing.[57] That is dignity as a 'trump'.

[52] *United States v Jones* (n 43) 413, 418 (Sotomayor, J, concurring) (Alito, J, concurring).
[53] *United States v Jones* (n 43) 415 (Sotomayor, J, concurring).
[54] ibid 416–18.
[55] *United States v Jones* (n 43) 430–31 (Alito, J, concurring).
[56] ibid 430.
[57] Art 1(1) Basic Law.

The Basic Law's inviolable protection of human dignity can take various forms. The most direct application involves what is referred to as the *Objektformel* (object formula).[58] This understanding draws on Kant's teachings, which insist that 'the dignity of every rational subject consists in being a legislative member in the realm of ends'.[59] Christian Starck explained that, according to the *Objektformel*,

> a person cannot be treated by the state or a fellow citizen as a mere object; that a person cannot be placed at the complete disposal of another person, be treated as a part of a sum, be regarded as a cog in a machine; and that in these ways a person be deprived of his or her individual mental-moral or even physical existence.[60]

For example, the Constitutional Court applied the *Objektformel* in a challenge to life-imprisonment as a criminal sentence.[61] The Court explained that 'placing people in the condition of a mere object conflicts with human dignity'.[62] Life-imprisonment was a permissible punishment, the Court concluded, because its implementation in Germany respects this mandate. These life-sentenced inmates, the Court explained, are provided with programming and treatment that aims at their resocialisation and at fostering their psychological well-being and independence.[63] Above all, through this programming, the law anticipates the possibility that the life-sentence might be reduced, permitting the inmate to return to society.[64] The Court emphasised that, faced as they are with a life-sentence, the inmates still had not been turned into 'mere objects of crime-control efforts in a manner that violates their constitutionally protected claims to value and respect from society … The fundamental preconditions for the individual and social existence of a person had been preserved'.[65] Had that not been the case, the Court would have been obliged to rule the life-sentence regime constitutionally out-of-bounds without regard for a balancing analysis. That is human dignity – conceived of as the *Objektformel* – with an absolute dimension.

A second application of the Basic Law's inviolable protection of human dignity has played a significant role in the security context. The Constitutional Court often resorts to the constitutional concept of human dignity as a way of framing the essence of other basic rights. This is necessary because Article 19(2) of the Basic Law demands that, despite the many limiting clauses that accompany them, 'in no case may the essence of a basic right be affected'.[66] One solution to this mandate

[58] See C Bumke and A Voβkuhle, *German Constitutional Law* (Oxford, Oxford University Press, 2019) 93. See also BVerfGE 109, 279 (312) [3 March 2004].

[59] I Kant, *Groundwork for the Metaphysics of Morals*, ed and trans A W Wood (New Haven CT, Yale University Press, 2002) 57.

[60] C Starck, 'Art 1' in H von Mangoldt, F Klein and C Starck (eds), *Das Bonner Grundgesetz*, vol 1, 4th edn (München, Vahlen, 1999) no 16.

[61] BVerfGE 45, 187 [21 June 1977].

[62] ibid 228.

[63] ibid 238.

[64] ibid 239.

[65] ibid 228–29.

[66] Art 19(2) Basic Law.

has been to understand that a basic right's essence consists of those features of the right that intersect with and help inform an understanding of human dignity. In these cases the Court speaks of a discrete dimension of a particular basic right as being 'connected with' human dignity.[67] When the government treads in these rarefied realms the Basic Law excludes those actions altogether. The essence of a right is a facet of dignity and dignity serves as a 'trump'.

Maybe the most sensational example of both understandings of human dignity (understandings that implicate its absolutist effect) involves the Court's decision in 2006 when it ruled the Aviation Security Act unconstitutional.[68] It is a bonus that, consistent with my broader thesis, this case involves a security law issue.

With the 11 September 2001 terrorist attacks in mind, the Aviation Security Act, among other provisions, gave German authorities the competence to shoot down hi-jacked aircraft that posed a threat to people on the ground.[69] The Constitutional Court struck the law because this response almost certainly would lead the government to kill the innocent passengers on the plane. But even if the constitutional protection owed to 'life and physical integrity' under Article 2(2) sentence 1 of the Basic Law can be interfered with 'pursuant to law' under Article 2(2) sentence 3,[70] the Court reasoned that the shoot-down provision of the Act intruded on the essence of the right to life when seen in connection with the Article 1(1) guarantee of human dignity.[71] And why would the dignitarian essence of the right to life be implicated by a shoot-down order? The *Objektformel* provided the answer. Bringing down the hi-jacked aircraft, the Court explained, would convert the innocent passengers to mere objects in the law: the sacrifice of their lives would be a means to the end of protecting the lives and physical integrity of those on the ground who might be killed or harmed by the hi-jacked plane. The Court insisted:

> By using their deaths as a means of rescuing others, the state simultaneously objectifies them and deprives them of rights; by unilaterally deciding over their lives, the state deprives them of the protection they are entitled to as aircraft passengers, and the value that, as humans, they have in and of themselves.[72]

A second version of the German Court's absolutist jurisprudence builds on a separate effort to preserve the 'essence' of an otherwise limitable basic right, even without the benefit of an intersection with inviolable human dignity. As if it were sequencing the basic rights' DNA, the Court has sought to identify the inviolable, absolutely protected core of the liberties protected by the Basic Law.

[67] Bumke and Voβkule (n 58) 110. See, eg, BVerfGE 65, 1 (41) [15 December 1983].

[68] BVerfGE 115, 118 [15 February 2006].

[69] Gesetz zur Neuregelung von Luftsicherheitsaufgaben [LuftSiG] [Civil Aviation Security Act], 11 January 2005, Bundesgesetzblatt [BGBl] I 78, §14(3).

[70] Art 2 Basic Law.

[71] BVerfGE 115, 118 (151–52) [15 February 2006] [translation from Bumke and Voβkule (n 58) 95].

[72] ibid 154.

The Court hinted at this approach in its ground-breaking *Elfes* case (1957).[73] Wilhelm Elfes was an outspoken post-War Christian Socialist and opponent of Chancellor Adenauer's policies seeking the reintegration of the newly-formed Federal Republic of Germany into the Western economic and defence framework.[74] Elfes advanced his agenda for greater understanding with the Soviet Union and rapid reunification with East Germany through the *Bund der Deutschen* (Alliance of Germans or BdD), a political movement closely aligned with the Soviet Communist Party and the East German *Sozialistische Einheitspartei Deutschlands* (Socialist Unity Party of Germany or SED). Elfes' application to renew his passport in 1953 was rejected by the authorities who concluded that his foreign travel posed a threat to the internal or external security of West Germany.[75] Without a valid passport Elfes no longer could travel freely abroad.

A range of courts upheld the denial of Elfes' passport application, including, ultimately, the Federal Constitutional Court.[76] The Court found that the case did not involve the right to freedom of movement secured by Article 11 of the Basic Law.[77] Article 11, the Court explained, only applied to free movement within the Federal Republic and did not guarantee a right to travel outside the country.[78] But the Court found that the freedom to travel abroad would be covered by the scope of the general right to freely develop one's personality that is secured by Article 2(1) of the Basic Law.[79] The Court explained that Article 2(1) applies to the 'core-area of personality'.[80] But the right to personality, the Court reasoned, also applies to a broader and more comprehensive understanding of 'freedom of action'.[81] Having documented these gradients of freedom, however, the Court found that the denial of Elfes' passport was not a violation of the less-central constitutional interest covered by 'freedom of action'.[82] For our purposes, the remarkable achievement of the *Elfes* case was the Court's suggestion that Article 2(1) consisted of a spectrum of constitutionally protected interests, including a *Kernbereich der Persönlichkeit* (core-area of freedom of personality), which naturally merits greater – perhaps even absolute – protection.[83]

The Constitutional Court has constructed from this framework the 'sphere theory' of the right to personality that is codified in Article 2(1).[84] This theory envisions three spheres of constitutional protection that coincide with various dimensions of the human-social condition. The innermost sphere of personal

[73] BVerfGE 6, 32 [6 January 1957].
[74] ibid 32–33.
[75] ibid.
[76] ibid 33, 44.
[77] ibid 35–36. See Art 11 Basic Law.
[78] BVerfGE 6, 32 (35–36) [6 January 1957].
[79] ibid 43–44.
[80] ibid 36–37.
[81] ibid.
[82] ibid 44–45.
[83] ibid 36.
[84] Bumke and Voβkule (n 58) 115.

privacy and integrity is associated with human singularity and intimacy, 'where feelings and thoughts are located'.[85] This is the core-area of personality that the Court in the *Elfes* case imagined. The Court has described this intimate sphere as a/the 'last, inviolable area of private life that simply is not subject to any interferences by public authority'.[86] If that sounds like American rights as 'trumps' that is because that is exactly what it is. As the Court explained, 'Even important general interests cannot justify interferences in this area; a weighing procedure conducted according to the principle of proportionality does not take place'.[87] The other spheres, moving outward through the human-social condition include the 'private sphere' ('where non-public life takes place' such as among family or close friends)[88] and the 'social sphere' ('in which public life takes place').[89] These spheres are owed a declining measure of constitutional protection. This framework 'lends structure to the requirements of the principle of proportionality'.[90]

B. Perplexing Priorities: America

While the German Federal Constitutional Court has developed a parallel absolutist rights jurisprudence through Article 1's protection of human dignity and the 'core-area' doctrine, the US Supreme Court has experimented with a proportionality analysis in America's constitutional rights framework. The American developments have been documented and thoughtfully critiqued by a number of scholars. Vicki Jackson sees evidence of balancing across a number of constitutional areas, including the First Amendment, the Second Amendment, the Fourth Amendment, the due process clauses of the Fifth and Fourteenth Amendments, the Eighth Amendment and the legislative empowerment clause of the Fourteenth Amendment.[91]

Many regard Chief Justice Vinson's majority opinion in *Dennis v US* (1951) as an early staging-ground for American constitutional balancing.[92] It is an important example because the case involved a First Amendment free speech claim, which is thought to be America's most sacrosanct constitutional liberty protection, and it's most absolute.[93] The idea is that, if balancing can make a 'beachhead' in the First Amendment context, where the Constitution permits 'no law'

[85] ibid.

[86] BVerfGE 80, 367 (373) [14 September 1989].

[87] ibid.

[88] Bumke and Voβkule (n 58) 115.

[89] ibid.

[90] ibid.

[91] V C Jackson, 'Constitutional Law in an Age of Proportionality' (2015) 124 *Yale Law Journal* 3094, 3104–6.

[92] *Dennis v United States*, 341 US 494 (1951). See, eg, Bomhoff (n 4) 134–37; Jackson (n 91) 3128.

[93] It is also a terrific parallel to the German *Elfes* case because *Dennis* also involves attempts at restricting the rights of communist sympathisers in the 1950s. Once again, this is subtle evidence of my over-arching thesis: when it comes to security issues, you can toss out the proportionality paradigm.

interfering with speech and religious freedoms, then it would have little trouble spreading to other constitutional rights. *Dennis* also is an important example of constitutional balancing because the dissenting opinions from Justices Black and Douglas were motivated by the sense that balancing was a novel approach to First Amendment jurisprudence that departed dangerously from a stricter, absolutist tradition of speech rights. The dispute between the majority and the dissenters in *Dennis* confirms, as Jacco Bomhoff noted, that American constitutional balancing is uniquely characterised by a controversy between 'so-called balancers and their opponents, the so-called absolutists'.[94] *Dennis* is a prominent first volley for the balancers.

Dennis, the General Secretary of the United States Communist Party, had been prosecuted under the Smith Act (Alien Registration Act of 1940) for wilfully and knowingly conspiring to teach or advocate the overthrow of the government by force and violence. The majority ruled that the law did not violate the First Amendment, despite the fact that it involved 'an element of speech'.[95] First, the majority insisted that 'nothing is more certain in modern society than the principle that there are no absolutes', including the free speech guarantee of the First Amendment.[96] Second, the majority found that the more pragmatic understanding of the First Amendment that had been fashioned in earlier opinions by Justices Holmes and Brandeis, also should be flexibly applied to take account of the distinct 'circumstances of each case'.[97] Third, having cleared away these barriers to a proportionality analysis, the majority engaged with the concerns that perennially inform a balancing approach to rights adjudication: it recognised the inherent value of free discourse, on the one hand, while considering the substantiality of the state's interest in restricting speech, on the other hand. On this scale, the majority concluded that the 'overthrow of the government by force or violence is certainly a substantial enough interest for the Government to limit speech'.[98] The majority approvingly invoked the standard articulated in the lower court by the respected Judge Learned Hand, who reasoned: 'In each case, [courts] must ask whether the gravity of the "evil", discounted by its improbability, justifies such invasion of free speech as is necessary to avoid the danger'.[99]

It may not matter that *Dennis*, and its balancing approach, were later overturned by the more absolutist interpretation of the First Amendment announced in *Brandenburg v Ohio* (1969).[100] The balancing cat was out of the bag. The logic of proportionality began to surface elsewhere in American constitutional law.

[94] See Bomhoff (n 4) 126.
[95] *Dennis v United States* (n 92) 502–3.
[96] ibid 508.
[97] ibid 513.
[98] ibid 509.
[99] ibid 510 (quoting *United States v Dennis et al*, 183 F2d 201, 212 (2d Cir 1950)).
[100] The Court held that the government cannot punish inflammatory speech unless that speech is 'directed to inciting or producing imminent lawless action and is likely to incite or produce such action'. *Brandenburg v Ohio*, 395 US 444, 448 (1969).

Famously, in *Mathews v Eldridge* (1976) the Court relied on a three-factor test to determine whether the government's termination of social welfare benefits violated the Fifth Amendment's due process protection.[101] Essentially, the factors pointed to the significance of the welfare benefits to the claimant, to the significance of the government's interest in the efficiency of terminating benefits with minimal process, and to the significance of the costs the government would incur if it were to provide more procedures to ensure the integrity of a termination decision. After balancing those concerns, the Court ruled that the claimant was not entitled to an evidentiary hearing to challenge the termination of benefits.[102] *Tennessee v Garner* (1985) provides another example of American constitutional rights balancing.[103] The Court found that a Tennessee law permitting the police to use deadly force in an attempt to capture a fleeing suspect was a violation of the Fourth Amendment. The Fourth Amendment requires that the government act 'reasonably' when seizing property or making an arrest.[104] The Court explained that determining reasonableness requires a consideration of the totality of the circumstances and calls on the judge to 'weigh' the nature of the intrusion on Fourth Amendment rights against the government's interest in seizing property or making an arrest.[105] In *Garner* the Court concluded that the state's interest in shooting unarmed fleeing suspects was not greater that the suspect's interest in life.[106]

Balancing even has managed to stage a comeback in the First Amendment setting. Justice Breyer, a serial balancer,[107] wrote a concurring opinion in *US v Alvarez* (2012) in which he joined the majority's conclusion that the Stolen Valor Act violated the First Amendment.[108] The Act criminalised false statements about military service and honours. Justice Breyer, joined by Justice Kagan in a concurring opinion, argued that the problem with the law was that it was disproportionate when assessed under the Court's intermediate scrutiny analysis. The relevant questions, Justice Breyer explained, are: (i) whether the law creates speech limits that are out-of-proportion to its justifications; and (ii) whether less restrictive alternatives – short of criminalisation – existed to advance the government's purposes.[109]

The American foray into proportionality is distinguished by an overall lack of conceptual consistency and systematisation. Bomhoff explains that 'the picture in the US is largely of a patchwork of doctrines and subdivisions' that never developed

[101] *Mathews v Eldridge*, 424 US 319 (1976). Writing for the majority, Justice Powell described the Court's challenge as 'striking the appropriate due process balance', at 347.

[102] ibid 349.

[103] *Tennessee v Garner*, 471 US 1 (1985).

[104] US Constitution, Amendment IV.

[105] *Tennessee v Garner* (n 103) 11.

[106] ibid.

[107] See Jackson (n 91) 3096–97.

[108] *United States v Alvarez*, 567 US 709 (2012).

[109] ibid 730 (Breyer, J, concurring). Justice Breyer explained: 'We must therefore ask whether it is possible substantially to achieve the Government's objective in less burdensome ways', at 737.

into a 'fully coherent approach'.[110] Still, if one pays close enough attention, it is possible to see variations on balancing operating in a wide-range of American constitutional contexts.

IV. Protect and Preserve

The proportionality paradigm tells us something. But it does not paint anything like an accurate picture of rights jurisprudence in the United States and Germany. Playing against its absolutist reputation, balancing has some traction in the United States. And contradicting the proportionality stereotype, German rights jurisprudence is coloured by some absolutism.

The paradigm shift is particularly evident in national security cases. This is clear from the discussion so far. The two GPS cases involved law enforcement investigations that relied on surveillance measures with obvious value to national security and counter-terrorism initiatives. The German *Elfes* case and the American *Dennis* case involved anti-communist measures undertaken in the name of (supposed) national security interests. In the following I offer a few additional examples of this phenomenon from each system.

A. Pre-empted Permissiveness: Germany

The German Constitutional Court has made the absolutism associated with its core-area jurisprudence a central part of its security law judgments. In these cases the Court conducts its usual proportionality analysis, allowing a challenged government policy to stand while demanding mitigating concessions from the legislature in order to remedy the policy's disproportionate intrusions on constitutionally-protected liberty interests. But proportionality does not tell the whole story. In many security cases the Court also demands concrete measures to ensure absolute protection for an inviolable core-area of privacy.

The Court's *BKA-Act* case (2016) is typical.[111] Involving one of Germany's recent, most significant security law and policy reforms, the case also can be taken as representative of German security law jurisprudence and the role absolutism plays in those cases.

Germany's Federal Criminal Police Office (*Bundeskriminalamt* or BKA) originally was envisioned as a national clearinghouse for the facilitation of the federal States' nearly exclusive competence over law enforcement.[112] The enforcement of the criminal law – prevention, investigation and prosecution – is meant to be

[110] Bomhoff (n 4) 125 and 129.
[111] BVerfGE 141, 220 [20 April 2016].
[112] See Miller (n 34) 1546, 1551–56, 1569–70.

carried out by the States' criminal police offices (*Landeskriminalämter*), public prosecutors' offices (*Staatsanwaltschaften*) and courts (*Gerichte*).[113] Nevertheless, the history of the BKA is a tale of the gradual expansion of the federal agency's mandate to include front-line law enforcement and security functions.[114] Often, the enhancement of the BKA's role was a response to significant events such as Germany's reunification in the early 1990s.[115] The agency acquired new authority in response to the 11 September 2001 terrorist attacks in the United States.[116] Despite the far-reaching BKA reforms implemented in the years after 9/11, the German States largely retained their entrenched priority over criminal law enforcement.[117]

That finally changed with the substantial amendments to the BKA-Act that were approved at the end of 2008.[118] The amended BKA-Act's provisions involved a significant aggrandisement of the agency's investigative powers, including:

- authority to collect personally-revealing data;[119]
- authority to subpoena information;[120]
- authority to take special measures to collect information (regular personal observation, use of technology to conduct surveillance outside the home and use of informants and undercover agents);[121]
- authority to use technology for surveillance inside and outside the home;[122]
- authority to conduct data-mining;[123]
- authority to secretly intrude on, manipulate and collect data from information-technology systems;[124]
- authority to conduct telecommunications surveillance;[125] and
- authority to collect telecommunications meta-data.[126]

The BKA's intrusive new powers were challenged in a set of constitutional complaints filed with the Federal Constitutional Court. As the paradigm would predict, the Court considered the proportionality of each new investigative tool.

[113] ibid 1569–70.
[114] ibid 1551–61.
[115] ibid.
[116] ibid.
[117] ibid.
[118] Gesetz zur Abwehr von Gefahren des internationalen Terrorismus durch das Bundeskriminalamt [BKATerrAbwG] [Act for the Federal Criminal Police Office's Role in the Defence Against the Threat of International Terrorism], 25 December 2008, BGBl I 3083 (amending the original 1997 BKA-Act).
[119] ibid §20b.
[120] ibid §20c.
[121] ibid §20g.
[122] ibid §20h.
[123] ibid §20j.
[124] ibid §20k.
[125] ibid §20l.
[126] ibid §20m.

It considered the weight to be accorded to the basic rights implicated, including rights to telecommunications privacy,[127] the inviolability of the home,[128] personal freedom[129] and human dignity.[130] Naturally, the Court found these to be very weighty liberty interests. The Court then considered the importance of the state's justification for intruding on those rights. The Court found that the new powers served the state's very weighty, paramount objectives in criminal law enforcement and threat prevention as a matter of domestic and foreign security. Finally, the Court concluded with a balancing of these interests in order to assess whether the Act's provisions were appropriately limited so that they would produce only the acceptably minimal degree of intrusion upon a basic right.

This is the archetypal proportionality analysis, involving an assessment of the legitimacy, suitability and necessity of the state's policy, followed by an inquiry into the policy's appropriateness (proportionality *stricto sensu*). It strives, as Alexy envisions it, to calibrate the application of a constitutional right (understood as a principle and not a rule) in order to maximise the potential realisation of both interests: the interests of the individual and the public's interest in the common good achieved by the law. Over and over, in a long and excruciatingly detailed judgment, the Court ruled that the BKA's new powers should be permitted but only with finely-modulated corrections to ensure proportional respect for basic rights. These corrections were very specific, often insisting upon an appropriate range of procedural protections involving judicial supervision, reporting requirements and strict rules for the retention and eventual deletion of information acquired through the use of the BKA's new powers.[131]

But the Court did something more. Throughout the decision it repeatedly found that the procedures demanded by the BKA-Act did not adequately protect the constitutionally sacrosanct 'core-area for the private arrangement of one's life'. In this mode, the Court was not demanding that a more finely-tuned calibration of the balance be maintained between liberty and security. The Court insisted on safeguards to ensure the absolute protection of the 'core-area of privacy'. In this absolutist mode liberty served as a 'trump' over security.

Consider the Court's analysis of the Act's provision granting the BKA the authority to take 'special measures' to collect information through regular personal observation, the use of technology to conduct surveillance outside the home and the use of informants and undercover agents.[132] With some detailed procedural improvements, the Court concluded that in many circumstances these measures could be proportional.[133] The Court had more profound reservations about the use of these surveillance measures in ways that involved intrusions that cut

[127] Art 10 Basic Law.
[128] Art 13 Basic Law.
[129] Art 2 Basic Law.
[130] Art 1 Basic Law.
[131] See Miller (n 34).
[132] BKATerrAbwG (n 118) §20g.
[133] BVerfGE 141, 220 (287) [20 April 2016].

perilously close to individuals' 'core-area of private life'.[134] Even where the activities subject to surveillance under these 'special measures' would occur outside the home and in full view of the public, the Court found that the 'core-area of privacy' also extends to a person's behaviour in a car, at a restaurant or during a secluded walk.[135] With that in mind, the Constitutional Court ordered the legislature to rewrite the Act so that it would provide clear rules ensuring the inviolability of this central privacy interest during the collection, analysis and use of information acquired as a result of the 'special investigative measures'.[136] The law, for example, must explicitly prohibit the collection of information from the 'core-area of private life' to the degree practicable, especially with respect to information acquired from conversations conducted between highly-trusted intimates.[137] These limits on the collection of information, the Constitutional Court insisted, also must include rules that require the BKA to suspend immediately all investigative measures as soon as it becomes evident that the 'core-area of private life' is concerned.[138] The Constitutional Court also demanded that, in order to protect the 'core-area of private life', an independent authority would pre-screen all information prior to it being analysed and used by law enforcement.[139] Finally, the Constitutional Court insisted that the law requires the immediate deletion of highly-personal information – a procedure that must be fully documented so that it can be subject to judicial review of these actions.[140]

The Court advanced a similar, absolutist agenda in its review of the Act's provision permitting the BKA to use technology for surveillance inside and outside the home.[141] The Court again ruled that the provision's proportionality could be salvaged with some fine-tuning.[142] But the Constitutional Court found that the deeply intrusive character of the surveillance measures authorised by this section of the law could have an impact on the human dignity elements of the right to privacy in the home that is secured by Article 13 of the Basic Law.[143] For this reason the Constitutional Court insisted that the strictest safeguards must be applied for the protection of the 'core-area of private life'.[144]

The Constitutional Court ruled that some elements of this part of the Act failed to meet this high standard.[145] Shortcomings were evident in the rules governing the *collection* of information via surveillance in the home.[146] Shortcomings also

[134] ibid 295.
[135] ibid.
[136] ibid.
[137] ibid 279.
[138] ibid.
[139] ibid 279–80.
[140] ibid.
[141] BKATerrAbwG (n 118) §20h.
[142] BVerfGE 141, 220 (295–96) [20 April 2016].
[143] ibid 299–300.
[144] ibid.
[145] ibid 299.
[146] ibid 300.

were evident in the rules governing the *analysis and use* of information collected via surveillance in the home.[147] The Court found, for example, that the Act clearly should have established a presumption against surveillance involving conversations between especially trusted confidants or intimates (*Personen des höchstpersönlichen Vertrauens*) that take place in the home.[148] The Court explained that this circle of people includes marital or life partners, siblings and direct relatives – especially when they are living in the same home – some professional service providers (such as criminal defence lawyers or doctors) and very close friends.[149] The privacy of conversations with these people in one's home must be given absolute protection, the Court insisted, as a way of satisfying the deeply human need to express one's dreams, sensitivities, feelings and thoughts.[150]

In the *BKA-Act* case the Constitutional Court repeatedly demanded absolute constitutional protection of the 'core-area of privacy'. In this realm, the Court seems to be following Dworkin's lead. Reading the basic rights as rules, the Court ruled: that the law must prohibit intrusions on the 'core-area of privacy'; that the law must provide procedures to ensure that measures that intrude on the 'core-area of privacy' immediately cease; that the law must provide procedures to ensure deletion of all data accidentally acquired from the 'core-area of privacy'; and that the law must require the state to maintain a protocol of all these measures in order to permit judicial review of their use. This is rights absolutism. This is rights as 'trumps'.

B. Permeable Positivism: America

Balancing has seeped into the American Supreme Court's security law jurisprudence. In these cases the Court skirts the expected rights absolutism and assesses the constitutionality of a government policy by weighing the state's law enforcement or security interests against the individual's constitutionally-protected liberty interests. This trend is facilitated by the Court's flexible – some might say 'opaque' – approach to the implementation of the standards of review that are meant to guide the justices' deference to or disregard for the will of the popularly-elected branches. More profoundly, the trend is attributable to the deeply American tradition of jurisprudential pragmatism.[151]

Carpenter v US is an example.[152] The case involved a challenge to the government's acquisition of cell-site location information from telecommunication services providers as part of an investigation into a string of armed robberies. With cell-site location information the government can pin-point everywhere a suspect

[147] ibid 301.
[148] ibid 300.
[149] ibid 266–77 (citing BVerfGE 109, 279 (321) [3 March 2004]).
[150] ibid.
[151] See, eg, R A Posner, 'Legal Pragmatism' (2004) 35 *Metaphilosophy* 147.
[152] *Carpenter v United States*, 138 S Ct 2206 (2018).

(and his or her cell-phone) has been and identify everyone (or at least every other cell-phone) a suspect has encountered. The government obtained the cell-site location information in *Carpenter* pursuant to statutory authority granting access to 'stored communications' records.[153] Requests for those records from law enforcement are liberally fulfilled by telecommunication services providers. Carpenter argued that the privacy implications of the cell-site location information merited the Fourth Amendment's more rigorous protection. The Fourth Amendment permits a government search or seizure only with the benefit of a judicially issued warrant that is supported by a finding that law enforcement has a probable cause to believe that the search will uncover criminal activity or contraband. Had it adopted a Dworkinian all-or-nothing posture in the case, then it would have been possible for the Court to summarily dismiss Carpenter's claims merely by concluding that the Fourth Amendment did not apply to cell-site location information. Well-established Fourth Amendment case law discounts privacy interests in information willingly shared with third parties, such as the telecommunication services providers who gathered the data in Carpenter's case.[154]

Writing for the majority, Chief Justice Roberts departed from the third-party doctrine. Instead, he engaged in a Fourth Amendment balancing analysis and concluded that the Fourth Amendment had been violated in *Carpenter*. On the one hand, Roberts implied that the government's interest in the case was modest. He suggested that the investigation and prosecution of armed robberies was not as weighty as national security concerns.[155] On the other hand, Roberts was concerned with the serious privacy intrusion involved in giving the government ready access to cell-site location information.[156] He reasoned that the cell-site location information was neither as discrete nor as static as something like banking records.[157] Balancing is clearly at the heart of Roberts' analysis as he places considerable weight on the side of Carpenter's privacy interests:

> The Government's position fails to contend with the seismic shifts in digital technology that made possible the tracking of not only Carpenter's location but also everyone else's, not for a short period but for years and years. Sprint Corporation and its competitors are not your typical witnesses. Unlike the nosy neighbor who keeps an eye on comings and goings, they are ever alert, and their memory is nearly infallible. There is a world of difference between the limited types of personal information addressed in *Smith* and *Miller* and the exhaustive chronicle of location information casually collected by wireless carriers today.[158]

There are clear echoes here of Justice Sotomayor's concern in the *Jones* case about the ways in which ubiquitous and invasive technology can give the state an

[153] Stored Communications Act, 18 USC §§2701–12 (1986).
[154] See *Smith v Maryland*, 442 US 735 (1979).
[155] *Carpenter v United States* (n 152) 2220.
[156] ibid 2217–18.
[157] ibid 2220.
[158] ibid 2219.

extremely revealing 'mosaic' picture of a suspect's life that raises new and disproportionate privacy issues.[159]

Chief Justice Roberts' opinion in *Carpenter* advances an embrace of balancing in the security context that already was evident in the ground-breaking *Holder* case from 2010.[160] *Holder v Humanitarian Law Project* is a particularly important example of America's departure from rights absolutism for several reasons.

First, the case involved the application of the First Amendment to so-called political speech. One commentator remarked that political speech – speech about government affairs – occupies the highest rung in the hierarchy of protected speech.[161] In terms surprisingly aligned with the German rights framework, political speech has been characterised as the 'core' of the First Amendment.[162] For this reason, the Supreme Court has given political speech the 'fullest and most urgent' protection under the First Amendment, strictly scrutinising government restrictions in a way that almost always is fatal for the state's policy.[163] The First Amendment secures political speech like a 'trump'. Adopting a balancing approach in the application of the First Amendment with respect to political speech is no small development.

Second, *Holder* is a worthy case-study of the Court's departure from its more absolutist tradition with respect to rights jurisprudence because, implicating the First Amendment as it does, it picks up the balancing trail on which the Supreme Court haltingly embarked in *Dennis* generations ago. *Dennis*, you will recall, also was a First Amendment case. The Court's turn towards balancing in *Holder* almost self-consciously involves a revival of the old debate between 'balancers and absolutists' from the 1950s and 1960s.[164] Of course, the balancing approach applied by the Court in *Dennis* eventually was put-down by the *Brandenburg* decision, which most commentators regard as one of the 'Supreme Court's most speech protective' judgments.[165] The *Brandenburg* standard permits government restrictions of speech only if several strictly construed requirements are satisfied. In fact, *Holder* is the first and only case in which the Court has upheld a government restriction of political speech since *Brandenburg* returned the Court to its First Amendment absolutism.

Finally, the Court's use of balancing in *Holder* merits our attention because it begs the question: what might justify the retreat from the deeply entrenched Dworkinian understanding of the First Amendment? The unorthodoxy can be explained by the fact that *Holder* involved a challenge to a key provision of

[159] *United States v Jones* (n 43) 416–18 (Sotomayor, J, concurring). See, eg, O S Kerr, 'The Mosaic Theory of the Fourth Amendment' (2012) 111 *Michigan Law Review* 311.

[160] *Holder v Humanitarian Law Project*, 561 US 1 (2010).

[161] E Chemerinsky, *Constitutional Law: Principles and Policies*, 6th edn (Alphen, Wolters Kluwer Law & Business, 2019) 1165–66.

[162] ibid.

[163] See *Eu v San Francisco County Democratic Central Committee*, 489 US 214, 223 (1989).

[164] Bomhoff (n 4) 126.

[165] Chemerinsky (n 161) 1089. See *Brandenburg v Ohio* (n 100).

the USA PATRIOT Act, which established one of America's most important, post-9/11 national security regimes. The same insight applies to *Dennis*. No matter how obscene the Smith Act appears to us now, its criminalisation of the act of advocating the overthrow of the government was seen as an essential part of the country's war-footing during WWII and later as a necessary tool for combatting the perceived existential threat of global communism. The Court's balancing analysis of the Smith Act in *Dennis* also was prompted, in its own uniquely historical way, by national security concerns. Of course, the role of national security interests in *Holder* and *Dennis* confirms my thesis about the breakdown of the proportionality paradigm in the security law context.

In *Holder* the Court was confronted with a challenge to the 'material support' provision of the USA PATRIOT Act.[166] This part of the law criminalises acts of support for or engagement with designated terrorist organisations if those acts facilitate or help to legitimate the terrorists' agenda.[167] The prohibition applies to training, providing expert advice or providing services.[168] The Humanitarian Law Project (HLP), a NGO dedicated to promoting the peaceful resolution of conflict, feared that its work with the Kurdistan Workers' Party (PKK) might expose its members to the risk of prosecution under the material support provisions of the USA PATRIOT Act. The PKK was a designated terrorist organisation. But the HLP argued that its contact with the PKK only involved instructional seminars that introduced the group to international law doctrine and the mechanisms available for peaceful conflict resolution at the United Nations. The HLP argued that teaching about these 'governmental affairs' was a classic form of political speech that should receive the strictest protection under the First Amendment.

In an opinion written by Chief Justice Roberts that relied on balancing, the majority of the Court disagreed. The Court ruled that the prosecution of HLP's members under the USA PATRIOT Act's material support provisions would not violate the First Amendment.

Chief Justice Roberts began his turn toward balancing in *Holder* by rejecting both parties' 'extreme positions' regarding the First Amendment issues in the case.[169] On the one hand, he refused to credit HLP's claim that the law constituted an outright ban on 'pure political speech'.[170] Roberts insisted, instead, that the Act merely prohibits 'support' for a terrorist organisation. Providing support, he explained, may not involve speaking at all.[171] But avoiding criminalised support for the listed organisations, Roberts reasoned, nevertheless leaves individuals free to speak and write about political issues about which they are concerned. Roberts embraced the government's portrayal of the Act: 'The statute does not prohibit

[166] 18 USC §2339B(a)(1).
[167] ibid.
[168] ibid.
[169] *Holder v Humanitarian Law Project* (n 160) 25.
[170] ibid 25.
[171] ibid 26.

independent advocacy or expression of any kind … it does not [even] prevent [plaintiffs] from becoming members of the suspect organisation'.[172] On the other hand, Roberts rejected the state's argument that the law only implicates conduct and not protected speech at all.[173] Roberts explained:

> Plaintiffs want to speak to the PKK … and whether they may do so under [the Act] depends on what they say. If plaintiffs' speech to those groups imparts a 'specific skill' or communicates advice derived from 'specialized knowledge' – for example, training on the use of international law or advice on petitioning the United Nations – then it is barred.[174]

Roberts recalled the Court's previous precedent in which it treated expressive conduct as protected political speech because the state sought to restrict the conduct because of what it communicated.[175]

By rejecting the parties' most extreme positions, Roberts found a way to animate the conflicting interests in the case: counter-terrorism initiatives versus free speech. He then turned to balancing those interests through a permissive application of the strict scrutiny standard of review that applies to restrictions on political speech.[176] The government's very weighty interest in combatting terrorism was on the one side of the scale. Roberts noted that 'everyone agrees [that this] is an urgent objective of the highest order'.[177] Even in pursuit of that pre-eminent interest, however, the Act's criminalisation of material support might have created constitutional problems if it was out of proportion to the *de minimis* security implications posed by the teaching and advice HLP sought to provide the PKK. But on the other side of the scale Roberts insisted that HLP's engagement with an extremely dangerous group such as the PKK was anything but a trivial or minor contribution to the group's terrorist agenda. Even 'ostensibly peaceful aid', such as training the PKK to use the United Nations' peaceful dispute resolution mechanisms, could have 'harmful effects'.[178] Roberts explained that HLP's activities could free-up fungible financial resources for the terrorist organisation.[179] It also might help to burnish the PKK's legitimacy, thereby making it 'easier for those groups to persist, recruit members, and to raise funds – all of which facilitate more terrorist attacks'.[180]

Roberts upheld the material support provisions of the USA PATRIOT Act because he assigned greater weight to the government's counter-terrorism policy than he did to the low-value speech in which HLP intended to engage. This was

[172] ibid 26.
[173] ibid 26.
[174] ibid 27.
[175] ibid 27–28.
[176] ibid 28.
[177] ibid 28.
[178] ibid 29.
[179] Ibid 30.
[180] ibid 30.

the more 'refined understanding' of the case that the majority detected.[181] Justice Breyer's dissent, Roberts complained, simply failed to give adequate weight to 'the real dangers at stake' while giving too much weight to the 'possible benefits of the plaintiffs' proposed activities'.[182]

The *Holder* decision was controversial. But one commentator suggested that the only consensus about the case was that 'the Court weighed the government's interest in fighting terrorism against the freedom of speech'.[183]

V. Postlude

I have documented the weak descriptive power of the proportionality paradigm, at least when it is applied to American and German security jurisprudence. In that constitutional context, Germany can be Dworkinian and America might channel Alexy. Proportional is absolute and absolute is proportional. In the following I suggest a few explanations for this surprising twist.

One straightforward answer is to note the inherent shortcomings in the comparative law functionalism that lies at the heart of most assertions of the proportionality paradigm. The contextualist critique of comparative law's functionalism is that the technique relies on abstractions and generalisations in order to make grand claims and construct crude classifications. Of course, no one believes that the proportionality paradigm depicts a reality about the nature of rights jurisprudence in the United States and Germany, let alone the rest of the wide world. Or do they? Comparative law's functionalism gives the metaphor life and it has been seized upon for its potential explanatory force. But that is only possible if the details of the practices of absolutism and balancing in any system are obscured; if the social, cultural, political and economic 'traces' weaving meaning into any legal phenomenon are ignored.[184]

This is an old debate in comparative law theory and method: forest or trees? My chapter makes a modest contribution to that debate by seeking to problematise the paradoxical practices of proportionality in the United States and Germany. Others have done profound work in this regard.[185] The contextualists would insist that proportionality has been overly generalised and that it is better understood as a quite diverse phenomenon as implemented around the world. Contrary to the triumphalist claims for proportionality: there are only 'proportionalities'.

Poorly done comparative law is surely a general explanation for the variations I have excavated here. But there is another possible explanation having more

[181] ibid 28.

[182] ibid 38.

[183] B J Smith, 'Protecting Citizens and their Speech: Balancing National Security and Free Speech When Prosecuting the Material Support of Terrorism' (2013) 59 *Loyola Law Review* 89, 97, 108.

[184] See P Legrand, 'Negative Comparative Law' (2015) 10 *Journal of Comparative Law* 405, 420.

[185] Bomhoff (n 4).

to do with my broader thesis. It may be that security concerns, like the glowing fires of the smelter, burn away the impurities exposing a constitution's essence, its identity.[186] This is a risky claim because it flirts so perilously with Carl Schmitt's insight that the 'state of exception' exposes a system's true constitutional order.[187] The constitution, Schmitt argued, is he who decides in the state of exception. Without endorsing Schmitt's normative conclusions on this point, it is a productive provocation to consider whether the existential nature of national security issues – whether real or perceived – exposes a constitutional order's essential character and identity.

Viewed in this way, the American embrace of proportionality in the security context looks like an expression of American constitutionalism's Lockean orientation.[188] Of course, the foremost purpose of Locke's social contract is to provide security (as much as possible) while leaving the citizen at liberty (as much as possible). The blind and blunt enforcement of constitutional rights as 'trumps' puts this fundamental constitutional commitment at risk. The constitution, we are told, is not a suicide pact.[189] Chief Justice Roberts captures this sentiment best in his opinion in *Holder*:

> The Preamble to the constitution proclaims that the people of the U.S. ordained and established the charter of government to 'provide for the common defence'. As Madison explained: 'Security from foreign danger is an avowed and essential object of the American union'.[190]

For its part, Germany's departure from the proportionality paradigm looks like an expression of post-War German constitutionalism's dignitarian orientation. This is the commitment to a substantive values order that promotes and protects dignity as a reaction to the National Socialist tyranny. The dogmatic application of proportionality to basic rights jurisprudence puts this fundamental constitutional commitment at risk. The Basic Law, we are told, expresses an objective order of values. The Constitutional Court captures this sentiment best in its *Wunsiedel* case:

> The Basic Law can virtually be regarded as a counter-concept to the totalitarianism of the national socialist regime. The experience gained from the destruction of all achievements of civilization by the National Socialist rule of arbitrary force has had a lasting and decisive effect on the entire post-war order.[191]

The two courts' departure from their expected modus in the security context provides palpable proof of the paltry prospects for the proportionality paradigm.

[186] G J Jacobsohn, *Constitutional Identity* (Cambridge MA, Harvard University Press, 2010).

[187] C Schmitt, *Political Theology: Four Chapters on the Concept of Sovereignty*, trans George Schwab (Chicago IL, University of Chicago Press, 2005).

[188] See M Sellers, *American Republicanism: Roman Ideology in the United States Constitution* (New York, New York University Press, 1994) 133–41.

[189] *Terminiello v City of Chicago*, 337 US 1, 37 (1949) (Jackson, J, dissenting).

[190] *Holder v Humanitarian Law Project* (n 160) 40 (quoting *The Federalist No 41: General View of the Powers Conferred by the Constitution* (James Madison, 1788)).

[191] BVerfGE 124, 300 (329) [4 November 2009].

11

Effectiveness, Proportionality and the Abstract and Concrete Forms of Decriminalisation. The Example of Italy

KONSTANZE JARVERS

> The more taboos and prohibitions there are in the world,
> The poorer the people will be …
> The more laws and orders are made prominent,
> The more thieves and robbers there will be.
>
> (Laozi, *Daodejing*)[1]

I. Introduction

The question of the proportionality and effectiveness of criminal law was addressed back in the nineteenth century by Franz von Liszt, who called punishment a double-edged sword aimed at the protection of legal interests (of potential victims) through the infringement of legal interests (of potential offenders). If punishment is to serve as a means to an end, it must, on the one hand, be tailored to that end (proportionality) and, on the other hand, economy in its use must be maximised (effectiveness).[2] In light of these considerations, this chapter examines whether and to what extent modern trends that limit the scope of criminal law by introducing both abstract and concrete forms of decriminalisation can lead to a more proportionate and, at the same time, a more effective criminal justice system.

[1] 57.2 and 57.3, available at: www.laterreinstitute.org/reading/non-being-tao-te-ching-daodejing-of-lao-tzu-laozi/.

[2] F von Liszt, 'Der Zweckgedanke im Strafrecht' (1883) 3 *Zeitschrift für die gesamte Strafrechtswissenschaft* 1, 31–32; C E Paliero, 'Il principio di effettività del diritto penale' (1990) *Rivista italiana di diritto e procedura penale* 430, 434.

Following an overview of the general concepts, the chapter focuses on Italy as a pertinent and complex example.

A. Effectiveness, Proportionality and the State's Power to Punish

Interference with individual freedom begins not just with the concrete imposition of punishment but rather earlier with the establishment, in the abstract, of a prohibition and the threat of criminal punishment for a violation.[3] That is why legislative as well as judicial action must be based on the principle of proportionality and its three components: suitability, necessity and appropriateness (or proportionality in the narrower sense).[4] Accordingly, the threat of criminal punishment for particular conduct must be a means well-suited to the achievement of legitimate state purposes, especially the protection of legal interests.[5] Furthermore, the legislature must always ascertain that it is necessary to make use of criminal law and that no other equally suitable but less severe legal[6] or extra-legal[7] measures are available. Finally, appropriateness is the benchmark for determining the severity of violations for which (suitable and necessary) recourse to criminal law is permitted. As the sharpest weapon in the arsenal of a given legal order, criminal law may only be used against objectively and subjectively serious violations of the social peace. In other words, 'don't use a sledgehammer to crack a nut'.[8]

For similar reasons, the legislature may neither enact nor retain ineffective or symbolic criminal provisions. Such provisions, which are clear manifestations of dysfunctionality, may even be unconstitutional (possible violations of the principles of *in dubio pro libertate*, equality and social solidarity).[9] A criminal judgment based on such a provision is largely unjust and, moreover, discriminatory. In fact, the price for ineffective legislation is paid primarily by outsiders and other socially

[3] Take, eg, the prohibition of incest in Germany (§173 Criminal Code, StGB). In most of these cases, proof of sexual intercourse is not possible in the absence of a pregnancy, making criminal prosecution extremely unlikely. Nevertheless, even the abstract threat of punishment means a considerable restriction on a couple's sexual freedom.

[4] With respect to Germany, see, eg, J Kaspar, *Verhältnismäßigkeit und Grundrechtsschutz im Präventionsstrafrecht* (Baden-Baden, Nomos, 2014) 398–433.

[5] ibid 214.

[6] Especially administrative law, but also tort law.

[7] Such as mediation or economic incentives.

[8] On the applicability of the principle of proportionality to the legislature, see in detail T Weigend, 'Der Grundsatz der Verhältnismäßigkeit als Grenze staatlicher Strafgewalt' in T Weigend (ed), *Festschrift für Hans-Joachim Hirsch zum 70. Geburtstag am 11. April 1999* (Berlin, de Gruyter, 1999) 925; E Hilgendorf, 'Punitivität und Rechtsgutslehre' (2010) *Neue Kriminalpolitik* 125, 127. See also Emmanouil Billis', Nandor Knust's and Jon Petter Rui's chapter 1 as well as Antony Duff's chapter 2 in this volume.

[9] In Italy: Art. 2, 3, 13 and 25 Costituzione della Repubblica Italiana; Paliero (n 2) 471.

disadvantaged individuals.[10] As a result, criminal laws that are merely symbolic must be categorically rejected.[11]

B. 'Inflation' of Criminal Law and the Need for 'Deflation'

Looking at the historical context, there are many European countries where the transition from an absolutist state to a state under the rule of law with a separation of powers had the effect of depriving the executive authority and the administration of the right to punish, assigning this right to the judiciary instead. As a result, many forms of conduct that formerly constituted administrative (police) offences were criminalised. The main purpose of criminalisation was to extend to these acts the judicial guarantees and defence rights that criminal law had begun to embrace during the Enlightenment. Later, as the welfare state developed and the reach of state power expanded into many areas of social life that had previously been entirely private (such as business activities), new criminal offences were created.[12]

But even today, criminal law tends to expand its boundaries over time.[13] In a natural, 'physiological' sense, this happens because criminal systems evolve and adapt to changes in society. A decisive influence on this development is the need to safeguard newly emerging legal interests[14] and to protect traditional legal interests against new forms[15] of assault.[16] However, there are also irrational, 'pathological' factors that contribute to the expansion of criminal law. One of them is the symbolic use of criminal law, namely the criminalisation of certain acts without any substantive basis and for illegitimate purposes.[17] Such legislation is frequently

[10] Paliero (n 2) 445, 472.

[11] Paliero (n 2) 472–73. See further Thomas Elholm's chapter 5 in this volume.

[12] See F Giunta, 'Depenalizzazione' in G Vassalli (ed), *Dizionario di diritto e procedura penale* (Giuffrè, Milano, 1986) 197. Frank complained back in the 19th century that criminal law was used as a panacea; R Frank, 'Die Überspannung der Staatlichen Strafgewalt' (1898) 18 *Zeitschrift für die gesamte Strafrechtswissenschaft* 733, 737. For a comprehensive historical overview of the hypertrophy of criminal law in various countries, see C E Paliero, *Minima non curat praetor* (Padova, Cedam, 1985) 3–78; European Committee on Crime Problems, 'Report on Decriminalisation' (Strasbourg, Council of Europe, 1980) 55–57.

[13] Hilgendorf (n 8) 125–31; J M Silva Sanchez, *Die Expansion des Strafrechts. Kriminalpolitik in Postindustriellen Gesellschaften* (Frankfurt am Main, Vittorio Klostermann, 2003) 1–6.

[14] Such as the right to data privacy protected in Germany by §§202c, 202d StGB or the fundamental right to informational self-determination; see the judgment of the Federal Constitutional Court, BVerfG, Urteil vom 15. Dezember 1983–1 BvR 209/83 in (1984) *Neue Juristische Wochenschrift* 419. The judgment BVerfG, Urteil vom 27. Februar 2008–1 BvR 370/07, 1 BvR 595/07 in (2008) *Neue Juristische Wochenschrift* 822 mentions the (new) fundamental right to ensure the confidentiality and integrity of information technology systems.

[15] eg, the commission of criminal offences via the Internet.

[16] Giunta (n 12) 197–98; I Zoda, *La deflazione penale in Italia* (Doctoral Thesis, University of Ferrara), available at: iris.unife.it/retrieve/handle/11392/2389156/123108/79.pdf, at 1.

[17] On the symbolic use of criminal law, see generally J Diez Ripolles, 'Symbolisches Strafrecht und die Wirkungen der Strafe' (2001) 113(3) *Zeitschrift für die gesamte Strafrechtswissenschaft* 516–38;

driven by public outcry; this was the case, for instance, after the series of mass sexual assaults, robberies and thefts in Cologne and Hamburg on New Year's Eve 2015.[18] Moreover, modern criminal law sometimes takes a proactive rather than a purely repressive approach, for example in cases where the source of danger is still unknown, such as preliminary conduct potentially causing pollution. Finally, the role of international and supranational law – which may also lead to a notable increase in the number of criminal offence definitions in the national law of states – must not be underestimated.[19]

Criminal law, however, as the sharpest weapon of a legal order and one that entails extensive infringements on a defendant's rights and freedoms, should only be used to protect legal interests that deserve such intense protection.[20] In addition, the application of criminal law as *ultima ratio* must be strictly necessary (subsidiarity principle) and effective (that is, enforced in practice), which leads to an ongoing demand for a decrease in its use.[21] Such a 'deflation' of criminal law – in response to the aforementioned 'inflation' – can occur at various levels: legislative, judicial and executive. As far as the legislative level (the focus of this chapter) is concerned, the main instrument for deflation is decriminalisation.[22]

C. Concept and Types of Decriminalisation

At first glance, decriminalisation may have a negative connotation because it entails a reduction in the scope of what is criminally relevant. Similarly to the natural, ongoing trend to criminalise, however, ongoing decriminalisation is also necessary so that criminal law can adapt to the changing needs of the legal system.[23] The concept of decriminalisation in its broadest sense encompasses a variety of substantive and procedural elements aimed at thinning out criminal law.[24]

S Bonini, 'Quali spazi per una funzione simbolica del diritto penale?' (2003) *L'Indice penale* 491, 533. See also Elholm's chapter 5 in this volume.

[18] For details, see BBC, 'Cologne Sex Attacks: Women describe "terrible" assaults', 7 January 2016: www.bbc.com/news/world-europe-35250903; 'Interview – R Steffes-enn', *tageschau*, 5 January 2016: www.tagesschau.de/inland/koeln-uebergriffe-interview-101.html; E Hoven, 'Das neue Sexualstrafrecht – Der Prozess einer Reform' (2018) *Kriminalpolitische Zeitschrift* 2–11, available at: kripoz.de/wp-content/uploads/2018/01/hoven-das-neue-sexualstrafrecht-der-prozess-einer-reform.pdf.

[19] For example, EU law not infrequently requires Member States to criminalise any of a broad variety of different kinds of conduct. The European Convention on Human Rights, in contrast, can require criminalisation only if the conduct at issue involves the violation of a fundamental human right, see Zoda (n 16) 1, 14–21.

[20] H Jescheck and T Weigend, *Lehrbuch des Strafrechts. Allgemeiner Teil*, 5th edn (Berlin, Duncker & Humblot, 1996) 2.

[21] Zoda (n 16) 8–9.

[22] At the judicial level, deflation takes place when criminal proceedings are avoided or curtailed with the goal of increasing procedural economy. The primary aim of deflationary mechanisms at the executive level is a reduction of the prison population. C Paliero, 'Depenalizzazione' (1989) *Digesto delle discipline penalistiche* 429; Zoda (n 16) 49, 75–81.

[23] Giunta (n 12) 192–93; Paliero (n 22) 426. See section I.B. above.

[24] Giunta (n 12) 193.

The most important of these in this context are de jure (abstract and concrete) decriminalisation, on the one hand, and de facto decriminalisation, on the other.

(i) Abstract Decriminalisation

Abstract decriminalisation[25] involves specific criminal offences usually located (at least in civil law systems) in the special part of a criminal code or in special laws. It consists in the repeal by the legislature of its own previously enacted criminalisations. The following three categories of abstract decriminalisation may be distinguished:

First, decriminalisation may aim at the full legal and social acceptance and recognition of previously criminalised behaviour. For example, homosexual behaviour among consenting adults was fully legalised in many western countries in the twentieth century. This implies a new-found respect for the legal right to choose a way of life that was previously subject to punishment. Such decriminalisations[26] necessarily have an impact on administrative and civil law as well, since all such behaviour must be considered entirely lawful.[27]

Second, the objective may not be a complete legalisation of the decriminalised behaviour but rather a shift in the state's position regarding the conduct at issue, for example in the form of greater neutrality. Take the example of incest between consenting adults. Even if many societies consider this conduct undesirable, it is still private, consensual behaviour between adults, in which the state – at least in the author's opinion – should not interfere.[28]

Finally, decriminalisation may involve conduct that is unwanted but which the state chooses to regulate by means more appropriate than criminal law – such as through the health system, the social welfare system, the educational system or by means of civil or administrative law. In fact, such conduct often remains unlawful as an administrative wrong even if it is decriminalised.[29]

(ii) Concrete Decriminalisation

In contrast, concrete decriminalisation leads to 'impunity' on a case-by-case basis for acts that, in the abstract, fulfil the definitional elements of an offence.[30] These types of deflationary mechanisms contain a legal 'filter' for use in court

[25] Paliero (n 12) 381–83. See in detail section II. below.

[26] In Italy this is also called 'dry decriminalisation' (*depenalizzazione secca*).

[27] The fact that homosexual conduct is legal, however, does not necessarily lead to the recognition of other rights, such as the right to adopt (administrative law) or the right to marry (civil law).

[28] Such conduct constitutes a criminal offence in many countries, however, including Germany (§173 StGB) and Italy (Art 564 cp).

[29] On the various categories of decriminalisation, see European Committee on Crime Problems (n 12) 15–17.

[30] L De Liguori, *La legge penale. Problemi e prassi applicative* (Milano, Giuffrè, 2008) 90–91; R Bartoli, 'L'esclusione della punibilità per particolare tenuità del fatto' (2015) *Diritto penale e processo* 659, 661.

proceedings: they require a concrete action by those who apply the law; that is the judge, the public prosecutor or even the victim.[31] Forms of concrete decriminalisation are typically included in the general part of substantive criminal law, but they may also be located in the special part as exceptions in individual offence definitions. In addition, there are mechanisms in procedural law that, under certain circumstances, lead to impunity for certain types of conduct. Of particular interest in this context are decriminalisation mechanisms based on the minor severity attached to the act and those designed to reward offenders who engage in good behaviour after committing an offence.[32]

(iii) De Facto Decriminalisation

Finally, looking at the broader picture, there is also what is called 'de facto' decriminalisation. Unlike the abstract and concrete forms of 'de jure' decriminalisation discussed above, 'de facto' decriminalisations refer to phenomena, namely factual elements considered in the selection of behaviours to be prosecuted, that may arise in many different ways in practice.[33] For example, problems of interpretation, application and evidence as well as short statutory limitation periods[34] may in fact lead to the non-prosecution of certain offences. A similar effect can be observed in offences that frequently go unreported by the victim, such as sexual offences. However, de facto decriminalisation is related to socio-political factors rather than legal issues and will not be discussed here in greater detail. Instead, the following analysis will concentrate on forms of abstract and concrete decriminalisation with a special focus on Italy.

D. The Italian Situation

Italian criminal law is particularly interesting with regard to proportionality and effectiveness and to the abstract and concrete forms of decriminalisation. The Italian Penal Code of 1930 (*codice penale*, cp), which dates from the time of fascism and has so far only been amended in a piecemeal fashion, provides for extremely high (and therefore disproportionate) abstract punishments. These punishments are not consistently imposed and enforced in practice, however, and are

[31] Paliero (n 12) 382–83. In terms of the victim, eg, by submitting or withdrawing a criminal complaint.

[32] See in detail section III. below.

[33] Giunta (n 12) 195; Paliero (n 22) 428; on de facto decriminalisations in detail, see Paliero (n 12) 203–347.

[34] In Italy, the maximum or absolute limitation period for ordinary crimes including suspensions and interruptions – that is, the period after whose expiration punishability is always expunged – is only 25% longer than the regular statutory time limit (Art 161 para 2 cp). See K Jarvers, 'Verjährung in Italien' in U Sieber and K Cornils (eds), *Nationales Strafrecht in Rechtsvergleichender Darstellung, Teilband 5* (Berlin, Duncker & Humblot, 2010) 605.

therefore often ineffective. First of all, substantive criminal law already provides for numerous mitigating circumstances that may lead to significantly reduced punishments.[35] A further reduction in punishment can be achieved by procedural means through the choice of an alternative type of procedure under the Code of Criminal Procedure (*codice di procedura penale*, cpp).[36] Finally, considerable reductions in prison terms are possible even during the execution of sentence.[37]

Furthermore, the inflation–deflation problem of criminal law is particularly pronounced in modern Italy. Since 1994, when Silvio Berlusconi came to power for the first time, Italy has been governed time and again by populist parties. During these periods, as a result of current events debated in the press and the general public, many sectoral 'front door' reforms – popularised by slogans in the media – were put into place for political purposes.[38] In an attempt to respond to the assumed or real public need for security, these reforms led to a substantial tightening of criminal law in the form of numerous new criminal offences. Well-known examples are the so-called safety decrees (*decreto sicurezza*) that are aimed primarily at immigration issues.[39]

This somewhat draconian and authoritarian legislative approach caused congestion in the workloads of prosecutors and judges and, correspondingly, excessively long proceedings, on the one hand, and chronic prison overcrowding, on the other. As a result, Italy has repeatedly been found in violation of the European Convention by the European Court of Human Rights (ECtHR).[40] This in turn caused an opposite trend: under pressure to reduce the prison population and to relieve prosecutors and judges, the legislature adopted more general reforms to relax the criminal law system as a whole – but without any media hype and rather quietly – through the 'back door'. The most important reform took place in 2014 by means of a law[41] that, in addition to introducing the option of suspending criminal proceedings against untraceable persons

[35] Particularly by applying ordinary (Arts 62, 62-*bis* cp) or specific mitigating circumstances, which lead to a (possibly even repeatedly) reduced sentencing range.

[36] eg, by means of the summary trial (*giudizio abbreviato*, Arts 438–443 cpp) and the application of punishment upon request (the so-called *patteggiamento*, Arts 444–448 cpp).

[37] Especially in case of conditional release (*liberazione condizionale*, Arts 176, 177 cp) or early release (*liberazione anticipata*, Art 54 cp).

[38] See P Veneziani, 'La giustizia penale in Italia, tra pacchetti sicurezza e decreti svuotacarceri', at: www.youtube.com/watch?v=_bwNzvIL7lc.

[39] Decreto-legge 23 maggio 2008, n 92 ('primo decreto sicurezza'); Decreto-legge 23 febbraio 2009, n 11 ('secondo decreto sicurezza'); Decreto-legge 4 ottobre 2018, n 113 ('decreto Salvini'); Decreto-legge 14 giugno 2019, n 53 ('decreto sicurezza *bis*'). See K Jarvers, 'National Characteristics, Fundamental Principles, and History of Criminal Law in Italy' in U Sieber, K Jarvers and E Silverman (eds), *National Criminal Law in a Comparative Legal Context, Vol 1.5* (Berlin, Duncker & Humblot, 2018) 167–68.

[40] Of the 1830 violation judgments against Italy between 1959 and 2018, 1194 were for excessively long proceedings; see www.echr.coe.int/Documents/Overview_19592018_ENG.pdf, at 8. The *Torreggiani* judgment in 2013 was perhaps the most influential. Because of prison overcrowding, Italy was found to be in repeated violation of the prohibition of inhuman or degrading treatment (Art 3 European Convention on Human Rights) and ordered to remedy the situation within one year. *cf* pilot judgment *Torreggiani and Others v Italy* App no 43517/09 (ECtHR, 8 January 2013).

[41] L 28 aprile 2014, n 67. See Jarvers (n 39) 162–63 and 169–70.

(Articles 419–420-*quinquies* cpp) and the option of suspending criminal proceedings on 'probation' (Article 168-*bis* cp),[42] authorised the Italian Government to do three things: introduce house arrest as a main penalty;[43] create a ground for excluding criminal punishment for particularly 'trivial' offences;[44] and decriminalise specific criminal offences and turn them into administrative or civil offences.[45] Finally, in 2017 a more comprehensive (legislative) reform of the criminal justice system took place[46] that, inter alia, introduced into the Penal Code (Article 162-*ter*) a general ground for 'extinguishment' of an offence if the offender engages in reparative conduct.[47]

II. Abstract Decriminalisation of Minor Offences in Italy

A. General Issues

Abstract forms of decriminalisation completely eliminate the punishability of conduct, thus reducing the horizontal scope of criminal law.[48] They involve issues exactly opposite to criminalisation.[49] As mentioned, Italy is a good example of a state that makes excessive use of criminal law. In addition to the criminal provisions in the Penal Code, there is an abundance of criminal offences in special laws outside the Code. Assumed and real security needs have served as justification for further criminalisations. Consequently, the country has been faced for some time now with the need to reduce judicial overload and to empty overcrowded prisons. Accordingly, there have been decriminalisation projects on a regular basis in the last several decades.[50] The most important ones took place in 1981, 1993, 1999, and more recently in 2016.

The Law of 1981[51] represents a significant turning point and constitutes the centrepiece of a new category of offences. On the one hand, this law implemented the decriminalisation of most ancillary criminal offences punishable only by a monetary penalty and of some infractions in the Penal Code.[52] As a result, these

[42] See section III.B. below.
[43] The deadline for implementing this particular authorisation expired without any result.
[44] This was done in 2015, see section III.C. below.
[45] See section II. below.
[46] L 23 giugno 2017, n 103 (so-called *riforma Orlando*).
[47] See section III.D. below.
[48] Bartoli (n 30) 661.
[49] Giunta (n 12) 194.
[50] For an overview up to 1999, see A Bernardi, 'Brevi note sulle linee evolutive della depenalizzazione in Italia' (2001) *L'Indice penale* 727–54.
[51] L 24 novembre 1981, n 689 ('Changes to the criminal system').
[52] eg, illegal exercise of itinerant trades (Art 669 cp), consumption of alcohol during hours when sale is prohibited (Art 687 cp).

minor offences lost their criminal nature and are now subject only to monetary administrative sanctions. On the other hand, the law introduced a set of new principles intended to regulate systematically the matter of so-called decriminalised offences (*illecito depenalizzato*), from both the substantive and the procedural points of view. There is controversy over details concerning the legal nature of these offences. Some define them as a criminal subsystem; others position them between criminal and administrative law.[53] Nevertheless, in terms of efficiency, the new type of administrative offences seems to be a suitable replacement for criminal law mechanisms in response to minor violations of legal interests. And by providing an adequate system of safeguards, the protection of individuals is reasonably guaranteed.[54]

The second important decriminalisation drive occurred in 1993.[55] It focused on a number of heterogeneous offences,[56] converting them to administrative offences. The criteria applied in selecting these offences for decriminalisation were proportionality considerations related to the low impact of these offences as well as effectiveness considerations involving the hope for a significant decrease in the number of criminal proceedings (due to the considerable incidence of these offences in the overall judicial case-load).[57] In the following years, further decriminalisations were gradually implemented in various areas.[58] These efforts were rendered useless, however, because of the simultaneous creation of numerous new offences in other areas.[59] Additional far-reaching decriminalisations were enacted in 1999 in the areas of food, navigation, road traffic and financial infringements[60] and in 2000 concerning income and value added taxes.[61]

[53] M Siniscalco, *Depenalizzazione e garanzia* (Bologna, Il Mulino, 1983) 150; see generally G Fiandaca and E Musco, *Diritto penale. Parte generale*, 8th edn (Bologna, Zanichelli, 2019) 915.

[54] This system is, to a great extent, inspired by the principles and criteria of imputation that are typical for criminal law, such as the principle of legality and the criteria referring to responsibility, the mental element, parties to crime and formal multiplicity of offences. For details, see Fiandaca and Musco (n 53) 915–19.

[55] L 28 dicembre 1993, n 561 ('Transformation of minor offences into administrative offences').

[56] Such as offences related to car sales, lottery, manufacturing of ignition devices and household lighters, installation of telecommunications equipment, prohibited conduct on trains or at railway stations, and failure to submit an accident report.

[57] A Pompei, 'Considerazioni generali' in D Carcano (ed), *Depenalizzazione e particolare tenuità del fatto* (Milano, Giuffrè, 2016) 8; Bernardi (n 50) 738.

[58] D.Lgs. 1 settembre 1993, n 385 in banking and credit matters; D.Lgs. 13 luglio 1994, n 480 ('Reform of rules on sanctioning contained in the consolidated law on public security'); D.Lgs. 24 marzo 1994, n 21 ('Rules on the non-payment withholding taxes and social security contributions'); D.Lgs. 9 settembre 1994, n 566 ('Amendments to the rules on sanctions for the protection of child labour, working mothers and homeworkers'); D.Lgs. 19 dicembre 1994, n 758 ('Amendments to the rules on sanctions in the field of employment'); D.Lgs. 23 luglio 1996, n 415 in the field of securities and capital adequacy of investment firms and credit institutions; D.Lgs 24 febbraio 1998, n 58 with regard to financial brokerage.

[59] G Napolitano and F Piccioni, *Depenalizzazione e decriminalizzazione* (Santarcangelo di Romagna, Maggioli, 2016) 19.

[60] D.Lgs. 30 dicembre 1999, n 507 ('Decriminalisation of minor crimes and reform of the sanctioning system, pursuant to Art 1 of Law No 205 of 25 June 1999').

[61] D.Lgs. 10 marzo 2000, n 74 ('New rules on offences relating to income and value added tax, pursuant to Art 9 of Law No 205 of 25 June 1999').

After the ECtHR delivered the *Torreggiani* judgment in 2013, with its violation finding based on prison overcrowding and its order to remedy the situation within one year,[62] the Italian state was under even more pressure to act. Implementing the authorisation of 2014,[63] the government enacted two legislative decrees (*decreto legislativo*, D.Lgs.) on 15 January 2016. One decree[64] (D.Lgs. 8/2016) deals with offences that infringe on collective interests and transforms them into administrative offences (*illecito amministrativo*). The other decree[65] (D.Lgs. 7/2016) focuses on offences that violate private interests. It provides for the first time for the conversion of criminal offences to so-called civil offences (*illecito civile*).

B. Criminal Offences Converted to Administrative Offences

As mentioned above, D.Lgs. 8/2016 decriminalised criminal offences that infringe on supra-individual interests. To that end, two different legislative techniques were employed, both already known from previous legislation. First, this Decree applied a formal criterion for selecting offences to decriminalise: violations carrying only a monetary penalty are no longer considered criminal offences but are instead subject to monetary administrative sanctions. It should be noted that the maximum administrative sanction may exceed the former criminal penalty.[66] This technique is also called 'blind decriminalisation' (*depenalizzazione 'cieca'*) because it automatically affects offences that protect various legal interests, without considering the social significance of the individual behaviour decriminalised.[67] Examples of offences decriminalised in this way because they were punishable by fine are driving without a licence (Article 116 paragraph 15 D.Lgs. 285/1992), secret abortion (Article 19 L 194/1978) and violations of certain anti-money laundering provisions (Article 55 paragraph 1 D.Lgs. 321/2007). Due to numerous exceptions, however, this is not as massive an intervention as it might seem at first sight. In fact, the offences set out in the Penal Code (with very few exceptions) and also those involving particularly sensitive subjects remain excluded from this general rule.[68]

[62] See n 40 above.

[63] See n 41 above.

[64] D.Lgs. 15 gennaio 2016, n 8 ('Provisions on decriminalisation, pursuant to Art 2 para 2 of Law No 67 of 28 April 2014'). See section II.B. below.

[65] D.Lgs. 15 gennaio 2016, n 7 ('Provisions on the repeal of criminal offences and the introduction of offences with civil pecuniary sanctions, pursuant to Art 2 para 3 of Law No 67 of 28 April 2014'). See section II.C. below.

[66] The pecuniary administrative sanction amounts to: €5,000–€10,000 for offences previously punished with a monetary penalty not exceeding a maximum of €5,000; from €5,000 to €30,000 for offences previously punished with a monetary penalty not exceeding a maximum of €20,000; from €10,000 to €50,000 for offences previously punished with a monetary penalty not exceeding a maximum of €20,000 (Art 1 para 5 D.Lgs 8/2016).

[67] A Leopizzi, *Pacchetto depenalizzazioni (dd.lgs. 15 gennaio 2016, nn. 7 e 8)* (Milano, Giuffrè, 2016) 14.

[68] An extensive list of these exceptions in the annex includes laws in the following areas: building and urban planning; environment, territory and landscape; food and beverages; health and safety in the

Second, the 2016 Decree identified specific criminal offences inside and outside the Penal Code for decriminalisation, such as obscene acts (Article 527 cp), obscene publications and performances (Article 528 cp), refusing assistance during a riot (Article 652 cp), abusing popular credulity (Article 661 cp), unauthorised theatre and movie presentations (Article 668 cp) and the unauthorised leasing, lending, renting, downloading or recording of copyrighted works in return for payment (Article 171-*quater* L 633/1941).[69] Similarly to the technique described above, this so-called named decriminalisation (*depenalizzazione 'nominativa'*) also transforms criminal offences into administrative offences, but includes misconduct previously punishable by imprisonment. It should be noted that the government made an independent choice not to implement the authorisation given by law to decriminalise two additional offences.[70] There are legitimate doubts as to whether proportionality considerations played a role in this decision.

C. Criminal Offences Converted to Civil Offences

In scaling back criminal law with D.Lgs. 7/2016, a fresh approach to decriminalisation was adopted.[71] Five criminal offences in the Penal Code that protected public faith, honour and property were repealed: falsification of a private document (Article 485 cp), falsification of a document signed in blank (Article 486 cp), insult (Article 594 cp), taking jointly owned property (Article 627 cp) and appropriation of lost property or found treasures (Article 647 cp).[72] In addition, the prerequisites for property damage (Articles 635–635-*quater* cp) were tightened, so that minor property damage is no longer criminally punishable (Article 2 D.Lgs. 7/2016). What all these offences have in common is that they affect private interests and, until 2016, could only be prosecuted upon a criminal complaint by the victim.[73]

workplace; public security; gambling and betting; weapons and explosives; elections and party financing; intellectual and industrial property (Art 1 para 3 D.Lgs 8/2016). Also excluded are the immigration offences provided for in D.Lgs. 25 luglio 1998, n 286 (Art 1 para 4 D.Lgs 8/2016). Additionally, if a decriminalised offence includes an aggravated form punishable by imprisonment, the latter is considered an autonomous offence definition and, therefore, still a criminal offence (Art 1 paras 2 and 5 D.Lgs 8/2016).

[69] Leopizzi (n 67) 14.

[70] Illegal entry and residence in the territory (Art 10-*bis* D.Lgs. 286/1998) as well as disturbing the pursuits or the repose of individuals (Art 659 cp) have not been decriminalised because of the particularly 'sensitive' nature of the interests involved; see the explanatory report on the draft of D.Lgs. 8/2016, available at: www.governo.it/sites/governo.it/files/relazione_illustrativa_6.pdf, at 5.

[71] M Guerra, 'Il decreto legislativo 15 gennaio 2016, n 7 in materia di abrogazione di reati e introduzione di illeciti con sanzioni pecuniarie civili' in D Carcano (ed), *Depenalizzazione e particolare tenuità del fatto* (Milano, Giuffrè, 2016) 103.

[72] In spite of the authorisation provided by parliamentary law, however, three offences were not repealed: usurpation (Art 631 cp), diversion of water and changing the condition of sites (Art 632 cp) and invasion of lands or buildings (Art 633 cp). The reason was the 'dramatic expansion' of these phenomena of occupying private property; see the explanatory report on the draft of D.Lgs. 7/2016, available at: www.governo.it/sites/governo.it/files/relazione_illustrativa_5.pdf, at 3.

[73] Leopizzi (n 67) 52.

The repeal of these criminal offences does not make the respective conduct lawful, however, as they were reintroduced as civil offences. The legislative technique typically consisted in introducing civil offences with the same definition as the repealed criminal offences (Article 4 D.Lgs. 7/2016). If these civil offences are committed intentionally, the perpetrator must pay – in addition to restitution and compensation for tangible and intangible harm under civil law – a civil fine established by law.[74]

The difference between civil fines and administrative fines is that civil fines are imposed by a civil court on the initiative (namely the bringing of a civil action) of the injured party. Moreover, if the convicted person is insolvent, a civil fine can never be converted to a sanction restricting personal freedom.[75] Some consider this form of civil liability something of a hybrid between a non-contractual tort and a criminal wrongdoing, as it still contains features of public law, especially by providing a punitive fine for the benefit of the treasury.[76] The Decree therefore also provides substantive and procedural rules evoking those in the criminal law, for example for parties to crime (Article 7 D.Lgs. 7/2016) and the sentencing criteria (Article 5 D.Lgs. 7/2016).[77] Furthermore, the general grounds of justification provided for in the Penal Code apply, whereas attempt is not relevant in the context of these new civil offences.[78]

D. Abstract Decriminalisation as an Opportunity for a More Proportional and Effective Criminal Law

While abstract forms of decriminalisation perform a primarily deflationary function – thereby neutralising the inflationary tendencies described above[79] – they also tend to distort the effectiveness and credibility of criminal law: the more criminal sanctions are applied to regulate social life, the lower the level of confidence in their legitimacy and the lower their ability to fulfil general and special preventive functions. By relieving the judiciary of essentially irrelevant proceedings in order to promote the repression of the most serious crimes, the operating efficiency of the judiciary is improved.[80] In fact, currently many offences cannot be

[74] From €200 to €12,000 for the more serious civil offences and from €100 to €8,000 for the less serious civil offences (Arts 3 and 4 D.Lgs. 7/2016).

[75] Guerra (n 71) 105.

[76] In this case the '*cassa delle ammende*' (Art 10 D.Lgs. 7/2016), see Guerra (n 71) 117–19; Leopizzi (n 67) 62–67. On the legal nature, see further R Guerrini, 'Il D.lgs. 15 gennaio 2016, n. 7. I nuovi illeciti civili tipizzati e le relative sanzioni' in G M Baccari, C Bonzano, K La Regina, E M Mancuso (eds), *Le recenti riforme in materia penale* (Padova, Cedam, 2017) 12, 31–38.

[77] Guerra (n 71) 121–24; Leopizzi (n 67) 63.

[78] Guerra (n 71) 119.

[79] See sections I.B. and I.D. above.

[80] Napolitano and Piccioni (n 59) 21; R Mancini 'L'abrogazione dei reati e l'introduzione degli illeciti con sanzioni pecuniarie civili' in A Conz and L Levita (eds), *La Depenalizzazione* (Roma, Dike Giuridica Editrice, 2016) 93–94.

punished at all because they are already time-barred due to the notorious congestion in the Italian courts and the resulting excessive length of proceedings. This is why, for some offences, enforceable fines (administrative or civil), quickly and therefore reliably imposed, are considered more powerful and more effective for purposes of prevention than the threat of a long and expensive criminal trial, which may not even result in a criminal punishment.[81]

Simultaneously, abstract forms of decriminalisation aim to strengthen the constitutional principles of subsidiarity and proportionality in light of the doctrinal categories of deserving and requiring punishment (*meritevolezza e bisogno della pena*).[82] As already mentioned, criminal law must always remain a measure of last resort (*ultima ratio*) for the protection of society; its norms must not be too numerous, nor excessive, but must be clearly formulated and aimed at the protection of values that are at least of 'constitutional significance'.[83] The subsidiarity principle requires the renunciation of a criminal sanction if an administrative or civil sanction is likely to provide an equivalent level of protection.[84] The principle of proportionality requires that a sanction be appropriate to the act committed. An inappropriate sanction is neither suited for deterrence (in the sense of negative general and special prevention) nor for demonstrating that the sanction is in fact just (in the sense of positive general prevention).[85] In addition, the proportionality principle calls for the decriminalisation of acts with a low severity value.[86] In other words, the principle applies not only to the relationship between the act and the threatened punishment for each distinct offence but must also serve as a touchstone in selecting the conduct to be decriminalised. This is not only a matter of priority of the legal interests concerned but also of the particular manner in which they are infringed.[87] The Italian legislature has not been very successful in this very difficult and complex undertaking.[88] Take the example of driving without a licence, an act with potentially severe repercussions, that was decriminalised, while disturbing the peace continues to be a criminal offence. In fact, a case involving a dog barking all night recently ended in a (suspended) sentence of one-month of detention after the case had worked its way through three court instances.[89]

[81] Mancini (n 80) 94; I Leoncini, 'Il D.lgs. 15 gennaio 2016 n 8, recante "disposizioni in materia di depenalizzazione, a norma dell'articolo 2 comma 2 della legge 28 aprile 2014, n. 67"' in G M Baccari, C Bonzano, K La Regina and E M Mancuso (eds), *Le recenti riforme in materia penale* (Padova, Cedam, 2017) 40.

[82] Pompei (n 57) 6; Zoda (n 16) 89–90.

[83] Pursuant to the Italian Constitutional Court (Corte Costituzionale) 23 marzo 1988, n 364.

[84] Zoda (n 16) 97–99.

[85] Pompei (n 57) 6. In this respect, the consequences of excessive use of criminal law and disproportionate punishment are similar.

[86] Pompei (n 57) 7.

[87] Zoda (n 16) 95; F Palazzo, 'Bene giuridico e tipi di sanzioni' (1992) *L'Indice penale* 209, 212.

[88] This is especially true in case of 'blind' decriminalisations that lack any reflection of criminal policy, Giunta (n 12) 212–13; Napolitano and Piccioni (n 59) 61–62.

[89] Cass, Sez III, 29 novembre 2018, n 5800, with annotation by G Gatta, 'Il ripetuto abbaiare di un cane vale un mese di arresto e tre gradi di giudizio penale? Considerazioni a margine di una annunciata

III. Concrete Forms of Decriminalisation in Italy

A. General Issues

Concrete forms of decriminalisation do not affect the abstract punishability of conduct; instead, they lead to a vertical reduction in the scope of criminal law by waiving punishment in specific cases. They prevent punishment regardless of whether the definitional offence elements are fulfilled and despite the general principle of mandatory prosecution, which is of constitutional status in Italy (Article 112 of the Constitution of Italy, *Costituzione*).[90] Thus, it is not the legislative act itself that leads to decriminalisation but rather the decision of a legal practitioner who is responsible for determining, based on the criteria set by the legislature, whether the act in question deserves a 'sanctioning' or a 'decriminalising' response.[91] The goal is a more flexible criminal justice system and, consequently, increased fairness in individual cases. From a systematic point of view, these decriminalisations are frequently designed as legal obstacles to prosecution or as grounds for extinguishing an offence.[92] The variety of these mechanisms is great,[93] but those based on the minor severity of the act and those that are rewarding in nature are particularly interesting. The first group covers cases where the act itself, in the case at issue, does not deserve punishment. This means the respective ground for waiving punishment must already be present at the time the offence is committed.[94] In contrast, the second group waives punishment if the perpetrator's behaviour after the crime leads to the mitigation or elimination of the harm or danger associated with the crime.[95]

Since the late 1980s, the Italian legislature has introduced several important new mechanisms resulting in impunity in such cases. The first mechanisms, which

riforma del sistema penale: perché non depenalizzare ancora?' (2019) *Il diritto penale contemporaneo*, available at: archiviodpc.dirittopenaleuomo.org/d/6479-il-ripetuto-abbaiare-di-un-cane-vale-un-mese-di-arresto-e-tre-gradi-di-giudizio-penale-considerazio.

[90] Bartoli (n 30) 661.

[91] Paliero (n 22) 431–32.

[92] See the report of the previous Commission on the Revision of the Criminal Justice System (14 December 2012), whose proposal, however, did not become law, at: www.giustizia.it/giustizia/it/mg_1_12_1.page;jsessionid=CnrqkdgEhbOXrgVen91FlTUP?facetNode_1=3_1&facetNode_2=3_1_3&facetNode_3=3_1_3_1&facetNode_4=4_57&contentId=SPS914197&previsiousPage=mg_1_12.

[93] Zoda (n 16) 60–77 mentions in this context offences punishable upon a criminal complaint of the victim, mechanisms of diversion and mechanisms based on expediency considerations such as settlement of misdemeanours, immunity, objective conditions of criminal liability, time-limits and amnesties.

[94] The most important mechanism is the exemption from punishment due to particular triviality, see section III.C. below.

[95] Compelling examples are mechanisms leading to a waiver of punishment due to the offender's restorative conduct (see section III.D. below) or probation (section III.B.). Others are the extinguishment of the offence following conciliation before the Justice of the Peace (Art 29 para 4 D. Lgs. 274/2000), abandonment of attempt (Art 56 para 3 cp), some grounds for excluding criminal liability or extinguishing the offence due to clemency (amnesty, Art 151 cp; general and individual pardon, Art 174 cp) and grounds provided in the special part (eg, Arts 376, 308, 309, 641 cp).

were created for the newly adopted juvenile criminal justice system of 1989, took the juvenile's developing personality into account.[96] In 2002 similar provisions were introduced to the new Justice of the Peace system. The focus of this new system was on minor offences involving interpersonal relationships.[97] Finally, as a consequence of the aforementioned *Torreggiani* judgment, there are now three new mechanisms in the Penal Code that apply to adults in ordinary proceedings; these mechanisms will be discussed in more detail below.

B. Suspension of Proceedings on Probation

The mechanism of suspending proceedings on probation (*sospensione del procedimento con messa alla prova dell'imputato*, Article 168-*bis* cp), introduced in 2014,[98] is modelled on the regulation that applies to juveniles.[99] It provides the accused – at an early stage in the proceedings[100] – with an opportunity to obtain a declaration that the offence has been extinguished in exchange for a series of measures aimed at social reintegration and compensation of damage.[101] First, conditions of probation typically require the accused to engage in activity aimed at eliminating the harmful or dangerous consequences of the offence and, where possible, at compensating for the harm caused by the offence. The decisive factor in this context is the effort undertaken by the accused to provide restitution (his or her success in fulfilling, to the letter, the imposed conditions is less important).[102] In addition, the accused is assigned to social services[103] to complete a programme that may include, among other things, socially relevant volunteer work or other defined obligations and restrictions (such as residence restrictions or prohibitions on visiting certain public places such as restaurants, clubs and bars). The programme must be based on resocialisation needs and must take into account the family, the social life and the personal and economic circumstances of the accused.[104] Finally, the accused must complete at least 10 days of community

[96] See generally U Gatti and A Verde, *Juvenile Justice in Italy*, available at: www.oxfordhandbooks.com/view/10.1093/oxfordhb/9780199935383.001.0001/oxfordhb-9780199935383-e-66.

[97] On the Justice of the Peace system, see generally K Jarvers, 'Die Kleinen lässt man laufen. Funktionieren die alternativen Verfahrenserledigungen und Sanktionsformen des italienischen Friedensrichters?' (2018) 130(4) *Zeitschrift für die gesamte Strafrechtswissenschaft* 1223–63.

[98] See section I.D. above.

[99] Art 28 Decreto del Presidente della Repubblica (DPR) 22 settembre 1988, n 448 (*Codice processo penale minorile*).

[100] According to the prevailing opinion, the mechanism is also applicable in preliminary proceedings, see C Conti, 'Sospensione del processo con messa alla prova del maggiorenne' (2016) *Digesto delle discipline penalistiche* 691, 712.

[101] A Logli, 'La sospensione del processo per messa alla prova tra equivoci dogmatici e limiti operativi' in M Danile and P Paulesu (eds), *Strategie di deflazione penale e rimodulazioni del giudizio in absentia* (Torino, Giappichelli, 2015) 134.

[102] ibid 153.

[103] More precisely, the Office for Noncustodial Sentence Enforcement (*ufficio per l'esecuzione penale esterna*, UEPE).

[104] Logli (n 101) 156. See also Art 464-*bis* cpp.

service, which is regarded as the overriding measure and centrepiece of the entire mechanism.[105]

The request for suspension on probation is admissible in cases of offences that carry only a fine or a maximum of four years' imprisonment and offences listed in Article 550 paragraph 2 cpp.[106] The suspension of proceedings may only be granted once, and proceedings may not be suspended in cases involving habitual, professional or predisposed offenders (Article 168-*bis* paragraphs 4–5 cp). If probation is successful, meaning the accused has done everything he or she was obliged to do, the offence is extinguished.

A suspension on probation is both rewarding and punitive in nature. Although the punitive response in this case is different from the conventional criminal response, it is still a major subject of criticism, especially with regard to its legitimacy. The reason is that an order of suspension on probation depends on the consent of the accused at such an early stage in the proceedings that his or her culpability (and the extent of it) has not yet been determined.[107] Additional concerns involve the alternative mechanism's lack of 'attractiveness' for the accused and the vagueness of its elements.[108]

C. Particularly Trivial Offences

In juvenile criminal law and in offences within the competence of the Justice of the Peace,[109] the 'particular triviality' (*particolare tenuità*) of an act has been a ground for terminating criminal proceedings for some time already. But it was not until 2015[110] that a ground for excluding criminal punishment in similar situations (*esclusione della punibilità per particolare tenuità del fatto*) was introduced into the Penal Code (Article 131-*bis* cp).[111] This new Article permits the non-imposition of punishment but does not abolish the unlawful nature of the act. One of the consequences is that self-defence is still permitted even against such a minor offence.[112] While less serious cases are possible with respect to any offence (at least in theory), this particular ground for excluding criminal liability applies only to minor offences carrying a maximum of five years' imprisonment and/or a

[105] Logli (n 101) 157–58.

[106] These are cases of direct summons for trial, for example violence or threats against or resisting a public officer (Art. 336, 337 cp), tampering with seals (Art 349 cp), personal injuries in traffic accidents (Art 590-*bis* cp) and aggravated theft (Art 625 cp).

[107] A Della Bella, 'Un viaggio tra le misure sospensive: i nodi da sciogliere in attesa della promessa riforma del sistema sanzionatorio' (2016) *Diritto penale e processo* 377, 384.

[108] Logli (n 101) 158, 169.

[109] Art 28 DPR 448/1988 (n 99) and Art 34 D.Lgs. 274/2000 respectively.

[110] Implementing the authorisation of 2014, see section I.D. above.

[111] See in detail K Jarvers, 'Die "Entkriminalisierung" von Bagatelldelikten in Italien' (2016) 128(2) *Zeitschrift für die gesamte Strafrechtswissenschaft* 549–77.

[112] C Grosso, 'La non punibilità per particolare tenuità del fatto' (2015) *Diritto penale e processo* 517–18.

fine. Although the deflationary effect of this mechanism is stronger if it is applied at an early stage, it can be applied at any stage in of the proceedings (all the way up to the appeal to the Court of Cassation).[113]

There are two prerequisites: first, the infringement must be particularly trivial in view of the nature of the conduct and the minor nature of harm done; and second, the behaviour may not be habitual. Thus, it must be a petty offence committed by an occasional offender.

The legal consequence is that the offender cannot be punished. The proceedings are discontinued or, if the main trial has already ended, the offender is acquitted. According to the prevailing opinion, however, the application of Article 131-*bis* cp implies that the offender's responsibility for the crime has been determined;[114] consequently, a corresponding decision is entered in the criminal registry. This fact is less of an issue if the mechanism is applied after trial, during which the responsibility of the offender is determined. It is more of a problem, however, if the mechanism is applied during the preliminary stages of criminal proceedings. This is true particularly because the accused does not need to agree to the application of the mechanism and thus cannot compel the court to continue the proceedings (leading to the loss of the possibility of acquittal). In this respect, this mechanism raises questions in terms of the right to a fair trial and the presumption of innocence.[115]

D. Extinguishment of an Offence due to Restorative Conduct

The so-called *riforma Orlando* of 2017[116] introduced the possibility of 'extinguishing' an offence due to restorative conduct (*estinzione del reato per condotte riparatorie*, Article 162-*ter* cp). The new provision evokes a similar, pre-existing mechanism for offences under the jurisdiction of the Justice of the Peace[117] and applies to offences prosecutable on a withdrawable criminal complaint. This excludes all *ex-officio* offences and offences prosecutable on the complaint of the victim where the complaint cannot be withdrawn.[118]

As prerequisites, the accused must have fully 'restored' the harm caused by the offence through restitution or compensation and, where possible, must have undone the harmful or dangerous consequences of the offence. Thus, a mere

[113] ibid 521.

[114] ibid 517 and 519.

[115] Similarly, M Chiavario, 'L'espansione dell'istituto della "tenuità del fatto": frammenti di riflessione su alcuni aspetti chiaroscurali' in S Quattrocolo (ed), *I nuovi epiloghi del procedimento penale per particolare tenuità del fatto* (Torino, Giappichelli, 2015) 255; L Parlato, 'Il volto processuale della particolare tenuità del fatto' in G M Baccari and K La Regina (eds), *Il nuovo volto della giustizia penale* (Padova, Cedam, 2015) 226.

[116] See section I.D. above.

[117] Art 35 D.Lgs. 274/2000.

[118] Examples include several of the sexual assault offences (Art 609-*septies* para 3 cp) and repeated aggravated stalking (Art 612-*bis* para 4 cp).

effort to restore is typically not sufficient. If the accused makes a genuine offer to pay compensation pursuant to the Civil Code (Article 1208), however, and the victim does not accept this offer, this may be recognised as compensation for the harm if the amount offered was appropriate. The described restorative conduct must occur (or be offered) at the latest before the hearing in a court of first instance begins.

Before deciding, the judge must hear the accused and the victim. In other words, even though the victim is permitted to set out his or her needs and the court must take them into account, they are not binding. Thus, if the judge concludes that the requirements have been fulfilled, he or she has no choice[119] but to declare the offence extinguished, regardless of the victim's consent (or even against the victim's express will).[120]

The introduction of this new mechanism confirms the assumption that criminal policy is increasingly recognising the value of restorative conduct. It may have general and special preventive as well as deflationary effects.[121] But the mechanism does not aim at introducing true restorative justice in the sense of a constructive dialogue between offender and victim. Rather, it removes the decision-making authority regarding exemption from punishment from haggling parties and instead entrusts it entirely to the judge. This in turn has the advantage that a potentially stubborn victim cannot prevent the application of the mechanism.[122]

E. Concrete Decriminalisation as an Opportunity for a More Proportionate and Effective Criminal Law

By waiving the imposition of criminal punishment, the concrete forms of decriminalisation can have a deflationary effect that is similar to abstract decriminalisation – at least if they are applied at a relatively early stage of proceedings. But these modern mechanisms have a wider potential beyond simple deflation: they may also contribute to an enhancement of the overall effectiveness of the criminal justice system. Their aim is to increase both the flexibility of the system as a whole as well as its fairness in individual cases, a goal that is in line with current international trends towards alternative conflict resolutions. The focus is less on the need to punish and more on encouraging the offender to face up to his or her crime actively and not to commit criminal offences in the future.

The exclusion of criminal liability due to the particular triviality of the act is based on the minor severity of the conduct at issue. As such, this mechanism

[119] F Palazzo, 'La Riforma penale alza il tiro? Considerazioni sul disegno di legge A.S. 2067 e connessi' (2016) *Diritto penale contemporaneo* 52, 54.

[120] C Perini, 'Condotte riparatorie ed estinzione del reato ex art. 162 ter cp: deflazione senza Restorative Justice' (2017) *Diritto penale e processo* 1274, 1276. This is what distinguishes this mechanism from withdrawal of the complaint.

[121] Perini (n 120) 1277.

[122] See also Palazzo (n 119) 54.

can implement the principles of proportionality and subsidiarity in concrete terms. Its aim is precisely to avoid criminal punishment if the infringement is so minor that such a punishment appears to be unjustified. The other two mechanisms presented here seek to reward offenders for restoration or for fulfilling the conditions of probation. Any and all restorative efforts on the part of the offender contribute to the re-establishment of social peace; therefore, such mechanisms can be a more appropriate response to the offence than punishment. The same is true for effectiveness. Ideally, the offender will admit his or her wrongdoing, face it and try to make up for it in some way. If this happens, the probability that the offender will commit offences in the future is reduced, which in turn considerably increases the effectiveness of the system.

IV. Conclusion

The Italian mechanisms for decriminalisation can, at least in theory, contribute to a more effective and proportionate criminal law. The question is whether this goal has been achieved in practice. Abstract decriminalisation has been on the legislative agenda for some time; indeed, by 1999 a number of criminal offences had been decriminalised. But between 1999 and 2016 more than 300 new criminal offences were introduced.[123] This is a factor that contributed to the collapse of criminal justice, evidenced in millions of pending proceedings and, consequently, multiple daily violations of the principle of reasonable duration of criminal proceedings[124] (as laid down in Article 6 of the European Convention on Human Rights and Article 111 *Costituzione*).[125] But it is also a factor that contributes to the recurring problem of prison overcrowding.[126] If the Italian State continues to create new offences even after the latest wave of decriminalisation in 2016,[127] it will not be able to keep up despite ongoing decriminalisations. It means taking one step forward and two steps back. In addition, it is not certain that the principle of proportionality was taken into consideration during the process of selecting

[123] Napolitano and Piccioni (n 59) 20.

[124] In 2017 the average duration of proceedings for ordinary offences at the public prosecutor's office (*Procura della Repubblica*) was 409 days. Proceedings before the district courts had a mean length of 559 (sitting as a 'single' court) and 623 days (sitting as a 'collegial' court) respectively, see: reportistica.dgstat.giustizia.it/VisualizzatoreReport.Aspx?Report=/Pubblica/Statistiche%20della%20DGSTAT/Materia%20Penale/3.%20Durata%20dei%20procedimenti/1.%20Durata%20effettiva/1.%20dati%20nazionali/1.%20tutti%20gli%20uffici.

[125] Napolitano and Piccioni (n 59) 20.

[126] The number of inmates in Italian penal institutions now designed for 50,688 inmates (www.giustizia.it/giustizia/it/mg_1_14_1.page?facetNode_1=0_2&contentId=SST238877&previsiousPage=mg_1_14) decreased from 67,961 at the end of 2010 to 53,623 at the end of 2014 but increased again to 60,769 by 31 December 2019, see at: www.giustizia.it/giustizia/it/mg_1_14_1.page?facetNode_1=0_2&contentId=SST165666&previsiousPage=mg_1_14.

[127] And this seems to be the case, considering the number of laws that were tightened or pushed through by the former minister of the interior Matteo Salvini during his brief 13-month term of office.

offences to be decriminalised. In this respect, current measures leave much to be desired as well.

The concrete forms of decriminalisation are more promising. Although they also have a deflationary effect and therefore contribute to the effectiveness and proportionality for this reason alone, they go even further: they can be of concrete benefit to both crime victims and society. There are, however, considerable deficiencies in terms of fair trial in the way the Italian mechanisms are designed. Furthermore, they must be applied in practice. The experience in proceedings before the Justice of the Peace, where similar mechanisms are very rarely used, is not promising.[128] Unfortunately, statistics for the new provisions applicable in ordinary proceedings are not yet available.

First steps have been taken. For noticeable improvements to occur, however, two things are necessary: first, the courts must actually make use of the available mechanisms; and second, the legislature must no longer view criminal law as the default response to undesirable social developments. Instead, it must revive the ideal, established during the Enlightenment: laws must be few, simple, clear and stable.[129]

[128] See Jarvers (n 97) 1248.

[129] Napolitano and Piccioni (n 59) 21.

12

Promoting Retributive Proportionality Through Sentencing Guidelines*

JULIAN V ROBERTS

I. Introduction

Proportionality guides decision-making throughout the criminal justice systems of Western nations,[1] particularly at sentencing where the state's power to affect the liberty interests of citizens is at its height. The proportionality principle is central to sentencing in all common law jurisdictions[2] and over the years has attracted much scholarship.[3] Until now, however, the scholarly literature has largely focused on defining the concept and exploring its constituent elements.[4] This chapter addresses a question which has attracted insufficient attention: how can the principle be implemented? Promoting proportionality is an important modern challenge for legislatures, prosecutors and sentencing courts. This chapter focuses on the ways that sentencing guidelines can contribute to this goal.

* My thanks to Emmanouil Billis, Netanel Dagan, Andrew Ashworth and Jose Pina-Sanchez for comments on an earlier draft of this chapter.

[1] E T Sullivan and R S Frase, *Proportionality Principles in American Law: Controlling Excessive Government Actions* (New York, Oxford University Press, 2009).

[2] Proportionality is important in civil law countries too. For example, it is one of the main factors guiding courts in Italy, see A Corda, 'Sentencing and Penal Policies in Italy 1985–2015: The Tale of a Troubled Country' in M Tonry (ed), *Sentencing Policies and Practices in Western Countries* (Oxford, Oxford University Press, 2016) 135. In Germany, T Weigend notes that 'the harm done and the offender's blameworthiness are the primary considerations', in 'Criminal Sentencing in Germany since 2000' in M Tonry (ed), *Sentencing Policies and Practices in Western Countries* (Oxford, Oxford University Press, 2016) 88.

[3] R Frase, C Momsen, T O'Malley and S L Washington, 'Proportionality of Punishment in Common Law Jurisdictions and in Germany' in K Ambos, A Duff, J V Roberts, T Weigend and A Heinze (eds), *Core Concepts in Criminal Law and Criminal Justice* (Cambridge, Cambridge University Press, 2020) 213–60.

[4] A von Hirsch and A Ashworth, *Proportionate Sentencing. Exploring the Principles* (Oxford, Oxford University Press, 2005); A von Hirsch, *Censure and Sanction* (Oxford, Oxford University Press, 1993); M Tonry (ed), *Of One-Eyed and Toothless Miscreants. Making the Punishment Fit the Crime?* (New York, Oxford University Press, 2019).

Proportionality may be considered a near-universal sentencing principle in the adversarial systems of justice. One explanation for its prevalence is that it derives from an even more fundamental concept of desert in society. There is great intuitive appeal[5] to the principle that outcomes – rewards as well as punishments – should be allocated according to an individual's desert. Most people find it troubling when rewards in life are assigned on non-desert grounds – for example when salary increments or promotions are awarded on the basis of pulchritude or personal favouritism rather than achievement or effort.[6] With respect to legal punishment, harsh sentences for trivial offences or derisory punishments for serious criminal wrongs are equally troubling departures from a desert-based outcome.

However, whether in the workplace or the criminal courts, proportional outcomes are hard to define and implement. Implementing a proportionality-based salary bonus scheme may be relatively straightforward. An employer specifies the determinants of merit awards, including factors such as productivity, years of service, educational achievement and so on. The list of factors is likely to be limited (and relatively uncontroversial). Once the criteria are agreed, panels of adjudicators can score candidates with respect to the stated criteria and allocate salary increments accordingly. Yet even a scheme with a limited number of determining variables will have a subjective element; adjudicators may disagree on some issues. Should educational attainment carry more or less weight than longevity in the firm? Is the number of employees a good measure of level of a manager's level of responsibility? In contrast, the relevant factors to be considered at sentencing are potentially limitless, sometimes ambiguous, occasionally controversial, and they often contradict each other.[7]

This chapter explores how sentencing guidelines promote retributive proportionality at sentencing, while recognising that retributivism is not the only guiding philosophy in sentencing; most jurisdictions recognise utilitarian objectives as well. The purpose is to illustrate the ways that a guideline may promote proportionality – and not to advocate the regime in my own jurisdiction of England & Wales as the only model to follow or to argue that proportional sentencing provides a comprehensive solution to sentencing problems.[8] Section II identifies the key components of a proportional sentence. Section III discusses

[5] von Hirsch and Ashworth (n 4) 4 observe that proportional sentencing 'comports with common-sense notions of justice'. For research on proportional sentencing and the public, see J V Roberts and M Hough, *Understanding Public Attitudes to Criminal Justice* (Maidenhead (Berkshire), Open University Press, 2005).

[6] There are exceptions; no one objects to the random allocation of even very large amounts of money, when these rewards arise in the context of lotteries.

[7] For example, how should a court respond to a defendant who expresses remorse at sentencing yet who pleaded not guilty and was convicted following a trial? For discussion of the complexities of sentencing factors, see C Tata, 'Sentencing as Craftwork and the Binary Epistemologies of the Discretionary Decision Process' (2007) 16(3) *Social & Legal Studies* 425–47.

[8] For a recent discussion of the challenges and limitations of proportionality at sentencing, see M Tonry, 'Proportionality' in Tonry, *Doing Justice, Preventing Crime* (Oxford, Oxford University Press, 2020).

the traditional means of achieving proportional sentences, namely statutory law and judgments from the appellate courts.[9] Section IV uses the sentencing guidelines operating in England and Wales to illustrate the ways that guidelines may promote proportionality. The English guidelines were selected because they are retributively-oriented[10] and have also served as a model for other jurisdictions.[11] Section V draws attention to two possible weaknesses of the guidelines approach.

II. Components of a Proportional Sentence

Retributive proportionality relates crime seriousness to the severity of assigned punishments. A leading proportionality scholar writes that '[t]he seriousness of crime has two elements: the conduct's degree of harmfulness and the extent of the actor's culpability.'[12] The principle of proportionality[13] and its requirements are clear: punishments should progressively increase in severity to match corresponding increments in offence seriousness and offender culpability. How to implement the principle is less obvious. A court first needs to calibrate the seriousness of a crime and then select a sentence which is of commensurate severity. Yet crime seriousness is a plastic concept.[14] Research demonstrates that there is consensus around offence seriousness rankings involving common crimes[15] – most people would agree that rape is a more serious assault than common assault and that manslaughter is less serious than murder. For many offences in the mid-range of seriousness, however, there is much disagreement regarding seriousness ratings.[16]

[9] Unless stipulated otherwise, all judgments cited in the chapter derive from the Court of Appeal Criminal Division in England and Wales.

[10] A Ashworth notes that 'the emphasis on assessing harm and culpability indicates the centrality of proportionality judgments in English sentencing', in 'Re-Evaluating the Justifications for Aggravation and Mitigation at Sentencing' in J V Roberts (ed), *Mitigation and Aggravation at Sentencing* (Cambridge, Cambridge University Press, 2011) 25.

[11] Modified versions of the English guidelines now operate in South Korea, Scotland, Kenya, Uganda, the Republic of North Macedonia and several Gulf States. The guidelines have also been cited by appellate courts in foreign jurisdictions, eg, *R v SLW*, 2018 ABCA 235; 72 Alta LR (6th) 63 (Alberta Court of Appeal).

[12] A von Hirsch, *Deserved Criminal Sentences* (Oxford, Hart Publishing, 2017) 23. Other scholars share the view: R Fox, 'The Meaning of Proportionality in Sentencing' (1994) 19(3) *Melbourne University Law Review* 489, 498.

[13] This chapter addresses positive proportionality, rather than negative or limiting proportionality. The former is a broader concept. Limiting proportionality sets a limit upon the severity of sanctions; see discussion in R S Frase, 'Theories of Proportionality and Desert' in J Petersilia and K Reitz (eds), *The Oxford Handbook of Sentencing and Corrections* (Oxford, Oxford University Press, 2012) 131–49.

[14] Retributivism itself, the conceptual framework of proportionality, also comes in different forms.

[15] A Ashworth, *Sentencing and Criminal Justice*, 6th edn (Cambridge, Cambridge University Press, 2015) 114–16.

[16] M Tonry notes the 'widely shared intuitions about offense seriousness exist only at the extremes'; 'Is Proportionality in Punishment Possible?' in Tonry (n 8) 10.

If there was universal agreement on the absolute and relative seriousness of crimes, and the factors affecting harm and culpability, implementing proportionality would be straightforward. Without consensus on these issues, however, opinions about proportionality will vary between judges and across courts. Proportionality, parity and consistency will be harder to achieve, and some form of guidance becomes indispensable. Proportionality at sentencing can only be achieved if courts consistently apply factors relevant to harm and culpability, and disregard or downplay factors which have no bearing on these concepts. For example, many factors commonly invoked at sentencing are unrelated to proportionality, plea being the most common. Most defendants receive a sentence reduction, often substantial, in return for pleading guilty. Courts seeking to promote proportionality need to ensure that such factors do not eclipse factors which are central to harm and culpability. The question becomes one of methodology: what is the most effective way of achieving proportionality?

III. Evaluating Existing Sources of Guidance for Courts at Sentencing

A. Legislative Guidance Regarding Proportionality at Sentencing

Statutory law is the primary source of guidance. Many legislatures have placed the proportionality principle and its various sub-requirements on a statutory footing. In some regimes, the principle is explicitly stated in statute. In Canada, for example, section 718.1 of the Criminal Code states that a sentence must be proportionate to the seriousness of the offence and the offender's level of responsibility.[17] Even in jurisdictions without such an explicit direction to courts, proportionality may be inferred from key provisions relating to the use of sanctions and the definition of crime seriousness. For example, in England and Wales, section 152(2) of the Criminal Justice Act 2003 states that:

> The court must not pass a custodial sentence unless it is of the opinion that the offence, or the combination of the offence and one or more offences associated with it, was so serious that neither a fine alone nor a community sentence can be justified for the offence.

Thus, crime seriousness rather than risk of re-offending determines whether an offender is sent to prison. A related provision (section 153(2)) states that a

[17] Other jurisdictions take the same approach. Section 40b of the Sentencing Law of Israel notes that: 'The guiding principle in sentencing is proportionality between the seriousness of the offence and the degree of culpability and the type and severity of punishment', see J V Roberts and O Gazal-Ayal, 'Sentencing Reform in Israel: Exploring the Sentencing Law of 2012' (2013) 46(3) *Israel Law Review* 455.

custodial sentence 'must be for the shortest term … that in the opinion of the court is commensurate with the seriousness of the offence'. Finally, section 143(1) identifies the components of crime seriousness as harm and culpability:

> In considering the seriousness of any offence, the court must consider the offender's culpability in committing the offence and any harm which the offence caused, was intended to cause or might foreseeably have caused.

Some legislatures have gone further and codified the factors which are central to a proportional sentencing model – those related to harm and culpability. The statute could also *proscribe* consideration of certain factors which have no bearing on these components.[18] Directing courts to ignore factors which would undermine proportionality is another means by which the legislature can promote greater proportionality at sentencing. The legislature can also contribute to enhancing proportionality by establishing a coherent structure of maximum penalties which then place limits on trial courts. For example, if the maximum penalty structure is constructed so that crimes of different seriousness attract commensurately distinct maxima, this will help trial courts devise prison sentences which conform to proportionality requirements. At present this is seldom the case; having been created in the nineteenth century, the maximum penalty structure in most common law jurisdictions is outdated.[19] Offences of very different seriousness levels often share a common maximum penalty (despite great differences in the sentences actually imposed), and the maxima bear little relation to the seriousness of the crimes for which they may be imposed.[20] While the maximum penalties may be unrealistically high, they still set a framework which appeal courts refer to in their judgments.

There are limits, however, on the ability of the legislature to ensure proportionality in sentencing practices. One complication arises from the pluralistic nature of most sentencing regimes. In recent years legislatures have directed sentencers to prevent crime through mandatory sentences and other strategies which are inconsistent with proportionality. When proportionality is the primary goal, even the most detailed sentencing statute can only highlight the most important considerations for courts to follow. The Sentencing Act 2002 in New Zealand contains extensive lists of aggravating and mitigating factors, but as scholars have described

[18] eg, s 7(2) of the 1995 Sentencing Act in Western Australia directs courts not to aggravate sentence for the following factors: '(a) the offender pleaded not guilty to it; or (b) the offender has a criminal record; or (c) a previous sentence has not achieved the purpose for which it was imposed.' Another provision in the same Act (s 9AA(4)) limits the size of a sentence reduction which may be awarded for a guilty plea; this protects proportionality.

[19] Many codes (including the Canadian Code) derive from an English Bill drafted by James Fitzjames Stephen in 1883.

[20] The offence of domestic burglary is a good example. In Canada, this offence shares a maximum penalty (life imprisonment) with many far more serious crimes such as rape, although burglary convictions typically result in a non-custodial sanction or a short term of custody, while sentences for rape fall in the range of five to ten years' imprisonment.

the statute as 'a useful beginning', many questions remain, and more guidance is needed.[21] A final limitation concerns the ability of a legislature to respond expeditiously to emerging trends. Bills require legislative time for debate; comprehensive statutory reforms are relatively rare, and amendments sporadic. Sentencing is the area of law most susceptible to populist or reactive legislation, at the expense of principles such as proportionality.[22]

The consequence is that, across most Western nations, sentencing reform in recent decades has done little to promote proportionality. More often, legislative reforms either intentionally or inadvertently undermine the principle. Mandatory sentences of imprisonment which deprive courts of the discretion to consider the individual defendant are the best example of this tendency to undermine proportionality at sentencing.[23] A mandatory sentence is blind to the circumstances of the offence and the individual offender's level of culpability; under these circumstances, achieving proportional sentences will be difficult if not impossible.

B. Judicial Guidance Regarding Proportionality at Sentencing

Judicial guidance emerges from the apex or appellate courts. A number of judgments have articulated the meaning of proportionality and affirmed its significance at sentencing.[24] Over time, the steady accretion of judgments guides courts with respect to the kinds of sentences to be imposed for, say rape, and how these should differ from sentencing for serious assaults. In these judgments the court's attention is restricted to the specific offence (and offender) brought on appeal. More comprehensive guidance emerges from 'guideline' judgments where the court is concerned about more than simply addressing judicial error. Here the court issues guidance for sentencing a range or category of offences and the factors affecting sentencing for these crimes. Guideline judgments provide guidance on general issues. For example, the court may issue guidance on the magnitude of plea-based sentence reductions[25] or the use of victim impact

[21] 'The guidelines needed to specify what factors aggravate or mitigate each offence, why, when and to what extent' – W Young and A King, 'Addressing Problematic Sentencing Factors in the Development of Guidelines' in J V Roberts (ed), *Mitigation and Aggravation at Sentencing* (Cambridge, Cambridge University Press, 2011) 208, 212.

[22] Terrorism-related legislation in the area of sentencing offers examples. Following the terrorist attacks in the United Kingdom in 2018, Parliament rapidly approved amendments to the sentencing for terrorism offences. Section 7 of the Counter-Terrorism and Border Security Act 2019 more than doubled the maximum penalties for crimes such as inciting terrorism. This was done without any proportionality analysis or public consultation.

[23] Most Western nations operate mandatory sentences for some serious crimes and offences such as impaired driving. Section 51A(5)(a)(i) of the Firearms Act 1968 in England and Wales requires a court to impose a minimum term of five years for one of a number of enumerated offences if the offender is aged 18 or over when he committed the offence.

[24] See an important judgment from the Supreme Court of Canada in *Lacasse* 2015 SCC 64; [2015] SCR 1089.

[25] *R v Caley* [2012] EWCA (Crim) 2821, [8].

statements at sentencing.[26] In both contexts, the goal is to promote proportionality by highlighting factors central to the concept and by discouraging courts from taking into account circumstances which may undermine the principle.

However, as with statutes, there are important limits on the effectiveness of appellate guidance.

- First, appellate courts are reactive;[27] they issue guidance only when a sentence is appealed by one of the parties. Accordingly, guidance from higher courts is sporadic, particularly with respect to issues such as mitigation and aggravation.[28] As O'Malley notes, 'appellate review can seldom be relied upon to produce comprehensive and mutually consistent guidelines'.[29] One explanation for the limited and episodic nature of guidance is the high standard of review: appellate courts interfere with trial court sentences only when there has been an error in law or the sentence was 'manifestly unfit'.[30] Appellate review may be an effective remedy for unfit sentences, but broader issues often remain unaddressed.[31]

  Judges will differ in their perceptions of sentencing factors in terms of their relevance and weight at sentencing. The effect of precedent and appellate scrutiny will be limited, and some judicial cultures will exacerbate the variability by actively promoting the concept of 'instinctive synthesis'. This term – most closely associated with Australian courts[32] – rejects any structured approach, arguing that sentencing is best accomplished by judges intuitively considering all relevant circumstances.
- Second, an appellate court has no research function, capacity or expertise (beyond case law reviews). Judges' only access to research or wider sources of information comes from the parties, and under the adversarial model of justice these will not be disinterested submissions. Determining proportionate

[26] *R v Perkins* [2013] 2 Cr App R (S) 460.

[27] 'Appellate courts are primarily a reactive institution', see Report of the Canadian Sentencing Commission, *Sentencing Reform: A Canadian Approach* (Supply and Services Canada, 1987) 85.

[28] J V Roberts, 'Aggravating and Mitigating Factors at Sentencing: Towards Greater Consistency of Application' (2008) *Criminal Law Review* 264.

[29] T O'Malley, 'Living without Guidelines' in A Ashworth and J V Roberts (eds), *Sentencing Guidelines: Exploring the English Model* (Oxford, Oxford University Press, 2013) 234.

[30] A number of reports have noted the limited scope for appeal. The Sentencing Advisory Council in Victoria described the scope for appellate intervention to be 'narrowly confined', in *Sentencing Appeals in Victoria* (Melbourne, Sentencing Advisory Council, 2012) 7.

[31] Later in this chapter I discuss the issue of plea-based sentencing reductions. In many jurisdictions such as Canada, appellate courts have declined to offer guidance on the levels of reduction appropriate for defendants who enter a guilty plea, reflecting the view that this should be left to the discretion of trial courts; D Cole and J V Roberts, 'What's the Point of Pleading Guilty?' (2018) 44 *Criminal Reports* (7th Series) 44.

[32] According to this approach, a court should simultaneously consider all relevant sentencing factors, and this process should not be systematised in any way or broken down into steps. The instinctive synthesis has been endorsed by the Australian High Court, notably in *Markarian v The Queen* (2005) 228 CLR 357.

sentence ranges requires more than merely a trawl through the case law. For example, empirical research with crime victims can shed important light upon the relative seriousness of crimes, as evidenced in their impact on victims.[33] A similar argument can be made with respect to culpability. Since proportionality requires an equivalence between crimes and punishments, research on the impact of different sanctions will also result in a more accurate calibration of the relative experienced severity of sanctions. Without such research, judges will resort to their intuitions of whether, for example, six months in custody is more or less severe than an 18-month intensive community punishment.

- Third, appeal courts sit with a small number of judges, typically three or five. If an apex court issues a key judgment, it may deploy the full court but even this means few individuals, perhaps nine in total. A wider and larger group would likely generate better outcomes. Appellate judges may consult each other informally by seeking the views of colleagues not hearing the appeal, but there is no opportunity to 'road-test' a judgment or draw upon the views of a wider constituency of stakeholders. Appellate courts cannot hold public or professional consultations prior to issuing a judgment, although this exercise is possible for a Sentencing Commission (see discussion below).
- Fourth, if the appellate courts constitute the primary source of guidance, sentencing will evolve far more slowly in response to societal changes. It is trite to observe that the penal value of crimes evolves over time; some offences perceived as serious in the past are now regarded as relatively minor crimes; others have increased in perceived seriousness. Any changes in the actual or perceived seriousness of crimes (or the subjective or perceived severity of punishments) should result in changes to sentencing practices. For example, if the full harm of an offence is only now becoming apparent (possibly as a result of empirical research), the severity of assigned punishments should reflect this evolving awareness. Domestic violence, sexual offending and hate-motivated crimes illustrate this tendency; sentences for these forms of offending have become harsher in recent decades as a response to research upon their effects. In the opposite direction, courts have been increasingly sensitive to sources of offender mitigation such as childhood abuse and foetal alcohol syndrome, again, in response to growing awareness of their impact on an offender's level of culpability.
- The other component of the proportionality equation – sentence severity – also evolves over time. Until recently, the pains, and hence severity, of a prison sentence were deemed to end once the offender left prison. If this were the case, the calibration of severity can be closely modelled by the duration of

[33] Hate motivated crime against minority groups is an example of an aggravating circumstance which was codified in many jurisdictions following research which demonstrated the wider harm created by this form of offending. Research involving offenders can provide insight into the circumstances which diminish a person's level of blameworthiness in ways which may well have escaped the attention of the judiciary.

imprisonment. A four-year sentence would be twice as onerous as a two-year sentence, and once an equivalence was created between say, *x* months of custody and *y* months of home confinement, these 'exchange rates' would not change. However, research has demonstrated the lasting adverse effects of imprisonment on a range of variables post-release, including health, income, employment opportunities, family stability and much else. This more comprehensive awareness of the effects of imprisonment should lead to a recalibration of sentence lengths in order to ensure proportionality.[34] When the courts are the only source of guidance, sentencing practices will evolve only to the extent that the judiciary assimilate these developments into their judgments and sentences. Individual judges will follow their own views and be guided by their own knowledge, although submissions from the parties may also have some influence.

Many of these limitations are avoided when guidance emanates from a Commission empowered to issue guidelines and equipped with an adequate research capacity. Fresh challenges may arise of course, relating primarily to the independence of the guidelines Commission and judicial confidence in, and compliance with, its guidelines.[35] I return to these at the conclusion of the chapter.

IV. Implementing Sentencing Proportionality Through Guidelines

A. The Sentencing Council and the Stepped Approach to Determining a Sentence

Before describing the proportionality-based guidelines operating in England and Wales, readers may benefit from a brief description of the body that devises these guidelines and the general approach to guideline development in this jurisdiction. The guidelines are issued by the Sentencing Council, which was created in 2010.[36]

[34] One of the lessons of this research is that the long-term adverse effects of imprisonment are not linear: very short and very long sentences of imprisonment have more negative effects; see A Ramakers, P Nieuwbeerta, J van Wilsem, R Apel and A Dirkzwager, 'The Past and Future Labor Market Careers of Dutch Prisoners' in A Blokland and V van der Geest (eds), *The Routledge International Handbook of Life-Course Criminology* (New York, Taylor & Francis, 2017) 377–96.

[35] Limitations on space preclude a thorough discussion of the perceived legitimacy of such a body. Sentencing statutes – primary legislation – carry the legitimacy of the democratically elected legislature. Some may regard a professional body which issues guidelines as lacking this level of legitimacy. The response would be that Parliament has devolved authority to issue guidelines to the Council, and the judicial majority of its members ensures the legitimacy which arises from independence of the current government.

[36] The Sentencing Council replaced two previous statutory bodies, the Sentencing Guidelines Council and the Sentencing Advisory Panel, both of which had played a pivotal role in the evolution

The Lord Chief Justice serves as President and the membership of the Council has a judicial majority. This significant degree of judicial involvement was critical to ensuring acceptance by sentencers. The Council has a broad mandate,[37] which includes issuing guidelines for courts.

Although some US guideline systems are advisory,[38] in England and Wales there is a statutory duty on courts to follow the guidelines. Systems of guidance will only achieve or promote the goal of proportionality if courts apply the guidelines. A purely advisory scheme is unlikely to contribute more than the guidance issued by appellate courts.[39] Judicial compliance is therefore necessary. In England and Wales, the statutory compliance requirement is found in section 125(1) of the Coroners and Justice Act 2009 which states that:

> (1) Every court—
> (a) must, in sentencing an offender, follow any sentencing guidelines which are relevant to the offender's case, and
> (b) must, in exercising any other function relating to the sentencing of offenders, follow any sentencing guidelines which are relevant to the exercise of that function, unless the court is satisfied that it would be contrary to the interests of justice to do so.[40]

B. Types of Guidelines: Offence-Specific and Generic

Most US guidelines employ a single grid. Minnesota started with one but now operates three.[41] All State offences are assigned to a row of the grid, with the result that many hundreds of crimes will share the same seriousness level and hence presumptive sentences. Guidance from the Minnesota Sentencing Guidelines Commission is contained within the guidelines' manual and the three grids. No other guidance is issued, and this is typical of the US guidelines. The English

of guidelines; see A Ashworth and J V Roberts, 'The Origins and Nature of Sentencing Guidelines in England and Wales' in A Ashworth and J V Roberts (eds), *Sentencing Guidelines: Exploring the English Model* (Oxford, Oxford University Press, 2013) 1–14.

[37] Section 128 of The Coroners and Justice Act 2009 specifies a number of other duties for the Council. These include monitoring the operation and effect of its guidelines.

[38] eg, in the States of Arkansas, Delaware and Massachusetts; see R S Frase, 'Forty Years of American Sentencing Guidelines: What Have We Learned?' (2019) 48 *Crime and Justice* 79, 99.

[39] Research on advisory or voluntary guidelines in the US has shown they fail to change sentencing practices as effectively as presumptively binding schemes; guidelines need to be enforceable and need to be enforced; G Edwards, S Rushin and J Colquitt, 'The Effects of Voluntary and Presumptive Sentencing Guidelines' (2019) 98(1) *Texas Law Review* 1; M Tonry, *Sentencing Matters* (Oxford, Oxford University Press, 1996) 193.

[40] This wording suggests a relatively restrictive regime. However, a subsequent provision makes it clear that the constraint upon courts is to impose a sentence within the total *offence* range rather than the much narrower *category* sentence range: 'nothing in this section imposes on the court a separate duty … to impose a sentence which is within the category range.' See A Ashworth, 'Coroners and Justice Act 2009: Sentencing Guidelines and the Sentencing Council' (2010) *Criminal Law Review* 389.

[41] mn.gov/sentencing-guidelines/.

guidelines offer more guidance. First, each offence category has its own guideline. The use of offence-specific guidelines allows the Council to reflect differences in the relative seriousness of offences by adjusting the starting-point sentences and sentence ranges contained in the guidelines (discussed below). In addition to its offence-specific guidelines, the English Council has issued several 'generic' guidelines which apply across cases. These cover issues such as: multiple offence sentencing, plea-based sentence discounts, sentencing for domestic abuse, the seriousness of offences and sentencing mentally ill offenders. Proportionality considerations and constraints should guide offence-specific guidelines which apply across all offences. With respect to the former, the starting point for sentences and sentence ranges should be determined by harm and culpability. If proportionality is the guiding principle of the sentencing regime, the generic guidelines should also be shaped by proportionality, promoting relevant circumstances and constraining courts from giving significant weight to non-retributive factors.

C. Devising Guidelines

As noted, an appellate court establishes proportionality over time and across judgments. A sentencing commission has far greater capacity and more time to consider the issues.[42] In practice, the appellate courts work in conjunction with the commission issuing guidelines. This is the case in England and Wales. The Court of Appeal provides guidance on the application of the guidelines and occasionally issues guideline judgments.

When preparing an offence-specific guideline, the Sentencing Council begins by reviewing judgments from the Court of Appeal. These furnish the foundation for the sentence ranges, recommended starting points and factors to be included in the guideline. But the Council will go beyond the case law to review and possibly conduct empirical research on issues relevant to the sentencing of this specific offence. The process will be iterative, allowing for reflection, consultation and modification of a draft guideline. Council discusses a draft guideline on several occasions and then 'road-tests' draft guidelines with practitioners. Finally, there is a statutory consultation period, after which Council will revisit the guideline prior to issuing a definitive version.[43] The consultation period permits all stakeholders and the general public (if they so desire) to provide input into the guidelines. Guidelines can be devised (or revised) far more expeditiously than primary legislation. This permits them to be more reactive to evolving circumstances such

[42] O'Malley notes that 'it is difficult to achieve both cardinal and ordinal proportionality … sentencing commissions are at a distinct advantage in this regard by having the time, opportunity, and facilities to generate comprehensive guidance with due regard to the relative gravity [of crimes]'; O'Malley (n 29) 231.

[43] J V Roberts, 'The Evolution of Sentencing Guidelines in Minnesota and England and Wales' (2019) 48 *Crime and Justice* 187.

as emerging developments in our understanding of the effects of crimes and punishments.

D. Promoting Proportionality

The Council's offence-specific guidelines employ a 'step by step' approach. The guideline aims to ensure that all principal factors are given due consideration, and proportionality is promoted by assigning greater weight to factors related to harm and culpability. Medical diagnosis provides a useful analogy. Confronted with a common constellation of symptoms, experienced clinicians may be tempted to move directly towards what seems an obvious diagnosis. The danger is that they may overlook symptoms pointing towards a different diagnosis. Diagnostic protocols – now formalised into software – ensure a more uniform and systematic approach to diagnosis.

The English guidelines promote proportionality at sentencing by imposing a 'stepped' approach, which is guided by harm and culpability. Section 121(2), a key provision in the Coroners and Justice Act 2009 directs the Council that its guidelines should: 'describe, by reference to one or more of the factors mentioned in subsection (3), different categories of case … which illustrate in general terms the varying degrees of seriousness':

> (3) Those factors are—
> (a) the offender's culpability in committing the offence;
> (b) the harm caused, or intended to be caused or which might foreseeably have been caused, by the offence;
> (c) such other factors as the Council considers to be particularly relevant to the seriousness of the offence in question.

This explicit statutory direction sets the English guidelines apart from other guideline regimes. The provision identifies harm and culpability as the primary determinants of the guidelines, and, as will be seen, this structure emerges clearly from the guidelines themselves. Other guidelines take an approach which reflects less well the twin components of proportionality. In Minnesota, for example, crime seriousness and the offender's criminal history constitute the two dimensions of the sentencing grid.[44] Culpability is absorbed into the axis of seriousness and a non-retributive factor – prior crimes – assumes central importance.

The English guidelines are not purely proportionate or retributive in nature. The objectives of sentencing enunciated in the Criminal Justice Act 2003 include preventive and retributive goals.[45] In addition, other provisions direct courts to

[44] See mn.gov/sentencing-guidelines/; R S Frase, 'Sentencing Guidelines in Minnesota, 1978–2003' in M Tonry (ed), *Crime and Justice* (Chicago, University of Chicago Press, 2005) and for comparative analysis, see Roberts (n 43).

[45] Section 142(1) states that: 'Any court dealing with an offender in respect of his offence must have regard to the following purposes of sentencing – (a) the punishment of offenders, (b) the reduction of

consider factors which are not relevant to proportionality. For example, section 144 of the 2003 Act directs courts to consider a defendant's plea and the stage at which it was entered, while sections 73 and 74 of the Serious Organised Crime and Police Act 2005 direct courts to take into account any assistance offered or provided to the prosecutor or police. The guidelines could not disregard these elements of English sentencing law. Steps 3 and 4 of the guidelines require courts to offer sentence reductions in return for any assistance the defendant provided the prosecution and for the guilty plea. In addition, the lists of mitigating and aggravating factors at Step 2 include factors which are unrelated to proportionality.[46] For these reasons, the guidelines reflect an imperfect proportionality scheme. Given the sentencing framework in this (and other common law jurisdictions), this seems inevitable.

E. Example of an English Guideline

Examining a typical offence-specific guideline illustrates the ways in which proportionality is encouraged. The Street Robbery Guideline[47] lays down nine separate steps for courts to follow.[48] (The Appendix to this chapter contains an extract from the Robbery Guideline consisting of the offence categories at Step 1 and the factors which determine which category is appropriate for the case being sentenced.)

The first step is the most important as it determines the limits of the sentence range that the court will work within as it proceeds through the remaining steps of the guideline. At Step 1 the court assigns the offence to one of three levels of harm and the defendant to one of three levels of culpability (high, medium and lesser). The guideline provides a list of factors which a court should consider to determine the appropriate category of harm and culpability. This list of factors is short, reflecting the fact that these are the most important circumstances[49] and courts should consider only these factors when determining the appropriate category of harm and culpability. Other (less central) factors may be taken into account only later, at Step 2. The exclusive nature of this list is one of the most restrictive elements of the English guidelines and aims to promote a more uniform and proportionate approach across courts.

crime (including its reduction by deterrence), (c) the reform and rehabilitation of offenders, (d) the protection of the public, and (e) the making of reparation by offenders to persons affected by their offences.'

[46] Examples include: 'exemplary conduct', 'determination and/or demonstration of steps having been taken to address addiction or offending behaviour'.

[47] See www.sentencingcouncil.org.uk/publications/item/robbery-definitive-guideline-2/.

[48] In discussing the methodology, we assume that courts do in fact work through all the steps. There is no reason to question the professionalism of sentencers in this respect, but equally there is no way of knowing how faithfully they follow the guideline's methodology. A court could, presumably, ignore the step-by-step structure, decide upon sentence and then work backwards to justify the decision. The use of the methodology must therefore be taken on trust.

[49] The Street Robbery Guideline contains only six harm and five culpability factors (see Appendix).

Once a court has determined the appropriate categories of harm and culpability (applying only the factors listed in the guideline), it moves to Step 2, which provides starting-point sentences and sentence ranges for each category. For example, if the court decides the robbery involved 'intermediate' harm (category 2) committed by an individual of the lowest culpability, the starting point is two years' imprisonment, and the sentence range spans one to four years' custody. Since this sentence range is determined by harm and culpability, and not retributively extraneous factors such as plea, it may be considered a *proportionate* sentence range. The court uses the starting-point sentence and then moves up and down within the category range considering a non-exhaustive list of mitigating and aggravating factors (along with any other factors proposed by the advocates). This exercise results in a provisional sentence.

Thereafter, the court works through additional steps, including awarding credit for any assistance given to the police or prosecution (Step 3) or a reduction in return for a guilty plea (Step 4). These two considerations are external to considerations of harm or culpability, and for this reason they are considered at a separate step. For example, assuming the provisional sentence after considering all relevant sentencing factors was three years' imprisonment, the court would normally reduce this by one-third if the defendant had entered a guilty plea at his or her first court appearance. The one-third reduction arises from the recommendations contained in a separate guideline regulating plea-based discounts (discussed later in this chapter).

F. Proportionality and Sentencing Factors

Establishing proportionality requires courts to separate cases in terms of their relative seriousness, and this entails considering the relevant mitigating and aggravating factors. If proportionality-relevant factors are overlooked or non-retributive factors given excessive weight, the appropriate distinctions will not be made, and proportionality will be undermined.

The number of potential mitigating and aggravating factors is vast. Some factors are obvious: the extent of the victim's injuries; the amount of money stolen or defrauded. Other circumstances are less clearly relevant or are contested. In practice, many factors are cited in mitigation, only some of which attract consensus. In England and Wales, courts are directed to take into account 'any matters that in the opinion of the court, are relevant in mitigation'.[50] This permissive provision allows judges much discretion in deciding what to consider in terms of mitigation. Factors may be ambiguous or may operate as mitigation or aggravation. Intoxication may aggravate if the offender, a regular drinker, routinely uses alcohol as a prelude to offending. Yet a normally teetotal student who commits

[50] Section 166(1) Criminal Justice Act 2003.

a crime after consuming alcohol while celebrating his graduation may plausibly claim some 'out of character' mitigation.[51] Some factors may mitigate or aggravate, depending upon the individual circumstances of the case.

One goal of any system of guidance is to bring some order to the panoply of factors potentially relevant to the sentencing decision. In the case of the English guidelines there is a need to prioritise those directly related to proportionality. Many variables will influence crime seriousness and culpability, and advocates will make submissions on a wide range of factors. Defence advocates represent the best interests of the client and will appeal to all plausible mitigating factors, including those unrelated to proportionality.[52] Mercy is often regarded as the expression of unprincipled leniency; a court is urged to mitigate sentence out of sympathy for an offender on grounds unrelated to the harm caused or his level of blameworthiness for that harm. If judges act upon their personal sympathy for defendants to the disregard of the core components, proportionality will be undermined. A mechanism is needed therefore to ensure that courts do not lose sight of the determinants of a proportionate sanction or to prevent courts overweighting factors which are peripheral or extraneous with respect to proportionality.

The guideline structure provides some limited structure to mitigating and aggravating factors. The English guideline structure creates two tiers of factors, those of primary relevance[53] to harm or culpability (located at Step 1)[54] and those of more limited relevance (assigned to Step 2). Criminal history offers a good example of a sentencing factor which needs to be constrained in order to protect proportionality. Prior convictions carry great intuitive appeal as an aggravator at sentencing and are taken into account in all jurisdictions.[55] However, prior crimes are not considered relevant to a proportionate sentence by most retributive theories and scholars.[56] Accordingly, if they carry great weight at sentencing, they will result in a loss of proportionality. Frase notes that US guidelines which assign great

[51] The Sentencing Council's guidelines take a different view: 'commission of the offence whilst under the influence of drugs or alcohol' is an aggravating factor located at Step 2 across all guidelines.

[52] For example, the defendant may have made some important contribution to society, or served the country in some capacity, and this may be cited in mitigation; see discussion in M Wasik, *A Practical Approach to Sentencing*, 5th edn (Oxford, Oxford University Press, 2014) 3.

[53] The Council's first guideline described the Step 1 factors as those which 'comprise the principal factual elements of the offence'. See www.sentencingcouncil.org.uk/wp-content/uploads/Assault_definitive_guideline-Crown_Court.pdf, at 4.

[54] The Step 1–Step 2 distinction is helpful because it guides sentencers as to the relative importance of sentencing factors, but it is not without problems. One obvious difficulty is that the Council must be able to distinguish factors which should be at Step 1 rather than 2. Readers reviewing the factor placements may perceive some anomalies, namely factors placed at Step 1 which should be classified at Step 2 (and vice versa).

[55] R Hester, R S Frase, J V Roberts and K L Mitchell, 'Prior Record Enhancements at Sentencing: Unsettled Justifications and Unsettling Consequences' (2018) 47(1) *Crime and Justice* 209; J V Roberts, *Punishing Persistent Offenders* (Oxford, Oxford University Press, 2008).

[56] To oversimplify a complex theoretical debate, retributivists generally argue that previous crimes affect neither culpability for the current crime nor the seriousness of the offence for which the offender is now being sentenced. See discussion in ch 1 in R S Frase and J V Roberts, *Paying for the Past: Prior Record Enhancements in the US Sentencing Guidelines* (Oxford, Oxford University Press, 2019).

weight to an offender's previous crimes will suffer from a loss of offence-based proportionality.[57]

Previous convictions are a statutory aggravating factor in England and Wales[58] and a guidelines scheme could play an important role in constraining the effect of previous crimes, thus protecting proportionality. The English guidelines are ambivalent with respect to this issue. They constrain the aggravating effect of prior convictions by placing this factor at Step 2 rather than Step 1 of the guidelines methodology. On the other hand, for certain high-recidivism offences (such as burglary), the guidelines suggest that relevant recent convictions are likely to result in an upward adjustment[59] (to the sentence). The current guidelines may need to do more to restrict courts from sentencing on the offender's record, but at least the means to achieving this objective is at hand.

The purpose of providing a list of the most important factors is clear: if all courts have the same core set of factors to consider, this should promote more uniform and proportionate outcomes.[60] Finally, the English guidelines also give guidance regarding the cases where certain factors may carry less or more weight for specific offences. For example, in its Rape Guideline the Council notes that 'previous good character or exemplary conduct should not normally be given significant weight'.[61] Some may disagree with the direction that good conduct by the offender should carry less weight when the offence involves very significant harm. The point, however, (as with previous convictions) is that guidelines permit this kind of direction which otherwise only come from the appellate courts, subject to the limitations noted earlier.

G. 'Generic' Guidelines Applying to All Offences

Offence-specific guidance needs to be supplemented by additional guidelines regarding sentencing issues relevant to all cases. As noted, the Council has issued a number of generic guidelines dealing with general issues. The Council is unique

[57] Frase (n 38) 79. In some US jurisdictions prior crimes carry significantly more weight than the crime of conviction; see R S Frase, J V Roberts and R Hester, 'Adverse Impacts on Offense-based Proportionality and Prison-use Priorities', ch 6 in Frase and Roberts, *Paying for the Past* (n 56).

[58] Section 143(2) Criminal Justice Act 2003.

[59] www.sentencingcouncil.org.uk/wp-content/uploads/Burglary-definitive-guideline-Web.pdf, at 9.

[60] A Ashworth criticises statutes, and presumably by inference the guidelines, for not providing 'any guidance as to the relevant weight [of factors] or as to the impact they should have on sentence', in 'Re-evaluating the Justifications for Aggravation and Mitigation at Sentencing' in J V Roberts (ed), *Mitigation and Aggravation at Sentencing* (Cambridge, Cambridge University Press, 2011) 21. Weighting seems challenging, to say the least, for factors such as remorse and many other circumstances. Additional guidance may involve specifying which factors may (or may not) determine whether the offender is sentenced to imprisonment. As noted, the English guidelines do at least distinguish primary from secondary factors, even if they do not explicitly use these terms.

[61] www.sentencingcouncil.org.uk/wp-content/uploads/Sexual-offences-definitive-guideline-Web.pdf. A similar warning is contained in an overarching guideline on domestic abuse: www.sentencingcouncil.org.uk/wp-content/uploads/Overarching-Principles-Domestic-Abuse-definitive-guideline-Web.pdf, at 4.

among sentencing commissions in this respect; no other sentencing guidelines authority issues guidelines on general matters. Guidance in the grid-based guidelines found across the US, for example, is restricted to the sentence ranges and midpoints found in the grid, with some very limited additional material in the guidelines' manual.[62]

For example, how should courts ensure proportionality when the offender is to be sentenced for many crimes which vary in terms of their nature and seriousness? When this occurs, the complex task of determining sentence becomes even more challenging.[63] One approach favoured by courts of appeal around the world involves applying the principle of totality. This principle attempts to achieve an overall degree of proportionality in such cases, but as with other aspects of sentencing, a guideline may offer more detailed and comprehensive guidance. The English Council's Guideline on Sentencing in Multiple Offence Cases[64] has been criticised by scholars for providing insufficient guidance. Again, however, the point is rather that it provides an illustration of how a guidelines regime might enhance the proportionality principle at sentencing, even if this particular example is insufficient.

Guidelines can prescribe, proscribe or limit the effects of particular sentencing factors. In any pluralistic sentencing regime (such as that operating in England and Wales), factors extraneous to proportionality will play a role. The guidelines must limit the influence of such factors if proportionality is to be preserved. Plea is an example of a factor unrelated to harm and culpability and therefore to proportionality. Defendants in all common law jurisdictions benefit from a sentence reduction if they plead guilty, although the rationale and the magnitude of reductions vary widely.[65] Guidance is needed because this issue is particularly susceptible to judicial interpretation and judges may hold different views on the appropriate discount to be awarded as well as the circumstances determining the level of reduction. It is clear, however, that significant discounts will undermine proportionality. If offenders convicted of the same serious crime receive very different sentences because one pleaded guilty and the other was convicted after trial, proportionality and retributive parity will be affected.

Some method of constraining the power of plea to reduce sentence is therefore necessary. The English Council's Guilty Plea Guideline[66] offers some protection for the proportionality principle. Prior to the Guideline, guilty plea reductions were

[62] See, eg, mn.gov/sentencing-guidelines/.

[63] For discussion, see J Ryberg, J V Roberts and J de Keijser (eds), *Sentencing Multiple Crimes* (Oxford, Oxford University Press, 2019).

[64] Available at: www.sentencingcouncil.org.uk/publications/item/offences-taken-into-consideration-and-totality-definitive-guideline/.

[65] A Flynn and A Freiberg, 'Plea Negotiations and Sentencing' in Flynn and Freiberg, *Plea Negotiations. Pragmatic Justice in an Imperfect World* (London, Palgrave Macmillan, 2018) 147–83; M Langer, 'Plea Bargaining, Conviction without Trial, and the Global Administration of Criminal Convictions' (2021) 4 *Annual Review of Criminology*, in press.

[66] Sentencing Council of England and Wales, *Reduction in Sentence for a Guilty Plea. Definitive Guideline*, available at: www.sentencingcouncil.org.uk/publications/item/reduction-in-sentence-for-a-guilty-plea-definitive-guideline-2/.

less predictable, and courts periodically awarded very large reductions in order to 'crack' or resolve trials of great complexity or involving multiple defendants. The English Guideline[67] places a stricter limit on the reduction which normally[68] may be awarded. Defendants who plead guilty at their first court appearance receive a *maximum* reduction of one-third off their custodial sentence. A maximum of one-third may be still be too high for some fundamentalist retributivists. The point, again, is that a guideline offers a mechanism for protecting proportionality which is absent in non-guideline jurisdictions.

V. Concerns Regarding the Guideline Approach

Guidelines should be subject to critical scrutiny, and concerns have been expressed about the concept in general and the English guidelines.[69] There may be some dangers associated with the guideline approach to proportionality. It is sometimes argued that a structured (guideline) approach to sentencing encourages a less thorough consideration of case characteristics and of the relationship between different factors. This may lead to a reduction in individualisation at sentencing. Graeme Brown asserts that guidelines are responsible for 'sacrificing individualised justice'.[70] This remains an unproven hypothesis, however, and the only empirical research on the question found that individualisation increased rather than declined after the introduction of the guidelines in England and Wales.[71]

The use of guidelines may also have some less obvious adverse effects. Any transformative effect of the sentence may also be weakened when the outcome is – under the simpler and more rigid US schemes – largely determined in advance.[72] Defendants in Minnesota can predict their sentence in advance of the sentencing hearing. This makes sentencing in that jurisdiction more predictable and transparent, but it may also come at a cost. Defendants may perceive their sentence to have been determined by the Minnesota Sentencing Guidelines Commission rather than the presiding judge.

[67] The US guidelines have no equivalent to this Guideline, with the result that sentence discounts are likely to be less predictable and in practice much higher than in England and Wales.

[68] Courts retain some discretion to award higher (or lower) reductions than those stipulated in the Guideline; see J V Roberts and B Bradford, 'Sentence Reductions for a Guilty Plea: New Empirical Evidence from England and Wales' (2015) 12(2) *Journal of Empirical Legal Studies* 187.

[69] Critics of the English guidelines have generally focused on aspects other than proportionality, so they will not be discussed here.

[70] G Brown, *Criminal Sentencing as Practical Wisdom* (Oxford, Hart Publishing, 2017) 179.

[71] J V Roberts, J Pina-Sanchez and I Marder, 'Individualisation at Sentencing: The Effects of Sentencing Guidelines and "Preferred" Numbers' (2018) *Criminal Law Review* 123.

[72] 'The judge's power to weigh all of the circumstances of the particular case and all of the purposes of criminal punishment represented an important acknowledgment of the moral personhood of the defendant and of the moral dimension of crime and punishment', K Stith and J A Cabranes, 'Judging Under the Federal Sentencing Guidelines' (1996–97) 91 *Northwestern University Law Review* 1247, 1252.

Another potential weakness of a system in which an authority external to the courts determines sentence ranges is that it can become politicised and lose its judicial independence. In some US jurisdictions, appointments to the Commission and amendments of the guidelines fall within the jurisdiction of the legislature or the State Governor. This arrangement opens the door for populist influences to undermine the proportionality of the guidelines. The Minnesota Sentencing Guidelines Commission has been under political pressure since its creation, resulting in an escalation in sentence severity over time. In 1991, Richard Frase noted '[t]he pressure for increased sentence severity and legislative control'.[73] These threats are real, and enabling legislation should ensure that the Council or Commission which issues the guidelines is insulated from such pressures. One way of achieving this is to create a judicial majority on the Council, as is the case in England and Wales. There is no evidence that, in its 10-year existence, the Council has been influenced by the government. In short, judicial independence is critical to ensure the integrity of the guidelines.

VI. Conclusion: The Need for Empirical Research

The debate over the utility of sentencing guidelines versus the more discretionary alternative takes place largely at the conceptual level. Ideally, research would shed light on the relative effectiveness of different approaches to promoting proportionality. Do guidelines promote proportionality more effectively than a more discretionary regime guided only by the appellate courts? Empirical researchers have generally overlooked this aspect of sentencing. In contrast, consistency and disparity have been studied for almost a century now by empirical researchers in many jurisdictions.[74]

Difficulties in conceptualising and measuring the concept may explain the absence of empirical research on proportionality. Consistency is more straightforward.[75] With respect to prison sentences, the standard deviation which represents the variance or spread in a distribution constitutes a good measure of consistency. But how is proportionality measured? One possibility would involve a ranking of serious offences based on the mean or median lengths of imprisonment

[73] R S Frase, 'Sentencing Reform in Minnesota, Ten Years After: Reflections on Dale G. Parent's Structuring Criminal Sentences: The Evolution of Minnesota's Sentencing Guidelines' (1991) 75(3) *Minnesota Law Review* 727, 732.

[74] F Gaudet, G S Harris and C W St John, 'Individual Differences in the Sentencing Tendencies of Judges' (1933) 23(5) *Journal of Criminal Law & Criminology* 811.

[75] On the issue of defining consistency, see L Harris, *Consistency in Sentencing: Is the Current Guidance in England and Wales Adequate?* (PhD thesis, Oxford 2019), available at: ora.ox.ac.uk/objects/uuid:fdaa2e1f-21d0-4b9e-b2e6-7d103d6c1665, and J Pina-Sanchez, 'Defining and Measuring Consistency in Sentencing' in J V Roberts (ed), *Exploring Sentencing Practice in England and Wales* (London, Palgrave Macmillan, 2015) 76–92.

as a measure of severity.[76] This kind of analysis would be useful to see whether offences are punished proportionately. For example, are the various levels of assault separated by appropriate increments in sentence severity? An absence of proportionality could be inferred if two crimes of very different seriousness attracted a similar average sentence at the trial court level. This 'severity index' measures harm but not culpability;[77] it is a start, however. Researchers could then compare the degree to which proportionality is respected in jurisdictions with and without guidelines. Such analyses would help resolve disputes about the relative advantages of competing systems with respect to proportionality.

Proportionality guides the allocation of punishments across the common law jurisdictions. Yet simply declaring the principle is insufficient to ensure that the principle is observed in sentencing practices at the trial court level. There is too much subjectivity regarding the factors affecting crime seriousness and offender culpability. Some guidance is necessary, and there are well-documented limits on the effectiveness of the appellate courts in this respect. Guidelines issued by a sentencing council offer a more effective and responsive means of achieving proportionality at sentencing,[78] and this chapter has identified the ways that this is attempted by the English guidelines.

[76] Using custodial sentence lengths as the 'dependent variable' restricts the external validity of the research (only imprisonable offences would be included) but is necessary to avoid the complexities arising from the use of multiple sanctions.

[77] There are of course other complications. The proposed analysis assumes some measure of seriousness independent of the severity of assigned punishments. This may have to be created *de nouveau* by asking judges to rank the seriousness of offences, taking into account the typical case of each crime. Their rankings could then be correlated with a ranking of offences based upon sentence length.

[78] For many countries at least. O'Malley suggests that in small, less populous jurisdictions, such as Ireland, a more robust system of appellate review may be sufficient; O'Malley (n 29) 235. Guidelines may be indispensable in England and Wales where there are approximately 27,000 sentencers (including lay magistrates and professional judges).

APPENDIX:

Extract from Sentencing Council Robbery Guideline

STEP ONE
Determining the offence category

The court should determine the offence category with reference **only** to the factors listed in the tables below. In order to determine the category the court should assess **culpability** and **harm**.

The court should weigh all the factors set out below in determining the offender's culpability.

Where there are characteristics present which fall under different levels of culpability, the court should balance these characteristics to reach a fair assessment of the offender's culpability.

Culpability demonstrated by one or more of the following:	
A – High culpability	• Use of a weapon to inflict violence • Production of a bladed article or firearm or imitation firearm to threaten violence • Use of very significant force in the commission of the offence • Offence motivated by, or demonstrating hostility based on any of the following characteristics or presumed characteristics of the victim: religion, race, disability, sexual orientation or transgender identity
B – Medium culpability	• Production of a weapon other than a bladed article or firearm or imitation firearm to threaten violence • Threat of violence by any weapon (but which is not produced) • Other cases where characteristics for categories A or C are not present
C – Lesser culpability	• Involved through coercion, intimidation or exploitation • Threat or use of minimal force • Mental disability or learning disability where linked to the commission of the offence

Harm The court should consider the factors set out below to determine the level of harm that has been caused or was intended to be caused to the victim.	
Category 1	• Serious physical and/or psychological harm caused to the victim • Serious detrimental effect on the business
Category 2	• Other cases where characteristics for categories 1 or 3 are not present
Category 3	• No/minimal physical or psychological harm caused to the victim • No/minimal detrimental effect on the business

Source: Sentencing Council of England and Wales, available at: www.sentencingcouncil.org.uk/publications/item/robbery-definitive-guideline-2/.

13

Proportionality in Asset Confiscation Proceedings*

JOHAN BOUCHT

I. Introduction

Proportionality is an important concept in many areas of law. Its precise meaning varies, but common to all interpretational efforts is that it involves a degree of balancing between interests. Proportionality plays an important role under the law of the European Convention on Human Rights (ECHR) concerning restrictions, for example, on the right to property under Article 1 Protocol No 1 to the ECHR (ECHR-P1) or the rights defined in Articles 8–11 ECHR, but also under EU law, particularly Article 5(4) of the Treaty on European Union (TEU) and the Protocol on the Application of the Principles of Subsidiarity and Proportionality.[1] It is also an important methodological tool used in national jurisdictions for the constitutional assessment of restrictions of constitutionally protected rights, for example, criminalisations and administrative decisions or actions (eg, the use of force by police officers). Furthermore, proportionality is a major principle in criminal law, used to convey the idea that the severity of the punishment of an offender should fit the gravity of the offence. This aspect of proportionality is also a feature of EU criminal law (Article 49 of the Charter of Fundamental Rights of the EU).

Asset confiscation relates to the process of depriving offenders of assets that are or represent criminal proceeds, obtained through unlawful conduct.[2] As such, asset confiscation constitutes an important part of the criminal justice regime in most jurisdictions.

* I wish to thank Gustaf Almkvist, Antony Duff, Ingvild Bruce, Ian Smith and the editors for their valuable and constructive comments on earlier drafts of this chapter. All remaining errors are entirely my own responsibility.

[1] 2012/C 326/01.

[2] Asset confiscation should be kept distinct from, for example, forfeiture of instrumentalities (eg, the tools that were used for committing burglary) or criminal products (eg, illicitly produced alcohol), as the various forms of confiscation fulfil different purposes and are, thus, justified on different grounds.

This chapter considers the relevance of proportionality in asset confiscation proceedings.

II. Proportionality

The essence of proportionality lies in the balancing of interests. In a criminal law context, a distinction is sometimes made between prospective and retrospective proportionality.[3] This distinction can be explained in the following terms. Prospective proportionality is an instrument for determining the *validity* of a norm (or of a particular application of a norm to a certain set of factual circumstances) restricting a protected right in light of a superior set of norms (such as a national constitution, human rights or EU law) or on balance with other protected rights.[4] This assessment can be seen as being forward-looking in nature.

The exact formulation of this principle may vary among jurisdictions, but the balancing operation requires at least that the purpose of the measure be an element of the assessment. Its standard formulation, however, inspired by German administrative law, often comprises four different sub-principles: 1) legitimate aim, 2) suitability to achieve the goal (rational aim), 3) necessity for reaching the aim, and 4) proportionality *stricto sensu* in regard to the aim.[5]

[3] See, eg, A von Hirsch, *Proportionalitet och straffbestämning* (Uppsala, Iustus förlag, 2001) 28; P Asp, *The Substantive Criminal Law Competence of the EU* (Stockholm, Skrifter utgivna av Juridiska fakulteten vid Stockholms universitet, 2012) 188–90; J Boucht, *The Limits of Asset Confiscation. On Legitimising Extended Appropriation of Criminal Proceeds* (Oxford, Hart Publishing, 2017) 168–70 and R A Duff's chapter 2 in this volume. On the historical evolution of retributive proportionality in criminal law, see Nestor Courakis' and Vagia Polyzoidou's chapter 6 in this volume.

[4] For example, for German law, see the Federal Constitutional Court decision BVerfG, Beschluss des Zweiten Senats vom 9. März 1994 – 2 BvL 43/92 s 120; for Finnish law, see opinion GrUU 243/1997 ed, 5 of the Constitutional committee of the Finnish Parliament and for Swedish law, see s 21 of the Constitution (Regeringsformen); see also the Swedish Supreme Court's judgment *NJA 2012* s 400. Proportionality as a constitutional principle also plays an important role, eg, in Canada and South Africa. For an overview, see A Barak, *Proportionality. Constitutional Rights and Their Limitations* (Cambridge, Cambridge University Press, 2012) 181–202. Proportionality as a methodological tool was originally developed by the Prussian Oberverwaltungsgericht (Higher Administrative Court) as a means of controlling the administrative powers of the police. On this development of proportionality, see Barak (ibid) 175–81.

[5] See Barak (n 4) 131–33. As indicated, however, this is not a universal formulation. There is, for example, some discussion as to whether or not the purpose is an independent element or forms part of the actual balancing act. R Alexy, 'Proportionality and Rationality' in V C Jackson and M V Tushnet, *Proportionality: New Frontiers, New Challenges* (Cambridge, Cambridge University Press, 2017) 14, argues that the legitimate purpose as an independent element is in fact superfluous and may even pose a danger for the rationality of the proportionality test, as it forms an integral part of the actual balancing operation (ie, proportionality *stricto sensu*). Moreover, in ECHR law, the legitimate aim has traditionally not been included in the proportionality assessment but tends to be considered separately. See, eg, B Rainey, E Wicks and C Ovey, *Jacobs, White & Ovey. The European Convention on Human Rights*, 6th edn (Oxford, Oxford University Press, 2014) 324–25. Necessity can also either constitute an independent element (see Barak (n 4) 175–81) or form part of the actual balancing operation, as in ECHR law, see C Grabenwarter and K Pabel, *Europäische Menschenrechtskonvention. Ein Studienbuch*, 4th edn (München, CH Beck, 2012) 129 s 14.

Assessing whether or not a prospectively proportionate balance has been struck between the interests of the state and those of the individual can be based, not only on substantive aspects (for instance, how severe a prescribed sanction is), but also on procedural considerations.[6] This relates to the overall fairness of the proceedings, for example, leading up to a particular sanction, the availability of a fair hearing – where the aggrieved individual has the opportunity to effectively challenge the measures – as well as the standard and burden of proof applied in these proceedings etc.

Retrospective proportionality, by contrast, refers to the quantification principle used for sanctioning purposes. This principle sets forth a balancing act between the seriousness of the offence and the magnitude of the sanction and calls for the sentence to be proportionate, or at least not (grossly) disproportionate, in its severity to the gravity of the offence.[7] Focusing on the relationship between a past act and a fitting punishment, it may be seen as being backward-looking in nature.

First of all, as regards terminology, one may ask whether 'prospective' and 'retrospective' are ideal denominations for these two functions of proportionality. To the extent that a distinction is necessary, it might be more illuminating to base the terminology on the functional differences between the two, as described above. Terms such as 'norm proportionality' and 'quantification proportionality' may be more adequate. These terms will be used in the following.

Norm proportionality and quantification proportionality are often treated as two separate categories.[8] Asp notes that while both involve a balancing act, the focus differs: whereas prospective proportionality concerns the relationship between the measure and the aim, retrospective proportionality focuses on the correlation between the seriousness of the offence and the sanction.[9] Moreover, while retrospective proportionality is based on both objective and subjective elements, prospective proportionality is based mainly on objective elements.[10] Kaspar also observes that retrospective proportionality comes without any discussion of the purpose of the legislation; a reasonable degree of proportionality between the conduct in question and the punishment suffices.[11]

However, whether or not retrospective proportionality is a separate and independent proportionality category is in fact not quite clear, as the two proportionality types interact. In a criminal law context, norm proportionality is of

[6] For example, ancillary to the substantive proportionality requirement inherent in the right to property under Art 1 ECHR-P1 there is also a procedural requirement analogous to Art 6(1) ECHR. The purpose of this is to ensure that the operation of the system and its impact on the person's property rights are neither arbitrary nor unforeseeable. See, eg, *Borzhonov v Russia* App no 18274/04 (ECtHR, 22 September 2009) [60].

[7] A von Hirsch, *Censure and Sanctions* (Oxford, Oxford University Press, 1993) 1.

[8] See, eg, von Hirsch (n 3) 28, Asp (n 3) 188–90 and Duff's chapter 2 in this volume.

[9] Asp (n 3) 194.

[10] ibid.

[11] J Kaspar, *Verhältnismäßigkeit und Grundrechtsschutz im Präventionsstrafrecht* (Baden-Baden, Nomos, 2014) 332.

principal importance for the legislator but may also be relevant for the courts when they constitutionally assess the scope of a particular criminalisation in light of a protected right (for instance, the right to free speech).[12] Quantification proportionality, by contrast, is of principal importance for the courts when they assess the magnitude of a fitting punishment in view of the penal value of a particular criminal offence.[13] However, at the legislative phase, and as part of norm proportionality, quantification proportionality not only bears on the justification of criminalisation regarding whether the conduct in question is serious enough (wrongful enough, harmful enough) to merit criminalisation but also on the prescribed penal latitudes so as to facilitate equivalence in relation to prescribed penal latitudes for other (similar/dissimilar) offences.

Therefore, for purposes of norm proportionality, quantification proportionality can actually be seen as forming part (as a sub-category) of the final stage of that assessment, ie, proportionality *stricto sensu*. For example, the German Federal Constitutional Court held that in the field of criminal law, proportionality in combination with the guilt principle entail that the punishment must be proportionate to the harmfulness of the offence and the culpability of the offender.[14] The involvement of the guilt principle (*Schuldprinzip*) in the field of criminal punishment proper also explains why the assessment of quantification proportionality, unlike norm proportionality, is based on both objective and subjective elements. That quantification proportionality forms part of the final stage would also seem to explain why quantification proportionality comes without any discussion of the purpose of the legislation.

However, in order to find a deserved response to culpable wrongdoing, provided that norm proportionality does not become an issue, quantification proportionality will fulfil a function in its own right as a quantification principle.

Any reference to 'proportionality' in the text below should be understood against this background.

[12] One example is the Swedish Supreme Court's judgment *NJA 2012* s 212 concerning the scope of the criminalisation of possession of child pornography (ch 16 s 10a of the Swedish Penal Code). In this case, the defendant, who was a translator of Japanese literature and an expert on Japanese comic books, had 51 so-called Manga drawings with sexually explicit motifs. The majority of the drawings consisted of drawings of fantasy figures and were clearly not depictions of a person appearing to be child. The question was whether depictions of fantasy figures amounted to child pornography under the provision. In assessing whether or not it would amount to a violation of the freedom of speech and information under the Swedish Constitution to convict the defendant, the Court relied on the proportionality principle. It concluded that criminalisation of these drawings would go farther than necessary to satisfy the aim of the provision, and acquitted the defendant.

[13] Moreover, quantification proportionality may also be relevant, eg, to the police in deciding whether it is worth devoting resources to investigating particular crimes and to prosecutors in deciding whether it is worth prosecuting the crime in question.

[14] BVerfG, Beschluss des Zweiten Senats vom 26. Februar 2008 – 2 BvR 392/07 s 37: 'Im Bereich staatlichen Strafens folgt aus dem Schuldprinzip und aus dem Grundsatz der Verhältnismäßigkeit, dass die Schwere einer Straftat und das Verschulden des Täters zu der Strafe in einem gerechten Verhältnis stehen müssen.'

III. Three Generations of Asset Confiscation Schemes

The development of asset confiscation schemes can be described in terms of 'generations', whereby each generation of schemes takes the confiscation of assets one step further away from the predicate offence.[15]

First-generation asset confiscation schemes are represented by rules on what I refer to as regular (or ordinary) criminal confiscation.[16] This kind of confiscation follows upon the conviction of the offender of a criminal offence liable to give rise to economic benefit. Only proceeds that the state is able to link causally to the offence of which the defendant has been duly convicted may be confiscated (for example the profits from selling a certain amount of narcotic drugs).

Second-generation confiscation schemes are constituted by rules on so-called extended criminal confiscation.[17] Rather than focusing on the benefit from a particular offence, extended confiscation often targets assets stemming from indistinct prior 'criminal activity' that the defendant is suspected of having been involved in. Traditional criminal procedural safeguards are usually watered down, often by reversing the burden of proof, for example by means of statutory presumptions or by lowering the standard of proof. However, a trigger conviction is still required. The measure is far-reaching and may often facilitate the confiscation of the defendant's entire possessions.

Third-generation asset confiscation rules are represented by non-conviction-based confiscation (NCB confiscation).[18] Whereas first and second-generation confiscation rules are found in many (if not most) jurisdictions, rules on NCB confiscation are less common. There are different kinds of NCB confiscation schemes. One is a hybrid model, which forms part of the criminal confiscation regime, but often operates with a lower standard of proof and no requirement to concretise the offence(s) from which the assets allegedly originate. This kind of regime can be found, eg, in German law.

Another is the civil recovery model, which operates independently from the criminal process. In Europe, this kind of NCB confiscation scheme has been implemented, for example, in Bulgaria, Ireland, Italy and the UK. The civil model differs from its 'criminal' counterparts in several respects. First, whereas in criminal confiscation proceedings, the existence of a predicate criminal conviction

[15] See J Boucht, 'Asset Confiscation in Europe – Past, Present, and Future Challenges' (2019) 26 *Journal of Financial Crime* 526, 529–30.

[16] See, eg, Art 4 of Directive 2014/42/EU of the European Parliament and of the Council of 3 April 2014 on the freezing and confiscation of instrumentalities and proceeds of crime in the European Union, OJ 2014 L 127/39–50.

[17] See, eg, Art 5 of Directive 2014/42/EU (n 16).

[18] The development of unexplained wealth mechanisms may be seen as a fourth generation of schemes, Boucht (n 15) 530. These can have different meanings, but, for example, an unexplained wealth order under the UK regime, implemented under ss 262A–362J of the Proceeds of Crime Act (POCA) 2002, means that the burden of explanation will be placed on the respondent for the purpose of subsequent civil recovery proceedings.

is a necessary prerequisite for confiscation, NCB confiscation is often available irrespective of the existence of a criminal conviction or criminal proceedings in general. Secondly, whereas criminal confiscation is normally pursued in connection with criminal proceedings, NCB confiscation proceedings are often pursued as civil or administrative proceedings. Thirdly, whereas criminal confiscation proceedings, being part of the criminal process, are often *in personam*, ie, directed against an individual, NCB confiscation proceedings are often considered to be *in specie*, ie, directed against the property as such.

IV. Proportionality and Asset Confiscation

A. Introduction

In the following I wish to discuss, first, the relevance proportionality has, or should have, in confiscation proceedings; secondly, what proportionality means, or what it should mean, in such proceedings; and thirdly, how proportionality, understood in this way, can be applied to the three kinds of confiscation schemes referred to in section III.

B. The Relevance of Proportionality in Confiscation Proceedings

The European Court of Human Rights (ECtHR) case *Paulet v United Kingdom* concerned the confiscation of the applicant's wages following his conviction for obtaining employment using a false passport.[19] The applicant complained that the confiscation order against him was disproportionate as it amounted to the confiscation of his entire savings over nearly four years of genuine work, without any distinction being made between his case and those involving more serious criminal offences such as drug trafficking or organised crime. The majority of the ECtHR Chamber hearing the case held that there had been a violation of the right to property under Article 1 ECHR-P1, as the scope of the review carried out by the domestic courts was too narrow to satisfy the requirement of 'fair balance' inherent in the provision.

The dissenting Judge Wojtyczek was critical of the conclusions of the majority and argued that substantive proportionality has no place in confiscation

[19] *Paulet v United Kingdom* App no 6219/08 (ECtHR, 13 May 2014). *Paulet* was decided by the national courts before the ground-breaking judgment by the UK Supreme Court in *R v Waya* [2013] 1 AC 294, which introduced, by reference to Art 1 ECHR-P1, proportionality into the English confiscation regime. The ECtHR indicated in the judgment that the assessment introduced by the *Waya* judgment would have complied with the minimum standards laid down by the Convention.

proceedings. He maintained that the confiscation of the proceeds of crime is a criminal-law measure based on natural justice. Illegal gains should therefore not be considered to fall within the scope of application of Article 1 ECHR-P1. The paradox of the approach adopted by the majority, he argued, is that possessions obtained as a result of crime enjoy protection under Article 1 of ECHR-P1 against excessive interference and may thus be retained by a criminal if the confiscation measure does not strike a fair balance between the individual and the public interests at stake.

The *Paulet* case and Judge Wojtyczek's dissenting opinion bring to the fore the important question: what relevance does, or should, proportionality have in asset confiscation proceedings?

An important starting point for assessing the acceptability of an asset confiscation scheme is the right to property, protected, for example, under Article 1 ECHR-P1 and/or similar national constitutional provisions. Proportionality is an essential concept under human rights law, and also often under national constitutions, for determining whether or not an infringement was justified.[20] For instance, it is well-established case law under Article 1 ECHR-P1 that in determining whether an infringement of an individual's property may be justified, the interference must achieve a 'fair balance' between the demands of the general interest of the community and the requirements of the protection of the individual's fundamental rights.[21] The burden that falls on the individual must not be excessive.[22] In other words, the interference has to be proportionate.[23]

As there is no doubt that asset confiscation constitutes an interference with an individual's right to peaceful enjoyment of his possessions,[24] it would appear

[20] On proportionality and constitutional law, see generally Barak (n 4).

[21] See, eg, *Denisova and Moiseyeva v Russia* App no 16903/03 (ECtHR, 1 April 2010) [56]. See also *G.I.E.M. S.r.l. and Others v Italy* App nos 1828/06, 34163/07 and 19029/11 (ECtHR, 28 June 2018) [292]–[293]. Art 1 ECHR-P1 contains three rules. The first sentence of the first paragraph, as a statement of principle, asserts everyone's right to the peaceful enjoyment of their property. The second sentence articulates the second rule, according to which no one shall be permanently deprived by the state of his possessions except in certain circumstances. The third rule, articulated in the second paragraph, provides that necessary restrictions may be imposed in order to control property, either in accordance with the general interest or to secure the payment of taxes, other contributions or penalties.

[22] See *G.I.E.M. S.r.l. and Others* (n 21) at [300] and *Paulet* (n 19) at [67]. See also the seminal judgment *R v Waya* [2013] 1 AC 294, [2012] 3 WLR 1188.

[23] Indeed, both criminal and NCB asset confiscation have on a number of occasions been treated by the ECtHR as measures for the control of property under the third rule of Art 1 ECHR-P1. See, eg, *Denisova and Moiseyeva* (n 21) at [58] and *Air Canada v United Kingdom* App no 18465/91 (ECtHR, 5 May 1995). This approach awards states a wide margin of appreciation with regard both to choosing the means of enforcement and to ascertaining whether the consequences of enforcement are justified in the general interest for the purpose of achieving the objective of the law in question; see D J Harris, M O'Boyle and C Warbrick, *Law of the European Convention on Human Rights*, 3rd edn (Oxford, Oxford University Press, 2014) 895, who observe that states have a far-reaching, even 'unfettered', discretion to intervene 'by control' under the third rule. The Court has been fairly liberal in accepting even far-reaching asset confiscation schemes under Art 1 ECHR-P1.

[24] This is well-established under Art 1 of ECHR-P1. See, eg, *Phillips v United Kingdom* App no 41087/98 (ECtHR, 5 July 2001) [49] and *Paulet* (n 19) at [64].

clear that proportionality ought to, in principle, also apply to asset confiscation proceedings.

Whether or not the assets were obtained through unlawful conduct should not be decisive as such. Rather than framing the question in the way Judge Wojtyczek did, a more appropriate question would seem to be under which conditions proportionality considerations can, or should, restrict a particular confiscation order relating to the proceeds of crime on the basis that it represents a disproportionate interference with the right to property.

The role of proportionality is to assure that the balance struck between the interests of the state and those of the individual does not place an excessive burden on the latter. This involves not only procedural aspects (under Article 6 ECHR), but also substantive aspects. As such, proportionality should guard, inter alia, against excessive quantification rules that facilitate confiscation of potentially legitimate assets. This will be discussed further in section IV.C.(iii).

C. The Meaning of Proportionality in Asset Confiscation Proceedings

(i) Introduction

What does, or should, proportionality mean in asset confiscation proceedings, ie, when is a confiscation measure proportionate and when is it not? As indicated above, this is a complex assessment that may comprise many different considerations, both substantive and procedural. Discussing all these aspects would exceed the scope of this chapter. However, as suggested in section II, identifying the purpose (or aim) of a measure is a crucial reference point in any proportionality assessment. It is therefore necessary to explore and identify what the legitimate aim of asset confiscation is, or should be. I will now turn to this question.

(ii) Identifying the True Aim(s) of Asset Confiscation

A number of different objectives for asset confiscation regimes tend to feature in policy documents, judicial decisions and legal doctrine. Not all of them are necessarily invoked in every jurisdiction, but typically one or more of the following are featured:

- *Deterrence* of potential offenders (general prevention) and actual offenders (special prevention) from committing unlawful acts in the future;
- *Restoration* of the *status quo ante*, ie, returning the state of things to what it was before the relevant offence was committed (gain neutralisation);
- *Prevention*, ie, the removal of property from the defendant in order to prevent it from being used to further crime (safety measure); or

- *Remedy*, ie, the compensation either of the victim for damages/expenses incurred by the crime, or of the government for expenses related to law enforcement.

Deterrence is often referred to as an important justification for asset confiscation, both by the ECtHR and national jurisdictions.[25] However, I have in different contexts argued that it may be useful to distinguish, in line with Hart's classical distinction, between a general justifying aim and principles of distribution also in a confiscation context.[26] In an asset confiscation setting, the latter may perhaps be termed 'principles of quantification'. Why confiscation is a beneficial institution ('general justifying aim') and how a confiscation order should be quantified ('principles of quantification') are separate questions that call for separate justifications.

Confiscation – criminal and NCB – forms part of the criminal justice system. As such, it also shares the general justifying aim of that system, which is general prevention (deterrence).[27] Indeed, it would send an unfortunate message if criminals were permitted to retain the fruits of their crimes. In fact, if authorities were regularly to omit to investigate the plausibility of confiscation proceedings in connection with acquisitive crime, it might even be interpreted as silent approval of a criminal lifestyle. The general presumption at the general justifying level would thus be that confiscation of illegal gains, by reducing the expected benefit of unlawful conduct, promotes deterrence and law abidance.

General prevention (or deterrence) is not, however, a suitable guiding principle of distribution, or quantification, in confiscation proceedings. A fundamental problem is the inherent boundlessness of deterrence due to its forward-looking nature. Measuring the proportionality of a confiscation order against general preventative aims will render it difficult, if not virtually impossible, to impose any substantive limitations on confiscation schemes. Reliance on deterrence at the level of quantification therefore entails the risk of imposing ever harsher and more intrusive confiscation schemes in order to increase the deterrent effect,

[25] Crime control has repeatedly been considered by the ECtHR to constitute a legitimate aim for imposing confiscation measures. See, eg, *Phillips* (n 24) at [52] and *Butler v United Kingdom* App no 41661/98 (ECtHR, 27 June 2002). In the older English case *R v Rezvi* [2002] UKHL 1 [14], Lord Steyn explained that the purposes of confiscation are 'to punish convicted offenders, to deter the commission of further offences and to reduce the profits available to fund further criminal enterprises'. In Norway, deterrence is considered to be the main purpose of confiscation, see M Matningsdal, *Inndragning* (Oslo, Universitetsforlaget, 1987) 106–10.

[26] Boucht (n 3) 96–97 and J Boucht, 'Non-Conviction Based Confiscation: Moving the Confiscation of Criminal Proceeds from the Criminal to the 'Civil' Sphere – Benefits, Issues and Two Procedural Aspects' in V Franssen and C Harding (eds), *Quasi-Criminal Enforcement Mechanisms in Europe: Historical Origins, Contemporary Concepts and Future Perspectives* (Oxford, Hart Publishing, 2020 forthcoming).

[27] On the general justifying aim of the criminal justice system, see, eg, A Ashworth and J Horder, *Principles of Criminal Law* (Oxford, Oxford University Press, 2013) 16–17. However, it is not unthinkable that there might be several general justifications. The general justifying aims of confiscation might therefore be both general prevention and restoration.

thus creating an unfair(er) regime (see further below). Moreover, confiscating the respondent's assets beyond what is necessary for restoring the *status quo ante* and neutralising illicit gains, in order to disincentivise offending, is problematic for reasons of principle. Lastly, it is difficult to disregard the fact that there is empirical uncertainty as to the degree to which the presumption referred to above corresponds to the factual effects of confiscation on crime rates.[28]

The proper aim of confiscation, both criminal and NCB, at the distributive level ought instead to be to recover the illicit financial benefit that the respondent has obtained through unlawful conduct, ie, restoration.[29] Arguably, an individual who has enriched himself by way of criminal conduct has no moral right to the criminal gain thus obtained and should therefore not be allowed to retain it. Hence, the main distributive principle of asset confiscation ought to be restoration of the position the respondent occupied prior to having obtained criminal proceeds, ie, gain neutralisation of (past) criminal conduct (*restitutio ad integrum*).[30] An inherent limitation on the quantification of confiscation orders (and on the pursuit of general prevention) will thus be the reference, at the quantification stage, to

[28] For confiscation to have a deterrent effect, it must be known to offenders that such a sanction may be imposed on them. Research on the deterrent effects of punishment proper suggests that much less is known amongst potential perpetrators about the consequences of their actions than the law-makers would like to think. As J Ulph, 'Confiscation Orders, Human Rights, and Penal Measures' (2010) 126 *Law Quarterly Review* 278, rightly observes, it 'cannot be said with confidence that criminals understand the current confiscation regime and, foreseeing the consequences of the actions, will take steps to avoid these severe measures'. Moreover, research indicates that membership of a group might weaken the capacity to let consequences guide actions, due to group pressure; see P H Robinson and J M Darley, 'Does Criminal Law Deter? A Behavioural Science Investigation' (2004) 24 *Oxford Journal of Legal Studies* 180, 180f. For a general discussion, see Boucht (n 3) 101–9. T Friehe, 'A Note on the Deterrence Effects of the Forfeiture of Illegal Gains' (2011) 7 *Review of Law and Economics* 121, in fact argues that confiscation may have an effect to the contrary. The reduced expected benefit of crime due to the risk of confiscation enhances the desire amongst perpetrators to avoid detection. Higher ambitions to avoid detection may cancel out the negative effect on crime rates that the prospect of reduced expected benefit may have, and thus, he argues, confiscation may in fact increase crime.

[29] Confiscation measures can also be based on purely preventative considerations. Due to the inherent boundlessness of preventative aims alluded to above, such schemes should be used with restriction. A preventative asset confiscation scheme would require particular safeguards to be put in place because of the exorbitant potential of prevention as a principle of quantification. In such a scheme, proportionality would have to be measured against the offences that the scheme is designed to prevent. The legitimacy of a particular confiscation order would therefore be contingent on whether or not there is a reasonable balance between the magnitude of the confiscation order and the seriousness of the anticipated offence. In this context, the seriousness of the offence is likely to be assessed mainly on objective grounds.

[30] Gain neutralisation in this context merely refers to the process of depriving the perpetrator of illicit gains, not to the potential restoration of the assets to those from whom they were taken. For example, if D defrauds V of £10,000, but it costs him £4,000 to prepare and carry through the fraud, then the net principle would allow only the confiscation of £6,000 (see on this issue, section IV.C.(iii) below). This would restore the *status quo* as far as D is concerned in line with the purpose of confiscation proceedings. However, it would not restore the *status quo* as far as V is concerned, but this would in many cases be addressed in separate civil proceedings. Alternatively, the confiscated assets might be used to compensate the loser, but this would also likely follow in a separate process subsequent to the confiscation decision. The question of confiscation should therefore be kept separate from that of victim compensation or restitution.

particular past criminal conduct. A confiscation scheme based on such a principle will, however, also concurrently fulfil other purposes, such as deterrence, prevention and, depending on the scheme, remedy.

Such an understanding of the leading distributive principle of confiscation would resonate well with how Lord Walker and Sir Anthony Hughes, with whom the other Law Lords agreed, described the aim of asset confiscation in the groundbreaking UK Supreme Court case *R v Waya*:

> Nor is it to be doubted that the severity of the regime will have a deterrent effect on at least some would be criminals. It does not, however, follow that its deterrent qualities represent the essence (or the 'grain') of the legislation. They are, no doubt, an incident of it, but they are not its essence. Its essence, and its frequently declared purpose, is to remove from criminals the pecuniary proceeds of their crime.[31]

There is, hence, an interaction between the general justifying aim of general prevention (deterrence) and the restorative principle of quantification. The offender has no right to the proceeds of his crime, which makes it permissible to confiscate them; but what positively justifies confiscation, what gives the state good reason to expend the resources that confiscation involves, is that this will have beneficial consequences such as deterrence.[32]

(iii) Restoration and Proportionality: Towards a Net Principle

If the primary distributive purpose of confiscation is to restore the *status quo ante* (ie, gain neutralisation), it would be, for example, clearly disproportionate to confiscate the benefit a perpetrator had obtained by defrauding another when the perpetrator had repaid, or stood ready to repay, the victim in full. In this case, there would be no gain to neutralise. Where only a part of the assets was restored, it should likewise be disproportionate not to deduct from the confiscation order the part that was returned to the loser (in order to avoid double confiscation). The same should probably apply in analogous cases, for example where the defendant by deception induces someone else to trade with him in a manner that is otherwise lawful but nonetheless gives full value for goods or services obtained.[33] It would also be disproportionate to order double recovery of, for example, unpaid tax by way of both confiscation and a civil remedy obtained by the tax authorities. Moreover, proportionality issues may arise where a confiscation order is made for the full amount against several defendants. Particularly

[31] *R v Waya* [2012] 3 WLR 1188 [21]. See also Explanatory Notes to POCA 2002, para 4.

[32] Thus, there would be an analogy with the way in which 'negative retributivism' figures in 'mixed' theories of punishment. The offender's penal desert makes it permissible to punish him, but punishment is positively justified (we have good reason to punish) only if it will have beneficial effects.

[33] The question of bribery may be complicated, such as in this case: a large construction project worth millions of pounds has been awarded to entrepreneur A by corrupt practices. Having received the contract, A fulfils his part impeccably. How should the net gain be calculated? See also n 58 below.

when the defendants have substantial assets, issuing confiscation orders for the full benefit in each case would lead to recovering far more than the conspiracy or joint enterprise had realised.

However, it can be asked whether the position that confiscation should be proportionate to the aim of restoration, could, and should, be taken one step further so as to mean that quantification is to be limited to the actual enrichment of an offender.[34] To limit confiscation to actual enrichment – ie, neutralising the illicit gain obtained by the perpetrator – would mean that the net principle applies to calculating enrichment at the quantification stage. On this basis, costs connected with obtaining the benefit through unlawful conduct should, in principle, be deductible from the gross proceeds of crime obtained by an offender to an extent that realises the aim of gain neutralisation.[35] The net approach seems particularly important in cases of expense-heavy criminality where the respondent's net gain is considerably smaller than his gross gain.

A net principle does not necessarily mean that absolutely every cost connected with the offence should be deductible. Determining which costs ought to be deductible is a complex issue and cannot be dealt with in detail here, and may also vary among different kinds of offences. What is crucial is to strike a reasonable balance which creates a confiscation scheme that is overall fair by design. Moreover, considering that this may involve difficult problems for the confiscation judge in assessing the real benefit in concrete cases, it may be appropriate to apply a relatively broad brush to this task.

Why should quantification be limited to actual enrichment? There are several reasons. As already discussed, the distributive purpose of confiscation ought to be gain neutralisation, ie, to restore the *status quo ante*. It ought not to go beyond that. In practice, many seem to agree that confiscation neither is, nor should be, a fine.[36] However, if the confiscation order imposes a more far-reaching detriment upon the respondent than a restorative aim requires, which many jurisdictions do, for example by denying the deduction of costs, and thus places the respondent in a poorer position compared to the one he occupied prior to having obtained criminal proceeds, confiscation becomes precisely what it is not supposed to be,

[34] Boucht (n 3) 98. See also D Hodgson, *Profits of Crime and Their Recovery* (London, Heinemann, 1984) 74–75; the confiscation committee chaired by Derek Hodgson supported the view that confiscation should be based on actual enrichment in UK law. For a discussion of the net principle, see Boucht (n 3) 98–100.

[35] It follows that deductions that ultimately produce gain for the perpetrator would not be justifiable.

[36] Per Lord Bingham in *R v May* [2008] 1 AC 1028 [48] approved by Lord Walker and Sir Anthony Hughes in *R v Waya* [2012] 3 WLR 1188 [22]. Nevertheless, in *May*, Lord Bingham approves of the English confiscation schemes that clearly go further than what is necessary in order to neutralise gain. Also, for example, in Finnish law (see J Boucht and D Frände, *Finsk straffrätt. Grundkurs i straffrättens allmänna läror*, 2nd edn (Helsinki, Edita Prima, 2020), 171–72), Norwegian law (see s 30 of the Penal Code) and Swedish law (see ch 1 s 8 of the Penal Code), confiscation is formally not considered to constitute a criminal penalty but is classified as an additional legal sanction. Nonetheless, and particularly in Finnish and Norwegian confiscation law, confiscation may in fact constitute a penalty as it may go further than what a restorative aim requires. See further below.

a pecuniary penalty.[37] Consequently, if a measure constitutes a penalty, not only should the guilt principle apply, but also, following the principle of quantification proportionality, the exceeding part ought to be considered when determining the magnitude of the punishment proper.[38] Confiscation that is limited to actual enrichment does not, in contrast, constitute punishment but is simply a restorative measure.[39]

Punishing the perpetrator by communicating blame and imposing deserved hard-treatment that is proportionate to the seriousness of the offence and the perpetrator's culpability is the task of punishment proper. It neither is, nor should be, the task of asset confiscation.

Unfortunately, in many jurisdictions the net principle has not yet been embraced. For example, case law under part 2 of the UK's POCA 2002 has made it quite clear that the defendant cannot set off any expenses connected to the crime. In his endnote to the leading case *R v May*, Lord Bingham explained that 'the benefit gained is the total value of the property or advantage obtained, not the defendant's net profit after deduction of expenses or any amounts payable to co-conspirators.'[40] This position was confirmed by the UK Supreme Court in *R v Waya*, even though the Court acknowledged that this involves 'the possibility of removing from the defendant by way of confiscation order a sum larger than may in fact represent his net proceeds of crime'.[41] As regards civil recovery, part 5 section 242(2)(a) POCA 2002 is explicit in disallowing the deduction of costs.[42] The net principle is also denied in Norwegian confiscation law, where section 67(1) of the Penal Code 2005 explicitly states that expenses cannot be set off (although costs connected with lawful activity may still be set off on grounds of fairness).

Why then is the net principle so hard to digest? Two possible explanations come to mind. The first one relates to effectiveness. Effectiveness can mean different things, but I wish to point to two meanings. The first focuses on efficiency in

[37] It could be argued that, if the gross gain is confiscated in order to make sure that the victim receives full restitution, confiscation does not constitute a pecuniary penalty. However, as argued above, the question of confiscation should be kept separate from that of victim compensation (see n 30 above).

[38] On the application of the guilt principle to penalties, see *G.I.E.M. S.r.l. and Others* (n 21) 242.

[39] That the confiscation order is limited to actual enrichment constituted an important reason in the case law of the ECtHR for not finding a confiscation order to represent a penalty. In *Dassa Foundation and others v Lichtenstein* App no 696/05 (ECtHR, 10 July 2007), a case that concerned the seizure and subsequent confiscation of all assets held by two foundations because of suspicion of bribery by another individual, the Court concluded that the confiscation order did not amount to a penalty under Art 7 ECHR. One important factor emphasised by the Court, which also made the confiscation measure more comparable to a restitution of unjustified enrichment, was that, in any event, defendants facing criminal proceedings would surely welcome the general principle that they ought to be punished only once, namely by punishment proper, rather than be additionally punished in confiscation proceedings. In *Saliba v Malta* App no 4251/02 (ECtHR, 8 November 2005) [17], the Court maintained that a measure that merely restores the *status quo ante* does not constitute a penalty under Art 7.

[40] *R v May* [2008] 1 AC 1028 [48].

[41] *R v Waya* [2012] 3 WLR 1188 [26].

[42] Section 242(2) POCA 2002: 'In deciding whether any property was obtained through unlawful conduct … (a) it is immaterial whether or not any money, goods or services were provided in order to put the person in question in a position to carry out the conduct'.

terms of achieving the aim of the measure in question. The aim of confiscation as discussed earlier in this section thus becomes relevant. It becomes apparent that, as justifications, general prevention and restoration will give very different answers to this aspect of effectiveness. If general prevention is awarded relevance at the quantification stage or if the distinction between the general justifying aim and the principles of distribution is not recognised, general prevention may clearly be used as an argument in support of disallowing cost deductions, as this may be thought to reduce the deterrent effect of confiscation.[43] For reasons set out above, I do not find this argument convincing. Where, in contrast, restoration is accepted as the main quantifying principle, efficiency arguments concern the degree to which gain neutralisation is achieved. Refusal to permit deductions can therefore hardly be justified by reference to this principle.

Effectiveness can also be understood in procedural terms, so that by permitting the respondent to set off costs related to the obtaining of the benefit, the proceedings become ineffective. It can be argued that attempting to inquire into the financial dealings of criminals would usually be impracticable. It might not only place an unreasonable burden on the courts to assess what costs can be set off, but it might also create unnecessary litigation on behalf of the respondents, and in the worst case, as reasoned by Lord Walker and Sir Anthony Hughes in *R v Waya*, 'lay the process of confiscation wide open to simple avoidance'.[44]

Indeed, there is considerable force in this objection. However, it is questionable whether a procedural objection of this kind should determine the substantive fairness of a confiscation scheme. Suppose that the costs in a case can be satisfactorily determined; to deny deduction of these costs because it may be difficult to ascertain them in other cases would not seem fair. One possible solution (which is the solution adopted by Swedish law), at least in some kinds of cases, might be to empower the courts, where there is insufficient evidence of the costs incurred by the defendant or such evidence is irreconcilable with the privilege against self-incrimination, to estimate the expenses incurred and deduct them from the confiscation order.[45]

Effectiveness in a procedural sense may also serve to highlight the dilemma connected with the net principle: placing the burden of proving the costs incurred on the defendant is prima facie inconsistent with an effective defence, particularly where the defendant is called to answer the confiscation claim in the same proceedings as those connected with the predicate offence.[46] However, this problem could

[43] See, for example, para 12.179 of the Law Commission Consultation Paper No 249 (2020), *Confiscation of the proceeds of crime after conviction: A consultation paper*, where it is held that '[a]n approach which goes no further than is strictly necessary to remove the defendant's benefit from crime will likely have less of a deterrent effect than one which goes further'.

[44] *R v Waya* [2012] 3 WLR 1188 [26].

[45] In the Swedish Supreme Court's case *NJA 2016* s 202 it was held that although the burden of proof is on the prosecutor, the court may, where there is no evidence of the expenses incurred, estimate the expenses to a reasonable amount, which may then be set off.

[46] D J Fried, 'Rationalizing Criminal Forfeiture' (1988) 79 *Journal of Criminal Law and Criminology* 328, 377–78.

possibly be remedied by detaching the confiscation hearing from the proceedings related to the criminal offence, thus creating a 'firewall' between the two sets of proceedings for safeguarding the privilege against self-incrimination.

The second explanation may be that permitting cost deductions would simply be considered morally repugnant. For example, Lord Walker and Sir Anthony Hughes argue in *R v Waya*, that

> [t]o embark upon an accounting exercise in which the defendant is entitled to set off the cost of committing his crime would be to treat his criminal enterprise as if it were a legitimate business and confiscation a form of business taxation.[47]

Similar arguments are echoed in other jurisdictions.

But what would be so immoral about permitting deductions and thereby making a confiscation scheme fair(er)? Gain neutralisation based on the net principle would seem to resonate well with the basic moral position that no one should benefit, directly or indirectly, from unlawful conduct (*ex turpi causa non oritur actio*). It is difficult to understand, in principle, that there should be any moral imperative for confiscation schemes to go further than what is necessary to recover in order to achieve gain neutralisation. And, as noted above, a net principle does not necessarily imply that *every* cost has to be deductible.

From the fairness perspective of defendants facing criminal proceedings, it would be an important general principle that they ought to be punished only once, namely by punishment proper, rather than by additional punishment in confiscation proceedings. It is vital for the legitimacy of criminal law that it is perceived to be fair and just (or at least as little unfair and unjust as possible).[48] Not only can fairness be seen as a positive value as such, but research also suggests that the perceived fairness and reasonableness of the system may enhance compliance.[49] This refers not only to procedural justice, ie, the perceived fairness of the procedures involved in decision-making and the perceived treatment one receives from a decision-maker,[50] but also to substantive fairness. In other words, the fact that the substance of the rule to some degree resonates with the internal moral values of the individual may be seen as being closely linked to legitimacy and compliance. It is therefore not unreasonable to think that the fairer the confiscation system design, the more likely it is that a defendant will accept culpability for offending,

[47] *R v Waya* [2012] 3 WLR 1188 [26].

[48] See Boucht (n 3) 23.

[49] See, eg, K Murphy, 'Regulating More Effectively: The Relationship between Procedural Justice, Legitimacy, and Tax Non-Compliance' (2005) 32 *Journal of Law and Society* 562, 564–67 and J Braithwaite, *Restorative Justice and Responsive Regulation* (Oxford, Oxford University Press, 2002) 78–79.

[50] Murphy (n 49) 566–67. See also C Hodges, *Law and Corporate Behaviour. Integrating Theories of Regulation, Enforcement, Compliance and Ethics* (Oxford, Hart Publishing, 2015) 26. On social legitimacy and the fairness of proceedings, see E Billis and N Knust, 'Alternative Types of Procedure and the Formal Limits of National Criminal Justice: Aspects of Social Legitimacy' in U Sieber, V Mitsilegas, C Mylonopoulos, E Billis and N Knust (eds), *Alternative Systems of Crime Control. National, Transnational, and International Dimensions* (Berlin, Duncker & Humblot, 2018) 49–56.

whereas unfair procedures might decrease the likelihood of compliance and acceptance of culpability by accused persons.

A net principle is in fact in no way merely a utopic and unattainable state of law but is legally perfectly feasible. The net principle has been taken seriously in some jurisdictions. In Swedish confiscation law, for example, the traditional rule, confirmed by the Swedish Supreme Court in the case *NJA 2016* s 202, is that costs connected with obtaining the benefit are generally deductible. In this case, the Court held that purchase costs, even of illegal substances (in this case the cost of purchasing cannabis), were deductible, but that, for example, production costs can only marginally reduce the confiscation order (and, moreover, only as part of a fairness assessment).[51]

Finnish confiscation law also accepts the net principle, although the Finnish Supreme Court has been more restrictive than its Swedish counterpart in accepting deductions. Only costs connected with *lawful* activity may be deducted, for example the cost of purchasing alcohol when this was sold at a profit.[52] Although a position where all costs are deductible is preferable from a point of principle, a compromise such as the Finnish position which accepts deductions of all expenses with legal value (and consequently prohibits setting off costs without legal value, such as narcotics) is still clearly preferable to a gross gain principle.

Also, older Norwegian confiscation law explicitly accepted, until its amendment in 1999 when the gross principle became the main rule, the net principle, so that deductions were in principle permitted.[53] However, even today deductions of costs connected with *lawful* activity may be deducted on grounds of fairness.[54] The report that forms the basis for the discussions relating to the introduction of an NCB confiscation scheme in Norwegian law is, nevertheless, explicitly based on the net principle, so that deductions are intended to be made.[55]

In view of Judge Wojtyczek's objections in the ECtHR judgment in *Paulet v United Kingdom*, a crucial distinction concerning the relevance of proportionality should be made between restorative confiscation, which seeks to restore the *status quo ante*, and repressive confiscation, which imposes upon the individual a more far-reaching detriment than is required to achieve the aim of gain neutralisation.[56] Where confiscation is limited to net enrichment, confiscation should be presumed to be proportionate. However, where the confiscation scheme facilitates going

[51] See G Almkvist, 'Avdrag för inköpsutgifter vid utbytesförverkande' (2016–17) 3 *Juridisk Tidskrift* 708–9.

[52] See, eg, the Finnish Supreme Court's case *2017:56*. See further Boucht and Frände (n 36) 700, 708–9.

[53] However, over the years the Norwegian Supreme Court made so many exceptions to this point of departure that in practice the law came to be based on the gross principle as the main rule. See Bill Ot.prp. nr. 8 (1998–99) 21. For a discussion, see Matningsdal (n 25) 190–202.

[54] See, eg, Norwegian Supreme Court case *Rt. 2015* s 184.

[55] See J P Rui, *Betenkning: Sivilrettslig inndragning rettet direkte mot formuesgoder* (2017) (www.regjeringen.no/contentassets/563c5153753e41438ec0b6d047f3ab20/betenkning_sivilrettslig-inndragning.pdf). To what extent the formal bill, if it reaches that stage, will follow this recommendation, is yet to be seen.

[56] *Paulet* (n 19).

beyond actual enrichment, thus imposing a more far-reaching detriment than a restorative aim requires, proportionality should be a limiting force.

D. Proportionality Applied

(i) Proportionality in Regular Criminal Confiscation Proceedings

Satisfying the net principle, and therefore proportionality, as explained in this chapter, in regular criminal confiscation ought to be generally relatively straightforward. The confiscation order is proportionate when confiscation is limited to the actual enrichment that the perpetrator had obtained through the offence of which he was convicted. This means that, for example, the costs of purchasing the drugs subsequently sold at a profit should in principle be deducted when the proceeds from the sales are calculated.[57] The same applies to the costs of purchasing raw materials used in the production of illicit alcohol which is subsequently sold at a profit.[58]

The question of quantification proportionality also arises. Proportionality in a criminal law context means that the overall sanction has to be proportionate to the seriousness of the offence. As argued above, where the quantification of confiscation orders is based on the net principle, the confiscation order represents no additional penalty and does not have to be considered for proportionality purposes in relation to punishment proper. By contrast, if the net principle is not adhered to, and to the extent that the confiscation order exceeds what is necessary to place the respondent in the position he occupied prior to committing the criminal offence, the confiscation order represents an additional pecuniary penalty.

In line with the requirement that the overall sanction should be proportionate, this ought to mean that the exceeding part of the confiscation order is considered a mitigating circumstance in sentencing when the penalty proper is determined. Consequently, confiscation should be decided before punishment proper in order to facilitate the potential consideration of the confiscation order in the sentencing procedure.

(ii) Proportionality in Extended Criminal Confiscation and NCB Confiscation Proceedings

As explained in section III, many jurisdictions have expanded their confiscation regimes beyond regular criminal confiscation to include extended criminal

[57] See also the examples mentioned in the first paragraph of section IV.C.(iii).

[58] As indicated above, difficult legal issues may arise in applying the net principle. Examples are how to deal with: a) pecuniary advantages where the defendant obtained no factual benefit; b) benefit from various misrepresentations or corrupt practices where the subsequent contract was fulfilled satisfactorily; or c) pecuniary benefit that arises out of employment obtained by deception but where the work carried out was flawless. However, these issues cannot be addressed here.

confiscation and/or NCB confiscation. There is no doubt that proportionality is important also for assessing the legitimacy of these schemes. The main purpose of these schemes should also be restoration, ie, to restore the *status quo ante* by taking out of circulation illicit net gain accrued from unlawful conduct.

However, assessing proportionality can be problematic in extended criminal and NCB confiscation proceedings, as the relevant criminal conduct to which the confiscation measure relates does not have to be specified. As observed above (section III), extended criminal confiscation is based, in addition to the conviction of a 'trigger offence', on the presumption of previous acquisitive criminality, which does not in itself have to be identified. In NCB confiscation, the state is in principle only required to prove that the identified property was obtained through unlawful conduct, not what this conduct was. Consequently, the reach of proportionality as a substantive safeguard is diminished due to the innovative legislative structure of these schemes.

Indeed, in NCB confiscation, a distinction can be made between two types of cases. First are proceedings where the unlawful conduct in question is known and would have been dealt with in criminal proceedings had it not been for (i) the defendant's flight or illness, (ii) statutory limitations or (iii) insufficient evidence for a criminal conviction. In this case, where a specific offence is identified and criminal proceedings would in fact have been carried out had it not been for the defendant's absence, net confiscation might actually be achievable and should in this case be strived for. Again, if the costs involved cannot be satisfactorily proved, the court should have discretion to assess the reasonable costs connected with the offence and make a reasonable deduction.

The second type of NCB confiscation proceedings are where the criminal conduct from which the assets allegedly originate is unspecified. It is particularly in this type of proceedings that assessing proportionality becomes difficult (similarly as in extended criminal confiscation proceedings). In this case, confiscation will in practice be decided without having regard to any costs incurred (ie, based on a gross gain principle), as it is not possible to ascertain what the respondent's real benefit might be.

One option, for both NCB confiscation and extended criminal confiscation, would be to require that the assets be traced back to the relevant criminal conduct from which they originated (although at a lower standard of proof).[59] In this case, reaching net proportionality might be possible. Alternatively, if this were considered to set the requirements too high (and defeat the purpose of the measure), it could be required to specify the criminal activity from which the assets allegedly originate to a lower degree that still allows the court to reach the conclusion that past criminal conduct was involved (ie, a nexus between the assets and the kind of offences involved). For example, this could mean that the assets should be traced back to criminal conduct specified in kind (for example 'drug trafficking',

[59] On the standard of proof in NCB confiscation proceedings, see Boucht, 'Non-Conviction Based Confiscation' (n 26).

'corruption', etc).[60] Nonetheless, it is doubtful whether tracing the assets to a particular kind of criminality would also allow the court to estimate reasonable costs connected with that conduct and to subtract them from the confiscation order in order to achieve proportionality.

In NCB confiscation proceedings, there is an additional obstacle to achieving net proportionality. As the claim is *in specie* – ie, targets the property rather than the individual – there is no certainty about the current holder of the property having in any way been involved in the criminal conduct and therefore having any costs to deduct (or any information about such costs). He may, for example, have acquired the property by way of a gift or by purchase. In this case, it may not be unreasonable to argue that the causal link between the costs linked to the original acquisition and the current holder has been broken.[61]

If a net amount were to be ascertained, the next question would be how to give effect to such an order within a confiscation scheme based on *in specie* confiscation. This is a further aspect that can make net confiscation difficult (if not impossible) to achieve in NCB confiscation as well as in extended criminal confiscation schemes. It seems that the only solution to this would be that instead of transferring the property to the state, the respondent should have the option to pay the net amount in cash and keep the property as it is. At least from a restorative perspective, such an arrangement should be quite acceptable.[62]

[60] As regards NCB confiscation, the answer to whether or not a nexus between the assets and the criminal conduct has to be established varies. Under pt 5 of the UK's POCA 2002, part of the state's burden of proof is to describe the unlawful conduct from which the assets allegedly derive in such general terms that it will enable the court to reach a conclusion as to whether the conduct in question might properly be described as unlawful, for example, 'importing and supplying controlled drugs', 'trafficking women for the purpose of prostitution', etc. A nexus between that type of unlawful conduct and the property in respect of which the order is sought must thus be established. However, it is not required that that unlawful conduct be specified as regards, for example, details of when it was committed, who participated, etc (see, eg, *Serious Organised Crime Agency v Bosworth* [2010] EWHC 645 (QB)). Assets can therefore be confiscated as drug proceeds if it can be proved that they derive from drug trafficking generally; they do not have be linked to any particular drug offence. Under German law, particularly s 76a sentence (4) Strafgesetzbuch (StGB, German Criminal Code), 'identified property stemming from unlawful conduct which has been seized in proceedings brought on suspicion of a relevant offence shall also be seized independently if the person concerned cannot be prosecuted or convicted of the offence.' The relevant unlawful conduct that may give rise to NCB confiscation is described in sentence (4) no. 1 and includes, inter alia, terrorist-related offences, offences relating to human trafficking, child pornography, money laundering, tax evasion, smuggling, narcotics offences and so on. The main requirement is that the assets were seized in proceedings relating to a 'suspicion' of a relevant offence. Provided that the assets are seized in such proceedings, there is no requirement (at least not according to the wording of the provision) that the property in question actually derives from these offences; instead it would suffice (at least according to the wording) that they can derive from any offence. Consequently, there appears to be no requirement that the assets must be traced back to a relevant kind of criminal conduct, although it is possible that the courts will subsequently establish such a requirement in the same way the English courts established a tracing requirement under pt 5 POCA 2002.

[61] Where the current holder of the property obtained it in good faith (and/or for value), the question of bona fide protections arises. If bona fide protections apply, there will be no confiscation of the property at all.

[62] As confiscation aims at gain neutralisation, there should in principle be nothing in the way of also confiscating legitimate property if the illicit gains have been consumed. Say, for example, there is strong

What then of the other aspect of quantification proportionality alluded to in section IV.D.(i), ie, proportionality in regard to punishment proper? As NCB confiscation is not a criminal sanction, it will not be of relevance in such proceedings. Could this kind of proportionality then have a role to play regarding extended criminal confiscation?

It might, for example, be argued that even if the purpose of extended confiscation is to reach beyond the predicate offence, it should nonetheless not be grossly disproportionate to the predicate offence in connection with which the measure is imposed. Such an argument was advanced in the preparatory works for the implementation of the 2005 EU Framework Decision (212/2005/JHA) in Swedish law.[63] However, even if the confiscation order were totally out of proportion to the triggering offence, relating the magnitude of the confiscation order to the trigger offence would hardly be adequate in light of the fact that the purpose of extended confiscation is precisely to reach *beyond* that predicate offence. The predicate offence has no other function than to operate as a trigger for the application of a more severe confiscation regime.

Indeed, it could also be argued that to the extent that extended criminal confiscation goes beyond actual enrichment, the exceeding part should be considered in sentencing (of punishment proper). However, there are problems with this account as well. First of all, as discussed in the previous paragraph, the confiscation order does not relate to the trigger predicate offence of which the defendant is convicted but to previous unlawful conduct. Secondly, if only the part that contravenes the net principle is repressive but the previous unlawful conduct to which the assessment relates is unspecified, it is difficult to ascertain if, or to what degree, the confiscation order is in fact repressive.

(iii) Conclusions

It has been argued that substantive proportionality in confiscation proceedings should be assessed in light of the restorative aim of confiscation and the net principle. The analysis shows that the net principle is feasible to observe in regular criminal confiscation. However, applying the net principle in extended criminal confiscation and NCB confiscation proceedings is more difficult to realise, if at all. Not only is there a weaker causal connection between offences and confiscation in extended criminal and NCB confiscation proceedings, but there is also a weaker connection between the deemed level of enrichment and the real enrichment that must have occurred.

evidence that the respondent was involved in an armed robbery and obtained a benefit of £10,000. As the respondent spent his wealth on 'loose living', it should in principle be possible to confiscate legitimate property up to that amount even if it cannot be traced back to that conduct. The problem, however, is that evidential obstacles are likely to arise in this context.

[63] Council Framework Decision (212/2005/JHA) of 24 February 2005 on Confiscation of Crime-Related Proceeds, Instrumentalities and Property. See Ds 2006:17, 86. However, this position was not elaborated and not mentioned in the subsequent Bill Prop 2007/08:68.

If it is not possible to assess the substantive proportionality of a confiscation measure, whether or not a confiscation measure strikes a fair balance between the interests of the state and those of the individual will ultimately depend on procedural safeguards. Important procedural aspects would be the standard and the burden of proof, the right to a hearing where the claims can be challenged, etc. Procedural considerations might also include aspects such as the target area, or scope, of a particular scheme. A narrower target area, which, for example, limits the scope of application to only certain categories of offences/assets, can in principle make a far-reaching scheme less controversial.[64] The difficulty of assessing substantive proportionality in combination with the inherent risk that these measures target legitimate assets ought to mean that the procedural safeguards are relatively stringent.[65]

Using the terminology of section II, this would mean that quantification proportionality is not possible to assess, either in concrete cases or *in abstracto* at the legislative phase (as part of norm proportionality). This is regrettable, as the legitimacy of a confiscation regime ought to be assessed in light of both its procedural and substantive fairness, and a procedurally fair(er) scheme should not as such be able to compensate for a substantively unfair one.

Ultimately, does this mean that the original rationale for depriving the respondent of illicitly acquired gains for restorative purposes has vanished and, consequently, that a new rationale for justifying these two forms of confiscation (extended confiscation and NCB confiscation) is required? Possible alternative rationales are deterrence or prevention. However, as argued above, both are unsatisfactory as principles of distribution in confiscation proceedings, because they both suffer from a lack of inherent limitations (see section IV.C.(ii)). As shown, a focus on deterrence may trigger ever more far-reaching confiscation measures. Furthermore, if confiscation is based on prevention, how, for example, can it be determined which acts need to be prevented and which assets thus need to be confiscated? As the aim of prevention is to prevent assets from being used for criminal purposes, the focus easily turns on the individual holding the assets rather than on the unlawful nature of the assets.[66]

E. Proportionality as Equity?

In light of the difficulties in assessing substantive proportionality alluded to above, fairness (or justness) considerations should arguably form part of the safeguard regime in asset confiscation proceedings.

[64] See Boucht (n 3) 143.
[65] For a discussion of this, see Boucht (n 3) ch 5.IV and 5.VII. For a further discussion of the standard and burden of proof in NCB confiscation proceedings, see also Boucht (n 26).
[66] See further Boucht (n 3) 113.

What does fairness mean in this context? Although related to proportionality, the two concepts are distinct. Whereas proportionality refers to the (objective) relationship between the confiscation object and the restorative aim of the measure, fairness relates to circumstances linked to the confiscation subject, ie, the respondent. As such, fairness has a stronger moral charge. Therefore, even a proportionate measure may in principle be unfair in a given situation.

Fairness provisions exist in confiscation schemes of some jurisdictions. For example, under chapter 10 section 10(1) of the Finnish Penal Code, extended asset confiscation is optional rather than mandatory, inter alia in cases where it would be unfair to order confiscation in light of the respondent's economic situation. An extended confiscation order can, under the same provision, be mitigated if the result is unfair, considering the nature of the triggering offence and the property in question, the economic position of the offender and other relevant circumstances. Under chapter 36 section 1b of the Swedish Penal Code, an extended confiscation order must not be issued if it is unreasonable considering, for example, other payment obligations caused by the offence, that the property has been in the offender's possession for a very long time or that a third person, against whom the order is directed, has obtained the property in good faith. Under section 68 of the Norwegian Penal Code, the court can reduce or abandon the confiscation order if confiscation would be clearly unreasonable. However, under Norwegian law fairness considerations are not applicable in extended criminal confiscation proceedings.

One may, of course, ask why such a clause would be desirable, particularly since confiscation schemes should already be subject to a substantive proportionality requirement, limiting confiscation to actual enrichment. Arguably, a fairness clause can be justified by reference to the normative starting point that the criminal law and the sentencing system (broadly understood) should be just, or at least as little unjust as possible.[67] Thus, fairness would serve as a corrective where the result in certain situations, all things considered, would appear unjust in view of the defendant's position, even if the measure in itself were proportionate. It may also be argued that a certain degree of elasticity regarding the distribution of risk may be reasonable, particularly when considering the vertical nature of confiscation: the risk of losses to the state as a result of the liability being mitigated for reasons of justness is clearly lower.

A general fairness clause would thus function as a safety valve for cases where confiscation, as such, would be deemed proportionate but nevertheless unjust in full or in part. Fairness considerations should potentially be given relevance as a mitigating circumstance (as a safety valve), in all asset confiscation schemes, regardless of whether or not they are based on the net principle. However, where substantive proportionality is difficult to achieve, such as in extended criminal

[67] von Hirsch (n 7) 103.

confiscation and NCB confiscation proceedings, or where confiscation is based on the gross principle, fairness considerations should be awarded relatively greater importance. Where, however, the confiscation scheme is based on the net principle, fairness considerations should have only marginal relevance as mitigating factors.

Determining which considerations would be relevant requires a separate analysis that cannot be pursued here. However, fairness considerations may include, for example, general considerations relating to the economic situation of the confiscation subject and his closest family, in light of the magnitude of the confiscation order and the kind of assets targeted. For instance, confiscation of a flat or a house that is the subject's and his family's residence may be harsh not only for the subject but also for the whole family. Particularly the fact that persons other than the subject are affected, eg, children, appears to be relevant. Extended criminal confiscation orders that deprive subjects of their total wealth may be problematic from a fairness perspective, as they may, inter alia, impede the reintegration of the convicted offender into society and may in fact even encourage the commission of further criminal conduct.[68] Confiscation of objects of everyday use without considerable value could also be precluded on this ground as well as property that the defendant held for a long time.

Fairness may also become relevant in regard to certain bona fide parties. Without going into depth about how bona fide protections can be constructed, it may be reasonable to protect, for example, a person who obtained the relevant property in good faith and did so for value.[69] Protecting a bona fide respondent may also be fair where he was acting in good faith when he obtained the property, taking steps after or before obtaining the property in reliance on the title to that property (for example applying for a mortgage), which he would not have taken otherwise and a confiscation order would thus be detrimental to him.[70] There may also be situations where fairness considerations may arise in regard to bona fide recipients of property, but where the respondent, so to say, falls between two stools. He may, for example, have obtained the property in good faith but not for value, or he may not have taken steps in reliance on the title conferred on him. In such a case, circumstances may be such that it would nevertheless be fair to determine that no confiscation be ordered or that the confiscation order be mitigated.[71]

[68] See, eg, the Swedish Supreme Court's case *NJA 1977* s 735, where such considerations were made in regard to regular criminal confiscation.

[69] For a discussion of bona fide protections, see, eg, Boucht (n 3) 156–59 and 209–13.

[70] For example, these two grounds provide bona fide protection under ss 266(3) and 308(1) of POCA 2002.

[71] See, eg, *Sanam v National Crime Agency* [2015] EWCA Civ 1234, where it was not considered disproportionate to make a civil recovery order in respect of property a criminal husband gave to an innocent wife, who did not fall within any the statutory provisions under which property transferred to third parties could be excluded. It was indicated by both the High Court Judge and the Lords of Appeal

Lastly, one problematic aspect of extended confiscation schemes is the risk that property is made liable to confiscation beyond what is needed in order to achieve gain neutralisation, although this risk will always prevail due to the nature of both extended criminal confiscation and NCB confiscation. A fairness clause would facilitate consideration of this aspect when assets are quantified. If there is sufficient risk that some assets are licit, it may be fair to exempt that property from confiscation.[72] Although there may also be some room for mitigating a regular criminal confiscation order for fairness reasons, where quantification is based on the net principle, such a reduction should always require strong reasons.

V. Endnote

The analysis shows that proportionality is an important concept in many areas of law, including confiscation law. Proportionality in confiscation law should be assessed in light of the aim of restoring the *status quo ante* by neutralising illicit gain obtained by the perpetrator. This should mean that confiscation is limited to the respondent's real gain by applying the net principle as the guiding quantifying principle. While such a proportionality principle is feasible in regular (or ordinary) confiscation proceedings, it is difficult to apply in both extended criminal confiscation and non-conviction-based confiscation proceedings. This is regrettable, as an important issue that arises in the context of these kinds of confiscation – where the link to the underlying criminal conduct in which the assets allegedly originate is more obscure – is the risk of wrongful confiscation decisions. This means that licit property, ie, property that should not properly have been liable to confiscation, can be targeted. Although a certain risk in this respect will always be inherent in this kind of proceedings, it is important to consider what kind of risk may be acceptable within a liberal criminal law and to think of adequate mechanisms through which a more far-reaching risk may be mitigated. Proportionality could be one important safeguard against excessive confiscation.

The consequence is that the fairness of these schemes ultimately will have to be assessed in light of procedural safeguards. However, fairness considerations would nonetheless be a feasible option for implementing some kind of substantive safeguards in situations where other substantive safeguards are deficient.

that much could be said in favour of allowing the wife to keep the property in question in this situation. However, Parliament had left the courts with no such discretion (see at [22] and [71]).

[72] Here the English case *R v Deprince* [2004] 2 Cr App R (S) 91 may be recalled. The Court of Appeal reduced the value of the confiscation order by 25% with the purpose of safeguarding against the risk of an injustice being done due to a remote possibility that a small part of the fund might have been from a legitimate property business.

Potentially extensive approaches to asset confiscation can be useful in light of their important purpose, but as these measures contain elements that may not readily be reconciled with the basic principles of criminal law and criminal procedural law, legitimate implementation is contingent on effective protections of the individual interests being put in place and on the adequate restriction of the scope of the measures. It is crucial that a fair balance be struck between the interests of the state and those of the individual. The burden placed on the individual should not be excessive.

PART III

Applying Proportionality: International Paradigms

14

The Proportionality Principle in Comparative Public, European Union and International Law – Reflections on the 'Proportionality Equation'

MICHAEL BOTHE AND EMANUELA-CHIARA GILLARD

I. The Proportionality Problem

The contributions to this volume relate mainly to the application of the proportionality principle in criminal law and measures to ensure security. However, the scope of application of the proportionality principle is much broader: it is a general legal principle applicable in many legal contexts. The present contribution attempts to highlight some of the elements of the principle that are of general significance, by demonstrating, inter alia, how its application affects and limits the exercise of public authority on different levels. It is not the task of this contribution to draw concrete conclusions on criminal and security law, themes that are addressed in other chapters of the volume.

The proportionality principle constitutes a technique of legal reasoning based on the rule of reason: 'never too much' (*μηδέν ἄγαν*) is an ancient Greek principle. It is common to many legal orders. The proportionality concept consists of three elements:

(1) a liberty or other interest which must be protected or limited (A);
(2) another interest supposed to justify the limitation of the first interest (B); and
(3) the relation between the two, or the relative weight given to one or the other ($A < B$ or $A > B$). This is known as the proportionality equation. It requires a balancing of values and interests. This implies a value judgement, or rather three related value judgements. The crucial question is how these judgements are made.

As law-makers and courts in many legal orders use this equation, it is important to shed some light on this question by trying to show how it is used in a comparative perspective, in national constitutional and administrative law, in the law of the European Union and in international law, and to allow some lessons to be drawn from this comparison. Proportionality applies on two different levels: on the one hand, it limits the exercise of public authority. On the other, it limits restrictions to which the rights of the addressees of public authority acts may be subject.

II. Comparative Constitutional and Administrative Law

In national constitutional and administrative law systems, there are rules on the limitation of fundamental freedoms where proportionality plays a crucial role, although it is not always referred to by this term.[1]

Under the US Constitution, the rules on the limitation of the freedom of expression[2] are an example of judge-made rules based on the principle of proportionality. Only a 'compelling state interest' can justify its restriction. This means that the protected interest (freedom of expression, A in the equation above) must only cede in relation to another value (the compelling state interest, B in the equation) if the competing interest is of a certain importance. The concrete application of this approach is in the hands of the courts. Applying a standard of 'strict scrutiny' is a similarly structured argument.

Another example of the same type is the jurisprudence of the German Federal Constitutional Court, which held that only values of overriding importance can justify a limitation of the freedom of economic activities where it amounts to an objective barrier of access.[3] Russell Miller's chapter in this volume carries out a German-US comparison of a different aspect of proportionality: the limitation of measures taken to enhance public security.[4]

III. The Law of the European Union

The principle of proportionality became part of the law of what is now the European Union (EU), formerly the European Communities, by virtue of the fact that this law was from the beginning inspired by the common traditions of the Member

[1] See the contributions in G Huscroft, B W Miller and G Webber (eds), *Proportionality and the Rule of Law. Rights, Justification, Reasoning* (Cambridge, Cambridge University Press, 2014). A very thoughtful analysis of various forms of the proportionality discourse and of the application of the proportionality principle in different areas of international law is provided by T Franck, 'On Proportionality of Countermeasures in International Law' (2008) 102 *American Journal of International Law* 715.

[2] For a recent analysis with detailed references, see R R Kelso, 'The Structure of Modern Free Speech Doctrine: Strict Scrutiny, Intermediate Review, and "Reasonableness" Balancing' (2016) 8 *Elon Law Review* 291.

[3] BVerfGE (Federal Constitutional Court Reports) 7, 377 (405ff) [11 June 1958].

[4] See Russell Miller's chapter 10 in this volume.

States. General principles common to the law of the Member States have been expressly recognised as sources of Community law.[5] It meant a kind of migration of principles of national law into the law of the European Communities, now the European Union. It was this approach that led to the recognition of fundamental rights in the law of the Communities, first through decisions of the Court of Justice of the European Communities,[6] as it then was, long before the Charter of Fundamental Rights of the European Union came into force. This is how the principle of proportionality also became an important element of EU law.

The Court of Justice of the European Union (CJEU) has frequently used this type of argument.[7] In terms of limitations on rights,[8] the principle of proportionality is now enshrined in Article 52 of the Charter of Fundamental Rights of the EU:

> 1. Any limitation on the exercise of the rights and freedoms recognised by this Charter must be provided for by law and respect the essence of those rights and freedoms. Subject to the principle of proportionality, limitations may be made only if they are necessary and genuinely meet objectives of general interest recognised by the Union or the need to protect the rights and freedoms of others.

The provision is the fruit of a long history of the principle of proportionality in national legal systems[9] and in international human rights law.[10] The provision gives only limited guidance on the elements of the proportionality equation. On the one side of the equation, there are the rights protected by the Charter. On the other side, there are two different elements: first, 'objectives of general interest recognised by the Union'. This is an open formula that must be filled in concrete cases. This is also true for the second element, namely 'the rights and freedoms of others'. The relation between the two sides is that the limitations must be 'necessary'. The need to balance the two sides is indicated by the reference to the principle of proportionality. An additional restriction of the permissible limitation is the requirement that the 'essence of those rights and freedoms' must be respected.

Security interests are, of course, recognised as 'objectives of general interest'. Measures taken to protect security interests may restrict fundamental rights in a number of ways. They are thus only admissible if they are necessary to meet their objective and proportionate in relation to the freedom or right affected.

[5] For a comprehensive analysis, see the contributions in U Bernitz, J Nergelius and C Cardner (eds), *Principles of EC Law in a Process of Development* (Alphen aan den Rijn, Kluwer Law International, 2008).

[6] In particular, Case 11/70 *Internationale Handelsgesellschaft mbH v Einfuhr- und Vorratsstelle für Getreide und Futtermittel* ECLI:EU:C:1970:114 (Judgment of 17 December 1970).

[7] Case C-359/92 *Federal Republic of Germany v Council of the European Union* ECLI:EU:C:1994:306 (Judgment of 9 August 1994) 42ff; for an analysis of the Court's jurisprudence, see T J Harbo, 'The Function of the Proportionality Principle in EU Law' (2010) 16 *European Law Journal* 158. See also Franck (n 1) 752ff.

[8] In terms of criminal law and sentencing, the principle of proportionality is enshrined in Art 49(3) of the Charter of Fundamental Rights of the EU.

[9] See above section II.

[10] See below section IV.A.

This has in particular been emphasised by EU organs in relation to the fight against terrorism.[11]

In the law of the European Union, the principle of proportionality is not only a yardstick for the limitation of fundamental rights, it also limits the powers of the Union vis-à-vis Member States. According to Article 5(1) of the Treaty on European Union (TEU) the use of Union competences is governed by the principles of subsidiarity and proportionality. TEU Protocol 2 on the Application of the Principles of Subsidiarity and Proportionality lays down the details of the application of these principles. Their application can become highly controversial. In a recent judgment, the German Federal Constitutional Court held that the European Central Bank, in executing its programme of buying Member State bonds, had violated the principle of proportionality by what can be called a 'balancing deficit'. In the Court's view the Bank had failed to take into account the impact of its purchases on Member States' economic policy, ie, in a domain reserved to the States.[12] The ensuing controversy between the EU und the Federal Republic of Germany was solved by a political compromise.

IV. International Law

In international law, proportionality is considered a constitutional principle of the international order.[13] It is thus related to the phenomenon of constitutionalisation,[14] which is characterised by the recognition of overarching fundamental principles and values. As an overarching principle, proportionality applies in different areas of international law. The precise elements of the balancing process are different in the following areas:

- international human rights law;
- international investment law to the extent that it protects private property;
- international trade law;
- international law concerning countermeasures; and
- international law regulating the use of armed force.

In the first two areas, the balancing takes place between a state interest and individual freedom, a legal situation already described and known from

[11] Council Framework Decision on Combating Terrorism, 13 June 2002, 2002/475/JHA, OJ 2002 L164/3, introductory paras 9 and 10, on penal sanctions Arts 5 and 8. See also CJEU's judgment in Joined Cases C-584/10 P, C-593/10 P and C-595/10 P: *European Commission and Others v Yassin Abdullah Kadi*, ECLI:EU:C:2013:518 (Judgment of the Grand Chamber of 18 July 2013) [100ff].

[12] Federal Constitutional Court, Judgment of 5 May 2020 – 2 BvR 859/15, available at: www.bverfg.de/e/rs20200505_2bvr085915.html.

[13] A Peters, 'Proportionality as a Global Constitutional Principle' in A E Lang and A Wiener (eds), *Handbook on Global Constitutionalism* (Cheltenham, Elgar, 2017) 248; and Franck (n 1) 716.

[14] T Kleinlein, *Konstitutionalisierung im Völkerrecht* (Heidelberg, Springer, 2012) 667ff.

constitutional law. But in international and European law, the question also has an additional, vertical aspect: there must be a balancing between state interest and community interest, as a state's view on the limitation of an individual freedom is not necessarily the same as that of a competent international or European decision-maker. That problem can be partly solved by recognising a state's 'margin of appreciation', which means that, in applying the proportionality equation, the international decision-maker respects the balancing decision of the national decision-maker.[15]

A. Human Rights

In international human rights law, the principle of proportionality appears in provisions on the limitation of such rights, beginning with the Universal Declaration of 1948:

> In the exercise of his rights and freedoms, everyone shall be subject only to such limitations as are determined by law solely for the purpose of securing due recognition and respect for the rights and freedoms of others and of meeting the just requirements of morality, public order and the general welfare in a democratic society.[16]

This classical formulation served as the model for the corresponding provisions of the European Convention on Human Rights (ECHR)[17] and later the International Covenant on Civil and Political Rights (ICCPR)[18] and the American Convention on Human Rights (ACHR).[19] On the one side of the proportionality equation are all the rights and freedoms enshrined in the Declaration. The other side contains two elements circumscribed by open formulas, namely 'the rights and freedoms of others' and (very open) 'the just requirements of morality, public order and the general welfare in a democratic society'. The relationship between the two sides is determined by two elements. First, the limitation must serve 'the purpose of securing due recognition and respect' for the interest justifying the limitation, and second, it must be 'determined by law', which amounts to a definition of the limitation by the authority competent to prescribe limitations and provide for the balancing of the two sides of the equation.

[15] For a thorough analysis of the practice of human rights courts and treaty bodies, see A Legg, *The Margin of Appreciation in Human Rights Law – Deference and Proportionality* (Oxford, Oxford University Press, 2012). For a critical review of the ECtHR case law, see J Gerards, 'Margin of Appreciation and Incrementalism in the Case Law of the European Court of Human Rights' (2018) 18 *Human Rights Law Review* 495.

[16] Art 29(2) of the Universal Declaration of Human Rights, adopted by General Assembly Resolution 217 A(III) of 10 December 1948.

[17] European Convention for the Protection of Human Rights and Fundamental Freedoms, 4 November 1950, 213 UNTS 222 No 2889.

[18] International Covenant on Civil and Political Rights, 16 December 1966, 999 UNTS 171 No 14668.

[19] American Convention on Human Rights, 'Pact of San José, Costa Rica', 22 November 1969, 1144 I UNTS 123 No 17955.

The International Covenant on Social, Economic and Cultural Rights (ICSECR) contains in Article 4 a general limitation clause that follows the model of the Universal Declaration.[20] The ICCPR, the ECHR and the ACHR do not contain a general limitation clause, but introduce the possibility of limitation of various specific guarantees.[21] One example is the freedom of opinion, set out in Articles 19 ICCPR, 10 ECHR and 13 ACHR.

Article 19 ICCPR provides:

> (2) Everyone has the right to freedom of expression …
> (3) The exercise of the rights provided for in paragraph 2 … may … be subject to certain restrictions, but these shall only be such as are provided for by law and are necessary: (a) For respect of the rights and reputation of others; (b) For the protection of national security or public order (*ordre public*), or of public health or morals.

Article 10 ECHR provides:

> (1) Everyone has the right to freedom of expression. …
> (2) The exercise of these freedoms … may be subject to such formalities, conditions, restrictions or penalties as are prescribed by law and are necessary in a democratic society, in the interest of national security, territorial integrity or public safety, for the prevention of disorder or crime, for the protection of the reputation or rights of others, for preventing the disclosure of information received in confidence, or for maintaining the authority and impartiality of the judiciary.

Article 13 ACHR is a little more detailed.

Other examples are the freedoms of conscience (Article 18 ICCPR, Article 9 ECHR and Article 12 ACHR), assembly (Article 21 ICCPR, Article 11 ECHR and Article 15 ACHR), association (Article 22 ICCPR, Article 11 ECHR and Article 16 ACHR) and privacy (Article 8 ECHR). The structure of these limitation clauses is similar: they all state that limitations must be provided 'by law' and are permissible only for certain specific purposes, which vary for the different freedoms. These competing values (B in the equation) may be defined in a general way, as in Article 19 ICCPR, or in very narrow and specific terms, as in Article 10 ECHR. The limitations must be 'necessary' to protect the competing value. Article 10 ECHR is more restrictive in this regard, specifying that they must be 'necessary in a democratic society'. Underlying these provisions, there appears to be a general concept of proportionality in the limitation of fundamental rights and freedoms. In this field, too, we observe the migration of national legal principles to the international level.

[20] International Covenant on Social, Economic and Cultural Rights, 16 December 1966, 993 UNTS 3 No 14531.

[21] The African Charter on Human and Peoples' Rights does not contain a similar regime of limitation, but a number of guarantees is subject to highly problematic 'claw-back clauses'. See G J Naldi, 'Limitation of Rights Under the African Charter on Human and Peoples' Rights: The Contribution of the African Commission on Human and Peoples' Rights' (2001) 17 *South African Journal on Human Rights* 109.

Since the 1970s, this general concept has been developed and refined, and continues to be developed in the case law of the European Court of Human Rights (ECtHR).[22] The Court examines whether there is a 'fair balance' between the protected right and the legitimate aim pursued by the state in limiting that right, and/or whether the reasons claimed to justify a restriction are relevant and sufficient.

This concept has also been recognised by human rights treaty bodies. The Human Rights Committee stated:

> States Parties must refrain from violation of the rights recognized by the Covenant, and any restrictions on any of those rights must be permissible under the relevant provisions of the Covenant. Where such restrictions are made, States must demonstrate their necessity and only take such measures as are proportionate to the pursuance of legitimate aims in order to ensure continuous and effective protection of Covenant rights. In no case may the restrictions be applied or invoked in a manner that would impair the essence of a Covenant right.[23]

This statement shows that proportionality sets a general limit on restrictions of fundamental rights, and that safeguarding the core content of such rights (the 'essence') is part of that principle.

A stronger form of human rights limitation is the possibility for states to derogate from their international obligations to guarantee these rights, provided for in a number of human rights treaties (Article 15 ECHR, Article 4 ICCPR and Article 27 ACHR). There is a vast practice of states availing themselves of this possibility.[24] In this respect, too, the principle of proportionality plays a major role. Article 15 ECHR reads:

> (1) In time of war or other public emergency threatening the life of the nation any High Contracting Party may take measures derogating from its obligations under this Convention to the extent strictly required by the exigencies of the situation, provided that such measures are not inconsistent with its other obligations under international law.

Articles 4 ICCPR and 27 ACHR have a similar structure.[25] Seen in the light of the proportionality equation discussed in section I above, in terms of side A, derogation is generally possible with the exception of a list of certain guarantees that may not be derogated from (right to life (with exceptions), prohibition of torture,

[22] For a succinct overview, see C Grabenwarter and K Pabel, *Europäische Menschenrechtskonvention*, 6th edn (München, Beck, 2016) 146ff. For a recent application of the principle, see *López Ribalda and Others v Spain* App nos 1874/13 and 8567/13 (ECtHR GC, 17 October 2019) [132] and [134].

[23] Human Rights Committee, General Comment No 31: The Nature of the General Legal Obligation Imposed on States Parties to the Covenant, 29 March 2004, UN Doc CCPR/C/21/Rev.1/Add.13, para 6.

[24] On recent ECtHR practice, see M Polzin, 'Art. 15 EMRK und die Rolle des Europäischen Gerichtshofs für Menschenrechte' (2018) 78 *Zeitschrift für ausländisches öffentliches Recht und Völkerrecht* 635. On the ICCPR, see Human Rights Committee, General Comment No 29, Art 4: Derogations during a State of Emergency, 31 August 2001, UN Doc CCPR/C.2/Add.11.

[25] The ICSECR does not contain a derogation clause.

prohibition of slavery, *nullum crimen sine lege*, etc). In relation to side B, ie, the justification of limitations, two legal questions arise in particular: the determination of situations of emergency and the assessment of the proportionality *stricto sensu* ('to the extent strictly required by the exigencies of the situation'). As regards the first question, the ECtHR grants Member States a rather broad margin of appreciation.[26] As to the second requirement, the Court exercises a strict proportionality control.[27] As to the ICCPR, the Human Rights Committee has expressed 'concerns' with regard to state practice regarding both questions.[28] However, it is difficult to discern a different standard of scrutiny for both questions.

B. International Investment Law

In international investment law, balancing the protection of the interest of foreign private investors (a property interest) and the regulatory interest of the host state has been a difficult task in a number of situations. Typical regulatory interests to be taken into account are the protection of the environment and human rights. It is proposed that the principle of proportionality should serve as a tool to harmonise investment protection, on the one hand, and regimes protecting the environment or human rights, on the other.[29] In this context, it is, however, a matter of concern that investment protection arbitrators appear to tend to give priority to the interests of investors.[30]

C. International Trade Law

In international trade law, a balancing must take place between the general community interest and well understood interests of all states in free trade, and the interest of single states in adopting regulations for the protection of preferred national interests. This question is addressed by Article XX of the General Agreement on Tariffs and Trade (GATT),[31] which allows states to establish exceptions to the general rules of the GATT ensuring the freedom of trade (most favoured nation principle, national treatment, prohibition of quantitative restrictions), but only for certain purposes listed in Article XX and subject to a limitation (in the introductory sentence of Article XX, the 'chapeau').

[26] Polzin (n 24) 641ff, 649ff.

[27] ibid 643ff.

[28] General Comment No 29 (n 24) paras 3 and 4. On the practice of the Human Rights Committee, see Franck (n 1) 759.

[29] E Guntrip, 'International Human Rights Law, Investment Arbitration and Proportionality Analysis: Panacea or Pandora's Box', *EJIL Talk!*, 7 January 2014.

[30] See, eg, *Tecmed v Mexico*, ICSID award, 29 May 2003, Case no APB(AF)/00/2.

[31] General Agreement on Tariffs and Trade, 30 October 1947, 55 UNTS 194, 308; now GATT 1994, 15 April 1994, 1867 UNTS no. 31874, 190, 33 ILM 1125 (1994).

This is a particular variation of the proportionality principle.[32] On the one side of the equation are the various provisions of the GATT ensuring freedom of trade (Articles I, III and XI in particular). On the other side, Article XX contains a list of regulatory interests which may justify 'exceptions', in other words, limitations of the trade freedoms. The formulation of the list is somewhat old-fashioned (as it was drafted in 1947), but it has been possible to give the various items a modern interpretation, in particular with respect to the possibility to ensure the protection of the environment,[33] which is covered by sub-paragraph (b) of Article XX ('necessary to protect human, animal or plant life or health') and sub-paragraph (g) of Article XX ('relating to the conservation of exhaustible natural resources …'). The idea of proportionality is enshrined in the proviso of the chapeau, which prohibits measures which would constitute a 'disguised restriction on international trade' or which are discriminatory (a point of fundamental importance as non-discrimination is a central GATT rule). Thus, the effect of the chapeau resembles that of the guarantee of the 'essence' of fundamental rights in the limitation clauses of human rights instruments. This requires a balancing between the trade interest and the competing regulatory interest. Through the case law of the GATT/WTO dispute settlement system, the interpretation of the various items on the list of regulatory interests justifying an exception and the significance of the chapeau have been clarified and concretised, including in terms of the necessary balancing process.[34] The GATT/WTO dispute settlement system also resorted to the proportionality principle in relation to another, yet often related subject, namely the reaction to an alleged previous violation of GATT rules by taking countermeasures.[35]

D. Countermeasures

(i) The Law of State Responsibility

In international law relating to state responsibility[36] and, in particular, in setting out the scope of permissible countermeasures in response to a prior or continuing injury, the International Law Commission (ILC) formulated the principle of

[32] Franck (n 1) 749ff.

[33] S Gaines, 'The WTO's Reading of the GATT Article XX Chapeau: A Disguised Restriction of Environmental Measures' (2001) 22 *University of Pennsylvania Journal of International Economic Law* 739.

[34] The leading cases (Panel Reports or Appellate Body Reports) are *Tuna/Dolphin I, Mexico et al v US*, DS21/R – 39S/155, 3 September 1991; *Reformulated Gasoline, Venezuela & Brazil v US*, DS 2, 20 May 1996; *Hormones, US & Canada v EC*, DS26/48, 13 February 1998; *Shrimp/Turtles, India et al v US*, DS58, 12 October 1998; *Seal Products, Canada v EC*, DS400, 16 June 2014.

[35] See below section IV.D.(ii).

[36] See Franck (n 1) 738ff and E Canizzaro, 'The Role of Proportionality in the Law of International Countermeasures' (2001) 12 *European Journal of International Law* 889.

proportionality in its Articles on the Responsibility of States for Internationally Wrongful Acts in the following terms:

> Countermeasures must be commensurate with the injury suffered, taking into account the gravity of the internationally wrongful act and the rights in question.[37]

This is a classical formulation of the proportionality equation. It is generally recognised that this is a rule of customary international law. In its commentary to the Articles, the ILC gives a detailed account of international jurisprudence that relies on the principle of proportionality. In the framework of state responsibility, countermeasures are a means to ensure compliance with an international legal obligation.[38] The purpose of maintaining the rule of law is both a justification and a limitation of countermeasures. The ILC explains:

> Proportionality is concerned with the relationship between the internationally wrongful act and the countermeasure. … In every case a countermeasure must be *commensurate* with the injury suffered, including the importance of the issue of principle involved … (emphasis added).[39]

(ii) International Trade Law

While, in general, international law determining the proportionality of countermeasures may be problematic in light of the absence of binding third-party decisions, the GATT/WTO regime provides for a special facilitation and control of countermeasures against alleged violations of GATT rules by another party to the agreement.[40] The specific character of the system is that it works under the strict control of the WTO Dispute Settlement Body (DSB). No countermeasures may be taken before the DSB has adopted a report stating that there is a violation of GATT rules. The general rules on countermeasures are contained in Article 22 of the Dispute Settlement Understanding (DSU),[41] and special rules on reactions to different types of forbidden subsidies are found in Articles 4 and 7 of the Agreement on Subsidies and Countervailing Measures.[42]

If the DSB finds that a state is not in compliance with WTO rules, and if that state fails to bring the measure complained of into compliance, the DSB may,

[37] ILC, Draft articles on Responsibility of States for Internationally Wrongful Acts, with commentaries (2001), Report of the International Law Commission on the work of the fifty-third session, UN Doc A/56/10, at 134 (Art 51): legal.un.org/ilc/texts/instruments/english/commentaries/9_6_2001.pdf.

[38] Art 49 of the ILC Articles on State Responsibility.

[39] ILC Articles and Commentary (n 37) at 135.

[40] Franck (n 1) 742ff.

[41] Understanding on Rules and Procedures Governing the Settlement of Disputes, Marrakesh Agreement Establishing the World Trade Organization, Annex 2, 15 April 1994, 1869 UNTS 401, No 13874.

[42] Agreement on Subsidies and Countervailing Measures, Marrakesh Agreement Establishing the World Trade Organization, Annex 1A, 15 April 1994, 1869 UNTS 401, No 13874.

according to Article 22(6) DSU, grant the aggrieved state 'authorization to suspend concessions or other obligations'. If the non-complying state objects, an arbitrator shall 'determine whether the level of such suspension is *equivalent* to the level of nullification or impairment' (emphasis added).[43] This entails a specific application of the proportionality principle. The countermeasure lawfully taken by the aggrieved state must not produce an advantage to that state which is greater than the damage resulting from the violation complained of.

A special provision on countermeasures is contained in the Agreement on Subsidies and Countervailing Measures (SCM). If the DSB determines that there is a forbidden subsidy, it may grant the aggrieved State 'authorization to take countermeasures'. Pursuant to Article 4(10) of the Agreement this authorization relates to 'appropriate countermeasures', and a footnote clarifies this is not meant to allow 'countermeasures that are *disproportionate*' (emphasis added). According to Article 7(9) SCM, the authorisation relates to 'countermeasures *commensurate with the degree and nature* of the adverse effects determined to exist' (emphasis added).

Both Article 22(7) DSU and the provisions of the SCM are expressions of the proportionality principle, but they are, nevertheless, different. This was clarified by a number of DSB rulings.[44] The term 'equivalent' in the DSU implies equality between the damage inflicted by the violation and the burden caused to the non-complying state by the countermeasure. The aggrieved state must not obtain more than the compensation of the loss inflicted by the preceding violation. The expressions 'not disproportionate' or 'commensurate' in the SCM could be interpreted as allowing states, in the calibration of the countermeasure, to take into account the need to induce future compliance, an idea which is justified by the *erga omnes* character of the prohibition of subsidies. Neither formulation allows countermeasures of a punitive character.

(iii) The Proportionality Equation and Countermeasures

Countermeasures are value deprivations used by one or several states to induce another state to comply with international law by discontinuing an alleged violation or by redressing it. The principle of proportionality serves as a limitation of these value deprivations and thus ensures that there is an equitable balance between the allegedly unlawful measure and the countermeasure. It is this balance that determines the relationship between sides A and B of the equation and makes the countermeasure an appropriate tool for ensuring compliance. In general, in international law this balance is flawed by the uncertainties of the decentralised character of the international legal order. The uncertainties of this balancing reappear in the question of the proportionality of use of force in self-defence, treated

[43] Art 22(7) DSU.
[44] For references, see Franck (n 1) 744.

in greater detail below. In international trade law, this uncertainty is to a large extent removed by the obligatory control of the GATT/WTO dispute settlement system.

E. International Law Regulating the Use of Armed Force

Proportionality also plays a central role in the rules of public international law regulating the use of force: *ius ad bellum*, the rules on resort to force, and *ius in bello* – also referred to as international humanitarian law (IHL) or the law of armed conflict –, the rules that regulate the conduct of hostilities.

(i) *Ius Ad Bellum* Proportionality

Despite its direct relevance to the prohibition of the use of force, a peremptory norm of general international law,[45] the precise application of the principle of proportionality in this field of law is less than clear. While it is uncontested that it does apply – as repeatedly recognised by the International Court of Justice (ICJ) – there is a lack of clarity and divergence of views as to precisely *how*.

Contemporary rules regulating states' resort to armed force are enshrined in the Charter of the United Nations (UN Charter) and, in particular, in Article 2(4) thereof, which requires states to 'refrain in their international relations from the threat or use of force against the territorial integrity or political independence of any state, or in any other manner inconsistent with the Purposes of the United Nations'. This prohibition is subject to two exceptions: first, use of force that is authorised by the Security Council under Chapter VII of the UN Charter; and second, use of force in the exercise of states' 'inherent right' of self-defence (Article 51 UN Charter). This right entitles states to use force in response to an actual – and, possibly, imminent – armed attack.[46] This is where the proportionality principle comes into play. As stated by the ICJ, any such use of force must be 'proportional to the armed attack and necessary to respond to it'.[47]

[45] ICJ *Case concerning Military and Paramilitary Activities in and against Nicaragua (Nicaragua v US)* (Merits, 1986 ICJ Rep 14) [190].

[46] See, for example, C Kreß, 'The International Court of Justice and the "Principle of Non-Use of Force"' in M Weller (ed), *The Oxford Handbook of the Use of Force in International Law* (Oxford, Oxford University Press, 2015) 579. Divergent views exist with regard to a number of the core elements of the right of self-defence, including whether it only arises once an attack has actually occurred or whether it also exists in relation to attacks that are imminent or, even more broadly, whether a right of 'anticipatory' self-defence exists; as well as whether the right also exists in response to armed attacks by non-state armed groups. See, for example, D Bethlehem, 'Self-Defense Against an Imminent or Actual Armed Attack by Nonstate Actors' (2012) 106 *American Journal of International Law* 769 and the responses thereto in (2013) 107 *American Journal of International Law*.

[47] *Case concerning Military and Paramilitary Activities in and against Nicaragua* (n 45) at [176] and [194]. See also *Advisory Opinion on the Legality of the Threat or Use of Nuclear Weapons* (1996 ICJ Rep 226) [41] and *Oil Platforms (Islamic Republic of Iran v United States of America)* (2003 ICJ Rep 161) [74].

Thus, proportionality is only one element in determining whether a use of force, claimed to be exercised in self-defence, is really justified as self-defence. Logically, it is the last step of the legal reasoning. First, it must be determined whether there is a situation which triggers a right of self-defence, namely an armed attack. Second, the use of force in question must indeed constitute self-defence and not, for instance, simply retaliation or an 'armed reprisal'. The prevailing but not unanimous view is that the purpose of the use of force must be limited to halting or repelling an armed attack.[48]

Determining the scope of the right of self-defence is a necessary first step to understanding how the principle of proportionality applies.[49] To the extent that self-defence can be exercised to prevent an imminent armed attack, 'repelling' must be understood as also covering that situation.[50]

Once the right to self-defence thus comes into play, any use of force for this purpose is governed by the principles of necessity and proportionality. Divergences of view persist on the relationship between the requirements of 'necessity' and 'proportionality'. While the ICJ has asserted that the use of force in self-defence must comply with these two principles, it has not provided guidance on how they are to be interpreted, and its case law is susceptible to different interpretations.[51]

The requirement of 'necessity' means that the use of force must be a measure of last resort. It is also relevant to the choice of targets of such use of force: they must be relevant to halting or repelling the attack. Not only must it be permissible to target them under the rules of international humanitarian law, but they must also be connected to the force to be repelled.[52]

What does the requirement of proportionality add? What must the force used in self-defence be proportionate to? Should it be coterminous with the permissible purpose of the use of force, ie, repelling an ongoing attack? This approach, referred to by some as the 'functional approach',[53] was first articulated in the early discussions of the ILC on state responsibility.[54] However, under this interpretation it is

[48] See, for example, T Ruys, *'Armed Attack' and Article 51 of the UN Charter* (Cambridge, Cambridge University Press, 2010) 94–95. See also Chatham House, *Principles of International Law on the Use of Force by States in Self-Defence*, ILP WP 05/01 (2005) at 10.

[49] Concerning the conceptual ambiguities existing in this regard, see D Akande and T Liefländer, 'Clarifying Necessity, Imminence and Proportionality in the Law of Self-Defence' (2013) 107 *American Journal of International Law* 563, 569.

[50] See the exchange between D Kretzmer, 'The Inherent Right to Self-Defence and Proportionality in *Ius Ad Bellum*' (2013) 24 *European Journal of International Law* 235 and G Nolte, 'Multipurpose Self-Defence, Proportionality Disoriented: A Response to David Kretzmer' (2013) 24 *European Journal of International Law* 283.

[51] Kreß (n 46) 589.

[52] Ruys (n 48) 108.

[53] ibid 112.

[54] R Ago, Addendum to the Eighth Report on State Responsibility, UN Doc A/CN.4/318/Adds.5-7, para 121, *Yearbook of the International Law Commission 1980*, Vol II, Part One, p 69. Ago rejected 'a requirement of symmetry between the mode of the initial attack and the mode of response'. This approach was referred to and adopted by Judge Higgins in her Dissenting Opinion to the *Advisory Opinion on the Legality of the Threat or Use of Nuclear Weapons* (n 47) at [5].

difficult to see what the requirement of 'proportionality' adds to what is already covered by 'necessity', which already limits use of force in this way.

Necessity and proportionality are two distinct requirements and separate content must be given to each. As a matter of legal logic, necessity comes first in a line of arguments. A measure which is unnecessary is unlawful. Any examination of proportionality is then irrelevant. In view of this, alternative interpretations of the requirement of proportionality have been suggested, including a 'quantitative' approach which requires 'some sort of equation between the *gravity* of the attack and the defensive response',[55] or one that requires proportionality between the damage inflicted in the exercise of self-defence and the objective it pursues.[56] While both these approaches are quantitative and add a different dimension to necessity, their application in practice could lead to very different results.

Consider the example of a state subjected to a series of low-intensity attacks that can only be stopped by invading the state where the perpetrators are hiding. If proportionality is understood as requiring commensurability between the harm that will be caused in self-defence and that already caused to the state acting in self-defence, the latter state would only be entitled to use the same quantum of force as the 'attacker', which would disallow invasion. Under the second interpretation, the answer is not as clear, as it requires a comparison of the harm threatened and the benefit pursued.[57]

In this connection (side B of the proportionality equation), the law is far from clear. The issue has not been addressed in case law. Necessity probably sets a *maximum* threshold of force that may be used: it may not exceed what is necessary to halt and repel an attack. It is less clear whether the requirement of proportionality adds some further 'quantitative' restriction on the permissible response – ie, not only must the use of force be necessary, but it must also not exceed some lower threshold, set by reference to the harm caused by the initial armed attack.[58]

A further aspect of *ad bellum* proportionality that has not received attention is the nature of the 'harm' that must thus be considered for the purposes of the proportionality assessment. Should it be the actual *physical* damage caused by the initial armed attack and the use of force in self-defence? To what extent should 'reverberating' effects also be considered? Should other, less tangible types of harm also be considered, such as the consequences for a state's ongoing capacity to defend itself?

Finally, there has only been limited analysis of the interplay between *ad bellum* and *in bello* proportionality. Does *ad bellum* proportionality continue to play a role when use of force continues after the *initial armed attack-use of force in self-defence* exchange? And if it does, how precisely does it operate alongside the rather different rules of proportionality under IHL?

[55] Ruys (n 48) 111.
[56] Akande and Liefländer (n 49) 566.
[57] ibid 567.
[58] Kreß (n 46) 589.

(ii) Ius In Bello Proportionality

a. The Frame of Reference for the Proportionality Assessment

The international discourse in the relevant epistemic community has been much more detailed and sophisticated in relation to the principle of proportionality in *ius in bello* than in relation to *ius ad bellum*. Therefore, many questions appear to be clearer. All aspects of the application of proportionality in the rules on the conduct of hostilities in this body of law have been the subject of extensive analysis. This includes: the frame of reference for application of the principle; what precisely the two interests to be balanced are; and the various steps in the process for conducting proportionality assessments.[59]

Proportionality is a central element of the rules regulating the conduct of hostilities and is the most apparent manifestation of the balance between military necessity and considerations of humanity that underpins international humanitarian law. Its essence is clear: in the words of Article 51(5)(b) of Additional Protocol I to the Geneva Conventions of 1949,[60] belligerents must refrain from attacks

> which may be expected to cause incidental loss of civilian life, injury to civilians, damage to civilian objects, or a combination thereof, which would be excessive in relation to the concrete and direct military advantage anticipated.

Although the prohibition refers to 'excessive' harm, this clearly constitutes a proportionality assessment.[61] The use of the term 'excessive' instead of 'proportionate' is deliberate. It gives more weight to the military advantage, at least in the perception of some participants in the negotiations, than the word 'disproportionate'.[62]

[59] However, proportionality also plays a role in relation to other rules of IHL. See, eg, Israel Supreme Court, *Beit Sourik Village Council v Government of Israel* case (HCJ 2056/04, 43 ILM 1099 (2004)) at [34], discussed in M Koskenniemi, 'Occupation and Sovereignty – Still a Useful Distinction?' in O Engdahl and P Wrange (eds), *Law at War: The Law as it Was and the Law as it Should Be. Liber Amicorum Ove Bring* (Leiden, Nijhoff, 2008) 163, 167. In this connection (the law of belligerent occupation), the structure of the proportionality argument is the same as that used in the field of human rights, see above section IV.A.

[60] Protocol Additional to the Geneva Conventions of 12 August 1949, and Relating to the Protection of Victims of International Armed Conflicts of 8 June 1977, 1125 UNTS 3, No 17512 ('AP I'). The prohibition is considered a rule of customary law applicable in international and non-international armed conflicts. Rule 14, ICRC Customary Law Study, L Doswald-Beck and J-M Henckaerts, *Customary International Humanitarian Law, Volume I – Rules* (Cambridge, Cambridge University Press, 2005).

[61] The original draft of this provision submitted by the International Committee of the Red Cross (ICRC) in 1973 used the term 'disproportionate'. This was unacceptable to some States in the negotiations and was replaced by 'excessive' without leaving clear traces of the debate in the Conference documentation. See F Kalshoven, 'Reaffirmation and Development of International Humanitarian Law Applicable in Armed Conflicts: The Diplomatic Conference, Geneva, 1974–1977' (1978) 9 *Netherlands Yearbook of International Law* 107, 117. Modern interpreters insist on the difference between 'disproportionate' and 'excessive', see W Heintschel von Heinegg in K Ipsen, *Völkerrecht* (V Epping and W Heintschel von Heinegg (eds)), 7th edn (München, Beck, 2018) 1349ff and references therein. See also W Heintschel von Heinegg, 'Proportionality and Collateral Damage' in R Wolfrum (ed), *Max Planck Encyclopedia of Public International Law (MPEPIL)*, available at: www.mpepil.com.

[62] It is not clear whether the customary law rule is identical to the formulation in the AP I. Some suggest that proportionality is broader in nature under customary law, specific IHL protection regimes

As for *ius ad bellum* proportionality, the frame of reference for conducting the proportionality assessment must be determined. For proportionality to come into play in relation to the conduct of hostilities, a number of conditions need to be met. First, the harm must be *incidental* – that is, it must occur in the course of an attack directed against a military objective. Attacks directed against civilian objects are unlawful – it would be wrong to introduce a proportionality assessment. Second, the harm must be expected to arise as a result of an 'attack' as this term is understood in IHL.[63] Not every use of force or military operation in an armed conflict constitutes an 'attack'. This is, for instance, a problem in relation to cyber operations that cause harm to an enemy. Third, a problem arises from the fact that a military operation most often tends to consist of a plurality of smaller operations. In view of this, what is the appropriate frame of reference for the proportionality assessment? A number of states participating in the negotiations of the Additional Protocols declared that it is the military advantage anticipated from an attack considered *as a whole* and not only from isolated parts thereof that must be considered.[64] In determining whether a particular act of violence amounts to an 'attack as a whole' and, therefore, constitutes the entire frame of reference for a proportionality assessment, consideration must be given to the context in which the act is conducted. If the anticipated military advantage is not dependent on or affected by other acts, then that act should be considered an 'attack as a whole'. If the act at hand is an element in a larger operation in which other acts contribute to the military advantage – for example, coordinated air attacks on a particular target or a set of interdependent targets – then the operation in its entirety should be considered the 'attack as a whole'.[65] Whatever the precise parameters of 'an attack as a whole' in a given case, the same interpretation and, thus, the same frame of reference must be adopted for determining what falls within each of the two sides of the proportionality assessment. The incidental harm expected from a specific attack as a whole must be balanced against the military advantage anticipated from that *same* attack.

b. Elements of the Proportionality Assessment

Under IHL, proportionality assessments must be conducted by belligerents *ex ante* when planning and prior to launching an attack, based on information they have

or under proportionality as a 'general principle' of the law of armed conflict. See discussion and references in E-C Gillard, *Proportionality in the Conduct of Hostilities: the Incidental Harm Side of the Assessment* (2018) Chatham House Research Paper (Chatham House Report) para 16.

[63] Art 49(1) AP I defines attacks as 'acts of violence against the adversary, whether in offence or in defence'.

[64] See essentially identical declarations upon ratification of AP I made by Australia, Belgium, Canada, France, Germany, Italy, the Netherlands, New Zealand, Spain and the UK, available at: ihl-databases.icrc.org/applic/ihl/ihl.nsf/States.xsp?xp_viewStates=XPages_NORMStatesParties&xp_treatySelected=470.

[65] See, eg, W Solf, 'Civilian Population' in M Bothe, KJ Partsch and W Solf, *New Rules for Victims of Armed Conflicts*, 2nd edn (Leiden, Brill, 2013) 329.

or should reasonably be expected to have from all sources in given circumstances. If information reasonably available at the time of the decision to attack later proves to be incorrect, this does not affect the lawfulness of the action taken. It might provide important guidance for future assessments.

Proportionality requires balancing the concrete and direct military advantage (A), against certain specific types of incidental harm: death or injury of civilians and damage to civilian objects (B). The process for doing so consists of four key steps: identifying the nature of the harm and advantage to be considered; ensuring that requirements of causation and foreseeability are met; assigning a weight to harm and advantage; and determining whether the harm is excessive compared to the advantage.[66]

Nature of Military Advantage and Incidental Harm

The advantage must be of a military nature. Political, economic or other non-military benefits are not relevant; nor is weakening the morale of the civilian population under the enemy's control.[67] The expected advantage must be identifiable and quantifiable and flow directly from the attack.

As far as incidental harm is concerned, divergences of view currently exist as to whether certain types of harm should be considered, including the death or injury of 'voluntary' human shields or military medical personnel, mental harm, damage to dual-use objects and 'reverberating' or 'knock on' harm.[68]

Causation

Causation requires establishing a causal relation between an attack and particular incidental harm. If the attack is expected to be the *sole* cause of the harm, determining causation is straightforward; so much so that in practice the proportionality analysis focuses solely on foreseeability. In such situations, incidental harm can be considered as caused by the attack if it is the outcome that was expected to occur from the attack in the ordinary course of events.[69]

Establishing causation becomes more complicated when more than one actor is involved – this could be the opponent or some other actor not a party to the conflict, such as an intergovernmental organisation that imposes sanctions. Setting aside questions of foreseeability, the fact that a second actor intervened does not automatically preclude the ensuing incidental harm from being considered as caused by the attack.

[66] See discussion in Chatham House Report (n 62) s 3.

[67] For a recent discussion, see International Law Association Study Group, 'The Conduct of Hostilities and International Humanitarian Law – Challenges of 21st Century Warfare', Final Report, 25 June 2017, 'Part II: The Principle of Proportionality' (ILA Study Group Report).

[68] Chatham House Report (n 62) s 4; ILA Study Group Report (n 67); and, eg, J Kleffner, 'Military Collaterals and Ius In Bello Proportionality' (2018) 48 *Israel Yearbook on Human Rights* 43.

[69] This is the approach adopted in other areas of public international law. See, eg, B Cheng, *General Principles of Law as Applied by International Courts and Tribunals*, 2nd edn (Cambridge, Grotius, 1987) 245.

In such circumstances the incidental harm to be considered is that which would not occur *but for* the attack – with one limitation. Harm that results from the conduct of an actor other than the attacker and does not arise from the *physical effects* of the attack is excluded. For example, the death or injury of persons used as involuntary human shields is included in the incidental harm to be considered. Even though it is the conduct of the attacker's opponent that placed them at risk, the harm is a result of the *physical effects* of the attack. By contrast, if the opponent were to execute people in retaliation for an attack, the harm would not be considered as caused by the attack as it was not caused by the *physical effects* of the attack. This step of the analysis is particularly relevant for 'reverberating' harm.[70]

Foreseeability

The next element of the analysis is determining whether the harm was *foreseeable* when the attack was planned or launched. In other areas of international law, 'foreseeability' is interpreted as referring to *reasonable* foreseeability, ie, what *should* have been foreseen. This injects an objective dimension.[71] The same approach applies to the identification of the harm in proportionality assessments:[72] it is the incidental harm that a reasonable person in circumstances of the person planning or launching the attack should have foreseen.

Weight

Once the relevant military advantage and incidental harm have been identified, a value or weight must be assigned to them. This makes it possible to take into account a range of factors, starting from the likelihood that the harm or military advantage in question will occur. This is a different and additional question to its foreseeability. Foreseeability relates to whether something can be expected to occur. 'Likelihood' relates to the *probability* that it will do so. For example, while it is foreseeable that the use of cluster munitions may cause civilian injuries and death, the likelihood of it doing so will depend on the expected dud rate of the cluster sub-munitions and the location of the attack. The lower the likelihood of a particular harm or military advantage occurring, the less weight is to be given to it.[73]

Other factors that affect weight include the severity of the expected harm. Assigning weight to different types of incidental harm also allows consideration to be given to some of the adverse effects of attacks on civilians that do not fall within the scope of incidental harm. For example, displacement of civilians does not

[70] Chatham House Report (n 62) paras 61–69.

[71] Cheng (n 69) 249–51.

[72] See, eg, I Robinson and E Nohle, 'Proportionality and Precautions in Attack: The Reverberating Effects of Using Explosive Weapons in Populated Areas' (2016) 98 *International Review of the Red Cross* 107, 119–21.

[73] See, eg, *Prosecutor v Ante Gotovina et al*, ICTY, Prosecution's Public Redacted Final Trial Brief, 2 August 2010, [549].

constitute incidental harm per se. However, the fact that displacement is likely to occur *as a result* of an attack expected to destroy civilian homes affects the weight to be given to that destruction.

Excessive

The final step in proportionality assessments is determining whether the expected incidental harm is excessive compared to the concrete and direct military advantage anticipated. As in other areas of law, this requires comparing two incommensurable factors.

Neither Additional Protocol I nor military manuals provide guidance on how to interpret the notion of 'excessive'. There is no indication that the imbalance needs to be significant. When considering individual criminal responsibility for attacks that violate the rule of proportionality, the International Criminal Tribunal for the Former Yugoslavia (ICTY) held that it is necessary to determine whether 'a reasonably well-informed person in the circumstances of the actual perpetrator making reasonable use of the information available to him or her, could have expected excessive civilian casualties to result from the attack'.[74] This approach has been refined by replacing the notion of reasonable 'person' with that of reasonable 'commander'.[75]

'Excessive' is a wide but not indeterminate standard. Provided they do what is required to collect information on which to base their assessment and conduct the assessment in good faith and in a manner that is reasonable, belligerents have 'a fairly broad margin of judgment'[76] to determine whether the expected incidental harm would be excessive.

Some states' armed forces have developed sophisticated procedures and analytical matrices to assist commanders in identifying expected incidental harm and to promote objectivity and consistency in proportionality assessments.[77] These 'collateral-damage estimation' methodologies aim to ensure that commanders are provided with all necessary information, and assist in the assigning of values to the incidental harm to be considered. They do not, however, address the question of whether the expected harm would be *excessive*. This decision cannot result from the application of a mechanical formula but remains a value judgement to be made by the commander, in good faith and in a reasonable manner.

[74] *Prosecutor v Stanislav Galić*, ICTY, Trial Chamber, IT-98-29, Judgment, 5 December 2003, [58].

[75] See, eg, ICTY, *Final Report to the Prosecutor by the Committee Established to Review the NATO Bombing Campaign Against the Federal Republic of Yugoslavia* (2000) 39 *International Legal Materials* 1257, para 50.

[76] Y Sandoz, C Swinarski and B Zimmermann (eds), *Commentary on the Additional Protocols of 8 June 1977 to the Geneva Conventions of 12 August 1949* (Geneva, ICRC, 1987) para 2210.

[77] See, eg, Australian Defence Doctrine Publication 3.14, Targeting, para 4.16; and US Chairman of the Joint Chiefs of Staff Instruction, 'No-Strike and the Collateral Damage Estimation Methodology', CJCSI 3160.01, 13 February 2009.

V. Enforcing and Concretising the Proportionality Principle

The starting point of this chapter was the fact that the principle of proportionality is a technique of legal reasoning used in many legal orders. It is characterised by its indeterminate character, even by its vagueness. Nevertheless, its use in relevant discourses, some of which have been presented in this chapter, shows that it has practical strength, and that it is effective, even in the highly decentralised international legal order.[78]

In relevant discourses, the principle gains its practical shape. It is concretised to become effective. It has been shown that the central aspect of this concretisation of the proportionality principle is a balancing process which has two elements: the determination of the competing or contradictory interests at stake (the two sides of the equation) and the determination of their relative weight. The first determination lends itself to rule-making, whereas the latter means decision-making in concrete cases.[79] This entails a fundamental institutional problem: who is entitled to take this decision? Does this decision possess legitimacy and authority?

The practical application of the principle, ie, its concretisation in individual cases or types of cases, has never been easy, as in these cases it must be decided which interests and values must be put on each side of the equation and how these interests or values are to be balanced. This chapter has demonstrated that this can be done in a variety of ways and means. Institutions matter. There is the question called 'oversight'. At a certain point in the course of a controversy, one has to move from the 'arguable', the fuzzy logic, to the hard decision of a concrete case. In national law, in the law of the EU and under regional human rights conventions, the application of the principle is in the hands of courts, which, through their jurisprudence, give the principle concrete shape. In the field of international human rights law, treaty bodies have various procedures for exercising oversight and enforcement. In the field of trade law, the jurisprudence of the GATT/WTO Dispute Settlement Body is essential. In the field of investment law, there is arbitration, in particular under the International Centre for Settlement of Investment Disputes (ICSID) framework, but its approach is open to criticism.

In the other fields of international law just discussed, the role of judicial or quasi-judicial bodies is limited but, nevertheless, relevant. Certain cases have been brought before international courts or tribunals. Their jurisprudence provides orientation.

With regard to *ius ad bellum*, the ICJ has issued a small number of judgments which address the principle of proportionality in relation to self-defence

[78] On this counter-intuitive phenomenon, see Franck (n 1) 717ff and Canizzaro (n 36) 916.
[79] Kleinlein (n 14) 668.

in abstracto[80] and apply it to the case in question, but they provide little guidance as to rules on the standard of judicial scrutiny.

With regard to *ius in bello*, there are contexts where military commanders are constantly undertaking proportionality assessments during the conduct of hostilities. There has been an intense academic and political discourse on the elements of the proportionality equation in specific cases, in particular concerning the conflict in the former Yugoslavia and certain Israeli armed interventions in the Gaza Strip. Part of this discourse was conducted by groups of experts who tried to concretise certain elements of *ius in bello* and one focused specifically on proportionality. The practical effect of these (quite numerous) expert works depends on their ability to convince relevant actors, be they state decision makers, be they courts. The frequent resort to these expert groups indicates that international practice has assigned considerable practical impact to them.[81]

The development of international criminal law and, in particular, the establishment and jurisprudence of international criminal tribunals, has added a judicial element to the practical application of the principle of proportionality in *ius in bello*.[82] The rule of proportionality is also the basis of a war crime in the Statute of the International Criminal Court (ICC); the war crime is narrower in scope than the rule in Additional Protocol I, only covering attacks where the expected incidental harm is 'clearly excessive' compared to the anticipated military advantage,[83] a text which continues the debate concerning the words 'proportionate' and 'excessive'.[84] To date, investigations and prosecutions of this crime have been rare.[85] One of the reasons for this is no doubt the difficulty in determining whether the incidental harm is indeed 'clearly excessive'. Prosecutors are likely to find in other possible crimes easier and 'safer' bases for investigations.[86]

This is not an indication that proportionality in IHL serves no purpose – such a conclusion would be taking an overly narrow view of how IHL works. Even if intrinsically not amenable to external oversight, the rule plays a fundamental role in affecting the behaviour of parties to armed conflict. It requires them to ensure they have systems in place to gather and analyse information and to exercise

[80] ICJ, *Legality of the Use or Threat of Nuclear Weapons* (n 47) at [41]; *Military and Paramilitary Activities in and against Nicaragua* (n 45) at [176]; *Oil Platforms, Iran v US* (n 47) at [76ff], [194] and [237ff]; and *Armed Activities in the Territory of the Congo, DRC v Uganda*, 19 December 2005, [146ff].

[81] M Bothe, 'Private Normunternehmer im Völkerrecht: Gedanken zur Fortentwicklung des Völkerrechts durch nicht-staatliche Institutionen' in H Hestemeyer, D König, N Matz-Lück, V Röben, A Seibert-Fohr, P-T Stoll and S Vöneky (eds), *Coexistence, Cooperation and Solidarity. Liber Amicorum Rüdiger Wolfrum*, vol II (Leiden, Brill, 2012) 1399.

[82] ICTY, *Prosecutor v Gotovina* (n 73); ICTY, *Final Report* (n 75) 71ff; and Franck (n 1) 734ff.

[83] Art 8(2)(b)(iv) ICC Statute.

[84] See above section IV.E.(ii). and n 61.

[85] See, eg, R Bartels, 'Dealing with the Principle of Proportionality in Armed Conflict in Retrospect: The Application of the Principle in International Criminal Trials' (2013) 46 *Israel Law Review* 271.

[86] The question of proportionality of damage caused by an attack must be distinguished from that of the proportionality of a sanction imposed as a consequence of an allegedly criminal act; on the latter aspect, see *Prosecutor v Galić*, ICTY, Appeals Chamber, IT-98-29-A, Judgment, 30 November 2006, at 204–5, [6]–[7].

restraint in the conduct of hostilities. External oversight is probably best suited to looking at whether all feasible measures were taken by the relevant decision-makers to ensure compliance with the rule.

Most of these considerations apply mutatis mutandis to other contexts where proportionality matters. All these institutional elements give life and shape to the principle of proportionality in international relations.

15

Proportionality and Efficiency in Sentencing under International Criminal Law

THOMAS WEIGEND

I. Introduction: Proportionality, Efficiency and Sentencing

A. Proportionality

Much of the debate on sentencing concerns the issue of proportionality. But the focus has traditionally been placed on a rather elusive matter, that is, the proportionality of the offender's guilt to the severity of the sanction. Since these two items belong to different spheres (the one concerning individual moral blame, the other measured in years of imprisonment or in sums of money), the construction of a 'just proportion' between them is difficult if not impossible.[1] All that can be expected is an approximation to ordinal proportionality, that is, the rule that a more serious crime should draw more severe punishment than a less serious crime.[2] One may well call this rule a matter of proportionality; but it has little to do with proportionality as it is being understood in public law: a concept limiting the state's authority to use force or constraint upon citizens.[3]

[1] See N Lacey, 'The Metaphor of Proportionality' (2016) 43(1) *Journal of Law and Society* 27, 40, pointing out that empirical studies have found consensus among different cultures on ordinal assessment of the seriousness of crimes, but that cardinal proportionality (ie, what punishment 'fits' larceny or robbery or murder) remains controversial. For empirical research in this regard, see P H Robinson and J M Darley, 'Intuitions of Justice' (2007) 81 *Southern California Law Review* 1; P H Robinson, *Intuitions of Justice and the Utility of Desert* (Oxford, Oxford University Press, 2013).

[2] On the importance of ordinal justice in sentencing, see A von Hirsch 'Proportionality in the Philosophy of Punishment' (1992) 16 *Crime and Justice* 55, 79–83; A Ashworth and A von Hirsch, *Proportionate Sentencing: Exploring the Principles* (Oxford, Oxford University Press, 2005) 139.

[3] For an informative overview of the many usages of the metaphor of proportionality in modern philosophical and legal discourse, see Lacey (n 1) 27–38.

This chapter follows the traditional path of analysing proportionality in sentencing, albeit in a special area, namely in the rules of international criminal law (*stricto sensu*) and their application by international tribunals. It is worthwhile, however, to point out that there exists a connection between sentencing and the general debate on proportionality. As the editors of this volume wrote, criminal justice is Janus-faced: 'the positive obligation to actively protect freedom and human dignity' through implementing and enforcing minimal rules for living together peacefully 'clashes with the negative obligation to safeguard people's fundamental rights from institutional interferences'.[4] Proportionality, on a general level, thus describes the ideal of achieving a perfect balance between protecting people's basic rights and interests against predators, on the one hand, and respecting their autonomy to act (and not to act) at will, on the other hand. In other words, proportionality requires that the state extend its power to punish exactly so far as is necessary for safeguarding the citizens' and the community's legitimate interests in need of protection. For criminal policy, proportionality translates into the *ultima ratio* principle: the state may use its inherent authority to enact and enforce criminal laws only to the extent indispensable for the protection of legitimate interests. At the same time, the state would neglect its duty to protect its citizens from harm, if it did not react to perceived (new) threats to such interests: a too timid or outdated criminal code that fails to address, for example, new threats to privacy or to property interests would be disproportionate in relation to the state's obligation to maintain a peaceful and safe environment for its citizens.

Sentencing law makes a significant contribution to this general attempt to strike a balance between different liberty interests. Criminal sentences have both a practical and a symbolic function. Their practical function is to prevent crime both by physically incapacitating (would-be) offenders through incarcerating them and by deterring them from committing offences through the threat of punishment. The symbolic function of sentences is to rank various offences according to their seriousness. Through both functions, sentences reinforce and at the same differentiate the prohibitions inherent in criminal laws. The differentiating aspect has a direct bearing on proportionality: if a law punished a minor offence (for example, shoplifting of an inexpensive item) with life imprisonment, it would clearly be disproportionate, and a court applying it would likewise violate the principle of proportionality by inflicting more harm on the offender than necessary to reach the purpose of upholding the rule against shoplifting. At the same time, such a law would miss its function of ranking offences by their seriousness: providing the same sentence for murder and shoplifting would violate the principle of relative proportionality and thus undermine the symbolic function of sentencing law. The same consideration can be applied, mutatis mutandis, to overly lenient sentences: a maximum sentence of one year's imprisonment, for example, for the crime of

[4] See Emmanouil Billis', Nandor Knust's and Jon Petter Rui's chapter 1 in this volume.

genocide would not only fail to protect the population from highly dangerous offenders but would also wreak havoc on any system of relative proportionality of criminal sentences.

Sentencing is thus closely connected to criminal law's general function of balancing the liberty interests of potential perpetrators and potential victims. Severe sentences must be provided and imposed if vital interests of individuals or the community are at stake; for the protection of less important interests or in cases of minor violations, sentences must be moderate, lest the *ultima ratio* principle be violated.

B. Efficiency

Efficiency also plays a role in the proportionality calculus. The practical function of sentencing would be moot if in fact no crime preventive effect were reached. In other words, criminal sentences that neither deter anyone (including the sentenced offender) from committing crimes nor prevent recidivism through rehabilitation are reduced to their symbolic function; and even that function would be undermined if the sanction imposed were superfluous, for example because a mere public declaration that the offender is guilty would have the same symbolic effect. Punishment without a positive effect would be inherently disproportionate because it causes suffering for the sentenced person without achieving any positive purpose.

If a person unbiased by centuries-old traditions was given the task of devising a system for preventing crime in a way that is least restrictive and painful, he or she might not primarily think of resorting to criminal punishment, because it is counter-intuitive to expect positive effects on a rule-breaker from locking him up in a prison. What saves the present system of imposing punishment from the verdict of being inherently disproportionate – in the sense of making individuals suffer without any proven positive effect – is our lack of empirical knowledge about the effects of punishment. Only two extreme positions seem to be incompatible with empirical research: first, the proposition that imposing sanctions for crime has no preventive effect at all, and second, the hypothesis that there is a reverse-proportional relation between the severity of punishment and the incidence of crime.[5] What we are left with, then, is a reasonable assumption that the imposition and enforcement of criminal sanctions, as a whole, has *some* deterrent effect and helps to strengthen the social validity of the rules that criminal law is designed to protect. Except for extreme differences between sentences, however, we cannot say that more severe sanctions are more efficient in reducing crime than

[5] For findings on the lack of impact of sentencing decisions on reoffending, see C Tetal, 'Hat die Art der strafrechtlichen Sanktion Einfluss auf die Legalbewährung?' in K Boers and M Schaerff (eds), *Kriminologische Welt in Bewegung* (Mönchengladbach, Forum Verlag Godesberg, 2018) 445.

milder sanctions.[6] It is against this background that we now turn to sentencing in international criminal law.

II. Sentencing Law of International Criminal Tribunals

Because of their high impact on public opinion, sentencing practices of criminal courts 'must evidence the highest degree of internal integrity if they are to cultivate political and public support'.[7] Yet, sentencing by international criminal tribunals does not have a good press. After the conviction and sentencing of more than 150 individuals by the International Criminal Court (ICC) and the temporary international tribunals for the former Yugoslavia (International Criminal Tribunal for the former Yugoslavia, ICTY) and for Rwanda (International Criminal Tribunal for Rwanda, ICTR),[8] many observers think that sentencing at these courts is 'disparate, uncertain and inconsistent'.[9] One scholar criticised the 'confusion and obfuscation on the part of the ad hoc tribunals relating to the possible scope and meaning to be accorded to penal justifications',[10] and another author even claimed that sentences at the ICTY were picked randomly so that 'sentencing … has become a game of Russian roulette'.[11]

This impression may not be entirely accurate. And even if principled sentencing is indeed not the strongest feature of international criminal tribunals, one

[6] For a summary of the state of empirical research on the individually preventive effects of criminal sanctioning, see J Kaspar, 'Kriminologische Forschungsfelder' in E Hilgendorf, H Kudlich and B Valerius (eds), *Handbuch des Strafrechts*, vol 1 (Heidelberg, CF Müller, 2019) 953, 989–992 (noting that individualised rehabilitative measures may have a positive effect on prisoners).

[7] S Dana, 'Revisiting the Blaskic Sentence: Some Reflections on the Sentencing Jurisprudence of the ICTY' (2004) 4 *International Criminal Law Review* 321, 323. For a similar assessment, see M B Harmon and F Gaynor, 'Ordinary Sentences for Extraordinary Crimes' (2007) 5 *Journal of International Criminal Justice* 683, 707: 'Sentencing, therefore, arguably means more to victims, the accused, and the public at large than almost any other issue that arises during trial.'

[8] 90 persons have been convicted and sentenced by the ICTY (www.icty.org/node/9590), 62 by the ICTR (unictr.irmct.org/en/tribunal) and four individuals have been sentenced by the ICC. For an overview of sentencing outcomes at all international and hybrid courts as of 2013, see A Smeulers, B Hola and T van den Berg, 'Sixty-Five Years of International Criminal Justice: The Facts and Figures' (2013) 13 *International Criminal Law Review* 7, 21.

[9] K Ambos, *Treatise on International Criminal Law*, vol II (Oxford, Oxford University Press, 2014) 268 (with references in fn 166). See also M Bagaric and J Morss, 'International Sentencing Law: In Search of a Justification and Coherent Framework' (2006) 6 *International Criminal Law Review* 191, 193; R D Sloane, 'Sentencing for the "Crime of Crimes"' (2007) 5 *Journal of International Criminal Justice* 713, 716–17; S Szoke-Burke, 'Avoiding Belittlement of Human Suffering' (2012) 10 *Journal of International Criminal Justice* 561, 568 (criticising the perfunctory reasoning on sentencing in ICTR judgments).

[10] R Henham, 'The Philosophical Foundations of International Sentencing' (2003) 1(1) *Journal of International Criminal Justice* 64, 69.

[11] O Olusanya, *Sentencing War Crimes and Crimes against Humanity under the International Criminal Tribunal for the Former Yugoslavia* (Groningen, Europa Law Publishing, 2005) 139. See also D Scalia, 'Long-Term Sentences in International Criminal Law' (2011) 9 *Journal of International Criminal Justice* 669, 681–84, claiming that the (non-)regulation of sentence length at the ICTY and the ICTR violates the principle of legality.

should take into account the fact that sentencing judges at these tribunals are faced with some problems beyond those confronted by domestic judges.[12] Let us first take a brief look at the legal rules concerning the imposition of sentences, taking as an example the rules of the ICC, which are more extensive and sophisticated than the relevant provisions for the ICTY[13] and the ICTR.[14] Article 77 ICC Statute provides:

> Applicable penalties
>
> 1. … the Court may impose one of the following penalties on a person convicted of a crime referred to in article 5 of this Statute:
>
> (a) Imprisonment for a specified number of years, which may not exceed a maximum of 30 years; or
>
> (b) A term of life imprisonment when justified by the extreme gravity of the crime and the individual circumstances of the convicted person.

In addition, the Court may impose a fine and order forfeiture of the proceeds of the crime (Article 77(2) ICC Statute). With respect to the selection of sentence, Article 78(1) ICC Statute specifies that the Court should 'take into account such factors as the gravity of the crime and the individual circumstances of the convicted person'.

Further guidance is provided by Rule 145 of the ICC Rules of Procedure and Evidence. Sub-rule 1(c) of Rule 145 advises the Court to

> give consideration, *inter alia*, to the extent of the damage caused, in particular the harm caused to the victims and their families, the nature of the unlawful behaviour and the means employed to execute the crime; the degree of participation of the convicted person; the degree of intent; the circumstances of manner, time and location; and the age, education, social and economic condition of the convicted person.

As if these were not enough factors for the sentencing court to consider, Rule 145(2) further offers a list of two mitigating and six aggravating circumstances. Notably, any effort by the convicted person 'to compensate the victims and any cooperation with the Court'[15] are named as mitigating factors (Rule 145(2)(a)(ii)).

[12] For comprehensive monographs on sentencing by international criminal tribunals, see J C Nemitz, *Strafzumessung im Völkerstrafrecht* (Freiburg, Edition Iuscrim, 2002); F Melloh, *Einheitliche Strafzumessung in den Rechtsquellen des ICC-Statuts* (Berlin, Duncker & Humblot, 2010); S D'Ascoli, *Sentencing in International Criminal Law* (Oxford, Hart Publishing, 2011); A Epik, *Die Strafzumessung bei Taten nach dem Völkerstrafgesetzbuch* (Tübingen, Mohr Siebeck, 2017).

[13] According to Art 24 of the ICTY Statute, the trial chamber could impose (only) penalties of imprisonment. Art 24 sub-s 2 further specified that the judges, in imposing the sentences, 'should take into account such factors as the gravity of the offence and the individual circumstances of the convicted person'. For a thoughtful and critical account of ICTY sentencing practice, see Harmon and Gaynor (n 7).

[14] Art 23 of the ICTR Statute is almost identical to Art 24 ICTY Statute.

[15] This provision opens the door for rewarding guilty pleas and other types of procedural 'cooperation' of the defendant by reducing his sentence. On the influence on sentences of pleading guilty, see, eg, N A Combs, *Guilty Pleas in International Criminal Law* (Stanford CA, Stanford University Press, 2006); D'Ascoli (n 12) 315–17; J I Turner and T Weigend, 'Negotiated Justice' in G Sluiter, H Friman, S Linton,

The imposition of a life sentence is regarded as exceptional: Rule 145(3) permits it only 'when justified by the extreme gravity of the crime and the individual circumstances of the convicted person, as evidenced by the existence of one or more aggravating circumstances'.

Proportionality is not explicitly mentioned among the factors the sentencing court should take into account. However, Article 81(2)(a) ICC Statute provides that both the prosecutor and the defendant may appeal a sentence 'on the ground of disproportion between the crime and the sentence'.

III. Sentencing Rationales in International Criminal Law

ICC Judges are thus faced with a smorgasbord of sentencing factors, offered without any guidance on how they relate to each other and what relative weight they should be given in any individual sentencing judgment. In this situation, it may help to look for the overarching rationales and purposes of punishment in international criminal law.[16]

In general, sentencing by international tribunals is based on the same rationales as in domestic jurisdictions. These can be roughly divided into considerations regarding the instrumental purposes of punishment and considerations about a just proportion between the offence and the sanction. In making this distinction, one should keep in mind that a categorical borderline between these two groups of considerations does not exist. On the one hand, the imposition of a proportional sentence may – and normally does – fulfil the function of restoring social peace and deterring would-be offenders; on the other hand, a sentence designed to deter or rehabilitate the offender will often be commensurate with his culpability.[17]

S Vasiliev and S Zappalà (eds), *International Criminal Procedure* (Oxford, Oxford University Press, 2012) 1375; J I Turner, 'Plea Bargaining and International Criminal Justice' (2017) 48 *University of the Pacific Law Review* 219; A Petrig, 'Negotiated Justice and the Goals of International Criminal Tribunals' (2018) 8 *Chicago-Kent Journal of International and Comparative Law* 1. For a critical appreciation of plea bargaining, see E Hoven, 'Elf Stunden für ein Menschenleben' (2013) 125 *Zeitschrift für die gesamte Strafrechtswissenschaft* 137, 162–65. See also E Billis and N Knust, 'Alternative Types of Procedure' in U Sieber, V Mitsilegas, C Mylonopoulos, E Billis and N Knust (eds), *Alternative Systems of Crime Control* (Berlin, Duncker & Humblot, 2018) 43–48 (with further references). See also the discussion on using the defendant's behaviour during trial and even his choice to remain silent as aggravating factors in *Prosecutor v Delalic*, ICTY, Appeals Chamber, IT-96-21-A20, Judgment, 20 February 2001, [783], [788].

[16] For an overview, see G Werle and F Jeßberger, *Völkerstrafrecht*, 5th edn (Tübingen, Mohr Siebeck, 2020) 52–57; for a detailed analysis, see A Werkmeister, *Straftheorien im Völkerstrafrecht* (Baden-Baden, Nomos, 2015).

[17] *cf* T Walter, 'Das Absolute wird relativ – wie sich Vergeltung als Strafzweck soziologisch begründen lässt' in F Neubacher and M Kubink (eds), *Kriminologie – Jugendkriminalrecht – Strafvollzug. Gedächtnisschrift für Michael Walter* (Berlin, Duncker & Humblot, 2014) 831; T Walter, 'Die Vergeltungsidee als Grenze des Strafrechts' (2019) 74 *Juristenzeitung* 649.

A. Rehabilitation

The most constructive purpose of criminal punishment is the rehabilitation or resocialisation of the offender. Imprisoned offenders should be offered schooling and vocational training as well as psychological or therapeutic support so that they are fit upon their release to deal with the challenges of social life without committing further crimes. However, several features of international criminal law and its application argue against a primarily rehabilitative approach: first, offenders convicted by international tribunals are not normally young persons prone to be re-educated toward leading a law-abiding life. Second, trials before international tribunals often take place only after a lawless regime has been deposed, so that the leaders of the former regime will not have an opportunity to continue with their criminal activities. Third, leading personnel as well as ground soldiers carrying out unlawful orders may be persons who are in fact socially particularly well integrated and ready to abide by the social norms prevalent at the time.[18] Fourth, the very serious offences typically adjudicated by international tribunals cannot be characterised as mere indications of the offender's need for rehabilitation.[19]

Although international tribunals do not regard rehabilitation as the prime purpose of sentencing,[20] they sometimes mention an offender's personal hardship or positive features of his personality as factors for the mitigation of punishment, however without quantifying the impact of such factors. For example, the ICC in *Prosecutor v Katanga* took into account the defendant's young age at the time of committing the crimes in question, the fact that he had a large family and his protective disposition toward civilians, but accorded these factors only 'very limited weight'.[21]

B. Deterrence

Special deterrence; that is, making the offender desist from committing similar crimes for fear of being punished (again), has only a limited role to play in international criminal law, because a person convicted by an international tribunal

[18] See Hoven (n 15) 145–47.

[19] *cf Prosecutor v Delalic* (n 15) [805]–[806]; *Prosecutor v Milutinovic et al*, ICTY, Trial Chamber, IT-05-87-T, Judgment, 26 February 2009, [1146]. For a similar conclusion as to the minor role of rehabilitation in international criminal justice, see Harmon and Gaynor (n 7) 693–94. See, however, Epik (n 12) 123–28, arguing that rehabilitation of international offenders is both necessary and feasible.

[20] See *Prosecutor v Popovic et al*, ICTY, Appeals Chamber, IT-05-88-A, Judgment, 30 January 2015, [1966]; *Prosecutor v Katanga*, ICC, Trial Chamber, ICC-01/04-01/07, Decision on Sentence, 23 March 2014, [38]; *Prosecutor v Bemba Gombo*, ICC, Trial Chamber, ICC-01/05-01/08, Decision on Sentence, 21 June 2016, [11] (rehabilitation should not be given undue weight).

[21] *Prosecutor v Katanga* (n 20) [88]; see also at [91] and [117] considering efforts undertaken to promote peace and statements of remorse.

is hardly in a position to reoffend in similar ways after his release from prison.[22] There may be a ('general') deterrent effect, however, on others who consider committing war crimes when involved in an armed conflict: knowing that, although they are in power *now*, they may later be held responsible for their acts even outside their home country may make them think twice before resorting to prohibited methods of warfare.[23] Such deterrent effects are most likely among military and civilian leaders of generally law-abiding states, who strive to abide by the rules on warfare enforced by international criminal tribunals.[24] But it is less likely that warlords in failed states or leaders of terroristic regimes actually consider the risk of being turned over to the Hague before they decide on a course of action in an ongoing conflict.[25]

C. Retribution

Retribution as a rationale of punishment has its roots in theology as well as in nineteenth-century idealist philosophy. The 'absolute' character of these antecedents, ie, demanding punishment for metaphysical reasons and unrelated to any positive individual or social effects, has made them lose credit in today's secular rationalist states.[26] Modern theories of retribution have therefore linked retribution to society's expectations of fairness: punishment is to deprive the offender of the unfair advantage he obtained by breaking the law.[27] This notion suggests that the punishment should (symbolically) equal the seriousness of the offence. Proportionality thus is the key word in any concept of retributivism.[28]

Proportionality must be regarded as an indispensable element of sentencing if the decisions of international criminal tribunals are to be accepted by the international community.[29] Consequently, international criminal tribunals have emphasised the importance of establishing the correct proportion between the crime and the sanction. For example, the ICTY Appeals Chamber ruled in 2005 that 'the principle of proportionality implies that a sentence must reflect

[22] See, however, Epik (n 12) 111–15, arguing that some former members of the National Socialist regime returned to influential positions in Latin America.

[23] See the strong emphasis on deterrence in *Prosecutor v Blaskic*, ICTY, Trial Chamber, IT-95-14-T, Judgment, 3 March 2000, [761]; *Prosecutor v Rutaganda*, ICTR, Trial Chamber, ICTR-96-3, Judgment and Sentence, 2 February 1999, [456]. See generally on this issue D'Ascoli (n 12) 299–300; Melloh (n 12) 137–40, emphasising that leaders calculate the risk of their actions and therefore can be deterred by a credible threat of punishment.

[24] See Harmon and Gaynor (n 7) 695.

[25] For a similar view, see Hoven (n 15) 148.

[26] See T Hörnle, 'Straftheorien' in E Hilgendorf, H Kudlich and B Valerius (eds), *Handbuch des Strafrechts*, vol 1 (Heidelberg, CF Müller, 2019) 511.

[27] On this aspect of retribution and its limitations especially in international criminal law, see Melloh (n 12) 106–10.

[28] Human dignity, fairness and the protection against arbitrariness have been cited as further supporting the notion of proportionality of punishment, see D'Ascoli (n 12) 22.

[29] D'Ascoli (n 12) 298.

the predominant standard of proportionality between the gravity of the offence and the degree of responsibility of the offender'.[30] Seven years later, ICC Trial Chamber I stated that the 'gravity of the crime' is one of the principal factors to be considered in the determination of the sentence, which should be in proportion to the crime and should reflect the culpability of the convicted person.[31] In assessing gravity, the tribunals look not so much at the definition of the offence but at the particular circumstances of the case, including the nature and degree of participation of the convicted person in the commission of the crime.[32] Yet, the complexity of international crimes makes it particularly difficult to determine a 'just' sentence that reflects the gravity of the crime, especially in relation to non-international offences.[33]

D. Expression of Disapproval

In recent times, the symbolic expression of society's disapproval of the offender's misconduct has been most widely discussed among the non-instrumental rationales of criminal punishment.[34] Formally expressing disapproval and censure can have a healing effect on society by restoring the balance between the offender and the (individual and collective) victim. Punishment of the offender can thus lead to re-establishing social cohesion and the public's reliance on the continued validity of important social norms.[35]

The theory of expressive reprobation may indeed be regarded as a modern, secular version of retributive sentencing. Retribution and expressive reprobation are interconnected through the notion that only a sanction that reflects the

[30] *Prosecutor v Nikolic*, ICTY, Appeals Chamber, IT-94-2-A, Decision on Sentencing, 4 February 2005, [21]; see also *Prosecutor v Delalic* (n 15) [731].

[31] *Prosecutor v Lubanga Dyilo*, ICC, Trial Chamber, ICC-01/04-01/06, Decision on Sentence, 10 July 2012, [36]. See also *Prosecutor v Katanga* (n 20) [39]; *Prosecutor v Bemba Gombo* (n 20) [11].

[32] *Prosecutor v Katanga* (n 20) [43]. For further references to case law on this point, see Ambos (n 9) 292–95; B Hola, C Bijleveld and A Smeulers, 'Punishment for Genocide – Exploratory Analysis of ICTR Sentencing' (2011) 11 *International Criminal Law Review* 745, 752.

[33] M M deGuzman, 'Proportionate Sentencing at the ICC' in C Stahn (ed), *The Law and Practice of the International Criminal Court* (Oxford, Oxford University Press, 2015) 932, 953–55.

[34] See M Aksenova, 'Symbolism as a Constraint on International Criminal Law' (2017) 30 *Leiden Journal of International Law* 475–99. For German perspectives on the symbolic dimension of punishment, see, eg, K Günther, 'Die symbolisch-expressive Bedeutung der Strafe' in C Prittwitz (ed), *Festschrift für Klaus Lüderssen* (Baden-Baden, Nomos, 2002) 205; T Hörnle, 'Zwecke und Rechtfertigung staatlicher Strafe' in F Saliger, Y W Kim, S I Liu, C Mylonopoulos, K Yamanaka, Y Zheng, J Tavares and O Isfen (eds), *Rechtsstaatliches Strafrecht. Festschrift für Ulfrid Neumann* (Heidelberg, CF Müller, 2017) 593, 600–601; Hörnle (n 26) 525–27. For an overview of relevant Anglo-American literature, see deGuzman (n 33) 939–43.

[35] For a thorough discussion of this theory in international criminal law, see Epik (n 12) 140–49. Henham (n 10) 80–85 proposes restoration and reconciliation as legitimate purposes of international sentencing; see also R Henham, *Sentencing Policy and Social Justice* (Oxford, Oxford University Press, 2018) for a broader theory of sentencing as a tool of re-establishing social justice. But this theory will be difficult to apply to the most serious offences that are adjudicated by international criminal tribunals.

(relative) gravity of the offence and the offender's personal blameworthiness[36] can be accepted by society as adequately expressing its disapproval.[37] With regard to international crimes, this function of sentencing has an additional aspect: acknowledging the harm and suffering of victims, which in turn can contribute to the restoration of peace in the community or nation affected by the offender's crimes.[38] Although the expressive and reconciliatory functions of punishment cannot be directly translated into a sentence of a particular number of years in prison, they require a sentence level that reflects the gravity of the crime and does not appear to the victims as a depreciation of their suffering.[39] The ICTY Appeals Chamber referred to this rationale in its judgment in *Prosecutor v Aleksovski* in 2000:

> A sentence of the International Tribunal should make plain the condemnation of the international community of the behaviour in question and show 'that the international community was not ready to tolerate serious violations of international humanitarian law and human rights'.[40]

Since sentencing in international criminal law is geared toward the purpose of adequately expressing the gravity of the offender's criminal conduct, the judges emphasise the importance of imposing a sentence that is in proportion with the seriousness of the offence and the offender's blameworthiness. It must be kept in mind, however, that the enormous magnitude of many crimes adjudicated by international tribunals makes it difficult to determine a punishment that fits the crime. Or, as the ICTY succinctly put the problem: 'A sentence, however harsh, will never be able to rectify the wrongs, and will be able to soothe only to a limited extent the suffering of the victims, their feelings of deprivation, anguish, and hopelessness.'[41] Yet, ever since the abolition of the *lex talionis* the punishment has never been really 'equal' to the crime except by conventional agreement;[42] and even the most heinous crimes can be met by commensurate sentences, as long as the sentence reflects the maximum on the available severity scale.

[36] It is not quite clear to what extent the offender's individual blameworthiness (beyond the objective harm caused by the offence) enters the assessment of 'gravity' in the tribunals' case law, see Sloane (n 9) 723–24.

[37] *cf* Melloh (n 12) 114–17; Ambos (n 9) 86.

[38] See *Prosecutor v Katanga* (n 20) [38]; *Prosecutor v Bemba Gombo* (n 20) [11].

[39] For a more detailed analysis of translating 'expressive' considerations into sentences, see DeGuzman (n 33) 956–58. Hoven (n 15) 155 infers from an expressive rationale of punishment that life imprisonment should be regarded as the 'normal' sentence for international crimes. See, however, *Prosecutor v Karadzic*, International Residual Mechanism for Criminal Tribunals (IRMCT) MICT-13-55-A, Appeals Chamber, Judgment, 20 March 2019, Dissenting opinion of Judge de Prada Solaesa, [847]–[851] (arguing that life sentences should not be imposed because they violate the principle of humanity).

[40] *Prosecutor v Aleksovski*, ICTY, Appeals Chamber, IT-95-14/1-A, Judgment, 24 March 2000, [185], citing *Prosecutor v Kambanda*, ICTR, Judgment, 4 September 1998, [28].

[41] *Prosecutor v Krajisnik*, ICTY, Trial Chamber, IT-00-39-T, Judgment, 27 September 2006, [1146].

[42] Melloh (n 12) 118–19.

E. Efficiency?

What, then, is the role of efficiency in the sentencing considerations of international criminal tribunals?

We saw the close connection between considerations of efficiency and instrumental purposes of punishment (rehabilitation and deterrence). With regard to rehabilitation, a lack of known recidivism among offenders sentenced by international tribunals seems to indicate maximum efficiency. But we need to keep in mind that the numbers of convicted persons are small, many offenders are still serving their prison sentence, and the absence of reoffending may mostly be due to a change of political circumstances that prevents former leaders from returning to power and committing more crimes. Regarding general deterrence, it is notoriously difficult to establish in quantitative terms any specific impact of sentencing on potential offenders' likelihood to commit further crimes. All we can say with some confidence is that the activity of international criminal tribunals probably has a deterrent effect by demonstrating to everyone that international crimes will not go unpunished even where national jurisdictions are unwilling or unable to prosecute them.

We have seen, however, that neither rehabilitation nor special or general deterrence play a significant practical role in the determination of sentences by international criminal tribunals.[43] The judges mainly pursue symbolic functions, such as reprobation or retribution, and thus do not need to place much weight on practical outcomes for justifying the imposition of sanctions.

Efficiency on a large scale might be demonstrated by showing a general change of attitude in the international community. When international criminal tribunals were created, it was indeed hoped that their activity would reinforce the rejection of war crimes and crimes against humanity as means of conducting armed conflicts. One can say that international criminal tribunals have established themselves and that it has become common knowledge that those who are convicted of serious international crime tend to receive long-term prison sentences. But most defendants before the ICC have been unlucky losers in African armed conflicts, and the most powerful states (United States, China, Russia, India) have refrained from joining the ICC and at best half-heartedly support its activities.[44]

[43] Neither the ICC Statute nor Rule 145(1) of the ICC Rules of Procedure and Evidence provide for rehabilitation or special deterrence as purposes of imposing and enforcing penalties. Even decisions on early release (Art 110(4) ICC Statute) depend on the perpetrator's cooperation with the Court rather than his prospects of rehabilitation. This contrasts starkly with the emphasis that, for example, the European Court of Human Rights places on efforts to rehabilitate prisoners; see *Vinter and Others v United Kingdom* App nos 66069/09, 130/10 and 3896/10 (ECtHR, 9 July 2013) [110]–[118] (referencing numerous international instruments on prison law). One should bear in mind, however, that sentencing and treatment of prisoners are different issues that do not necessarily follow the same principles.

[44] For a similar assessment, see N Grono and A de Courcy Wheeler, 'The Deterrent Effect of the ICC on the Commission of International Crimes by Government Leaders' in C Stahn (ed), *The Law and Practice of the International Criminal Court* (Oxford, Oxford University Press, 2015) 1225, 1240–44.

It is therefore not surprising that the few cases that have been decided by the International Criminal Court since its inception seem not to have left much of an impression on persons in power. Given that many brutal conflicts are at this moment fought in different parts of the world, mostly without much concern for the rules of humanitarian law, it is difficult to maintain that adherence to the basic rules of armed conflict has increased as a result of the activity of international criminal tribunals, and it is unlikely that their impact will significantly increase in the foreseeable future. It should be kept in mind, however, that international criminal law is not limited to the cases brought before the ICC; it is, indeed, primarily the task of domestic courts to enforce it.

IV. Specific Problems of Determining Proportionality in International Criminal Law

When making sentencing decisions, international tribunals like domestic courts have to grapple with the problem of translating concrete, case-specific evaluations of gravity into years and months of prison time. Beyond this general challenge, the application of the proportionality principle in international criminal law is faced with some specific problems. Some of them will be addressed below.

A. High Rank of the Perpetrator in a Hierarchy – An Aggravating Factor?

International criminal tribunals primarily adjudicate cases involving high-ranking members of state or military hierarchies. Typically, these perpetrators do not personally carry out acts of physical violence; they cause them to be performed by subordinates, or even limit themselves to passively accepting the fact that offences are being committed by those under their command. International criminal law has adopted a variety of legal concepts for holding such leading members of a bureaucracy or a military hierarchy responsible as perpetrators of the crimes committed by their subordinates, for example the construct of Joint Criminal Enterprise[45] or – at the ICC – the notion of perpetration through another (criminally responsible) person (Article 25(3)(a) ICC Statute).

With respect to sentencing, the question arises whether the blameworthiness of leaders should be regarded as greater, equal or less than the guilt of the 'front men' who actually carried out the murders, rapes and acts of torture.

[45] See G Werle and F Jessberger, *Principles of International Criminal Law*, 3rd edn (Oxford, Oxford University Press, 2014) marginal notes 527–46; E van Sliedregt, 'Perpetration and Participation in Article 25 (3)' in C Stahn (ed), *The Law and Practice of the International Criminal Court* (Oxford, Oxford University Press, 2015) 499, 501–6.

The international criminal tribunals have uniformly come to the conclusion that a person's blameworthiness (and hence his or her sentence) increases with each step up in a chain of command. Thus, in its decision on sentencing Mr Bemba Gombo, an army leader whose soldiers had committed atrocities in the Central African Republic, ICC Trial Chamber II declared that

> … in accordance with the principle of gradation in sentencing, high-level leaders, regardless of the mode of liability, generally bear heavier criminal responsibility than those further down the scale. Although once or several times physically removed from the acts of his or her subordinates, the culpability of a superior and his or her degree of moral blameworthiness might, depending on the concrete circumstances, be greater than that of his or her subordinates.[46]

In line with this statement of principle, empirical studies of sentencing practice at the international tribunals have found that holding a position of leadership is a strong indicator of receiving a severe sentence.[47] This practice is in line with a retributive orientation that takes account of personal blameworthiness to a larger degree than the objective harm caused by the offence.[48] A perpetrator's low-level position does not, however, necessarily entail a reduction in blameworthiness and, consequently, in sentence. The fact that leaders bear special responsibility for preventing offences against international criminal law does not, by itself, reduce the culpability of those who carry out, often with excessive cruelty, orders to commit atrocities or even perpetrate them on their own initiative.[49]

B. Consistency

Comparing and assessing the relative responsibility of commanders and subordinates is only one aspect of the more general issue of relative or 'inter-personal' proportionality at sentencing. When arguing about matters of sentencing, parties tend to refer to cases of other defendants who had previously been sentenced by the same tribunal and demand that the present defendant's sentence should be equal, higher or lower, as the case may be, in comparison to the sentence passed earlier. ICTY Judges have generally been reluctant to enter into such comparisons. Their typical response was that each case must be decided on its own merits, and

[46] *Prosecutor v Bemba Gombo* (n 20) [17]. See also *Prosecutor v Aleksovski* (n 40) [183].

[47] See Hola, Bijleveld and Smeulers (n 32) 753, 755, 771; W R Pruitt, 'Aggravating and Mitigating Sentencing Factors at the ICTR – An Exploratory Analysis' (2014) 14 *International Criminal Law Review* 148, 161 (both concerning ICTR sentencing practice). For a thoughtful and critical assessment of the 'leadership bias', see Hoven (n 15) 157–58.

[48] This approach has been suggested by D'Ascoli (n 12) 293.

[49] See *Prosecutor v Delalic* (n 15) [847]: 'In certain circumstances, the gravity of the crime may be so great that even following consideration of any mitigating factors, and despite the fact that the accused was not senior in the so-called overall command structure, a very severe penalty is nevertheless justified.' For similar findings in relation to ICTR case law, see Hola, Bijleveld and Smeulers (n 32) 768.

that differences between defendants and their cases are often more significant than their similarities.[50]

At the same time, the ICTY declared that a sentence 'may be thought to be capricious or excessive if it is out of reasonable proportion with a line of sentences passed in similar circumstances for the same offences' and that such disparity may give rise to an inference that the judges disregarded applicable sentencing criteria.[51] In 2019 the International Residual Mechanism for Criminal Tribunals, presented with an appeal against the sentence of 40 years' imprisonment imposed in 2016 by the ICTY Trial Chamber on the Serb-Bosnian leader Radovan Karadzic, decided that the principle of relative proportionality had been violated: since some lower-level officials of the Bosnian-Serbian administration, who were subordinated to Mr Karadzic, had received life sentences, the Appeals Chamber concluded that Mr Karadzic's sentence 'was so unreasonable and plainly unjust' that the Trial Chamber must have failed to properly exercise its discretion.[52] This case may have been exceptional – but the judgment demonstrates that an evident and unexplained inconsistency between the sentences imposed on offenders engaged in related criminal activities may so violate an appellate chamber's sense of (proportional) justice that the lower chamber's sentencing decision will be overruled. This case may also support the thesis advanced by Uwe Ewald that judges – consciously or not – tend to anchor their sentencing decisions in sentences previously imposed (often by other courts) on defendants in positions similar to the defendant presently before them.[53]

Striving for relative proportionality among sentences is a challenge for any criminal court, and especially for international tribunals, whose judgments are discussed and scrutinised worldwide and are often regarded as political statements. The ICTY Appeals Chamber correctly pointed out that consistency in punishment is 'one of the fundamental elements in any rational and fair system of criminal justice.'[54] It further predicted that by and by a sentencing case law will develop that judges will have to consider in order to avoid 'an unjustified disparity which may erode public confidence in the integrity of the Tribunal's administration of criminal justice'.[55] This pragmatic approach toward consistency has much to recommend itself. It avoids the intractable problem of determining the single 'correct' sentence for each case[56] but still curbs excessive arbitrariness in sentencing.

Some authors suggested that, in order to enhance consistency, sentencing margins for international crimes should be reduced, for example by introducing

[50] See, eg, *Prosecutor v Delalic* (n 15) [719]; *Prosecutor v Nikolic* (n 30) [19]. For a critical view of this argument, see Sloane (n 9) 718–19.

[51] *Prosecutor v Jelisic*, ICTY, IT-95-10-A, Appeals Chamber, Judgment, 5 July 2001, [96]; *Prosecutor v Nikolic* (n 30) [16].

[52] *Prosecutor v Karadzic* (n 39) [766]–[767], [772]–[773].

[53] U Ewald, 'Predictably Irrational – International Sentencing and its Discourse' (2010) 10 *International Criminal Law Review* 365, 385, 388.

[54] *Prosecutor v Delalic* (n 15) [756]. For a similar statement, see Melloh (n 12) 37.

[55] *Prosecutor v Delalic* (n 15) [757].

[56] *cf* Ewald (n 53) 379–81.

statutory minimum and maximum sentences for individual offences[57] or by promulgating 'soft' sentencing guidelines that judges would have to discuss in their sentencing decisions.[58] It is doubtful, however, whether such measures could resolve the problem. As for fixed sentence ranges, the maximum for all international core crimes would probably have to be set at life imprisonment. For war crimes, statutory minima could not be very high since the list of war crimes contains a variety of heterogenous types of offences, not all of which are of great seriousness. One might set, for example, three years imprisonment as a minimum sentence for genocide and crimes against humanity;[59] but it would be unusual for an international tribunal to impose a lesser sentence even under present law.

'Soft' sentencing guidelines could not do much more than codify the present sentencing standards. To the extent that sentencing judges can deviate from them, the main effect of guidelines would be to further increase the obligation to give lengthy reasons for the court's decision. It might thus be preferable to leave the law as flexible as it is and place trust in appeals chambers to correct any inexplicable deviations from emerging sentencing standards.

C. Distinguishing Between the Most Egregious Crimes?

Probably the most difficult problem in sentencing offenders under international criminal law is rooted in the fact that each instance of genocide, each crime against humanity and many war crimes would typically draw the most severe sanctions under any national criminal legislation. Most of the offences adjudicated by international criminal tribunals involve the killing and/or severe maltreatment of persons, sometimes of thousands of civilians. Should a sentencing court then impose the maximum punishment (normally: imprisonment for life) on every convicted defendant?[60] Article 77 ICC Statute forecloses this option: it permits the imposition of life imprisonment only 'when justified by the extreme gravity of the crime and the individual circumstances of the convicted person'. ICC Judges are thus obliged to make distinctions even among the most serious offenders. In the first sentencing case before the ICC, the Prosecutor suggested a general baseline for sentencing, to be drawn at 80 per cent of the statutory maximum; that is 24 years' imprisonment, with aggravating and mitigating circumstances being

[57] D'Ascoli (n 12) 283–84; Hoven (n 15) 154, 167; Ambos (n 9) 286.

[58] Harmon and Gaynor (n 7) 710–11; Ambos (n 9) 302–3.

[59] Section 7 sub-s 1 of the German Code of Crimes against International Law provides for a minimum of three years for some instances of crimes against humanity, with the possibility of imposing only one to three years if there are mitigating circumstances.

[60] This solution has been suggested by Hoven (n 15) 157–59; for a similar view, see J D Ohlin, 'Proportional Sentences at the ICTY' in B Swart, A Zahar and G Sluiter (eds), *The Legacy of the International Criminal Tribunal for the Former Yugoslavia* (Oxford, Oxford University Press, 2011) 323. See also the criticism of lenient sentencing of the ICTR by Szoke-Burke (n 9) 566–72.

applied to permit deviations from that baseline. The ICC Judges, however, rejected that approach, arguing that it was not anchored in the ICC Statute or the Rules of Procedure and Evidence, and that it would limit too strictly the consideration of the individual circumstances of each case.[61]

If an international tribunal embraces the principle of relative proportionality and in sentencing seeks to distinguish between horrible and even more horrible crimes,[62] this implies the possibility to impose lesser sentences on some defendants compared to the sentence of life imprisonment these defendants would probably receive if their case were adjudicated by a domestic court, based on the mere fact that they were responsible[63] for the intentional killing of a least one person.[64] Those who strive for relative proportionality within the system of international criminal law are thus bound to violate the ideal of equal punishment for similar crimes when domestic criminal justice is included in the calculus.[65]

This dilemma cannot be resolved in a completely satisfactory way. Probably the better option is to treat international and national systems as separate entities and to aim at creating an inherently consistent sentencing scheme for international criminal tribunals, for example through guideline judgments by appeals chambers. It may be that individual defendants will then benefit from being tried by international rather than national tribunals. One should keep in mind, however, that the ICC, in accordance with the principle of complementarity, has jurisdiction over crimes only if the relevant national jurisdiction is unable or unwilling to conduct proceedings in this matter (Article 17(1)(a) ICC Statute), ie, only when sentencing by a domestic court would not be a realistic option for the defendants in question. Moreover, even temporary prison sentences imposed by the ICC can – and often will – be of long duration, up to a maximum of 30 years. Thus, the fact

[61] *Prosecutor v Lubanga Dyilo* (n 31) [92]–[93].

[62] See Hola, Bijleveld and Smeulers (n 32) 754 (ICTR distinguishing between 'serious and horrendous' and 'even more serious and horrendous' criminal acts).

[63] It should be noted that due to the broad interpretation of Art 25(3)(a) ICC Statute, many different persons involved in an offence under international criminal law are regarded as perpetrators; moreover, the sentencing scheme of the ICC does not provide for a mandatory reduction of sentence for mere accessories.

[64] *cf* Harmon and Gaynor (n 7) 686–88.

[65] Szoke-Burke (n 9) 576–77 therefore suggests that the ICTR should have tried to assimilate sentences to those provided by Rwandan law. But national sanctioning systems may not be compatible with principles of international criminal law, eg, with respect to acceptance of the death penalty. *cf* the problems of inconsistency between sentences imposed by the ICTR and Rwandan courts as highlighted by S Rugege and A M Karimunda, 'Domestic Prosecution of International Crimes: The Case of Rwanda' in G Werle, L Fernandez and M Vormbaum (eds), *Africa and the International Criminal Court* (The Hague, TMC Asser Press, 2014) 79–116; B Holá and H N Brehm, 'Punishing Genocide: A Comparative Empirical Analysis of Sentencing Laws and Practices at the International Criminal Tribunal for Rwanda (ICTR), Rwandan Domestic Courts, and Gacaca Courts' (2016) 10 *Genocide Studies and Prevention: An International Journal* 59–80. For a similar problem with regard to the ICTY and Bosnian courts, see B Holá, 'Vertical Inconsistency of International Sentencing? The ICTY and Domestic Courts in Bosnia and Herzegovina' in C Stahn, C Agius, S Brammertz and C Rohan (eds), *Legacies of the International Criminal Tribunal for the Former Yugoslavia* (Oxford, Oxford University Press, 2020).

that international tribunals adhere to a differentiated sentencing scheme does not mean that convicted defendants can expect to get off lightly.

V. Conclusion

International criminal justice presents special challenges for proportionality in sentencing. Provided with a 'laundry list' of sentencing factors but no clear guidelines as to how they should be applied, the international tribunals acknowledged the importance of consistency in sentencing but have also emphasised the prerogative and the obligation of sentencing judges to do justice to each individual defendant. They tried to make distinctions according to the gravity of the offence and the culpability of the offender, although most of the defendants were responsible for what would be a most serious crime under any domestic penal law. Given the fact that judges of international criminal tribunals come from vastly different legal backgrounds, it is not surprising that not all sentencing decisions have been plausible. But appeals chambers of the ad hoc tribunals for Yugoslavia and Rwanda have demonstrated their willingness to review sentencing decisions with a view toward minimal relative consistency, and it is to be hoped that a similar development will set in at the International Criminal Court.

16

Proportionality, Mass Surveillance and Criminal Investigation: The Strasbourg Court Facing Big Brother

LORENA BACHMAIER WINTER

I. Introduction

'Massive' and 'proportionate' look like two opposite concepts, especially when applied to the protection of human rights in the area of interception of communications. At first glance, trying to reconcile those two concepts may seem an aporia – it may appear ontologically impossible to consider a massive degree of intrusion into our privacy proportionate when it is not based on any prior element of suspicion of the commission of a criminal offence. It is therefore not surprising that issues involving the regulation and application of bulk surveillance measures by intelligence agencies for the protection of national security interests give rise to discussions and doubts about the compliance of those measures with the principle of proportionality.

We must bear in mind that the mass interception of communications and the retention of the data thereby obtained constitute a significant interference with the right to privacy, even if those data are not actually analysed.[1] The very existence of schemes of mass surveillance of communication metadata, even when no specific individual is initially affected, is per se an intrusion into our privacy, which may influence our behaviour and exert a chilling effect on the development

[1] There is agreement on this. See, eg, the judgment of the Court of Justice of the European Union (Grand Chamber) in Joined Cases C-293/12 and C-594/12 *Digital Rights Ireland v Minister for Communications, Marine and Natural Resources and Others and Kärntner Landesregierung and Others*, ECLI:EU:C:2014:238 (Judgment of 8 April 2014), where the Court held that EU Directive 2006/24/EC was incompatible with the principle of proportionality, and therefore the national legislation providing for the retention of communications data should be considered also in breach of Arts 7 and 8 of the Charter of Fundamental Rights of the EU unless such legislation was complemented with sufficient safeguards on access to data.

of our private life and our freedom of expression.[2] Beyond the possible violation of individual rights due to the enormous risks of abuse of secret technological surveillance, this has broader implications for the preservation of democracy and the rule of law.[3]

Naturally, the risks are even higher if, due to the selectors that were applied, specific individuals become targets and the content of their communications is monitored and analysed. We must not forget that these mechanisms are designed to detect threats and hence are activated on unknown targets; ie, they may affect any and every citizen although there is no previous suspicion about anyone in particular. This is precisely the factor that led to questioning of the proportionality of techniques which intervene and store all communications in order to select those worth being subjected to further analysis. The potential value of bulk interceptions for security operations is hardly discussed, and the proactive approach in identifying threats to the national security has been considered legitimate and reasonable.[4] However, considering that, unlike a criminal investigation, such an invasion of our privacy is untargeted and operates on the basis of selectors – and is thus not linked to a prior suspicion – it is understandable to question whether it complies with the principle of proportionality and also whether the test of proportionality in such cases should be different from that in ordinary criminal proceedings.

It is not my intention to cover here in detail the scope and meaning of the right to privacy, the various national systems of mass surveillance and their specific regulations,[5] or the controversial application of different standards to measures affecting foreign intelligence and national communications respectively. Each of these topics is extremely complex and multifaceted in itself, as demonstrated in the huge body of legal literature in these fields.

This chapter focuses on the analysis of certain aspects of the judgment of the European Court of Human Rights (ECtHR) in the landmark case *Big Brother Watch and others v United Kingdom*,[6] which involves questions of compliance of

[2] On the chilling effect, see the Council of Europe (CoE) Report of the Commissioner for Human Rights 'Democratic and effective oversight of national security services', May 2015, available at: rm.coe.int/1680487770, at 25. In the same sense, although highlighting the few empirical studies in this regard, D Murray and P Fussey, 'Bulk Surveillance in the Digital Age: Rethinking the Human Rights Law Approach to Bulk Monitoring of Communications Data' (2019) 52(1) *Israel Law Review* 31, 43–47.

[3] See CoE Report (n 2) 26.

[4] As recognised in the European Commission for Democracy through Law (Venice Commission) Report on the Democratic Oversight of Signals Intelligence Agencies of 15 December 2015, CDL-AD(2015)011, para 47.

[5] See the CoE Report (n 2).

[6] *Big Brother Watch and others v United Kingdom* App nos 58170/13, 62322/14 and 24960/15 (ECtHR, 13 September 2018). The Court decided to join the three applications filed between 2013 and 2015 by different applicants. As some of them filed their claims first with the national Investigatory Powers Tribunal but others did not, the inadmissibility question regarding the exhaustion of the national remedies was raised but finally rejected (see at [268]).

the UK Regulation of Investigatory Powers Act 2000 (RIPA) with the European Convention of Human Rights (ECHR).[7] This is not the first time where the ECtHR dealt with a possible breach of the Convention by intelligence regimes and the measures they can carry out to prevent national security risks.[8] But it is the first time[9] where the ECtHR assessed the implications of digital mass surveillance mechanisms, for its previous judgments had a more narrow scope, either legal or factual. The Chamber's decision was appealed and, on 4 February 2019, the case was referred to the Grand Chamber. A final decision is still pending at the time of writing this chapter.

In these pages I will focus on the Court's assessment of the compliance with Article 8 ECHR (the right to respect for private and family life) of bulk interception of communications for surveillance purposes within the realm of intelligence. I will further analyse whether the proportionality test used by the ECtHR in assessing the bulk surveillance of communications for reasons of national security differs from the tests used to evaluate the interception of communications as a criminal investigative measure. First, I will summarise those aspects of the *Big Brother* judgment that are of most interest for the purposes of this chapter. Second, I will try to explain – without entering into the complex debates on constitutional argumentation – which elements are usually considered within the framework of a proportionality assessment, as this is a necessary premise for a critical analysis of the ECtHR judgment. Finally, I will try to identify the differences between the criteria used in the proportionality assessment of interception of communications for *surveillance* and for *criminal investigation* purposes, and will address the question whether, with regard to the interception of communications, the analysis ex post of an interference with the right to respect for private life is different from the assessment *in abstracto* of the concept of 'quality of the law' (as part of the 'in accordance with the law' requirement under Article 8 ECHR).

[7] RIPA has been subject to consequential amendments, the last one by the Investigatory Powers (Consequential Amendments etc) Regulations 2018 (2018 No 682) of 6 June 2018, introducing new provisions under the Investigatory Powers Act 2016. It has to be underlined that the rules regarding the oversight mechanisms that were in force at the moment of filing the applications – and addressed in the judgment – were later amended in order to increase the level of safeguards. It is not my aim to discuss here either the precise provisions of RIPA or the amendments that were subsequently adopted. I will refer to those rules only to the extent necessary for the assessment of the proportionality test applied by the ECtHR.

[8] See *Gabriele Weber and Cesar Saravia v Germany* App no 54934/00 (ECtHR, 29 June 2006); *Liberty and others v United Kingdom* App no 58243/00 (ECtHR, 1 July 2008); *Roman Zakharov v Russia* App no 47143/06 (ECtHR GC, 4 December 2015); *Szabó and Vissy v Hungary* App no 37138/14 (ECtHR, 12 January 2016); *Centrum för rättvisa v Sweden* App no 35252/08 (ECtHR, 19 June 2018; as with *Big Brother*, the referral to the Grand Chamber was also decided on 4 February 2019).

[9] In addition to *Centrum för rättvisa* (n 8), a case which also dealt with a digital mass surveillance regime.

II. The ECtHR *Big Brother* Judgment of 13 September 2018

A. The Main Facts and Arguments

The judgment addresses three different surveillance regimes foreseen by the UK legislation: the bulk interception of communications; the sharing of intelligence with foreign governments, with respect to which the Court (by five votes to two) found no violation of the Convention;[10] and the obtaining of communications data from communications service providers (CSP). In this last case, the Court ruled that the acquisition of communications data from the CSP for the purpose of combatting crime is a targeted measure, which, in order to be in compliance with the Convention, should be subject to prior review by a court or an independent administrative body and limited to the investigation of serious crimes. These requirements have already been introduced to British legislation as of November 2018.[11] In the following I will therefore only discuss the issues related to the bulk interception of communications.

The applicants claim inter alia that the provisions under section 8(4) of the UK RIPA, which provides the legal framework for the mass interception of external communications (defined in section 20 as 'communication[s] sent or received outside the British Islands'), violate Article 8 ECHR.[12] They claim that the UK regime is in breach of the Convention by allowing the bulk interception of communications using specific programmes (KARMA, POLICE, Black Hole or TEMPORA). Their main allegation is that the interference lacks objective evidence of suspicion of a serious crime or a threat to national security in regard to the persons whose data are sought, that there is no prior independent judicial authorisation and, finally, that the lack of notification of the affected persons deprives them of the right to a judicial remedy to challenge the interception of their communications.

Under section 8(4) RIPA, the bulk interception of communications as an intelligence capability requires a warrant issued by the Secretary of State, accompanied by a certificate that ensures that a selection process will be applied and only material described in the certificate can be subject to analysis. This process is subject

[10] The Court held that the threshold that the material transferred should only be able to be searched if all the requirements under national law were fulfilled was met, see *Big Brother Watch v UK* (n 6) [447].

[11] The ECtHR follows here the principles set out by the CJEU case law in *Digital Rights Ireland* (n 1) and in Joined Cases C-203/15 and C-698/15 *Tele2 Sverige AB v Post- och telestyrelsen and Secretary of State for the Home Department v Tom Watson and Others* ECLI:EU:C:2017:222 (Order of the Grand Chamber of 16 March 2017).

[12] On the precise questions raised by the different applicants and the history of the legal proceedings, see *Big Brother Watch v UK* (n 6) [7]–[55]. For a short summary of the background, see B van der Sloot and E Kosta, 'Big Brother Watch and Others v UK: Lessons from the Latest Strasbourg Ruling on Bulk Surveillance' (2019) 5 *European Data Protection Law Review* 252, 253–55.

to internal audit and external oversight by the Interception of Communications Commissioner,[13] who carries out biannual inspections of each of the agencies and who is able to check the systems of interception as well as the relevant records kept. The application for a warrant needs to reflect sufficient background information and state the reasons why the interception is considered necessary and proportionate to the aim sought. Only if the interception is necessary 1) in the interest of national security, 2) for preventing or detecting a serious crime, or 3) for safeguarding the economic well-being of the UK, to the extent that those interests are also relevant to the national security interests, can interceptions under section 8(4) RIPA be authorised (sections 21 and 22 RIPA). The number of persons allowed access to the intercepted material within the agency is limited to a minimum. The ECtHR judgment includes a lengthy and detailed description of the domestic law and practice, supported by several reports on the implementation and exercise of oversight on the interception-of-communications scheme.[14]

In its judgment of 13 September 2018, the Court did not specifically address the issue of the legitimacy of the interference with respect to the aims of safeguarding national security interests, preventing crime and protecting the economic well-being of the country, as this was not disputed by the applicants – although the Court expressly declared that the aim was legitimate.[15] It can be argued that an aim as broad as the 'protection of national security' is a vague term that allows for a wide interpretation and thus risks abuse, but the Court already established in *Kennedy v United Kingdom* that it is a legitimate aim and complies with the legal requirement of foreseeability.[16]

The Strasbourg Court first addressed the question whether the bulk surveillance measure as provided under section 8(4) RIPA is 'in accordance with the law' under Article 8(2) ECHR, and, specifically, whether the legal basis complies with the requirements of foreseeability and accessibility. The Court held that the foreseeability requirement can be lowered in the context of secret surveillance, as citizens should not always be able to predict when the authorities will adopt surveillance measures targeting them, thus allowing them to adapt their conduct accordingly.[17] In well-established case law involving communications interceptions in the field of criminal investigations, the Court defined the requirements for compliance with the ECHR standards in order to give citizens clear and adequate indications as to the circumstances and conditions where the state has powers

[13] Now the Investigatory Powers Commissioner, under the Investigatory Powers Act 2016.

[14] Such a lengthy description of the national provisions and the functioning of the oversight mechanisms is not found in any other judgment of the ECtHR on mass surveillance; see *Big Brother Watch v UK* (n 6), [56] to [193], covering almost 80 of the 204 pages of the judgment.

[15] ibid [322]–[323].

[16] *Kennedy v United Kingdom* App no 26839/05 (ECtHR, 18 May 2010) [159].

[17] See *Big Brother Watch v UK* (n 6) [306]. See also *Kennedy v UK* (n 16) [152]; *Leander v Sweden* App no 9248/81 (ECtHR, 26 March 1987) [51].

to resort to such measures.[18] In *Weber and Saravia v Germany*, the ECtHR had already determined that the same minimum 'quality of the law' requirements are also applicable in cases of interception of communications for reasons of national security (known as the 'six *Weber* requirements').[19]

The Court undertook a thorough analysis of each of the national provisions to determine not only whether they fulfilled the requirements of accessibility and foreseeability but also whether the quality of the law ensured that secret surveillance measures are applied only when 'necessary in a democratic society'. In particular, the Court examined in detail the issue whether the safeguards accompanying the entire bulk surveillance procedure were enough to keep the interference to what was really necessary. In its analysis the Court focused on the oversight mechanisms provided in RIPA and their practical implementation. The Court stated that such oversight measures must be in place at all three stages of the mass surveillance procedure: at the beginning when first ordered, while being carried out, and when it is concluded.[20]

The Strasbourg Court found that the RIPA rules on bulk surveillance of telecommunications applicable at the time in question were in violation of Articles 8 and 10 of the Convention for lack of sufficient oversight of the entire selection process

> including the selection of bearers for interception, the selectors and search criteria for filtering intercepted communications and the selection of material for examination by an analyst; and secondly the absence of any real safeguards applicable to the selection of related communications data for examination.[21]

With regard to whether the bulk interception of communications for national security purposes is legitimate and necessary in a democratic society, the Court left the assessment and balancing of the interests at stake to the national authorities, who 'enjoy a certain margin of appreciation in choosing the means for achieving the legitimate aim of protecting national security'. However, it explicitly recognised that the reports provided by the British independent reviewer on terrorism legislation and by the CoE's Venice Commission show that the operation of a bulk interception regime to locate unknown or unidentified targets 'is a valuable means

[18] These minimum requirements concern: the nature of the offences which might give rise to the interception; categories of persons liable to have their communications intercepted; duration and conditions for renewal; procedure to be followed for examining, using and storing the data intercepted; precautions to be taken when communicating the data to other parties; and rules on deleting and destroying the data. See *Huvig v France* App no 11105/84 (ECtHR, 24 April 1990); *Kopp v Switzerland* App no 23224/94 (ECtHR, 25 March 1998); *Valenzuela Contreras v Spain* App no 27671/95 (ECtHR, 30 July 1998); *Amann v Switzerland* App no 27798/95 (ECtHR GC, 16 February 2000); *Rotaru v Romania* App no 28341/95 (ECtHR GC, 4 May 2000); *Prado Bugallo v Spain* App no 58496/00 (ECtHR, 18 February 2003); *Copland v United Kingdom* App no 62617/00 (ECtHR, 3 April 2007); *Dumitru Popescu v Romania (no 2)* App no 71525/01 (ECtHR, 26 April 2007); *Liberty and others v UK* (n 8).

[19] See *Weber and Saravia v Germany* (n 8) [84], [92ff], [95]; *Roman Zakharov v Russia* (n 8) [238].

[20] See *Big Brother Watch v UK* (n 6) [309].

[21] ibid [387].

to achieve the legitimate aims pursued, particularly given the current threat level from both global terrorism and serious crime',[22] and expressly confirmed that the decision to operate a bulk interception regime to identify unknown targets falls within the state's margin of appreciation.[23]

B. The Two Partly Dissenting Opinions

It is interesting to see that the two separate opinions in the 2018 *Big Brother* judgment arrive at diametrically different conclusions: the first holding that more safeguards should have been required, and the second holding that there was no violation of the Convention. They show that despite all the theoretical elaboration of legal argumentation on human rights, the assessment on the sufficiency of oversight measures in the realm of mass surveillance measures can lead to opposing conclusions. The first partly dissenting opinion, delivered by Judge Koskelo (Finland) and joined by Judge Turkovic (Croatia), starts by underlining that the risks of secret surveillance have increased in the 'technological sea change' and concludes that the safeguards provided in the previous ECtHR case law assessing strategic surveillance measures (mainly in *Klass v Germany* and *Weber and Saravia v Germany*) are not sufficient. The Judges advocate increasing the standards by reducing the states' margin of appreciation on the basis that the factual circumstances have changed. Judge Koskelo questions 'the approach according to which prior independent control by a judicial authority should not be a necessary requirement in the system of safeguards' (paragraph [20]) and reckons that it cannot be appropriate to leave all the ex ante control in the hands of the executive (paragraph [23]). The possibility for such a mechanism of prior judicial or independent authorisation is illustrated by the Swedish legislation, as seen in the ECtHR judgment in *Centrum för rättvisa* of 19 June 2018.

The second partly dissenting opinion of Judges Pardalos (San Marino ad hoc judge) and Eicke (the United Kingdom) in the part dealing with the bulk interception of communications under Article 8(4) RIPA, rather than considering the safeguards insufficient, argues the opposite: despite the identified areas for improvement in the oversight of the selection process, these 'are not, in themselves, sufficiently significant' to allow the conclusion that the law does not meet the 'quality of law' standards (paragraph [23]). Comparing the present case with the ruling in the judgment in *Centrum för rättvisa*, the two Judges consider that the British law on bulk interception for reasons of national security provides sufficient guarantees against arbitrariness and risk of abuse, and thus they do not find a violation of Article 8 ECHR.

[22] ibid [386].
[23] ibid [314].

III. Understanding the Principle of Proportionality

Before addressing the relevant issues raised in the ECtHR judgment in *Big Brother* it is necessary to explain, succinctly and without entering into detailed analyses, the principle of proportionality. In the French tradition, the proportionality test has been widely applied in administrative law, with the principle being understood as based on the fair assessment of different interests converging in the field of discretionary policy decisions and functioning as a safeguard against unlimited legislative or administrative powers. The origins of the concept of proportionality as a prohibition of abuse with regard to fundamental rights can be found in the evolution of administrative law at the end of the eighteenth century. The notion developed throughout the nineteenth century, together with the growing awareness for fundamental rights as protective guarantees against the arbitrary exercise of state powers.[24]

Proportionality refers to the relationship between means and ends.[25] The greater the degree of non-satisfaction of, or detriment to, one interest, the greater must be the importance of satisfying the other.[26] Some authors link this assessment to a cost-benefit analysis (the cost being the means and the benefit the ends).[27] The principle of proportionality entails the need to balance conflicting interests in a particular case, usually with the aim of setting limits on possible excesses of the power exercised by public authorities. It is sometimes defined as a technique of special legal reasoning, where diverse factors have to be weighed to form a specific kind of rational legal discourse.[28] Other scholars consider balancing to be a part of any reasonable and prudential judicial reasoning, which requires taking into account all relevant factors and weighing them against each other.[29] For Endicott, proportionality requires the judges to reconcile incommensurable interests, but

[24] JI López González, *El principio general de proporcionalidad en el derecho administrativo* (Sevilla, Universidad de Sevilla, 1988) 17ff; W Degener, *Grundsatz der Verhältnismäßigkeit und strafprozessuale Zwangsmaßnahme* (Berlin, Duncker & Humblot, 1985) 43; J Barnes Vázquez, 'Introducción al principio de proporcionalidad en el derecho comparado y comunitario' (1994) 135 *Revista de Actualidad Penal* 531ff.

[25] See, eg, N Emiliou, *The Principle of Proportionality in European Law: A Comparative Study* (London, Kluwer International, 1996) 23–24.

[26] R Alexy, *A Theory of Constitutional Rights* (Oxford, Oxford University Press, 1986) 102.

[27] This is criticised by M Luterán, 'The Lost Meaning of Proportionality' in G Huscroft, B Miller and G Webber (eds), *Proportionality and the Rule of Law: Rights, Justification, Reasoning* (Cambridge, Cambridge University Press, 2014) 28. This author argues that the particular means cannot be wholly explained by its costs but only with regard to its contribution to the achievement of the end.

[28] See R Alexy and his repeatedly explained weight formula, for instance in *Teoría de la argumentación jurídica* (Madrid, CEPC, 2014) 356ff; also in 'Constitutional Rights and Proportionality' (2014) 22 *REVUS* 51, 63–64. Following Alexy, see, in Spain, C Bernal Pulido, *El principio de proporcionalidad y los derechos fundamentales* (Madrid, CEPC, 2003). For further details, see Ralf Poscher's and Christos Mylonopoulos' chapters 3 and 4 respectively in this volume.

[29] See T J Gunn, 'Deconstructing Proportionality in Limitations Analysis' (2005) 19 *Emory International Law Review* 465, 494ff.

conflicting interests at stake cannot be weighed on any sort of scales. In the end, the judge will 'have to throw the scales out of the window, and just choose'.[30] It is interesting that the authors who are more sceptical about the proportionality principle often come from a common law background.[31]

Some constitutions expressly recognise proportionality as a constitutional principle. One example is the German *Grundgesetz* (Basic Law).[32] German constitutional case law on the meaning and elements of the proportionality principle has clearly influenced the jurisprudence of the Court of Justice of the EU (CJEU) and of the ECtHR. It is considered a principle implicit in the very notion of human rights and the rule of law or *Rechtstaatsprinzip*.[33] Proportionality is also established as a basic principle of EU law, together with the principle of subsidiarity – 'the content and form of Union action shall not exceed what is necessary to achieve the objectives of the Treaties.'[34]

Proportionality has also been a crucial principle in the field of criminal law, at least since Beccaria set it out in his work *Dei delitti e delle pene*, for assessing the reasonableness of the penalties and the need to avoid excessive punishments in relation to the aim pursued.[35] This is explicitly recognised in Article 49(3) of the EU Charter of Fundamental Rights ('The severity of penalties must not be disproportionate to the criminal offence'). Proportionality is also anchored in

[30] T Endicott, 'Proportionality and Incommensurability' in G Huscroft, B Miller and G Webber (eds), *Proportionality and the Rule of Law: Rights, Justification, Reasoning* (Cambridge, Cambridge University Press, 2014) 315.

[31] This may be explained by the fact that the doctrines of necessity and of reasonableness assume comparable, although not identical functions; see T Cottier, R Echandi, R Leal-Arcas, R Liechti, T Payosova and C Sieber-Gasser, 'The Principle of Proportionality in International Law' (2012) 38 *SSRN Electronic Journal* 1–34, available at: www.researchgate.net/publication/275347556_The_Principle_of_Proportionality_in_International_Law.

[32] For details, see Ralf Poscher's chapter 3 in this volume. The principle of proportionality is not expressly mentioned in the Spanish Constitution of 1978, but Art 106(1) recognises it as a guiding principle of administrative law by stating: 'The Courts control the power to issue regulations and to ensure that the rule of law prevails in administrative action, as well as to ensure that the latter is subordinated to the ends which justify it.' On the constitutional judicial doctrine regarding the principle of proportionality, see, eg, M González Beilfuss, *El principio de proporcionalidad en la jurisprudencia del Tribunal Constitucional* (Cizur Menor, Aranzadi, 2003).

[33] See Degener (n 24) 46; Barnes Vázquez (n 24) 531ff. See also Emmanouil Billis', Nandor Knust's and Jon Petter Rui's chapter 1 in this volume.

[34] Art 5(4) of the Treaty on European Union. See also TFEU Protocol (No 2) on the Application of the Principles of Subsidiarity and Proportionality, OJ 2008 C 115/206. According to Art 52(1) of the EU Charter of Fundamental Rights: 'Any limitation on the exercise of the rights and freedoms recognised by this Charter must be provided for by law and respect the essence of those rights and freedoms. Subject to the principle of proportionality, limitations may be made only if they are necessary and genuinely meet objectives of general interest recognised by the Union or the need to protect the rights and freedoms of others.'

[35] See, eg, A Toscano, *La funzione della pena e le garanzie dei diritti fondamentali* (Milano, Giuffrè, 2012) 29ff. For a historical overview on this aspect of proportionality, see Nestor Courakis' and Vagia Polyzoidou's chapter 6 in this volume.

international law within but also beyond the context of the protection of human rights.[36]

When a state action interferes with citizens' fundamental rights – be it in the application of administrative (sanctioning) law, criminal law, surveillance or investigative measures – it becomes necessary to determine whether the interference is reasonable and justified by the aims pursued. For reviewing the proportionality of any measure, the following questions – corresponding to proportionality's three main sub-principles – should be taken into account:[37] 1) does the measure adopted pursue a legitimate aim? (legitimacy); 2) can it serve to further that aim at least to a certain degree? (suitability); 3) is it the least restrictive measure for fundamental rights to achieve that aim? (necessity); and 4) all in all, do the ends justify the means? (proportionality in a strict or narrow sense). The last one is also called the law of balancing or balancing test between the compelling rights and interests. The ECtHR enters into balancing only when the measure is legitimate, adequate and necessary (in the sense of being the least intrusive means).

It is precisely the notion of proportionality *stricto sensu* that offers a more blurred profile. To assess whether this criterion has been met, it is customary to refer to undetermined legal concepts such as the *reasonable proportion* between the gravity of the interference with fundamental rights and the aim pursued. It has also been suggested that the proportionality principle is a sort of *rule of common sense*, applied to prevent excessive harms that are not justified by the aims. And this is where we face a major definitional problem when addressing the issue of proportionality: what is 'common sense' in this context? What shall be considered 'reasonable' or excessive? With respect to interferences with the right to privacy caused by surveillance or investigative measures, it is a *petitio principii* or circular reasoning to define the proportionality of these measures by making use of equally broad or undetermined terms such as 'adequate balance', 'reasonability', 'common sense' or 'prohibition of excess'.

We are facing a broad legal concept comparable to classical notions such as 'the good paterfamilias' (reasonably cautious person) or 'due diligence'. These are notions that are not immutable and whose precise content can be defined only in each particular case, by taking into account the aims pursued, the precise circumstances, the interests at stake, the prevailing values in that particular legal system, the social context and the sensibility of that society to the protection of fundamental rights and values at the time in which the rule has to be applied.

[36] Although the principle of proportionality has not been considered part of the general principles of customary law, it is embedded in many fields of international law beyond the protection of human rights, as, for example, in the conduct of war and self-defence, finding its roots in the law of reprisals. See, eg, T M Franck, 'On Proportionality of Countermeasures in International Law' (2008) 102 *American Journal of International Law* 715–67. See also Michael Bothe's and Emanuela-Chiara Gillard's chapter 14 in this volume.

[37] See M Fordham and T De La Mare, 'Identifying the Principles of Proportionality' in J Jowell and J Cooper (eds), *Understanding Human Rights Principles* (Oxford, Hart Publishing, 2001) 27, 28.

However, this balancing test with respect to the reasonableness of the mass interception of communications for surveillance and security aims is absent from the *Big Brother* judgment of the Strasbourg Court. The ECtHR, when determining the proportionality of the interception of communications (either in the context of intelligence schemes or of criminal investigation), systematically avoids proceeding to the balancing of the interests at stake and resorts instead to the doctrine of the states' margin of appreciation, reasoning that national authorities are in a better position to decide whether such measures are reasonable in the precise context where they are or will be applied. This is completely logical given the specific circumstances of every country, although this practice has been criticised for the risk of uneven application and for refraining from setting truly objective standards.[38]

For the European Court of Human Rights, the national judges are the ones who shall control whether measures interfering with fundamental rights, once prescribed by the law, are applied correctly and are not excessive in the light of the conflicting interests at stake: namely, the protection of national security and the prevention/prosecution of crime, on the one hand, and the protection of the fundamental rights of citizens, on the other. Nonetheless, as will be shown, the Court focuses on ensuring that the states comply with the requirements of the Convention by reviewing the effectiveness of the existing oversight mechanisms.

IV. Mass Surveillance and Criminal Investigation: Different Approaches in Assessing Proportionality?

It is widely known that measures of bulk interception of communications for national security reasons have caused a huge debate and even met rejection. This is logical, taking into account the potential risk of abuse, especially after the information disseminated by Edward Snowden's leak confirmed that such abuses were not only a possibility but also a fact. In this context, it is important to examine: first, whether in this particular field the ECtHR's approach is different from the one adopted by the Court with respect to interceptions of communications as a criminal investigative measure; and second, whether there has been any change with regard to the requisites established by the ECtHR for measures of targeted surveillance. In other words, I will try to analyse here to what extent the Court actually modified its approach or introduced new requirements when assessing the proportionality of communication interceptions in the context of mass digital surveillance for intelligence aims. To this end, we should bear in mind that, in order to comply with the ECHR as interpreted by the Strasbourg Court, any

[38] J McBride, 'Proportionality and the European Convention on Human Rights' in E Ellis (ed), *The Principle of Proportionality in the Laws of Europe* (Oxford, Hart Publishing, 1999) 23, 29.

measure that is restrictive of fundamental rights must be necessary in a democratic society[39] and respond to a *pressing social need*.[40] This obviously applies both to criminal investigation and mass surveillance.

A. Legitimate Aim

First, it is a proportionality requirement in both regimes (criminal investigation and intelligence) that the aim sought be legitimate. Only on a case-by-case basis, looking at the particular circumstances of a case, it is possible to draw conclusions about the legitimacy or the pressing social need that may justify the interference with the fundamental rights of citizens. In particular, the case law of the ECtHR has recognised that the prosecution of a serious crime is a legitimate aim for purposes of Article 8 ECHR. The legitimacy of mass surveillance for protecting national security or preventing serious crimes has not been questioned either. The Court in *Big Brother* underlined that 'terrorist violence constitutes, in itself, a grave threat to human rights' and, 'faced with such a threat, the Court has considered it legitimate for Contracting States to take a firm stand against those who contribute to terrorist acts'.[41] This approach seems to be appropriate, even if questions as to what should be defined as 'national security' or a 'serious offence' justifying the interference with the fundamental right to privacy cannot be answered in a clear and generally accepted manner. Both concepts are indeed very broad and it is probably not for the Court to define them. But it must be admitted that accepting, as legitimate aims, purposes that are too general or too vague does not add anything substantial to the judicial reasoning.[42]

B. Suitability and Effectiveness

Second, the suitability/effectiveness of communication interception for the investigation of crimes and the detection of national security threats is hardly discussed in the case law of the ECtHR. The Court accepts for both regimes that the interception of communications is adequate to achieve the aim sought. It is generally confirmed that such measures contribute to the aim sought. However, the Court does not test to what extent they are effective in achieving the aim sought.

[39] See K Reid, *A Practitioner's Guide to the European Convention on Human Rights* (London, Sweet & Maxwell, 2019) 430ff; L Bachmaier, 'Criminal Investigation and the Right to Privacy in the Case Law of the European Court of Human Rights' (2009) 2 *Lex et Scientia (Lesij)* 9, 12.

[40] See *Silver and others v United Kingdom* App nos 5947/72, 6205/73, 7052/75, 7061/75, 7107/75, 7113/75 and 7136/75 (ECHR, 11 October 1980); *Camenzind v Switzerland* App no 21353/93 (ECtHR, 16 December 1997).

[41] *Big Brother Watch v UK* (n 6) [445]–[446].

[42] See J Gerards, 'How to Improve the Necessity Test of the European Court of Human Rights' (2013) 11(2) *International Journal of Constitutional Law* 466, 480, available at: doi.org/10.1093/icon/mot004.

This assessment would require in each case that the causal link between the means and the end be established, something that is not possible because there are usually multiple sources of information both in terms of investigating crime and identifying threats to the national security. For the ECtHR, a deferential test of effectiveness may be used when it has left the states a wide margin of appreciation,[43] meaning that, unless there are clear indications of *un*suitability (negative test of suitability), the Court will not enter into a factual, empirical or statistical analysis of the effectiveness of the restrictive measure. The Court followed this approach in the *Big Brother* case, relying on the reports of international and national bodies.

C. Necessity

Third, analysis of the ECtHR's approach to the necessity test shows, as the point of departure, that any criminal investigative measure restricting the rights protected under Article 8 ECHR must be deemed strictly necessary in the sense that there are no less intrusive means to reach the same or equivalent results. In the Court's case law, the measure need not be absolutely indispensable to fulfil this requirement;[44] it is enough if it is reasonably necessary and convenient. The necessity test requires analysis of the possible existence of equally effective alternatives; to satisfy the necessity test, it is not required to undertake an investigation of *all* possible hypothetical alternatives. The problem in determining whether there exists an equally effective but less intrusive measure than the interception of communications is how to gather and evaluate information on the measure's effectiveness. As seen above, establishing the causal link between measure and achievement of the aim is not easy in the field of criminal investigation or national security.

An ex post assessment of a particular criminal investigation may show that the interception of communications was not strictly necessary or that the judicial warrant did not provide enough information in this regard. The necessity requirement applies also to bulk interception of communications within an intelligence scheme but, as alleged by the applicants in *Big Brother*, its ex post control by the affected persons will in most cases be absent.

Thus, the difference between the criminal procedure and the intelligence regime is that in the latter case the utility test (how useful the mechanism is for detecting national security threats) and the necessity test (whether there is a less restrictive measure to achieve the same results) cannot, as a rule, be applied to individual cases (as it can in the criminal procedure), albeit on the basis of the information included in internal auditing reports and reports prepared by national

[43] ibid 475.

[44] See *Handyside v United Kingdom* App no 5493/72 (ECtHR, 7 December 1976) [48]; *The Sunday Times v United Kingdom* App no 6538/74 (ECtHR, 26 April 1979) [59]; and specifically with regard to Art 8 ECHR, see, eg, *Dudgeon v United Kingdom* App no 7525/76 (ECtHR, 22 October 1981) [51]–[53].

independent commissioners. The ex post control by an independent commissioner fulfilling this task clearly cannot cover all files or records. The ECtHR is completely aware of this: not being able to determine whether the same preventive aim could have been achieved by other means less intrusive compared to the bulk interception of communications, the Court has to rely on the assessment by the national legislator and the reports of the independent oversight bodies.

D. Quality of the Law

Fourth, with regard to the 'quality of the law' requirement, the ECtHR has long since defined the aspects the law has to regulate to ensure that the secret interception of communications within the framework of a criminal investigation meets the necessary conditions to be in conformity with the Convention. As seen above, the same '*Weber* requirements' are to be applied to the legislation on bulk interception of communications for national security purposes.

E. Proportionality in the Narrow Sense

Fifth, the measure in question must also comply with the proportionality principle in the narrow sense. For assessing this element of the proportionality principle in the context of criminal investigation, the following aspects must be taken into account: the seriousness of the crime, the intensity of the suspicions, the perspective of the measure's success, and the harm caused to the individual vis-à-vis the usefulness of the results.[45] Within the mass surveillance regime, the circumstances considered in the overall assessment are 'the nature, scope and duration of the possible measures, the grounds required for ordering them, the authorities competent to authorise, carry out and supervise them, and the kind of remedy provided by the national law'.[46]

F. Margin of Appreciation

The Strasbourg Court has consistently held that the principle of proportionality is inherent in balancing the protection of individual rights against other general

[45] These are the elements of the so-called 'test of proportionality', which can be found already in the common law of England and Wales and are expressly stated in the 1948 case of *Associated Provincial Picture Houses Ltd v Wednesbury Corp* [1948] 1 KB 223. On this, see Fordham and De La Mare (n 37) 30ff. These criteria are thoroughly analysed by Degener (n 24) 224ff.

[46] See *Big Brother Watch v UK* (n 6) [308]. The same elements are required under the Interception of Communications Code of Practice with respect to the application of RIPA bulk surveillance interception of communications.

public interests in society.[47] The margin-of-appreciation doctrine allows national authorities wide discretionary powers to assess the necessity and proportionality of both surveillance and investigative measures that interfere with fundamental rights. Since *Klass and others* in 1978 the Court has recognised the states' margin of appreciation in the field of interception of communications and of surveillance within intelligence schemes.[48]

The precise extent of the margin of appreciation and whether such margin should be reduced in cases where the fundamental right to privacy is at stake are questions under debate.[49] A very broad discretionary power would be contrary to the essence of the fundamental rights; but excessively trying to lessen the states' discretionary powers in this field would imply that a supranational court should decide, in each and every single case, on the suitability, necessity and proportionality of the preventive or investigative measures, thereby running the risk of becoming some kind of fourth extraordinary instance.

The unavoidable ambiguities present in the ECtHR case law with respect to the evaluation of the necessity and proportionality of the measure in a democratic society correspond to the search for an adjustment between the supranational protection of human rights and the respect for the features and principles of national legal systems. In any event, the exercise of the margin of appreciation is subject to supervision by the Court

> embracing both legislation and decisions applying it. In view of the risk that a system of secret surveillance set up to protect national security may undermine or even destroy democracy under the cloak of defending it, the Court must be satisfied that there are adequate and effective guarantees against abuse.[50]

In order to determine whether the interference with the right under Article 8 ECHR is 'necessary in a democratic society', the Court requires an effective adequate oversight scheme to be in place. And this points to one of the main differences we can find between the criminal investigative context and the intelligence regime: how and when the safeguards apply.

G. Judicial Safeguards and Oversight

The two elements denoting the main distinction as to the safeguards are: the requirement of a previous suspicion in the criminal investigation field and the ex ante judicial warrant. The interception of communications within the

[47] Y Arai-Takahashi, *The Margin of Appreciation Doctrine and the Principle of Proportionality in the Jurisprudence of the ECHR* (Antwerp, Intersentia, 2002) 190ff.

[48] *Klass and others v Germany* App no 5029/71 (ECtHR, 6 September 1978); *Leander v Sweden* (n 17); *Liberty and others v UK* (n 8).

[49] See Arai-Takahashi (n 47) 60ff.

[50] See *Big Brother Watch v UK* (n 6) [308].

framework of a criminal investigation requires a justified judicial warrant that controls the lawfulness of the measure and the proportionality elements, and considers the existence of a suspicion against a particular individual. The targeted interception for investigative purposes is subject to judicial control at all stages and, in addition, the possibility for ex post control is open to the defendant and the adjudicating court.

The approach in the case of non-targeted surveillance differs completely from that adopted for targeted interceptions. In non-targeted surveillance, an initial judicial decision based on previous suspicion against concrete individuals is absent, simply because there *is* no specific target. This seems logical, once the suitability and necessity requirements are assessed. The minimum requirements of indications or suspicions necessary to allow a targeted interception of communication are not applicable to the situation of unknown targets subjected to bulk interceptions.[51]

As the ECtHR stated,

> bulk interception is by definition untargeted, and to require 'reasonable suspicion' would render the operation of such a scheme impossible. Similarly, the requirement of 'subsequent notification' assumes the existence of clearly defined surveillance targets, which is simply not the case in a bulk interception regime.[52]

The argument is plausible, and the request of the applicants, demanding – as an additional safeguard – that the existence of a previous suspicion be checked, in my view, does not seem to be compatible with the scheme of untargeted surveillance for detecting national security threats.

The next step, however, is crucial: the use of selectors to identify the threats and the possibility that, following the selection process, the untargeted surveillance is transformed into a targeted analysis. When it comes to the oversight of mass surveillance measures for intelligence purposes, the ECtHR emphasised that such oversight has to be in place at all stages of the interception procedure. This is where the Court in *Big Brother* was not satisfied with the oversight measures provided by RIPA at the crucial time. Therefore, although the requirement of reasonable suspicion as known within the criminal sphere is not applicable to the preventive (security) realm, it can be agreed that additional controls should be in place whenever the decision is made to analyse the communications of particular individuals.

With regard to the issue of ex ante judicial authorisation, which, as we have seen, is present in the criminal procedure, the applicants in the *Big Brother* case claimed that, due to the intrusiveness of the surveillance, additional guarantees should be in place and an ex ante judicial warrant should be required also within the intelligence regime of bulk surveillance.[53] The applicants' argument that the

[51] ibid [317].
[52] ibid.
[53] See ibid [280].

criteria the ECtHR had adopted until now should be revised in the new digital context is shared by Judge Koskelo in her dissenting opinion (joined by Judge Pardalos).[54]

Regarding the authorisation of surveillance measures, the Court had expressed in previous judgments a clear preference for an authorisation by a judicial body but did not establish this as a requirement for compliance with Article 8 ECHR;[55] however, oversight by an independent authority is required.[56] In the case at hand, the Court recognised that judicial authorisation is not inherently incompatible with the effective functioning of bulk interception (as illustrated by the Swedish system of surveillance) and it is an important and 'highly desirable' safeguard against arbitrariness; nevertheless, the Court added that 'to date [the Court] has not considered it to be a "necessary requirement" or the exclusion of judicial control to be outside "the limits of what may be deemed necessary in a democratic society"'.[57] On this basis, the Court concluded that the lack of prior judicial authorisation in the RIPA regime does not constitute in itself a violation of the Convention,[58] following its previous ruling in *Kennedy*, where the Court clearly held that judicial authorisation could be either ex ante or ex post facto.[59]

In view of the safeguards foreseen by the British intelligence regime, it may not be totally indispensable to require prior judicial warrant. However, the Court used surprising and unconvincing arguments in this regard, as when it held that a prior judicial authorisation can fail, recalling that in the *Roman Zakharov* case the prior judicial scrutiny had provided limited or no protection against abuse.[60] The argument is weak and redundant, for nobody questions that an ex ante judicial authorisation may not be sufficient and abuses can nevertheless occur.

The fact is that the ECtHR utilised this argument to emphasise the idea that the crucial point is not only that safeguards are in place but that they must also be adequately implemented; and in the United Kingdom, the ex post control might have proved to be a sufficient safeguard. A further point is whether the Court, after finding the oversight mechanism under RIPA sufficient, should have then exceeded its powers by imposing an additional guarantee such as the ex ante judicial authorisation. I share the Court's opinion that such a safeguard would

[54] 'I do not believe that the necessary safeguard in the circumstances of surveillance based on bulk interception of communications can be sufficient without including an independent ex ante judicial control', see the dissenting opinion, at [29].

[55] See *Klass and others* (n 48) [56]; *Kennedy v UK* (n 16) [167].

[56] See *Association for European Integration and Human Rights and Ekimdzhiev v Bulgaria* App no 62540/00 (ECtHR, 28 June 2007) [85] and [87].

[57] See *Big Brother Watch* (n 6) [318] and [381].

[58] See ibid [381].

[59] *Kennedy v UK* (n 16) 166.

[60] See *Big Brother Watch v UK* (n 6) [319]. Abuses were found also in *Association for European Integration v Bulgaria* (n 56) and *Mustafa Sezgin Tanrıkulu v Turkey* App no 27473/06 (ECtHR, 18 July 2017), despite prior judicial authorisation.

be desirable in this particular case but that there were no substantial reasons to impose a judicial ex ante control on the UK legislator.[61]

Finally, when it comes to the ex post control, the British law also includes the possibility for an individual to trigger an ex post assessment by the Investigatory Powers Tribunal. The fact that individuals will probably not resort to such a tribunal, claiming an unlawful interference with their rights, because they typically will not know whether their communications were intercepted or not does not reduce its importance as an ex post individual oversight mechanism, although its effectiveness might be called into question.

After having examined in detail the oversight system put in place by the British law, the ECtHR in *Big Brother* concluded that, except at the intermediate stage, there was an adequate system providing effective guarantees to prevent abuses, and there were also elements that demonstrated that its practical implementation was in conformity with the European Convention. Therefore, albeit recognising that all systems of secret interception of communications are susceptible to potential abuses, the Court reached the conclusion that the United Kingdom was compliant with its obligations under the Convention.

V. Final Remarks

Due to the increased potential for causing harm and the manifest risks of abuse connected with bulk interception of communications and secret intelligence mechanisms, it is logical that some tend to find such measures disproportionate, or at least expect the ECtHR to apply a more stringent proportionality test than the one adopted for the individual (targeted) interception of communications or for pre-digital surveillance schemes. As the potential harm increases, proportionality tests have to evolve accordingly. However, this is not reflected in the *Big Brother* judgment. Here, the Court focuses on the oversight of the security services. Axiomatically, an efficient oversight scheme is fundamental for ensuring that intelligence agencies contribute effectively to the protection of the populations they are bound to serve and at the same time respect the rule of law and human rights guarantees in undertaking this task. As for the remaining contentious issues, the Strasbourg Court defers to the reasonableness of the choices made by the national decision-making bodies. Is this right?

Even if at first glance one could argue that the methods for checking the proportionality of criminal investigation interceptions, on the one hand, and mass surveillance measures, on the other, should differ, this must not be taken for granted. Certainly, the elements that need to be weighed in the areas of criminal investigation and intelligence, respectively, are dissimilar; and the same applies

[61] To my mind there is no contradiction with the decision taken in *Digital Rights Ireland* (n 1), as the retention of data under the EU 2006/24/EC Directive also contemplated the investigation of crimes, which is not the case in terms of the intelligence scheme.

with respect to the oversight system. Nonetheless, the method for assessing proportionality followed by the ECtHR in both cases is not substantially different. Both in the area of mass surveillance and in that of interceptions of communications within the ordinary criminal process the ECtHR resorted to the doctrine of the margin of appreciation, without itself properly dealing with the question whether there is an actual need for mass interceptions of communications for national security reasons. Thus, the Court avoided an evaluation with respect to the justification of the means in relation to the end pursued. The proportionality test *stricto sensu*, which entails in the present case a balancing between privacy and security (costs-benefits), was once again replaced by deference to the national authorities' discretionary appreciation. This notwithstanding, the ECtHR accepted that the means were justified by the aim pursued. Still, it is striking that in a landmark case like *Big Brother* and after recognising that the current digital sphere represents a 'sea change', the effectiveness and necessity tests were not substantiated by the Court. There is definitely room for improvement in that regard.

While some may consider this approach disappointing and demand that the ECtHR adopt a more active role in setting limits on the states' powers, especially in areas that pose vast risks to human rights, it is also understandable that the Court decided to continue applying the margin-of-appreciation doctrine. The resulting differences in terms of the Strasbourg Court's stance regarding both the interception of communications in the criminal investigative field and the bulk surveillance intelligence regime are not significant. It is true that when addressing interceptions of communications within criminal investigations, the Court carries out an ex post assessment. Due to the fact that in reviewing such cases the focus was put on the 'quality of the law' requirement, this approach ultimately resembles the assessment carried out in the *Big Brother* case. Foreseeability, quality of the law and sufficient oversight mechanisms: these are what matter to the Court in this field. Even if this may be insufficient for many, in the end the *Big Brother* judgment remains consistent with the role the Council of Europe Member States assigned to, and the operational limits they set on, the ECtHR.

17

Proportionality Issues in European Arrest Warrant Proceedings – Three Stories from the Field

ILIAS ANAGNOSTOPOULOS

I. The European Arrest Warrant 2004–20: A Success Story, at a Cost

The European Arrest Warrant (EAW) was, and still is, the first and the most powerful legal instrument of criminal justice cooperation in the EU area. Its adoption in 2002[1] in the aftermath of the terrorist attacks of 9/11 marks a new era of efficiency-oriented simplified procedures between States Parties. Its proclaimed aim was to tackle serious cross-border crime which was thought to be on the rise.[2] Hailed as a success by Member States and EU institutions, the EAW was also met with sharp criticism.[3] Critics argue that the speedier enforcement of criminal decisions in the area of freedom, security and justice has been achieved at the cost of fundamental rights of individuals.[4]

Indeed, persons who are subjected to EAW surrender procedures have seen their rights minimised, losing the protection offered by such long-cherished principles as the dual criminality rule or the non-extradition of nationals. Moreover, ousting the executive power from the decision-making process bars a flexible approach to each individual case at the final stage of surrender, where

[1] Council Framework Decision 2002/584/JHA of 13 June 2020 on the European arrest warrant and surrender procedures between Member States, OJ 2002 L 190/1.

[2] See Explanatory Memorandum to the European Commission's Proposal on the EAW of 19 September 2001, COM(2001) final at 3., 4.1.

[3] For an overview of the debate on the EAW, see A Weyembergh, I Armada and C Brière, *Critical Assessment of the Existing European Arrest Warrant Framework Decision* (Brussels, Research Paper for DG European Parliamentary Research Service, European Parliament, 2014) 7.

[4] See, eg, S Alegre and M Leaf, *European Arrest Warrant – A Solution ahead of its Time?* (London, JUSTICE, 2003) 8.

humanitarian, personal, political or other relevant aspects may be weighed against the need for transnational criminal enforcement.[5]

In the decade following the EU-Presidency Conclusions in Tampere (1999), which declared the mutual recognition of criminal judgments and decisions as the 'cornerstone' of cooperation in the common judicial area,[6] the EU institutions focused on maximising the efficiency of police and prosecuting authorities across Europe. At the same time, the European Commission's initiative to introduce a comprehensive set of procedural rights in criminal and EAW proceedings via a Framework Decision ultimately failed.[7]

It was not until the Stockholm Programme and the Roadmap on Strengthening Procedural Rights in Criminal Proceedings,[8] which was launched by the Swedish Presidency in 2009, that the EU turned its attention to the rights of suspects and accused persons. In the words of EU Justice Commissioner Viviane Reding: 'Before 2010, Lady Justice was holding two swords and no scales. Since then the Commission has taken action to bring a new balance into justice policies by strengthening the rights and freedoms of our citizens.'[9]

From 2010 to 2016 six Directives on minimum procedural rights have been adopted on a step-by-step basis following the ordinary legislative procedure in accordance with Article 82(2) of the Treaty on the Functioning of the European Union (TFEU). The Directives establish minimum standards in criminal and EAW proceedings for suspects and accused persons in relation to their rights to interpretation and translation, information, access to a lawyer, the presumption of innocence and the right to be present at trial, legal aid and the protection of child defendants.[10]

The above package of procedural rights, though far from perfect, has strengthened the position of defendants in criminal procedures across the European Union including the EAW surrender proceedings. The Council Framework Decision 2009/299/JHA of 26 February 2009, which introduced a number of

[5] I Anagnostopoulos, 'Criminal Justice Cooperation in the European Union after the First Few "Steps": A Defence View' (2014) *ERA Forum* 9, 10.

[6] Tampere Council Presidency Conclusions of 15/16 October 1999, para 33. See, eg, L Salazar, 'Twenty Years since Tampere – The Development of Mutual Recognition in Criminal Matters' (2020) *Eucrim: The European Criminal Law Associations' Forum* 255; A Erbežnik, 'The Principle of Mutual Recognition as a Utilitarian Solution, and the Way Forward' (2012) 2(1) *European Criminal Law Review* 4, 7.

[7] Proposal for a Framework Decision on certain procedural rights of 28 April 2004, COM(2004) 328 final.

[8] The Stockholm Programme – An Open and Secure Europe Serving and Protecting the Citizens, OJ 2010 C 115/1. The Roadmap was adopted by the Council of the European Union on 30 November 2009, OJ 2009 C 295/1.

[9] European Commission Press Release of 27 November 2013 (IP/13/1157). See V Mitsilegas, *EU Criminal Law after Lisbon, Rights, Trust and the Transformation of Justice in Europe* (Oxford, Hart Publishing, 2016) 156ff.

[10] For an overview of the six Directives and the respective CJEU case law, see Fair Trials International, 'Mapping CJEU Case Law on EU Criminal Justice Measures', 2020, available at: www.fairtrials.org/sites/default/files/Mapping-CJEU-Case-Law-on-EU-Criminal-Justice-Measures-February-2020.pdf.

amendments to the EAW Framework Decision (FD EAW) as well as to other FDs in the area of judicial cooperation, with a view to reinforcing the position of individuals against decisions rendered *in absentia*, shall also be mentioned in this respect.[11]

One of the main areas of criticism against the EAW law and practice throughout its 16 years of operation has been the lack of respect for the fundamental principle of proportionality, which in some Member States seems to be widespread.[12] Two aspects are within the focus of the EAW proportionality debate. First, it is noted that arrest warrants are issued for less serious offences with no proper assessment of their potentially devastating impact on arrestees.[13] Second, it is argued that significant numbers of arrest warrants are issued in cases which are not trial-ready, ie, for investigative purposes, with no prior consideration of equally suitable and less intrusive measures such as the summons of the suspect or the use of alternative mutual assistance tools, for example, interrogation of suspects by a competent authority in the executing state, interrogation via video-link, etc.[14]

In its Report on the implementation of the EAW of 2011 the European Commission welcomed the EAW as 'a successful mutual recognition instrument in practice',[15] but it also expressed concern over the fact that '[c]onfidence in the application of the EAW has been undermined by the systematic issue of EAWs … in respect to often very minor offences' and emphasised the need for a uniform application of a proportionality check in all issuing Member States in accordance with the 2010 amended version of the *Handbook on How to Issue and Execute a European Arrest Warrant*[16] (the Handbook). In the Commission's view, a soft law

[11] For a critical assessment of the EU legal framework regarding *in absentia* trials, see E Sellier and A Weyembergh, *Criminal Procedural Laws across the European Union – A Comparative Analysis of Selected Main Differences and the Impact They Have over the Development of EU Legislation* (Brussels, Research paper requested by the LIBE Committee of the European Parliament, 2018) 131ff.

[12] See, eg, E Xanthopoulou, 'The Quest for Proportionality for the European Arrest Warrant: Fundamental Rights Protection in a Mutual Recognition Environment' (2015) 6(1) *New Journal of European Criminal Law* 32; T Hammarberg (Commissioner for Human Rights of the Council of Europe), *Overuse of the European Arrest Warrant – a Threat to Human Rights*, available at: www.coe.int/en/web/commissioner/-/overuse-of-the-european-arrest-warrant-a-threat-to-human-righ-1; S Haggenmüller, 'The Principle of Proportionality and the European Arrest Warrant' (2013) 3(1) *Oñati Socio-legal Series* 95, 100 (available at: www.ssrn.com/abstract=2200874).

[13] R Davidson, 'A Sledgehammer to Crack a Nut? Should there be a Bar of Triviality in European Arrest Warrant Cases?' (2009) *Criminal Law Review* 31; M Plachta, 'Evaluation of the European Arrest Warrant: Quantitative and Practical Aspects' (2011) 27 *International Enforcement Law Reporter* 681, 683.

[14] Weyembergh, Armada and Brière (n 3) 37; S Carrera, E Guild and N Hernanz, 'Europe's Most Wanted? Recalibrating Trust in the European Arrest Warrant System', CEPS Paper (2013) 55 *Liberty and Security in Europe* 16, available at: www.ceps.eu/ceps-publications/europes-most-wanted-recalibrating-trust-european-arrest-warrant-system/.

[15] Report from the Commission to the European Parliament and the Council of 11 April 2011, COM(2011) 175 final at 7–8.

[16] The Handbook was revised in 2017, see Commission Notice of 28 September 2017, *Handbook on How to Issue and Execute a European Arrest Warrant*, C(2017) 6389 final, available at: e-justice.europa.eu/fileDownload.do?id=db28c045-9f92-472e-9452-518b4ce84712.

instrument such as the Handbook in conjunction with the applicable statutory provisions in national laws would provide a good basis for a proportionate – in all the circumstances of each case – use of the EAW and thus ensure mutual trust between Member States.

In the following years, the European Parliament took a more critical approach towards the EAW. In its Resolution on the review of the European Arrest Warrant of 27 February 2014,[17] the Parliament highlighted the importance of respect for the fundamental rights of suspects and accused persons as the basis upon which mutual trust can be achieved, and pointed out gaps in the FD EAW 'such as failing to explicitly include fundamental rights safeguards or a proportionality check'.[18] In the same Resolution concern was expressed about 'the disproportionate use of the EAW for minor offences or in circumstances where less intrusive alternatives might be applied, leading to unwarranted arrests and unjustified and extensive time spent in pre-trial detention'.[19]

The European Parliament's Resolution called on Member States to 'exhaust all possible alternative mechanisms before issuing an EAW'. Most importantly, it requested the Commission, according to Article 225 TFEU, to submit legislative proposals including, inter alia,

> a proportionality check when issuing mutual recognition decisions, based on all the relevant factors and circumstances such as the seriousness of the offence, whether the case is trial-ready, the impact on the rights of the requested person, including the protection of private and family life, the cost implications and the availability of an appropriate less intrusive alternative measure.

It also recommended

> a standardised consultation procedure whereby the competent authorities in the issuing and executing Member State can exchange information regarding the execution of judicial decisions such as on the assessment of proportionality and specifically in regard to the EAW to ascertain trial-readiness,

as well as

> a mandatory refusal ground where there are substantial grounds to believe that the execution of the measure would be incompatible with the executing Member State's obligation in accordance with Article 6 of the TEU and the Charter, notably Article 52(1) thereof with its reference to the principle of proportionality.[20]

The Commission did not agree with the Parliament on the necessity of a legislative initiative. In its Response of 28 May 2014 the Commission noted that the EAW is

[17] P7_TA (2014)0174; the Resolution followed a Report of the LIBE Committee dated 28 January 2014 (A7-0039/2014, Rapporteur Baroness Sarah Ludford).

[18] ibid point C.

[19] ibid point F(v).

[20] ibid points 7(b), 7(c) and 7(d) respectively.

'Europe's most successful criminal justice instrument' and that it 'does not share the Parliament's view that improving the European arrest warrant system requires a revision of the Framework Decision either alone or in conjunction with a revision of other mutual recognition instruments'.[21] In the Commission's view,

> [g]iven the risks of interference with a largely successful system and the fact that the issues identified by the Parliament are already and can be further addressed and improvements achieved without re-opening the core legislation, ... the best course of action for improving the European arrest warrant is to continue the work that is already on-going to address the issues raised by the Parliament.

The EAW figures compiled by the Commission until the year 2017 do not indicate significant changes in the Member States' practice.[22] The number of EAWs issued from 2015 to 2017 increased moderately (16144, 16636 and 17491 respectively) and the same holds true for those executed (5304, 5812 and 6317 respectively). Poland, a country which has been criticised in the past for the overuse of the new instrument, still remains one of the most EAW-friendly Member States (2432 EAWs issued in 2017) despite a significant decrease compared to previous years (4844 EAWs were issued in Poland in 2009, which represents the highest number of all countries since 2005), while the UK makes very moderate use of this instrument throughout its operation (approximately 200–300 EAWs per year).[23] The number of refusals to execute EAWs is remarkably low (796 for 2017 across 24 Member States and 719 for 2016 across 25 Member States), the more so given that the most common refusal ground is the execution of the custodial sentence, the enforcement of which is sought by the EAW, in the requested state (229 out of 719 refusal cases in 2017). Only in rare cases do the fundamental rights of the arrestee appear to be the reason for non-execution of the EAW (109 cases in 2017), the vast majority of which were recorded in Germany (87).

II. Three Stories from the Field

Three recent EAW cases are presented and discussed in this chapter, which involve three EU Member States (Greece, United Kingdom and Cyprus) as the issuing or executing states of the warrant.[24] On initial inspection, these cases do not seem to raise serious proportionality issues, because they refer to allegedly serious offences

[21] Follow up to the European Parliament Resolution with recommendations to the Commission on the review of the European arrest warrant adopted by the Commission on 28 May 2014.

[22] See Commission Staff Working Document, Replies to questionnaire on quantitative information on the practical operation of the European arrest warrant – Year 2017, 28 August 2019, SWD(2019) 318 final.

[23] Hungary, with a population of c 9.7 million, also appears to be EAW-friendly (1376 EAWs in 2017).

[24] In all three cases I acted as counsel for the defendants and had access to the documents of the case file.

(bribery, financial fraud, market abuse and tax fraud) and the EAWs appear to be legally correct. However, closer scrutiny reveals specific troubling aspects of the persistently disproportionate use of the EAW across the EU, despite laudable efforts to counter it. In the common EU area security seems to trump liberty and justice.

A. The Case of LB

(i) The Facts of the Case

LB is a well-known Greek businessman who holds a high-ranking position within a group of companies with notable international activity in the construction, energy, recycling and other sectors. The group holds a subsidiary in Cyprus, against which an investigation was opened due to alleged bribery practices by the subsidiary, involving public officials of Cyprus.

In 2016 a court in Nicosia issued an EAW against LB and an alert for execution was entered into the Schengen Information System (SIS). After LB learned about the EAW against him from press reports, he appeared voluntarily before the Extradition Prosecutor's Office in Athens, Greece, but did not consent to his surrender to Cyprus. No detention or other restrictive measures were imposed on LB, who had a permanent residence in Athens, except a prohibition to leave the country. The EAW against LB had been issued for investigative purposes, as the case was still in the hands of the police, and no effort was made by the authorities of Cyprus prior to the issue of the EAW to summon him at his known residence in Greece in order to appear for interrogation.

The EAW hearing took place before the Extradition Chamber of the Court of Appeal Athens,[25] which issued an interim decision asking the issuing state to describe more accurately the offences for which LB was sought, including a clear definition of the place where these offences had taken place. Cyprus did not respond to the above decision, leading to the rejection of the initial EAW by the Greek authorities. Instead, the authorities in Cyprus withdrew the first EAW and issued a new one which included more details on the offences. In this context it is worthwhile to note that the Court of Justice of the EU (CJEU) had ruled in *AY*[26] that the issuing Member State is not prevented from issuing more than one EAW against the same person for the same acts during the various procedural stages, and that the executing Member State has a duty to consider each one of them irrespective of a prior refusal.

[25] Under the Greek statute (Law No 3251, 9 July 2004) implementing the FD EAW, the Court of Appeal sits as a first instance court, while appeals against judgments of the latter are heard by Areios Pagos, ie, Greece's Cassation Court.

[26] Case C-268/17 *AY* ECLI:EU:C:2018:602 (Judgment of 25 July 2018); the case concerned two successive EAWs from Croatia against a Hungarian citizen.

Following the hearing on the second EAW the Court of Appeal Athens issued its judgment no 69/2016,[27] refusing to execute the warrant on the grounds that the most significant part of LB's acts as described in the EAW had taken place in Greece. It should be noted that under the Greek law which implemented the FD EAW,[28] territoriality is a mandatory refusal ground, ie, the execution of the EAW must be rejected if the offence, or parts thereof, was committed on Greek territory.[29] With the same judgment the Court of Appeal Athens lifted the *ne exeat republica* order of the Extradition Prosecutor's Office in Athens against LB and forwarded the case file to the Public Prosecutor's Office in Athens, requesting it to assume jurisdiction over the alleged offences of LB.

Thereafter, the Athens Prosecutor opened a preliminary investigation against LB and other individuals, in the course of which LB was interrogated as a suspect and answered questions put to him. The Prosecutor also submitted a request to the Cypriot authorities to forward all evidence in their possession relevant to the alleged acts of LB. After the closing of the preliminary investigation, the Prosecutor ordered the opening of a formal investigation to be conducted by an Investigating Judge. Under Greek law the Investigating Judge has broad powers regarding the gathering of evidence, the interrogation of witnesses and suspects, etc.[30]

In 2018, while the above formal investigation in Athens was still pending against him, LB filed a request with the Nicosia District Court asking for a withdrawal of the EAW issued by the authorities in Cyprus. He argued, inter alia, that the withdrawal should be granted on grounds of proportionality. It should be noted that, in the applicant's view, Cyprus had no reasonable grounds to insist on his cross-border prosecution given that the competent authorities in his home country (Greece) had assumed jurisdiction and were actively investigating the bribery offences in question.

Furthermore, LB argued that the proceedings against him opened in Athens, in which he actively participated, would necessarily result in a final decision on the case, ie, either in a final acquittal (non-indictment) decision to be issued by the indicting chamber or in a judgment by a trial court in the event of an indictment after the closing of the formal investigation. Such decisions would subsequently bar any other prosecution in all Member States including Cyprus according to the *non bis in idem* rule.[31]

[27] Athens Court of Appeal, *Bobolas v Cyprus*, judgment no 69/2016 (unreported).

[28] See n 25.

[29] Art 11(h) Law 3251/2004.

[30] For a brief overview of the pre-trial stages in Greece, see I Anagnostopoulos, J Zapanti and A Tsagkalidis, 'Procedure Before Criminal Courts' in *Greek Law Digest*, 3rd edn (Athens, Nomiki Bibliothiki, 2019) 57 (also available at: www.greeklawdigest.gr/topics/judicial-system/item/299-procedure-before-criminal-courts).

[31] Art 4(3) FD EAW (2009/299/JHA of 26 February 2009); see Joined Cases C-187/01 and C-385/01 *Hüseyin Gözütok and Klaus Brügge* ECLI:EU:C:2003:87 (Judgment of 11 February 2003); Case C-467/04 *Giuseppe Francesco Gasparini and Others* ECLI:EU:C:2006:610 (Judgment of September 2006); Case C-398/12 *M* ECLI:EU:C:2014:1057 (Judgment of 5 June 2014); Case C-486/14 *Piotr Kossowski* ECLI:EU:C:2016:483 (Judgment of 29 June 2016).

Given these circumstances the non-withdrawal of the EAW by Cyprus appeared, in the applicant's view grossly disproportionate, as it confined him for an extensive period (starting in 2016) to Greek territory, even though he was not considered a flight risk, resulting in his inability to fulfil his professional obligations around the world and also negatively affecting his family obligations regarding his two children, who were studying abroad, and of whom he was sole guardian, as his wife was deceased. He claimed the disproportionality of the Cypriot EAW was even more evident, considering that there was no real prospect of him being tried in Cyprus after he had submitted himself to the jurisdiction of the Greek authorities who would finally judge the case. In the applicant's view, Cyprus's insistence on the EAW revealed itself as a purposeless punitive measure, which infringed on his fundamental right of free movement as an EU citizen.

The Nicosia Court disagreed. In its decision of 29 June 2018,[32] the Court held that under both domestic and EU law the proceedings pending in Greece on the same matter did not oblige Cyprus to withdraw its EAW against the applicant; such an obligation would arise under Article 54 of the Schengen Convention and Article 50 of the EU Charter of Fundamental Rights (EU Charter) only after issuance of a final judgment in Greece. Moreover, the Court found that a proportionality test as described in paragraph 10.3. of the European Commission's Handbook on the EAW did not reveal a violation of this principle in the case at hand in view of the seriousness of the offences and the strong public interest in their prosecution in Cyprus.

LB filed an appeal against the decision of the Nicosia Court before the Supreme Court of Cyprus. The Supreme Court rejected the appeal. In its judgment of 26 September 2019,[33] the Supreme Court held that Cyprus, as a sovereign state, is under no obligation to withdraw its EAW against the appellant simply because parallel proceedings for the same acts had been initiated in Greece. The Court invoked in this respect Recital 11 of the Framework Decision on Conflicts of Jurisdictions in Criminal Proceedings, which states:

> No Member State should be obliged to waive or to exercise jurisdiction unless it wishes to do so. As long as consensus on the concentration of criminal proceedings has not been reached, the competent authorities of the Member States should be able to continue criminal proceedings for any criminal offence which falls within their national jurisdiction.[34]

In the Cyprus Supreme Court's view, the applicant's interests do not override the interests of society in the good administration of justice and the sovereign state's

[32] Nicosia District Court, 29 June 2018 (unreported).

[33] Cyprus Court of Appeal, Civil Appeal 239/2018, *Bobolas v Cyprus*, 26 September 2019, available at: www.cylaw.org/cgi-bin/open.pl?file=/apofaseis/aad/meros_1/2019/1-201909-239-18PolEf.htm (in Greek).

[34] Council Framework Decision on the prevention and settlement of conflicts of exercise of jurisdictions in criminal proceedings, 2009/948/JHA, OJ 2009 L 328/42, at 43.

power not to withdraw an EAW regarding serious acts of corruption falling within its jurisdiction. The Court concluded that neither the principle of proportionality nor the fundamental rights of the applicant, which are not absolute, had been breached.

(ii) Discussion

LB's case demonstrates deficiencies in the operation of the EAW mechanism. The authorities of Cyprus did not notify LB of the investigation against him or their intention to interrogate him as a suspect in any manner available to them. Instead, they opted to issue an EAW at a relatively early procedural stage, ie, before the case was trial-ready, therefore denying him any chance of voluntarily appearing for questioning (either in Cyprus or in Greece), using the usual channels of judicial assistance. This would have been a straightforward procedure, which would have been accelerated by the fact that both countries use the same official language.

Moreover, no compelling reasons were officially stated as to why the Cypriot authorities considered LB a flight risk despite his known permanent residence in Greece and the absence of a criminal past. In this respect, there is also a striking discrepancy between the approach of the Greek authorities, which did not consider it necessary to detain or even to bail LB regarding this matter throughout their investigation, and that of the Cypriot authorities, which insisted on his arrest for many years.

It is also noteworthy that Cyprus did not enter into consultations with Greece on the parallel proceedings in question, even though such an obligation arises under Article 10(1) of the FD on conflicts of jurisdictions, which states:

> When it is established that parallel proceedings exist, the competent authorities of the Member States concerned shall enter into direct consultations in order to reach consensus on any effective solution aimed at avoiding the adverse consequences arising from such parallel proceedings, which may, where appropriate, lead to the concentration of the criminal proceedings in one Member State.[35]

Member States are reminded of their duty to resolve conflicts of jurisdiction in case of multiple EAWs for the same acts in parallel proceedings also in the Handbook on the EAW.[36]

Finally, in assessing the proportionality of the EAW the courts in Cyprus did not specifically address the question of its duration. The EAW in question was issued on 3 May 2016 and was still in force more than three years later when the case was heard by the Cyprus Supreme Court. In this context the Handbook on the EAW invites Member States to reconsider its necessity and proportionality after a refusal to execute it by another Member State, taking into account,

[35] ibid, at 46.
[36] See n 16, para 5.10.2.

inter alia, fundamental rights and other available less coercive measures.[37] The Handbook[38] also makes reference to the SIS II Decision,[39] stipulating in Article 44(4)–(5) that, as a rule, alerts shall be removed after three years of their entry and allows states to exceptionally decide to keep an alert longer 'following a comprehensive individual assessment, which shall be recorded, … should this prove necessary for the purposes for which the alert was issued'.

On the face of it, the EAW by Cyprus against LB seems to be in full compliance with existing legislation. It was issued by a competent judicial authority, which is presumed to have conducted a prior, proper proportionality check, and it refers to serious punishable acts committed in part in the issuing state.[40] Following the CJEU judgment in *Radu*,[41] where the Court ruled that the issuing state is under no obligation to summon a suspect of known residence before issuing an arrest warrant against him/her for purposes of prosecution, the competent authorities in Cyprus had the right to decide at their own discretion whether they would first summon LB to appear for interrogation or instead issue an arrest warrant, and, therefore, their opting for the latter did not render the EAW invalid. Moreover, the parallel proceedings opened in Greece for the same acts did not create a *non bis in idem* bar until the conclusion of the case by final judgment, while Cyprus had the power not to withdraw the SIS alert against LB as long as it deemed it necessary in accordance with the criteria under its national law.

At the same time, the existing EU soft law provisions, particularly those included in the Handbook on the EAW and the SIS II Decision, as well as the non-compulsory consultations between the concurring Member States provided for in the FD on Conflicts of Jurisdiction[42] did not offer a solution in LB's case. They did not motivate Cyprus as the issuing state to enter into consultations with Greece with a view to concentrating the proceedings against LB in one country, where Greece might have had priority as the *forum conveniens* given the place where LB's alleged acts primarily took place, his nationality, his permanent residence, his

[37] ibid para 10.3.

[38] ibid para 10.4.

[39] Council Decision 2007/533/JHA of 12 June 2007 on the establishment, operation and use of the second-generation Schengen Information System (SIS II), OJ 2007 L 205/63.

[40] *cf* T Christou, 'The European Arrest Warrant and Human Rights in the Context of the Republic of Cyprus' (2012) 1(1) *Cyprus Human Rights Law Review* 57, 63.

[41] Case C-396/11 *Cyprian Radu* ECLI:EU:C:2013:39 (Judgment of the Grand Chamber of 29 January 2013) 39–40; for a critical assessment of the *Radu* judgment and of Case C-399/11 *Stefano Melloni v Ministerio Fiscal* ECLI:EU:2013:107, CJEU, see, eg, K Gaede, 'Minimalistischer EU-Grundrechtsschutz bei der Kooperation im Strafverfahren' (2013) 66 *Neue Juristische Wochenschrift* 1279.

[42] The gaps in the EU legislation in respect of conflicts of jurisdiction are addressed in the European Law Institute's 'Draft Legislative Proposals for the prevention and resolution of conflicts of jurisdiction in criminal matters in the European Union legal framework', 2017, available at: www.europeanlawinstitute.eu/fileadmin/user_upload/p_eli/Publications/Conflict_of_Jurisdiction_in_Criminal_Law_FINAL.pdf. See also M Kaiafa-Gbandi, 'Jurisdictional Conflicts in Criminal Matters and their Settlement within EU's Supranational Settings' (2018) 8(1) *European Criminal Law Review* 30, 40.

professional obligations, family relations, etc. In the course of such consultations Cyprus might have had to reconsider the necessity of arresting LB, taking into account the different approach of the Greek authorities in conjunction with the demonstrated willingness of LB to submit to the proceedings opened in Greece.

LB's case illustrates how a prima facie legally correct EAW may in reality disregard the interests of the individual, whose freedom is disproportionally restricted for years. The above thoughts beg the question whether the available EU legal framework sufficiently addresses such problems arising in the operation of the EAW or whether legislative action is needed to counter the persisting overuse of this highly intrusive instrument, as the European Parliament had recommended to the Commission to no avail in 2014.[43] This question will be addressed in the final part of this chapter after the presentation of the other two EAW cases.

B. The Case of KP

(i) The Facts of the Case

KP was the CEO of a group of companies ('G') based in Athens, Greece, which operated in the digital technology sector in various countries. G had been admitted for share trading to the London Stock Exchange's Alternative Investment Market (AIM) and had a UK-registered head office. In October 2015 G's shares were suspended from trading on allegations of misstating the company's financial position. The UK Financial Conduct Authority (FCA) opened a criminal investigation in the same year, in the course of which it requested judicial assistance from Greece, including the search and seizure of records and other documents on the premises of G. These investigative acts were conducted by competent Greek authorities, and KP made no objection to the seizure of the company's records. In 2016 the FCA filed a request for the purposes of interrogating KP. Both requests were made under the 1959 European Convention on Mutual Assistance in Criminal Matters,[44] to which the UK and Greece are parties.

The FCA's request for KP's interrogation was handled by the Investigating Judge of the Extradition and Judicial Assistance Division of the First Instance Court in Athens, who scheduled an interrogation of KP in the presence of three FCA officers based on a list of questions drafted by said agency. KP consented to his examination, prior to which he asked to exercise his rights as a suspect under the applicable Greek law, ie, the Code of Criminal Procedure, which grants the suspect access to the case file before his interrogation.[45] However, FCA officers

[43] See n 17.

[44] European Convention on Mutual Assistance in Criminal Matters, Strasbourg, April 1959, ETS No 030, available at: www.coe.int/en/web/conventions/full-list/-/conventions/treaty/030.

[45] Art 31 of the Code of Criminal Procedure in force at that time.

objected to KP's full access to the case file and declared that they would only allow limited access to the evidence in their possession, because this would be the case under UK law. Following the FCA's refusal to consent to KP's full access to the evidence, the latter appeared with counsel before the Investigating Judge on the scheduled day and declared in respect of all questions put to him that he was not in a position to answer them in view of the violation of his fundamental procedural rights under applicable Greek law.

KP received no other notification or information from the UK authorities on his case until the beginning of 2019. Nor did the latter contact KP's attorney in London, who had notified the FCA of his appointment and his client's willingness to respond to possible future requests in this matter. In February 2019 the District Judge of the Westminster Magistrates' Court issued, upon an FCA request, an EAW against KP in relation to four offences, namely making misleading statements on G's performance and revenue figures and its cash reserve figures to its auditors and the public, defrauding London Barclay's for the purpose of obtaining a credit facility, hiding of share dealing by KP, and a failed attempt to issue a high-yield bond on false financial data. A similar EAW was issued against the CFO of G.

When KP learned of the EAW, he appeared voluntarily at the Extradition Prosecutor's Office in Athens, where he was officially informed of the EAW and was released on the condition that he did not leave the country, surrendered his passport and appeared twice a month at the police station of his residence. KP declared that he did not consent to his surrender to the UK authorities.

The initial EAW hearing took place on 21 May 2019 before the Extradition Chamber of the Athens Court of Appeal, which issued an interim decision requesting further information from the UK authorities, including more details in relation to the place where the alleged offences had been committed. In response, the FCA provided a detailed answer including the requested supplementary information. The final hearing was held on 27 August and 6 September 2019. The Athens Court of Appeal declined to execute the EAW with respect to the aforementioned misleading statements on the grounds that the offences were time-barred under the corresponding provisions of Greek law.[46] It also rejected the EAW with respect to the fraud and market abuse counts, because KP's acts had been partly committed in Greece. As mentioned above, the Greek law implementing the FD EAW provides for a mandatory ground for refusal where part of the offences took place in Greece.[47] The FCA did not dispute that KP had partly committed the offences in Greece, where he was based. However, it argued that the UK was the most suitable forum for trying KP's case given that the alleged offences were related to a UK-registered company, which was admitted to the UK stock market for trading.

[46] Judgment no 129/2019, (2020) *Poinika Chronika* 46 (in Greek).
[47] See text to nn 25, 29.

It also expressed criticism against the Greek legislation for turning an optional EAW refusal ground into a mandatory one.

It should be noted that the Greek Court did not accept KP's claims that the EAW violated the proportionality principle and/or his fair trial rights under Article 6 European Convention on Human Rights (ECHR) or the EU Charter. Instead, it based the refusal to execute the EAW solely on the above grounds (statute of limitations and territoriality). Subsequently, the Athens Court of Appeal lifted the aforementioned restrictions imposed on KP by the Extradition Prosecutor and forwarded KP's file to the Public Prosecutor's Office in Athens, requesting it to assume jurisdiction over the case.

(ii) Discussion

KP's case is indicative of the problems that may arise in judicial assistance and EAW procedures. The Greek authorities responded at all stages without delay to the UK authorities' requests. They searched G's premises in Athens and seized documents and records which were made available to the FCA. They also responded to the request for KP's interrogation, allowing it to take place in the presence of three FCA officers and on the basis of their prepared list of questions. The FCA officers were made aware of the Greek provisions regarding access to evidence, which, as they knew, was the applicable law under the 1959 European Convention on Mutual Assistance in Criminal Matters. However, the FCA decided not to allow KP to exercise his procedural rights under Greek law; this decision resulted in KP's examination being fruitless.

Furthermore, the UK authorities moved ahead with issuing an EAW against KP rather than summoning him at his residence in Athens, which was known to them, and they did not at any stage notify his attorney in London of their intention to have KP appear in the UK. KP did not attempt at any time to escape justice; on the contrary, he did not oppose the above search and seizure and appeared for interrogation, while his application for access to the evidence was fully legitimate under the applicable laws.

It should also be pointed out that as of 22 May 2019, the European Investigation Order (EIO) entered into force, to which both Greece and the UK are parties.[48] This innovative legal instrument ensures a speedier and more flexible approach to the gathering of evidence between Member States compared to the traditional mutual assistance tools.[49] Indeed, Article 9 of the EIO Directive allows the execution of the issuing state's request to take place according to its own legislation and not that of the executing state except in situations where grounds of non-recognition

[48] Directive 2014/41/EU of the European Parliament and of the Council of 3 April 2014 regarding the European Investigation Order in criminal matters, OJ 2014 L 130/1.

[49] See, eg, R Belfiore, 'The European Investigation Order in Criminal Matters: Developments in Evidence-gathering across the EU' (2015) *European Criminal Law Review* 312.

or non-execution under Article 11 apply. In KP's case the EIO would have enabled the UK authorities to pursue his interrogation in Greece in accordance with English law to the extent that this would not be deemed incompatible with Greece's obligations under Article 6 TEU or the EU Charter. In case of a dispute in this respect, this would have been resolved by the Greek courts. The EIO also offers alternative measures such as the hearing of a suspect by videoconference (Article 24), which greatly facilitates and accelerates the proceedings between Member States. It is true that the EAW in question was issued in February 2019 before the entry into force of the EIO. However, such implementation had been expected in the coming months, and the new instrument was made applicable months before the EAW hearing at the Athens Court of Appeal. Apparently, the EIO's entry into force had not led the UK authorities to reconsider the available options including less intrusive measures against KP.

As already mentioned, the Greek judicial authorities assumed jurisdiction over KP and opened an investigation into his alleged acts as described in the EAW, with the exception of the offences that were time-barred under Greek law. These proceedings shall be concluded by a final judgment, which, as explained above,[50] will bar a prosecution for the same acts in any other Member State on *non bis in idem* grounds. Notwithstanding, the UK has full discretion as to the future of the EAW against KP. In particular, it may or may not withdraw it from the SIS alerts, while KP has no EU remedy available to him with a view to compelling the UK to withdraw the EAW. Also, there are no indications of consultations between the UK and the Greek authorities for the purpose of resolving their concurrent jurisdictions in this matter.

Given these circumstances, KP will de facto be confined to Greece for as long as the UK's EAW remains in force, even though he submitted to the jurisdiction of his home country and is not considered a flight risk by its authorities. As in LB's case, the EAW against KP, though legally correct on its face, disregards the interests of the affected individual, whose freedom of movement is disproportionally restricted.

C. The Case of FC

(i) The Facts of the Case

FC, a high-ranking officer of a global investment group, holds dual UK–US citizenship and resides primarily in these two countries. In 2008 he served on the board of the chemical products company 'N' in Greece with the aim of ensuring the smooth acquisition of the shares of the Greek company by the investment group. Having acquired the shares of the Greek company, the group then decided to reverse the share deal due to various irregularities revealed within the acquired

[50] See above at section II.A.(i).

company. FC, however, had left the board before the end of 2008 and had no other involvement in the business activities of N.

In 2013 the Greek tax authorities conducted an audit of N, during the course of which they asked the administrators of the company (which in the meantime had been placed in receivership) to present its books and records. In the tax authorities' view, the administrators did not comply with their request and therefore they proceeded to conduct a so-called 'out of books calculation' of the company's revenue, including the year 2008. According to the tax audit report, the value added taxes which N had failed to pay in 2008, based on the above method of calculation, amounted to approximately EUR 30 million.

Following the tax audit, a criminal complaint report was filed with the Prosecutor's Office in Athens and a criminal investigation was opened on allegations of VAT fraud. When FC was unofficially informed of the pending investigation, he mandated an attorney in Athens to contact the competent authorities and notify them of his current address in London, should they need to question him as a witness or a suspect. In March 2014 FC's Greek attorney filed on his behalf a declaration of residence with the Investigating Judge in Athens who was handling the case.

The Investigating Judge did not attempt to summon FC for interrogation at his London address through the UK authorities. Instead, she issued in June 2015 an arrest warrant against him, stating that FC 'easily qualifies as a flight risk'.[51] In the Investigating Judge's view, the fact that FC had filed the above declaration of his permanent residence in London through his attorney without simultaneously authorising him to receive summonses or other documents addressed to FC on his behalf indicated his unwillingness to appear for questioning and his intention to delay the investigation given that 'the judicial assistance, especially from the aforementioned country [viz, the UK] takes time and requests are not executed for a year or more at best'. In her view, his filing of the above residence declaration 'mask[ed] delaying tactics in order to avoid investigation and judicial scrutiny and therefore he is a flight risk'.

A European Arrest Warrant against FC was subsequently issued in September 2015, which was then executed in the UK in October 2015 at London Heathrow Airport, where FC was arrested. He was released on bail and was required to wear an electronic device, pending extradition proceedings in London. At the same time, FC's counsel in Athens submitted a request to the Investigating Judge to withdraw the arrest warrant and allow FC to travel to Greece and be questioned without being arrested. This request was rejected. Subsequently, FC's counsel filed, in December 2015, an application with the Judicial Council at the Athens Court of Appeal requesting the lifting of the arrest warrant or, alternatively, its replacement

[51] Arrest Warrant no 16/26 June 2015 of the Investigating Judge of the 25th Department with the Athens First Instance Court; the parts of the Arrest Warrant which are cited in the text have been translated into English by the author.

by less restrictive measures. In their application it was argued that it had been wrong to consider FC a flight risk in view of his declared willingness to participate in the proceedings, his permanent residence in London and his overall status, including the lack of any criminal record.

By its decision no 336 of 10 March 2016,[52] the Judicial Council at the Athens Court of Appeal lifted the arrest warrant against FC following a positive recommendation from the Prosecutor and replaced it with a surety of EUR 10,000, which was deposited by FC. As a result, the EAW was withdrawn shortly before the extradition hearing in London was due to take place. In March 2019 a trial hearing on the case was held before the Athens Court of Appeal sitting as a first instance court, which was attended by FC. At this hearing FC was acquitted of the charges. The Court held that he had no personal involvement and no criminal intent with respect to the alleged offences.[53]

(ii) Discussion

FC's case is a worrying example of the overuse of domestic and European arrest warrants. The Investigating Judge who handled the case in Greece demonstrated not only an unwarranted mistrust towards the defendant but also towards the UK authorities. In her effort to avoid 'delays' in the investigation, she made a deliberate decision not to request the cooperation of the UK authorities and opted instead for an arrest warrant against FC, disregarding the severe consequences for him.

FC was unexpectedly arrested at Heathrow Airport, was compelled to deposit a substantial surety of GBP 70,000 and to accept an electronic device and was subjected to the uncertainty of extradition proceedings in the UK, which, in case of a negative outcome, would most likely result in pre-trial detention of several months in Greece until the hearing. It was not until March 2016, ie, six months after his arrest in London, that a judicial council in Athens lifted the arrest warrant, even though his counsel had filed a request to this end in December 2015.

For their part, the UK authorities duly executed the EAW from Greece following the principle of mutual recognition of criminal decisions in the EU common area. The UK authorities most likely acted on the presumption that competent Greek authorities had conducted a proportionality test before issuing the EAW. In reality the Greek authorities had disregarded the proportionality principle, while their actions were at the same time motivated by mistrust towards the UK authorities and their potential willingness to offer judicial assistance during the investigation. Again, an ostensibly correct EAW grossly disrespected the individual's fundamental rights in an area declared as an area of freedom and justice.

[52] Judicial Council, Athens Court of Appeal, decision no 336 of 10 March 2016 (unreported).
[53] Court of Appeal Athens, Judgment no 1162/2019 of 8 March 2019 (unreported).

III. Perspectives on Future Initiatives

The three cases presented above demonstrate that the European Parliament's call for legislative action on the EAW deserves support. The Commission's view that the proportionality problems arising in the operation of this highly intrusive instrument may be tackled by using the existing legal framework in conjunction with soft law rules and the encouragement of best practices among Member States does not seem to provide an effective cure for the persisting overuse of the EAW. Future EU initiatives on the EAW (or, if necessary, on a horizontal level covering more judicial assistance instruments) may include the following legislative amendments:

– *Proportionality Test in the Issuing State*

The insertion of an explicit proportionality clause in respect of the issuance of EAWs seems necessary. The existing FD does not include a proportionality test provision. However, some national laws implementing the EAW *do* contain such a clause (for example, Germany, Italy, United Kingdom, Estonia and Belgium).[54] Moreover, the fundamental character of the proportionality principle, which is enshrined in various EU and/or national statutes, enables the national courts to find a legal basis for such a test despite the lack of an explicit regulation in the FD.[55] The added value of an explicit proportionality clause at EU level, which could be modelled on the existing provisions of the Handbook, would remedy the uncertainty in the current legal landscape and create an EU-wide uniform proportionality test that would encourage a more moderate use of the EAW, based on common standards, and simultaneously support the adoption of less intrusive alternative measures.[56]

– *Proportionality Test in the Executing State*

Admittedly, the proportionality check is primarily a duty of the issuing state and the executing state is supposed to act on the presumption that such a test has been conducted in the requesting state. The insertion of a ground for non-execution of incoming EAWs on proportionality grounds, provided that the courts of the executing Member State find that exceptional circumstances justify such refusal, is, nevertheless, also recommended.

Specifically, exceptional situations might arise in which the courts of the executing state take the view that the execution of the EAW is unacceptable, especially in cases where, during the executing state's EAW proceedings, additional

[54] See Weyembergh, Armada and Brière (n 3) 35.

[55] See the Opinion of Advocate General Yves Bot in Joint Cases C-404/15 and C-659/15 PPU *Aranyosi and Căldăraru v Generalstaatsanwaltschaft Bremen* ECLI:EU:C:2016:140 (delivered on 3 March 2016) [147ff].

[56] Weyembergh, Armada and Brière (n 3) 35.

evidence adduced justifies this conclusion. In such cases the courts must be able to refuse the execution of the EAW on proportionality grounds.[57] A refusal decision of this kind in exceptional circumstances would not undermine the principle of mutual recognition, as it would not entail the expression of a general lack of trust towards the issuing state but would be based on the specific circumstances surrounding the individual case.

In some Member States the courts do perform a proportionality test of the incoming EAWs based on their legislation on the EAW or other provisions of domestic legislation. This is the case, for example, in Germany, where courts assess the incoming EAWs from a proportionality perspective and abstain from executing them if their execution appears to be 'intolerable'.[58] The establishment of the proposed refusal ground at EU level would advance a uniform practice in all Member States in this area.

Prior to refusing the execution of the EAW on proportionality grounds, however, the executing state should enter into consultations with the issuing state with a view to exchanging information and considering possible alternatives. Such an approach is highly recommended in cases of EAWs for investigation purposes, ie, in cases not ready for trial where the individual was not summoned to be questioned by the issuing state. The EIO could provide acceptable solutions in this respect (for example, use of videoconferencing).

In its *Aranyosi and Căldăraru* judgment[59] as well as in those that followed the same approach,[60] the CJEU has been highly supportive of a consultations model among Member States. This approach is in line with the principle of mutual trust and contributes to the better understanding of the different legal systems of Member States.

– *Mandatory Withdrawal of SIS Alerts*

Introducing an obligation of the issuing state to withdraw the SIS alert following the refusal to execute the EAW by another Member State should be considered in those cases where the executing state exercises its jurisdiction over the acts for which the EAW was issued, either already prior to its issuance or after its refusal. The provision of a mandatory withdrawal of the EAW in the above cases would turn the existing soft law provisions of the SIS II Decision and the Handbook[61]

[57] See, eg, J Vogel and J R Spencer, 'Proportionality and the European Arrest Warrant' (2010) *Criminal Law Review* 474.

[58] See ibid. See also UK Supreme Court *F-K v Polish Judicial Authority* [2012] UKSC 25 (Judgment of 20 June 2012) [44]–[48] (non-execution of a Polish arrest warrant on Art 8 ECHR grounds).

[59] Joined Cases C-404/15 and C-659/15 PPU *Pal Aranyosi and Robert Căldăraru v Generalstaatsanwaltschaft Bremen* ECLI:EU:C:2016:198 (Judgment of the Grand Chamber of 5 April 2016) [95ff]. On the wider implications of this judgment, see, eg, Sellier and Weyembergh (n 11) 106ff; W van Ballegooij, 'Mutual Recognition and Individual Rights: Did the Court get it Right?' (2016) 7(4) *New Journal of European Criminal Law* 439, 446.

[60] Case C-220/18 PPU *ML* ECLI:EU:C:2018:589 (Judgment of 25 July 2018) and Case C-128/18 *Dumitru-Tudor Dorobantu* ECLI:EU:C:2019:857 (Judgment of October 2019).

[61] See text to nn 38, 39.

into hard law and result in the termination of parallel proceedings, which unnecessarily double prosecution and investigation costs and unfairly expose the affected individuals to multiple prosecutions. In the proposed mandatory EAW withdrawal model, the issuing Member State would be entitled to reinstate the alert if the executing Member State decides to discontinue the proceedings with no final decision on the case. The term 'final decision' shall be understood in accordance with the case law of the CJEU on *non bis in idem*.[62]

Moreover, a duty of Member States to withdraw the SIS alert at the latest three years after its entry should be envisaged. A reinstatement of the alert would be possible only in a formalised procedure, in which the competent judicial authorities of the issuing state decide that the prolongation of the alert is justified on exceptional grounds. This could be coupled with a mandatory review of the duration of the alert on an annual basis in the above formalised procedure. Overall, the establishment of an explicit withdrawal obligation would strengthen the current provisions of the SIS II Decision and the Handbook and, in conjunction with the proposed prolongation procedure, would motivate states to reconsider the proportionality of their EAWs and make use of available less intrusive alternatives.

– *Refusal on the Grounds of Fundamental Rights*

The insertion of an explicit human rights ground for refusing the execution of EAWs seems necessary. This would allow the courts of the executing Member State to refuse the execution of the EAW in exceptional situations where there are serious grounds to believe that its enforcement would violate fundamental rights of the arrestee under the ECHR and/or the EU Charter.

The human rights debate in the context of the EAW took a positive turn after the CJEU had ruled in *Aranyosi and Căldăraru* that Article 1(3) of the FD EAW – which refers directly to the fundamental rights and fundamental legal principles as enshrined in Article 6 TEU – may offer in exceptional circumstances a basis to address potential human rights concerns in the execution of EAWs.[63] Moreover, in its judgment in *LM* of 25 July 2018 the Court ruled that the opening of an Article 7 TEU procedure against a Member State (in this case Poland) by the Commission may provide grounds for refusing the execution of an EAW issued in that state when the independence of the judiciary cannot be guaranteed in the case at hand.[64]

[62] See the references in n 31; for an overview of the CJEU case law on *non bis in idem*, see Commission's Handbook on the EAW (n 16) 115.

[63] *Aranyosi and Căldăraru* (n 59) [81ff]. See L Mancano, 'A New Hope? The Court of Justice Restores the Balance Between Fundamental Rights Protection and the Enforcement Demands in the European Arrest Warrant System' in C Brière and A Weyembergh (eds), *The Needed Balances in EU Criminal Law – Past, Present and Future* (Oxford, Hart Publishing, 2018) 285, 297.

[64] Case C-216/18 PPU *LM* ECLI:EU:C:2018:586 (Judgment of the Grand Chamber of 25 July 2018) [48ff]. See H Satzger, 'Mutual Recognition in Times of Crisis – Mutual Recognition in Crisis? An Analysis of the New Jurisprudence on the European Arrest Warrant' (2018) 8 *European Criminal Law Review* 317, 325; M A Simonelli, '"… And Justice for All?" The Right to an Independent Tribunal after the Ruling of the Court of Justice in *LM*' (2019) 10(4) *New Journal of European Criminal Law* 329, 333.

The Commission's Handbook on the EAW states the following with respect to a human rights-based refusal ground:

> The Framework Decision on EAW does not contain any provision on non-execution on the basis of a breach of the requested person's fundamental rights in the issuing Member State. However, Article 1(3), read together with recitals 12 and 13 of the Framework Decision on EAW clarify that fundamental rights and fundamental legal principles should be respected in the context of the EAW … If the judicial authority of the executing Member State is in possession of evidence of a real risk of inhuman or degrading treatment of individuals detained in the issuing Member State because of general detention conditions, it must follow the procedure as set out in the judgment of the Court of Justice in Joined Cases C-404/15 and C-659/15 PPU *Aranyosi and Căldăraru* (paragraphs 89 to 104).[65]

It is true that in some Member States the courts apply a human rights-based refusal ground expressly provided for in their domestic legislation.[66] Moreover, reliance on Article 1(3) of the FD EAW may offer a solution where such special provisions do not exist.[67] However, neither the positive developments in case law nor the alternatives offered in the current legislation render the insertion of a human rights clause into the EAW legal framework superfluous. The suggested clause would enhance legal certainty in a sensitive area and would encourage a kind of continuous 'peer review' of human rights standards among Member States.[68] The EAW provision could follow the model of Article 11(f) of the EIO, which states that the recognition or execution of an EIO may be refused in the executing state 'where there are substantial grounds to believe that the execution of the investigative measure indicated in the EIO would be incompatible with the executing State's obligations in accordance with Article 6 TEU and the Charter'. A provision along these lines would broaden the scope of the human rights

[65] Commission's Handbook on the EAW (n 16) para 5.6.

[66] See, eg, Irish European Arrest Warrant Act 2003 s 37(1)(a); Act (2003:1156) on surrender from Sweden s 4(2); UK Extradition Act 2003 s 21(1). See also A Willems, 'Extradition on the Two Sides of the Atlantic: The U.S. Model as Blueprint for the European Arrest Warrant?' (2016) 27 *Criminal Law Forum* 443, 466.

[67] See the Opinion of Advocate General M Paolo Mengozzi in the EAW Case C-42/11 *João Pedro Da Silva Jorge* ECLI:EU:C:2012:151 (delivered on 20 March 2012), in which he states [28]: 'The reference to fundamental rights and principles made by Art 1(3) … must act as a safeguard … in the area of police and judicial cooperation in criminal matters, the principle of mutual recognition … cannot be applied in the same way as it is in the case of a university qualification or a driving licence … the protection of fundamental rights … must be the overriding concern … the free movement of judgments in criminal matters must not only be guaranteed but also, where appropriate, limited'. On the recent case law of German courts, see K M Böhm, 'Aktuelle Entwicklungen im Auslieferungsrecht' (2020) *Neue Zeitschrift für Strafrecht* 197, 204, 207; T Wahl, 'Fair Trial Concerns: German Court Suspends Execution of Polish EAW' (2020) *Eucrim: The European Criminal Law Associations' Forum* (available at: eucrim.eu/news/fair-trial-concerns-german-court-suspends-execution-polish-eaw/).

[68] Anagnostopoulos (n 5) 19; T Marguery, 'La confiance mutuelle sous pression dans le cadre du transfert de personnes condamnés au sein de L'Union Européenne' (2018) *Eucrim: The European Criminal Law Associations' Forum* 182, 186. See also, in a more general context, Mitsilegas (n 9) 125ff; J Öberg, 'Trust in the Law? Mutual Recognition as a Justification to Domestic Criminal Procedure' (2020) 16(1) *European Constitutional Law Review* 1, 23.

bar beyond the narrow area of Article 3 ECHR and Article 4 EU Charter, and include other violations as well, especially those of Articles 5, 6 and 8 ECHR and Articles 47 and 48 EU Charter.[69]

– *Legal Remedies*

Finally, it would be helpful to provide a special EAW legal remedy which would enable affected individuals to challenge the EAW and ask for its withdrawal on proportionality and/or human rights grounds. Such a remedy should not be conditional on the surrender of the individual and should be available both in the issuing state and the executing state. Moreover, the provision of a special legal remedy at EU level would strengthen the position of individuals by restoring the balance in the relevant procedures and would allow national courts to submit preliminary questions more easily to the CJEU where appropriate.

Though national legislation allows the arrestee to challenge the lawfulness of the domestic warrant and/or the EAW according to the existing provisions, there are significant variations in the way they shape the respective rights, which do not always ensure easy access to the relevant procedures. It is noteworthy in this respect that in *LB's* case the General Prosecutor of Cyprus went to great lengths to rebut on grounds of admissibility the applicant's request that the EAW be withdrawn, arguing that the case must not be examined on the merits. The General Prosecutor's argument was not shared by the courts; however, the existing domestic provisions were rather far from producing clarity in this area.

The above tentative list of potential legislative initiatives, which builds upon the European Parliament's recommendations of 2014,[70] may encourage an EU-wide dialogue among stakeholders with a view to remedying deficiencies in the operation of the EAW. 'Europe's most successful criminal justice instrument'[71] is in need of reform. In Europe's common judicial area, freedom and justice should not be traded for security.[72]

IV. *Postscriptum*

After submission of the manuscript of this chapter three important documents have been released.

[69] See Satzger (n 64) 327, who argues for a European *ordre public* refusal ground; A Torres Pérez, 'A Predicament for Domestic Courts: Caught between the European Arrest Warrant and Fundamental Rights' in B de Witte, J A Mayoral, U Jaremba, M Wind and K Podstawa (eds), *National Courts and EU Law. New Issues, Theories and Methods* (Cheltenham, Edward Elgar Publishing, 2016) 191, 207ff.

[70] See n 17.

[71] See n 21.

[72] See H Satzger, 'The European Arrest Warrant in German-Italian Practice – Not a Success Story without Problems' (2019) 9(3) *European Criminal Law Review* 285, 287, 298. In a more general context, see D López Garrido and A López Castillo, *The EU Framework for Enforcing the Respect of the Rule of Law and the Union's Fundamental Principles and Values* (Study for the AFCO Committee, European Parliament, Brussels, January 2019) 9ff.

The European Commission issued its 2020 Report on the implementation of the FD EAW. The Report concludes[73] that in some Member States the level of implementation 'is still not satisfactory' and announces that 'the Commission will take appropriate measures to ensure compliance … including, where necessary, initiating infringement proceedings under Article 258' TFEU.

Meanwhile, the European Parliament published an In-Depth Analysis with preliminary findings on the FD EAW implementation[74] and a comprehensive Study including a European implementation assessment and tentative recommendations on how to overcome the shortcomings identified.[75] Both publications are the result of an own-initiative implementation report by the European Parliament's LIBE Committee (rapporteur: Javier Zarzalejos, EPP, Spain) and are intended to contribute to the EAW reform discussion. The recommendations seek to improve the effective implementation of the FD EAW, its efficiency and proportionality, as well as compliance with EU values and fundamental rights. In the medium term, for reasons of democratic legitimacy, legal certainty and coherence with other judicial cooperation instruments, a 'Lisbonisation' of the FD EAW is recommended as part of a proposed EU judicial cooperation code in criminal matters.

It remains to be seen whether this ambitious initiative of the European Parliament will lead to a broader 'fitness check' of the existing judicial cooperation instruments in criminal matters with a view to supplementing, simplifying and streamlining the current legislative framework in this rapidly developing area.

[73] Report from the Commission to the European Parliament and the Council of 2 July 2020, COM(2020) final at 22–23. The EAW figures compiled by the Commission for the year 2018 are similar to those for the previous years, see Commission Staff Working Document, Replies to questionnaire on quantitative information on the practical operation of the European arrest warrant – Year 2018, 2 July 2020, SWD(2020) 1278 final.

[74] See W van Ballegooij and I Kiendl Krišto, *European Arrest Warrant, Framework for Analysis and Preliminary Findings on its Implementation* (Brussels, In-Depth Analysis for DG European Parliamentary Research Service, February 2020).

[75] See W van Ballegooij, *European Arrest Warrant, European Implementation Assessment* (Brussels, Study for DG European Parliamentary Research Service, June 2020).

BIBLIOGRAPHY

A

Aarnio, A, *The Rational as Reasonable. A Treatise on Legal Justification* (Dordrecht, D Reidel Publishing Company, 1987).

Ackerman, B, 'The Emergency Constitutions' (2004) 113 *Yale Law Journal* 1029.

Akande, D and Liefländer, T, 'Clarifying Necessity, Imminence and Proportionality in the Law of Self-Defence' (2013) 107 *American Journal of International Law* 563.

Aksenova, M, 'Symbolism as a Constraint on International Criminal Law' (2017) 30 *Leiden Journal of International Law* 475.

Alder, J, 'The Sublime and the Beautiful: Incommensurability and Human Rights' (2006) *Public Law* 697.

Alegre, S and Leaf, M, *European Arrest Warrant – A Solution ahead of its Time?* (London, JUSTICE, 2003).

Aleinikoff, A T, 'Constitutional Law in the Age of Balancing' (1987) 96 *Yale Law Journal* 943.

Alexy, R, *A Theory of Constitutional Rights* (Oxford, Oxford University Press, 1985, 1986, 2002).

—— *Theorie der Grundrechte* (Frankfurt am Main, Suhrkamp, 1986).

—— 'On Balancing and Subsumption. A Structural Comparison' (2003) 16 *Ratio Juris* 433.

—— 'The Weight Formula' in J Stelmach, B Brożek, W Załuski (eds), *Studies in the Philosophy of Law: Frontiers of the Economic Analysis of Law* (Krakow, Jagiellonian University Press, 2007) 9–27.

—— 'The Construction of Constitutional Rights' (2010) 4 *Law & Ethics of Human Rights* 21.

—— 'Constitutional Rights and Proportionality' (2014) 22 *Revus – Journal for Constitutional Theory and Philosophy of Law* 51.

—— *Teoría de la argumentación jurídica* (Madrid, CEPC, 2014).

—— 'Proportionality and Rationality' in V C Jackson and M Tushnet (eds), *Proportionality: New Frontiers, New Challenges* (Cambridge, Cambridge University Press, 2018) 13–29.

Allan, T R S, 'Procedural Fairness and the Duty of Respect' (1998) 18 *Oxford Journal of Legal Studies* 497.

—— *Constitutional Justice: A Liberal Theory of the Rule of Law* (Oxford, Oxford University Press, 2003).

Almkvist, G, 'Avdrag för inköpsutgifter vid utbytesförverkande' (2016–17) 3 *Juridisk Tidskrift* 708.

Amankonah, J, *Crime and Punishment, Examining Proportionality Issues within Criminal Law* (LLM thesis in University of South California, 2012).

Ambos, K, *Treatise on International Criminal Law*, vol II (Oxford, Oxford University Press, 2014).

American Law Institute, Model Penal Code and Commentaries, Commentary vol 1, revised edn (Philadelphia PA, American Law Institute, 1985).

Anagnostopoulos, I, 'Criminal Justice Cooperation in the European Union after the First Few "Steps": A Defence View' (2014) *ERA Forum* 9.

Anagnostopoulos, I, Zapanti, J and Tsagkalidis, A, 'Procedure Before Criminal Courts' in *Greek Law Digest*, 3rd edn (Athens, Nomiki Bibliothiki, 2019), available at: www.greeklawdigest.gr/topics/judicial-system/item/299-procedure-before-criminal-courts.

Andenæs, J, *Punishment and Deterrence* (Ann Arbor MI, University of Michigan Press, 1974).

—— 'Nyere forskning om almenprevensjonen – status og kommentar' (1977) *Scandinavian Journal of Criminal Law and Criminology* 61.

Anderson, D, 'Shielding the Compass: How to Fight Terrorism without Defeating the Law' (2013) 3 *European Human Rights Law Review* 233.

—— 'Shades of Independent Review' in G Lennon, C King and C McCartney (eds), *Counter-Terrorism, Constitutionalism and Miscarriages of Justice* (Oxford, Hart Publishing, 2019) 81–98.

Androulakis, N, 'Abschied vom Rechtsgut – Einzug der Moralität?' in U Neumann and F Herzog (eds), *Festschrift für Winfried Hassemer* (Heidelberg, CF Müller Verlag, 2010) 271–86.

Arai-Takahashi, Y, *The Margin of Appreciation Doctrine and the Principle of Proportionality in the Jurisprudence of the ECHR* (Antwerp, Intersentia, 2002).

Aristotle, 'Nicomachean Ethics' in the edition of the Loeb Classical Library with a translation by H Rackham (Cambridge MA, Harvard University Press, 1968).

Arnardóttir, O M, 'The "Procedural Turn" under the European Convention on Human Rights and Presumptions of Convention Compliance' (2017) 15 *International Journal of Constitutional Law* 9.

Arnauld, A, 'Zur Rhetorik der Verhältnismäßigkeit' in M Jestaedt and O Lepsius (eds), *Verhältnismäßigkeit: Zur Tragfähigkeit eines verfassungsrechtlichen Schlüsselkonzepts* (Tübingen, Mohr Siebeck, 2016) 276–92.

Ashworth, A, 'Coroners and Justice Act 2009: Sentencing Guidelines and the Sentencing Council' (2010) *Criminal Law Review* 389.

—— 'Re-evaluating the Justifications for Aggravation and Mitigation at Sentencing' in J V Roberts (ed), *Mitigation and Aggravation at Sentencing* (Cambridge, Cambridge University Press, 2011) 21–39.

—— *Sentencing and Criminal Justice*, 6th edn (Cambridge, Cambridge University Press, 2015).

Ashworth, A and Horder, J, *Principles of Criminal Law*, 7th edn (Oxford, Oxford University Press, 2013).

Ashworth, A and Roberts, J V, 'The Origins and Nature of Sentencing Guidelines in England and Wales' in A Ashworth and J V Roberts (eds), *Sentencing Guidelines: Exploring the English Model* (Oxford, Oxford University Press, 2013) 1–14.

Ashworth, A and Zedner, L, *Preventive Justice* (Oxford, Oxford University Press, 2014).

Asp, P, 'Two Notions of Proportionality' in N Kimmo (ed), *Festschrift in Honour of Raimo Lahti* (Helsinki, Publications of the Faculty of Law – University of Helsinki, 2007) 207–19.

—— *The Substantive Criminal Law Competence of the EU* (Stockholm, Skrifter utgivna av Juridiska fakulteten vid Stockholms universitet, 2012).

Aubert, W, Eckhoff, T and Sveri, K, *En lov i søkelyset, sosialpsykologisk undersøkelse av den norske hushjelplov* (Oslo, Akademisk forlag, 1952).

Azmeh, U, 'Exemplary Sentencing for Terrorist Offenders: The Counter-Terrorism and Sentencing Bill 2020' (2021) 1 *Criminal Law Review* 5.

B

Baade, B, *Der Europäische Gerichtshof für Menschenrechte als Diskurswächter: Zur Methodik, Legitimität und Rolle des Gerichtshofs im demokratisch-rechtsstaatlichen Entscheidungsprozess* (Berlin, Springer, 2017).

Bachmaier Winter, L, 'Criminal Investigation and the Right to Privacy in the Case Law of the European Court of Human Rights' (2009) 2 *Lex et Scientia* (Lesij) 9.

—— 'The Role of the Proportionality Principle in Cross-Border Investigations Involving Fundamental Rights' in S Ruggeri (ed), *Transnational Inquiries and the Protection of Fundamental Rights in Criminal Proceedings* (Berlin, Springer, 2013) 85–110.

Bagaric, M and Morss, J, 'International Sentencing Law: In Search of a Justification and Coherent Framework' (2006) 6 *International Criminal Law Review* 191.

Baier, K, *Der Standpunkt der Moral. Eine rationale Grundlegung der Ethik* (Düsseldorf, Patmos Verlag, 1974).

Ball, K S and Murakami-Wood, D, 'Political Economies of Surveillance' (2013) 11(1) *Surveillance & Society* 1.

Barak, A, 'Proportionality and Principled Balancing' (2010) 4 *Law & Ethics of Human Rights* 1.

—— *Proportionality. Constitutional Rights and Their Limitations* (Cambridge, Cambridge University Press, 2012).

Barnes Vázquez, J, 'Introducción al principio de proporcionalidad en el derecho comparado y comunitario' (1994) 135 *Revista de Actualidad Penal* 531.

Bartels, R, 'Dealing with the Principle of Proportionality in Armed Conflict in Retrospect: The Application of the Principle in International Criminal Trials' (2013) 46 *Israel Law Review* 271.

Bartoli, R, 'L'esclusione della punibilità per particolare tenuità del fatto' (2015) *Diritto penale e processo* 659.

Beatty, D M, *The Ultimate Rule of Law* (Oxford, Oxford University Press, 2004, 2010).

Beccaria, C, *On Crimes and Punishments* 1764, available at: www.laits.utexas.edu/poltheory/beccaria/delitti/index.html.

Beck, U, *Risikogesellschaft: Auf dem Weg in eine andere Moderne* (Frankfurt, Suhrkamp 1986).

Belfiore, R, 'The European Investigation Order in Criminal Matters: Developments in Evidence-gathering Across the EU' (2015) *European Criminal Law Review* 312.

Bentham, J, *Traités de législation civile et pénale*, vol 1 (Paris, 1820), available at: isidore.science/document/ark:/12148/bpt6k5696197f.

Bernal Pulido, C, *El principio de proporcionalidad y los derechos fundamentales* (Madrid, CEPC, 2003).

Bernardi, A, 'Brevi note sulle linee evolutive della depenalizzazione in Italia' (2001) *L'Indice penale* 727.

Bernitz, U, Nergelius, J and Cardner, C (eds), *Principles of EC Law in a Process of Development* (Alphen aan den Rijn, Kluwer Law International, 2008).

Bethge, H, 'Grundrechtsverwirklichung und Grundrechtssicherung durch Organisation und Verfahren: Zu einigen Aspekten der aktuellen Grundrechtsdiskussion' (1982) *Neue Juristische Wochenschrift* 1.

Bethlehem, D, 'Self-Defense Against an Imminent or Actual Armed Attack by Nonstate Actors' (2012) 106 *American Journal of International Law* 769.

Bibas, S, *The Machinery of Criminal Justice* (Oxford, Oxford University Press, 2012).

Billis, E, 'On the Methodology of Comparative Criminal Law Research: Paradigmatic Approaches to the Research Method of Functional Comparison and the Heuristic Device of Ideal Types' (2017) 24 *Maastricht Journal of European and Comparative Law* 864.

Billis, E and Knust, N, 'Alternative Types of Procedure and the Formal Limits of National Criminal Justice: Aspects of Social Legitimacy' in U Sieber, V Mitsilegas, C Mylonopoulos, E Billis and N Knust (eds), *Alternative Systems of Crime Control. National, Transnational, and International Dimensions* (Berlin, Duncker & Humblot, 2018) 39–58.

Billis, E, Knust, N and Rui, J P, 'Künstliche Intelligenz und der Grundsatz der Verhältnismäßigkeit' in H Kudlich, M Engelhart and B Vogel (eds), *Festschrift für Ulrich Sieber* (Berlin, Duncker & Humblot, 2020).

Blackbourn, J, 'Accountability, Counter-Terrorism and Civil Liberties' (2018) 29 *King's Law Journal* 297.

—— 'Excluding Terrorists' in G Lennon, C King and C McCartney (eds), *Counter-Terrorism, Constitutionalism and Miscarriages of Justice* (Oxford, Hart Publishing, 2019) 135–50.

Blankenburg, E, 'Über die Unwirksamkeit von Gesetzen' (1977) 63 *Archiv für Rechts- und Sozialphilosophie* 43.

Böhm, K M, 'Aktuelle Entwicklungen im Auslieferungsrecht' (2020) *Neue Zeitschrift für Strafrecht* 197.

Bomhoff, J, *Balancing Constitutional Rights* (Cambridge, Cambridge University Press, 2013).

Bonini, S, 'Quali spazi per una funzione simbolica del diritto penale?' (2003) *L'Indice penale* 491.

Bonner, D, *Executive Measures, Terrorism and National Security* (Aldershot, Ashgate, 2007).

Böse, M, 'The Principle of Proportionality and the Protection of Legal Interests' (2011) 1(1) *European Criminal Law Review* 35.

Bothe, M, 'Private Normunternehmer im Völkerrecht: Gedanken zur Fortentwicklung des Völkerrechts durch nicht-staatliche Institutionen' in H Hestemeyer, D König, N Matz-Lück, V Röben, A Seibert-Fohr, P-T Stoll and S Vöneky (eds), *Coexistence, Cooperation and Solidarity. Liber Amicorum Rüdiger Wolfrum*, vol II (Leiden, Brill, 2012) 1399–412.

Bothe, M, Partsch, K J and Solf, W, *New Rules for Victims of Armed Conflicts*, 2nd edn (Leiden, Brill, 2013).

Boucht, J, *The Limits of Asset Confiscation. On Legitimising Extended Appropriation of Criminal Proceeds* (Oxford, Hart Publishing, 2017).

—— 'Asset Confiscation in Europe – Past, Present, and Future Challenges' (2019) 26 *Journal of Financial Crime* 526.

—— 'Non-Conviction Based Confiscation: Moving the Confiscation of Criminal Proceeds from the Criminal to the 'Civil' Sphere – Benefits, Issues and Two Procedural Aspects' in V Franssen and C Harding (eds), *Quasi-Criminal Enforcement Mechanisms in Europe: Historical Origins, Contemporary Concepts and Future Perspectives* (Oxford, Hart Publishing, 2020).

Boucht, J and Frände, D, *Finsk straffrätt. Grundkurs i straffrättens allmänna läror*, 2nd edn (Helsinki, Edita Prima, 2020).

Bowling, B and Phillips, C, 'Disproportionate and Discriminatory: Reviewing the Evidence on Police Stop and Search' (2007) 70 *Modern Law Review* 936.

Boyd, J P (ed), *The Papers of Thomas Jefferson*, vol 2 (A Bill for Proportioning Crimes and Punishments in Cases Heretofore Capital), (Princeton NJ, Princeton University Press, 1950).

Braithwaite, J, *Restorative Justice and Responsive Regulation* (Oxford, Oxford University Press, 2002).

Braithwaite, J and Pettit, P, *Not Just Deserts* (Oxford, Oxford University Press, 1990).

Brauneis, R and Goodman, E, 'Algorithmic Transparency for the Smart City' (2018) 20 *Yale Journal of Law and Technology* 103.

Brayne, S, 'Big Data Surveillance: The Case of Policing' (2017) 82(5) *American Sociological Review* 977.

Brems, E and Lavrysen, L, '"Don't Use a Sledgehammer to Crack a Nut": Less Restrictive Means in the Case Law of the European Court of Human Rights' (2015) 15 *Human Rights Law Review* 139.

Broome, J, 'Is Incommensurability Vagueness?' in R Chang (ed), *Incommensurability, Incomparability, and Practical Reason* (Cambridge MA, Harvard University Press, 1997) 67–89.

Brown, G, *Criminal Sentencing as Practical Wisdom* (Oxford, Hart Publishing, 2017).

Brown, I and Korff, D, 'Terrorism and the Proportionality of Internet Surveillance' (2009) 6(2) *European Journal of Criminology* 119.

Bumke, C, *Der Grundrechtsvorbehalt* (Baden-Baden, Nomos, 1998).

Bumke, C and Voβkuhle, A, *German Constitutional Law* (Oxford, Oxford University Press, 2019).

Busch, T A, 'Noen utviklingstrekk I norsk kriminalpolitikk basert på 40 år I påtalemyndigheten' 2018 (4) *Tidsskrift for strafferett* 265.

C

Canizzaro, E, 'The Role of Proportionality in the Law of International Countermeasures' (2001) 12 *European Journal of International Law* 889.

Carrera, S, Guild, E and Hernanz, N, 'Europe's Most Wanted? Recalibrating Trust in the European Arrest Warrant System', CEPS Paper (2013) 55 *Liberty and Security in Europe* 16, available at: www.ceps.eu/ceps-publications/europes-most-wanted-recalibrating-trust-european-arrest-warrant-system/.

Caudill, M, 'Using Neural Sets: Fuzzy Decisions' (1990) 5 *AI Expert* 59.

Celiksoy, E, 'Overruling "the *Salduz* Doctrine" in *Beuze v Belgium*: The ECtHR's Further Retreat from the *Salduz* Principles on the Right to Access to Lawyer' (2019) 10 *New Journal of European Criminal Law* 342.

Chang, R, 'The Possibility of Parity' (2002) 112 *Ethics* 659.

—— *Making Comparisons Count* (Hoboken NJ, Routledge, 2014).

Chapman, B, 'Law, Incommensurability, and Conceptually Sequenced Argument' (1998) 146 *University of Pennsylvania Law Review* 1487.

Chemerinsky, E, *Constitutional Law: Principles and Policies*, 6th edn (Alphen, Wolters Kluwer Law & Business, 2019).

Cheng, B, *General Principles of Law as Applied by International Courts and Tribunals*, 2nd edn (Cambridge, Grotius, 1987).

Chiavario, M, 'L'espansione dell'istituto della "tenuità del fatto": frammenti di riflessione su alcuni aspetti chiaro-scurali' in S Quattrocolo (ed), *I nuovi epiloghi del procedimento penale per particolare tenuità del fatto* (Torino, Giappichelli, 2015) 235–64.

Christoffersen, J, *Fair Balance: Proportionality, Subsidiarity and Primarity in the European Convention on Human Rights* (Leiden, Martinus Nijhoff Publishers, 2009).

Christou, T, 'The European Arrest Warrant and Human Rights in the Context of the Republic of Cyprus' (2012) 1(1) *Cyprus Human Rights Law Review* 57.

Coaffee, J, *Terrorism, Risk and the City: The Making of a Contemporary Urban Landscape* (London, Routledge, 2009).

Cohen-Eliya, M and Porat, I, 'Proportionality and the Culture of Justification' (2011) 59 *American Journal of Comparative Law* 463.

Cole, D, 'The Priority of Morality: The Emergency Constitution's Blind Spot' (2004) 113 *Yale Law Journal* 1753.

Cole, D and Roberts, J V, 'What's the Point of Pleading Guilty?' (2018) 44 *Criminal Reports* (7th Series) 44.

Combs, N A, *Guilty Pleas in International Criminal Law* (Stanford CA, Stanford University Press, 2006).

Conti, C, 'Sospensione del processo con messa alla prova del maggiorenne' (2016) *Digesto delle discipline penalistiche* 691.

Cooper, N, 'Scale Words' (1967) 27 *Analysis* 153.

Corda, A, 'Sentencing and Penal Policies in Italy 1985–2015: The Tale of a Troubled Country' in M Tonry (ed), *Sentencing Policies and Practices in Western Countries* (Oxford, Oxford University Press, 2016) 107–74.

Corlett, A, 'The Philosophy of Joel Feinberg' (2006) 10 *The Journal of Ethics* 131.

Cottier, T, Echandi, R, Leal-Arcas, R, Liechti, R, Payosova, T and Sieber-Gasser, C, 'The Principle of Proportionality in International Law' (2012) 38 *SSRN Electronic Journal* 1, available at: www.researchgate.net/publication/275347556_The_Principle_of_Proportionality_in_International_Law.

Courakis, N, *Zur sozialethischen Begründung der Notwehr* (Baden-Baden, Nomos, 1978).

—— 'Self-Defense as a Domain of Moderate Paternalism: The Need for Social Solidarity and Cohesion' in C Papacharalambous (ed), *Paternalism and Criminal Law. Modern Problems of an Old Query* (Athens, Sakkoulas, 2018), 135–45.

Courakis, N and Gavrielides, T, 'Beyond Restorative Justice. Social Justice as a New Objective for Criminal Justice' in T Gavrielides (ed), *Routledge International Handbook of Restorative Justice* (London, Routledge, 2019) 43–55.

Craig, P and de Búrca, G, *EU Law: Text, Cases, and Materials*, 5th edn (Oxford, Oxford University Press, 2015).

Creemers, R, 'Cyber China: Upgrading Propaganda, Public Opinion Work and Social Management for the Twenty-First Century' (2017) 26(103) *Journal of Contemporary China* 85.

D

D'Ascoli, S, *Sentencing in International Criminal Law* (Oxford, Hart Publishing, 2011).

Dana, S, 'Revisiting the Blaskic Sentence: Some Reflections on the Sentencing Jurisprudence of the ICTY' (2004) 4 *International Criminal Law Review* 321.

Davidson, R, 'A Sledgehammer to Crack a Nut? Should there be a Bar of Triviality in European Arrest Warrant Cases?' (2009) *Criminal Law Review* 31.

de Hert, P, 'Balancing Security and Liberty Within the European Human Rights Framework. A Critical Reading of the Court's Case Law in the Light of Surveillance and Criminal Law Enforcement Strategies After 9/11' (2005) 1(1) *Utrecht Law Review* 68.

de Jong, F, 'Symbolic and Diabolic Forces in Criminal Law' (2016) 81 *Pompe Reeks* 31.

de Liguori, L, *La legge penale. Problemi e prassi applicative* (Milano, Giuffrè, 2008).

de Londras, F, 'Prevention, Detention, and Extraordinariness' in F Ní Aoláin and O Gross (eds), *Guantanamo and Beyond: Exceptional Courts and Military Commissions in a Comparative Perspective* (Cambridge, Cambridge University Press, 2013) 117–36.

—— 'Evaluation and Effectiveness of Counterterrorism' in J P Burgess, G Reniers, K Ponnet, W Hardyns and W Smit (eds), *Socially Responsible Innovation in Security: Critical Reflections* (London, Routledge, 2018) 117–28.

de Londras, F and Davis, F, 'Controlling the Executive in Times of Terrorism: Competing Perspectives on Effective Oversight Mechanisms' (2010) 30 *Oxford Journal of Legal Studies* 19.

de Schutter, O and Tulkens, F, 'Rights in Conflict: The European Court of Human Rights as a Pragmatic Institution' in E Brems (ed), *Conflicts between Fundamental Rights* (Antwerp, Intersentia, 2008) 169–216.
Degener, W, *Grundsatz der Verhältnismäßigkeit und strafprozessuale Zwangsmaßnahme* (Berlin, Duncker & Humblot, 1985).
DeGuzman, M M, 'Proportionate Sentencing at the ICC' in C Stahn (ed), *The Law and Practice of the International Criminal Court* (Oxford, Oxford University Press, 2015) 932–62.
Deleuze, G, 'Postscript on the Societies of Control' (1992) 59 *October* 3.
Della Bella, A, 'Un viaggio tra le misure sospensive: i nodi da sciogliere in attesa della promessa riforma del sistema sanzionatorio' (2016) (3) *Diritto penale e processo* 377.
Dencik, L, Hintz, A and Carey, Z, 'Prediction, Pre-Emption and Limits to Dissent: Social Media and Big Data Uses for Policing Protests in the United Kingdom' (2017) 20(4) *New Media & Society* 1433.
Dickson, B, 'The House of Lords and the Northern Ireland Conflict – a Sequel' (2006) 57 *Modern Law Review* 383.
Diez Ripolles, J, 'Symbolisches Strafrecht und die Wirkungen der Strafe' (2001) 113(3) *Zeitschrift für die gesamte Strafrechtswissenschaft* 516.
Doswald-Beck, L and Henckaerts, J-M, *Customary International Humanitarian Law, Volume I – Rules* (Cambridge, Cambridge University Press, 2005).
Dreier, H, 'Die Zwischenkriegszeit' in D Merten and H-J Papier (eds), *Handbuch der Grundrechte, Band I* (Heidelberg, CF Müller, 2004) 153–200.
Dressler, J, 'The Jurisprudence of Death by Another: Accessories and Capital Punishment' (1979–1980) 51 *University of Colorado Law Review* 17.
Duff, R A, 'Penal Communications: Recent Work in the Philosophy of Punishment' (1996) 20 *Crime and Justice: A Review of Research* 1.
—— *Punishment, Communication and Community* (Oxford, Oxford University Press, 2001, 2003).
—— 'Perversions and Subversions of the Criminal Law' in R A Duff, L Farmer, S E Marshall, M Renzo and V Tadros (eds), *The Boundaries of the Criminal Law* (Oxford, Oxford University Press, 2010) 88–112.
—— *The Realm of Criminal Law* (Oxford, Oxford University Press, 2018).
Duff, R A and Marshall, S E, 'Benefits, Burdens and Responsibilities: Some Ethical Dimensions of Situational Crime Prevention' in A von Hirsch, D Garland and A Wakefield (eds), *Ethical and Social Perspectives on Situational Crime Prevention* (Oxford, Hart Publishing, 2000) 17–36.
Duff, R A, Farmer, L, Marshall, S E, Renzo, M and Tadros, V (eds), *The Constitution of the Criminal Law* (Oxford, Oxford University Press, 2013).
Durkheim, E, 'Deux lois de l'évolution pénale' (1899–1900) 4 *Année sociologique* 65–95, reprinted as ch 4, 'The Evolution of Punishment' in S Lukes and A Scull (eds), *Durkheim and the Law*, 2nd edn (London, Palgrave Macmillan, 2013) 78–102.
—— *De la division du travail social*, trans by G Simpson (Paris, Alcan, 1893).
—— *The Division of Labor in Society*, trans by G Simpson (New York, Macmillan, 1933).
—— *L'Éducation morale* (Cours dispensé en 1902–1903 à la Sorbonne) (Paris, Alcan, 1934) (*Moral Education*, trans by E K Wilson (New York, Dover Publications, 2011)).
Duroché, J-P and Pédron, P, *Droit pénitentiaire*, 2nd edn (Paris, Vuibert, 2013).
Dworkin, R, *Taking Rights Seriously* (Boston MA, Harvard University Press, 1977; London, Duckworth, 1987).
—— 'Rights as Trumps' in J Waldron (ed), *Theories of Rights* (Oxford, Oxford University Press, 1984) 153–67.
Dyzenhaus, D, 'Deference, Security and Human Rights' in B Goold and L Lazarus (eds), *Security and Human Rights* (Oxford, Hart Publishing, 2007) 125–55.

E

Edwards, G, Rushin, S and Colquitt, J, 'The Effects of Voluntary and Presumptive Sentencing Guidelines' (2019) 98(1) *Texas Law Review* 1.

Ehmke, H, 'Prinzipien der Verfassungsinterpretation: Mitbericht von Professor Dr. Horst Ehmke, Freiburg' (1963) 20 *Veröffentlichungen der Vereinigung der Deutschen Staatsrechtslehrer* (VVDStRL) 53.

Elholm, T, 'The Symbolic Purpose of Criminal Law – A Danish Perspective' in S Reindl-Krauskopf, I Zerbes, W Brandstetter, P Lewisch and A Tipold (eds), Festschrift für Helmut Fuchs (Wien, Verlag der Österreichischen Akademie der Wissenschaft, 2014) 137–52.

Elholm, T and Colson, R, 'The Symbolic Purpose of EU Criminal Law' in R Colson and S Field (eds), *EU Criminal Justice and the Challenges of Diversity: Legal Cultures in the Area of Freedom, Security and Justice* (Cambridge, Cambridge University Press, 2016) 48–64.

Emiliou, N, *The Principle of Proportionality in European Law: A Comparative Study* (London, Kluwer International, 1996).

Enders, C, 'Sozialstaatlichkeit im Spannungsfeld von Eigenverantwortung und Fürsorge' (2004) 64 *Veröffentlichungen der Vereinigung der Deutschen Staatsrechtslehrer* (VVDStRL) 7.

Endicott, T, 'Proportionality and Incommensurability' in G Huscroft, B Miller and G Webber (eds), *Proportionality and the Rule of Law: Rights, Justification, Reasoning* (Cambridge, Cambridge University Press, 2015) 311–42.

Engle, E, 'The General Principle of Proportionality and Aristotle' in L Huppes-Cluysenaer and N Coelho (eds), *Aristotle and The Philosophy of Law: Theory, Practice and Justice* (Dordrecht, Springer, 2013) 265–76.

Epik, A, *Die Strafzumessung bei Taten nach dem Völkerstrafgesetzbuch* (Tübingen, Mohr Siebeck, 2017).

Erbežnik, A, 'The Principle of Mutual Recognition as a Utilitarian Solution, and the Way Forward' (2012) 2(1) *European Criminal Law Review* 4.

Evangelista, G F and Jones, S (eds), *Mean Streets: A Report on the Criminalisation of Homelessness in Europe* (Belgium, European Federation of National Organisations working with the Homeless, 2013), available at: www.housingrightswatch.org/sites/default/files/Mean%20Streets%20-%20Full.pdf.

F

Fan, M D, 'Justice Visualized: Courts and the Body Camera Revolution' (2017) 50(3) *University of California Davis Law Review* 897.

—— 'Body Cameras, Big Data, and Police Accountability' (2018) 43(4) *Law & Social Inquiry* 1236.

Feeley, M and Simon, J, 'Actuarial Justice. The Emerging New Criminal Law' in D Nelken (ed), *The Futures of Criminology* (London, Sage, 1994) 173–201.

Feinberg, J, 'The Expressive Function of Punishment' (1965) 49(3) *The Monist* 397.

—— *Doing and Deserving: Essays in the Theory of Responsibility* (Princeton NJ, Princeton University Press, 1970).

—— *Harm to Others – The Moral Limits of the Criminal Law*, vol 1 (New York, Oxford University Press, 1984).

—— *Offense to Others – The Moral Limits of the Criminal Law*, vol 2 (Oxford, Oxford University Press, 1985).

—— *Harmless Wrongdoing – The Moral Limits of the Criminal Law*, vol 4 (New York, Oxford University Press, 1990).

Feldman, D, 'Proportionality and Discrimination in Anti-Terrorism Legislation' (2005) 64 *Cambridge Law Journal* 271.

Fenwick, H, 'The Anti-Terrorism, Crime and Security Act 2001: A Proportionate Response to 11 September?' (2002) 65 *Modern Law Review* 724.

Fiandaca, G and Musco, E, *Diritto penale. Parte generale*, 8th edn (Bologna, Zanichelli, 2019).

Fish, M, 'An Eye for an Eye: Proportionality as a Moral Principle of Punishment' (2008) 28(1) *Oxford Journal of Legal Studies* 57.

Flynn, A and Freiberg, A, *Plea Negotiations. Pragmatic Justice in an Imperfect World* (London, Palgrave Macmillan, 2018).

Fontanelli, F, 'The Mythology of Proportionality in Judgments of the Court of Justice of the European Union on Internet and Fundamental Rights' (2016) 36(3) *Oxford Journal of Legal Studies* 630.

Fordham, M and De La Mare, T, 'Identifying the Principles of Proportionality' in J Jowell and J Cooper (eds), *Understanding Human Rights Principles* (Oxford, Hart Publishing, 2001) 27–90.

Forst, R, *Das Recht auf Rechtfertigung: Elemente einer konstruktivistischen Theorie der Gerechtigkeit* (Frankfurt am Main, Suhrkamp, 2007).

Forsthoff, E, *Der Staat der Industriegesellschaft: Dargestellt am Beispiel der Bundesrepublik Deutschland* (München, CH Beck, 1971).

Foucault, M, *Surveiller et Punir. Naissance de la Prison* (Paris, Gallimard, 1975).

Fox, R, 'The Meaning of Proportionality in Sentencing' (1994) 19(3) *Melbourne University Law Review* 489.

Franck, T M, 'On Proportionality of Countermeasures in International Law' (2008) 102 *American Journal of International Law* 715.

Frank, R, 'Die Überspannung der Staatlichen Strafgewalt' (1898) 18 *Zeitschrift für die gesamte Strafrechtswissenschaft* 733.

Frase, R S, 'Sentencing Reform in Minnesota, Ten Years After: Reflections on Dale G. Parent's Structuring Criminal Sentences: The Evolution of Minnesota's Sentencing Guidelines' (1991) 75(3) *Minnesota Law Review* 727.

—— 'Limiting Retributivism' in M Tonry (ed), *The Future of Imprisonment* (New York, Oxford University Press, 2004) 83–120.

—— 'Sentencing Guidelines in Minnesota, 1978–2003' in M Tonry (ed), *Crime and Justice* (Chicago IL, University of Chicago Press, 2005) 131–219.

—— *Just Sentencing: Principles and Procedures for a Workable System* (Oxford, Oxford University Press, 2012).

—— 'Theories of Proportionality and Desert' in J Petersilia and K Reitz (eds), *The Oxford Handbook of Sentencing and Corrections* (Oxford, Oxford University Press, 2012) 131–49.

—— 'Forty Years of American Sentencing Guidelines: What Have We Learned?' (2019) 48 *Crime and Justice* 79.

Frase, R S, Momsen, C, O'Malley, T and Washington, S L, 'Proportionality of Punishment in Common Law Jurisdictions and in Germany' in K Ambos, R A Duff, J V Roberts, T Weigend and A Heinze (eds), *Core Concepts in Criminal Law and Criminal Justice* (Cambridge, Cambridge University Press, 2020) 213–60.

Frase, R S and Roberts, J V, *Paying for the Past: Prior Record Enhancements in the US Sentencing Guidelines* (Oxford, Oxford University Press, 2019).

Frase, R S, Roberts, J V and Hester, R, 'Adverse Impacts on Offense-based Proportionality and Prison-use Priorities' in R S Frase and J V Roberts (eds), *Paying for the Past: Prior Record Enhancements in the US Sentencing Guidelines* (Oxford, Oxford University Press, 2019) 114–27.

Fried, D J, 'Rationalizing Criminal Forfeiture' (1988) 79 *Journal of Criminal Law and Criminology* 328.

Friedman, M and Friedman, R, *Tyranny of the Status Quo* (San Diego CA, Harcourt Brace Jovanovich, 1984).

Friehe, T, 'A Note on the Deterrence Effects of the Forfeiture of Illegal Gains' (2011) 7 *Review of Law and Economics* 118.

Fröhlich, M, Gassmann, F, Becker, S, Backfisch, M and Emrich, E, '30 Jahre Bewertungstabelle im Zehnkampf: Ist eine Revision nötig?' (2016) 57 *Leipziger Sportwissenschaftliche Beiträge* 81.

Fussey, P and Murray, D, *Independent Report on the London Metropolitan Police Service's Trial of Live Facial Recognition Technology* (Essex, University of Essex, 2019).

G

Gaede, K, 'Minimalistischer EU-Grundrechtsschutz bei der Kooperation im Strafverfahren' (2013) 66 *Neue Juristische Wochenschrift* 1279.

Gaines, S, 'The WTO's Reading of the GATT Article XX Chapeau: A Disguised Restriction of Environmental Measures' (2001) 22 *University of Pennsylvania Journal of International Economic Law* 739.

Galič, M, Timan, T and Koops, B J, 'Bentham, Deleuze and Beyond: An Overview of Surveillance Theories from the Panopticon to Participation' (2017) 30 *Philosophy & Technology* 9.

Gardiner, C, 'Principles of Internet Contracting: Illuminating the Shadows' (2019) 48(4) *Common Law World Review* 208.

Garland, D, 'Durkheim's Theory of Punishment: A Critique' in D Garland and P Young (eds), *The Power to Punish* (London, Heinemann, 1983) 37–61.

—— *Punishment and Welfare* (Aldershot, Gower, 1985).

—— *Punishment and Modern Society – A Study in Social Theory* (Chicago IL, The University of Chicago Press, 1993).

—— 'The Limits of the Sovereign State, Strategies of Crime Control in Contemporary Society' (1996) 36(4) *The British Journal of Criminology* 445.

—— 'Sociological Perspectives on Punishment' in A von Hirsch and A Ashworth (eds), *Principled Sentencing. Readings on Theory and Policy* (Oxford, Hart Publishing, 1998) 381–93.

—— *The Culture of Control* (Oxford, Oxford University Press, 2001).

Garnsey, P, *Social Status and Legal Privilege in the Roman Empire* (Oxford, Clarendon Press, 1970).

Garvie, C, Bedoya, A and Frankle, J, *The Perpetual Line-Up: Unregulated Police Face Recognition in America* (Georgetown Law, Center on Privacy & Technology, 2016).

Gatta, G, 'Il ripetuto abbaiare di un cane vale un mese di arresto e tre gradi di giudizio penale? Considerazioni a margine di una annunciata riforma del sistema penale: perché non depenalizzare ancora?' (2019) *Il diritto penale contemporaneo*, at: archiviodpc.dirittopenaleuomo.org/d/6479-il-ripetuto-abbaiare-di-un-cane-vale-un-mese-di-arresto-e-tre-gradi-di-giudizio-penale-considerazio.

Gatti, U and Verde, A, *Juvenile Justice in Italy*, available at: www.oxfordhandbooks.com/view/10.1093/oxfordhb/9780199935383.001.0001/oxfordhb-9780199935383-e-66.

Gaudet, F, Harris, G S and St John, C W, 'Individual Differences in the Sentencing Tendencies of Judges' (1933) 23(5) *Journal of Criminal Law & Criminology* 811.

Gearty, C, 'Human Rights in an Age of Counter-Terrorism: Injurious, Irrelevant or Indispensable?' (2005) 58 *Current Legal Problems* 25.

Gerapetritis, G, *Proportionality in Administrative Law* (Athens, Ant N Sakkoulas, 1997).

Gerards, J, 'How to Improve the Necessity Test of the European Court of Human Rights' (2013) 11(2) *International Journal of Constitutional Law* 466.

—— 'Margin of Appreciation and Incrementalism in the Case Law of the European Court of Human Rights' (2018) 18 *Human Rights Law Review* 495.

Gerards, J and Brems, E, 'Procedural Review in European Fundamental Rights Cases: Introduction' in J Gerards and E Brems (eds), *Procedural Review in European Fundamental Rights Cases* (Cambridge, Cambridge University Press, 2017) 1–14.

Giannoulis, G, *Studien zur Strafzumessung* (Tübingen, Mohr Siebeck, 2014).

Giannoulopoulos, D, *Improperly Obtained Evidence in Anglo-American and Continental Law* (Oxford, Hart Publishing, 2019).

Gibbs, L, *Aesop's Fables* (New York, Oxford University Press, 2002).

Gill, C, Postlethwaite, N and Seaford, R (eds), *Reciprocity in Ancient Greece* (Oxford, Oxford University Press, 1998).

Gillard, E-C, Proportionality in the Conduct of Hostilities: The Incidental Harm Side of the Assessment (2018) *Chatham House Research Paper* (Chatham House Report).

Giunta, F, 'Depenalizzazione' in G Vassalli (ed), *Dizionario di diritto e procedura penale* (Giuffrè, Milano, 1986).

Glas, L R, 'From Interlaken to Copenhagen: What Has Become of the Proposals Aiming to Reform the Functioning of the European Court of Human Rights?' (2020) 20 *Human Rights Law Review* 121.

Goerlich, H, *Grundrechte als Verfahrensgarantien: Ein Beitrag zum Verständnis des Grundgesetzes für die Bundesrepublik Deutschland* (Baden-Baden, Nomos, 1981).

Goh, J, 'Proportionality – An Unattainable Ideal in the Criminal Justice System' (2013) 2 *Manchester Student Law Review* 41, available at: hummedia.manchester.ac.uk/schools/law/main/research/MSLR_Vol2_4(Goh).pdf.

Gomez-Jara Diez, C, 'Enemy Combatants Versus Enemy Criminal Law' (2008) 11 *New Criminal Law Review* 529.

González Beilfuss, M, *El principio de proporcionalidad en la jurisprudencia del Tribunal Constitucional* (Cizur Menor, Aranzadi, 2003).
Goss, R, '"To the Serious Detriment of the Public": Secret Evidence and Closed Material Procedures' in L Lazarus and J C McCrudden (eds), *Reasoning Rights: Comparative Judicial Engagement* (Oxford, Hart Publishing, 2014) 117–34.
—— 'Out of Many, One? Strasbourg's *Ibrahim* Decision' (2017) 80 *Modern Law Review* 1137.
Grabenwarter, C and Pabel, K, *Europäische Menschenrechtskonvention*, 4th edn (München, Beck, 2012).
—— *Europäische Menschenrechtskonvention*, 6th edn (München, Beck, 2016).
Greene, J, 'Rights as Trumps?' (2018) 132 *Harvard Law Review* 28.
Greer, S, 'Terrorism and Counter-Terrorism in the UK: From Northern Irish Troubles to Global Islamist Jihad' in G Lennon, C King and C McCartney (eds), *Counter-Terrorism, Constitutionalism and Miscarriages of Justice* (Oxford, Hart Publishing, 2019) 45–62.
Grono, N and de Courcy Wheeler, A, 'The Deterrent Effect of the ICC on the Commission of International Crimes by Government Leaders' in C Stahn (ed), *The Law and Practice of the International Criminal Court* (Oxford, Oxford University Press, 2015) 1225–44.
Grosso, C, 'La non punibilità per particolare tenuità del fatto' (2015) *Diritto penale e processo* 517.
Grotius, H, *The Rights of War and Peace* (*De jure belli ac pacis*, 1625) Book II, available at: oll.libertyfund.org/titles/grotius-the-rights-of-war-and-peace-1901-ed.
Grzeszick, B, 'Art. 20 GG' in T Maunz and G Dürig (eds), *Grundgesetz: Kommentar* (München, Beck, 2020).
Guerra, M, 'Il decreto legislativo 15 gennaio 2016, n 7 in materia di abrogazione di reati e introduzione di illeciti con sanzioni pecuniarie civili' in D Carcano (ed), *Depenalizzazione e particolare tenuità del fatto* (Milano, Giuffrè, 2016) 103–52.
Guerrini, R, 'Il D.lgs. 15 gennaio 2016, n. 7. I nuovi illeciti civili tipizzati e le relative sanzioni' in G M Baccari, C Bonzano, K La Regina, E M Mancuso (eds), *Le recenti riforme in materia penale* (Padova, Cedam, 2017) 3–38.
Gunn, T J, 'Deconstructing Proportionality in Limitations Analysis' (2005) 19 *Emory International Law Review* 465.
Günther, K, 'Die symbolisch-expressive Bedeutung der Strafe' in C Prittwitz (ed), *Festschrift für Klaus Lüderssen* (Baden-Baden, Nomos, 2002) 205–20.
Guthrie Ferguson, A, 'Big Data and Predictive Reasonable Suspicion' (2015) 163(2) *University of Pennsylvania Law Review* 327.

H

Habermas, J, *Between Facts and Norms: Contributions to a Discourse Theory of Law and Democracy*, trans by W Rehg (Cambridge MA, MIT Press, 1996).
Haggenmüller, S, 'The Principle of Proportionality and the European Arrest Warrant' in (2013) 3(1) *Oñati Socio-legal Series* 95, available at: www.ssrn.com/abstract=2200874.
Haggerty, K D and Ericson, R V, 'The Surveillant Assemblage' (2000) 51(4) *British Journal of Sociology* 605.
Hammarberg, T (Commissioner for Human Rights of the Council of Europe), *Overuse of the European Arrest Warrant – a Threat to Human Rights*, available at: www.coe.int/en/web/commissioner/-/overuse-of-the-european-arrest-warrant-a-threat-to-human-righ-1.
Hampton, J, *Political Philosophy* (Oxford, Westview Press, 1997).
Hannah-Moffat, K, 'Algorithmic Risk Governance: Big Data Analytics, Race and Information Activism in Criminal Justice Debates' (2019) 23(4) *Theoretical Criminology* 453.
Harbo, T J, 'The Function of the Proportionality Principle in EU Law' (2010) 16 *European Law Journal* 158.
Hardy, K, 'Preventive Justice Principles for Countering Violent Extremism' in T Tulich, R Ananian-Welsh, S Bronitt and S Murray (eds), *Regulating Preventive Justice: Principle, Policy and Paradox* (London, Routledge, 2017) 117–35.

Hardyns, W and Rummens, A, 'Predictive Policing as a New Tool for Law Enforcement? Recent Developments and Challenges' (2018) 24 *European Journal on Criminal Policy and Research* 201.

Harmon, M B and Gaynor, F, 'Ordinary Sentences for Extraordinary Crimes' (2007) 5 *Journal of International Criminal Justice* 683.

Harris, D J, O'Boyle, M and Warbrick, C, *Law of the European Convention on Human Rights*, 3rd edn (Oxford, Oxford University Press, 2014).

Harris, L, *Consistency in Sentencing: Is the Current Guidance in England and Wales Adequate?* (PhD Thesis, University of Oxford, 2019), available at: ora.ox.ac.uk/objects/uuid:fdaa2e1f-21d0-4b9e-b2e6-7d103d6c1665.

Hart, H L A, 'Legal Responsibility and Excuses' in H L A Hart, *Punishment and Responsibility*, 2nd edn (Oxford, Oxford University Press, 2008) 28–53.

—— *Punishment and Responsibility* (Oxford, Clarendon Press, 1968, 2008).

Hassemer, W, 'Symbolisches Strafrecht und Rechtsgüterschutz' (1989) (9) *Neue Zeitschrift für Strafrecht* 556.

Hefendehl, R, 'Enron, WorldCom, and the Consequences: Business Criminal Law Between Doctrinal Requirements and the Hopes of Crime Policy' (2004) 8 *Buffalo Criminal Law Review* 51.

Hegel, G W F, *Grundlinien der Philosophie des Rechts*, ed by H Reichelt (Frankfurt am Main, Ullstein, 1972 [1821]).

Heintschel von Heinegg, W, 'Proportionality and Collateral Damage' in R Wolfrum (ed), *Max Planck Encyclopedia of Public International Law (MPEPIL)*, available at: www.mpepil.com.

—— 'Die völkerrechtlichen Verträge als Hauptrechtsquelle des Völkerrechts' in K Ipsen, *Völkerrecht* (V Epping and W Heintschel von Heinegg (eds)), 7th edn (München, Beck, 2018) 453–521.

Helenius, D, 'Mutual Recognition in Criminal Matters and the Principle of Proportionality. Effective Proportionality or Proportionate Effectiveness?' (2014) 5 *New Journal of European Criminal Law* 349.

Hempel, C G, 'Typologische Methoden in den Sozialwissenschaften' in E Topisch (ed), *Logik der Sozialwissenschaften*, 8th edn (Köln, Kiepenheuer & Witsch, 1972) 85–103.

Henham, R, 'The Philosophical Foundations of International Sentencing' (2003) 1(1) *Journal of International Criminal Justice* 64.

—— *Sentencing Policy and Social Justice* (Oxford, Oxford University Press, 2018).

Hensel, A, 'Die Rangordnung der Rechtsquellen' in G Anschütz and R Thoma (eds), *Handbuch des deutschen Staatsrechts* (Tübingen, Mohr Siebeck, 1932) 313–29.

Herberger, M and Dieter, S, *Wissenschaftstheorie für Juristen. Logik, Semiotik, Erfahrungswissenschaften* (Frankfurt am Main, Alfred Metzner Verlag, 1980).

Herman, B, 'Feinberg on Luck and Failed Attempts' (1995) 37(1) *Arizona Law Review* 143.

Hesse, K, *Grundzüge des Verfassungsrechts der Bundesrepublik Deutschland* (Karlsruhe, Müller, 1967).

Hester, R, Frase, R S, Roberts, J V and Mitchell, K L, 'Prior Record Enhancements at Sentencing: Unsettled Justifications and Unsettling Consequences' (2018) 47(1) *Crime and Justice* 209.

Hilgendorf, E, 'Punitivität und Rechtsgutslehre: Skeptische Anmerkungen zu einigen Leitbegriffen der heutigen Strafrechtstheorie' (2010) 22(4) *Neue Kriminalpolitik* 125.

Hodges, C, *Law and Corporate Behaviour. Integrating Theories of Regulation, Enforcement, Compliance and Ethics* (Oxford, Hart Publishing, 2015).

Hodgson, D, *Profits of Crime and Their Recovery* (London, Heinemann, 1984).

Höffling, W, 'Grundrechtstatbestand – Grundrechtsschranken – Grundrechtsschrankenschranken' (1994) *Jura* 169.

Hoffman, S, 'Managing the State: Social Credit, Surveillance and the CCP's Plan for China' (2017) 17 *China Brief* 21.

—— *Social Credit: Technology-enhanced Authoritarian Control with Global Consequences* (Barton ACT, Australian Strategic Policy Institute, International Cyber Policy Centre, 2018).

Holá, B, 'Vertical Inconsistency of International Sentencing? The ICTY and Domestic Courts in Bosnia and Herzegovina' in C Stahn, C Agius, S Brammertz and C Rohan (eds), *Legacies of the International Criminal Tribunal for the Former Yugoslavia* (Oxford, Oxford University Press, 2020) 405–23.

Holá, B, Bijleveld, C and Smeulers, A, 'Punishment for Genocide – Exploratory Analysis of ICTR Sentencing' (2011) 11 *International Criminal Law Review* 745.

Holá, B and Brehm, H N, 'Punishing Genocide: A Comparative Empirical Analysis of Sentencing Laws and Practices at the International Criminal Tribunal for Rwanda (ICTR), Rwandan Domestic Courts, and Gacaca Courts' (2016) 10 *Genocide Studies and Prevention: An International Journal* 59.

Honneth, A, *Kampf um Anerkennung: Zur moralischen Grammatik sozialer Konflikte, Sonderausgabe* (Frankfurt am Main, Suhrkamp, 2003).

Hörnle, T, *Tatproportionale Strafzumessung* (Berlin, Duncker & Humblot, 1998).

—— 'Zwecke und Rechtfertigung staatlicher Strafe' in F Saliger, YW Kim, S I Liu, C Mylonopoulos, K Yamanaka, Y Zheng, J Tavares and O Isfen (eds), *Rechtsstaatliches Strafrecht. Festschrift für Ulfrid Neumann* (Heidelberg, CF Müller, 2017) 593–606.

—— 'Straftheorien' in E Hilgendorf, H Kudlich and B Valerius (eds), *Handbuch des Strafrechts*, vol 1 (Heidelberg, CF Müller, 2019) 507–38.

Hoskins, Z, *Beyond Punishment? A Normative Account of the Collateral Legal Consequences of Conviction* (New York, Oxford University Press, 2019).

Hoven, E, 'Elf Stunden für ein Menschenleben' (2013) 125 *Zeitschrift für die gesamte Strafrechtswissenschaft* 137.

—— 'Das Neue Sexualstrafrecht – Der Prozess einer Reform' (2018) *Kriminalpolitische Zeitschrift* 2.

Husak, D N, *Overcriminalization: The Limits of the Criminal Law* (Oxford, Oxford University Press, 2007).

Huscroft, G, Miller, B W and Webber, G (eds), *Proportionality and the Rule of Law. Rights, Justification, Reasoning* (Cambridge, Cambridge University Press, 2014).

I

Ienilieieva, A E, *Basic Approaches to the History of the Principle of Proportionality* (Simferopol, Taurida National V I. Vernadsky University, 2013).

J

Jackson, J, 'Recent Developments in Criminal Evidence' (1989) 40 *Northern Ireland Legal Quarterly* 105.

—— 'Curtailing the Right of Silence in Northern Ireland: Lessons from Northern Ireland' (1991) *Criminal Law Review* 404.

—— 'Common Law Evidence and the Common Law of Human Rights: Towards a Harmonic Convergence?' (2019) 27 *William & Mary Bill of Rights Journal* 689.

—— *Special Advocates in the Adversarial System* (Abingdon (Oxon), Routledge, 2020).

Jackson, V C, 'Constitutional Law in an Age of Proportionality' (2015) 124 *Yale Law Journal* 3094.

Jacobs, J B and Potter, K A, 'Hate Crimes: A Critical Perspective' (1997) 22 *Crime and Justice* 1.

Jacobsen, J, 'Is the Last Laugh on Liszt? – The Development of the Norwegian Criminal Sanctions' (2020) 132(1) *Zeitschrift für die gesamte Strafrechtswissenschaft* 223.

Jacobsohn, G J, *Constitutional Identity* (Cambridge MA, Harvard University Press, 2010).

Jakobs, G, *Strafrecht, Allgemeiner Teil: Die Grundlagen und ihre Zurechnumg* (Berlin, De Gruyter, 1991).

—— 'Bürgerstrafrecht und Feindstrafrecht' (2004) (3) *Höchstrichterliche Rechtsprechung Strafrecht* 88.

Jarvers, K, 'Verjährung in Italien' in U Sieber and K Cornils (eds), *Nationales Strafrecht in Rechtsvergleichender Darstellung, Teilband 5* (Berlin, Duncker & Humblot, 2010) 277–340.

—— 'Die "Entkriminalisierung" von Bagatelldelikten in Italien' (2016) 128(2) *Zeitschrift für die gesamte Strafrechtswissenschaft* 549.

—— 'Die Kleinen lässt man laufen. Funktionieren die alternativen Verfahrenserledigungen und Sanktionsformen des italienischen Friedensrichters?' (2018) 130(4) *Zeitschrift für die gesamte Strafrechtswissenschaft* 1223.

—— 'National Characteristics, Fundamental Principles, and History of Criminal Law in Italy' in U Sieber, K Jarvers and E Silverman (eds), *National Criminal Law in a Comparative Legal Context, vol 1.5* (Berlin, Duncker & Humblot, 2018).

Jescheck, H and Weigend, T, *Lehrbuch des Strafrechts. Allgemeiner Teil*, 5th edn (Berlin, Duncker & Humblot, 1996).

Joh, E, 'The New Surveillance Discretion: Automated Suspicion, Big Data, and Policing' (2016) 10 *Harvard Law and Policy Review* 15.

—— 'Policing the Smart City' (2019) 15 (Special Issue 2) *International Journal of Law in Context* 177.

Jolls, C, Sunstein, C and Thaler, R, 'A Behavioral Approach to Law and Economics' (1998) 50 *Stanford Law Review* 1471.

K

Kahn, D, *Sacred Violence: Torture, Terror and Sovereignty* (Ann Arbor MI, University of Michigan, 2008).

Kaiafa-Gbandi, M, 'Jurisdictional Conflicts in Criminal Matters and their Settlement within EU's Supranational Settings' (2018) 8(1) *European Criminal Law Review* 30.

Kalshoven, F, 'Reaffirmation and Development of International Humanitarian Law Applicable in Armed Conflicts: The Diplomatic Conference, Geneva, 1974–1977' (1978) 9 *Netherlands Yearbook of International Law* 107.

Kant, I, 'Metaphysik der Sitten (1798)' in W Weischedel (ed), *Kant Werke, Bd 7* (Darmstadt, Wissenschaftliche Buchgesellschaft, 1975).

—— *Groundwork for the Metaphysics of Morals*, ed and trans by A W Wood (New Haven CT, Yale University Press, 2002).

Kaspar, J, *Verhältnismäßigkeit und Grundrechtsschutz im Präventionsstrafrecht* (Baden-Baden, Nomos, 2014).

—— 'Kriminologische Forschungsfelder' in E Hilgendorf, H Kudlich and B Valerius (eds), *Handbuch des Strafrechts*, vol 1 (Heidelberg, CF Müller, 2019) 953–1002.

Kaufmann, E, 'Die Grenzen der Verfassungsgerichtsbarkeit' (1952) 9 *Veröffentlichungen der Vereinigung der Deutschen Staatsrechtslehrer* (VVDStRL) 1.

Kavanagh, A, 'Special Advocates, Control Orders and the Right to a Fair Trial' (2010) 73 *Modern Law Review* 836.

Kelman, M, 'Behavioral Economics as Part of a Rhetorical Duet: A Response to Jolls, Sunstein, and Thaler' (1998) 50 *Stanford Law Review* 1577.

Kelso, R R, 'The Structure of Modern Free Speech Doctrine: Strict Scrutiny, Intermediate Review, and "Reasonableness" Balancing' (2016) 8 *Elon Law Review* 291.

Kennedy, D, *Of War and Law* (Princeton NJ, Princeton University Press, 2006).

Kerr, O S, 'The Mosaic Theory of the Fourth Amendment' (2012) 111 *Michigan Law Review* 311.

Kim, N, 'Relative Consent and Contract Law' (2017) 18(1) *Nevada Law Journal* 165.

Kitchin, R and Dodge, M, *Code/Space: Software and Everyday Life* (Cambridge MA, MIT Press, 2011).

Kleffner, J, 'Military Collaterals and Ius In Bello Proportionality' (2018) 48 *Israel Yearbook on Human Rights* 43.

Kleinig, J, 'The Ethical Perils of Knowledge Acquisition' (2009) 28(2) *Criminal Justice Ethics* 201.

Kleinlein, T, *Konstitutionalisierung im Völkerrecht* (Heidelberg, Springer, 2012).

—— 'The Procedural Approach of the European Court of Human Rights: Between Subsidiarity and Dynamic Evolution' (2019) 68 *International & Comparative Law Quarterly* 91.

Knust, N, *Strafrecht und Gacaca* (Berlin, Dunker & Humblot, 2013).

Koch, H-J and Rüßmann, H, *Juristische Begründungslehre. Eine Einführung in die Grundprobleme der Rechtswissenschaft* (München, CH Beck, 1982).

Koch, O, *Der Grundsatz der Verhältnismäßigkeit in der Rechtsprechung des Gerichtshofs der Europäischen Gemeinschaften* (Berlin, Duncker & Humblot, 2003).

Kolber, A, 'The Comparative Nature of Punishment' (2009) 89 *Boston University Law Review* 1565.

Kosco, B, *Fuzzy Thinking. The New Science of Fuzzy Logic* (London, Harper Collins, 1994).

Koskenniemi, M, 'Occupation and Sovereignty – Still a Useful Distinction?' in O Engdahl and P Wrange (eds), *Law at War: The Law as it Was and the Law as it Should Be. Liber Amicorum Ove Bring* (Leiden, Nijhoff, 2008) 175–86.

Kostka, G, 'China's Social Credit Systems and Public Opinion: Explaining High Levels of Approval' (2019) 21(7) *New Media & Society* 1565.

Kramer, M, *Torture and Moral Integrity: A Philosophical Inquiry* (Oxford, Oxford University Press, 2014).

Kremnitzer, M, Steiner, T and Lang, A (eds), *Proportionality in Action: Comparative and Empirical Perspectives on the Judicial Practice* (Cambridge, Cambridge University Press, 2020).

Kreß, C, 'The International Court of Justice and the "Principle of Non-Use of Force"' in M Weller (ed), *The Oxford Handbook of the Use of Force in International Law* (Oxford, Oxford University Press, 2015) 562–604.

Kretzmer, D, 'The Inherent Right to Self-Defence and Proportionality in Ius Ad Bellum' (2013) 24 *European Journal of International Law* 235.

Kuhlen, L, *Typuskonzeptionen in der Rechtstheorie* (Berlin, Duncker & Humblot, 1977).

Kumm, M, 'Political Liberalism and the Structure of Rights: On the Place and Limits of the Proportionality Requirement' in G Pavlakos (ed), *Law, Rights and Discourse: The Legal Philosophy of Robert Alexy* (Oxford, Hart Publishing, 2007) 131–66.

—— 'The Idea of Socratic Contestation and the Right to Justification: The Point of Rights-Based Proportionality Review' (2010) 4 *Law & Ethics of Human Rights* 141.

Kyvsgaard, B, '100 års nordisk kriminalpolitik. Indlæg ved Svensk Kriminalistforenings 100-års jubilæum' (2012) 2 *Nordisk Tidsskrift for Kriminalvidenskab* 128.

L

Lacey, N, 'The Metaphor of Proportionality' (2016) 43(1) *Journal of Law and Society* 27.

Lacey, N and Pickard, H, 'The Chimera of Proportionality: Institutionalising Limits on Punishment in Contemporary Social and Political Systems' (2015) 78(2) *Modern Law Review* 216.

Langenbacher, E and Conradt, D P, *The German Polity*, 11th edn (London, Rowan & Littlefield, 2017).

Langer, M, 'Plea Bargaining, Conviction without Trial, and the Global Administration of Criminal Convictions' (2021) 4 *Annual Review of Criminology*, in press.

Langer, M and Sklansky, D (eds), *Prosecutors and Democracy* (Cambridge, Cambridge University Press, 2017).

Lauterwein, C, *Symbolische Gesetzgebung. Eine Untersuchung am Beispiel Strafrecht* (München, Verlag Ernst Vögel, 2006).

Lavrysen, L, 'System of Restrictions' in P van Dijk, F van Hoof, A van Rijn and L Zwaak (eds), *Theory and Practice of the European Convention on Human Rights*, 5th edn (Cambridge, Intersentia, 2018) 307–30.

Lee, Y, 'Why Proportionality Matters' (2012) 160 *University of Pennsylvania Law Review* 1835.

Legg, A, *The Margin of Appreciation in Human Rights Law – Deference and Proportionality* (Oxford, Oxford University Press, 2012).

Legrand, P, 'Negative Comparative Law' (2015) 10(2) *Journal of Comparative Law* 405.

Leoncini, I, 'Il D.lgs. 15 gennaio 2016 n 8, recante "disposizioni in materia di depenalizzazione, a norma dell'articolo 2 comma 2 della legge 28 aprile 2014, n. 67"' in G M Baccari, C Bonzano, K La Regina and E M Mancuso (eds), *Le recenti riforme in materia penale* (Padova, Cedam, 2017) 39–60.

Leopizzi, A, *Pacchetto depenalizzazioni (dd.lgs. 15 gennaio 2016, nn. 7 e 8)* (Milano, Giuffrè, 2016).

Lepsius, O, 'Die Grenzen der präventivpolizeilichen Telefonüberwachung' (2006) *Jura* 929.

—— 'Chancen und Grenzen des Grundsatzes der Verhältnismäßigkeit' in M Jestaedt and O Lepsius (eds), *Verhältnismäßigkeit: Zur Tragfähigkeit eines verfassungsrechtlichen Schlüsselkonzepts* (Tübingen, Mohr Siebeck, 2016) 1–41.

Lerche, P, *Übermaß und Verfassungsrecht: Zur Bindung des Gesetzgebers an die Grundsätze der Verhältnismässigkeit und der Erforderlichkeit* (Köln, Heymann, 1961).

Liang, F, Das, V, Kostyuk, N and Hussain, M, 'Constructing a Data-Driven Society: China's Social Credit System as a State Surveillance Infrastructure' (2018) 10(4) *Policy & Internet* 415.

Linder, T, 'Surveillance Capitalism and Platform Policing: The Surveillant Assemblage-as-a-Service' (2019) 17(1/2) *Surveillance & Society* 76.

Livingstone, S, 'The House of Lords and the Northern Ireland Conflict' (1994) 57 *Modern Law Review* 333.

Logli, A, 'La sospensione del processo per messa alla prova tra equivoci dogmatici e limiti operativi' in M Danile and P Paulesu (eds), *Strategie di deflazione penale e rimodulazioni del giudizio in absentia* (Torino, Giappichelli, 2015) 133–80.

López Garrido, D and López Castillo, A, *The EU Framework for Enforcing the Respect of the Rule of Law and the Union's Fundamental Principles and Values* (Study for the AFCO Committee, European Parliament, Brussels, January 2019).

López González, J I, *El principio general de proporcionalidad en el derecho administrativo* (Sevilla, Universidad de Sevilla, 1988).

Luban, D, 'Eight Fallacies About Liberty and Security' in RA Wilson (ed), *Human Rights in the War on Terror* (Cambridge, Cambridge University Press, 2005) 242–57.

Lübbe, W, 'Abwägen: Warnung vor einer Metapher der normativen Urteilsbildung' (2018) *Information Philosophie* 26.

Lübbe-Wolff, G, 'The Principle of Proportionality in the Case-Law of the German Federal Constitutional Court' (2014) 34 *Human Rights Law Journal* 12.

Luhmann, N, *Legitimation durch Verfahren* (Frankfurt am Main, Suhrkamp Verlag, 1983).

—— *Rechtssoziologie*, 3rd edn (Opladen, Westdeutscher Verlag, 1987).

—— *Das Recht der Gesellschaft* (Frankfurt am Main, Suhrkamp Verlag, 1995).

Lum, K and Isaac, W, 'To Predict and Serve?' (2016) 13(5) *Significance* 14.

Luterán, M, 'The Lost Meaning of Proportionality' in G Huscroft, B Miller and G Webber (eds), *Proportionality and the Rule of Law: Rights, Justification, Reasoning* (Cambridge, Cambridge University Press, 2014) 21–42.

Lyon, D, 'Facing the Future: Seeking Ethics for Everyday Surveillance' (2001) 3 *Ethics and Information Technology* 171.

M

Macdonald, S, 'The Role of the Courts in Imposing Terrorism Prevention and Investigation Measures: Normative Duality and Legal Realism' (2015) 9 *Criminal Law and Philosophy* 265.

Macnish, K, 'An Eye for an Eye: Proportionality and Surveillance' (2015) 18(3) *Ethical Theory and Moral Practice* 529.

Mager, U, *Einrichtungsgarantien: Entstehung, Wurzeln, Wandlungen und grundgesetzgemäße Neubestimmung einer dogmatischen Figur des Verfassungsrechts* (Tübingen, Mohr Siebeck, 2003).

Mancano, L, 'A New Hope? The Court of Justice Restores the Balance Between Fundamental Rights Protection and the Enforcement Demands in the European Arrest Warrant System' in C Brière and A Weyembergh (eds), *The Needed Balances in EU Criminal Law – Past, Present and Future* (Oxford, Hart Publishing, 2018) 285–312.

Mancini, R, 'L'abrogazione dei reati e l'introduzione degli illeciti con sanzioni pecuniarie civili' in A Conz and L Levita (eds), *La Depenalizzazione* (Roma, Dike Giuridica Editrice, 2016) 93–97.

Mantello, P, 'The Machine that Ate Bad People: The Ontopolitics of the Precrime Assemblage' (2016) 3(2) *Big Data & Society* 1.

Maras, M H and Wandt, A S, 'Enabling Mass Surveillance: Data Aggregation in the Age of Big Data and the Internet of Things' (2019) 4(2) *Journal of Cyber Policy* 160.

Marat, J-P, *Plan de législation criminelle. Introduction, notes, postface de Daniel Hamiche* (Paris, Aubier Montaigne, 1974).

Marguery, T, 'La confiance mutuelle sous pression dans le cadre du transfert de personnes condamnés au sein de L'Union Européenne' (2018) *Eucrim: The European Criminal Law Associations' Forum* 182.

Martinson, R, 'What works? – Questions and Answers about Prison Reform' (1974) 35 *The Public Interest* 22.

—— 'New Findings, New Views: A Note of Caution Regarding Sentencing Reform' (1979) 7(2) *Hofstra Law Review* 242.

Marx, G, 'Ethics for the New Surveillance' (1998) 14(3) *The Information Society* 171.
Matningsdal, M, *Inndragning* (Oslo, Universitetsforlaget, 1987).
McBride, J, 'Proportionality and the European Convention on Human Rights' in E Ellis (ed), *The Principle of Proportionality in the Laws of Europe* (London, Hart Publishing, 1999) 23–36.
McKittrick, D and McVea, D, *Making Sense of the Troubles* (London, Penguin, 2001).
Melia, MC, 'Terrorism and Criminal Law: The Dream of Prevention, the Nightmare of the Rule of Law' (2011) 14 *New Criminal Law Review* 108.
Melloh, F, *Einheitliche Strafzumessung in den Rechtsquellen des ICC-Statuts* (Berlin, Duncker & Humblot, 2010).
Miceli, T, 'On Proportionality of Punishments and the Economic Theory of Crime' (2018) 46 *European Journal of Law and Economics* 303.
Michaelsen, C, 'The Proportionality Principle, Counter-Terrorism Laws and Human Rights: A German-Australian Comparison' (2010) 2 *City University of Hong Kong Law Review* 19.
Milaj, J, 'Privacy, Surveillance, and the Proportionality Principle: The Need for a Method of Assessing Privacy Implications of Technologies Used for Surveillance' (2016) 30(6) *International Review of Law, Computers & Technology* 115.
Mill, J S, *The Subjection of Women* (London, 1869).
Miller, R A, 'Pantomime of Privacy: Terrorism and Investigative Powers in German Constitutional Law' (2017) 58 *Boston College Law Review* 1545.
Mitsilegas, V, *EU Criminal Law after Lisbon, Rights, Trust and the Transformation of Justice in Europe* (Oxford, Hart Publishing, 2016).
Mitsilegas, V and Billis, E, 'Article 49 – Principles of Legality and Proportionality of Criminal Offences and Penalties' in S Peers, T Hervey, J Kenner and A Ward (eds), *The EU Charter of Fundamental Rights. A Commentary*, 2nd edn (Oxford, Hart Publishing, 2021).
Möller, K, 'Proportionality: Challenging the Critics' (2012) 10 *International Journal of Constitutional Law* 709.
Mommsen, T, *Römisches Strafrecht* (Leipzig, Duncker & Humblot, 1899 and reprinted in Graz, 1955).
Monahan, J, 'The Individual Risk Assessment of Terrorism: Recent Developments' in G LaFree and J D Freilich (eds), *The Handbook of the Criminology of Terrorism* (London, Wiley, 2017) 520–34.
Montesquieu, *De l'esprit des lois* (Paris, Garnier Frères, 1927 [1748]).
—— *Lettres persanes* (Cologne, Pierre Marteau, 1721), available at: vousnousils.fr/casden/pdf/id00233.pdf.
Moore, M S, *Placing Blame: A Theory of Criminal Law* (Oxford, Oxford University Press, 1997).
Mori, T, 'Wirkt in der Abwägung wirklich das formelle Prinzip?' (2019) 58 *Der Staat* 555.
Morris, N, 'Punishment, Desert and Rehabilitation' in H Gross and A von Hirsch, *Sentencing* (Oxford, Oxford University Press, 1981) 257–71.
Murphy, K, 'Regulating More Effectively: The Relationship between Procedural Justice, Legitimacy, and Tax Non-Compliance' (2005) 32 *Journal of Law and Society* 562.
Murray, D and Fussey, P, 'Bulk Surveillance in the Digital Age: Rethinking the Human Rights Law Approach to Bulk Monitoring of Communications Data' (2019) 52(1) *Israel Law Review* 31.
Mylonopoulos, C, 'Das Verhältnis von Vorsatz und Fahrlässigkeit und der Grundsatz in dubio pro reo' (1987) 99 *Zeitschrift für die gesamte Strafrechtswissenschaft* 685.
—— *Komparative und Dispositionsbegriffe im Strafrecht* (Frankfurt am Main, Peter Lang, 1998).
—— *Poiniko Dikaio: Geniko Meros* (Criminal Law: The General Part), vol I (Athens, PN Sakkoulas, 2007).
—— 'Bargain Practices and the Fundamental Values of the ECHR' in U Sieber, V Mitsilegas, C Mylonopoulos, E Billis and N Knust (eds), *Alternative Systems of Crime Control. National, Transnational, and International Dimensions* (Berlin, Duncker & Humblot, 2018) 89–105.

N

Naldi, G J, 'Limitation of Rights Under the African Charter on Human and Peoples' Rights: The Contribution of the African Commission on Human and Peoples' Rights' (2001) 17 *South African Journal on Human Rights* 109.

Napolitano, G and Piccioni, F, *Depenalizzazione e decriminalizzazione* (Santarcangelo di Romagna, Maggioli, 2016).

Nemerofsky, J, 'What is a "Trifle" Anyway?' (2002) 37 *Gonzaga Law Review* 315.

Nemitz, J C, *Strafzumessung im Völkerstrafrecht* (Freiburg, Edition Iuscrim, 2002).

Neumann, P, 'The Trouble with Radicalization' (2013) 89 *International Affairs* 873.

Neumann, U, *Wahrheit im Recht: Zur Problematik und Legitimität einer fragwürdigen Denkform* (Baden-Baden, Nomos, 2004).

Ní Aoláin, F and Gross, O (eds), *Guantanamo and Beyond: Exceptional Courts and Military Commissions in a Comparative Perspective* (Cambridge, Cambridge University Press, 2013).

Noll, P, 'Symbolische Gesetzgebung' (1981) 100 *Zeitschrift für Schweizerisches Recht* 355.

Nolte, G, 'Multipurpose Self-Defence, Proportionality Disoriented: A Response to David Kretzmer' (2013) 24 *European Journal of International Law* 283.

Nozick, R, *Anarchy, State and Utopia* (Oxford, Blackwell, 1974).

—— *Philosophical Explanations* (Oxford, Clarendon Press, 1981).

O

Öberg, J, 'Trust in the Law? Mutual Recognition as a Justification to Domestic Criminal Procedure' (2020) 16(1) *European Constitutional Law Review* 1.

O'Day, K, 'Some Thoughts on Joel Feinberg's Modest Proposal: Is it Really Such a Modest Proposal After All?' (1995) 37(1) *Arizona Law Review* 243.

O'Donovan, O, *The Just War Revisited* (Cambridge, Cambridge University Press 2003).

Ohlin, J D, 'Proportional Sentences at the ICTY' in B Swart, A Zahar and G Sluiter (eds), *The Legacy of the International Criminal Tribunal for the Former Yugoslavia* (Oxford, Oxford University Press, 2011) 322–44.

Olusanya, O, *Sentencing War Crimes and Crimes against Humanity under the International Criminal Tribunal for the Former Yugoslavia* (Groningen, Europa Law Publishing, 2005).

O'Malley, T, 'Living without Guidelines' in A Ashworth and J V Roberts (eds), *Sentencing Guidelines: Exploring the English Model* (Oxford, Oxford University Press, 2013) 218–35.

Ossenbühl, F, 'Grundrechtsschutz im und durch Verfahrensrecht' in K Eichenberger and G Müller (eds), *Staatsorganisation und Staatsfunktionen im Wandel: Festschrift für Kurt Eichenberger zum 60. Geburtstag* (Basel, Helbing & Lichtenhahn, 1982) 183–96.

Otte, G, 'Komparative Sätze im Recht. Zur Logik eines beweglichen Systems' in A Hans (ed), *Jahrbuch für Rechtssoziologie und Rechtstheorie*, vol 2 (Düsseldorf, Bertelsmann Universitätsverlag, 1972) 301–21.

P

Palazzo, F, 'Bene giuridico e tipi di sanzioni' (1992) *L'Indice penale* 209.

—— 'La Riforma penale alza il tiro? Considerazioni sul disegno di legge A.S. 2067 e connessi' (2016) *Diritto penale contemporaneo* 52.

Paliero, C E, *Minima non curat praetor* (Padova, Cedam, 1985).

—— 'Depenalizzazione' (1989) *Digesto delle discipline penalistiche* 429.

—— 'Il principio di effettività del diritto penale' (1990) *Rivista italiana di diritto e procedura penale* 430.

Parlato, L, 'Il volto processuale della particolare tenuità del fatto' in G Baccari and K La Regina (eds), *Il nuovo volto della giustizia penale* (Padova, Cedam, 2015) 225–82.

Parmar, A, 'Stop and Search in London: Counter-Terrorist or Counter-Productive?' (2011) 21(4) *Policing and Society* 369.

Peeters, R and Schuilenburg, M, 'Machine Justice: Governing Security Through the Bureaucracy of Algorithms' (2018) 23(3) *Information Polity* 267.

Perini, C, 'Condotte riparatorie ed estinzione del reato ex art. 162 ter c.p.: deflazione senza Restorative Justice' (2017) *Diritto penale e processo* 1274.

Peters, A, 'Proportionality as a Global Constitutional Principle' in A E Lang and A Wiener (eds), *Handbook on Global Constitutionalism* (Cheltenham, Edward Elgar, 2017) 248–64.

Petersen, N, 'Proportionality and the Incommensurability Challenge: Some Lessons from the South African Constitutional Court' (2013) *New York University Public Law and Legal Theory Working Papers* 1.

—— *Verhältnismäßigkeit als Rationalitätskontrolle: Eine rechtsempirische Studie verfassungsgerichtlicher Rechtsprechung zu den Freiheitsgrundrechten* (Tübingen, Mohr Siebeck, 2015).

Petrig, A, 'Negotiated Justice and the Goals of International Criminal Tribunals' (2018) 8 *Chicago-Kent Journal of International and Comparative Law* 1.

Pettit, P, *Republicanism: A Theory of Freedom and Government* (Oxford, Oxford University Press 1997).

Pina-Sanchez, J, 'Defining and Measuring Consistency in Sentencing' in J V Roberts (ed), *Exploring Sentencing Practice in England and Wales* (London, Palgrave Macmillan, 2015) 76–92.

Philipps, L, 'Auf die Entsprechung kommt es an! Die Logik der je/desto-Sätze im Recht' in L Philipps, *Endliche Rechtsbegriffe mit unendlichen Grenzen. Rechtslogische Aufsätze* (Bern, Editions Weblaw, 2012) 127–40.

Plachta, M, 'Evaluation of the European Arrest Warrant: Quantitative and Practical Aspects' (2011) 27 *International Enforcement Law Reporter* 681.

Poetzsch-Heffter, F, *Handkommentar der Reichsverfassung vom 11. August 1919: Ein Handbuch für Verfassungsrecht und Verfassungspolitik*, 3rd edn (Berlin, Liebmann, 1928).

Pohl, O, *Ist der Gesetzgeber bei Eingriffen in die Grundrechte an den Grundsatz der Verhältnismäßigkeit gebunden?* (Köln, Dissertation Universität Köln, 1959).

Pompei, A, 'Considerazioni generali' in D Carcano (ed), *Depenalizzazione e particolare tenuità del fatto* (Milano, Giuffrè, 2016) 1–12.

Porat, I and Cohen-Eliya, M, *Proportionality and Constitutional Culture* (Cambridge, Cambridge University Press, 2013).

Poscher, R, 'Eingriffsschwellen im Recht der inneren Sicherheit: Ihr System im Licht der neueren Verfassungsrechtsprechung' (2008) 41 *Die Verwaltung* 345.

—— 'Menschenwürde und Kernbereichsschutz: Von den Gefahren einer Verräumlichung des Grundrechtsdenkens' (2009) 64 *Juristenzeitung* 269.

—— 'The Hermeneutic Character of Legal Construction' in S Glanert and F Girard (eds), *Law's Hermeneutics: Other Investigations* (New York, Routledge, 2017) 207–28.

Posner, R A, 'Legal Pragmatism' (2004) 35 *Metaphilosophy* 147.

Pritchard, J B (ed), *The Ancient Near East. An Anthology of Texts and Pictures* (Princeton NJ, Princeton University Press, 1958).

Pruitt, W R, 'Aggravating and Mitigating Sentencing Factors at the ICTR – An Exploratory Analysis' (2014) 14 *International Criminal Law Review* 148.

Purshouse, J and Campbell, L, 'Privacy, Crime Control and Police Use of Automated Facial Recognition Technology' (2019) *Criminal Law Review* 188.

Q

Qiang, X, 'The Road to Digital Unfreedom: President Xi's Surveillance State' (2019) 30(1) *Journal of Democracy* 53.

R

Rachels, J, 'Kantian Theory: The Idea of Human Dignity' in J Rachels, *The Elements of Moral Philosophy* (New York, Random House Inc, 1986), available at: https://public.callutheran.edu/~chenxi/phil345_022.pdf.

Radin, M, 'Boilerplate Today: The Rise of Modularity and the Waning of Consent' (2006) 104(5) *Michigan Law Review* 1223.

Rainey, B, Wicks, E and Ovey, C, *Jacobs, White & Ovey. The European Convention on Human Rights*, 6th edn (Oxford, Oxford University Press, 2014).

Ramakers, A, Nieuwbeerta, P, van Wilsem, J, Apel, R and Dirkzwager, A, 'The Past and Future Labor Market Careers of Dutch Prisoners' in A Blokland and V van der Geest (eds), *The Routledge International Handbook of Life-Course Criminology* (New York, Taylor & Francis, 2017) 377–96.

Ramsay, P, *The Insecurity State: Vulnerable Autonomy and the Right to Security in the Criminal Law* (Oxford, Oxford University Press, 2012).
Rawls, J, *A Theory of Justice* (Cambridge MA, Harvard University Press, 1971).
Raz, J, *The Morality of Freedom* (Oxford, Clarendon Press, 1986).
Redeker, K, 'Grundgesetzliche Rechte auf Verfahrensteilhabe: Bemerkungen zu einem status activus processualis' (1980) *Neue Juristische Wochenschrift* 1593.
Regan, D, 'Value, Comparability, and Choice' in R Chang (ed), *Incommensurability, Incomparability, and Practical Reason* (Cambridge MA, Harvard University Press, 1997) 129–50.
Reid, K, *A Practitioner's Guide to the European Convention on Human Rights* (London, Sweet & Maxwell, 2019).
Reimer, P, 'Verhältnismäßigkeit im Verfassungsrecht: Ein heterogenes Konzept' in M Jestaedt and O Lepsius (eds), *Verhältnismäßigkeit: Zur Tragfähigkeit eines verfassungsrechtlichen Schlüsselkonzepts* (Tübingen, Mohr Siebeck, 2016) 60–76.
Reisig, M D, 'Community and Problem-Oriented Policing' in M Tonry (ed), *The Oxford Handbook of Crime and Criminal Justice* (Oxford, Oxford University Press, 2011) 538–76.
Remmert, B, *Verfassungs- und verwaltungsrechtsgeschichtliche Grundlagen des Übermaßverbotes* (Heidelberg, Müller Juristischer Verlag, 1995).
Remy, H, *Les principes généraux du Code Pénal de 1791* (Thèse Paris, 1910).
Reuter, T, 'Die Verhältnismässigkeit im engeren Sinne – Das unbekannte Wesen' (2009) *Jura* 511.
Richards, J, 'Needles in Haystacks: Law, Capability, Ethics, and Proportionality in Big Data Intelligence-Gathering' in A Bunnik, A Cawley, M Mulqueen and A Zwitter (eds), *Big Data Challenges: Society, Security, Innovation and Ethics* (London, Palgrave Macmillan, 2016) 73–84.
Rigoni, C, 'Crime, Diversity, Culture and Cultural Defence' in H N Pontell (ed), *Oxford Research Encyclopedia of Criminology and Criminal Justice* (Oxford, Oxford University Press, 2018).
Roberts, J V, *Punishing Persistent Offenders* (Oxford, Oxford University Press, 2008).
—— 'Aggravating and Mitigating Factors at Sentencing: Towards Greater Consistency of Application' (2008) *Criminal Law Review* 264.
—— 'The Evolution of Sentencing Guidelines in Minnesota and England and Wales' (2019) 48 *Crime and Justice* 187.
Roberts, J V and Bradford, B, 'Sentence Reductions for a Guilty Plea: New Empirical Evidence from England and Wales' (2015) 12(2) *Journal of Empirical Legal Studies* 187.
Roberts, J V and Gazal-Ayal, O, 'Sentencing Reform in Israel: Exploring the Sentencing Law of 2012' (2013) 46(3) *Israel Law Review* 455.
Roberts, J V and Hough, M, *Understanding Public Attitudes to Criminal Justice* (Maidenhead (Berkshire), Open University Press, 2005).
Roberts, J V, Pina-Sanchez, J and Marder, I, 'Individualisation at Sentencing: The Effects of Sentencing Guidelines and "Preferred" Numbers' (2018) *Criminal Law Review* 123.
Roberts, P, 'The Priority of Procedure and the Neglect of Evidence and Proof: Finding Facts in International Criminal Law' (2015) 13 *Journal of International Criminal Justice* 479.
Robinson, I and Nohle, E, 'Proportionality and Precautions in Attack: The Reverberating Effects of Using Explosive Weapons in Populated Areas' (2016) 98 *International Review of the Red Cross* 107.
Robinson, P H, *Intuitions of Justice and the Utility of Desert* (Oxford, Oxford University Press, 2013).
Robinson, P H and Darley, J M, 'Does Criminal Law Deter? A Behavioural Science Investigation' (2004) 24 *Oxford Journal of Legal Studies* 173.
—— 'Intuitions of Justice' (2007) 81 *Southern California Law Review* 1.
Rønn, K V and Lippert-Rasmussen, K, 'Out of Proportion? On Surveillance and the Proportionality Requirement' (2020) 23 *Ethical Theory and Moral Practice* 181.
Roxin, C, 'Zur jüngsten Diskussion über Schuld, Prävention und Verantwortlichkeit im Strafrecht' in A Kaufmann (ed), *Festschrift für Paul Bockelmann* (München, CH Beck, 1979), 279–309.
Rugege, S and Karimunda, A M, 'Domestic Prosecution of International Crimes: The Case of Rwanda' in G Werle, L Fernandez and M Vormbaum (eds), *Africa and the International Criminal Court* (The Hague, TMC Asser Press, 2014) 79–116.

Rui, J P, 'The Interlaken, Izmir and Brighton Declarations: Towards a Paradigm Shift in the Strasbourg Court's Interpretation of the European Convention of Human Rights?' (2013) 31 *Nordic Journal of Human Rights* 28.

—— *Betenkning: Sivilrettslig inndragning rettet direkte mot formuesgoder* (2017), available at: www.regjeringen.no/contentassets/563c5153753e41438ec0b6d047f3ab20/betenkning_sivilrettslig-inndragning.pdf.

Ruys, T, *'Armed Attack' and Article 51 of the UN Charter* (Cambridge, Cambridge University Press, 2010).

Ryberg, J and Roberts, J V (eds), *Popular Punishment. On the Normative Significance of Public Opinion* (Oxford, Oxford University Press, 2014).

Ryberg, J, Roberts, J V and de Keijser, J (eds), *Sentencing Multiple Crimes* (Oxford, Oxford University Press, 2019).

S

Salazar, L, 'Twenty Years since Tampere – The Development of Mutual Recognition in Criminal Matters' (2020) *Eucrim: The European Criminal Law Associations' Forum* 255.

Sanders, C B and Sheptycki, J, 'Policing, Crime and "Big Data"; Towards A Critique of the Moral Economy of Stochastic Governance' (2017) 68(1) *Crime, Law and Social Change* 1.

Sandoz, Y, Swinarski, C and Zimmermann, B (eds), *Commentary to the Additional Protocols of 8 June 1977 to the Geneva Conventions of 12 August 1949* (Geneva, ICRC, 1987).

Sapir, E, 'Grading, A Study in Semantics' (1944) 11 *Philosophy of Science* 93.

Satzger, H, 'Mutual Recognition in Times of Crisis – Mutual Recognition in Crisis? An Analysis of the New Jurisprudence on the European Arrest Warrant' (2018) 8 *European Criminal Law Review* 317.

—— 'The European Arrest Warrant in German-Italian Practice – Not a Success Story without Problems' (2019) 9(3) *European Criminal Law Review* 285.

Saurer, J, 'Die Globalisierung des Verhältnismäßigkeitsgrundsatzes' (2012) 43 *Der Staat* 3.

Savigny, E, *Grundkurs im wissenschaftlichen Definieren* (München, Deutscher Taschenbuch Verlag, 1970).

—— 'Die heterogene Basis als wissenschaftstheoretisch bedeutsames Merkmal der strafrechtsdogmatischen Argumentation' in U Neumann, J Rahlf and E Savigny (eds), *Juristische Dogmatik und Wissenschaftstheorie* (München, CH Beck, 1976).

Scalia, D, 'Long-Term Sentences in International Criminal Law' (2011) 9 *Journal of International Criminal Justice* 669.

Schabas, W A, *The European Convention on Human Rights. A Commentary* (Oxford, Oxford University Press, 2015).

Scheuner, U, 'Die Rechtsprechung des Bundesverfassungsgerichts und das Verfassungsrecht der Bundesrepublik' (1952) 67 *Deutsches Verwaltungsblatt* 613.

Schinkel, W, 'Prepression: The Actuarial Archive and New Technologies of Security' (2011) 15(4) *Theoretical Criminology* 365.

Schlink, B, *Abwägung im Verfassungsrecht* (Berlin, Duncker & Humblot, 1976).

Schmitt, C, *Verfassungsrechtliche Aufsätze aus den Jahren 1924–1954* (Berlin, Duncker & Humblot, 1958).

—— *Political Theology: Four Chapters on the Concept of Sovereignty*, trans by George Schwab (Chicago IL, University of Chicago Press, 2005).

Schneier, B, *Beyond Fear. Thinking Sensible about Security in an Uncertain World* (New York, Copernicus Books, 2003, 2006).

Sellers, M, *American Republicanism: Roman Ideology in the United States Constitution* (New York, New York University Press, 1994).

Sellier, E and Weyembergh, A, *Criminal Procedural Laws across the European Union – A Comparative Analysis of Selected Main Differences and the Impact They Have over the Development of EU Legislation* (Brussels, Research paper requested by the LIBE Committee of the European Parliament, 2018).

Sellin, T and Wolfgang, M E, *The Measurement of Delinquency* (New York, Wiley, 1978).
Seungeun Lee, C, 'Datafication, Dataveillance, and the Social Credit System as China's New Normal' (2019) 43(6) *Online Information Review* 952.
Shah, S, 'From Westminster to Strasbourg: *A and Others v United Kingdom*' (2009) 9 *Human Rights Law Review* 473.
Sharma, S and Nijjar, J, 'The Racialized Surveillant Assemblage: Islam and the Fear of Terrorism' (2018) 16(1) *Popular Communication* 72.
Sieber, U, 'The New Architecture of Security Law – Crime Control in the Global Risk Society' in U Sieber, V Mitsilegas, C Mylonopoulos, E Billis and N Knust (eds), *Alternative Systems of Crime Control. National, Transnational, and International Dimensions* (Berlin, Duncker & Humblot, 2018) 3–35.
Siehr, A, 'Symbolic Legislation and the Need for Legislative Jurisprudence: The Example of the Federal Republic of Germany' (2008) 2 *Legisprudence* 271.
Silva Sanchez, J M, *Die Expansion des Strafrechts. Kriminalpolitik in Postindustriellen Gesellschaften* (Frankfurt am Main, Vittorio Klostermann, 2003).
Simmons, R, 'Quantifying Criminal Procedure: How to Unlock the Potential of Big Data in Our Criminal Justice System' (2016) *Michigan State Law Review* 947.
Simonelli, M A, '"... And Justice for All?" The Right to an Independent Tribunal after the Ruling of the Court of Justice in LM' (2019) 10(4) *New Journal of European Criminal Law* 329.
Siniscalco, M, *Depenalizzazione e garanzia* (Bologna, Il Mulino, 1983).
Sloane, R D, 'Sentencing for the "Crime of Crimes"' (2007) 5 *Journal of International Criminal Justice* 713.
Slobogin, C, 'Limiting Retributivism and Individual Prevention' in F Focquaert, E Shawn and B Wallace (eds), *The Routledge Handbook of the Philosophy and Science of Punishment* (London, Routledge, 2020).
Smend, R, 'Das Recht der freien Meinungsäußerung' (1928) 4 *Veröffentlichungen der Vereinigung der Deutschen Staatsrechtslehrer* (VVDStRL) 44.
Smeulers, A, Hola, B and van den Berg, T, 'Sixty-Five Years of International Criminal Justice: The Facts and Figures' (2013) 13 *International Criminal Law Review* 7.
Smith, B J, 'Protecting Citizens and their Speech: Balancing National Security and Free Speech When Prosecuting the Material Support of Terrorism' (2013) 59 *Loyola Law Review* 89.
Spano, R, 'Universality or Diversity of Human Rights? Strasbourg in the Age of Subsidiarity' (2014) 14 *Human Rights Law Review* 487.
—— 'The Future of the European Court of Human Rights – Subsidiarity, Process-Based Review and the Rule of Law' (2018) 18 *Human Rights Law Review* 473.
Staihar, J, 'Proportionality and Punishment' (2015) 100 *Iowa Law Review* 1209.
Starck, C, 'Art 1' in H von Mangoldt, F Klein and C Starck (eds), *Das Bonner Grundgesetz*, vol 1, 4th edn (München, Vahlen, 1999).
Stegmüller, W, *Probleme und Resultate der Wissenschaftstheorie und analytischen Philosophie, Theorie und Erfahrung*, vol 2a (Berlin, Springer, 1973).
Steiker, C, 'Proportionality as a Limit on Preventive Justice: Promises and Pitfalls' in A Ashworth, L Zedner and P Tomlin (eds), *Prevention and the Limits of the Criminal Law* (Oxford, Oxford University Press, 2013) 194–213.
Stern, K, 'Zur Entstehung und Ableitung des Übermaßverbotes' in P Badura (ed), *Wege und Verfahren des Verfassungslebens: Festschrift für Peter Lerche zum 65. Geburtstag* (München, Beck, 1993) 165–78.
Stith, K and Cabranes, J A, 'Judging Under the Federal Sentencing Guidelines' (1996–97) 91(4) *Northwestern University Law Review* 1247.
Stoddart, E, 'Challenging "Just Surveillance Theory": A Response to Kevin Macnish's "Just Surveillance? Towards a Normative Theory of Surveillance"' (2014) 12(1) *Surveillance & Society* 158.
Stone Sweet, A and Mathews, J, 'Proportionality Balancing and Global Constitutionalism' (2008) 47 *Columbia Journal of Transnational Law* 68.
Stuntz, W, *The Collapse of American Criminal Justice* (Cambridge MA, Belknap Press, 2011).

Sullivan, E T and Frase, R S, *Proportionality Principles in American Law: Controlling Excessive Government Actions* (New York, Oxford University Press, 2009).
Sumner, M, 'Retribution' in E McLaughlin and J Muncie (eds), *The Sage Dictionary of Criminology* (London, Sage, 2013) 456.
Szoke-Burke, S, 'Avoiding Belittlement of Human Suffering' (2012) 10 *Journal of International Criminal Justice* 561.

T

Tata, C, 'Sentencing as Craftwork and the Binary Epistemologies of the Discretionary Decision Process' (2007) 16(3) *Social & Legal Studies* 425–47.
Tetal, C, 'Hat die Art der strafrechtlichen Sanktion Einfluss auf die Legalbewährung?' in K Boers and M Schaerff (eds), *Kriminologische Welt in Bewegung* (Mönchengladbach, Forum Verlag Godesberg, 2018) 445–50.
Thomas, P, 'Emergency and Anti-Terrorist Powers: 9/11: USA and UK' (2003) 26 *Fordham International Law Journal* 1193.
Thorburn, M, 'Constitutionalism and the Limits of the Criminal Law' in R A Duff, L Farmer, S E Marshall, M Renzo and V Tadros (eds), *The Structures of the Criminal Law* (Oxford, Oxford University Press, 2011) 85–105.
—— 'Proportionate Sentencing and the Rule of Law' in L Zedner and J V Roberts (eds), *Principles and Values in Criminal Law and Criminal Justice* (Oxford, Oxford University Press, 2012) 269–84.
Tomkins, A, 'Readings of A v Secretary of State for the Home Department' (2005) *Public Law* 259.
Tonry, M, *Sentencing Matters* (Oxford, Oxford University Press, 1996).
—— (ed), *Why Punish? How Much? A Reader on Punishment* (Oxford, Oxford University Press, 2011).
—— (ed), *Of One-eyed and Toothless Miscreants: Making the Punishment Fit the Crime?* (New York, Oxford University Press, 2019).
—— 'Fairness, Equality, Proportionality, and Parsimony: Towards a Comprehensive Jurisprudence of Just Punishment' in A du Bois-Pedain and A E Bottoms (eds), *Penal Censure. Engagements Within and Beyond Desert Theory* (Oxford, Hart Publishing, 2019).
—— *Doing Justice, Preventing Crime* (Oxford, Oxford University Press, 2020).
Torres Pérez, A, 'A Predicament for Domestic Courts: Caught between the European Arrest Warrant and Fundamental Rights' in B de Witte, J A Mayoral, U Jaremba, M Wind and K Podstawa (eds), *National Courts and EU Law, New Issues, Theories and Methods* (Cheltenham, Edward Elgar Publishing, 2016) 191–216.
Toscano, A, *La funzione della pena e le garanzie dei diritti fondamentali* (Milano, Giuffrè, 2012).
Tsakyrakis, S, 'Proportionality: An Assault on Human Rights?' (2009) 7(3) *International Journal of Constitutional Law* 468.
Turner, J I, 'Plea Bargaining and International Criminal Justice' (2017) 48 *University of the Pacific Law Review* 219.
Turner, J I and Weigend, T, 'Negotiated Justice' in G Sluiter, H Friman, S Linton, S Vasiliev and S Zappalà (eds), *International Criminal Procedure* (Oxford, Oxford University Press, 2012) 1375–414.

U

Ulph, J, 'Confiscation Orders, Human Rights, and Penal Measures' (2010) 126 *Law Quarterly Review* 251.
Uniacke, S, 'Proportionality and Self-Defense' (2011) 30(3) *Law and Philosophy* 253.
Urbina, F, 'A Critique of Proportionality' (2012) 57 *American Journal of Jurisprudence* 49.

V

van Ballegooij, W, 'Mutual Recognition and Individual Rights: Did the Court get it Right?' (2016) 7(4) *New Journal of European Criminal Law* 439.
—— *European Arrest Warrant, European Implementation Assessment* (Brussels, Study for DG European Parliamentary Research Service, June 2020).

van Ballegooij, W and Kiendl Krišto, I, *European Arrest Warrant, Framework for Analysis and Preliminary Findings on its Implementation* (Brussels, In-Depth Analysis for DG European Parliamentary Research Service, February 2020).

van der Sloot, B and Kosta, E, 'Big Brother Watch and Others v UK: Lessons from the Latest Strasbourg Ruling on Bulk Surveillance' (2019) 5 *European Data Protection Law Review* 252.

van Sliedregt, E, 'Perpetration and Participation in Article 25 (3)' in C Stahn (ed), *The Law and Practice of the International Criminal Court* (Oxford, Oxford University Press, 2015) 499–516.

Veel, P-E N, 'Incommensurability, Proportionality, and Rational Legal Decision-Making' (2010) 4 *Law & Ethics of Human Rights* 177.

Venter, F, 'The Politics of Constitutional Adjudication' (2005) 65 *Zeitschrift für ausländisches öffentliches Recht und Völkerrecht* 129.

Venturi, F, *Utopia and Reform in the Enlightenment* (Cambridge, Cambridge University Press, 1971).

Victor, D, 'Från behandlingsideologi till nyklassicism' (2012) 2 *Nordisk Tidsskrift for Kriminalvidenskab* 114.

Vogel, J and Spencer, J R, 'Proportionality and the European Arrest Warrant' (2010) *Criminal Law Review* 474.

Volkmann, U, 'Anmerkung zur BVerfGE Rasterfahndung' (2006) 61 *Juristenzeitung* 906.

von Bogdandy, A and Venzke, I, *In wessen Namen? – Internationale Gerichte in Zeiten globalen Regierens* (Berlin, Suhrkamp Verlag, 2014).

von Hirsch, A, *Doing Justice: The Choice of Punishments* (New York, Hill & Wang, 1976).

—— 'Neoclassicism, Proportionality, and the Rationale for Punishment: Thoughts on the Scandinavian Debate' (1983) 29(1) *Crime & Delinquency* 52.

—— *Past and Future Crimes* (Manchester, Manchester University Press, 1985).

—— 'Proportionality in the Philosophy of Punishment' (1992) 16 *Crime and Justice* 55.

—— *Censure and Sanctions* (Oxford, Oxford University Press, 1993).

—— *Proportionalitet och straffbestämning* (Uppsala, Iustus förlag, 2001).

—— 'The "Desert" Model for Sentencing: Its Influence, Prospects, and Alternatives' (2007) 74(2) *Social Research: An International Quarterly* 413.

—— 'Ein grundrechtliches Verbot exzessiver Strafen? – Versuch einer Begründung' in U Neumann and F Herzog (eds), *Festschrift für Winfried Hassemer* (Heidelberg, CF Müller Verlag, 2010) 373–82.

—— *Deserved Criminal Sentences* (Oxford, Hart Publishing, 2017).

von Hirsch, A and Ashworth, A, *Proportionate Sentencing: Exploring the Principles* (Oxford, Oxford University Press, 2005).

von Hirsch, A, Garland, D and Wakefield, A (eds), *Ethical and Social Perspectives on Situational Crime Prevention* (Oxford, Hart Publishing, 2000).

von Hirsch, A and Hörnle, T, 'Positive Generalprävention und Tadel' in A von Hirsch (ed), *Fairness, Verbrechen und Strafe: Strafrechtstheoretische Abhandlungen* (Berlin, Berliner Wissenschafts-Verlag, 2005) 19–40.

von Hirsch, A and Jareborg, N, 'Gauging Criminal Harm. A Living-Standard Analysis' (1991) 11(1) *Oxford Journal of Legal Studies* 1.

von Krauss, R, *Der Grundsatz der Verhältnismäßigkeit: In seiner Bedeutung für die Notwendigkeit des Mittels im Verwaltungsrecht* (Hamburg, Kommissionsverlag Ludwig Appel, 1955).

von Liszt, F, 'Der Zweckgedanke im Strafrecht' (1883) 3 *Zeitschrift für die gesamte Strafrechtswissenschaft* 1.

von Scherenberg, C F, *Die sozialethischen Einschränkungen der Notwehr* (Frankfurt am Main, Peter Lang, 2009).

W

Wagstaff, R, *Terror Detentions and the Rule of Law* (Oxford, Oxford University Press, 2014).

Wahl, R, 'Der Grundsatz der Verhältnismäßigkeit: Ausgangslage und Gegenwartsproblematik' in D Heckmann, R P Schenke and G Sydow (eds), *Verfassungsstaatlichkeit im Wandel: Festschrift für Thomas Würtenberger zum 70. Geburtstag* (Berlin, Duncker & Humblot, 2013) 823–54.

Wahl, T, 'Fair Trial Concerns: German Court Suspends Execution of Polish EAW' (2020) *Eucrim: The European Criminal Law Associations' Forum*, available at: eucrim.eu/news/fair-trial-concerns-german-court-suspends-execution-polish-eaw/.

Waldron, J, 'Fake Incommensurability: A Response to Professor Schauer' (1993) 45 *Hastings Law Journal* 813.

—— 'Security and Liberty: The Image of Balance' (2003) 11 *Journal of Political Philosophy* 191.

—— 'Safety and Security' (2006) 85 *Nebraska Law Review* 454.

—— *Torture, Terror and Trade-offs: Philosophy for the White House* (Oxford, Oxford University Press, 2010).

Walen, A, 'A Punitive Precondition for Preventive Detention: Lost Status as an Element of a Just Punishment' (2011) 63 *San Diego Law Review* 1229.

—— 'Retributive Punishment' in the *Stanford Encyclopedia of Philosophy*, available at: plato.stanford.edu/entries/justice-retributive/.

Walker, C, *The Prevention of Terrorism in British Law*, 2nd edn (Manchester, Manchester University Press, 1992).

—— 'Terrorism Prosecution in the United Kingdom' in F Ní Aoláin and O Gross (eds), *Guantanamo and Beyond: Exceptional Courts and Military Commissions in a Comparative Perspective* (Cambridge, Cambridge University Press, 2013) 245–66.

—— *Blackstone's Guide to the Anti-Terrorism Legislation*, 3rd edn (Oxford, Oxford University Press, 2014).

—— 'Counter-Terrorism Laws and their Discontents' in G Lennon, C King and C McCartney (eds), *Counter-Terrorism, Constitutionalism and Miscarriages of Justice* (Oxford, Hart Publishing, 2019) 307–26.

Walker, C and Blackbourn, J, 'Interdiction and Indoctrination: The Counter-Terrorism and Security Act 2015' (2016) 79 *Modern Law Review* 840.

Walker, N, *Punishment, Danger and Stigma* (Oxford, Oxford University Press, 1980).

Walklate, S and Mythen, G, *Contradictions of Terrorism: Security, Risk and Resilience* (London, Routledge, 2015).

Walls, S M, *Individualism in the United States* (New York, Bloomsbury Academic, 2015).

Walsh, D, 'Beyond the Ordinary: Criminal Law and Terrorism' in G Lennon, C King and C McCartney (eds), *Counter-Terrorism, Constitutionalism and Miscarriages of Justice* (Oxford, Hart Publishing, 2019) 27–44.

Walter, T, 'Das Absolute wird relativ – wie sich Vergeltung als Strafzweck soziologisch begründen lässt' in F Neubacher and M Kubink (eds), *Kriminologie – Jugendkriminalrecht – Strafvollzug. Gedächtnisschrift für Michael Walter* (Berlin, Duncker & Humblot, 2014) 831–52.

—— 'Die Vergeltungsidee als Grenze des Strafrechts' (2019) 74 *Juristenzeitung* 649.

Wasik, M, *A Practical Approach to Sentencing*, 5th edn (Oxford, Oxford University Press, 2014).

Weber, M, *Wirtschaft und Gesellschaft*, 5th edn (Tübingen, Mohr, 1980). [English translation: G Roth and C Wittich (eds), *Max Weber's Economy and Society* (Berkeley CA, University of California Press, 1978)].

Weigend, T, 'Der Grundsatz der Verhältnismäßigkeit als Grenze staatlicher Strafgewalt' in T Weigend (ed), *Festschrift für Hans-Joachim Hirsch zum 70. Geburtstag am 11. April 1999* (Berlin, de Gruyter, 1999) 917–38.

Weinreb, L L, *Criminal Law: Cases, Comment, Questions*, 7th edn (New York, Foundation Press, 2003).

Weisburd, D, Mastrofski, S, McNally, A M, Greenspan, R and Willis, J, 'Reforming to Preserve: Compstat and Strategic Problem Solving in American Policing' (2003) 2(3) *Criminology & Public Policy* 421.

Werkmeister, A, *Straftheorien im Völkerstrafrecht* (Baden-Baden, Nomos, 2015).

Werle, G and Jessberger, F, *Principles of International Criminal Law*, 3rd edn (Oxford, Oxford University Press, 2014).

—— *Völkerstrafrecht*, 5th edn (Tübingen, Mohr Siebeck, 2020).

Wexler, R, 'Life, Liberty, and Trade Secrets: Intellectual Property in the Criminal Justice System' (2018) 70 *Stanford Law Review* 1343.

Weyembergh, A, Armada, I and Brière, C, *Critical Assessment of the Existing European Arrest Warrant Framework Decision* (Brussels, Research Paper for DG EPRS, European Parliament, 2014).

Willems, A, 'Extradition on the Two Sides of the Atlantic: The U.S. Model as Blueprint for the European Arrest Warrant?' (2016) 27 *Criminal Law Forum* 443.

X

Xanthopoulou, E, 'The Quest for Proportionality for the European Arrest Warrant: Fundamental Rights Protection in a Mutual Recognition Environment' (2015) 6(1) *New Journal of European Criminal Law* 32.

Y

Young, W and King, A, 'Addressing Problematic Sentencing Factors in the Development of Guidelines' in J V Roberts (ed), *Mitigation and Aggravation at Sentencing* (Cambridge, Cambridge University Press, 2011) 208–27.

Z

Zadeh, L A, 'Fuzzy Sets' (1965) 8 *Information and Control* 338.

—— 'Fuzzy Logic' (1988) 21 *Computer* 83.

Završnik, A, 'Algorithmic Justice: Algorithms and Big Data in Criminal Justice Settings' (2019) *European Journal of Criminology* 1.

Zedner, L, 'Securing Liberty in the Face of Terror: Reflections from Criminal Justice' (2005) 32 *Journal of Law and Society* 507.

—— 'Pre-Crime and Post-Criminology?' (2007) 11(2) *Theoretical Criminology* 261.

—— *Security* (London, Routledge, 2009).

—— 'Pre-Crime and Pre-Punishment: A Health Warning: Lucia Zedner Calls for Restraint' (2010) 81 *Criminal Justice Matters* 24.

—— 'Criminal Justice in the Service of Security' in M Bosworth, C Hoyle and L Zedner (eds), *Changing Contours of Criminal Justice* (Oxford, Oxford University Press, 2016) 152–68.

—— 'Security against Arbitrary Government in Criminal Justice' in A du Bois-Pedain, M Ulväng and P Asp (eds), *Criminal Law and the Authority of the State* (Oxford, Hart Publishing, 2017) 89–110.

—— 'Curtailing Citizenship Rights as Counterterrorism' in B Goold and L Lazarus (eds), *Security and Human Rights*, 2nd edn (Oxford, Hart Publishing, 2019) 99–124.

—— 'The Hostile Border: Crimmigration, Counter-Terrorism or Crossing the Line on Rights?' (2019) 22 *New Criminal Law Review* 318.

—— 'Countering Terrorism or Criminalising Curiosity? The Troubled History of UK Responses to Right-Wing and Other Extremism' (2020) 49(4) *Common Law World Review* (forthcoming).

Zedner, L and Stuckenberg, C-F, 'Due Process' in K Ambos, R A Duff, J V Roberts, T Weigend and A Heinze (eds), *Core Concepts in Criminal Law and Criminal Justice: Volume 1, Anglo-German Dialogues* (Cambridge, Cambridge University Press, 2020) 304–42.

Zimmermann, H J, *Fuzzy Sets Theory and its Applications*, 2nd edn (New York, Springer Science+Business Media, 1991).

Zoda, I, *La deflazione penale in Italia* (Doctoral Thesis, University of Ferrara), available at: iris.unife.it/retrieve/handle/11392/2389156/123108/79.pdf.

Zoppei, V, *Anti-Money Laundering Law: Socio-Legal Perspectives on the Effectiveness of German Practices* (The Hague, TMC Asser Press, 2017).

Zuboff, S, 'Big Other: Surveillance Capitalism and the Prospects of an Information Civilization' (2015) 30(1) *Journal of Information Technology* 75.

—— 'Surveillance Capitalism and the Challenge of Collective Action' (2019) 28(1) *New Labor Forum* 10.

INDEX